INVESTMENTS

THIRD EDITION

INVESTMENTS

William F. Sharpe

Timken Professor of Finance
Graduate School of Business
Stanford University

Prentice-Hall, Inc., Englewood Cliffs, New Jersey 07632

Library of Congress Cataloging in Publication Data

SHARPE, WILLIAM F.
    Investments.

    Includes index.
    1. Investments.   2. Investment analysis.
I. Title.
HG4521.S48 1985   332.6   84–26264
ISBN 0–13–504697–1

Editorial/production supervision Pamela Wilder
Interior and cover design: Jayne Conte
Manufacturing buyer: Ed O'Dougherty

Printed in the United States of America
10 9 8 7 6 5 4 3 2 1

ISBN 0-13-504697-1 01

Prentice-Hall International, Inc., *London*

Prentice-Hall of Australia Pty. Limited, *Sydney*

Editora Prentice-Hall do Brasil, Ltda., *Rio de Janeiro*

Prentice-Hall Canada Inc., *Toronto*

Prentice-Hall Hispanoamericana, S.A., *Mexico*

Prentice-Hall of India Private Limited, *New Delhi*

Prentice-Hall of Japan, Inc., *Tokyo*

Prentice-Hall of Southeast Asia Pte. Ltd., *Singapore*

Whitehall Books Limited, *Wellington, New Zealand*

to Robbie, Debbie, and Jon

CONTENTS

3 Investment Value and Market Price 54

4 The Valuation of Riskless Securities 70

5 The Valuation of Risky Securities 93

6 Portfolio Analysis 118

7 Capital Asset Pricing Models 145

8 Factor Models and the Arbitrage Pricing Theory 182

9 Taxes 202

10 Inflation 240

11 Fixed-Income Securities 269

12 Bond Prices, Yields, and Returns 312

13 Common Stocks 355

14 The Valuation of Common Stocks 413

Contents

18 Investment Companies 564

19 Financial Analysis 595

22 Extended Diversification 705

Index 729

PREFACE

The field of investments is in the midst of a continuing revolution.

Not too many years ago, investments textbooks were devoted primarily to discussions of the art of security analysis. Readers were introduced to the mysteries of accounting, some of the details of the operations of major industries, and various rules of thumb for selecting "good" or "bad" securities. Institutional details of securities markets, types of investment instruments, transactions costs, and the like were presented, along with historic data, but the reader was provided no framework for understanding such phenomena. A theory of the formation of prices in capital markets was lacking.

Harry Markowitz published his seminal work on portfolio theory in the 1950s. This provided a way to deal with risk and return methodically. The original Capital Asset Pricing Model was developed by the present author, John Lintner, and Jan Mossin in the 1960s. It provided a model of the relationships among risks and returns in an efficient market. Fischer Black and Myron Scholes published their work on option pricing in the 1970s. It showed that some securities can be valued by considering the values of related instruments, under the assumption that riskless arbitrage is impossible in a well-functioning capital market.

With this array of theories, it was possible to approach the field of investments in a rigorous manner. The first edition of this text reflected these changes.

Unlike many fields, investments is blessed with a wealth of quantitative data. Thus theories can be subjected to empirical tests. Early investigations suggested that the new theories conformed well with reality. A few deviations were found, but they were accommodated by extending the basic theories.

The second edition of this text reflected the situation at the beginning of the 1980s. Markets were assumed to be highly efficient and to conform reasonably well to the specifications given by extended versions of the original Capital Asset Pricing Model. Deviations of prices from corresponding "intrinsic values" were assumed to be small, temporary, unsystematic, and difficult to identify.

Recent empirical work has cast some doubt on this comforting view of the world. Earlier statistical tests have been found to be relatively weak, suggesting that they may have been unable to identify important disparities between theory and reality. Moreover, systematic "anomalies" have been found, calling into question at least some aspects of the standard theories.

In reaction to these findings, investigators have turned their attention with renewed vigor to models of the factors determining security returns. Some work is limited to statistical analysis of historic data, but much of it goes further, to include fundamental economic analysis of the interrelationships among firms and between firms and major aspects of the overall economy. Associated with such factor models is the Arbitrage Pricing Theory, developed by Stephen Ross.

This edition differs considerably from its two predecessors.

It is more eclectic—encompassing both utility-based theories (i.e. Capital Asset Pricing Models) and factor-model-based theories (i.e. the Arbitrage Pricing Theory). It emphasizes the fact that one need not choose one or the other of these approaches—indeed, both may hold at the same time. The strengths and weaknesses of each are given, along with challenges associated with using them in practice.

Empirical work is given substantial attention—especially that connected with factor models and with "anomalies" such as the returns from small stocks, the behavior of security prices in January, and so on.

Much of the work comes from professionals working in the investment industry. In the early phases of the revolution in investment theory, there tended to be an attitude of confrontation between academicians and practitioners. This has long since ceased. The flow of ideas (and people) between the two groups is perhaps greater than that in any business field. This should not be surprising—after all, *research* is the key ingredient in investment management.

The structure of the book is similar to that of the second edition. An overall framework is provided at the outset in sufficient detail to provide a needed base for the remaining material. Following a discussion of taxes and inflation, particular instruments are described and analyzed. The remaining chapters cover financial analysis, investment management, performance measurement, and extended diversification. Throughout, factual and institutional details are discussed in the context of an overall marketplace that provides investors with a relatively efficient means for participating, in whole or in part, in future prospects for the economy.

The book is intended to be encyclopedic without excessive or insignificant detail, rigorous without the use of needless analytic apparatus, and as integrated as possible.

Many readers will choose to cover only a portion of the material. To facilitate this approach, the chapters have been written in a modular manner.

No one can undertake a project of this magnitude without a great deal of help. I am especially grateful for all that I have learned from my colleagues (past and present) at the Stanford Graduate School of Business and at Wells Fargo Investment Advisors. El Vera Fisher at Stanford and Linda Frascino, Robert Lentz, and Pam Wilder at Prentice-Hall played key roles in the production of this edition. These are only a few of my many debts, but the rest of the list is far too long for publication. It must suffice for me to offer my thanks to all who have been my teachers (formal and informal) over the years and to express my appreciation to my wife, my son and daughter, and to my parents for providing the environment and encouragement necessary to support the kind of work represented in this book.

1

Introduction

INVESTMENT

General Motors invests millions of dollars in a new model car. A wealthy doctor invests over a hundred thousand dollars in a new apartment house. A successful professor invests thousands of dollars by purchasing shares of General Motors stock from someone else. His secretary invests her savings by taking them to a federally insured savings and loan association, which in turn invests the money by purchasing a mortgage on the doctor's apartment house. Nearby a young businesswoman is investing money in commodity futures, based on her belief that others have misestimated the price of corn some months hence. A lawyer is studying the racing form, considering the investment of some money in a promising three-year-old in the second race at a local track. Meanwhile, a pawnbroker is investing by loaning money to a man who has fallen on hard times, but only after carefully appraising the gold watch to be held as security.

Do all these actions qualify as *investment*? By some people's definitions, yes. By others', no. Each case involves the sacrifice of something *now* for the prospect of something *later*. And this, in the broadest sense, is investment. Two different attributes may be involved: *time* and *risk*. The sacrifice takes place in the present and is certain. The reward comes later, if at all, and the magnitude may be uncertain. In some cases the element of time predominates (e.g., government bonds). In others, risk is the dominant attribute (e.g., parimutuel tickets). In yet others, both are important (e.g., shares of General Motors stock).

In this book we will use the term *investment* in its broadest sense:

Investment is the sacrifice of certain present value for (possibly uncertain) future value.

INVESTMENT VERSUS SAVINGS

A distinction is often made between investment and savings. The latter is defined as foregone consumption, with the former restricted to "real" investment of the sort that increases national output in the future. While this definition may prove useful in other contexts, it is not especially helpful for analyzing the specifics of particular investments or even large classes of investment media. A deposit in a "savings" account at a bank is investment in the eyes of the depositor. Even cash stored in the proverbial mattress can be viewed as an investment: one yielding a dollar for every dollar invested (or less in the event of fire or theft). For our purposes, investment can be viewed broadly, as the sacrifice of certain present consumption for (possibly uncertain) future consumption.

REAL VERSUS FINANCIAL INVESTMENT

Semantics aside, there is still a difference between an "investment" in a ticket on a horse and the construction of a new plant; between the pawning of a watch and the planting of a field of corn. Some investments are simply transactions among people; others involve nature. The latter are "real" investment; the former are not.

While this distinction may be too harsh, it is nonetheless useful. Every investment can be conceived as an asset held by someone: the prospect of future returns. Some investments involve liabilities as well: someone else may have to provide the returns. A loan is a classic example. It is an asset to the lender, who will receive the required payments when and if they are made. But it is a liability to the borrower, who must make the payments. The lender has invested money, but the investment is strictly financial in nature.

At the other extreme lies the harried executive's agrarian dream. An investor buys a plot of land, some seeds, fertilizer, and so on and becomes a farmer. The newly sown land is an asset to the investor, but there is no corresponding liability (unless it be nature's). No other person must pay corn, wheat, grapes, or whatever. This is real investment.

In a complex modern economy, much investment is of the financial rather than the real variety. But highly developed institutions for financial investment greatly facilitate real investment. By and large, the forms are complementary, not competitive.

The financing of an apartment house provides a good example. Apartments are sufficiently tangible ("bricks and mortar") to be considered real investment. But where do the resources come from? Some may come from direct investment—for example, from the wealthy doctor mentioned earlier. But the majority of the required money is usually provided through a mortgage. In essence, someone loans money for construction, with repayment promised in fixed amounts on a specified schedule over many years. In the typical case the "someone" is not a person at all, but an institution acting as a financial intermediary. In the earlier example, it was a savings and loan association, using money obtained from many of its investors, none of whom might be willing or able to invest in the apartment directly.

The "secondary" market for securities provides another example. At some time General Motors finds itself in need of resources for, say, plant construction. This real investment may be financed by the sale of new common stock in the "primary" market for securities (this is not a physical location, only a convenient fiction). Subsequently, people buy and sell these shares of stock, trading among themselves in the "secondary" market (for example, on the New York Stock Exchange). These transactions generate no money for General Motors. But the fact that a secondary market exists makes the original purchase more attractive and thus facilitates real investment. People would pay less for a new share of stock if there were no way to sell it quickly and inexpensively later on, if and when the initial owners' circumstances or expectations warrant it.

SECURITIES

When a nearly destitute man borrows money from a pawnbroker, he must leave some item or items of value as *security*. If he fails to repay the loan, plus interest, the lender can then sell the pawned item(s) to recover his or her costs, plus perhaps a profit or loss. The terms of the agreement are recorded via "pawn tickets." When a college student borrows money to buy a car, the lender usually holds the formal title to the car until the loan is repaid. In the event of default, the lender can repossess the car and attempt to sell it to recover his or her costs. In this case the official certificate of title, issued by the state, serves as the tangible *security* for the loan. When someone borrows money for a vacation, he or she may simply sign a piece of paper promising repayment with interest. The loan is *unsecured* in the sense that no specific asset or *collateral* is promised the lender in the event of default. In such a situation, the lender would have to take the borrower to court and share the borrower's assets with other lenders in a similar position. Only a piece of paper or *promissory note* stands as tangible evidence of such a loan.

When a corporation borrows money, it may or may not offer collateral. For example, some firms back certain loans with specific pieces of property (buildings and so on). Such loans are represented by *mortgage bonds*, which indicate the terms of repayment and the particular assets pledged to the holder of the certificate in the event of default.

However, it is much more common for a corporation to simply pledge its overall assets, perhaps with some provision for the manner in which the division will take place in the event of default. Such a promise is represented by a *debenture bond*.

Finally, a corporation may promise a "piece of the action" in return for an investor's funds. Nothing is pledged, and no irrevocable promises are made. The corporation simply pays whatever its directors deem reasonable from time to time. However, to protect against serious malfeasance, the original investor is given the right to help determine the members of the board of directors. His or her property right is represented by a share of *common stock*, which can be sold to someone else, who will then be able to exercise the right. The holder of common stock is said to be an *owner* of the corporation and can, in theory, exercise control over its operation through periodic votes.

In all these cases but the first, only a piece of paper represents the original investor's rights to certain prospects and/or property and the conditions under which he or she may exercise those rights. In general, the piece of paper may be transferred to another, and with it all the associated property rights. Although the word is often clearly inappropriate in its strictest sense, the evidence of any property right is generally termed a *security*. Thus everything from a pawn ticket to a share of IBM stock is a security. We will use the term in this broad sense: *a legal representation of the right to receive prospective future benefits under stated conditions*. The task of *security analysis* is to determine *these prospective future benefits, the conditions under which they will be received, and the likelihood of such conditions*.

By and large, we will focus on securities that may be easily and efficiently transferred from one owner to another. Thus we will be more concerned with common stocks than with pawn tickets, although much of the material in this book applies to both types of instruments.

INVESTMENT, SPECULATION, AND GAMBLING

Webster's New Collegiate Dictionary contains the following definitions:[1]

investment To commit (money) in order to earn a financial return.

speculate To assume a business risk in hope of gain; especially: to buy or sell in expectation of profiting from market fluctuations.

gamble To bet on an uncertain outcome.

All three definitions fall within the scope of *investment* as we have defined it. And as the dictionary definitions show, distinctions among the three kinds of activity are subtle at best.

---

[1] By permission, from *Webster's New Collegiate Dictionary,* © 1980 by G. & C. Merriam Co., publishers of the Merriam-Webster dictionaries.

The term *speculate* is sometimes used to identify the horizon of the investor. Thus someone who buys a piece of land on which to build a house in which to live might be termed an investor, while a real estate agent who buys the land and builds a house for almost immediate resale might be termed a speculator. The former is concerned primarily with the direct benefits provided by the asset over the long run, the latter with others' evaluations of those benefits (i.e., the price of the asset) in the relatively near future. Similarly, the widow who buys a stock for its dividends may be termed an investor, while a young businesswoman who buys in anticipation that good news about the company will shortly drive the price up, enabling her to sell at a gain, may be termed a speculator. While this sort of distinction is sometimes useful, the dividing line is seldom obvious. Few investors are oblivious to price movement. And since price is at base a reflection of future benefits, anyone wishing to speculate on price movements must analyze the prospects for future benefits.

A better approach concentrates on motivation: a speculator trades on the basis of information that he or she believes is not yet known to or properly evaluated by other investors; an investor makes no such assumption.

Some use the term "speculative" to refer to high-risk investments, possibly without commensurately high return. Thus a new stock issue may be denoted a "speculative investment."

A final use of the term "speculative" is simply to denote activities of which the speaker disapproves. One's friends are investors, one's enemies speculators.

Turning to the term *gamble*, we encounter similar difficulties. The word is often used in a derogatory sense, perhaps even more than "speculate." Certainly the dictionary definition would apply it to any investment other than the very safest possible.

Perhaps the most useful distinction has to do with the relationship between risk and return. A person might be considered a gambler if he or she takes on risk that is greater than commensurate with expected return. Thus playing roulette at Las Vegas could be termed gambling; the risk is great, yet on average the players' return is negative, to allow for the house "take." Investment in the stock market also entails risk, but the return is positive on average.

Here, too, the dividing line is sometimes difficult to draw. Is the knowledgeable horse player a gambler if he or she has sufficient inside knowledge to expect a positive return commensurate with the associated risk? Is the knowledgeable "investor" in commodity futures a gambler? Although many would term people who "play" in the commodity futures market speculators, common usage and legal status refrain from identifying them as gamblers. Gambling is, *de facto*, whatever the law says it is. One of the differences between betting on the future price of corn and betting on the point spread in a football game is that the former is legal in all states, the latter only in some.

RISK AND RETURN

Figures 1-1(a), (b), and (c) show the year-by-year results obtained from three different types of investments over the 57-year period from 1926 through 1982. In each case, the percentage change in an investor's wealth from the beginning to the end of year is shown. This amount, the annual *return*, reflects both payments received in cash and any change in the value of the investment.

The first type of investment involves loaning money on a short-term basis to the U.S. Treasury Department. Such a loan carries little if any risk that payment will not be made as promised. Moreover, while the rate of return varies from period to period, at the beginning of any given period it is known with certainty. The return on such investments ranged from a high of 14.71% per year (in 1981) to a low of virtually zero (in 1938) with an average value of 3.18% during the period. While this type of investment has little if any risk, it provides a rather modest return.

The second type of investment involves the purchase of a group of corporate bonds, each of which represents a fairly long-term commitment on the part of the issuer to make cash payments each year (the "coupon" amount) up to some point ("maturity"), at which point a single, final cash payment (the "principal") will be made. The amount for which such a bond can be bought or sold varies from time to time, so the overall return over a year's time is difficult to predict in advance. While coupon payments are easily determined, changes in value are not. The figure shows the overall return on a (changing) group of bonds selected by the firm of Salomon Brothers[2] to represent long-term corporate bonds. Return varied from a high of 43.76% per year (in 1982) to a low of −8.09% per year (in 1969), averaging 4.44% per year during the period. While this type of investment has considerable risk, on average it provides somewhat more return than short-term loans.

The final type of investment involves the purchase of a group of common stocks, each of which represents a commitment on the part of a corporation to periodically pay whatever its board of directors deems appropriate as a cash dividend. While the amount of cash dividends to be paid in a year is subject to some uncertainty, it is relatively predictable. However, the amount for which a stock can be bought or sold varies considerably from time to time, making overall return

---

[2] Values produced by Standard and Poor's Corporation were used to derive the returns for the period before 1946.

FIGURE 1-1
Annual Returns, 1926-1982

SOURCE: Roger G. Ibbotson and Rex A. Sinquefield, *Stocks, Bonds, Bills and Inflation*: *1926-1982*, (Charlottesville, Va.: Financial Analysts Research Foundation, 1983).

highly unpredictable. The figure shows the return from a portfolio of stocks (currently 500 different issues) selected by Standard and Poor's Corporation to represent the performance of the typical dollar invested in common stocks. Returns ranged from an exhilarating 53.99% per year (in 1933) to a depressing −43.34% per year (in 1931), and averaged 11.58% per year during the period. Such investments provide substantial returns on average, but with substantial risk.

Table 1-1 provides more detail. Year-by-year returns are shown

TABLE 1-1
Annual Returns: Stocks, Bonds and Treasury Bills and Change in the Consumer Price Index

TOTAL RETURNS					
Year	Stocks	Long-Term Corporate Bonds	Long-Term Government Bonds	Treasury Bills	Change in the Consumer Price Index
1926	11.62	7.37	7.77	3.27	1.49
1927	37.49	7.44	8.93	3.12	−2.08
1928	43.61	2.84	.10	3.24	−.97
1929	−8.42	3.27	3.42	4.75	.19
1930	−24.90	7.98	4.66	2.41	−6.03
1931	−43.34	−1.85	−5.31	1.07	−9.52
1932	−8.19	10.82	16.84	.96	−10.30
1933	53.99	10.38	.08	.30	.51
1934	−1.44	13.84	10.02	.16	2.03
1935	47.67	9.61	4.98	.17	2.99
1936	33.92	6.74	7.51	.18	1.21
1937	−35.03	2.75	.23	.31	3.10
1938	31.12	6.13	5.53	−.02	−2.78
1939	−.41	3.97	5.94	.02	−.48
1940	−9.78	3.39	6.09	.00	.96
1941	−11.59	2.73	.93	.06	9.72
1942	20.34	2.60	3.22	.27	9.29
1943	25.90	2.83	2.08	.35	3.16
1944	19.75	4.73	2.81	.33	2.11
1945	36.44	4.08	10.73	.33	2.25
1946	−8.07	1.72	.10	.35	18.17
1947	5.71	−2.34	−2.63	.50	9.01
1948	5.50	4.14	3.40	.81	2.71
1949	18.79	3.31	6.45	1.10	−1.80
1950	31.71	2.12	.06	1.20	5.79
1951	24.02	−2.69	−3.94	1.49	5.87
1952	18.37	3.52	1.16	1.66	.88
1953	−.99	3.41	3.63	1.82	.62
1954	52.62	5.39	7.19	.86	−.50
1955	31.56	.48	−1.30	1.57	.37
1956	6.56	−6.81	−5.59	2.46	2.86

TABLE 1-1 (Cont.)

Year	Stocks	Long-Term Corporate Bonds	Long-Term Government Bonds	Treasury Bills	Change in the Consumer Price Index
1957	−10.78	8.71	7.45	3.14	3.02
1958	43.36	−2.22	−6.10	1.54	1.76
1959	11.95	−.97	−2.26	2.95	1.50
1960	.47	9.07	13.78	2.66	1.48
1961	26.89	4.82	.97	2.13	.67
1962	−8.73	7.95	6.89	2.73	1.22
1963	22.80	2.19	1.21	3.12	1.65
1964	16.48	4.77	3.51	3.54	1.19
1965	12.45	−.46	.71	3.93	1.92
1966	−10.06	.20	3.65	4.76	3.35
1967	23.98	−4.95	−9.19	4.21	3.04
1968	11.06	2.57	−.26	5.21	4.72
1969	−8.50	−8.09	−5.08	6.58	6.11
1970	4.01	18.37	12.10	6.53	5.49
1971	14.31	11.01	13.23	4.39	3.36
1972	18.98	7.26	5.68	3.84	3.41
1973	−14.66	1.14	−1.11	6.93	8.80
1974	−26.47	−3.06	4.35	8.00	12.20
1975	37.20	14.64	9.19	5.80	7.01
1976	23.84	18.65	16.75	5.08	4.81
1977	−7.18	1.71	−.67	5.12	6.77
1978	6.56	−.07	−1.16	7.18	9.03
1979	18.44	−4.18	−1.22	10.38	13.31
1980	32.42	−2.62	−3.95	11.24	12.40
1981	−4.91	−.96	1.85	14.71	8.94
1982	21.41	43.76	40.37	10.53	3.87
Average:	11.58	4.44	3.78	3.18	3.19
Std. Dev.:	21.52	7.62	7.41	3.20	4.96

SOURCE: Roger G. Ibbotson and Rex A. Sinquefield, *Stocks, Bonds, Bills and Inflation, 1926-1982* (Charlottesville, Va.: Financial Analysts Research Foundation, 1983).

for the three types of investments plotted in Figure 1-1. The table also includes return on long-term U.S. government bonds and the percentage change in the Consumer Price Index as an indicator of variations in the "cost of living." Average yearly values are shown at the bottom of the table, along with values of the standard deviation—a measure of year-to-year variability that will be described in Chapter 6.

The record illustrates a general principle: *when sensible investment strategies are compared with one another, risk and expected return tend to go together.*

It is important to note that *variability* is not necessarily an indication of *risk*. The former deals with the record over some past period; the latter has to do with uncertainty about the future. The pattern of returns on short-term loans provides one example. Although the values vary from period to period, in any given period the amount to be earned is known in advance. On the other hand, the annual return on a common stock is very difficult to predict. For such an investment, variability in the past may provide a fairly good measure of the uncertainty surrounding future return.

To see how difficult it is to predict common stock return, cover the portion of Table 1-1 from 1941 on, then try to guess the return in 1941. Having done this, uncover the value for 1941 and try to guess the return in 1942. Proceed in this manner a year at a time, keeping track of your overall predictive accuracy. Unless you are very clever or very lucky, you will conclude that the past pattern of stock returns provides little help in predicting next year's return. We will see that this is a characteristic of an *efficient market*. At this stage, it is enough to indicate that past variability of stock returns can be taken as a rough approximation of future risk.

Is one of these three major types of investment obviously "the best"? No. To oversimplify: the right investment or combination of investments depends on the ultimate beneficiary's situation and preference for return relative to his or her distaste for risk. There may be "right" or "wrong" investments for a particular person or purpose. But it would be surprising indeed to find an investment that is clearly wrong for everyone and every purpose. Such situations are simply not present in an efficient market.

ASSET OWNERSHIP

Who owns securities in the United States? According to the most recent New York Stock Exchange survey, approximately 32 million U.S. residents directly owned shares of common stock in 1981; but many more had an interest in securities via indirect holdings. Table 1-2 shows the changes in direct ownership from 1952 through 1981, while Table 1-3 provides some breakdowns of the total in 1981. The typical stockholder has a higher-than-average income, some college education, and is or was in a skilled profession.

As Table 1-2 shows, a smaller percentage of the population held NYSE stock in 1981 than in 1970. Figure 1-2 shows the other side; during the first half of the 1970s the percentage of such stock held by institutions increased, reaching over 35% in 1975. Since then the percentage has remained approximately the same. Nonetheless, indirect ownership of common stock through financial intermediaries is substantial. Table 1-4 provides a breakdown. In 1980 institutional investors held NYSE

TABLE 1-2
Shareholders of Public Corporations, 1952-1981

Year	Shareowners as Percent of U.S. Adult Population
1952	6
1956	8
1959	13
1962	17
1965	17
1970	25
1975	17
1980	19
1981	19

SOURCE: *The New York Stock Exchange Fact Book, 1976, 1983.*

stock with a total value of more than 440 billion dollars. While this is large, the total amount under professional management is even greater, since many individuals receive professional advice concerning their own investment decisions.

As might be expected, there is substantial concentration in common stock ownership, both direct and indirect. In the last detailed survey (completed in 1972), the richest .5% of the population was estimated to own 49.3% and the richest 1% to own 56.5% of the stock held by individuals.[3] Figure 1-3 uses Lorenz curves to show the distributions in each of four years for which careful estimates have been made. The horizontal axis plots the percentage of total families, arrayed from the poorest (on the left end of the axis) to the richest (on the right end); the vertical axis plots the percentage of the total value of stock owned by these families. Although the equality of distribution has increased over time, even the most recent curve is far from the 45-degree line, which represents complete equality. The extent of "people's capitalism" in the United States is still rather limited.

The existence of complex financial institutions makes the link between "real" assets and the ownership of securities very difficult to trace. Tables 1-5 and 1-6 provide two extreme views of assets owned by individuals.

Table 1-5 shows the most recent set of estimates of overall national wealth, all of which is ultimately owned by individuals. Note

---

[3] *Statistical Abstract of the United States, 1978* (Washington, D.C.: U.S. Department of Commerce, Bureau of the Census), p. 476.

TABLE 1-3
Shareholders of Public Corporations,
1981

Age	
Under 21 years	7.2%
21 to 34 years	23.7%
35 to 44 years	17.4%
45 to 54 years	16.9%
55 to 64 years	19.0%
65 years and older	15.7%
Household income	
Under $9,999	7.4%
$10,000-$14,999	8.7%
$15,000-$24,999	23.5%
$25,000-$49,999	41.6%
$50,000 and over	18.8%
Education	
Three years high school or less	6.2%
Four years high school	20.3%
One to three years college	33.7%
Four years college or more	39.8%
Occupation	
Professional and technical	23.1%
Managers and proprietors	20.1%
Clerical and sales	14.2%
Craftsmen and foremen	5.7%
Operatives and laborers	3.9%
Service workers	1.0%
Farmers and farm laborers	0.4%
Housewives, retired persons, and nonemployed adults	31.5%

SOURCE: *The New York Stock Exchange Fact Book, 1983.*

that each individual "owns" substantial assets in his or her role as a citizen. Particularly important classes are private residential housing and land. Investment in consumer durables (refrigerators, television sets, and so on but, most importantly, automobiles) is also substantial: at the time of the survey it was almost as large as that in producer durables (turret lathes, riveting machines, computers, and the like) and publicly owned equipment. Moreover, even these figures include only a portion of the total national wealth. By far the most important item is omitted entirely: human capital, representing the value of the population as producers of future income.

Table 1-6 looks at wealth from the viewpoint of individual households, but only financial assets and liabilities are included. The assets require little comment, but the liabilities merit some discussion. The large value of home mortgages outstanding is not surprising, given the considerably larger value of homes owned. Although some mortgages are held as assets by individuals (as shown in the table), most are held by banks and savings and loan companies, who obtain them by lending money provided by individuals (reflected in the table by the values of the first two assets listed). Consumer credit is also large, but not overly so, given the value of consumer durables owned. Other sources of credit include banks, security brokers, and life insurance companies.

The difference between assets and liabilities in Table 1-6 is large, but it is nonetheless considerably less than the true net worth of all households, since nonfinancial assets have been omitted. For example, the total national wealth shown in Table 1-5 was over five times as

FIGURE 1-2
Percentage of NYSE-listed Stock Held by Institutions

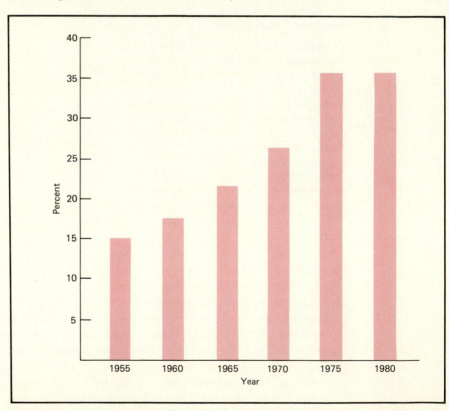

SOURCE: The New York Stock Exchange Fact Book, 1983.

Introduction

TABLE 1-4

Estimated Holdings of New York Stock Exchange listed Stocks by Institutional Investors, 1980 (all figures in $ billions)

Type of Institution	Holdings
Insurance companies:	
Life	38.1
Nonlife	26.9
Investment companies	43.2
Noninsured pension funds:	
Private	166.0
State and local government	53.0
Nonprofit institutions:	
Foundations	32.4
Educational endowments	12.1
Trust funds	9.5
Mutual savings banks	1.5
Foreign institutions	57.5
Total	440.2

SOURCE: *The New York Stock Exchange Fact Book*, 1983.

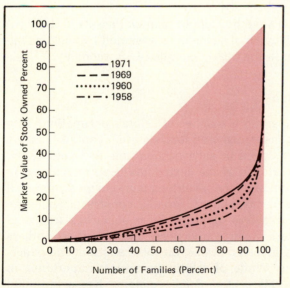

FIGURE 1-3

Trends in the Distribution of Stock Ownership 1958-1971

SOURCE: Marshall E. Blume, Jean Crockett, and Irwin Friend, "Stock Ownership in the United States: Characteristics and Trends," *Survey of Current Business*, November 1974.

Introduction

TABLE 1-5
National Wealth, 1975 ($ billions)

Category	Value
Structures	
Nonfarm structures:	
Public nonresidential	745.4
Institutional	125.6
Other private nonresidential	710.5
Residential	952.9
Farm structures	20.9
Equipment	
Private business and public equipment	543.7
Consumer durables	496.6
Inventories	
Private, farm	43.9
Private, nonfarm	555.8
Public	107.5
Land	
Private, farm	336.2
Private, nonfarm	705.6
Public	243.0
Total	5587.6

SOURCE: *Statistical Abstract of the United States, 1982-83.*

great as the difference between household financial assets and liabilities at the time. Although much of value is represented by such instruments, much is not, even in the highly complex U.S. economy.

The Investment Industry

Government statisticians group a number of related occupations into a sector called "Finance, Insurance, and Real Estate." Table 1-7 shows the number of people employed in such occupations in recent years. As can be seen, the importance of the sector has been increasing. In 1981 approximately one out of every seventeen workers was employed in this sector. All deal with investment, broadly construed. Some are in sales, some arrange transfers of property or securities from one investor to another, others manage investors' funds, and still others handle the recordkeeping involved in this, the most abstract and paper-oriented of all industries. While of relatively modest importance in the employment figures, this sector of the economy has a profound impact on virtually everyone's life. A clear understanding of investments is obviously valuable for the one in seventeen who will work

TABLE 1-6
Financial Assets and Liabilities of Households, 1981 ($ billions)

Category	Value
Assets	
Checkable deposits and currency	290.3
Time and savings deposits	1365.2
Money market fund shares	181.9
Value of life insurance policies	232.6
Value of pension funds	788.7
Investment company shares	64.0
Other corporate shares	1020.2
U.S. government securities	313.4
State and local government obligations	89.1
Corporate and foreign bonds	76.5
Mortgages	130.2
Miscellaneous financial assets	134.4
Total financial assets	4686.7
Liabilities	
Mortgages	1038.9
Consumer credit	413.6
Other loans	147.4
Total liabilities	1599.9
Financial assets less liabilities	3086.8

SOURCE: Statistical Abstract of the United States, 1982-83.

TABLE 1-7
Number of Employees: Finance, Insurance, and Real Estate

EMPLOYER	NUMBER OF EMPLOYEES (thousands)					
	1960	1965	1970	1975	1980	1981
Banking	673	792	1,044	1,274	1,571	1,627
Credit agencies, other than banks	261	327	361	432	570	585
Security and commodity brokerages and services	114	129	205	170	227	261
Insurance carriers	832	893	1,031	1,085	1,224	1,233
Insurance agents, brokers, and services	196	233	274	339	452	466
Real estate	517	569	680	748	981	990
Other finance, insurance, and real estate	76	80	91	117	135	140
Total	2,669	3,023	3,687	4,165	5,160	5,301
Employees in this sector as a percent of total employees in nonagricultural industries	4.92%	4.97%	5.14%	5.41%	5.71%	5.82%

Introduction

in the field, but it is also worthwhile for the sixteen who will not. While most people obtain the majority of their income in the form of salary and wages, income from investments is also important. This book is intended to provide an understanding of investment for both those whose interest is professional and those whose interest is strictly personal.

Problems

1. In how many years since 1926 did investors lose money in stocks? What does this imply about the probability that those who invest in stocks may lose money next year?

2. In how many years since 1926 did those who invested in long-term government bonds lose money? How does this compare with the record for long-term corporate bonds? Does this imply that government bonds are riskier than corporate bonds?

3. In terms of total return, what was the worst single calendar year for stock investors? What was the worst year in the 1970s? Compare the two years in terms of return in "constant dollars" (purchasing power). Does this show that the stock market "slump" in the 1970s was not at all as serious as the "crash" associated with the Great Depression?

4. List two phenomena for which past variability is not entirely relevant for estimating uncertainty about next period's value.

5. In the Second World War, some Allied cargo ships adopted courses based on a chart of the level of the British stock market in the period from 1910 onward. Why was this thought to be a good strategy against German submarines? What were the possible dangers?

6. List your assets and liabilities and estimate the value of each. Which assets are real? Which are financial?

2

Securities
and Markets

BROKERS AND DEALERS

When a security is sold, many people are likely to be involved. Although it is possible for two investors to trade with each other directly, the usual transaction employs the services provided by brokers, dealers, or markets.

A *broker* acts as an agent and is compensated via commission. Like a marriage broker or real estate broker, an investment broker tries to bring two parties together and to obtain the best possible terms for his or her customer. Many individual investors deal with brokers in large *retail* or "*wire*" houses—firms with many offices connected by private wires with their own headquarters and, through the headquarters, with major markets. The people in brokerage firms with prime responsibility for individual accounts are termed *account executives*, *registered representatives*, or (in the vernacular) *customer's men and women*.

Institutional investors deal with both large firms offering retail brokerage service and smaller firms that maintain only one or two offices and specialize in institutional business. There are also *regional* brokerage firms and *discount* brokers. The former concentrate on transactions in a geographic area; the latter provide "bare-bones" services at low cost.

An account executive's compensation is typically determined in part by the amount of commissions paid by his or her customers—an amount that is usually greater, the greater the *turnover* in an account. This provides some temptation to recommend changes in investors' holdings and, since the commission rates on various types of investments differ, to recommend particular types of changes. In the long run, account executives who encourage excessive churning should lose customers. Nonetheless, such behavior may be advantageous for them in the short run.

It is a simple matter to open an account with a brokerage firm: simply appear at (or call) the local office. An account executive will be assigned to you and will take care of the formalities. Transactions will be posted to your account as they would to a bank account. You may deposit money, purchase securities using money from the account, add the proceeds from security sales to the account, borrow money, and so on. After the initial forms have been signed, everything can be done by mail or telephone. Brokers exist (and charge fees) to make securities transactions as simple as possible.

A broker acts as an agent for investors, but a *dealer* (or *market-maker*) buys and sells securities for his or her own account, taking at least temporary positions and maintaining at least small and transitory inventories of securities. Like a used-car dealer, a security dealer runs risks and ties up capital in order to make it easy for individuals to buy or sell on a moment's notice. Dealers are usually compensated by the *spread* between the *bid* price at which they buy a security and the *ask* price at which they sell it. The percentage spread is typically larger, the smaller the amount of trading activity and the greater the volatility in a security's price.

To facilitate the coming together of traders (be they investors, brokers, or dealers), physical locations or communications facilities or both are required. *Security exchanges* are physical locations where trading is done on a person-to-person basis (usually by brokers and dealers) under specified rules. Communications networks, formal or informal, are often termed *markets*. Some have clearly defined boundaries; others do not.

Often a firm or even an individual will play more than one role in this process. Most retail brokerage firms hold some inventories of securities and may thus act as dealers (but the law requires that they inform their customers if they do so). Some exchanges have *specialists*, who serve as brokers for some trades and as dealers for others. Brokers may employ other brokers, dealers may deal with other dealers, and so on.

TYPES OF ORDERS

Brokers will accept instructions of various types concerning the conditions under which a security is to be purchased or sold. Some of the procedures are institutionalized; others are simply agreements between the investor and his or her account executive.

By far the most common procedure is that used for a *market order*. The broker is instructed to buy or sell a stated number of securities at the best available price or prices (as low as possible for a purchase, as high as possible for a sale). It is incumbent on the broker in such a situation to act on a "best-efforts" basis to get the best possible deal at the time.

In most cases there is fairly good information concerning the likely price at which a market order might be executed. If this is unacceptable, a *limit order* may be placed instead. Both a quantity and an acceptable price are specified. The broker is to purchase or sell the stated number of shares only at the indicated price or better (higher for a sale, lower for a purchase). If a limit order cannot be executed immediately, it is usually kept by the broker or placed by the broker on the books of another broker (e.g., an exchange specialist) to be executed as soon as the requisite price can be obtained.

Some limit orders are *day orders*—canceled if not executed by the end of the day they are placed. However, an investor may specify that an order be considered *good-till-canceled* (*GTC*) or that it be canceled immediately if not executed [this is termed a *fill-or-kill* (*FOK*) order].

A limit order "on the books" is executed only when a security's price becomes more favorable. A *stop-loss* order operates in the opposite direction. For example, a stop-loss order at $30 per share might be placed to *sell* 100 shares of a stock currently trading at $40 per share. As long as the price remains above $30, nothing happens. But as soon as the price reaches (or drops below) $30, the order is converted to a market order, to be executed on the best possible terms. A stop-loss order to *purchase* shares becomes a market order when the price reaches or rises above the level indicated.

The standard unit in which a stock is traded is termed a *round lot* (usually 100 shares). Any smaller quantity is an *odd lot*. An investor who wishes to purchase or sell an odd lot generally does business with a dealer instead of another investor. For example, certain brokerage firms will usually purchase an odd lot of a stock listed on the New York Stock Exchange at the price of the first round-lot transaction on the Exchange following receipt of the odd-lot order (possibly minus a small differential) or sell an odd lot for the same price (possibly plus a small differential).

MARGIN ACCOUNTS

A *cash account* with a brokerage firm is like a regular checking account: deposits (cash and the proceeds from security sales) must cover withdrawals (cash and the costs of security purchases). A margin account is like a bank account with overdraft privileges: within limits, if more money is needed, a loan is automatically made by the broker.

All securities purchased on margin must be left with the brokerage firm and registered in its name (i.e., "street name"). Moreover, the account holder must sign a *hypothecation* agreement, which grants the broker the right to pledge margined securities as collateral for bank loans. Most firms also expect customers to allow them to lend securities to others who wish to sell them short (a procedure described in the next section). Such lending is done by the broker; the account holder is generally not even notified when it takes place.

The interest charged on loans advanced by a broker for a margin account is usually calculated by adding a service charge (e.g., 1%) to the broker's current *call money* rate. The latter is the rate paid by the broker to one or more banks for money used to finance margin purchases. Securities in margin accounts serve as collateral for the bank loans. The call money rate changes from time to time, and with it the interest charged for margin loans.

The Securities and Exchange Act of 1934 prohibits any broker (or bank) from making an initial loan for the purchase of a security in excess of the *loan value* of the collateral (e.g., the security to be purchased). This *initial margin* requirement differs for different types of investments—e.g., it is usually higher for stocks than for bonds—and is changed from time to time by the Board of Governors of the Federal Reserve System as an instrument of economic policy. Since 1934 the initial margin required for exchange-listed stocks has ranged from 40% to 100%. In 1983 it was 50%.

The *percentage margin* in an account can be calculated as follows:

$$\text{percentage margin} = \frac{\text{equity in the account}}{\text{market value of all positions}} \quad \textbf{(2-1)}$$

For example, assume an investor wishes to buy 100 shares of ABC stock at $40 per share but has only $3,000. If a broker loans the remaining $1,000 for the purchase, the account's balance sheet will be:

| 100 shares of ABC at $40 per share = $4,000 | Loan from broker = $1,000 |
| | Equity = $3,000 |

The percentage margin will be $3,000/$4,000, or 75%. If this exceeds the current initial margin requirement, the purchase can be made.

After the purchase, if ABC slips to $30 per share, the account's balance sheet will be:

| 100 shares of ABC at $30 per share = $3,000 | Loan from broker = $1,000 |
| | Equity = $2,000 |

The percentage margin has fallen to $2,000/$3,000, or 66⅔%. If the price of the stock falls farther, and the margin with it, the broker may become nervous, since an additional sudden price decline could bring the value of the collateral below the amount of the loan. To protect against such an occurrence, a broker will require that margin be kept above a *maintenance margin* level. The New York Stock Exchange requires its member firms to insist on at least 25%, but many require a larger amount.

If an account falls below the maintenance margin requirement, the broker will issue a *margin call*, requesting the account holder to add cash or securities to the account or to sell some securities currently in the account; this will raise the numerator or lower the denominator of the fraction in formula (2-1), thus increasing the margin. If a customer does not act (or cannot be reached), in accordance with the terms of the original agreement the broker will sell securities from the account to restore the margin to the required maintenance level.

If ABC rises to $50 per share, the picture will be brighter:

---

100 shares of ABC at $50 per share = $5,000   Loan from broker = $1,000
                                                          Equity = $4,000

Here the percentage margin is $4,000/$5,000, or 80%. If the initial margin requirement is 75%, the account's current equity can support positions worth $5,333 (= $4,000/.75); if desired, securities worth up to $333 could be purchased and financed entirely with an additional loan from the broker. Alternatively, since only $3,750 (= .75 × $5,000) of equity is required to support positions worth $5,000, an additional $250 could be borrowed from the broker, taken as cash, and removed from the account.

When the percentage margin of an account falls below the initial margin requirement, no action need be taken. However, the account will be *restricted*. When an account is in this status, transactions will generally not be allowed if their net effect is to decrease the actual percentage margin; however, transactions occurring within a single trading day may be combined for this calculation.[1]

SHORT SALES

Most investors purchase securities first and sell them later. However, the process can be reversed: one can sell a security now and buy it back later. This is accomplished by borrowing certificates for use in

---

[1] To meet legal requirements, more than one type of account may have to be maintained and funds transferred between accounts from time to time to allow the maximum possible amount of margin loans.

the initial trade, then repaying the loan with certificates obtained in the later trade.

Any order for a *short sale* must be identified as such. The Securities and Exchange Commission has ruled that short sales may not be made when the market for the security is falling, on the assumption that the short-seller could exacerbate the situation, cause a panic, and profit therefrom—an assumption inappropriate for an efficient market with astute, alert traders. The precise rule is that a short sale must be made on an *up-tick* (for a price higher than that of the previous trade) or on a *zero-plus tick* (for a price equal to that of the previous trade but higher than that of the last trade at a different price).

At the end of the day on which a short sale is made, the seller's broker must borrow securities for delivery to the purchaser, unless the short-seller has already purchased them. Borrowed securities may come from the brokerage firm's own inventory or from that of another firm, but they are more likely to be securities held in street name for an investor with a margin account. Both the borrower and the lender have the option to terminate the agreement at any time—that is, the lender may call for securities or the borrower may return them.

To protect the security lender against default, the borrower (short-seller) must deposit cash equal to the value of the securities involved. Initially, the proceeds from the short sale must be deposited with the security lender. When the market value rises, more cash must be deposited; when it falls, some of the deposit may be removed—that is, the deposit is *marked to market*. When the securities are returned, the deposit is refunded.

The possible loss from a normal (*long*) position in a security is limited: only the original investment can be lost. But the potential loss from a short sale is unlimited, since a security's price can rise to several times its initial amount. Moreover, an increase in price can jeopardize the position of the lender of the security, since it may make it impossible for the borrower (short-seller) to buy the certificates required to pay back the loan. For this reason short-sellers are required to maintain a certain amount of equity in their accounts to serve as an additional cushion against adverse price changes.

Judicious use of accounts makes it possible to apply formula (2-1) to both long and short positions. For example, consider the following account:

Securities held long: market value = $100,000	Short positions: market value = $40,000
Cash deposited with security lenders = $40,000	Loan from broker = $30,000 Equity = $70,000

The current percentage margin is $70,000/(\$100,000 + \$40,000)$, or 50%. Adverse moves greater than this amount in the positions (i.e., price declines for long positions, price increases for short positions) would wipe out the equity and place in jeopardy the loan from the broker or the loaned securities or both. For this reason all the rules concerning initial and maintenance margins, restricted accounts, and so on apply when short positions are maintained; the current market value of such positions is simply added to that of the long positions when computing the account's current margin.

A short sale neither generates cash (since the proceeds must be deposited with the security lender) nor requires it. Subsequent price increases do require cash, while declines generate cash. Although margin is required for a short sale, this means only that assets must be kept in the account to guard against default on the loan of the borrowed securities.

At times securities may be lent only on the payment of a premium; at other times lenders may pay interest on the money deposited with them. Usually, however, securities are loaned "flat"—the lending broker keeps the deposits and enjoys the use of the money, and neither the short-seller nor the investor who owns the securities (in principle, but not in fact) receives any direct compensation.

During the period in which a security is "on loan," the borrower must pay to the lender amounts equal to the values of all the dividends or interest payments that would otherwise have been received. Such payments are not returned when the short position is *covered* (i.e., when securities are purchased and the loan repaid).

CONTINUOUS VERSUS CALL MARKETS

No market is ever truly continuous, for trades occur at discrete times. However, some markets are explicitly organized to group trades at specific times. In such *call markets*, when a security is called, all who wish to buy and sell are brought together. Enough time is allowed to elapse between calls (e.g., an hour or more) to accumulate a substantial number of offers to buy and sell. In some call markets there is an explicit *auction* in which prices are called out until the quantity demanded is as close as possible to the quantity supplied (this procedure is used by the Paris Bourse for major stocks). In other call markets, orders are left with a clerk between calls and "crossed" at a price that allows the maximum number to be executed (this procedure is used for some stocks by the Paris Bourse and the Tokyo Stock Exchange).

In a *continuous market* trades may occur at any time. While such a market could function with only investors and brokers, it would not be very effective, for an individual who wished to consummate a sale or purchase very quickly would either have to spend a great deal of money searching for a good offer or run the risk of accepting a poor one. Since orders from investors arrive more or less randomly, prices in such a market would vary considerably, depending on transitory relationships between desired purchases and sales. Such a situation could be exploited by anyone willing to take temporary positions in securities, ironing out transitory variations in demand and supply and making a profit thereby. This is the role of a *dealer* or *market-maker*, whether officially identified as such or not. Only greed and avarice are required to attract such people, but in the pursuit of personal gain they generally reduce fluctuations in price unrelated to changes in value, thereby providing liquidity for investors.

In some markets dealers compete with each other in order to offer the best possible terms for a given security. The London Stock Exchange is, in essence, a physical location where dealers ("jobbers") take orders from brokers. In the over-the-counter market in the United States, dealers' bid and ask prices are communicated to brokers via a computer network. On the floor of the Chicago Board of Trade dealers in commodities mingle with brokers in the "pits."

The New York Stock Exchange, to facilitate a continuous market, assigns *specialists* to stocks. The specialist is allowed to deal for his or her own account, but only if no better offer is forthcoming from "the floor"—that is, from brokers acting for their customers or themselves. The specialist is allowed to make a profit but is also charged with maintaining a "fair and orderly market"—a requirement both ill-defined and difficult, if not impossible, to enforce. In return, specialists are allowed to maintain books of unexecuted limit (and stop-loss) orders. Whenever possible, a specialist executes orders from the book, crossing them with orders from the floor, or simply trading directly, using his or her own account, receiving in return a commission for serving as a "broker's broker."

INFORMATION-MOTIVATED AND LIQUIDITY-MOTIVATED TRANSACTIONS

There are two major reasons for security transactions. An investor may believe that a security has become mispriced—that is, that its value is outside the current range between (1) the total *proceeds* from a sale and (2) the total *cost* of a purchase. One who feels this way believes that he or she has information not known to (or understood by) the market in general and may be termed an *information-motivated* trader. On the other hand, an investor may simply want to sell securities to buy a new car, buy some securities with recently inherited money, alter a portfolio to better conform to a recent change in job, or the like. Such a person may be termed *liquidity-motivated*: although feeling that value is also outside the proceeds/cost range, he or she does not presume that others in the market have evaluated the prospects for the security incorrectly.

Dealers can make money by trading with liquidity-motivated traders or with stupid information-motivated traders. But, on average, they can only lose money by trading with clever information-motivated traders. The larger a dealer's bid-ask spread, the less business he or she will do; but whatever the spread, when a clever information-motivated investor makes a trade, the dealer may expect to lose. In the absence of foolish investors, the very existence of a dealer market depends on investors' desires for liquidity. A dealer must select a bid-ask spread wide enough to limit the number of trades with customers possessing superior information, but narrow enough to attract an adequate number of liquidity-motivated transactions.

A dealer can take either a passive or an active role. For example, a bid-ask spread can be established and a tentative price set. As orders come in and are filled, the dealer's inventory (position) will vary and may even become negative when promises to deliver securities exceed promises to accept delivery. But any clear trend suggests that the price should be altered. In effect, a *passive dealer* lets the market indicate the appropriate price.

An *active dealer* tries to get as much information as possible and to alter bid and ask prices in advance to keep the flow of orders more in balance. The better a dealer's information, the smaller the bid-ask spread required to make a profit.

When there is competition among dealers, those who are not well informed either price themselves out of the market by requiring too high a bid-ask spread or go out of business after incurring heavy losses. In general, the interests of investors are best served by a market in which dealers with unlimited access to all sources of information compete with one another.

PRICES AS INFORMATION SOURCES

The usual description of a market assumes that every trader wishes to purchase or sell a known quantity at each possible price. All the traders come together, and in one way or another a price is found that clears the market—that is, makes the quantity demanded as close as possible to the quantity supplied.

This may or may not be an adequate description of the markets for consumer goods, but it is clearly inadequate when describing security markets. The value of any capital asset depends on future prospects that are almost always uncertain. Any information that bears on such prospects may lead to a revised estimate of value. The fact that a knowledgeable trader is willing to buy or sell some quantity of a security at a particular price is likely to be information of just this sort. Offers to trade may thus affect other offers. Prices may both clear markets and convey information.

The dual role of prices has a number of implications. For example, it behooves the liquidity-motivated trader to publicize his or her motives and thereby avoid an adverse effect on the market. Thus an institution purchasing securities for a fund intended to simply hold a representative cross section of securities should make it clear that it does not consider the securities underpriced. On the other hand, any firm trying to buy or sell a large number of shares that it considers mispriced should try to conceal either its motives, its identity, or both (and many do try). Such attempts may be ineffective, however, as those asked to take the other side of such trades try to find out exactly what is going on (and many succeed).

Since offers may affect other offers, the way in which a market functions can affect the prices at which trades are made. And different markets function in different ways. For example, the New York Stock Exchange specialist's "books" contain information on both the prices and the quantities specified in standing orders, but only the lowest ask price and the highest bid price and the quantities associated with each are revealed to the general market. In the over-the-counter market, dealers publicly announce bid and ask prices that are firm for small quantities, but they negotiate prices for larger quantities. Orders for some stocks on the Paris Bourse are placed in a book with both prices and quantities specified, while for other stocks the book contains only the prices of orders.

The extent to which standing orders are made public may thus affect the prices at which such orders are executed, the extent to which investors will place them with brokers, and the extent to which brokers will place them in a central "book" where they can be seen by others.

Some investors depend almost entirely on price for information about value. This raises the possibility that a clever trader could make money by placing orders to trigger foolish responses from such investors. While this may occur in isolated instances, it is limited by the presence of informed traders who use external information sources to assess value. Given a large enough number of people who study fundamental aspects, it is possible for most investors to assume that market price reflects value.

MAJOR MARKETS IN THE UNITED STATES

The New York Stock Exchange

Many individual investors maintain an account with a retail brokerage firm that is a member of the New York Stock Exchange, by far the most important stock exchange.

At the end of 1982, 1,499 stocks with a market value of $1.7 trillion were listed for trading on the New York Stock Exchange. In the course of that year 16.5 billion shares (worth $488.4 billion) changed hands on the Exchange. This compares with 4.2 billion shares traded on all other exchanges, and 8.4 billion shares traded over-the-counter using the NASDAQ system.[2] For the individual investor the New York Stock Exchange is the major market place for actively traded stocks.

The decision to list a company's stock on the Exchange is based on "(1) the degree of national interest in the company, (2) its relative position and stability in the industry, and (3) whether it is engaged in an expanding industry, with prospects of at least maintaining its relative position." The company must apply for listing and agree to provide certain information to the public. After listing, if trading interest in a security declines substantially, it may be *delisted* by the Exchange. Companies may apply for listing on more than one exchange, and under certain conditions an exchange may set up "unlimited trading privileges" for transactions in a stock already listed on another exchange.

The operation of the New York Stock Exchange is best described by example. Mr. A asks his broker for the current price of General Motors shares. The broker punches a few buttons on a televisionlike quotation machine and finds that the current bid and ask prices on the New York Stock Exchange are 61 and 61¼ and that the specialist in GM will buy at least 100 shares at 61 and sell at least 500 shares at 61¼ (either as dealer, for his own account, or as a broker, for an investor whose order is in the book). Moreover, the quotation machine indicates that the prices on the New York Stock Exchange are as favorable as any others available at present. Mr. A instructs his broker to "buy 100 at market." The broker transmits the order to his firm's New York headquarters, which communicates it to the "post" where General Motors is traded. Since the order is a small one, it will be "exposed" to the market via the Exchange's Designated Order Turnaround System (DOT).

The existence of a standing order to buy at 61 means that no one else is prepared to sell at that price; and the existence of a standing order to sell at 61¼ means that no higher price need be paid. This leaves only the gap between the two prices for possible negotiation. If Mr. A is lucky, another broker (for example, one with a market order to sell 100 shares for Ms. B) will "take" the order at a price "between the quotes" (here, at 61⅛). Information will be exchanged between the two brokers and the sale consummated.

If the gap between quoted bid and ask prices is wide enough, a little auction may even occur among brokers, with trades consummated at one or more prices between the specialist's quoted values.

---

[2] *The New York Stock Exchange Fact Book, 1983* and the *National Association of Securities Dealers 1982 Fact Book.*

What if no response had been forthcoming from the floor when Mr. A's order arrived? In such a case the specialist would "take the other side," selling 100 shares to Mr. A's broker. The actual seller might be the specialist or another investor, whose limit order is being executed by the specialist.

If the bid-ask spread on a stock is no larger than the standard unit in which prices are quoted (typically ⅛ of a point, or 12.5 cents), market orders are generally executed directly by the specialist.

If Mr. A places a limit order with his broker, the latter's representative will not even try to execute it if the stated price is outside the current bid-ask spread on the available markets. Instead, the order will likely be sent directly to the specialist who handles the stock at the NYSE, who will enter it in a "book" (probably computerized) for subsequent execution when possible. If there are several limit orders in the book at the same price, they are executed in order of arrival (i.e., first-in first-out).

It may not be possible to fill an entire order at a single price. Thus a broker with an order to buy 500 shares at market might obtain 300 shares at 61⅛ and have to pay 61¼ for the remaining 200. A limit order to buy 500 shares at 61⅛ or better might result in the purchase of 300 shares at 61⅛ and the entry of a limit order in the specialist's book for the other 200 shares. And so on.

Large orders (e.g., those for 1,000 shares or more) are typically handled by representatives on the floor of the Exchange, acting as agents for the brokerage firm, rather than indirectly, via the Designated Order Turnaround system.

Especially large orders (typically placed by institutional customers) are likely to be handled in the "upstairs dealer market." For example, the XYZ pension fund may wish to sell 20,000 shares of General Motors. It negotiates with major brokerage firms for the sale of the entire "block" at a fixed price (plus commission). The winning bidder buys all the shares for its own account, then proceeds to sell them in smaller units, as buyers are found.

Other Exchanges

Table 2-1 shows the total dollar value of stocks, options, rights and warrants traded on each of the active exchanges in the United States in 1981. Not surprisingly, the New York Stock Exchange dominates the list. Second in importance is the American Stock Exchange (AMEX), which lists shares of somewhat smaller companies of national interest (a few of which are also listed on the New York Stock Exchange). All the others (with the exception of the Chicago Board Options Exchange) are termed *regional exchanges,* since historically each served as the sole location for trading securities primarily of interest to investors in its region. However, the major regional exchanges now depend

Exchange	Volume ($ billions)
New York	416.1
American	40.4
Midwest	24.7
Chicago Board Options	22.4
Pacific Coast	13.3
Philadelphia	11.4
Boston	2.4
Cincinnati	2.0
Spokane	.014
Intermountain	.001

SOURCE: U.S. Securities and Exchange Commission,
Annual Report, 1982.

to a substantial extent on transactions in securities that are also listed on a national exchange.

A relative newcomer to the list is The Chicago Board of Options Exchange, which lists only stock options and dominates this portion of the market (accounting for approximately 54% of the volume in 1981).[3]

Other stock exchanges use procedures similar to those of the New York Stock Exchange. The roles of specialists and the extent of automation may differ, but the basic approach is the same.

Options exchanges and commodities exchanges utilize some procedures that differ significantly from those employed by stock exchanges. Commodities exchanges substitute daily price limits for the presence of a specialist with orders to maintain a "fair and orderly market." The Chicago Board Options Exchange separates the two functions of the specialist; a "board broker" is charged with the maintenance of the book of limit orders, with one or more registered "market-makers" assigned the role of dealer.

The Over-the-Counter Market

In the early days of the United States, banks acted as the primary dealers for bonds and stocks, and investors literally bought and sold securities "over the counter" there. Transactions are more impersonal

---

[3] U.S. Securities and Exchange Commission, *Annual Report, 1982*.

now, but the designation remains in use for transactions that are not consummated on an organized exchange. Most bonds are sold over-the-counter, as are mutual funds, many bank and finance stocks, and the securities of small (and some not-so-small) companies.

The over-the-counter market for stocks is highly automated. In 1971 the National Association of Securities Dealers (NASD), which serves as a "self-regulating" agency for its members, put into operation the NASD Automated Quotations System (NASDAQ). This nationwide communications network allows brokers to know virtually instantly the terms currently offered by all major dealers in securities covered by the system.

Dealers who subscribe to Level III of NASDAQ are given terminals with which to enter firm bid and ask prices for any stock for which they make a market. Such dealers must be prepared to execute trades for at least one "normal unit of trading" (usually 100 shares) at the prices quoted. As soon as a bid or ask price is entered for a security, it is placed in a central computer file and may be seen by other subscribers (including other dealers) on their own terminals. When new quotations are entered, they replace the dealer's former prices.

Most brokerage firms subscribe to Level II of NASDAQ for their trading rooms, obtaining terminals that can display the current quotations on any security in the system. All bid and ask quotations are displayed, with the dealer offering each quotation identified.

Level I of NASDAQ is used by individual account executives to get a feel for the market. It shows the highest bid and the lowest ask price for each security.

Stocks with larger trading volumes are classified as *National Market Issues*. Every transaction made by a dealer for such a stock is reported directly, providing up-to-date detailed trading information to NASDAQ users. For the less active issues, dealers report only total transactions at the close of each day.

NASDAQ is primarily a quotation system. Actual transactions are made via direct negotiation between broker and dealer. However, the system could easily be adapted to cross orders and thus provide "automatic execution."

To be included in NASDAQ, a security must have at least two registered market-makers and a minimum number of publicly held shares; moreover, the issuing firm must meet stated capital and asset requirements. At the end of 1982, 3,664 issues were included in the system.[4]

The NASDAQ system covers only a portion of the outstanding OTC stocks, and no bonds. Brokers with orders to buy or sell noncovered securities rely on quotation sheets and less formal communications networks to obtain "best execution" for their clients.

---

[4] *National Association of Securities Dealers 1982 Fact Book.*

The Third and Fourth Markets

Until the 1970s the New York Stock Exchange required its member firms to trade all NYSE-listed stocks at the Exchange and to charge fixed commissions. For large institutions this was both cumbersome and expensive. Typically, a brokerage firm with a large transaction to complete would serve as a *block positioner* (i.e., an "upstairs dealer"), seeking out institutions willing to take at least part of the other side of the trade but also prepared to take at least part for its own account. After both sides had been lined up, the block would be brought to the floor of the Exchange for formal execution, any public orders at the previously negotiated price would be taken, and the broker's buy and sell orders then crossed.

The requirement that NYSE member firms bring such blocks to the Exchange floor was at most a nuisance. But the required minimum commission rate was a serious problem, since it exceeded the marginal cost of arranging trades of such size. Brokerage firms that were not members of the Exchange faced no such restrictions and could thus compete effectively for trades in NYSE-listed stocks. Such transactions were said to take place in the *third market*.

Many institutions dispense with brokers and exchanges entirely for transactions in New York Stock Exchange-listed stocks and other securities. Trades of this type are sometimes said to take place in the *fourth market*. In the United States some of these transactions are facilitated by an automated computer/communications system called *Instinet*, which provides quotations and execution automatically.[5] A subscriber can enter a limit order in the computerized "book," where it can be seen by other subscribers who can, in turn, signal their desire to take it. Whenever two orders are crossed, the system automatically records the transaction and sets up the paperwork for its completion. Subscribers can also use the system to find likely partners for a trade, then conduct negotiations by telephone. A similar system, called *Ariel,* is used in the United Kingdom.

Some New York Stock Exchange-listed stocks are traded on other exchanges or through the NASDAQ system. However, most trades in such securities are at least formally made on the NYSE (over 78% in early 1982).[6]

THE CENTRAL MARKET

The *Securities Acts Amendments of 1975* mandated that the U.S. Securities and Exchange Commission move as rapidly as possible toward

---

[5] The use of an intermediary system makes it difficult to categorize such trades (perhaps they occur in a 3.5 market).

[6] *New York Stock Exchange Fact Book, 1983.*

the implementation of a truly nationwide competitive central securities market:

> The linking of all markets for qualified securities through communication and data processing facilities will foster efficiency, enhance competition, increase the information available to brokers, dealers, and investors, facilitate the offsetting of investors' orders, and contribute to best execution of such orders.[7]

Implementation of these objectives has proceeded in steps. In 1975 a *Consolidated Tape* began to report trades in New York and American Stock Exchange-listed stocks that took place on the two exchanges, on major regional exchanges, over-the-counter using the NASDAQ system, and in the fourth market using the Instinet system. Since 1976 this information has been used to produce the *composite stock price tables* published in the daily press.

Another step involves quotations. To obtain the best possible terms for a client, a broker must know the prices currently available on all major markets. To facilitate this, the Securities and Exchange Commission instructed stock exchanges to make their quotations available for use in a *Consolidated Quotations Service* (CQS). With the implementation of this system in 1978, bid and ask prices were made more accessible to those subscribing to quotation services. Increasingly, a broker is able to rely on electronics to determine the best available terms for a trade, thus avoiding the need for extensive "shopping around."

In 1978, the Intermarket Trading System (ITS) was inaugurated. This electronic communications network links seven exchanges (the NYSE, Amex, Boston, Cincinnati, Midwest, Pacific, and Philadelphia exchanges) and over-the-counter securities dealers, enabling brokers and dealers at various locations to interact with one another. In 1982, over 1,000 exchange-listed stocks were included on the system.

The final step in the process would be the establishment of a single centralized limit order book (CLOB), with associated procedures for linking markets electronically and the setting of rules concerning its use and disclosure. Other issues must be settled as well: should there be specialists, and if so, how should they operate? What requirements (if any) should be imposed on market-makers? Who should operate the central market system? And so on.

It is easy to envision a truly modern approach. For example, the centralized computer system might operate with a completely open book of orders. However, subscribers' computers could communicate with the central computer, interrogate it for information on recent trades in a stock and the current book, and automatically place, remove, or change orders based on such information. A subscribing firm could

---

[7] *Securities Acts Amendments of 1975,* section 11A.

program its computer system to maintain a private book, fill various types of orders (e.g., stop-loss) automatically, follow certain technical rules, alter its own limit orders based on changes in the market, and so on. Competition among brokerage firms would eventually weed out the bad ideas and institutionalize the good ones, but the central market's role would be limited to facilitating procedures of all types.

There are many long-entrenched and powerful institutions in the securities industry. The eventual nature of the central market will undoubtedly depend in part on the relative political power of the various vested interests. But the goals seem relatively clear, and on net, the changes are likely to benefit investors.

CLEARING PROCEDURES

Most securities are sold the "regular way," which requires delivery of certificates within five business days. On rare occasions a sale may be made as a "cash" transaction, requiring delivery the same day, or as a "seller's option," giving the seller the choice of any delivery day within a specified period (typically, no more than 60 days).

It would be extremely inefficient if every security transaction had to end with the physical transfer of certificates from the seller to the buyer. On a given day, a brokerage firm might sell 500 shares of American Telephone and Telegraph stock for Mr. A and buy 300 shares for Ms. B. The firm could deliver Mr. A's 500 shares to the buyer's broker and obtain Ms. B's 300 shares by accepting delivery from the seller's broker. But it would be much easier for the firm to transfer 300 of Mr. A's shares to Ms. B, send the other 200 to the buyer's broker, and instruct the seller's broker to deliver the 300 shares directly to the buyer's broker. This would be especially helpful if the firm's clients maintained their securities in street name, for the 300 shares kept within the firm would not have to be moved or have their ownership transferred on the books of the issuing corporation.

The process can be facilitated even more by a *clearing house*, the members of which are security brokerage firms, banks, and the like. Records of transactions made by members during a day are sent there. At the end of the day both sides of the trades are verified for consistency, then all transactions are netted out. Each member receives a list of the net amounts of securities to be delivered or received along with the net amount of money to be paid or collected. Every day each member settles once with the clearing house instead of many times with various other firms.

A centralized clearing house, operated by the National Securities Clearing Corporation, handles trades made on the New York and American stock exchanges and in the over-the-counter market. Some regional exchanges also maintain clearing houses. Not all exchange members join such organizations; some choose to use the services of other members. Some banks belong, in order to facilitate delivery of securities which serve as collateral for call loans and so on.

By holding securities in street name and using clearing houses, brokers can reduce the cost of transfer operations. But even more can be done: certificates can be *immobilized* almost completely. The *Depository Trust Company* (*DTC*) accomplishes this by maintaining computerized records of the securities "owned" by its member firms (brokers, banks, and so on). Members deposit certificates, which are credited to their accounts. The certificates are transferred to the DTC on the books of the issuing corporation and remain registered in its name unless a member subsequently withdraws them. Whenever possible, one member will "deliver" securities to another by initiating a simple bookkeeping entry in which one account is credited and the other debited for the shares involved. Dividends paid on securities held by DTC are simply credited to members' accounts based on their holdings and may be withdrawn in cash.

The Securities Acts Amendments of 1975 instruct the Securities and Exchange Commission to develop a central system of this sort to eliminate the movement of stock certificates and possibly eliminate stock certificates entirely. Eventually, at dividend time, corporations' computers may deal directly with other computers that are in touch with still other computers in banks, brokerage firms, and so on. Moreover, the central market system may be integrated with the central clearing system, so that agreement of two parties to the terms of a transaction will automatically bring about the transfer of ownership required to complete the trade.

INSURANCE

In the late 1960s many brokerage firms were confronted with an unexpectedly large volume of transactions and a lack of proven computerized systems able to handle the workload. This gave rise to back-office problems and resulted in a rash of "fails to deliver"—situations in which a seller's broker did not deliver certificates to a buyer's broker on or before the required settlement date.

Worse yet, several brokerage firms subsequently failed, and some of their clients discovered for the first time that certificates "in their accounts" were not necessarily physically available. Such events led to serious concern about the desirability of any procedure that kept certificates out of the hands of the investor. To avoid erosion of investor confidence, member firms of the New York Stock Exchange spent substantial sums to cover the losses of failed firms or to merge them into successful firms. But such remedies were only temporary; insurance provided a more permanent solution.

The Securities Investor Protection Act of 1970 established the *Securities Investor Protection Corporation* (SIPC), a quasi-governmental agency that insures the accounts of clients of all broker-dealers and members of exchanges registered with the Securities and Exchange Commission against loss due to the firms' failure. Each account is insured up to a stated amount ($500,000 per customer in 1983). The cost of the insurance is supposed to be borne by the covered brokers and dealers through premiums, but up to $1 billion may be borrowed from the U.S. Treasury.

A number of brokerage firms have gone farther, arranging for additional coverage from private insurance companies.

COMMISSIONS

In the 1770s people interested in buying and selling stocks and bonds met under a buttonwood tree at 68 Wall Street in New York City. In May 1792 a group of brokers pledged "not to buy or sell from this day for any person whatsoever, any kind of public stock at a less rate than one quarter per cent commission on the specie value, and that we will give preference to each other in our negotiations."[8] A visitor to the New York Stock Exchange in the early 1970s could see this "buttonwood agreement" publicly displayed. This was not surprising, since the Exchange is a lineal descendant of the group that met under the buttonwood tree. And until 1968 the Exchange required its member brokers to charge fixed minimum commissions for stocks, with no "rebates, returns, discounts or allowances in 'any shape or manner,' direct or indirect."[9] The terms had changed, but the principle established 180 years earlier remained in effect.

In the United States most cartels designed to limit competition by fixing prices are illegal. But this one was exempted from prosecution under the antitrust laws. Before 1934 the Exchange was, in essence, considered a private club for its members. This changed with passage of the *Securities and Exchange Act of 1934,* which required most exchanges to be registered with and controlled by the Securities and Exchange Commission (SEC). The Commission, in turn, encouraged "self-regulation" by the exchanges of most of their activities, including the setting of minimum commissions.

After repeated challenges, the system of fixed commissions was finally terminated by the Securities Acts Amendments of 1975. Since May 1, 1975 (known in the trade as "May day"), brokers have been free to set commissions at any desired rate or to negotiate with custom-

---

[8] Wilford J. Eiteman, Charles A. Dice, and David K. Eiteman, *The Stock Market* (New York: McGraw-Hill Book Company, 1969), p. 19.

[9] Eiteman, Dice, and Eiteman, *The Stock Market,* p. 138.

ers concerning the fees charged for particular trades. The former procedure is more commonly employed in "retail" trades executed for small investors, while the latter is used more often by institutional investors and others who engage in large trades.

In the era of fixed commissions only competition in terms of prices was completely restricted. Brokerage firms that belonged to the New York Stock Exchange competed with one another by offering a panoply of services to customers. Large institutions were provided with security analysis, performance measurement services, and the like in return for "soft dollars"—brokerage commissions designated as payment for services rendered. Some brokers would accept as little as $3 in commissions in lieu of $2 in cash; apparently, up to two-thirds of the fixed commission rate ($2 out of $3) on such large orders was pure (marginal) profit.

Experience after May day provided confirmation. Rates for large trades fell substantially. So did those charged for small trades by firms offering only "bare-bones" brokerage services. On the other hand, broad-line firms that provided extensive services to small investors for no additional fee continued to charge commissions similar to those specified in the earlier fixed schedules. In succeeding years, as costs have risen, charges for smaller transactions have increased, while those for large trades have not.

During the 1960s and 1970s a number of procedures were used to subvert the fixed commission rates: the third market prospered, regional exchanges invented ways to serve as conduits to return a portion of the fixed commissions to institutional investors, and so on.

No legal restriction gave the New York Stock Exchange its monopoly power in the first instance. Instead, the situation has been attributed to the natural monopoly arising from economies of scale in bringing many people together (either physically or via modern communication technology) to trade with each other. The potential profits from such a monopoly are, of course, limited by the advantages it confers. The increasing institutionalization of security holdings and progress in communications and computer technology have diminished the advantages associated with a centralized physical exchange. The removal of legal protection for this particular type of price-fixing may thus have only accelerated a trend already under way.

Increased competition among brokerage houses has resulted in a wide range of alternatives for investors. Following May day, some firms "unbundled"—pricing execution and other services separately; others "went discount"—dropping almost all ancillary services and cutting commissions accordingly. Still others "bundled" new services into comprehensive packages. Some of these approaches have not stood the test of time, but just as mail-order firms, discount houses, department stores, and expensive boutiques coexist in retail trade, many different combinations are viable in the brokerage industry.

Figure 2-1 shows typical commission rates charged by retail brokerage firms for small to medium-sized trades. These rates are representative of those charged by full-line retail brokers that provide offices with quotation boards, research reports, account executives available for advice and information, and the like. They also apply to trades

FIGURE 2-1
Typical Commission Rates for Selected Transactions; Dollar Commission as a Percentage of the Value of the Order

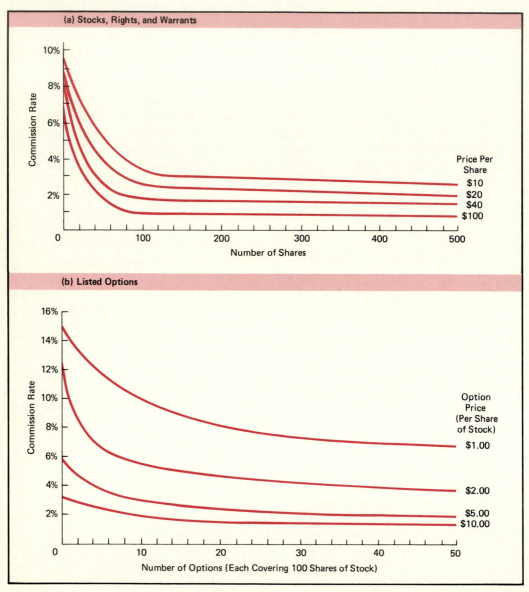

made by customers whose volume of business is small. Discount firms with little but execution capability typically charge 30% to 70% less.

As in any other competitive industry, it behooves the customer to decide what is worth paying for and then shop around to obtain the best possible price.

TRANSACTIONS COSTS

Commission costs are only a portion of the total cost associated with buying or selling a security. Consider a "round-trip" transaction in which a stock is purchased, then sold during a period in which no new information causes investors to collectively reassess the value of the stock (more concretely: the bid and ask prices quoted by dealers do not change). The stock will typically be purchased at the dealers' ask price and sold at the bid price, which is lower. The *bid-ask spread* thus constitutes a portion of the round-trip transactions costs.

How large is the spread between the bid and ask prices for a typical stock? According to one study: approximately 30 cents per share for the securities of large, actively traded companies. This amounts to less than 1% of the price per share for most stocks of this type—a reasonably small amount to pay for the ability to buy or sell in a hurry.

But not all securities enjoy this type of liquidity. Shares of smaller firms tend to sell at lower prices but at similar bid-ask spreads. As a result, the *percentage* transactions cost is considerably larger. This is shown in Table 2-2(a). Stocks were assigned to *capitalization sectors*, based on the market value of outstanding equity. If the total market value of the shares of a company was less than $10 million, it was considered to be in sector 1; if the market value was greater than $1.5 billion, the company was included in sector 9; and so on. As the table shows, the higher the capitalization, the greater was the average price per share. Note also that the average spread in *dollars* was actually higher for the smallest capitalization stocks than for the largest. Most importantly, the *ratio* of the average spread to the average price was smaller, the higher the capitalization, falling from 6.55% for the smallest sector to .52% for the largest.

Brokerage commissions and bid/ask spreads represent transactions costs for small orders (typically 100 shares). For larger orders, one must consider the possibility of a *price impact*. The larger the order, the more likely that price will be higher (for a purchase) or lower (for a sale). The more rapidly the order is to be completed, and the more knowledgeable the individual or organization placing the order, the greater the price concession required by the dealer.

Table 2-2(b) provides estimates of average costs for transactions in the "upstairs dealer" market. All three sources of costs are included:

TABLE 2-2(a)
Common Stock Bid/Ask Spreads: Small Orders

	CAPITALIZATION						
Sector	From ($ millions)	To ($ millions)	Number of Issues	Percent of U.S. Market	Average Price ($)	Average Spread ($)	Spread Price
1 (small)	0	10	1,009	.36	4.58	.30	6.55%
2	10	25	754	.89	10.30	.42	4.07%
3	25	50	613	1.59	15.16	.46	3.03%
4	50	75	362	1.60	18.27	.34	1.86%
5	75	100	202	1.27	21.85	.32	1.46%
6	100	500	956	15.65	28.31	.32	1.13%
7	500	1,000	238	12.29	35.43	.27	.76%
8	1,000	1,500	102	8.87	44.34	.29	.65%
9 (large)	1,500	99,999	180	57.48	52.40	.27	.52%

Round-Trip Transactions Costs, Common Stock

	CAPITALIZATION								
	Dollar Value of Block ($ thousands)								
Sector	5	25	250	500	1,000	2,500	5,000	10,000	20,000
1 (small)	17.3	27.3	43.8						
2	8.9	12.0	23.8	33.4					
3	5.0	7.6	18.8	25.9	30.0				
4	4.3	5.8	9.6	16.9	25.4	31.5			
5	2.8	3.9	5.9	8.1	11.5	15.7	25.7		
6	1.8	2.1	3.2	4.4	5.6	7.9	11.0	16.2	
7	1.9	2.0	3.1	4.0	5.6	7.7	10.4	14.3	20.0
8	1.9	1.9	2.7	3.3	4.6	6.2	8.9	13.6	18.1
9 (large)	1.1	1.2	1.3	1.7	2.1	2.8	4.1	5.9	8.0

SOURCE: Thomas F. Loeb, "Trading Cost: The Critical Link Between Investment Information and Results," *Financial Analysts Journal*, 39, no. 3 (May/June 1983), 39–44.

bid/ask spreads, brokerage commissions, and price concessions. The figures refer to the total cost for a "round trip"—a purchase followed by a sale.

Figure 2-2(a) plots the costs for transactions in blocks of $25,000 each. Values range from over 27% (for small-capitalization stocks) to 1.2% (for large capitalization stocks). Figure 2-2(b) shows the relationship between order size and transaction cost for each of the three largest-capitalization sectors. As indicated, the impact of a very large order on price can be substantial, and the impact is greater, the smaller the capitalization of the stock.

FIGURE 2-2
Round-Trip Transactions Costs

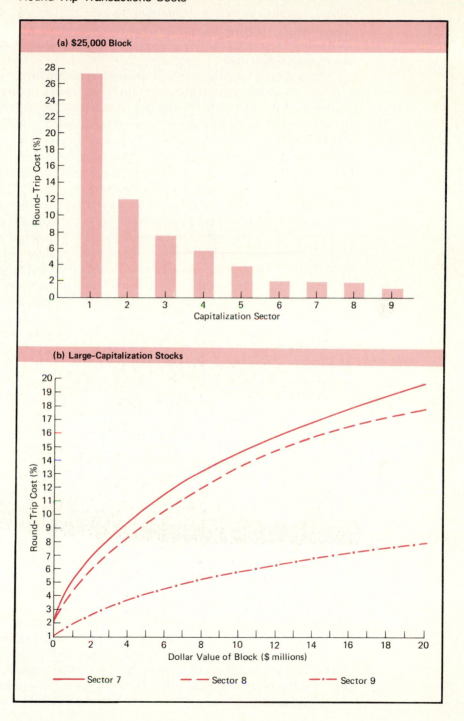

Investment Banking

New securities are said to be sold in the *primary market*. Some issuers deal directly with purchasers, but many rely on *investment bankers*, who serve as intermediaries between issuers and the ultimate purchasers of their securities.

Investment banking services are performed by brokers and dealers and, for tax-exempt general obligation bond issues, by banks. In some instances only a few large institutional investors are solicited, and the entire issue is sold to one or more of them. Such *private placements* are frequently used for bond issues. As long as relatively few potential buyers are contacted (e.g., less than 25), requirements for detailed disclosure, public notice, and so on may be waived, considerably reducing the cost of floating an issue. Such placements are often announced after the fact, via advertisements in the financial press.

When public sale is contemplated, much more must be done. Many firms may serve as intermediaries in the process. One, acting as the "lead" investment banker, will put together a *purchase group* or *syndicate* and a *selling group*. The former includes firms that purchase the securities from the issuing corporation and *underwrite* the offering; the latter includes firms that contact potential buyers and do the actual selling, usually on a commission basis.

The process begins with discussions between the issuing corporation and one or more investment bankers. Some issuers utilize *competitive bidding*, then select the investment banker offering the best overall terms. This procedure is used for many government bond issues and is required by law for securities issued by firms in certain regulated industries. However, many corporations maintain a continuing relationship with a single investment banker and *negotiate* the terms of each new offering with that firm. The investment banker is likely to be heavily involved in the planning of an offering, the terms involved, the amount to be offered, and so on, serving, in effect, as a financial consultant to the corporation.

Once the basic characteristics of an offering have been established, a *registration statement* is filed with the Securities and Exchange Commission, and a preliminary prospectus disclosing material relevant to the prospective buyer is issued. The actual price of the security is not included in the preliminary prospectus, and no final sales may be made until the registration becomes *effective* and a *final prospectus* issued, indicating the "offer" price at which the stock will be sold. The final prospectus may be issued as soon as, in the opinion of the Securities and Exchange Commission, there has been adequate disclosure and a reasonable waiting period has passed (usually, 20 days). The Commission, however, does not take a position regarding the investment merits of an offering or the reasonableness of the price.

A security issue may be completely underwritten by an investment banker and the other members of the purchasing group. If it is, the issuing corporation receives the public offering price less a stated percentage spread (although underwriters will occasionally be compensated with shares, warrants, and so on). The underwriters, in turn, sell the securities at the public offering price or less and may take some of the securities themselves. Underwriters who provide this sort of *firm commitment* bear all the risk, once the price and underwriting spread have been determined.

Not all agreements are of this type. In the case of a rights offering an underwriter may agree to purchase at a fixed price all securities not taken by current stockholders; this is termed a *standby agreement*. In the case of a nonrights offering, members of an investment banking group may serve as agents instead of dealers, agreeing only to handle an offering on a *best-efforts* basis.

During the period when new securities remain unsold, the investment banker is allowed to attempt to "stabilize" the price of the security in the secondary market by standing ready to make purchases at or above the offering price. Such *pegging* may continue for up to ten days after the official offering date. There is a limit to the amount that can be purchased in this manner, usually stated in the agreement under which the underwriting syndicate is formed, since the members typically share the cost of such transactions. If there is to be any pegging, a statement to that effect must be included in the prospectus.

In any security transaction there may be explicit and implicit costs. In a primary distribution the explicit cost is the underwriting spread, and the implicit cost is any difference between the public offering price and the price that might have been obtained otherwise. The spread provides compensation for both marketing services and risk-bearing. The lower the public offering price, the smaller the risk that the issue will not be sold quickly at that price. If an issue is substantially underpriced, the investment banking syndicate can be assured that the securities will sell rapidly, requiring little or no support in the secondary market. Since many corporations deal with only one investment banker, and since the larger investment banking firms rely on each other for inclusion in syndicates, it has been alleged that issuers pay too much in spreads, given the prices at which their securities are offered. In other words, the returns to underwriting are asserted to be overly large relative to the risks involved, owing to ignorance on the part of issuers or the existence of an informal cartel among investment bankers.

Whether or not this is the case, a number of new issues do appear to have been underpriced. Figure 2-3 shows the *abnormal returns* for a group of common stock new issues. For each of the first 60 months after the initial offering (horizontal axis) the return over and above that of stocks of equal risk is shown (vertical axis). The leftmost point indicates the abnormal return obtained by an investor who purchased

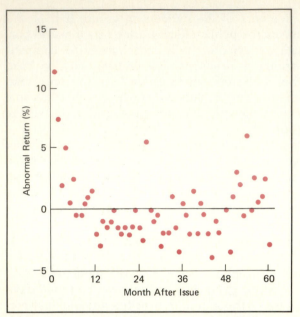

FIGURE 2-3
Abnormal Returns: 112 Common Stock
New Issues, 1960-1969

SOURCE: Roger G. Ibbotson, "Price Performance of Common Stock New Issues," *Journal of Financial Economics*, *2*, no. 3 (September 1975), 252. By permission of North-Holland Publishing Co., Amsterdam.

such stock at its offering price and sold it for the bid price at the end of the month during which it was offered. The amount was substantial: 11.4% in a month or less (and significantly different from zero in a statistical sense). The remaining points show the returns that could have been obtained by an investor who was able to purchase the security at the bid price at the end of the next month. Some of these were positive, but only one was significantly different from zero. Moreover, none was large enough to overcome the transactions costs associated with in-and-out trades on the secondary market—that is, the fact that the ask prices, at which sales would be made, were 6% to 7% greater than the bid prices.

On average, new issues of "unseasoned" securities appear to have been underpriced. Investors able to purchase a cross section of such shares at their offering prices might thus expect better performance than those holding other securities of equal risk. It is not surprising that such offerings are often rationed by the members of the selling group to "favored" customers. It is "not uncommon for underwriters to receive, prior to the effective date, public 'indication of interest' for five times the number of shares available."[10] Unfavored customers are presumably allowed to buy only the new issues that are not substan-

---

[10] Securities and Exchange Commission, *Report of Special Study on Security Markets*, 1973.

tially underpriced. And since costs may be incurred in becoming a "favored" customer, it is not clear that even such an investor obtains abnormally large returns overall.

While the return obtained by the purchaser of a new issue may be substantial on average, the amount may be very good or very bad in any particular instance, as Figure 2-4 shows. While the odds may be in the purchaser's favor, a single investment of this type is far from a sure bet.

A relatively recent change in regulations has made it possible for large corporations to foster greater competition among underwriters. Starting in 1982, the Securities and Exchange Commission allowed firms to register securities in advance of issuance under Rule 415. With such "shelf registration" (in which the firm registers securities, then places them on a shelf) securities may be sold up to a year later. With securities "on the shelf," a corporation can require investment bankers to bid competitively, simply refusing to sell shares if desirable bids are not forthcoming.

FIGURE 2-4

Abnormal Return from Offering Price to Bid Price at the End of the Offering Month, 112 Common Stock New Issues, 1960-1969

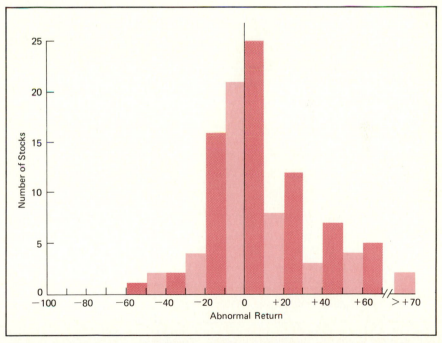

SOURCE: Roger G. Ibbotson, "Price Performance of Common Stock New Issues," *Journal of Financial Economics*, *2*, no. 3 (September 1975), 235-72. By permission of North-Holland Publishing Co., Amsterdam.

BLOCK SALES

An individual or institution wishing to sell a large block of stock can do so in either of two ways. A brokerage firm may be asked to find one or more buyers and perhaps to take some of the position itself, or the stock may be sold through a *secondary distribution*. An investment banking group buys the block from the seller and then offers the shares publicly at a stated price; in a typical case the shares are first offered after normal trading hours at the day's closing price. The buyer of shares in a secondary distribution usually pays no commission, and the original seller receives the total proceeds less an underwriting spread.

The Securities and Exchange Commission requires that a secondary distribution be registered, with public announcement and disclosure and a 20-day waiting period, if the seller has a "control relationship" with the firm that issued the securities. Otherwise the distribution may be unregistered.

The impact of the sale of a large block on a stock's price provides information on the resiliency of the capital market. As might be expected, the information that someone is selling tends to lower the price. But one would not expect a block sale to depress price so much that it later bounces back significantly, as the market "absorbs" the shares.

Figure 2-5 provides confirmation for this hypothesis. It shows the average price adjusted for market changes for 345 secondary distributions, with the price 25 days prior to the distribution taken as 1.0. On average, a secondary distribution leads to 2% to 3% once-and-for-all reduction in price. This is undoubtedly due to the information content of the fact that someone has decided to sell. Additional analysis of

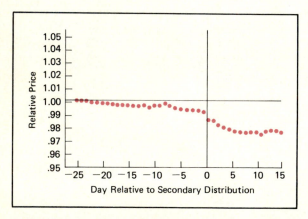

FIGURE 2-5
Prices for 345 Secondary Distributions, 1961-1965

SOURCE: Myron S. Scholes, "The Market for Securities: Substitution versus Price Pressure and the Effects of Information on Share Prices." *The Journal of Business*, 45, no. 2 (April 1972). 179-211. © 1972 by the University of Chicago. All Rights Reserved.

Securities and Markets

TABLE 2-3
Average Price Decline versus Type of Seller: 345 Secondary Distributions,
1961-1965

Type of Seller	Percentage Change in Adjusted Price from Ten Days before the Distribution to Ten Days after the Distribution
Corporations and officers	2.9
Investment companies and mutual funds	2.5
Individuals	1.1
Estates	.7
Banks and insurance companies	.3

SOURCE: Myron S. Scholes, "The Market for Securities: Substitution versus Price Pressure and the Effects of Information on Share Prices," *The Journal of Business,* 45, no. 2 (April 1972), 179-211. © 1972 by the University of Chicago. All Rights Reserved.

these results supports the assertion. The size of the decline was related to the identity of the seller—being the greatest for sellers likely to be information-motivated and smallest for sellers likely to be liquidity-motivated, as shown in Table 2-3.

A similar picture was obtained when blocks of stock traded on the New York Stock Exchange were examined. To select transactions likely to have been initiated by a seller, blocks sold on a "minus tick"— at a price below that of the previous trade—were used. Figure 2-6 shows the results. The vertical axis plots the average price, adjusted for market moves, relative to that 20 days before the block trade. There appears to be a once-and-for-all decline of about 2% due to the information content of the knowledge that someone wishes to sell a large block.

Examination of the price behavior during the day on which a block is sold does reveal a small price-pressure effect, however. As Figure 2-7 shows, a block sale appears to depress price temporarily by an average amount of about .7%.

REGULATION OF SECURITY MARKETS

Directly or indirectly, security markets in the United States are regulated under both federal and state laws.

The *Securities Act of 1933* was the first major legislation at the federal level. Sometimes called the "truth in securities" law, it requires registration of new issues and disclosure of relevant information by the issuer and prohibits misrepresentation and fraud in security sales.

The *Securities Exchange Act of 1934* extended the principles of

FIGURE 2-6
Prices for 1,121 Large-Block Trades on Minus Ticks, Traded on the New York Stock Exchange, 1968-1969

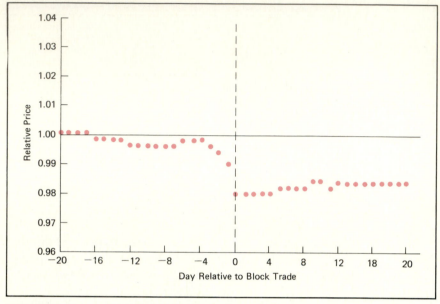

SOURCE: Alan Kraus and Hans Stoll, "Price Impacts of Block Trading on the New York Stock Exchange," *The Journal of Finance*, XXVII, no. 3 (June 1972), 580.

the earlier act to cover secondary markets and required national exchanges and brokers and dealers to be registered.

Since 1934, both acts (and subsequent amendments to them) have been administered by the *Securities and Exchange Commission (SEC)*, a quasi-judicial agency of the U.S. government. It is run by five Commissioners appointed by the President and confirmed by the Senate; each Commissioner serves for a five-year term. The Commission is aided by a large permanent staff of lawyers, accountants, economists, and others.

The SEC is the prime administrative agency for a number of other pieces of federal legislation. The *Public Utility Holding Company Act of 1935* brought such corporations under the Commission's jurisdiction. The *Bankruptcy Act of 1938* specified that the Commission should advise the court in any reorganization of a firm under Chapter X whenever there is substantial public interest in the firm's securities. The *Trust Indenture Act of 1939* gave the Commission power to insure that bond indenture trustees were free from conflict of interest. The *Investment Company Act of 1940* extended disclosure and registration requirements to investment companies. The *Investment Advisers Act of 1940* required the registration of most advisers and the disclosure of any

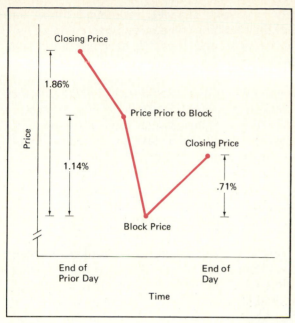

SOURCE: Alan Kraus and Hans Stoll, "Price Impacts of Block Trading on the New York Stock Exchange," *The Journal of Finance*, XXVII, no. 3 (June 1972), 575.

FIGURE 2-7
Within-Day Prices for 1,121 Large Block Trades on Minus Ticks, Traded on the New York Stock Exchange, 1968-1969

potential conflicts of interest. The *Securities Investor Protection Act of 1970* provided for the coverage of losses in the event of failure of a brokerage firm.

Federal securities legislation relies heavily on the principle of *self-regulation*. The SEC has delegated to exchanges its power to control trading practices for listed securities, while retaining, however, the power to alter or supplement any resulting rules or regulations. The Commission's power to control trading in over-the-counter securities has been delegated similarly to the *National Association of Securities Dealers* (NASD), a private association of brokers and dealers in OTC securities. In practice the SEC staff usually discusses proposed changes with both the NASD and the exchanges in advance, and few rules are formally altered or rejected by the Commission.

An important piece of legislation that makes security markets in the United States different from those in many other countries is the (Glass-Steagall) *Banking Act of 1933*, which separated commercial banking from investment banking. Because of this act, banks have not played as prominent a role in security markets in the United States as elsewhere. Recently, however, a major move has begun toward greater competition among financial institutions. Two key pieces of legislation were the *Depository Institutions Deregulation and Monetary Control Act* of 1980 and the *Depository Institution Act* of 1982. Many

Securities and Markets

banks now offer security brokerage services, retirement funds, and the like via subsidiaries of their holding companies. Long-standing limitations on rates paid on deposits and checking accounts have been removed, and so on. The line between commercial banking and investment activity is becoming more blurred every day.

Initially, security regulation in the United States was the province of state governments. Beginning in 1911, state *blue sky laws* were passed to prevent "speculative schemes which have no more basis than so many feet of blue sky."[11] While such statutes vary substantially from state to state, most of them outlaw fraud in security sales and require registration of brokers and dealers (and, in some cases, investment advisers) and of nonexempt securities. Some order has been brought by the passage in many states of all or part of the *Uniform Securities Acts* proposed by the National Conference of Commissions on Uniform State Laws in 1956.

Securities traded in interstate commerce, and brokers, dealers, and exchanges trading in interstate commerce, fall under the provisions of federal legislation (although some have been explicitly exempted under its terms). A considerable domain still comes under the exclusive jurisdiction of the states. Moreover, federal legislation only supplements state legislation, it does not supplant it. Some argue that the investor is overprotected as a result, while others suggest that regulatory agencies in general, and especially those that rely on "self-regulation" by powerful industry organizations, in fact protect the members of the regulated industry against competition, thereby damaging the interests of their customers, rather than promoting them. Both positions undoubtedly contain elements of truth.

Problems

1. New York Stock Exchange specialists are expected to make trades to maintain a "fair and orderly market." This is sometimes taken to mean that they should trade for their own accounts as required to avoid sudden and substantial price changes. Under what conditions would this be desirable? Under what conditions would it be profitable for the specialist?

2. What dangers are associated with placing a market order? A limit order?

3. Ted Turner wants to buy 100 shares of Silicon Valley Products, which is currently selling for $31 per share. Assume that initial margin requirements permit him to borrow 40% of the current stock price, and maintenance margin regulations require him to have a 25% equity position in the account at all times. If he borrows

---

[11] *Hall* v. *Geiger-Jones Co.*, 242 U.S. 539 (1917).

initially as much as possible in buying the 100 shares, at what price would he be subject to a margin call?

4. Some time after Ted Turner bought Silicon Valley Products, Sally Stanford sold 100 shares short at $31 per share. Initial margin on short sales was then 50%, and maintenance margin regulations required that she have an equity position equal to 40% of the value of the shorted stock. If she put up as little cash as possible at the time she sold SVP short, at what price would she be subject to a margin call?

5. What is the justification for the rule that short sales should not be made in falling markets? What is the counterargument?

6. As a practical matter, who gets the proceeds from a short sale? What are the costs of such a sale to the short-seller?

7. Commissions on large trades are typically a smaller percentage of the value of the trade than are commissions on small trades. Is this discriminatory?

8. There is some evidence that stocks of companies with small amounts of stock (measured by market value) outstanding "do better" than other stocks, taking such things as differences in risk into account. If this is so, should one hold only small-capitalization stocks? Could this situation prevail in an efficient market of sophisticated investors?

3

Investment Value and Market Price

INVESTMENT VALUE: AN OVERVIEW

Payments provided by securities may differ in both timing and riskiness. Thus a security analyst must estimate *when* and *under what conditions* payments will be received (and, of course, the magnitude of such payments). This typically requires detailed analysis of the company involved, the industry or industries in which the company operates, and the economy as a whole. Once such estimates have been made, the overall value of the security must be determined. This generally requires conversion of *uncertain future* values to equivalent *certain present* values. The current prices of other securities can usually be utilized in this process. If it is possible to obtain a similar set of prospects in some other way, the going market price of doing so provides a benchmark for the investment value of the security being analyzed, since one would not want to pay more than this for the security nor sell it for less. In some cases, however, equivalent alternatives may not exist, or the mere act of buying or selling the security in question in the quantities being considered might substantially affect the price. Under these conditions the preferences of the investor may have to be utilized explicitly in the process of estimating the security's investment value.

The next few chapters discuss in detail the manner in which estimated future prospects can be used to determine investment value. Methods for estimating prospects and finding equivalent alternatives will be discussed in later chapters, after the characteristics of relevant investment media have been introduced. We thus deal first with the general principles of investment value, leaving procedures designed for specific types of securities for later.

Although there are almost 900 million shares of American Telephone and Telegraph common stock outstanding, on an average day only 1 million shares will be traded. What determines the prices at which such trades take place? A simple (and correct) answer is: demand and supply. A more fundamental (and also correct) answer is: investors' estimates of A.T.&T.'s future prospects, for such estimates greatly influence demand and supply. Before dealing with such influences, it is useful to examine the role of demand and supply in price determination.

As we have seen, securities are traded by many people in many different ways. While the forces that determine price are similar in all markets, they are slightly more obvious in markets using periodic "calls"; one such is the Paris Bourse (stock exchange).

At a designated time, all brokers holding orders to buy or sell a given stock for customers gather at a specified location on the floor of the exchange. Some of the orders are "market" orders. For example, Mr. Ricard may have instructed his broker to buy 100 shares of Michelin at the lowest possible price, whatever it might be. His demand to buy shares at the time is shown by the solid line in Figure 3-1(a): he wishes to buy 100 shares no matter what the price. While this captures the contractual nature of a market buy order, Mr. Ricard undoubtedly has a good idea that the price of Michelin will be near its previous day's value, say 950 francs per share. His true demand curve might be more like the dashed line in the figure, indicating his desire to buy more shares, the lower the price. But to simplify his and his broker's tasks, he has guessed that the price will be in the range in which he would choose to buy 100 shares.

Other customers may place limit orders. Thus Mr. Dufour may have instructed his broker to buy 200 shares at the lowest possible price if and only if that price is below 940 francs per share. His demand to buy shares is plotted in Figure 3-1(b).

Brokers will also hold market and limit orders to sell shares of Michelin. The solid vertical line in Figure 3-1(c) plots the supply curve for a customer who has placed a market order for 100 shares—that is, asked her broker to sell 100 of her shares at the highest possible price. As with market buy orders, customers generally place such orders on the supposition that the actual price will be in the range in which their true desire is to sell the stated number of shares. Thus the customer's actual supply curve might appear more like the dashed line in Figure 3-1(c), indicating her willingness to sell more shares, the higher the price. Figure 3-1(d) plots the supply curve for a customer who has placed a limit order to sell 300 shares at the highest possible price, but only if the price exceeds 960 francs per share.

Some customers may give their broker two or more orders for the same security. Thus Madame Point may wish to buy 100 shares

FIGURE 3-1
Individuals' Demand-to-Buy and Supply-to-Sell Curves

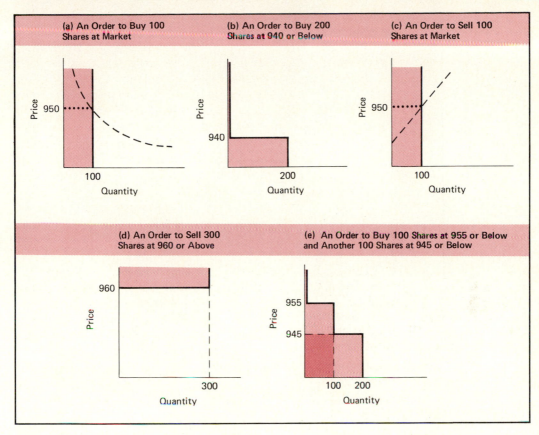

at a price of 955 and 200 shares if the price falls below 945. To do this, she places a limit order for 100 shares at 955 and a second limit order for 100 shares at 945. Her total demand to buy shares is plotted in Figure 3-1(e).

If one could look at all the brokers' books and summarize all the orders to buy (both market and limit orders), it would be possible to determine how many shares would be bought at every possible price. The resulting *demand-to-buy* curve would have an appearance like that of Figure 3-2(a): at lower prices, more shares would be demanded. Similarly, all the orders to sell (both market and limit) could be used to determine how many shares would be sold at every possible price. The resulting *supply-to-sell* curve would have an appearance like that of Figure 3-2(b): at higher prices, more shares would be supplied.

The demand and supply curves are both shown in Figure 3-2(c).

FIGURE 3-2
Aggregate Demand-to-Buy and Supply-to-Sell Curves

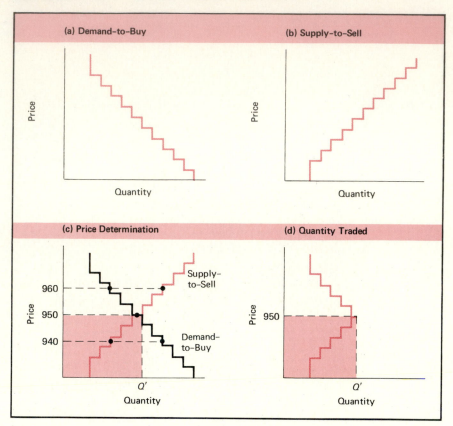

Generally, no one will have enough information to draw the actual curves. But this in no way diminishes their usefulness as representations of the underlying forces acting to determine price.

What actually happens when all the brokers gather together with their order books in hand? A clerk of the exchange "calls out" a price—for example, 940 francs per share. Brokers proceed to try to complete transactions with one another. Those with orders to buy at that price signify the number of shares they wish to buy. Those with orders to sell do likewise. Some deals will be made, but as Figure 3-2(c) shows, more shares will be demanded at 940 than will be supplied. When trading dies down, a number of brokers will be calling "buy" and none will stand ready to sell to them. The price was too low.

The clerk, seeing this, will cry out a different price, say 960. The brokers then consult their order books and signify the extent to which they are willing to buy or sell shares at this price. In this case, as the figure shows, when trading dies down, there will be a number of brokers calling "sell" and none will stand ready to buy from them. The price was too high.

Undaunted, the clerk will try again. And again, if necessary. Only when there are relatively few unsatisfied brokers will the price be declared final. As Figure 3-2(c) shows, 950 is such a price. At 950, customers collectively wish to sell Q' shares. Quantity demanded equals quantity supplied. The price was "just right."

Another way to view this process focuses on the quantity actually traded. This will be the *smaller* of (1) the quantity people are willing to buy and (2) the quantity others are willing to sell. This is shown in Figure 3-2(d). At a price of 950 the quantity traded is maximized. The procedure used to determine the price thus maximizes trading and equates the quantity demanded with the quantity supplied.

Trading procedures employed in security markets vary from auction markets to dealer markets and from periodic to almost continuous trading. But the similarities are more important than the differences. In the United States, for example, specialists at the New York Stock Exchange and dealers in the over-the-counter market provide some of the functions of the clerk at the Paris Bourse, and trades can take place at any time. But the basic principles of price determination still operate. In general, market price equates quantity demanded with quantity supplied.

THE DEMAND TO HOLD SECURITIES

While brokers' order books reflect some customers' attitudes at a particular time, not all relevant information is contained there. For example, many holders of a security who would be delighted to sell it at prices substantially higher than those obtained in recent trades simply do not bother placing corresponding limit orders with their brokers, since they think it unlikely that such orders would be executed under current conditions. Thus order books may indicate a supply to sell shares such as that shown by the solid curve in Figure 3-3(a), while the full situation is that shown by the dashed curve. At prices substantially higher than the current range (around P in the figure), more sell orders would be placed. And, as indicated earlier, if sellers thought price might fall substantially below P, some of the current market orders might be withdrawn.

A similar argument applies to the demand to buy shares. Many who would be willing to buy shares under current conditions at substantially lower prices than experienced in recent trades do not bother to place corresponding limit orders. And if substantially higher prices were likely, some customers would withdraw their market orders. Thus the

FIGURE 3-3
Actual versus Potential Orders

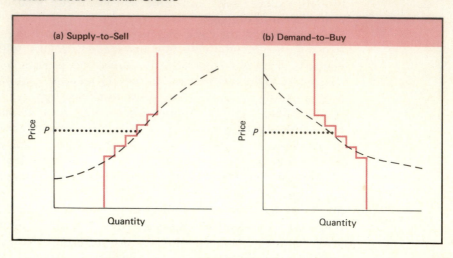

FIGURE 3-4
NYSE Annual Average Daily Volume, Millions of Shares

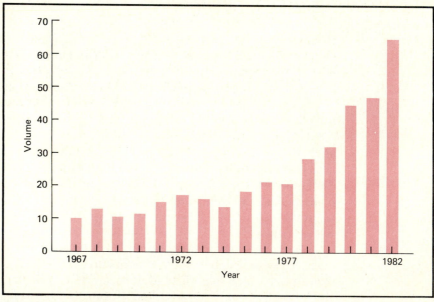

SOURCE: New York Stock Exchange Fact Book, 1983.

Investment Value and Market Price

full demand-to-buy curve would appear more like the dashed curve in Figure 3-3(b) than the solid curve, which reflects only the current orders on the books.

Demand and supply curves based on unexecuted orders on the books have another characteristic: they change frequently, as orders are executed. This is of major importance for understanding the forces determining the *volume* of trading. However, there need be no direct relationship between such volume and price. For example, if a new tax law redistributes income from one group to another, the former may sell shares to the latter, causing great volume but little or no overall impact on price. Similarly, a piece of information may be regarded by some as bad news and by others as good news; members of the former group may sell shares to members of the latter group, enriching brokers but affecting price little if at all. On the other hand, if a piece of good news about a company is released, people may raise their estimates of the value of the company's stock by similar amounts, generating little trading. These are, however, extreme examples. Usually a change in price will be accompanied by larger-than-normal volume. For instance, some investors will value good news more highly than others, leading to a situation in which substantial trading can and will take place. Major price changes (in either direction) are usually accompanied by abnormally large trading volume.

Without question, the volume of trading on exchanges and over-the-counter has increased significantly in the last decade. Figure 3-4 shows the annual average daily volume of shares traded on the New York Stock Exchange from 1967 through 1982. Similar increases took place in other markets. Some of the increase may be attributable to decreases in the costs of trading for institutional investors and to a shift from public to private savings vehicles. But it is entirely possible that greater uncertainty, with accompanying increases in the diversity of opinions concerning economic news, has played a significant role.

For some purposes it is useful to abstract entirely from moment-to-moment changes in customers' orders and focus instead on the fundamental forces at work. Instead of asking how many shares an investor wishes to *buy* at a given price, we seek to determine the number of shares he or she wishes to *hold* at that price. There is, of course, a close relationship between the two quantities. If an investor wishes to hold more shares than he or she currently has, the difference is his or her demand to buy. Conversely, if he or she wishes to hold fewer shares than currently owned, the difference is his or her supply to sell.

In Figure 3-5 one investor's *demand-to-hold* curve for a security is shown by curve *dd*. This simply plots the number of shares he or she wishes to hold at each possible price. The lower the price, in general, the larger the number of shares. Of course, the entire curve is

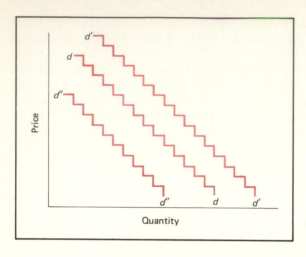

FIGURE 3-5
An Individual's Demand-to-Hold Curve

predicated on the investor's current feelings about the security's future prospects. If something makes one more optimistic, he or she will generally wish to hold more shares at any given price—the entire curve may shift to the right, as shown by curve $d'd'$. On the other hand, if something makes one more pessimistic, the entire curve may shift to the left, as shown by curve $d''d''$.

A factor that complicates analysis of this type is the tendency for some investors to regard sudden and substantial price changes as indicators of changes in a company's future prospects. In the absence of further information, an investor may well interpret such a change as an indication that "someone knows something." While exploring the situation, he or she may at least temporarily revise his or her own assessment of the company's prospects and *demand-to-hold* curve in the same direction. For this reason, few investors place limit orders at prices substantially different from the current trading range, for fear that such orders would be executed only if prospects changed significantly, giving recognition to the idea that a careful reevaluation would be in order before buying or selling shares under such conditions.

Despite this complication, it is possible to construct an aggregate curve indicating the total number of shares that investors will wish to hold at any given price, assuming no change in their current views of the relevant prospects. This overall demand-to-hold curve, obtained by adding the amounts investors wish to hold at each possible price, would have an appearance like that of curve DD in Figure 3-6. In the short run, at least, the available stock of any security to be held is fixed—for example, at Q in the figure. Only one free-market price will equate the demand-to-hold with the available number of shares. In Figure 3-6 it is P. At any higher price, current holders will collectively wish to hold fewer shares than are outstanding. In their attempts to

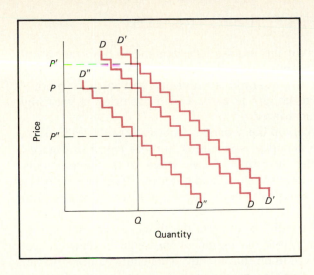

FIGURE 3-6
Aggregate Demand-to-Hold and Available
Quantity

sell such shares, they will drive price down until they or others are willing to hold the stock. Conversely, if price is below P, investors will collectively wish to hold more shares than are outstanding. In their attempts to buy such shares, they will drive price up until they no longer want additional shares or others are no longer willing to provide them.

How flat will be the demand-to-hold curve for a security? The answer depends in part on the extent to which it is regarded as unique. The closer the available substitutes, the more elastic (flat) will be the demand curve: at lower-than-competitive prices the security will be in great demand. The poorer the substitutes, the less elastic will be the demand curve: given future prospects, a fall in price will make the security more attractive and investors will want to increase their holdings, but doing so will typically make their portfolios more risky, since the new shares cannot simply be substituted for others with similar prospects and higher prices. The dangers associated with putting all one's eggs into the same basket limit the magnitude of an investor's response to changes in a security's price. The response to a given price change will thus be smaller, the more unique the security.

If one investor becomes more optimistic about the prospects for a security while another becomes more pessimistic, they may very likely trade with one another with no effect on the overall demand-to-hold and thus on the price. On the other hand, if some investors become more optimistic and no one becomes more pessimistic, the curve may shift to the right, for example to $D'D'$, causing an increase in price, to P'. An increase in pessimism, not offset by concurrent increases in optimism, would be likely to shift the curve to the left, for example to $D''D''$, causing a decrease in price, to P''.

Thus far we have drawn the individual's demand-to-hold curve only in the region of positive quantities. But there is more to it: the higher the price, the smaller the quantity an investor will wish to hold. At some point the desired amount is zero. And if the price is very high, a short sale will be considered.

If short-sellers received the proceeds from such sales, an individual's demand-to-hold a security would look like the curve in Figure 3-7(a), which can be read in either of two ways: as a *demand curve* (i.e., at price A the person wishes to hold quantity B) or as a *marginal-value curve* (i.e., if quantity B is held, the marginal value of one share more or less will be A).

In fact, short-sellers do not receive the proceeds of such sales—they are escrowed to protect the lender of the security. And in most instances no interest is paid on that money. This changes the situation. Selling a security one owns generates cash that can be used for other purposes (e.g., it could earn interest). But selling a security one doesn't own generates no cash. Thus the decision to go short requires a higher price than it would otherwise. The effective demand-to-hold curve looks like the curve in Figure 3-7(b). To the right of the vertical axis it is the same as the original marginal-value curve, but to the left it is above it.

Two effects of this are shown in Figure 3-7(c). The solid curve is the effective demand-to-hold curve. The dashed curve is the original demand and marginal-value curve. If the current price of the security is P^*, this person will go short only Q_1^* shares, instead of Q_2^*. His or her pessimism about the security will thus not have as much impact on the market as it would otherwise. In a sense the person chooses a holding (Q_1^*) at which he or she considers the marginal value (M^*) to be less than the current market price (P^*).

PRICE AS A CONSENSUS

However one chooses to analyze price determination, it is important to remember that a free-market price for a security reflects a kind of consensus. This can be seen in Figure 3-8. The current price is P^*. Some individuals hold the security. For each of them the situation is like that shown in Figure 3-8(a), they will have adjusted their portfolios so that the marginal value of a share equals its market price. A few individuals will be short the security. Their situation is like that shown in Figure 3-8(b). Because of the short-sales rules each will have taken a position at which the marginal value of a share is in a sense less than the price. Many investors will choose to hold no shares. Their

FIGURE 3-7
Demand-to-Hold Curves

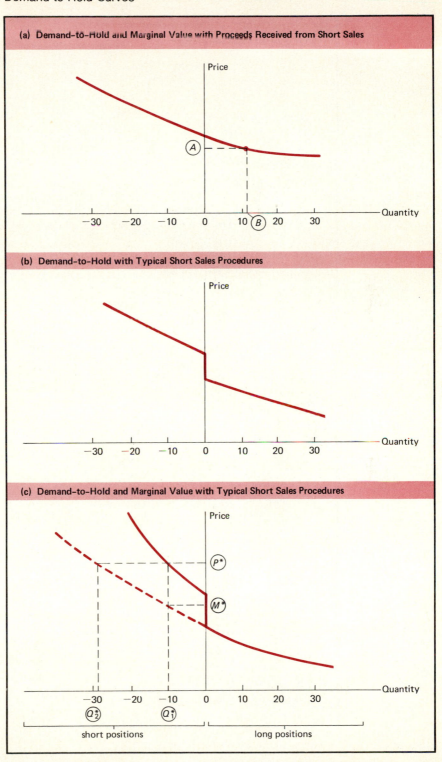

(a) Demand-to-Hold and Marginal Value with Proceeds Received from Short Sales

(b) Demand-to-Hold with Typical Short Sales Procedures

(c) Demand-to-Hold and Marginal Value with Typical Short Sales Procedures

FIGURE 3-8
Price of a Security as a Consensus

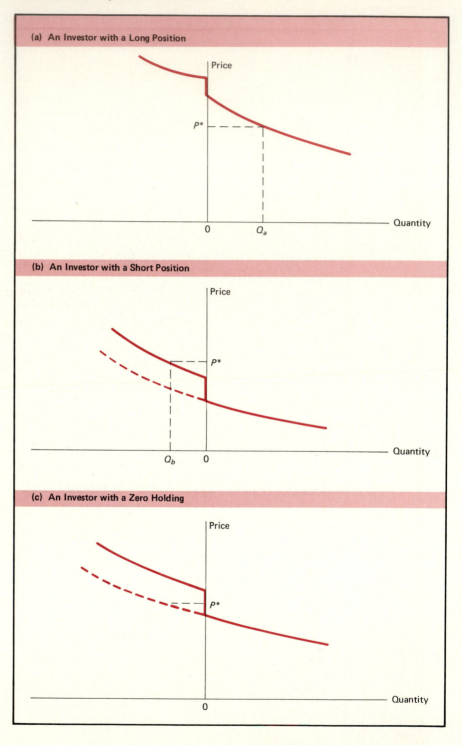

situation is shown in Figure 3-8(c). For each of them marginal value is equal to or (in the case shown) somewhat below the price.

Were it not for the short-selling rules, every investor would adjust portfolio holdings until the marginal value of a security to him or her equaled its price. Since the going price is the same for everyone, so would be the marginal value for all investors (at least all who paid attention to the market). Price would clearly represent a consensus of investor opinion about value.

The short-selling rules change the situation, but only slightly. Since some investors (primarily pessimists) might choose holdings at which marginal value is below the market price, the price could be slightly higher than an average of investors' marginal values.

The impact of the rules for short sales is, however, likely to be small in practice. Even for the short-seller, the disparity between price and marginal value may be small. For those who hold no shares it will be smaller yet (or zero). And for those who hold shares it will be zero. Moreover, short positions are typically a small fraction of long positions. For practical purposes price can reasonably be considered equal to a consensus opinion of investors concerning marginal investment value. For it to be seriously in error as an estimate of that value, many investors must be poorly informed or poor analysts. Moreover, there must be either (1) a preponderance of such investors with overly optimistic forecasts or (2) a preponderance of such investors with overly pessimistic forecasts. Otherwise, the actions of the poorly informed and foolish will cancel each other, making the consensus opinion—price—a good estimate of the value of the future prospects of the security (certain or uncertain).

MARKET EFFICIENCY

Imagine a world in which (1) all investors have access to currently available information about the future, (2) all are good analysts, and (3) all pay close attention to market prices and adjust their holdings appropriately. The prices that would lead to an equilibrium in such a market can be termed the *investment values* of the securities.

We can now define an *efficient market*:

A (perfectly) efficient market is one in which every security's price equals its investment value at all times.

In an efficient market a set of information is fully and immediately reflected in prices. But what information? A popular taxonomy is the following:[1]

---

[1] Eugene Fama, "Efficient Capital Markets: A Review of Theory and Empirical Work," *Journal of Finance*, May 1970.

Form of Efficiency	Information Fully Reflected in Security Prices
Strong	All currently known
Semistrong	All publicly available
Weak	Previous prices of securities

As we will see, major securities markets appear to conform quite well to the model of weak-form efficiency and somewhat less well to the model of semistrong efficiency (although lack of a precise meaning for "publicly available" makes this definition slightly ambiguous). The strong form is, as the term suggests, strong, and we will see that markets are not generally efficient in this sense.

In an efficient market any *new* information would be immediately and fully reflected in prices. New information is just that: *new*—a *surprise* (anything that is not a surprise is predictable and should have been predicted before the fact). Since happy surprises are about as likely as unhappy ones, *price changes* in an efficient market are about as likely to be positive as negative. While one might *expect* a security's price to move enough to give (in conjunction with dividend or interest payments) a reasonable return on capital, anything above or below this would, in such a market, be *unpredictable*. In a perfectly efficient market, price changes would be more or less *random*.

Now consider a crazy market, in which prices never bear any particular relationship to investment value. In such a world, price changes would also be random!

Major securities markets are certainly not crazy. They may not attain perfect efficiency, but they are certainly much closer to it than to craziness. To understand real markets, it is important to understand perfectly efficient markets.

In an *efficient market*, a security's price will be a good estimate of its investment value—that is, the present value of its future prospects as estimated by well-informed and clever analysts. Any substantial disparity between price and value would reflect market inefficiency. In a well-developed and free market, major inefficiencies are rare. The reason is not hard to find. Major disparities between price and investment value will be noted by alert analysts, who will seek to take advantage of their discoveries. Securities priced below value will be purchased, creating pressure for price increases due to increased demand-to-buy. Securities priced above value will be sold, creating pressure for price decreases due to increased supply-to-sell. As investors seek to exploit opportunities created by temporary inefficiencies, they will cause the inefficiencies to be reduced, denying the less alert and the less informed a chance to obtain large abnormal profits.

In the United States there are thousands of professional security analysts and more amateurs. Not surprisingly, the major U.S. securities market appear to be closer to efficiency than to craziness, as do those of other major countries.

Problems

1. On the day that Congress passed by a small margin a bill increasing the tax on oil companies, the prices of the stocks of such companies actually went up, even though most stocks fell on that day. Does this suggest that the market is inefficient?

2. Is bad news always bad for stocks in the sense that it will cause their prices to fall?

3. If short-sale rules make price larger than the average marginal value as assessed by investors, then one might assume that the disparity would be greater for stocks about which there is the greatest diversity of opinion. If so, might such stocks continually be overpriced relative to others?

4. When a firm reports its earnings for a period, the volume of transactions in its stock typically increases, but often there is no significant change in price. How can this be explained?

5. Major officers and directors of corporations often make abnormally large profits from trades in the stocks of their own companies. Is this inconsistent with market efficiency?

4

The Valuation of Riskless Securities

TIME AND RISK

In this world, it seems, nothing is riskless. Philosophically this may well be an appropriate position. However, some securities are clearly less risky than others, and as a useful first step in understanding valuation it is worthwhile to consider investments that are totally riskless, whether or not such extreme examples really exist.

In terms of *dollar* returns, the obvious candidates for this classification are the instruments representing the debt of the U.S. government. Since the government can print money whenever it chooses, the promised payments are virtually certain to be made on schedule. However, the ability and perhaps too frequent willingness of the government to create money raises the possibility of only partially predictable increases in the overall level of prices, with attendant uncertainty as to the purchasing power of the promised payments. While U.S. government bonds may be riskless in terms of dollar returns, they may be quite risky in terms of *real* returns—that is, purchasing power.

This source of risk can be dealt with. For example, a number of governments have issued bonds whose payments are adjusted to compensate for changes in an index of their country's overall price level.

Of course, not all government debt is riskless with respect to nominal payments, let alone purchasing power, as holders of the bonds of Czarist Russia will testify.

Despite these important questions, in this chapter we will assume that there are securities whose returns are certain, and we will consider the factors that determine their values. To the extent that inflation is relevant, we will assume that its magnitude can be predicted. Such abstractions make it possible to focus on the impact of *time* on security valuation. Having accomplished this, we will then be in a position to expand our view to include *risk* as well.

INVESTMENT

To begin with the simplest possible case, let us analyze the plight of Robinson Crusoe. Poor Mr. Crusoe has been shipwrecked on an uninhabited island with little but a store of 20 bushels of corn. His knowledge of shipping leads him to expect to be saved in two years. In the meantime he must decide how much corn to eat this year and how much to plant (i.e., invest) to obtain corn to eat next year. In keeping with the goals of this chapter, we assume the island is not subject to the vagaries of nature that plague most farmers; Crusoe can be certain of the results of whatever planting he undertakes.

After carefully surveying the island, Crusoe decides that there are 20 plots of arable land, each capable of taking one bushel of corn. The plots differ in exposure, soil quality, and so on. This is shown in Table 4-1, in which the plots are listed in decreasing order of yield. The best plot offers a return of 36% on an investment of one bushel of corn; the worst plot offers a negative return of −2%.

TABLE 4-1
Productivity of Crusoe's Land

Plot Number	Bushels of Corn Planted This Year on Plot	Yield in Bushels of Corn Harvested Next Year on Plot	Return on Investment on Plot (%)	Cumulative Yield from This Plus All Previous Plots
1	1	1.36	36	1.36
2	1	1.34	34	2.70
3	1	1.32	32	4.02
4	1	1.30	30	5.32
5	1	1.28	28	6.60
6	1	1.26	26	7.86
7	1	1.24	24	9.10
8	1	1.22	22	10.32
9	1	1.20	20	11.52
10	1	1.18	18	12.70
11	1	1.16	16	13.86
12	1	1.14	14	15.00
13	1	1.12	12	16.12
14	1	1.10	10	17.22
15	1	1.08	8	18.30
16	1	1.06	6	19.36
17	1	1.04	4	20.40
18	1	1.02	2	21.42
19	1	1.00	0	22.42
20	1	.98	−2	23.40

The Valuation of Riskless Securities

The shaded region in Figure 4-1 shows Crusoe's alternatives. He could, of course, eat all 20 bushels of corn this year, leaving him nothing to eat next year; this strategy plots at point A in the field. If Crusoe chooses instead to plant one of his bushels of corn, reducing the amount eaten to 19 bushels, he can look forward to eating next year; the amount will be 1.36 bushels if he uses the best plot of land, keeps the birds from eating the corn, and so on.

If Crusoe chooses to invest two of his bushels of corn, he will, unhappily, get less than twice as great a return. The incremental investment of one additional bushel of corn today yields only 1.34 bushels of corn next year. Why? Because poorer land must be used. This is simply a special case of the more general principle of diminishing returns. The more invested in an economy, the smaller is likely to be the return on each additional unit of investment. Since Crusoe is the entire economy of his island, the situation is quite typical.

The shaded region in the figure portrays all the productive opportunities shown in Table 4-1 for this simple economy. Which point will

FIGURE 4-1
Consumption and Investment Selection

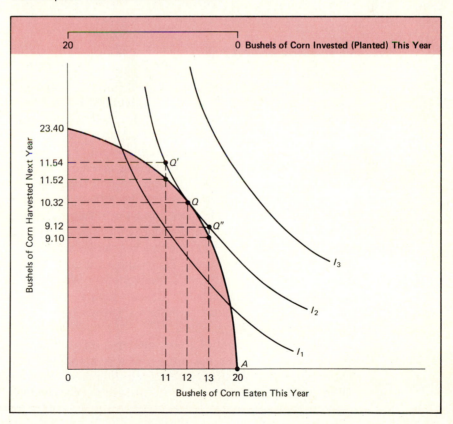

Crusoe choose? The answer clearly depends on his feelings about present versus future consumption. These feelings can be shown graphically by a series of *indifference curves*, each of which connects combinations among which Crusoe is indifferent. For example, he considers any combination on curve I_1 as good as any other on that curve. Similarly, he considers any combination on curve I_2 as good as any other on that curve. Of course, he would prefer a combination on I_2 over one on I_1, and a combination on I_3 over one on either I_2 or I_1. To keep from cluttering up the figure, only three of Crusoe's indifference curves have been drawn; many more could, of course, be added.

What will Crusoe do? From his available opportunities he will pick the one he prefers. Graphically, this is the opportunity on the highest (best) indifference curve, and it lies at a point where the curve touches but does not cut (i.e., is tangent to) the opportunity region. In the figure, this is shown by point Q: Crusoe chooses to eat 12 bushels of corn this year, invest (plant) 8 ($20 - 12$) bushels of his initial stock, and look forward to harvesting 10.32 bushels, all of which he will eat next year while waiting for his ship to come in.

What is the return on Crusoe's investment? He plants eight bushels of corn and harvests 10.32 bushels a year later. The rate of return is thus:

$$\frac{10.32 - 8}{8} = .29$$

or 29% per year.

This is the *overall* or *average* return on investment in the economy as a whole. But it is not the *incremental* or *marginal* rate of return. And the latter corresponds to the interest rate in a complex economy, as we will see.

Look closely at the area around point Q in Figure 4-1. What would happen if Crusoe decided to eat one more or one less bushel of corn this year? If he decided to eat one less bushel, the return on the extra bushel planted (invested) would be 20%—he could plan to eat 1.20 ($11.52 - 10.32$) bushels more next year. However, it would take 1.22 ($11.54 - 10.32$) bushels to keep him as happy as he is with combination Q, as shown by point Q'; for this reason he will not make the change. Looking the other way, the figure shows that if one more bushel were eaten this year, next year's consumption would be reduced by 1.22 ($10.32 - 9.10$) bushels, while Crusoe would be willing to reduce it by only 1.20 ($10.32 - 9.12$) bushels, as shown by point Q''; thus he will not make this change either.

While the effect of a change depends on both the type of change (up or down) and its magnitude, in the region of the chosen point the marginal effects are fairly similar. In this case Crusoe chooses a situation in which the marginal rate of return on investment is about 21%

per year. Moreover, after he chooses the best available combination, the rate at which he is willing to trade present for future consumption is also about 21%.

INVESTMENT AND INTEREST

Let us move a step closer to reality by assuming that Crusoe is not alone. He has been preceded by Mr. Friday, who owns all the land on the island outright. However, Crusoe owns all the corn. If no one else were to intrude, the final outcome could depend on bargaining, cheating, skulduggery, or even war. To avoid such unpleasantries, let us assume that one of the clerks from the Paris Bourse is scheduled to drop by and "call out" a rate at which Crusoe and Friday can trade present corn for corn one year hence. Moreover, let us assume that both Crusoe and Friday take this rate as given, and they engage in no form of ruse trying to obtain a better rate by concealing their true desires. While this is hardly likely to be the case with two traders in a very small market, it is quite representative of most people's situation in a developed economy: for example, the interest rate at the local savings and loan is not likely to be affected by the magnitude of any single person's transactions. Since we are using Crusoe and Friday only to illustrate more complex economies, it makes sense to avoid diversion into matters of gamesmanship and potential violence.

Given a rate at which Friday can get corn, how much will he take? Assume that Crusoe will provide corn at a (corn) interest rate of 31%. In other words, for every bushel Friday takes, he must pay back 1.31 bushels next year. Referring to Table 4-1, one bushel clearly makes sense; Friday can clear a profit of .05 bushels (1.36 − 1.31) using his best plot of land. A second bushel will add .03 bushels (1.34 − 1.31) to his profit, if he plants it on his second-best plot. A third bushel will add another .01 bushels (1.32 − 1.31) to his profit. But any more would clearly be unprofitable. At an interest rate of 31%, Friday will take three bushels of corn. Figure 4-2 shows this, as well as the amount he will take at other interest rates. Not surprisingly, this is simply the information from Table 4-1, plotted in a different form. It shows the *marginal efficiency of* (*corn*) *capital* and is also the *demand for* (*corn*) *capital*. The lower the interest rate, the more investment will be profitable for producers such as Friday and the greater will be the quantity of capital demanded.

How much (corn) capital will Crusoe offer at various interest rates? The answer depends on his initial stock and his attitudes toward present versus future consumption. However, the situation shown in Figure 4-2 is typical: the higher the interest rate, the greater the amount of present consumption people are willing to forego in favor of future consumption. The *supply-of-capital* curve is upward-sloping.

FIGURE 4-2
Demand and Supply of Capital

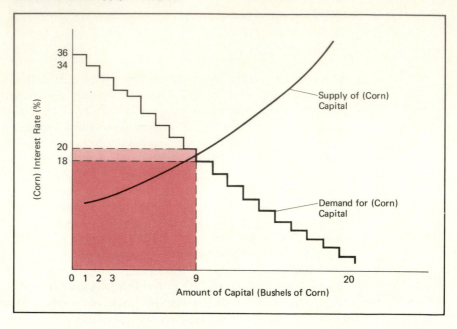

As in Paris, our visiting clerk wants to maximize the amount invested. Since this will be the smaller of (1) the amount Friday will take and (2) the amount Crusoe will provide, the appropriate interest rate, as shown in Figure 4-2, is about 19%. At this rate Crusoe will wish to supply nine bushels of corn in return for 10.71 (9 plus 19% of $9 = 1.9 \times 9$) bushels next year. Moreover, at this rate Friday will wish to take just nine bushels, knowing he will obtain a total yield of 11.52 bushels, leaving .81 bushels (11.52 − 10.71) in profit for his undertaking (not much, but a welcome supplement to his usual diet of fish). Having arranged such a compatible situation, the clerk can steal silently away and return home.

THE INTEREST RATE

In the real world, there can be a little Friday and a little Crusoe in each of us. We all own some assets (if nothing else, ourselves) that can be invested or consumed. Further, most of us engage to some extent in production. However, this does not alter the key conclusions reached in the previous section. *In a free economy, interest rates will adjust until the total amount of capital demanded by producers equals the amount that owners of wealth are willing to supply.* Demand depends, at base, on productive opportunities, supply on preferences for present versus future consumptions and on the ownership of wealth. Both affect the outcome and together determine the interest rate.

This is often difficult to see, since the day-to-day forces affecting interest rates appear to relate more to government policy, flotations of new securities by corporations, and so on. While such activities do impact real interest rates, they are usually only ripples on the surface; the underlying forces of productive opportunities and preferences for present versus future consumption are the major determinants.

Two extreme cases illustrate the influence of demand and supply conditions. At one end of the spectrum are the interest rates paid to depositors (investors) by savings and loan associations. These change fairly frequently, but no single association is likely to adjust its rate as the demand and supply for its funds varies from day to day. As in any other competitive industry, rates are fairly consistent from firm (association) to firm (association). Only when overall demand changes relative to supply will firms find it desirable to change interest rates. And this does happen from time to time. Within any limits allowed by government regulation, demand and supply determine the rates paid by savings and loans.

At the other end of the spectrum lie the 90-day Treasury bills sold by the U.S. government every week. Each bill entitles the holders to receive $1,000 ninety days from the date of issue. The quantity issued (supplied) each week depends primarily on the government's financing needs. Individuals and businesses can bid for (demand) the bills. The effective interest rate thus depends directly on the bid prices (demand) relative to the quantity available (supply). Not surprisingly, the resulting values vary from week to week.

MONETARY VERSUS REAL INTEREST RATES

In real economies there is, of course, more to life than corn. One can trade present corn for future corn, present wheat for future wheat, present wine for future automobiles, and so on.

Modern economies gain much of their efficiency through the use of money—a generally agreed-upon medium of exchange. Instead of trading present corn for a future Honda, as in a barter economy, the citizen of a modern economy can trade his corn for money (i.e., "sell" it), trade the money for future money (i.e., "invest" it), then trade the future proceeds for a Honda (i.e., "buy" it). The rate at which he or she can trade present money for future money is the *monetary* interest rate—usually called simply *the* interest rate.

In periods of changing prices the monetary interest rate may prove a poor guide to the real return obtained by the investor. While there is no completely satisfactory way to summarize the myriad of price changes that take place in such periods, most governments attempt to do so by measuring the cost of a specified mix of major items. The "overall" price level computed for this representative combination of items is usually termed a *cost-of-living index* or *consumer price index*. Whether or not it is relevant for a given individual depends to a major extent on the similarity of his or her purchases to the mix of goods and services used to construct the index. Moreover, such indices tend to overstate increases in the cost of living and understate decreases for people who do begin by purchasing the chosen mix of products. There are two reasons for this. First, improvements in quality are seldom taken adequately into account. Perhaps more important, little or no adjustment is made in the mix as relative prices change. The rational consumer can reduce the cost of attaining a given standard of living as prices change by substituting relatively less expensive goods for those that have become relatively more expensive.

Despite these drawbacks, cost-of-living indices provide at least rough estimates of changes in prices. And such indices can be used to determine an overall *real* rate of interest. For example, assume that during a year in which the monetary rate of interest is 8%, the cost-of-living index increases from 121 to 124. This means that the combination of goods and services that cost $100 in some base year cost $121 at the beginning of the year and $124 at the end of the year. The owner of such a bundle could have sold it for $121 at the start of the year, invested the proceeds at 8% to obtain $1.08 \times 121 = \$130.68$ at the end, then purchased $130.68/124 = 1.05387$ bundles. The real interest was thus 5.387%.

These calculations can be summarized in the following formula:

$$\frac{C_0 \times (1 + i_m)}{C_1} = 1 + i_r$$

where:

$C_0 = $ cost-of-living index at the beginning of the year

$C_1 = $ cost-of-living index at the end of the year

$i_m = $ the monetary interest rate, expressed as a decimal number (e.g., .08)

$i_r = $ the real interest rate, expressed as a decimal number (e.g., .05387)

An alternative version is:

$$\frac{1 + i_m}{1 + c} = 1 + i_r$$

where

$1 + c = C_1/C_0$

$c = $ the change in the cost of living, expressed as a decimal number

In this case, $C_1/C_0 = 124/121 = 1.02479$, so prices increased by about 2.5% ($c = .02479$).

For quick calculation, the real interest rate can be estimated by simply subtracting the rate of change in the cost of living from the interest rate:

$$i_r \approx i_m - c$$

where $\approx$ means "is approximately equal to." In this case, the quick calculation results in an estimate of $.08 - .02479 = .05521$ or 5.521%, reasonably close to the true value of 5.387%.

Sad to say, in this world the fact of inflation seems to be fairly predictable, but its precise magnitude is hard to estimate in advance. For this reason we defer further discussion of real versus monetary interest rates until Chapter 10. Suffice it to say here that it may be best to view the expected real interest rate as determined by the underlying forces described in earlier sections, with the monetary interest rate approximately equal to this amount plus the likely change in prices.

FORWARD RATES

Unlike Robinson Crusoe, most of us make plans extending well beyond the coming year: no ship is likely to come in and solve all our economic problems. People thus consider investments that will pay off next year, those that will pay off in the following year, and so on. Since interest rates are associated with investments, and investments differ in longevity, there are thus many interest rates, not just one.

To take a simple case, assume that two U.S. government bonds can be purchased at present. The first matures in a year, at which time the holder will receive $1,000. The second matures in two years, at which time the holder will receive $1,000. Although U.S. bonds of such duration entitle the holder to periodic interest payments, we will ignore this for now to keep the calculations simple. The prices asked by dealers for the two bonds are:

One-year bond: $934.58
Two-year bond: $865.35

It is a simple matter to determine the effective interest rate on the one-year bond. An investment of $934.58 will pay $1,000 one year hence. The return is thus:

$$\frac{1,000 - 934.58}{934.58} = .07$$

—that is, an interest rate of 7% per year.

But what is the interest rate on the two-year bond? Or should one even think of an interest rate in this case? Three approaches merit discussion.

The first is the simplest of all. One simply expresses the rate in terms of the actual life of the bond:

$$\frac{1,000 - 865.35}{865.35} = .1556$$

or 15.56% for two years. The obvious disadvantage of this measure is its inability to provide comparisons among bonds of different maturities. Moreover, it cannot be used for even a single bond with intermediate interest payments. It is little used, and with good reason.

A second method calculates the so-called "yield-to-maturity." This is the single interest rate (with interest compounded at some specified intervals) that, if paid by a bank on the amount invested, could enable the investor to obtain all the payments made by the bond in question. For example, assuming annual compounding at a rate r [expressed as a decimal], an account with $865.35 invested initially would grow to $(1 + r) \times \$865.35$ in one year. Leaving this total intact, the account would grow to $(1 + r)[(1 + r) \times \$865.35]$ by the end of the second year. The interest rate we seek must bring the account to $1,000 at the end of the second year. In other words, r must be selected so that:

$$(1 + r)^2 \times 865.35 = 1,000$$

or

$$1 + r = \sqrt{\frac{1,000}{865.35}}$$

The required value of r is .07499, so the yield-to-maturity of this bond is 7.499% per year.

Yield-to-maturity is the most commonly used measure of a bond's return. It can be computed for any investment, and it facilitates comparisons among investments of different lives and other characteristics. However, it has some serious drawbacks. In the attempt to express a complex instrument's return in a single number, it raises the possibility of serious oversimplification. It is thus desirable to look behind the yield-to-maturity to examine the fundamental determinants of value. The third method does just this.

The payment on a two-year bond can be considered the result of investment for two years at two potentially quite different rates. Thus the initial investment of $865.35 could have grown to $(1 + r_1) \times \$865.35$ at the end of the first year, and this total could then have grown to $(1 + r_2) \times [(1 + r_1) \times 865.35]$ at the end of the second year. We could thus describe the bond with any of the many pairs of one-year rates r_1 and r_2 that would let the account grow to $1,000 at the end of the second year. We need only select a pair of values that satisfies the equation:

$$(1 + r_1)(1 + r_2)865.35 = 1,000$$

The yield-to-maturity is simply a special case of this in which a further requirement is imposed: that the rates be the same.

But there is no reason for the rates to be the same. In fact, they seldom are. This case is no exception. We know from the price of the one-year bond that the interest rate for money loaned now and paid back a year from now is 7%. The appropriate value for r_1 is thus .07. But what is the value of r_2? The answer can be determined readily. We seek the value that will make:

$$1.07(1 + r_2)865.35 = 1,000$$

It is .08 or 8%. This is the implied *forward rate* for year two: the interest rate for money loaned a year from now and paid back two years from now, *with the contract made now*. It is important to distinguish this from the rate for one-year loans that will prevail for deals made a year from now (the *spot* rate at that time). A forward rate applies to contracts made for a period "forward" in time. By the nature of the contract, the terms are certain now, even though the actual transaction will occur later. If, instead, one were to wait until next year to borrow money, the terms might prove better or worse than today's forward rate; in any event future spot rates are generally not perfectly predictable.

Forward contracts are sometimes made explicitly. For example, a contractor might obtain a commitment from a bank for a one-year construction loan a year hence at a fixed rate of interest. *Financial futures markets* (discussed in Chapter 17) provide standardized agreements similar to forward contracts. For example, in January 1984 one could contract to pay $976.08 in September 1984 to purchase a 90-day U.S. Treasury bill that would pay $1,000 in December 1984.

PRESENT VALUE

Given the interest rates determined in the market at any given time, it is fairly straightforward to find the present value of any investment offering future payments with certainty. As before, let us use r_1 to represent the interest rate on a one-year loan maturing in a year, and r_2 to represent the forward interest rate on a one-year loan maturing in two years. Similarly, r_3, r_4, . . . will represent one-year loans maturing in three, four, . . . years. Thus r_1 is today's spot rate and r_2, r_3, . . . are forward rates. As before, all values are expressed as decimals.

By proper use of existing instruments it is possible to arrange for P dollars today to grow to F_2 dollars in two years, where P and F_2 satisfy the equation:

$$[(1 + r_1)(1 + r_2)]P = F_2$$

By extension, if we let t represent any year, P dollars today can be made to grow to F_t dollars t years from now, where P and F_t satisfy the equation:

$$[(1 + r_1)(1 + r_2) \cdots (1 + r_t)]P = F_t$$

[The term in the brackets is simply a shorthand representation of the product of all the terms from $(1 + r_1)$ to $(1 + r_t)$, inclusive.]

This equation can be used to find the *present* value, P, that is equivalent to a future value of F_t, received t years in the future. Simple rearrangement provides the answer:

$$P = \left[\frac{1}{(1 + r_1)(1 + r_2) \cdots (1 + r_t)} \right] F_t$$

or:

$$P = d_t F_t \tag{4-1}$$

The term in brackets (d_t) is the *discount factor* for year t. The multiplication of F_t by d_t is termed *discounting*: converting the given future value into an equivalent present value. The latter is equivalent in the sense that P present dollars can be converted into F_t dollars in year t via available investment instruments, given the currently prevailing interest rates. An investment promising F_t dollars in year t with certainty should sell for P dollars today. If it sells for more, it is overvalued; if it sells for less, it is undervalued. These statements rest solely on comparisons with equivalent opportunities in the marketplace. Valuation of riskless investments thus requires no assessment of individual preferences, only careful analysis of available opportunities in the market.

The simplest and, in a sense, most fundamental characterization of the structure of the market for default-free bonds is given by the current set of discount factors, known as the *discount function*. With this set of values it is a simple matter to value a riskless bond that provides more than one payment, for it is, in effect, a package of bonds, each of which provides only one payment. Each amount is simply discounted using formula (4-1), and the resultant present values summed. For example, take a bond paying a coupon of $100 at the end of the current year and $1,000 at maturity, two years hence. Assume the values from our previous example hold. Thus:

$$d_1 = \frac{1}{1 + r_1} = .9346 = \frac{1}{1.07}$$

TABLE 4-2
Present Value of a Bond

Time	Payment ($)	Discount Factor	Present Value ($)
One year hence	100	.9346	93.46
Two years hence	1,000	.8654	865.40
		Total present value:	$958.86

and

$$d_2 = \frac{1}{(1 + r_1)(1 + r_2)} = .8654 = \frac{1}{1.07 \times 1.08}$$

The present value of the bond is thus $958.86, as shown in Table 4-2.

No matter how complex the pattern of payments, this procedure can be used to determine the value of a riskless bond of this type. The general formula is:

$$PV = \sum_t d_t F_t$$

where

PV = present value

F_t = the (certain) payment to be made at time t

d_t = the present value of a dollar paid (with certainty) at time t

$\sum_t$ = the sum of all relevant values (e.g., $d_1F_1 + d_2F_2 + d_3F_3 + \cdots$)

YIELD-TO-MATURITY

As we have seen, if P dollars grows to F_t dollars in year t:

$$[(1 + r_1)(1 + r_2) \cdots (1 + r_t)]P = F_t$$

or

$$[(1 + r_1)(1 + r_2) \cdots (1 + r_t)] = \frac{F_t}{P}$$

The yield-to-maturity, also called the internal rate of return, is the constant rate of interest that would have the same effect. In this case, we must find a value r for which:

$$[(1 + r)(1 + r) \cdots (1 + r)]P = F_t$$

where there are t values of $(1 + r)$ in the brackets. Simplifying:

$$(1 + r)^t = \frac{F_t}{P}$$

Since we know that F_t/P will also equal the product of the true interest rates, we can simply find the value of r that satisfies:

$$(1 + r)^t = (1 + r_1)(1 + r_2) \cdots (1 + r_t)$$

Taking the tth root of each side:

$$(1 + r) = \sqrt[t]{(1 + r_1)(1 + r_2) \cdots (1 + r_t)}$$

This shows that $(1 + r)$ is a kind of average of the values $(1 + r_1)$, $(1 + r_2)$, and so on. It is called the *geometric mean*, as contrasted with the more common *arithmetic mean* or simple average. The two values will usually differ; recall that in our earlier example the yield-to-maturity was 7.499%, while a simple average of the two rates would be 7.5%. In more realistic examples the two rates can differ by a substantial amount.

For more complex (and common) cases in which payments are made at different times, it is more difficult to calculate the yield-to-maturity. Generally a trial-and-error procedure must be followed. The goal is to find a value of r that will discount all future payments to present values that sum to the present price. The discount factors are, for payments one year hence:

$$\frac{1}{1 + r}$$

for payments two years hence:

$$\frac{1}{(1 + r)(1 + r)}$$

for payments t years hence:

$$\frac{1}{(1 + r)^t}$$

An example will show how the process works. In this case we wish to analyze a bond that will pay $100 one year hence and $1,000 two years hence. Imagine that it sells for $930. What is its yield-to-maturity?

To get started, let us guess 10% and calculate the implied present value. The results are shown in Table 4-3. The present value is too small. We have discounted the payments by too much. Clearly a lower interest rate is in order. Let us guess 5%. The results are shown in Table 4-4. Now the present value is too large. We have not discounted the future payments enough. We need to try some rate between 5% and 10%.

And so it would go, until the calculated present value came sufficiently close to the actual price of the bond. Here, this will happen when the discount factors are computed at a rate of about 9.21%; this is the bond's yield-to-maturity.

TABLE 4-3
Present Value of a Bond at 10%

Time	Payment ($)	Discount Factor at 10%	Present Value ($) Using a Discount Factor of 10%
One year hence	100	.9091	90.91
Two years hence	1,000	.8264	826.40
		Total present value:	$917.31

Happily, computers are good at trial-and-error. One can describe a very complex series of payments to a computer and get an answer concerning yield-to-maturity in short order. In fact, some hand-held calculators come with built-in programs to find yields-to-maturity (and do present-value and compound-interest calculations). To calculate yield-to-maturity one simply enters the number of days to maturity, the annual payment, and the present price, then presses the key or keys that indicate yield-to-maturity is desired. The lights blink as the calculator engages in its trial-and-error procedure, then in a few seconds the answer appears.

DURATION

Most bonds provide "coupon" (interest) payments in addition to a final ("par") payment at maturity. Depending on the relative magnitudes of these payments, a bond may be more or less like others with the same maturity date. A measure of the average time prior to the receipt of payment is obtained by calculating the bond's *duration*. This is simply a weighted average of the lengths of time prior to the payments, using the relative present values of the payments as weights.

The bond analyzed earlier provides an illustration. Recall from

TABLE 4-4
Present Value of a Bond at 5%

Time	Payment ($)	Discount Factor at 5%	Present Value ($) Using a Discount Factor of 5%
One year hence	100	.9524	95.24
Two years hence	1,000	.9070	907.00
		Total present value:	$1,002.24

TABLE 4-5
Calculating the Duration of a Bond

(1) Time (Years from Now)	(2) Present Value of Payment ($)	(3) Present Value of Payment as Proportion of Present Value of Bond	(4) Column 1 Times Column 3
1	93.46	.0975	.0975
2	865.40	.9025	1.8050
	$958.86	1.0000	1.9025

Table 4-2 that the payment of $100 one year hence had a present value of $93.46, while the final payment of $1,000 two years hence had a present value of $865.40, making the total present value of the bond $958.86. As shown in Table 4-5 this bond has a duration of 1.9025 years.

Bonds of similar duration are more likely to react in similar ways to changes in interest rates than are bonds of similar maturity but different durations. This should not be surprising. Maturity measures only the time over which a bond provides payments; it takes no account of the pattern of those payments over time. Duration takes both factors into account and thus measures a bond's characteristics more accurately.[1]

COMPOUNDING

Thus far we have concentrated on annual interest rates and assumed that funds are compounded annually. This is often appropriate, but for more precise calculations a shorter period may be more desirable. Moreover, some lenders explicitly compound funds more often than once each year.

Compounding is, of course, the payment of "interest on interest." At the end of each compounding interval, interest is computed and added to principal. This sum becomes the principal on which interest is computed at the end of the next interval. The process continues until the final compounding interval is reached.

No problem is involved in adapting our formulas to compounding intervals other than a year. The simplest procedure is to count in units of the chosen interval. Thus, if quarterly compounding is to be used,

---

[1] As we will see in Chapter 12, even more accurate measures can be obtained.

The Valuation of Riskless Securities

r_t can represent the rate of interest per quarter for a three-month loan due t quarters from now, with terms contracted now.

The yield-to-maturity can also be calculated using any chosen compounding interval. If payment of P dollars now will result in a receipt of F dollars ten years from now, the yield-to-maturity can be calculated using annual compounding by finding a value r_a that satisfies the equation:

$$(1 + r_a)^{10} P = F$$

since F will be received ten annual periods from now. The result, r_a, will of course be expressed as an interest rate per year.

Alternatively, yield-to-maturity can be calculated using semiannual compounding, by finding a value r_s that satisfies the equation:

$$(1 + r_s)^{20} P = F$$

since F will be received 20 semiannual periods from now. The result, r_s, will be expressed as an interest rate per semiannual period. It can be doubled to give an annualized figure; better yet, an annualized value can be computed on the assumption of semiannual compounding—that is:

$$1 + r_a = (1 + r_s)^2$$

To reduce the massive confusion caused by the many different methods that can be used to express interest rates, the Federal Truth-in-Lending Act requires every lender to compute and disclose the *annual percentage rate (APR)* implied by the terms of a loan. This is simply the yield-to-maturity, computed using the most frequent time between payments on the loan as the compounding interval. While some complications arise when payments are required at irregular intervals, the use of APR's has clearly simplified the task of comparing lenders' terms.

Semiannual compounding is commonly used to determine the yield-to-maturity for bonds, since interest payments are usually made twice each year. Most preprogrammed calculators and computers use this approach.

THE BANK DISCOUNT METHOD

Despite the truth-in-lending law, other methods are still used to summarize interest rates. One time-honored procedure is the "bank discount" method. If someone "borrows" $100 from a bank, to be repaid a year hence, the bank will discount the interest of, say $8 and pay the borrower $92. According to the bank discount calculation, this is an interest rate of 8%. Not so. The borrower only receives $92, for which he or she must pay $8 in interest. The true interest rate (APR) must be based on the money the borrower actually gets to use. In this case the rate is 8.7%, since:

$$\frac{8}{92} = .087$$

It is a simple matter to convert an interest rate quoted on a bank discount basis to a true interest rate. If the bank discount rate is r_d, the true rate is simply:

$$\frac{r_d}{1 - r_d}$$

where both values are expressed as decimal numbers. The previous example provides an illustration:

$$\frac{.08}{1 - .08} = .087$$

CONTINUOUS COMPOUNDING

When we compute an investment's return, the compounding interval can make a difference. For example, regulations may limit a savings institution to paying a fixed rate of interest but make no specifications about the compounding interval. For example, in early 1975 the legal limit on interest paid by savings and loan companies on deposits committed from six to ten years was 7.75% per year. Initially, most companies paid "simple interest"—thus $1 deposited at the beginning of the year would grow to $1.0775 by the end of the year. But then some enterprising companies announced that they would pay 7.75% per year, compounded semiannually. This meant that $1 deposited at the beginning of the year would grow to $1.03875 at the end of six months, and the total would then grow to 1.03875 × 1.03875, or 1.079 by the end of the year: an increase of 7.9%. This procedure was considered within the letter, if not the spirit, of the law.

Before long, other competitors offered 7.75% per year compounded quarterly (i.e., 1.938% per quarter), giving an effective increase of 7.978% by the end of one year. Then others offered to compound monthly (at .646% per month), for an effective increase of 8.031%. The denouement was reached when one company offered *continuous compounding* at an annual rate of 7.75%. This rather abstract procedure represents the limit approached as interest is compounded more and more frequently. If r represents the annual rate of interest (in this case, .0775) and n the number of times compounding takes place per year, the effective rate of increase, r_e, is given by:

$$\left(1 + \frac{r}{n}\right)^n = 1 + r_e$$

Thus with semiannual compounding:

$$(1.03875)^2 = 1.079$$

With quarterly compounding:

$$(1.01938)^4 = 1.07978$$

and so on. As the compounding interval grows shorter, the number of times compounding takes place (n) grows larger, as does the effective rate, r_e.

Mathematicians can prove that as n grows larger, $[1 + (r/n)]^n$ becomes increasingly close to e^r, where e stands for the number 2.71828 (to five-place accuracy). In this case, $e^{.0775} = 1.0806$ or an effective rate of 8.06% per year.[2]

A more general formula for continuous compounding can also be derived. At an annual rate of r, P dollars will grow to F_t dollars t years from now, with continuous compounding, if the values satisfy the equation:

$$e^{rt}P = F_t$$

Similarly, the present value of F_t dollars received t years hence at an annual rate of r, continuously compounded, will be:

$$P = \frac{F_t}{e^{rt}}$$

The discount factor (d_t) is thus $1/e^{rt}$ or e^{-rt}. These formulas can be used for any value of t, including fractional amounts (e.g., $t = 2.5$ for two years, six months).

Continuous compounding is sometimes used for the analysis of interest-rate formation and change because the formulas lend themselves to algebraic treatment more readily than do those describing periodic compounding. The use of continuous compounding in practice is, however, relatively rare.

THE YIELD CURVE

At any time riskless securities will be priced more or less in accord with a set of discount factors and the associated implied forward interest rates. There is no necessary relationship among these rates. At some times rates are higher, the farther in the future the period to which they apply; at other times they are lower; at still other times, the same. It obviously behooves the security analyst to know which case prevails at present.

---

[2] Tables of natural logarithms may be used for such calculations. The natural logarithm of 1.0806 is .0775, and the antilogarithm of .0775 is 1.0806.

FIGURE 4-3
Yields of Treasury Securities, September 30, 1983 (based on closing bid quotations)

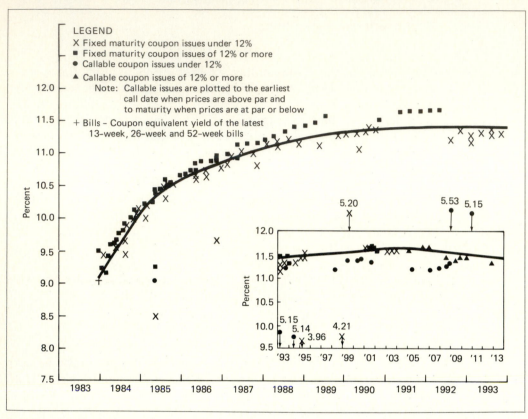

Note: The curve is fitted by eye and based only on the most actively traded issues. Market yields on coupon issues due in less than three months are excluded.

This is, unhappily, easier said than done. Only the bonds of the U.S. government are clearly riskless in dollar terms, and even they are not usually considered riskless in real terms. Moreover, such bonds differ in tax advantages, the ability of the government to select the effective date of maturity, and other features. Despite these problems, the U.S. Treasury Department summarizes the approximate relationship between short- and long-term yields with a *yield curve* in each issue of the *Treasury Bulletin*. This provides an estimate of the current *term structure* of interest rates. Figure 4-3 shows an example.

Unfortunately, the yield curve does not relate forward interest rates to the applicable time periods. Instead it plots the yield-to-maturity for actual bonds versus their maturity.[3] As the figure shows, the relationship is less than perfect. Part of the imperfection is due to

---

[3] Or, in some cases, the earliest date at which they can be "called" by the government.

The Valuation of Riskless Securities

differences in taxability and the like. Part is due to the fact that yield-to-maturity figures represent averages of actual forward rates and thus obscure the underlying determinants of bond prices.

Historically, a "rising yield curve" such as that shown in Figure 4-3 is the most common: long-term yields exceed short-term, implying that forward rates are higher, the farther in the future is the period for which a contract is drawn. Rising yield curves tend to be associated with periods of normal or low short-term interest rates.

When short-term interest rates are fairly high, the yield curve may be "flat," implying that all forward rates are roughly the same.

In periods of very high short-term rates the yield curve may be "falling" throughout or even "humped." A downward-sloping curve implies that forward rates are generally smaller, the farther in the future is the period for which the contract is drawn.

The determinants of the yield curve are many and complex. Moreover, risk may play a role. For this reason, we will defer further discussion until Chapter 12.

The current yield curve provides some information on the manner in which bonds are priced in the market. More fundamental values are the discount factors and associated forward rates, for they can be used to evaluate any investment. If the investment is truly riskless, its value can be determined directly. If it is risky, additional aspects must be taken into account. But that is the subject of the next three chapters.

Problems

1. Explain why the indifference curves in Figure 4-1 cannot cross.
2. a. In August 1979 one could buy a U.S. Treasury bill that would pay $1,000 in six months for a price of $954.10. What was the effective interest rate on the bill, expressed as a rate per six months?
   b. At the same time one could buy a U.S. Treasury bill paying $1,000 in twelve months for $910.10. What was the effective interest rate on this bill, expressed as a rate per twelve months?
   c. Assume that you wanted to express the return on the twelve-month bill in terms of an interest rate per six months, compounded every six months. What would be the resulting yield-to-maturity expressed as a rate per six months?
   d. Given the prices of these bills, can you determine the implicit forward rate for the second six-month period? If so, what is it (expressed as a rate per six months)?
3. A savings account that yields 8% per year compounded monthly has a higher effective annual yield than an account that offers 8% per year compounded quarterly. An account that offers 8% per year compounded daily has an even

higher effective yield. What would be the effective yearly yield (the yield equivalent to a one-time yearly compounding) for an account offering 8% per year with continuous compounding?

4. The Beneficent Loan Company has agreed to lend you funds to complete the last year of an M.B.A. program. The company will give you $10,000 today if you agree to repay the loan four years from now with a lump-sum payment of $20,164. What annual rate of interest is Beneficent charging you?

5. Assume default-free bonds are currently priced in accordance with the following set of discount factors:

Year (*t*)	Discount Factor (*dt*)
1	.9259
2	.8534
3	.7829
4	.7150

a. What are the implicit forward rates of interest?
b. What is the present value of a 10% coupon four-year bond that pays $100 in each year up to and including year 4 plus an additional $1,000 in year 4?
c. What is the present value of a 5% coupon four-year bond that pays $50 in each year up to and including year 4 plus an additional $1,000 in year 4?
d. What are the durations of the two bonds in (b) and (c)? What accounts for the nature of the difference in the two values?

5

The Valuation of Risky Securities

INTRODUCTION

Payments received from riskless securities can be accurately predicted: neither their amounts nor their timing is uncertain. But many securities do not meet such high standards. Some or all of their payments are *contingent* on events with respect to amount, timing, or both. A bankrupt corporation may not make its promised bond payments in full. A worker who is laid off may pay his bills late (or not at all). A corporation may reduce or eliminate its dividend if its business becomes unprofitable. And so on.

The security analyst must try to evaluate these circumstances affecting a risky investment's payments and enumerate the key events upon which such payments are contingent. For example, an aircraft manufacturer's fortunes may depend on whether or not the firm is awarded a major contract by the government, whether or not its recently introduced commercial aircraft is accepted by the airlines, whether or not there is an upturn in the economy with a concomitant increase in demand for airline travel, and so on. To properly value the stock of such a company the analyst must consider each of these contingencies and estimate the corresponding effect on the firm and its stock.

The identification of important influences and the evaluation of the impact of each one is exceedingly difficult. Among other things, the appropriate level of detail must be determined. The number of potentially relevant events is almost always very large, and the analyst must attempt to focus on the relatively few that appear to be most important. In some cases it may be best to differentiate only a few alternatives (for example, whether the economy will turn up, turn down, or stay the same). In other cases, finer distinctions may be needed (for example, whether the gross national product will be up 1%, 2%, 3%, and so on).

The process of identifying and evaluating key influences is central to security analysis. Here we will concentrate on the *use* of such estimates. After the contingencies have been identified and the corresponding payments estimated, how can the value of the security be determined?

MARKET VERSUS PERSONAL VALUATION

One approach to the valuation of risky securities focuses on the investor's personal attitudes and circumstances. Given his or her assessment of the likelihood of various contingencies, and feelings about the corresponding risks involved in an investment, an investor might determine the amount he or she would be willing to pay, by some sort of introspection. This would be a "personal" valuation of the security.

Such an approach would be appropriate if there were only one investment in the world. But such is not the case. A security need not and should not be valued without considering available alternatives. Current market values of other securities provide important information, since a security is seldom so unique that nothing else is even comparable. Security valuation should not be done in a vacuum; it should instead be performed in a market context.

Key to this approach is the comparison of one investment or combination of investments with another having comparable characteristics. For example, assume that A and B in Figure 5-1(a) are similar in this respect; then the two should be equal in value.

Now imagine that alternative B includes a security we wish to value—call it X. Moreover, assume that all other securities included in A and B are regularly traded and that their market values (prices) are widely reported and easily determined. Combination B can be thought to have two components: security X and the rest, which we

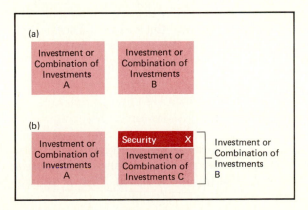

(a)

Investment or Combination of Investments A

Investment or Combination of Investments B

(b)

Investment or Combination of Investments A

Security X

Investment or Combination of Investments C

Investment or Combination of Investments B

FIGURE 5-1

Comparing Combinations of Investments

will represent by C, as in Figure 5-1(b). Combination C might include many securities, only one, or, as a very special case, none at all.

If people are willing to purchase combination A for a present value of PV_A, they should be willing to purchase combination B for the same amount, since the two provide comparable prospects. Thus:

$$PV_A = PV_B$$

The present value of B will, however, be simply the sum of the present values of its components:

$$PV_B = PV_X + PV_C$$

This implies that the present value of security X can be determined solely by reference to market values placed on the securities comprising combinations A and C. Since:

$$PV_A = PV_X + PV_C$$

then:

$$PV_X = PV_A - PV_C$$

APPROACHES TO SECURITY VALUATION

It is reasonable enough to say that market prices of "comparable investments" should be used to determine the value of a security. But when are two investments truly comparable?

An obvious case arises when investments provide identical payments in every possible contingency. If an investment's outcome is affected by relatively few events, it may be possible to purchase a set of other investments, each of which pays off in only one of the relevant contingencies. A properly selected mix of such investments may thus be completely comparable to the one to be valued. The next section illustrates this approach with an example drawn from the field of insurance.

A much more common approach to valuation is less detailed but more useful. Two alternatives are considered comparable if they offer similar expected returns and contribute equally to portfolio risk. Central to this view is the need to assess the probabilities of various contingencies. The remainder of this chapter and the next two chapters are devoted to this more widely used *risk-return approach*.

EXPLICIT VALUATION OF CONTINGENT PAYMENTS

Insurance

Insurance policies are highly explicit examples of contingent payments. One can buy a $100,000 one-year "term" life insurance policy on a reasonably healthy 60-year-old male for about $2,300. This, of course,

The Valuation of Risky Securities

can be viewed as an investment (albeit a morbid one): the sum of $100,000 will be paid by the insurance company if the insured dies within a year; otherwise nothing at will be paid. Involved is the sacrifice of a present certain value ($2,300) for a future uncertain value. The only relevant event is the possible death of the insured, and the relationship between that event and the amount to be paid is crystal clear.

Now imagine that a reasonably healthy 60-year-old male executive asks you to loan him some money for a year. He would like as much as possible now; in return he promises to pay you $100,000 at the end of the year. Your problem is to determine the present value of that promise—that is, how much to advance now. Put somewhat differently, you must determine an appropriate interest rate for the loan.

To keep the example simple, assume that the only source of uncertainty is the borrower's ability to remain in this position and thus earn the requisite money, and that this depends only on his continued presence among the living. In other words, if he lives he can and will repay the $100,000 in full; otherwise neither he nor his heirs will pay you anything.

The piece of paper representing the executive's promise to pay $100,000 is our security X. What is it worth? The answer clearly depends in an important way on the available alternatives. And a crucial factor is the current rate of interest.

Assume that the going rate for riskless one-year loans is 8%. If there were no doubt whatever that the executive would repay the loan, it would be reasonable to advance $92,592.59 (since $100,000/$92,592.59 = 1.08). However, the uncertainty connected with the loan makes this inadvisable. The appropriate amount is obviously less. But how much less?

In this case an answer can easily be determined. It would be entirely reasonable to advance at least $90,292.59, making the *promised* interest rate on the loan approximately 10.75% (since 100,000/90,292.59 = 1.1075). The basis for this calculation is quite simple. It relies on the fact that an investor can insure against the relevant risk, obtaining an overall position that is completely riskless.

Table 5-1 provides the details. The relevant event is whether or not the executive survives the year. The loan is thus a risky investment, paying $100,000 only if he lives. The life insurance policy is also a risky investment, paying $100,000 only if he dies. But a *portfolio* that includes both investments is totally riskless: its owner will receive $100,000, no matter what happens! By paying $90,292.59 for the loan and $2,300 for the insurance policy, an investor could give up $92,592.59 now for a certain payment of $100,000 a year hence—obtaining a riskless return of 8%, which is the going rate on other riskless ventures.

This is, of course, an application of the general procedure de-

The Valuation of Risky Securities

TABLE 5-1

Costs and Payments for a Loan and an Insurance Policy

ITEM	EVENT		COST
	Executive Dies	Executive Lives	
Loan	0	$100,000	$90,292.59
Insurance policy	$100,000	0	2,300.00
Total	$100,000	$100,000	$92,592.59

scribed in the previous section. Figure 5-2 summarizes the details in the format used earlier, for purposes of comparison.

Valuation in a Complete Market

Assume, for the present, that market values can be used to estimate the present value of any contingent payment. A market in which such detailed quotations are available is termed *complete*. While no real market conforms to this specification, it is useful to see how valuation would be done in such circumstances.

First, we need a way to represent the present value of a guaranteed commitment to pay $1 at a specified time if (and only if) a specified event or "state of the world" occurs. The following will suffice:

$$PV(\$1, t, e)$$

where

t = the time at which the dollar is to be paid
e = the event that must occur if the dollar is to be paid

FIGURE 5-2

Comparing Two Riskless Investments

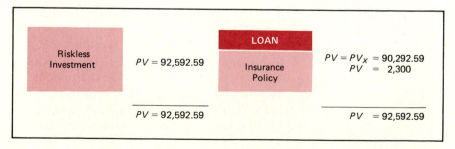

Armed with this notation, we can show how one might analyze any risky investment. Every possible contingency could, in theory, be considered separately, giving a (probably very lengthy) list of contingent payments of the following form:

Time of Payment	Event on Which Payment Is Contingent	Amount of Payment
t_1	e_1	D_1
t_2	e_2	D_2
.	.	.
.	.	.
.	.	.

Of course, some of the events might be the same, as might some of the times and amounts.

To find the present value of the investment, we need to find the present value of each of its contingent payments, then add them up. In tabular form:

(1) Time of Payment	(2) Event on Which Payment Is Contingent	(3) Amount of Payment	(4) Discount Factor	(5) = (3) × (4) Present Value
t_1	e_1	D_1	$PV(\$1, t_1, e_1)$	$D_1 \times PV(\$1, t_1, e_1)$
t_2	e_2	D_2	$PV(\$1, t_2, e_2)$	$D_2 \times PV(\$1, t_2, e_2)$
.	.	.	.	.
.	.	.	.	.
.	.	.	.	.

Total value = _____

This method of valuation is commonly termed the *state-preference* approach, since it begins with the assumption that people's preferences are for *state-contingent claims* and concludes that securities will be valued on the basis of their payoffs in different "states of the world."

Some believe that Lloyd's of London will insure almost anything. Perhaps so. This could ease the security analyst's task considerably. He or she would only (!) have to determine the payments $(D_1, D_2, \ldots)$ associated with an investment, the times at which they could be made $(t_1, t_2, \ldots)$, and the events on which they were contingent $(e_1, e_2, \ldots)$. The analyst could then use the premiums specified for the relevant insurance policies as estimates of appropriate discount factors $[PV(\$1, t_1, e_1), PV(\$1, t_2, e_2), \ldots]$, and perform the required calculations.

But even if Lloyd's will insure anything, the premiums charged for many policies might attract no takers. There are a number of interrelated reasons for this. As a case in point, imagine an aerospace company, the future profits of which depend heavily on whether or not the firm will be awarded a major government contract. Why not buy an appropriate insurance policy from Lloyd's, guaranteed to pay off if the firm loses the contract? Then only Lloyd's and the other firms in the industry would care about the outcome.

The idea is obviously whimsical. If Lloyd's were even willing to issue such a policy, the cost would be more than anyone would be likely to pay. But why?

First, because of differences in *information*. Those familiar with the company or the government or both have better information about the likely outcome and can better assess the likelihood of various alternatives. Lloyd's operates at least partly in the dark. To protect itself, it will charge more than otherwise.

Second, there is the likelihood of *adverse selection*. If a policy of this sort is offered at a price low enough to attract anyone at all, the insurer can expect the firms that are least likely to win the contract to buy insurance, while those most likely to get the contract take their chances. This occurs frequently with life insurance. The less healthy an individual, the more likely he or she is to buy a policy; for this reason, the insured is usually required to pass a medical examination as a condition of sale. An examination of the health of a company's bid to win a government award might be much more difficult or expensive, so an insurance company must set its fees for such a policy on the assumption that it would end up insuring the riskiest client or clients.

Another factor is the thoroughly modern phenomenon described by the old-fashioned term *moral hazard*. The purchase of insurance may affect the likelihood of the event in question. If the manager of a firm is insured against the loss of the contract, he or she may well put less effort into the attempt to win it, increasing the likelihood of its loss and the insurance company's obligation to pay off. This explains the reluctance of an insurance company to insure a house or car for more than its replacement value, and the desire of many stockholders to have a corporation's officers own some of the firm's stock and none of its competitors' issues. Here again, the insurance company will account for this effect when setting prices.

Finally, there is the simple matter of *overhead*. Insurance people like to eat, as do investors who provide the capital that insurance companies need. The costs of doing business will, over the long pull, be reflected in the prices charged for that business. No financial service is free, and insurance is no exception.

For all these reasons securities markets do not conform to the specifications of the complete-market state-preference model. While the approach is helpful for addressing certain theoretical issues, it is less useful for investment purposes than the risk-return (or "mean-variance") approach, to which we now turn.

PROBABILISTIC FORECASTING

Assessing Probabilities

Lacking a plethora of widely available and low-cost insurance policies, it is not possible to value an investment without explicitly considering the likelihood of various outcomes. Instead, the analyst must attempt to assess directly the likelihood of each major event that can affect an investment. In short, he or she must engage in *probabilistic forecasting*.

The idea is simple enough, although its implementation is exceedingly difficult. The analyst expresses his or her assessment of the likelihood of every relevant event as a *probability*. If he or she feels that the chances of an event's taking place are 50-50, a probability of .50 is attached to the event. If the chances seem to be 3 out of 4, the probability is ¾, or .75 (another way of expressing this is to say that the *odds* are 3-to-1 that the event will take place). If the analyst considers an event to be absolutely *certain*, a probability of 1.0 should be assigned. If he or she feels an event is completely impossible, its probability of occurrence is zero.

It is important, of course, to be consistent in one's estimates. For example, if the events on a list are *mutually exclusive* and *exhaustive* (i.e., one of them, but only one, will take place), the probabilities should sum to one.

Probability is, at base, a *subjective* concept. Even simple cases fall under this heading. For example, a gambler may assess the probability of a coin's coming up heads at .5, based on knowledge of coins and observations of the coin in question over the past. But the estimate is still subjective, involving the implicit assumption that the coin really is "fair" and that the past is an appropriate guide to the future. Similar cases arise frequently in security analysis. Relative *frequencies* of various returns in the past are sometimes used as estimates of the *probabilities* of such returns in the future. Clearly this procedure relies on assumptions that require subjective judgment and may in some circumstances be totally inappropriate. Forecasts based on the extrapolation of past relationships are neither wholly objective nor necessarily to be preferred over predictions obtained in more subtle ways.

Probabilistic forecasting entails a decision to confront uncertainty head-on, acknowledge its existence, and try to measure its extent. Instead of attempting to answer a question such as "What will General Motors earn next year?" the analyst explicitly considers some of the more likely alternatives and the likelihood of each one. This brings the analysis out in the open, allowing both the estimator and the user or users of such estimates to assess the reasonableness of the values. Insistence on a single number for each estimate, with no measure of associated uncertainty, would suggest naiveté or insecurity on the part of the producer or the consumer of such predictions.

In some organizations analysts engage in explicit probabilistic forecasting, passing on all their detailed assessments to others charged with bringing together the estimates made within the group. In other organizations the analysts make explicit probabilistic forecasts but summarize their evaluations in a relatively few key estimates, sending only the latter to others. In still other organizations analysts do not engage in explicit probabilistic forecasting; instead, they produce estimates that summarize their implicit beliefs about the probabilities of various events. As always, it is not the form but the substance that matters.

PROBABILITY DISTRIBUTIONS

It is often convenient to portray probabilistic forecasts graphically. The possible outcomes are represented on the horizontal axis and the associated probabilities on the vertical axis. Figure 5-3 provides an example.

In this case the outcomes are qualitatively different in nature and can only be listed on the horizontal axis: the ordering and spacing are arbitrary.

Figure 5-4 shows a somewhat different case. Here the alternative outcomes differ quantitatively, and with regard to only one variable: earnings next year. In this instance the analyst has chosen to group together all possibilities from $.90 to $.99, assess the probability that the actual amount will fall within that range, then repeat the process for the range from $1.00 to $1.09, the range from $1.10 to $1.19, and so on.

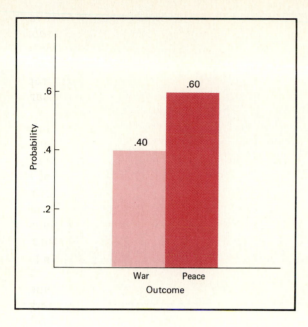

FIGURE 5-3
Probabilities of War and Peace

The analysis could, of course, have been conducted at a more detailed level, with probabilities estimated for outcomes in the ranges from $.90 to $.94, $.95 to $.99, and so on. An even more detailed analysis would assign a probability to every possible outcome. In this case the bars would be numerous, and each would be very thin, as shown in Figure 5-5.

FIGURE 5-4
Probabilities of Next Year's Earnings (using wide ranges)

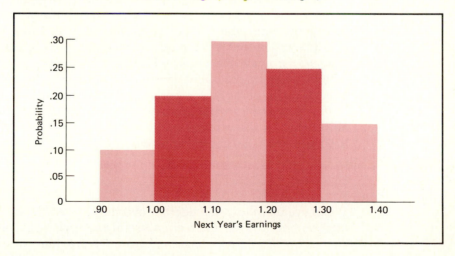

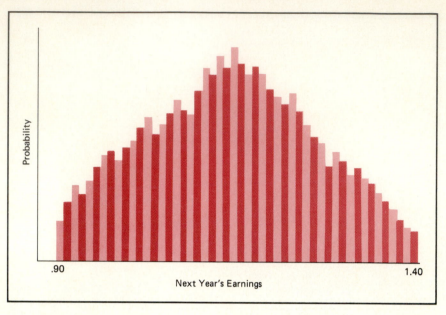

FIGURE 5-5
Probabilities of Next Year's Earnings (using narrow ranges)

The ultimate in a detailed prediction is represented by a continuous curve, or *probability distribution*. Such a curve represents, in effect, the tops of many very thin bars, such as those shown in Figure 5-5. Three examples of curves of this type are shown in Figure 5-6(a), (b), and (c).

If probability distributions are to be used, the analyst can forego explicitly assessing particular outcomes, simply drawing a curve that seems to best represent the situation as he or she sees it. The relative likelihood of any outcomes is indicated by the height of the curve at the appropriate point. If the outcomes portrayed are the only ones possible, the probabilities must, of course, sum to one. In practice the analyst can draw the curve without regard to the probability scale, as only *relative* probabilities are important. The height of the curve at each major point on the horizontal axis (measured in grid squares) can be read and the sum then used to determine the appropriate probability scale for the vertical axis. For example, if the sum of the heights is 50 grid units, each unit represents a probability of .02 ($\frac{1}{50}$).

Event Trees

When events follow one another over time, or are in any sense dependent on one another, it is often useful to describe the alternative sequences with a "tree" diagram. Figure 5-7 provides an example.

The Valuation of Risky Securities

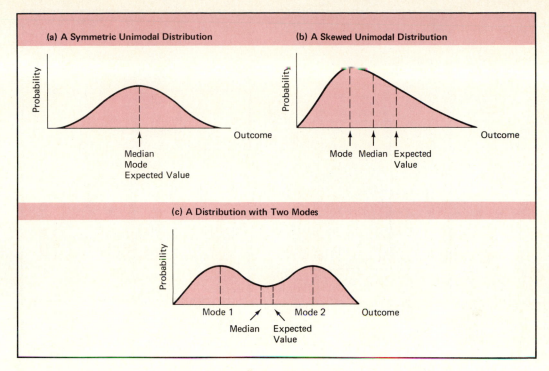

FIGURE 5-6
Continuous Probability Distributions

A borrower has promised to pay $15 one year hence and $8 two years hence, if possible. The analyst feels the odds are only 40-60 that the first payment will in fact be made in full. Otherwise, she feels the borrower will be able to pay only $10 one year hence.

As far as the second year is concerned, the likely situation depends, in this analyst's judgment, on the outcome in the first year. If the borrower manages to pay the full $15 in the first year, the analyst feels the odds are only 1 in 10 that he will be able to meet his commitment to pay $8 at the end of two years. Otherwise, he will pay less: $6. On the other hand, if the borrower pays out $10 in the first year, although there appears to be no chance of recovering the $5 shortfall, the analyst feels the odds are about even that the promised $8 will be paid in the second year. If this does not happen, she feels that $4 will be paid instead.

Figure 5-7 also shows the probability of each of the four possible sequences, or paths, through the tree. For example, the probability that both payments will be made in full is only .04, since there are only 40 chances out of 100 that the first payment will be made, and of those, only 1 out of 10 is expected to be followed by payment in

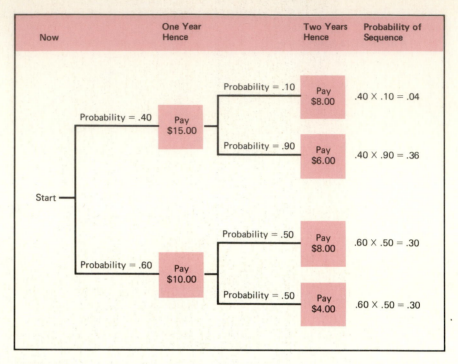

Now	One Year Hence	Two Years Hence	Probability of Sequence
		Probability = .10 → Pay $8.00	.40 X .10 = .04
Probability = .40 → Pay $15.00			
		Probability = .90 → Pay $6.00	.40 X .90 = .36
Start			
		Probability = .50 → Pay $8.00	.60 X .50 = .30
Probability = .60 → Pay $10.00			
		Probability = .50 → Pay $4.00	.60 X .50 = .30

FIGURE 5-7
An Event Tree

full of the final obligation. This gives 4 out of 100 chances for the sequence: a probability of .04.

EXPECTED VALUE

Often an analyst is uncertain about an outcome but wishes, or is required, to summarize the situation with one or two numbers—one indicating the *central tendency* of the distribution of outcomes, and one measuring *relevant risk*. Both return and risk are discussed in subsequent chapters; the remainder of this chapter concentrates on the former.

How might a single number intended to summarize a set of possible outcomes be obtained? Obviously no satisfactory way can be found if the alternative outcomes differ qualitatively (for example, war versus peace). But if the outcomes differ quantitatively, and especially if they differ in only one dimension, a number of possibilities present themselves.

Perhaps the most common procedure is to adopt the *most likely* value. This is known as the *mode* of the probability distribution. Figure

106   The Valuation of Risky Securities

5-6 shows the mode of each of the distributions. Note that in Figure 5-6(c) there are two modes: in this case, no single number can be used to answer the question in this manner.

Another alternative is to provide a "50-50" number—a value that is as likely to be too low as to be too high. This is called the *median* of the probability distribution. As shown in Figure 5-6, it may differ significantly from the mode(s).

A third alternative is to use an *expected value*, a *weighted average of all the possible outcomes, using the associated probabilities as weights*. It takes into account all the information expressed in the distribution, both the *magnitude* and the *probability* of occurrence of each possible outcome. Almost any change in an investment's prospects or probabilities will affect the expected value of its outcomes (as it should).

In many instances there are no differences among these three measures. If the distribution is symmetric (each half is a mirror image of the other) and unimodal (there is one most likely value), then the median, mode, and expected value coincide, as in the case shown in Figure 5-6(a). Thus an analyst may choose to think in terms of, say, a 50-50 (median) value, even though the number wanted is the expected value. Only if the underlying probability distribution is highly skewed might this procedure lead to difficulties.

In those cases in which the values do differ, there are good reasons to prefer the expected value. As stated earlier, it takes all the estimates into account. But it has another advantage. Estimates about the prospects for securities serve as inputs for the process of portfolio construction or revision. The expected value for a portfolio is related in a straightforward way to the expected values for its securities, but neither the median nor the mode for a portfolio can, in general, be determined from comparable values for its securities.

Table 5-2 provides an example of the computation of expected values. An analyst is trying to predict the impact on the prices of two securities of a surprise television address scheduled by the President. He has delineated a number of possible announcements, ranging from changes in the situation in the Mideast through a decision concerning the federal deficit. The alternatives represented in the table have been defined to be mutually exclusive and exhaustive (i.e., every possible combination is shown in a different row). After much thought and with some trepidation, the analyst has also estimated the probability of each announcement and the resultant effect on the prices of the two securities. Finally, he has computed the associated values of a portfolio containing one share of each stock.

The expected values are shown at the bottom of the table. Each is obtained by multiplying the probability of every announcement by the associated price, then summing. For example, the expected price of security A is determined by computing $[(.10 \times 40.00) +$

TABLE 5-2
Analysis of Effects of Announcements on Two Securities and a Portfolio of Both
Securities

Announcement	Probability	Predicted Price ($) of Security A	Predicted (Price ($) of Security B	Predicted Value ($) of a Portfolio of A and B
a	.10	40.00	62.00	102.00
b	.20	42.00	65.00	107.00
c	.10	40.50	60.00	100.50
d	.25	41.00	61.00	102.00
e	.15	38.00	65.00	103.00
f	.10	40.50	59.00	99.50
g	.05	45.00	58.00	103.00
h	.05	40.50	58.00	98.50
	Expected Values:	$40.73	$61.90	$102.63

$(.20 \times 42.00) + \cdots$]; that of security B by computing [$(.10 \times 62.00) + (.20 \times 65.00) + \cdots$]; and that of the portfolio by computing [$(.10 \times 102.00) + (.20 \times 107.00) + \cdots$]. Not surprisingly, the expected value of the portfolio equals the sum of the expected values of its component securities. When the expected values for the securities are added together, one is, in effect, adding ($.10 \times 40.00 + \ldots$) to ($.10 \times 62.00 + \ldots$). Clearly, this will give the expected value of the portfolio, which is $.10 \times (40.00 + 62.00) + \cdots$.

EXPECTED VERSUS PROMISED YIELD-TO-MATURITY

If payments from a bond are certain, there is no difference between the expected yield-to-maturity and the promised amount. However, many bonds fail to meet these standards. Two types of risk may be involved. First, the issuer may defer some payments. A dollar received farther in the future is, of course, worth less in present value than a dollar received on schedule; thus the present value of a bond will be smaller, the greater the likelihood that this might happen. The second type of risk is potentially more serious. The borrower may default, in whole or in part, on some of the interest payments or on the principal at maturity. A firm becomes bankrupt when it is clearly unable to meet such obligations; the courts then divide the remaining assets among the various creditors in accordance with provisions agreed upon when the debts were issued.

To estimate the expected yield-to-maturity for a risky debt instrument, one should in principle consider all possible outcomes and the probability of each one. The simple example shown in Figure 5-7 can be used to illustrate the procedure. Assume the security in question costs $15; that is, the borrower wants $15 now in return for a commitment to pay $15 one year hence and $8 two years hence. The promised yield-to-maturity is the interest rate that makes the present value of these payments equal $15. In this case it is 38.51% per year, a substantial figure indeed.

But the analyst feels that the probability of actually receiving this yield-to-maturity is only .04. Table 5-3 shows the possible sequences (paths in the event tree), as well as the probability and the yield-to-maturity for each one. The expected yield-to-maturity is simply the weighted average of these values, using the probabilities as weights (e.g., [(.04 × 38.51%) + (.36 × 30.62% + · · ·].

The expected yield-to-maturity is considerably less than the promised amount: 15.09% as opposed to 38.51%. And the former is clearly the more relevant figure for investment analysis.

This is an important point. The yield-to-maturity, as normally calculated, is based on promised payments, made at the promised times. If there is any risk that the borrower's commitments will not be fully met, the expected yield-to-maturity is less than this figure; and the greater the risk, the greater the disparity. This is illustrated in Table 5-4, which shows the (promised) yield-to-maturity values for four groups of bonds classified by Standard and Poor's, a major rating service, as having different degrees of risk. While the *levels* of all four yields reflect general interest rates at the time, the *differences* among them are primarily due to differences in risk. If promised yields of all bonds were the same, the expected yields of high-risk bonds would be less than those of low-risk ones—an unlikely situation indeed. Instead, riskier bonds promise higher yields so that their expected yields can be at least as large as those of less risky ones.

TABLE 5-3
Promised Versus Expected Yield-to-Maturity

Payment One Year Hence ($)	Payment Two Years Hence ($)	Probability	Yield-to-Maturity (%)
15	8	.04	38.51
15	6	.36	30.62
10	8	.30	13.61
10	4	.30	−5.20
		Expected Yield-to-Maturity:	15.09%

TABLE 5-4
Standard and Poor's Composite Bond Yields, December 28, 1983

Rating	Yield-to-Maturity (%)
AAA	12.34
AA	12.50
A	12.70
BBB	13.41

SOURCE: Standard and Poor's *Bond Guide*, January 1984.

The nature of most debt obligations would be more obvious if contracts were written somewhat differently. At present, a standard bond with no extra features "guarantees" that the borrower will pay the lender, say, $90 per year for twenty years, then $1,000 twenty years hence. A more appropriate statement would indicate that the borrower guarantees to pay *no more than* $90 per year for twenty years, and $1,000 twenty years hence.

EXPECTED HOLDING-PERIOD RETURN

Calculating Holding-Period Return

Yield-to-maturity calculations do not take into account any changes in the market value of a security prior to maturity. This might be interpreted as implying that the owner has no interest in selling the instrument prior to maturity, no matter what happens to its price or his or her situation. The calculation also fails to treat intermediate payments in a fully satisfactory way. If the owner does not wish to spend interest payments, he or she might choose to buy more of these securities. But the number that can be bought at any time depends on the price at that time, and yield-to-maturity calculations fail to take this into account.

While few dispute the value of yield-to-maturity as at least an indicator of bond's overall return, it should be recognized as no more than this. For some purposes other measures may prove more useful. Moreover, for other types of securities there is no maturity: common stocks provide the most important example.

A measure that can be used for any investment is *holding-period return*. The idea is to specify a holding period of major interest, then assume that any payments received during the period are reinvested.

While assumptions may differ from case to case, the usual procedure assumes that any payment received from a security (e.g., a dividend from a stock, a coupon payment from a bond) is used to purchase more units of that security at the then current market price. Using this procedure, the performance of a security can be measured by comparing the value obtained in this manner at the end of the holding period with the value at the beginning. This *value-relative* can be converted to a holding-period return simply enough. The latter is just the value that satisfies the relationship:

$$1 + r_{hp} = \frac{\text{value at the end of the holding period}}{\text{value at the beginning of the holding period}}$$

Put another way: the *holding-period return is the holding-period value-relative minus one*.

Holding-period return can, of course, be converted to an equivalent return per period. Allowing for the effect of compounding, the appropriate procedure would be to find the value that satisfies the relationship:

$$(1 + r_g)^N = 1 + r_{hp}$$

or

$$r_g = (\sqrt[N]{1 + r_{hp}}) - 1$$

where:

$N =$ the number of periods in the holding period

$r_{hp} =$ the holding-period return

$r_g =$ the equivalent return per period, compounded every period

Suppose that a stock sold for $46 per share at the beginning of one year, paid dividends of $1.50 during that year, sold for $50 at the end of the year, paid dividends of $2 during the next year, and sold for $56 at the end of that year. What was the return over the two-year holding period?

To simplify the calculations, assume that all dividend payments are received at year-end. Then the $1.50 received during the first year could have bought $1.50/$50 or .03 shares of the stock at the end of the first year. In practice, of course, this would be feasible only if the money were pooled with other funds similarly invested—for example, in a mutual fund, or simply in an investor's own portfolio (for example, the dividends from 100 shares could have been used to buy three additional shares). In any event, for each share originally held, the investor would have obtained 1.03 × $2, or $2.06 in dividends in the second year, and have had stock with value of 1.03 × $56, or $57.68 at the end of the second year. The ending value would thus have been $57.68 + $2.06, giving a value-relative of:

$$\frac{\$59.74}{\$46.00} = 1.2987$$

The holding-period return was thus 29.87% per two years. This is equivalent to $\sqrt{1.2987} - 1$ (= .1396), or 13.96% per year.

An alternative method of computation treats the overall value-relative as the product of value-relatives for the individual periods. For example, if V_0 is the value at the beginning, V_1 the value at the end of the first year, and V_2 the value at the end of the second year:

$$\frac{V_2}{V_0} = \frac{V_2}{V_1} \times \frac{V_1}{V_0}$$

Moreover, there is no need to carry the expansion in number of shares from period to period, since the factor (1.03 in our example) will simply cancel out in the subsequent periods' value-relatives. Each period can be analyzed in isolation, an appropriate value-relative calculated, and the set of such value-relatives multiplied together.

In our example, during the first year, ownership of a stock with an initial value of $46 led to stock and cash with a value of $50 + $1.50 at the end of the year. Thus:

$$\frac{V_1}{V_0} = \frac{\$51.50}{\$46.00} = 1.1196$$

During the second year, ownership of stock with an initial value of $50 led to stock and cash with a value of $56 + $2 at year-end. Thus:

$$\frac{V_2}{V_1} = \frac{\$58}{\$50} = 1.16$$

The two-year holding-period value-relative was therefore:

$$1.1196 \times 1.16 = 1.2987$$

which is, of course, exactly equal to the value obtained earlier.

The value-relative for each period can be viewed as 1 plus the return for that period. Thus the return on the stock being analyzed was 11.96% in the first year and 16% in the second. The holding-period value-relative is the product of 1 plus each return. If N periods are involved:

$$\frac{V_N}{V_0} = (1 + r_1)(1 + r_2) \cdots (1 + r_N)$$

To convert the result to a holding-period return stated as an amount per period, with compounding, one can take the *geometric mean* of the periodic returns:

$$1 + r_g = \sqrt[N]{(1 + r_1)(1 + r_2) \cdots (1 + r_N)}$$

The Valuation of Risky Securities

More sophisticated calculations may be employed within this overall framework. Each dividend payment can be used to purchase shares immediately upon receipt, or, alternatively, allowed to earn interest in a savings account until year end. Brokerage and other costs associated with reinvestment of dividends can also be taken into account, although the magnitude of such costs will undoubtedly depend on the overall size of the holdings in question. The appropriate degree of complexity will, as always, be a function of the use for which the values are obtained.

Unhappily, the most appropriate holding period is often at least as uncertain as the return over any given holding period. Neither an investor's situation nor his or her preferences can usually be predicted with certainty. Moreover, from a strategic view, an investment manager would like to hold a given security only as long as it outperforms available alternatives. Attempts to identify such periods in advance are seldom completely successful, but managers quite naturally continue to try to discover them.

Holding-period return, like yield-to-maturity, provides a useful device for simplifying the complex reality of investment analysis. While no panacea, it allows an analyst to focus on the most relevant horizon in a given instance and offers a good measure of performance over such a period.

Some of the discussion of "return" in this book applies strictly only to return per holding period [i.e., $(V_N/V_0) - 1$]. Although the relationships may not apply exactly to other measures of return, the differences will, in most cases, be slight. *Quantitative* conclusions may sometimes apply strictly only to holding-period returns, but the *qualitative* conclusions will usually apply quite generally.

Estimating Expected Holding-Period Return

It is a relatively straightforward matter to calculate holding-period return after the fact. It is quite another thing to estimate it in advance. Any uncertainty surrounding payments by the issuer of a security during the period must be taken into account, but this is usually much simpler than the task of estimating the market values, which often constitute a large portion of overall return. For example, it might seem a simple matter to estimate the return over the next year for a share of Xerox stock. Dividends to be paid are relatively easy to predict. But the price at year-end will depend on investors' attitudes toward the company and its stock at that time. To predict even a one-year holding-period return one must consider a much longer period and assess not only the company's future but also investors' future attitudes about that future—a formidable task indeed.

Quite clearly, estimation of holding-period return must account in some way for uncertainty. If a single estimate is required, it should conform to the principles stated earlier. Explicitly or implicitly, an *expected value* should be provided. The various possibilities should be considered along with their probabilities.

Expected holding-period return is a weighted average of possible holding-period returns, using probabilities as weights.[1]

Estimating a Bond's Expected Holding-Period Return

Once the importance of market values is recognized, the presence of a new kind of risk becomes obvious. And the idea of a truly riskless investment becomes a relative matter.

Assume that an investor is interested in a holding period of five years. What sort of investment would be riskless for these purposes? Obviously, one with no default risk, which promises a payment at the end of five years and at no other time. Any other investment will involve some risk. The five-year holding-period return from a bond that provides semiannual coupon payments will depend on the prices at which such payments can be used to purchase additional units of the bond (or some other instrument). The return on a bond with a maturity in excess of five years will depend on the price at which it can be sold at the end of the fifth year. The return on a shorter-maturity bond will depend on the instruments that are available when the proceeds must be reinvested, and their prices at those times.

Since bond prices depend in large part on interest rates, this source of uncertainty is sometimes termed *interest-rate risk*. In many cases it is far more important than default risk. Moreover, it makes even U.S. government debt risky, unless there is a perfect correspondence between the investor's desire for cash and the payments promised by the bond in question.

Interest-rate risk should be incorporated in any analysis of expected holding-period return. For U.S. government securities this requires estimates of possible future interest rates and their associated probabilities. For other securities the likely future differentials for various levels of risk must also be taken into account.

EXPECTED RETURN AND SECURITY VALUATION

There is a very simple relationship between expected holding-period return, expected end-of-period value, and current value:

---

[1] Expected return is also the *mean* of the probability distribution of holding-period returns— hence the "mean" in the term "mean-variance approach."

$$\text{expected holding-period return} = \frac{\text{expected end-of-period value}}{\text{current value}} - 1$$

Thus:

$$\text{current value} = \frac{\text{expected end-of period value}}{1 + \text{expected holding-period return}}$$

In words: to value a security, one need only (!) estimate the expected value at the end of a holding period and the expected return for the holding period that is appropriate for such a security.

The final phase is crucial. What is the "appropriate" expected return, and on what does it depend? Therein lies the remainder of the theory of valuation.

One possible answer is that the appropriate expected return is that available from an investment that provides a riskless return over the period in question. However desirable such a relatively simple answer might be, it is simply inconsistent with the general behavior of investors.

By and large, investors are *risk averse*. Other things equal, they prefer less risk to more. However, other things equal, they also prefer more expected return to less. Not surprisingly, this implies that in the process of valuation one should require a higher expected return on a security, the greater the relevant risk involved.

Risk is not a simple concept: it thus requires extended discussion. The next two chapters provide it.

Problems

1. The arithmetic average annual return on Standard and Poor's index of common stocks from 1926 through 1978 was 11.18%. If, on January 1, 1979, you had been required to provide an estimate of the expected return on the S&P 500 over the coming year, would you have chosen 11.18%? Why or why not?

2. The probability distribution in Figure 5-6(b) is "skewed to the right." If a distribution is skewed to the left, which will be larger—the expected value or the median?

3. Calculate the expected return, mode, and median for a stock having the following probability distribution:

Return (5)	Probability of Occurrence
−40	.03
−10	.07
0	.30
15	.10
30	.05
40	.20
50	.25

4. At the beginning of the year the market price of Tulipmania stock was $45. At the end of the year the stock was selling for $40. During the year the company paid a cash dividend of $1. What was the stock's holding-period return for the year?

5. Charles Ponzi purchased 100 shares of Postal Reply Coupons, Incorporated, (PRC) and held the securities for a total of four years. Ponzi's holding-period returns in these four years were as follows:

Year	Return (%)
1	+20
2	+30
3	+50
4	−90

   a. What was the value-relative for the four-year period?
   b. What was the geometric mean return for the four-year period?

6. In August of 1979 Harrah's Casino in Reno, Nevada, accepted bets on the teams that would eventually go to the Superbowl to play for the National Football League championship. For example, one could pay $10 at that time to bet that the (then) Oakland Raiders would represent the American Football Conference in the Superbowl. The payoff on such a bet was set at $60 if the Raiders did go to the Superbowl, and zero otherwise. Payoffs for bets on all the teams in the Western Division of the American Football Conference were:

Team	Payoff per $1 Bet
Seattle Seahawks	$ 13
Oakland Raiders	6
San Diego Chargers	5
Denver Broncos	11
Kansas City Chiefs	101

a. What was the present value of $1 contingent on the event (state of the world) "The Raiders go to the Superbowl"?
b. What was the present value of $1 contingent on the event "The Seahawks go to the Superbowl"?
c. Why did the answers for (a) and (b) differ?
d. If someone had offered to pay you $1 if *any* team in the Western Division of the American Football Conference went to the Superbowl, how much would you have paid for this bet ("security")? If you had been virtually certain that one of these teams would go to the Superbowl, would your answer differ? Why or why not?

6

Portfolio
Analysis

PORTFOLIO AND SECURITY RETURNS

A major thesis of investment management is the need to consider individual investments as components of an overall investment plan. Without limiting the range of instruments covered, it is convenient to call individual investments *securities* and the totality the *portfolio*. Since it is rarely desirable to invest the entire funds of an individual or an institution in a single security, it is essential that every security be viewed in a portfolio context. This implies, for example, that a security's *total* risk is not of prime importance, only its *contribution* to the total risk of a portfolio. This distinction will be treated at length later. First, we consider the simpler case of return.

For expected return, the two measures coincide: a security's expected return *is* its contribution to portfolio expected return.

The example of a portfolio with three securities shown in Table 6-1(a) illustrates the point. The expected holding-period value-relative for the portfolio is clearly:

$$\frac{\$19,200}{17,200} = 1.1163$$

giving an expected holding-period return of 11.63%.

Table 6-1(b) combines the information in a somewhat different manner. As shown, the portfolio's expected holding-period value-relative is simply a *weighted average* of the expected value-relatives of its component securities, using *current market values* as weights.

This is not too surprising. Let us represent the current market value of security 1 by v_1^c, that of security 2 by v_2^c, and that of security 3 by v_3^c. Expected end-of-period values can be represented by v_1^e, v_2^e,

TABLE 6-1(a)
Security and Portfolio Values

(1) Security	(2) No. of Shares	(3) Current Price per Share	(4) Current Value = (2) × (3)	(5) Expected End-of-Period Value per Share	(6) Expected End-of-Period Value = (2) × (5)
ABC	100	$40	$ 4,000	$42	$ 4,200
DEF	200	35	7,000	40	8,000
XYZ	100	62	6,200	70	7,000
			$17,200		$19,200

TABLE 6-1(b)
Security and Portfolio Value-Relatives

(1) Security	(2) Current Value	(3) Proportion of Current Value of Portfolio = (2)/$17,200	(4) Current Price per Share	(5) Expected End-of-Period Value per Share	(6) Expected Holding-Period Value-Relative = (5)/(4)	(7) Contribution to Portfolio Expected Holding-Period Value-Relative = (3) × (6)
ABC	$ 4,000	.2325	$40	$42	1.0500	.2441
DEF	7,000	.4070	35	40	1.1429	.4652
XYZ	6,200	.3605	62	70	1.1290	.4070
	$17,200	1.0000				1.1163

TABLE 6-1(c)
Security and Portfolio Holding-Period Returns

(1) Security	(2) Proportion of Current Value of Portfolio	(3) Expected Holding-Period Return (%)	(4) Contribution to Portfolio Expected Holding-Period Return (%)
ABC	.2325	5.00	1.16
DEF	.4070	14.29	5.82
XYZ	.3605	12.90	4.65
	1.0000		11.63

and v_3^e. The current market value of the portfolio is, of course, $v_1^c + v_2^c + v_3^c$, while its expected end-of-period value is $v_1^e + v_2^e + v_3^e$. The expected value-relatives for the securities are just v_1^e/v_1^c, v_2^e/v_2^c, and v_3^e/v_3^c, while the relative market proportions are $v_1^c/(v_1^c + v_2^c + v_3^c)$, $v_2^c/(v_1^c + v_2^c + v_3^c)$, and $v_3^c/(v_1^c + v_2^c + v_3^c)$. The portfolio's expected value-relative is:

$$\frac{v_1^e + v_2^e + v_3^e}{v_1^c + v_2^c + v_3^c} \tag{6-1}$$

This value is computed directly in Table 6-1(a).

In Table 6-1(b) each security's expected value-relative is multiplied by its relative market value and these products are summed. Using the current notation:

$$\left(\frac{v_1^c}{v_1^c + v_2^c + v_3^c} \cdot \frac{v_1^e}{v_1^c}\right) + \left(\frac{v_2^c}{v_1^c + v_2^c + v_3^c} \cdot \frac{v_2^e}{v_2^c}\right) + \left(\frac{v_3^c}{v_1^c + v_2^c + v_3^c} \cdot \frac{v_3^e}{v_3^c}\right) \tag{6-2}$$

After canceling and simplifying, this reduces to formula (6-1).

The relationship is perfectly general. A portfolio's expected holding-period value-relative will be a weighted average of its component securities' expected holding-period value-relatives, using current market values as weights.

The procedure can be used as easily with holding-period returns. Table 6-1(c) provides an illustration. Holding-period return is simply 100 times the value obtained by subtracting 1 from the holding-period value-relative. Thus a weighted average of the former will have the same characteristics as a weighted average of the latter:

The expected return of a portfolio is a weighted average of the expected returns of its component securities, using relative market values as weights.

In symbols:

$$E_p = \sum_{i=1}^{N} X_i E_i$$

where

E_p = the expected return of the portfolio
X_i = the proportion of the portfolio's value invested in security i
E_i = the expected return of security i
N = the number of securities

The summation sign means that every security must be included in the total (i.e., $E_p = X_1 E_1 + X_2 E_2 + \cdots + X_N E_N$).

Since a portfolio's expected return is a weighted average of the expected returns of its securities, the contribution of each security to portfolio expected return depends on its expected return and its proportionate share of the current portfolio's market value. Nothing else is relevant.

An investor who simply wants the greatest possible expected return should hold one security: the one he or she considers to have the greatest expected return. In case of ties, a coin could be flipped to decide which of the group of top candidates to hold. Very few investors do this, and very few investment advisers would counsel such an extreme policy. Instead investors should, and do, *diversify*: their portfolios include more than one security. Why? Because diversification can reduce *risk*.

RISK

The *Webster's New Collegiate Dictionary* definition of risk includes the following meanings: "possibility of loss or injury . . . the degree of probability of such loss."[1] This conforms to the connotation put on the term by most investors. Professionals often speak of "downside risk" and "upside potential" on the grounds that risk has to do with bad outcomes, potential with good ones.

As formal measures of risk, such notions can be criticized on two grounds: vagueness and excessive simplicity. One might measure risk by the probability that return will fall below the expected value. But this could characterize many different investments as equally risky. (For example, the probability in question is .50 for all symmetric distributions.) A more common procedure would focus on the probability of any *negative* return. But even this is an extremely blunt measure. Which is riskier: an investment with a .30 probability of a slight loss or one with a .29 probability of a very large loss? Most investors would specify the latter.

A more useful measure of risk takes into account both the probability of an outcome and its magnitude. Instead of measuring the probability of a range of outcomes, one estimates the extent to which the actual outcome is likely to *diverge* from the expected value.

Two measures are used for this purpose: the average (or mean) absolute deviation and the standard deviation.

Table 6-2(a) shows how the average absolute deviation can be calculated. First the expected return is determined in the usual way.[2] In this case it is 6.50%. Next each possible outcome is analyzed to determine the amount by which its value deviates from the expected amount. These figures, shown in column (5) of the table, include both positive and negative values. As shown in column (6), a weighted average, using probabilities as weights, will equal zero. This is a mathematical necessity, given the way the expected value is calculated. To assess

---

[1] By permission. From *Webster's New Collegiate Dictionary*, copyright 1980 by G. & C. Merriam Co., Publishers of the Merriam-Webster dictionaries.

[2] A more consistent approach uses the median return instead of the expected return when calculating the mean absolute deviation.

TABLE 6-2(a)
Calculating the Mean Absolute Deviation

(1) Event	(2) Probability	(3) Return (%)	(4) = (2) × (3) Probability × Return
a	.20	−10	−2.00
b	.35	5	1.75
c	.45	15	6.75
		Expected return =	6.50

(5) = (3) − 6.50 Deviation	(6) = (2) × (5) Probability × Deviation	(7) Probability × Absolute Deviation
−16.50	−3.300	3.300
− 1.50	− .525	.525
8.50	3.825	3.825
	0	

Average absolute deviation = 7.65

risk, the signs of the deviations can simply be ignored. As shown in column (7), the weighted average of the absolute values of the deviations, using the probabilities as weights, is 7.65%. This constitutes the first measure of "likely" deviation.

The second measure is slightly more complex but preferable analytically. As shown in Table 6-2(b), the deviations are squared (making the values all positive), then a weighted average of these amounts is taken, using the probabilities as weights. The result is termed the *variance*. We convert it to the original units by taking the square root. The result [in Table 6-2(b), 9.3675%] is termed the *standard deviation*.

TABLE 6-2(b)
Calculating the Standard Deviation

(1) Event	(2) Probability	(3) Deviation	(4) = (3)² Deviation Squared	(5) = (2) × (4) Probability × Deviation Squared
a	.20	−16.50	272.25	54.45
b	.35	1.50	2.25	.7875
c	.45	8.50	72.25	32.5125

Variance = probability weighted average squared deviation = 87.75
Standard deviation = square root of variance = 9.3675

In the examples shown in Tables 6-2(a) and (b) any single measure of likely deviation would provide at best a very crude idea of the possibilities. But in the more common case in which a portfolio's prospects are being assessed, either of the measures described earlier may prove to be a very good guide to the analyst's degree of uncertainty. The clearest example arises when the situation can be reasonably well represented by the familiar bell-shaped curve: that is, the analyst is willing to use a *normal probability distribution*. This is often considered a plausible assumption for analyzing returns on diversified portfolios when the holding period being studied is relatively short (say a quarter or less). For longer holding periods, a more appropriate procedure assumes that the portfolio's *continuously compounded rate of return* is distributed in this manner (equivalently: that the return itself follows a "log-normal" distribution). Such an approach may be applied for any holding period; but for short holding periods, since actual return differs little from the continuously compounded return, either procedure may be used.

For a normal distribution the standard deviation is about 125% of the average absolute deviation. Either value may thus be determined, once the other is known. In general, a list of portfolios ordered from highest to lowest on the basis of the standard deviation of return would differ little if at all from a list ordered on the basis of average absolute deviation.

But why count happy surprises (those above the expected value) at all in a measure of risk? Why not just consider the deviations *below* the expected return? Measures that do so have much to recommend them. But if a distribution is symmetric, the results will be the same, since the left side is a mirror image of the right! And in general, a list of portfolios ordered on the basis of "downside risk" will differ little if at all from one ordered on the basis of standard deviation. A similar statement can be made about many other reasonable measures of risk.

Although different measures of risk are often virtually interchangeable, the standard deviation is generally preferred for investment analysis. The reason is simple: the standard deviation of a portfolio's return can be determined from (among other things) the standard deviations of the returns of its component securities, no matter what the distributions. No relationship of comparable simplicity exists for most other measures.

Let us emphasize the meaning of this measure of risk:

The standard deviation is an estimate of the likely divergence of an *actual* amount from an *expected* amount.

For working purposes, the returns are often assumed to follow a normal distribution, giving the relationship shown in Table 6-3. Thus

TABLE 6-3
Probabilities of Divergence for a Normal Distribution

Divergence, in Terms of Standard Deviation Units	Probability That Divergence Will Be Less Than This Amount
0	0
.10	.08
.20	.16
.30	.24
.40	.31
.50	.38
.60	.45
.70	.52
.80	.58
.90	.63
1.00	.68
1.10	.73
1.20	.77
1.30	.81
1.40	.84
1.50	.87
1.60	.89
1.70	.91
1.80	.93
1.90	.94
2.00	.95
2.10	.96
2.30	.97
2.40	.98
2.50	.99

the odds are thought to be about 2 out of 3 that the actual outcome will lie within one standard deviation of the expectation and about 95 out of 100 that the actual outcome will lie within two standard deviations of the expectation.

When an analyst predicts that a stock will return 12% next year, he or she is presumably stating something comparable to an expected value. If asked to express the *uncertainty* about the outcome, the analyst might reply that the odds are about 2 out of 3 that the actual return will be within 8% of the estimate (i.e., between 4% and 20%). The standard deviation is a formal measure of uncertainty, or risk, expressed in this manner, just as the expected value is a formal measure of a "best-guess" estimate. Most analysts make such predictions directly, without explicitly assessing probabilities and making the requisite computations. No matter. The point is to consider uncertainty or risk and to measure its extent as best one can.

PORTFOLIO RISK

What is the relationship between the risk of a portfolio and the risks of its component securities? An answer that covers all possible cases is both complex and of limited practical importance. We will develop the general relationship briefly, then turn to some special cases that are both relatively simple and extremely important for investment analysis.

Table 6-4(a) shows the returns on two securities and on a portfolio that includes both of them. Each row in the table indicates an analyst's assessment of the likely outcomes if a particular event takes place; the probability of the event is also shown.

TABLE 6-4
Portfolio and Security Risks

(a) RETURNS				
(1) Event	(2) Probability	(3) Return on Security A	(4) Return on Security B	(5) = .6 × (3) + .4 × (4) Return on Portfolio
a	.10	5.0%	−1.0%	2.6%
b	.40	7.0	6.0	6.6
c	.30	−4.0	2.0	−1.6
d	.20	15.0	20.0	17.0

(b) SUMMARY MEASURES			
	Security A	Security B	Portfolio
Expected return	5.10%	6.90%	5.82%
Variance of return	45.89	48.09	42.7956
Standard deviation of return	6.7742	6.9347	6.5418

(c) COVARIANCE AND CORRELATION					
(1) Event	(2) Probability	(3) Deviation of Return for Sec. A	(4) Deviation of Return for Sec. B	(5) = (3) × (4) Product of Deviations	(6) = (2) × (5) Probability Times Product of Deviations
a	.10	−.1%	−7.90%	.79	.079
b	.40	1.90	−.9	−1.71	−.684
c	.30	−9.10	−4.9	44.59	13.377
d	.20	9.90	13.1	129.69	25.938
				Covariance =	38.71

$$\text{Correlation coefficient} = \frac{38.71}{6.7742 \times 6.9347} = .824$$

In Table 6-4(a), security A constitutes 60% of the market value of the portfolio and security B the other 40%. The predicted return on the portfolio in each row is simply a weighted average of the predicted returns on the securities, using the proportionate values as weights.

Table 6-4(b) shows values computed from the estimates in Table 6-4(a), using the procedures described in previous sections. As always, the expected return for the portfolio is simply the weighted average of the expected returns on its securities, using the proportionate values as weights (5.82% = .6 × 5.10% + .4 × 6.90%). However, this is not true for either the variance or the standard deviation of returns. The risk of a portfolio is not typically equal to the weighted average of the risks of its component securities. In this case, both the variance and the standard deviation of return for the portfolio are smaller than the corresponding values for either of the component securities!

This rather surprising result has a simple explanation. The risk of a portfolio depends not only on the risks of its securities, considered in isolation, but also on the extent to which they are affected similarly by underlying events. To illustrate this, two extreme cases are shown in Table 6-5.

In the first case both the variance and the standard deviation of the portfolio are the same as the corresponding values for the securities. Here diversification has no effect at all on risk.

In the second case the situation is very different. Here the security's returns offset one another in such a manner that the particular combination that makes up this portfolio has no risk at all! Diversification has completely eliminated risk.

The difference between these cases concerns the extent to which the security's returns are *correlated*—that is, tend to "go together." Either of two measures can be used to state the degree of such a relationship: the *covariance* or the *correlation coefficient*.

Table 6-4(c) shows the computations required to obtain the covariance for the two securities considered earlier. The deviation of each security's return from its expected value is determined and the product of the two obtained [column (5)]:

> The *covariance* of two securities' returns is a weighted average of the products of the deviations of the returns from their expected values, using the probabilities of the deviations as weights.

A positive value for covariance indicates that the securities' returns tend to go together—for example, a better-than-expected return for one is likely to occur along with a better-than-expected return for the other. A negative covariance indicates a tendency for the returns to offset one another—for example, a better-than-expected return for one is likely to occur along with a worse-than-expected return for the other. A small or zero value for the covariance indicates that there is little or no relationship between the two returns.

TABLE 6-5

Risk and Return for a Two-Security Portfolio

(a) TWO SECURITIES WITH EQUAL RETURNS				
(1) Event	(2) Probability	(3) Return on Security A (%)	(4) Return on Security B (%)	(5) = .6 × (3) + .4 × (4) Return on Portfolio (%)
a	.10	5.0	5.0	5.0
b	.40	7.0	7.0	7.0
c	.30	6.0	6.0	6.0
d	.20	−2.0	−2.0	−2.0
Expected return (%)		4.70	4.70	4.70
Variance of return		11.61	11.61	11.61
Standard deviation of return		3.4073	3.4073	3.4073

(b) TWO SECURITIES WITH OFFSETTING RETURNS				
(1) Event	(2) Probability	(3) Return on Security A (%)	(4) Return on Security B (%)	(5) = .6 × (3) + .4 × (4) Return on Portfolio (%)
a	.10	5.0	2.5	4.0
b	.40	7.0	−.5	4.0
c	.30	6.0	1.0	4.0
d	.20	−2.0	13.0	4.0
Expected return (%)		4.70	2.95	4.0
Variance of return		11.61	26.1225	0
Standard deviation of return		3.4073	5.1110	0

A related measure is the *correlation coefficient*:

The *correlation* of two securities' returns equals their covariance divided by the product of their standard deviations.

As shown in Table 6-4(c), in this case the value is .824. The procedure used to obtain the correlation coefficient rescales the covariance to facilitate comparison with corresponding values for other pairs of variables. *Correlation coefficients always lie between −1.0 and +1.0, inclusive*. The former value represents perfect *negative* correlation of the type shown in the example in Table 6-5(b); the latter, perfect positive correlation of the type shown in the example in Table 6-5(a). Most cases lie between, as does the example shown in Table 6-4.

The relationship between covariance and correlation can be represented as follows:

Portfolio Analysis

$$C_{AB} = r_{AB}S_AS_B \qquad \textbf{(6-3)}$$

or

$$r_{AB} = \frac{C_{AB}}{S_AS_B} \qquad \textbf{(6-4)}$$

where

C_{AB} = covariance between return on A and return on B
r_{AB} = coefficient of correlation between return on A and return on B
S_A = standard deviation of return for A
S_B = standard deviation of return for B

Armed with measures of correlation between two returns, we can now show the relationship between the risk of a portfolio of two securities and the relevant variables. The formula is:

$$V_p = X_A^2 V_A + 2X_AX_BC_{AB} + X_B^2 V_B \qquad \textbf{(6-5)}$$

where

V_p = the variance of return for the portfolio
V_A = the variance of return for security A
V_B = the variance of return for security B
C_{AB} = the covariance between the return on security A and the return on security B
X_A = the proportion of the portfolio's value invested in security A
X_B = the proportion of the portfolio's value invested in security B

For the case shown in Table 6-4:

$X_A = .6$
$X_B = .4$
$V_A = 45.89$
$V_B = 48.09$
$C_{AB} = 38.71$

Inserting these values in formula (6-5) gives 42.7956, which is the variance for the portfolio as a whole.

The relationship that gives the variance for a portfolio with more than two securities is similar in nature but more extensive. Both the risks of the securities and all their correlations have to be taken into account. The formula is:

$$V_p = \sum_{i=1}^{N} \sum_{j=1}^{N} X_iX_jC_{ij} \qquad \textbf{(6-6)}$$

where

V_p = the variance of return for the portfolio

X_i = the proportion of the portfolio's value invested in security i

X_j = the proportion of the portfolio's value invested in security j

C_{ij} = the covariance between the return on security i and the return on security j

N = the number of securities

The two summation signs mean that every possible combination must be included in the total, with a value between 1 and N substituted where i appears and a value between 1 and N substituted where j appears. In those cases in which the values are the same, the relevant covariance is that between a security's return and itself. This is the variance of the security's return, as reexamination of the procedure described before will show.

Since formula (6-6) is rather formidable, it is fortunate that the key ideas about portfolio risk can be obtained from an examination of important special cases, to which we now turn.

WHEN DIVERSIFICATION DOESN'T HELP: PERFECTLY POSITIVELY CORRELATED RETURNS

The returns from two securities are perfectly positively correlated when a cross-plot gives points lying precisely on an upward-sloping straight line, as shown in Figure 6-1(a). Each point indicates the return on security A (horizontal axis) and the return on security B (vertical axis) corresponding to one event. The example shown in Table 6-5(a) conforms to this pattern.

What is the effect on risk when two securities of this type are combined? The general formula (6-5) is:

$$V_p = X_A^2 V_A + 2X_A X_B C_{AB} + X_B^2 V_B$$

The covariance term can, of course, be replaced, using formula (6-3):

$$C_{AB} = r_{AB} S_A S_B$$

However, in this case there is perfect positive correlation, so $r_{AB} = +1$ and $C_{AB} = S_A S_B$. As always, $V_A = S_A^2$, $V_B = S_B^2$, and $V_p = S_p^2$. Substituting all these values in the general formula gives:

$$S_p^2 = X_A^2 S_A^2 + 2X_A X_B S_A S_B + X_B^2 S_B^2$$

The right-hand side can be factored into a single term squared:

$$S_p^2 = (X_A S_A + X_B S_B)^2$$

As long as the value in parentheses is not negative:

$$S_p = X_A S_A + X_B S_B \quad \text{when } r_{AB} = +1 \qquad \textbf{(6-7)}$$

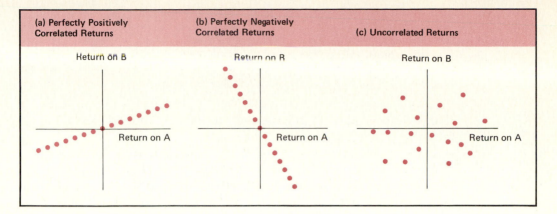

FIGURE 6-1
Returns on Two Securities

This is an important result. *When two securities' returns are perfectly positively correlated, the risk of a combination, measured by the standard deviation of return, is just a weighted average of the risks by the component securities, using market values as weights.* The principle holds as well if more than two securities are included in a portfolio. In such cases, diversification does not provide risk *reduction*, only risk *averaging*.

WHEN DIVERSIFICATION CAN ELIMINATE RISK: PERFECTLY NEGATIVELY CORRELATED RETURNS

The returns from two securities will be perfectly negatively correlated when a cross-plot gives points lying precisely on a downward-sloping straight line, as shown in Figure 6-1(b). The example shown in Table 6-5(b) conforms to this pattern.

Since $r_{AB} = -1$ in such a situation, the general formula becomes:

$$S_p^2 = X_A^2 S_A^2 - 2X_A X_B S_A S_B + X_B^2 S_B^2$$

This can be factored to obtain:

$$S_p^2 = (X_A S_A - X_B S_B)^2 \quad \text{when } r_{AB} = -1 \qquad \textbf{(6-8)}$$

Now, imagine a portfolio in which the proportionate holdings are inversely related to the relative risks of the two securities. That is:

$$\frac{X_A}{X_B} = \frac{S_B}{S_A}$$

Rearranging:

$$X_A = \frac{S_B X_B}{S_A}$$

For this combination the parenthesized term in formula (6-8) will be:

$$X_A S_A - X_B S_B = \frac{S_B X_B}{S_A} S_A - X_B S_B = 0$$

If this term is zero, of course, the portfolio's standard deviation of return must be zero as well.

When two securities' returns are perfectly negatively correlated, it is possible to combine them in a manner that will eliminate all risk. This principle motivates all *hedging* strategies. The object is to take positions that will offset each other with regard to certain kinds of risk, reducing or completely eliminating such sources of uncertainty.

Hedging strategies, used extensively in the futures markets, by certain bond managers, and in the markets for options on common stocks, will be discussed at length in later chapters.

THE INSURANCE PRINCIPLE: UNCORRELATED RETURNS

A special case of extreme importance arises when a cross-plot of security returns shows no pattern that can be represented even approximately by an upward-sloping or downward-sloping line. In such an instance, the returns are uncorrelated. The correlation coefficient, r_{AB}, is zero, as is the covariance. Figure 6-1(c) provides an example.

In this situation, the general formula (6-5) becomes:

$$S_p^2 = X_A^2 S_A^2 + X_B^2 S_B^2 \quad \text{when } r_{AB} = 0 \qquad \textbf{(6-9)}$$

At first glance it might appear that diversification has no effect here. But this is not at all the case. To see this, consider a portfolio divided equally between two securities of equal risk, say 10.0%. That is:

$$X_A = .5, \quad X_B = .5, \quad S_A = 10, \quad S_B = 10$$

Substituting these values in formula (6-9) gives:

$$(.5)^2(10)^2 + (.5)^2(10)^2 = (.25 \times 100) + (.25 \times 100)$$

Thus:

$$S_p^2 = 50 \quad \text{and} \quad S_p = 7.07$$

The risk of the portfolio is less than the risk of either of its component securities. Diversification has indeed helped. If more than two securities with uncorrelated returns are included in a portfolio, the result is similar. In such a case the complete formula (6-6) becomes:

$$S_p^2 = X_1^2 S_1^2 + X_2^2 S_2^2 + \cdots + X_N^2 S_N^2 \qquad \textbf{(6-10)}$$

when all returns are uncorrelated. In this formula:

S_p = the standard deviation of the return on the portfolio

$X_1, X_2, \ldots$ = the proportions invested in securities 1, 2, etc.

$S_1, S_2, \ldots$ = the standard deviations of the returns for securities 1, 2, etc.

N = the number of securities included

This is an extremely important relationship for investment analysis. It also provides the basis for insurance, or *risk-pooling*.

We can see this by extending the previous example. Imagine a portfolio of equal parts of a number of securities, each with a risk (standard deviation of return) of 10%. If two securities are included:

$$S_p^2 = (½)^2 10^2 + (½)^2 10^2$$
$$= 2(½)^2 10^2$$

If three securities are included:

$$S_p^2 = (⅓)^2 10^2 + (⅓)^2 10^2 + (⅓)^2 10^2$$
$$= 3(⅓)^2 10^2$$

To generalize, represent the number of securities by N. Then:

$$S_p^2 = \left(\frac{1}{N}\right)^2 10^2 + \left(\frac{1}{N}\right)^2 10^2 + \cdots$$
$$= N\left(\frac{1}{N}\right)^2 10^2$$

Simplifying:

$$S_p^2 = \frac{N}{N^2} 10^2 = \frac{10^2}{N}$$
$$S_p = \frac{10}{\sqrt{N}}$$

Table 6-6 shows the relationship between the number of securities included and the risk of the corresponding portfolio, while Figure 6-2 provides a graphical representation.

Diversification provides substantial risk reduction if the components of a portfolio are uncorrelated. In fact, *if enough are included, the overall risk of the portfolio will be almost (but not quite) zero!* This is why insurance companies attempt to write many individual policies and spread their coverage so as to minimize overall risk. Death from natural causes can be insured at low cost, since payments on various policies are virtually uncorrelated. On the other hand, death arising from a major war cannot be insured at low cost, since payments are likely to be correlated, at least to some extent.

Some risks can be substantially reduced by pooling, and others

TABLE 6-6
Risk of Portfolios with Different Numbers of Securities When Returns Are Uncorrelated and All $S_i =$ 10%

Number of Securities	Standard Deviation of Return
1	10.00
2	7.07
3	5.77
4	5.00
5	4.47
10	3.16
20	2.24
50	1.41
100	1.00
1,000	.32
5,000	.14
10,000	.10
100,000	.03

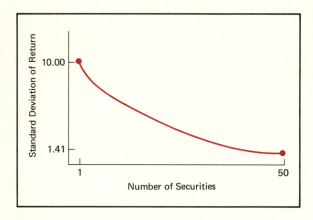

FIGURE 6-2
Risk versus Number of Securities, When Returns Are Uncorrelated and All $S_i =$ 10%

cannot. This has crucial implications for investment management. Most importantly, it provides the basis for understanding the relationship between risk and return, as will be shown in the next chapter.

BORROWING AND LENDING: COMBINING RISKY AND RISKLESS SECURITIES

What happens to risk when a risky security (or portfolio) is combined with a riskless one? Once again we can find the answer by adapting the general formula (6-5) in the appropriate manner. If security A's return is certain, while that of security B is uncertain, $S_A = 0$, as does C_{AB}, and the relationship becomes:

$$S_p^2 = X_A^2 0 + 2X_A X_B 0 + X_B^2 S_B^2$$
$$= X_B^2 S_B^2$$

Thus:

$$S_p = X_B S_B \quad \text{when} \quad S_A = 0 \qquad \text{(6-11)}$$

When a risky security or portfolio is combined with a riskless one, the risk of the combination is proportional to the amount invested in the risky component.

An obvious case of this sort arises when an investor splits his or her funds between a common stock portfolio and a savings account. Table 6-7 shows some representative values. Cases C and D involve splitting funds between the risky alternative (B) and the riskless one (A). *Investing in a riskless security is equivalent to lending money.* For example, by investing in U.S. Treasury bills, one is in effect lending money to the U.S. government.

Combinations C and D are plotted in Figure 6-3, along with the original alternatives, A and B. Each point shows the expected return and risk (standard deviation) of an alternative combination. Since both risk and return will be proportional to the investment proportions in a case of this sort, both point C and point D lie on the straight line connecting points A and B. This relationship is quite general: by combining riskless lending (A) with investment in any risky situation (B), an investor can obtain any risk-return combination plotting along the straight line (AB) connecting the two points in a risk-return diagram such as that shown in Figure 6-3.

When formulas involving investment proportions are used, the proportions must, of course, sum to 1, since the whole must equal the sum of its parts. Moreover, thus far we have focused on cases in which

TABLE 6-7
Combining a Risky and a Riskless Investment

	Security A (Savings Account)	Security B (Common Stock Portfolio)	Combination C	Combination D	Combination E
Proportion in A (X_B)	1.0	0	.6	.4	−.2
Proportion in B (X_B)	0	1.0	.4	.6	1.2
Expected return	5.0%	10.0%	7.0%	8.0%	11.0%
Standard deviation of return	0%	20.0%	8.0%	12.0%	24.0%

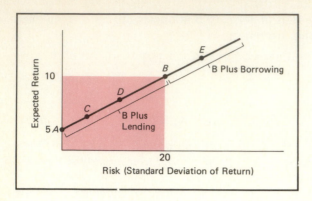

FIGURE 6-3
Risk and Return for Combinations of a
Risky and Riskless Investment

the individual proportions are all positive. But this need not be the case. For example, X_A could equal $-.20$ and X_B could equal $+1.20$, as shown by combination E in Table 6-7 and point E in Figure 6-3.

What does this mean? Imagine a person with $10,000 to invest. If willing to take the risk involved, such an investor might invest all his or her own money and also borrow additional money to take advantage of some (hopefully profitable) opportunity. For example, $2,000 might be borrowed, with a promise to repay the loan plus interest at 5%. A total of $12,000 could then be invested in the project. Everything left over after repaying the loan would belong to the investor.

Table 6-8(a) shows the effect of this sort of leverage under favorable circumstances. Here the investment returns 10%, leaving the investor with a profit on his or her own investment and a net contribution from the investment of the borrowed funds. The result is a total return of 11.0% on the investor's own capital.

The final column of Table 6-7 shows a similar set of computations for combination E. If borrowed funds are invested in a risky alternative with an expected return in excess of the interest rate to be paid, the result is an increase in the expected return on the investor's capital. This is the good news about *leverage:* point E lies above point B in Figure 6-3.

However, leverage can also bring bad news. This is shown in Table 6-8(b), which indicates the outcome when the investment in question returns less than the rate paid on borrowed funds. The investor must make up the difference, reducing the return on his or her own capital to an amount below that on the investment itself. Clearly, he or she would have been better off without borrowing. This sort of outcome constitutes the *risk* associated with leverage.

The effect of leverage on risk is shown in the fourth line of Table 6-7. Borrowing increases risk. This is also shown in Figure 6-3: point E is to the right of point B.

Investors can and do borrow from a number of sources. Banks

TABLE 6-8
The Effects of Leverage

(a) With a Favorable Outcome:

Investment return	10%
Dollar return on total investment	$.10 \times \$12,000 = \$1,200$
Interest rate on loan	5%
Dollar amount of interest	$.05 \times \$2,000 \quad = \underline{\quad 100}$
	Net proceeds $= \$1,100$

$$\text{Return on investor's capital} = \frac{1,100}{10,000} = .110 = 11.0\%$$

(b) With an Unfavorable Outcome:

Investment return	2%
Dollar return on total investment	$.02 \times \$12,000 \quad = \$240$
Interest rate on loan	5%
Dollar amount of interest	$.05 \times \$2,000 \quad = \underline{\quad 100}$
	Net proceeds $= \$140$

$$\text{Return on investor's capital} = \frac{140}{10,000} = .014 = 1.4\%$$

will loan money, using cars, houses, or securities as collateral. Credit unions often loan money with no explicit collateral at all. Security brokers loan money on margin accounts, using securities as collateral.

Interest rates charged for loans differ from time to time. Moreover, at any time the amount charged may depend on the borrower, the lender, the collateral, the purpose for which the loan is made, the length of time involved, and the amount of money borrowed. If there is a chance that the loan will not be repaid in full and on time, the rate charged will, of course, be higher, and the loan will not be riskless, making the use of formula (6-11) inappropriate.

In those cases in which leverage is used within the limits required to keep the loan riskless, the relationship will be that shown in Figure 6-3. Margined or leveraged purchases of any risky investment (e.g., B) can be used to obtain a combination of risk and return plotting above and to the right of point B on the straight line connecting the points representing the two components (A and B). The prospect obtained in this manner will depend on the amount of leverage: the greater the leverage, the farther to the right of the risky investment's point will be the point representing the new combination.

Leverage is commonly used by corporations. For example, point B in Figure 6-3 might represent the risk and return obtained by a firm on its total assets. If, however, the corporation has issued debt, both the risk and return of its common stock should be greater than this.

For example, if the firm had obtained an initial capital of $12,000 by issuing $2,000 worth of debt and $10,000 worth of equity, the results would conform to the example shown in Table 6-7 and Figure 6-3.

Many corporations issue sufficient debt to make at least some of it risky. Thus the relationship is more complex than this. But the point remains: *leverage generally increases both risk and expected return*. It is thus neither obviously desirable nor obviously undesirable.

WHEN LEVERAGE MAY NOT MATTER: MARKET ALTERNATIVES

One of the great debates in the field of corporate finance concerns the appropriate amount of debt in a firm's capital structure. In essence, the question is whether or not to lever the firm's assets and, if so, to what extent. Putting it slightly differently, the issue concerns the appropriate "packaging" of the firm's overall prospects.

One answer to this question was provided in 1938 by John Burr Williams.[3] His *law of the conservation of investment value* asserts that it simply doesn't matter. As long as investors can make deals among themselves, the initial packaging may be irrelevant. For example, if an investor would like a leveraged version of a firm's prospects, and the firm has chosen to issue no debt, the investor can accomplish his or her goal by margined purchase of the firm's stock. On the other hand, if he or she would like an unleveraged version and the firm has issued debt, the investor can simply hold proportionate shares of the firm's debt and equity, thus "putting the firm back together."

An extended analysis of this relationship, provided by Modigliani and Miller [4] in 1958, is now generally known as the *M–M hypothesis*. Subsequent discussion has centered on tax effects, bankruptcy costs, and other factors that may make it more efficient for firms to provide certain combinations than for investors to do so.

Many investment institutions exist solely to allow low-cost packaging, unpackaging, or repackaging of various investment projects. Their very existence is evidence that such a function is not costless. However, these institutions make such activity possible and relatively inexpensive. If a firm packages its prospects inappropriately, some other procedure may be used to repackage the outcomes. A firm's choice of leverage may matter, but much less than it would in a less well-developed capital market.

---

[3] John Burr Williams, *The Theory of Investment Value* (Cambridge: Harvard University Press, 1938).

[4] Franco Modigliani and Merton Miller, "The Cost of Capital, Corporation Finance, and the Theory of Investment," *American Economic Review*, 48, no. 3 (June 1958), 261–97.

WHEN LEVERAGE DOES MATTER: PERSONAL INVESTMENT POLICY

Eventually everyone must select an overall investment policy. In doing so, one should consider all sources of future income: salary, savings, insurance, social security, pension, stocks and bonds, etc. The sum total can be viewed as a total portfolio. Alternatively, all the risky elements can be considered one portfolio and the riskless elements another. Figure 6-4 shows the latter view, highlighting the decision concerning the appropriate amount of borrowing or lending. This particular investor's attitudes toward risk and return are summarized in a family of indifference curves. He or she is indifferent among combinations lying on curve I_1. He or she is also indifferent among combinations lying on curve I_2 but would prefer any of them to any combination lying on I_1. The curves are upward-sloping, indicating the common preference for higher expected return and aversion to risk. Thus, if a person considers two combinations equally good, the one with the greater expected return must also be more risky.

A typical characteristic of such indifference curves is also shown in Figure 6-4: *each curve becomes steeper as one goes from left to right.* This indicates that the more risk involved, the greater the added expected return required to keep the investor "equally happy."

While the curves in Figure 6-4(a) and those in Figure 6-4(b) both (1) are upward-sloping and (2) become steeper as one goes from left

FIGURE 6-4
Selecting a Personal Investment Policy

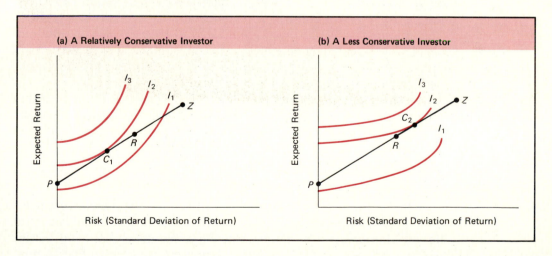

to right, they nonetheless are quite different, reflecting significant differences in the preferences of the two investors.

The particular shape of the indifference curves reflecting a given investor's preferences depends on his or her unique attitudes, circumstances, and general psychology. The investor shown in Figure 6-4(a) prefers to split funds between the risky combination shown by point R and the riskless alternative shown by point P. The preferred combination is C_1—it lies on his or her highest (best) attainable indifference curve, which says nothing more than that he or she prefers it over all the available alternatives on line PRZ.

The investor shown in Figure 6-4(b), presented with the same alternatives, chooses to borrow funds. His or her preferred combination is C_2—which lies on the highest (best) attainable indifference curve. Such a person may be richer, younger, or simply more adventuresome. But no one can say that he or she is right and the other investor is wrong. The ultimate choice between risk and return is up to the person who will bear the consequences of that choice. Investment advisers can help a client obtain the best possible alternatives, understand the prospects for those alternatives, and think carefully about his or her feelings about those prospects. But the final decision must depend on the client's preferences.

INVESTMENT SELECTION: AN OVERVIEW

Figure 6-5 provides a graphical summary of the conceptual steps involved in investment selection.

The first step requires analysis of the prospects of potential investment media. This is traditionally known as *security analysis*. Both the expected return and the risk of each alternative must be assessed. This information is portrayed graphically in Figure 6-5(a). In addition, some assessment must be made of the correlations among the various returns. As discussed in the later chapters, this process can be simplified considerably, but it cannot be ignored.

The second step is *portfolio analysis*. In essence, the predictions obtained in the first step must be combined to determine the prospects of alternative portfolios (combinations). From these a set of *efficient* alternatives can be identified.

An efficient portfolio has less risk than any other with comparable expected return and more return than any other with comparable risk.

In Figure 6-5(b1) no riskless alternatives are available. Every point in the shaded area, or opportunity set, represents an attainable portfolio, and the *efficient portfolios* plot along the upper left-hand border of this area. This is the *efficient risk-return trade-off*. To find it, relatively sophisticated computer analysis may have to be performed. For

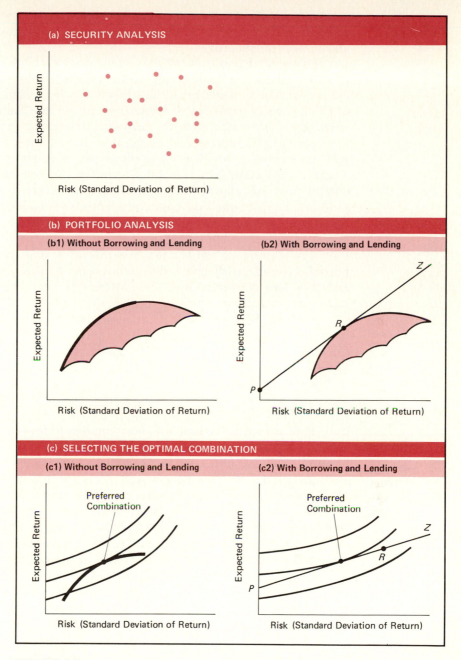

FIGURE 6-5
Investment Selection

present purposes it suffices to state that, given the estimates of security analysts, determination of the efficient set of portfolios is a strictly mechanical procedure.

Figure 6-5(b2) shows the results of portfolio analysis when it is possible to both lend and borrow (within reason) at some riskless interest rate P. The procedure can be broken into two parts. First, the set of efficient risky portfolios is determined, as before. Then one of these is chosen to be combined with borrowing or lending; in Figure 6-5(b2) it is the portfolio represented by point R. By combining this portfolio with borrowing or lending, an investor can obtain any desired risk-return combination lying on the relevant portion of line PRZ. Such combinations are clearly better than any shown in the original shaded area and any obtained by combining borrowing or lending with any other risky portfolio. Graphically, the preferred combination of risky securities is obtained by swinging a line from point P until it just touches the upper border of the shaded area. Combining P with any other portfolio would clearly give a risk-return combination lying on a lower, and thus less desirable, line. The portfolio plotting at point R is the *optimum combination of risky securities.*

The final step in the overall process is the selection of the preferred investment strategy for the investor in question. If borrowing and lending are available, this simply requires a decision regarding the amount to be borrowed or lent to purchase the optimal risky portfolio identified in the previous stage, as shown in Figure 6-5(c2). If this is not the case, the combination must be chosen from a more complex set of efficient portfolios, as shown in Figure 6-5(c1).

This overall procedure is at least implicit in investment selection, whether the client is a person or an institution. In many cases constraints or alterations must be included to reflect the circumstances surrounding the ultimate beneficiary. Some institutional investors are more concerned with long-run returns than many private investors. Tax status differs considerably. Some investors may require a minimum level of current income from their portfolios, and so on.

Other differences occur in the final step. In some cases a professional adviser will present a client with at least a rough idea of his or her assessment of the risk-return trade-off, then ask the client to choose a preferred portfolio. In other cases the adviser will attempt in advance to assess the client's circumstances and attitudes, then make the complete choice. In yet other cases a money management organization may describe a set of attitudes that it plans to assume in its portfolio management, then invite those with similar attitudes to provide funds for investment. Mutual funds provide a good example of the latter procedure.

The three stages of investment selection are often performed by different people. One or more *security analysts* may be responsible for stage 1, a *portfolio manager* for stage 2, and an *investment counselor* (*or adviser*), plus the client, for stage 3. Some investors fill some or all of the roles. Even in organizations with large staffs, there is often some overlap in functions.

Whatever procedure is followed, it is important to recognize that conceptually different functions are involved and that rather different skills may be required for successful performance. Properly accounting for this provides a challenge and an opportunity for both investors and money managers.

Problems

1. If portfolio expected return is always equal to the weighted average of the expected returns of the component securities, why is not portfolio risk always equal to the weighted average of security risks?
2. What assumptions lie behind the notion that only efficient portfolios are worthy of consideration?
3. An investment has the following possible returns and associated probabilities:

Return	Probability
−10%	.24
0	.16
+10%	.36
+25%	.24

Compute the expected return and standard deviation of return for this investment.
4. Two investments (A and B) have the following returns for the specified events:

	EVENT		
Returns	1	2	3
Security A	10	5	−20
Security B	0	2	−10
Event Probability	.5	.4	.1

Calculate the variances (V_A and V_B), standard deviations (S_A and S_B), the covariance (C_{AB}), and the correlation (r_{AB}).

5. Three securities have the following expected returns, variances, and covariances:

EXPECTED RETURNS (%)	
Security	Expected Return
1	6
2	8
3	12

VARIANCES AND COVARIANCES

		Security		
		1	2	3
Security	1	500	100	100
	2	100	700	200
	3	100	200	900

Find the expected return, variance of return, and standard deviation of return for a portfolio having proportions $X_1 = .5$, $X_2 = .3$, and $X_3 = .2$.

6. Why might an insurance company limit the number of homes it would insure against loss by fire or flood in a given area while remaining willing to write such policies in many different areas?

7. Mr. Hartford estimates the risk of security A to be 20% (return per year) and the risk of security B to be the same. He also believes their returns will be determined by completely unrelated events (i.e., that their returns are uncorrelated).
   a. Assuming he is right, what will be the risk of a portfolio divided equally between the two securities?
   b. What about a portfolio with 60% invested in security A and 40% in B?
   c. What combination of the two securities is likely to have the smallest risk?
   d. Is the combination in (c) the one that Mr. Hartford should choose?

8. A successful investment consultant has decided that he prefers sailing in the Caribbean to any other possible type of vacation. He can charter (rent) a boat when he wishes to go there or he can purchase a boat, lease it to the chartering company, and use it when he goes. Why might he choose the latter alternative?

9. A professor purchased a house for $100,000, using $20,000 of her own money and $80,000 borrowed at an interest rate of 12%. A year later she sold the house for $120,000 and paid off the mortgage.
   a. What was the return on the total investment?
   b. What was the return on her investment?
   c. How would you have answered (a) and (b) if the sales price had been $110,000?
   d. *Before the fact*, would you have advised the professor to obtain a larger or smaller mortgage? Why?

7

Capital Asset Pricing Models

RISK AND RETURN

Risk and return are the two key features of investment media and investment strategy. It is thus important to know their sources. The major factors contributing to each must be identified and evaluated. This is the primary task of security analysis, and the results are crucial ingredients for portfolio construction, revision, and evaluation, as well as for setting long-range investment policy.

The analysis of risk and return should not be undertaken without careful consideration of the impact of other investors' actions on security prices. In an efficient capital market there will be likely relationships between risk and return; investment analysis should begin by considering such relationships, then proceed to assess the possible extent of deviations in particular cases.

To repeat: ways must be found to think about the sources of risk and return and the likely relationships among them. These two tasks are almost inextricably intertwined and can rarely be completely separated. One issue lies in the realm of *descriptive* analysis: how are risk and return likely to be related? The other issue lies in the realm of *decision-making*: how should risk and return be taken into account in investment management? This chapter and the next deal with the former question; both aspects are covered in subsequent chapters.

THE NEED FOR SIMPLIFICATION

The discussion of risk and return in previous chapters provides the conceptual basis for investment analysis. However, it is far from usable at the practical level. No analyst can be expected to delineate every relevant possible contingency, then estimate its probability of occurrence and the effect it will have on every possible investment alternative. This can be avoided to some extent if expected returns are estimated directly, along with the likely divergence of each security's return from its expected value.

But a problem still remains. To estimate the risk of a portfolio, one must estimate the likely degrees of correlation for all possible pairs of securities. This is too much. *Simplification* is required. The analyst must *abstract* from the full complexity of the situation, focusing instead on the most important elements.

A mathematician would describe this process as building a *model* of the world, the market, and the security or securities in question. This is a useful view and one that well describes a number of valuation methods developed and used by members of the investment community. In each case the assumptions are necessarily simplistic, in order to provide a sufficient degree of abstraction to allow some success in the analytic process. The "reasonableness" of the assumptions (or the lack thereof) is, in the final analysis, of little direct relevance. Just as the test of a cake is in the eating, so the test of a model is in its ability to help one understand (and perhaps predict) the process being modeled. At the very least, it is useful to know how analysts simplify the valuation process simply because their actions influence prices.

We proceed then with the process of abstraction, moving from some very simple views (or "models") to somewhat more complex alternatives. Models intended to apply to most or all types of investment media will be described in this chapter and the next, while those designed primarily for the valuation of specific types of securities will be described in later chapters.

CAPITAL ASSET PRICING MODELS

Security prices are the result of different analyses of somewhat different sets of information, along with different conditions and preferences relevant for various investors. One analyst's estimates of risk and return for a security are likely to differ from those of other analysts. Since both risk and return are subjective estimates dealing with the future, there is ample room for disagreement. People differ in their predictions of the future, be it the future of the economy or the return from a single security. Moreover, a single analyst's predictions will change over time, as he or she receives news of relevance for the situation being predicted. These differences make the security markets exciting, unpredictable, and profitable for brokers and others. They also make it impossible to categorically measure risk and return and the relationship between them.

However, it is useful to consider the *consensus* opinion of analysts regarding these matters. Votes in the marketplace are not taken democratically: those managing the most money have the most influence on prices. The majority of dollar votes is under the control of a rather well-informed and careful group of analysts and money managers. To the extent that they share similar information and use similar types of analysis, their consensus opinion is likely to reflect as good a set of estimates of risk and return as one can find.

But will this opinion be reflected in prices? What about the ill-informed and the incompetent? Might they artificially inflate prices of "fad" stocks or depress those of securities currently "out of favor"? They can, and upon occasion they may. But the net effect may be fairly small. First, lack of information or poor analysis will lead some investors to overly optimistic assessments of future prospects, and others to overly pessimistic assessments. Such people will tend to cancel each other out, in terms of impact on the market. Second, any substantial divergence of price from the value estimated by the professional investment community will set in motion powerful forces. If a price seems unreasonably low to those in the know, purchase orders will flood in, driving the price back up. If the price seems unreasonably high, many orders to sell will appear, driving the price back down.

In short, prices may not diverge much or for long from those consistent with a consensus professional view of risk and return. This makes it both possible and necessary to analyze the manner in which such a view is likely to affect security prices.

A simple, yet powerful description of the relationship between risk and return in an efficient market is provided by the *Capital Asset Pricing Model* (*CAPM*), developed in the mid-1960s. It provides the intellectual basis for a number of the current practices in the investment industry. Since the introduction of the model a number of extensions and modifications have been proposed. We will describe these later. Initially, we concentrate on the original version.

To focus on risk and return, the CAPM reduces the situation to an extreme case. Every investor is assumed to have the same information and to analyze and process it in the same way. Everyone thus agrees about the future prospects for securities. Moreover, investors are assumed to be concerned *only* with risk and return. Since risk and return relate present price to future prospects, every investor in such a never-never land agrees with every other regarding all ingredients required for portfolio analysis. And, since everyone knows all the relevant aspects of portfolio analysis, all will process the available information in the same way.

To complete the scenario, transactions costs are ignored (brokers are assumed to work for nothing) and every investor is able to borrow or lend money at the Treasury bill rate. Moreover, taxes are assumed to have no noticeable effect on investment policy. This constitutes the world of the (original) Capital Asset Pricing Model.

What would happen in such a world? First, everyone would analyze the situation and determine a set of efficient risky portfolios, but *everyone would obtain the same set*. Since borrowing and lending at the same rate of interest are possible, no adviser need stop at this point, since he or she can proceed to select one of the efficient portfolios as the preferred combination of risky securities, regardless of a client's preferences. Moreover, *each adviser would recommend the same combination of risky securities*. Each investor would thus be advised to spread his or her funds "at risk" among securities in the same indicated proportions, adding borrowing or lending to taste to achieve a personally preferred combination of risk and return.

But what if it won't work? In this world every adviser will recommend the same proportionate holdings of risky securities. What if shares of the Little Gem Mining Company are not included on the list? No one will want to hold them, and orders to sell will be received in substantial quantities. Prices will fall, as brokers try to find someone who will buy. But now all the analysts must go back to their drawing boards. If Little Gem's future prospects are unchanged, but the current price is lower, expected return will be greater than before. This alone makes a new analysis necessary. Eventually, of course, when the price has fallen far enough, analysts will recommend the stock to their clients after all.

The converse situation could also arise. What if all analysts conclude that 20% of every investor's funds at risk should be invested in Ford Motors stock, but at current prices Ford shares constitute considerably less than 20% of total market value? Orders to buy will flood in, and brokers will raise the price in search of sellers. This will alleviate the problem in two ways. First, Ford will represent an increasing share of market value. Second, it will be less and less attractive as its price rises, causing analysts to recommend smaller proportionate holdings.

How can everything balance out? When will all the adjustment stop, bringing the markets into *equilibrium*? First, *when there is consistency between the total amount one group of investors wishes to borrow and the amount another group wishes to lend*. Second, *when the preferred combination of risky securities contains every such security, each in proportion to its outstanding market value*.

THE MARKET PORTFOLIO

A combination of all securities, each in proportion to market value outstanding, is called the *market portfolio*. Included may be stocks, bonds, real estate, and so on. Such a portfolio plays a central role:

Under the assumptions of the original Capital Asset Pricing Model, efficient investment strategies include *only* the market portfolio, borrowing, and/ or lending.

While no counterpart for the overall market portfolio is described in the daily press, indices intended to measure the performance of major components are available. One of the most widely known is Standard and Poor's 500-stock index, a value-weighted average of 500 important stocks. Since each stock is weighted by the market value of outstanding shares, and since primarily stocks with large values outstanding are included, this index represents reasonably well the results obtained in the stock market segment of the overall capital market.

Complete coverage of the stocks listed on the New York Stock Exchange is provided by the Exchange's composite index, which also weights stocks in proportion to total value outstanding. The American Stock Exchange computes a similar index for the stocks it lists, and the National Association of Security Dealers provides a value-weighted index of over-the-counter stocks traded via the NASDAQ system. The Wilshire 5000 index, covering 5,000 stocks, is the most comprehensive index of this type published regularly and should thus be closer than others to a representation of the true market portfolio.

Without question the most widely quoted market index is the Dow Jones Industrial Average. Although based on the performance of only 30 stocks, and utilizing a less satisfactory averaging procedure, the "DJIA" provides at least a fair idea of what is happening to stock values.

Table 7-1 shows the top 50 stocks in Standard and Poor's 500-stock index, based on total market values in early 1984. Although relative rankings change from time to time, these securities, representing ownership of large, widely known firms, continue to make up a large portion of this index of the overall market portfolio.

Table 7-2 provides another view of the composition of Standard and Poor's 500-stock index. Each security has been classified as belonging to a given *economic sector;* in the table, the relative values in

TABLE 7-1

The Top 50 Securities in Standard and Poor's 500-Stock Index (based on total market value outstanding, February 29, 1984)

Company	Percent of Total Value	Cumulative Percent of Total Value
International Business Machs.	5.86%	5.86%
Exxon Corp.	2.85	8.71
General Elec Co.	2.05	10.76
General Mtrs Corp.	1.86	12.62
Shell Oil Co.	1.50	14.11
American Tel & Teleg Co.	1.41	15.52
Standard Oil Co Ind.	1.32	16.84

TABLE 7-1 (*Continued*)

Company	Percent of Total Value	Cumulative Percent of Total Value
Schlumberger Ltd.	1.24	18.08
Royal Dutch Pete Co.	1.16	19.24
Mobil Corp.	1.05	20.29
Sears Roebuck & Co.	1.04	21.33
Standard Oil Co. Calif.	1.01	22.34
Eastman Kodak Co.	0.98	23.32
Standard Oil Co. Ohio	0.97	24.29
Atlantic Richfield Co.	0.97	25.26
Du Pont E I De Nemours & Co.	0.96	26.23
Gulf Corp.	0.94	27.16
Texaco Inc.	0.87	28.03
Hewlett Packard Co.	0.80	28.84
Bellsouth Corp.	0.78	29.62
Minnesota Mng & Mfg Co.	0.77	30.39
American Home Prods Corp.	0.71	31.10
Philip Morris Inc.	0.71	31.81
Procter & Gamble Co.	0.68	32.49
Coca Cola Co.	0.63	33.12
GTE Corp.	0.62	33.74
Ford Mtr Co. Del.	0.61	34.35
Merck & Co. Inc.	0.60	34.95
Bell Atlantic Corp.	0.59	35.54
Johnson & Johnson	0.57	36.11
Ameritech	0.56	36.67
Reynolds R J Inds. Inc.	0.54	37.21
Bristol Myers Co.	0.54	37.75
Pfizer Inc.	0.53	38.28
Dow Chem Co.	0.51	38.79
American Express Co.	0.51	39.31
Nynex Corp.	0.51	39.82
US West Inc.	0.50	40.32
Southwestern Bell Corp.	0.50	40.81
Phillips Pete Co.	0.50	41.31
Unocal Corp.	0.49	41.80
ITT Corp.	0.48	42.28
Tenneco Inc.	0.48	42.76
Pacific Telesis Group	0.47	43.23
Digital Equip Corp.	0.45	43.67
Abbott Labs	0.44	44.12
Texas Oil & Gas Corp.	0.44	44.56
Sun Inc.	0.44	45.00
Union Pac Corp.	0.44	45.43
Superior Oil Co.	0.42	45.85

SOURCE: Wells Fargo Investment Advisors.

TABLE 7-2
Economic Sectors in Standard and Poor's
500-Stock Index (based on total market
value outstanding, February 29, 1984)

Economic Sector	Percent of Total Value
Basic Industries	5.99
Consumer Basic Goods	11.08
Consumer Discretionary Goods	17.62
Capital Goods	16.97
Electronics	2.59
Finance	5.34
Energy	19.13
Shelter	3.89
Transportation	2.55
Utilities	11.11
Multiple Industries	3.74

SOURCE: Wells Fargo Investment Advisors.

early 1984 have been summed by sector. While any such classification involves elements of arbitrariness, the figures do suggest the relative importance of major economic sectors in the economy.

THE CAPITAL MARKET LINE

In the fictional world of the Capital Asset Pricing Model it is a simple matter to determine the relationship between risk and return for efficient investment strategies. Figure 7-1 portrays it graphically. Point M represents the market portfolio and point P a riskless security returning R_f. Preferred investment strategies plot along line PMZ, representing alternative combinations of risk and return obtainable by combining the market portfolio with borrowing or lending. This is known as the *Capital Market Line*.

All investment strategies other than those employing the market portfolio and borrowing or lending would lie below the Capital Market Line, although some might plot very close to it. In such a world, any investor could devise an appropriate strategy alone; no security analysts, portfolio manager, or investment adviser would be needed. This may seem paradoxical, but it is not. The activities of professional analysts help make the market efficient. Their *total* value to investors and to the economy as a whole is thus very great indeed. However, the major results of their analysis are reflected in current security prices.

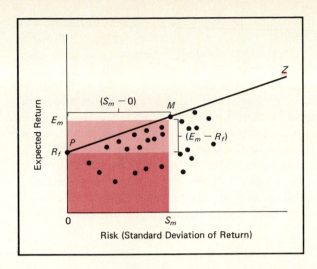

FIGURE 7-1
The Capital Market Line

The investor need pay only a small amount for a newspaper to obtain the results of millions of dollars of analysis. The *marginal* value of additional analysis may thus be rather small: in the world of the original Capital Asset Pricing Model it would be zero. In the real world, where analysts do not work for nothing, the marginal value of additional analysis should be positive but, given adequate competition in the investment industry, should just equal the cost of doing such analysis in the most efficient manner.

The slope of the Capital Market Line can be regarded as the *reward per unit of risk borne*. As Figure 7-1 shows, this equals the difference between the expected return on the market portfolio and that of the riskless security $(E_m - R_f)$ divided by the difference in their risks $(S_m - O)$.

Equilibrium in the capital market can be characterized by two key numbers. The first is the *reward for waiting* or riskless interest rate, shown by the vertical intercept of the Capital Market Line (point *P* in Figure 7-1).

The second is the reward per unit of risk borne, shown by the slope of the line. In essence, the capital market provides a place where time and risk can be traded and their prices determined by the forces of demand and supply. The interest rate can be thought of as the *price of time,* and the slope of the Capital Market Line as the *price of risk.*

MARGINAL EFFECTS OF CHANGES IN PORTFOLIO HOLDINGS

The Capital Market Line posits a relationship between expected return and a measure of risk (standard deviation of return) for *efficient portfolios.* Individual securities will generally plot below the line: a single security, held by itself, is almost certainly an *in*efficient portfolio. The Capital Asset Pricing Model implies nothing about any relationship between the expected returns of individual securities and their *total* risks (standard deviations of return). To say more about *securities'* expected returns we must probe deeper.

Key is consideration of changes in the risk and return of an efficient portfolio when security holdings are changed.

What will happen to the characteristics of a portfolio if the amount invested in security *i* is changed by a small amount? Assume that the current portfolio is *p*. Imagine adding to the portfolio, or subtracting from it, a small amount of security *i*. If the security is already included in the portfolio, total holdings will simply be increased or reduced. If not, either a new position will be established or a short position will be taken.

The "new" portfolio will have:

X_i in security *i*

X_p in portfolio *p*

The current portfolio has:

$X_i = 0$
$X_p = 1$

Marginal Expected Return

The expected return of the portfolio will (as usual) be a weighted average of the expected returns of the components:

$$E_i = X_i E_i + X_p E_p$$

If X_i were changed to $X_i + \Delta X_i$, the expected return would become:

$$E'_i = (X_i + \Delta X_i)E_i + X_p E_p$$

The *change* in expected return would be:

$$\Delta E_i = E'_i - E_i = \Delta X_i E_i$$

while the change in expected return per unit change in ΔX_i would be:

$$\frac{\Delta E}{\Delta X_i} = E_i$$

As smaller and smaller changes in X_i are considered, the closer a ratio such as this gets to a value known as the *first derivative*. In this case:

$$\frac{dE}{dX_i} = E_i$$

where:

$$\frac{dE}{dX_i} = \text{the first derivative of } E \text{ with respect to } X_i$$

The term on the left-hand side of the equation represents the marginal contribution of security i to the expected return of portfolio p. More succinctly, it is the security's *marginal expected return*.

Note that nothing about portfolio p is included on the right-hand side of the equation. The marginal contribution of a security to the expected return of *any* portfolio is given by its expected return. Simply put: marginal expected return equals expected return. As we will see, a comparable situation does not hold for risk.

Marginal Variance

The variance of a combination of security i and portfolio p will (as usual) depend on the variances of the two portfolios, the covariance between their returns, and the proportions invested in each:

$$V = X_i^2 V_i + 2X_i X_p C_{ip} + X_p^2 V_p$$

If X_i were changed to $X_i + \Delta X_i$, the variance would become:

$$V' = (X_i + \Delta X_i)^2 V_i + 2(X_i + \Delta X_i) X_p C_{ip} + X_p^2 V_p$$

The *change* in variance would be:

$$\Delta V = V' - V = 2X_i \, \Delta X_i V_i + (\Delta X_i)^2 V_i + 2\Delta X_i X_p C_{ip}$$

while the change in variance per unit change in ΔX_i would be:

$$\frac{\Delta V}{\Delta X_i} = 2X_i V_i + \Delta X_i V_i + 2X_p C_{ip}$$

As smaller and smaller changes in X_i are considered, the middle term grows smaller. If the change in X_i is very small, the term will be insignificant, and:

$$\frac{\Delta V}{\Delta X_i} \approx 2X_i V_i + 2X_p C_{ip}$$

where $\approx$ means "is approximately equal to."

As ΔX_i gets smaller and smaller, the value of $\Delta V/\Delta X_i$ approaches the *first derivative of V with respect to X_i. It represents the marginal contribution of security i to the risk of portfolio p. More succinctly, it is the security's marginal variance.*

In the current portfolio, $X_i = 0$ and $X_p = 1$. Thus:

$$\frac{dV}{dX_i} = 2C_{ip}$$

where:

$$\frac{dV}{dX_i} = \text{the first derivative of } V \text{ with respect to } X_i$$

In words: the marginal effect of a change in the amount of security *i* held in portfolio *p* on the variance of that portfolio depends on the *covariance between the return of the security and the return of the portfolio*.

Note that the effect of a change in the holdings of a security on the risk of a portfolio depends on characteristics of *both* the security and the portfolio. For example, a change in holdings of General Motors stock might have a very different impact on the risk of a portfolio of automotive stocks than on the risk of a portfolio of electronic stocks.

CONDITIONS FOR PORTFOLIO OPTIMALITY

Marginal expected return and marginal variance indicate the effects on portfolio characteristics of changes in the holdings of one security. In practice, of course, one cannot alter only the amount of one security: to buy a security, another must be sold (for this purpose, cash is simply another security). Algebraically: all the X_is must sum to 1.

Assume that someone seeks your counsel concerning the desirability of a portfolio. Given estimates of security expected returns, risks, and correlations, you compute the marginal expected return and marginal variance for each security. Looking down the list, you discover the following:

Security	Marginal Expected Return	Marginal Variance
i	15	400
j	12	400

The portfolio can clearly be improved by selling some shares of security *j* and using the proceeds to purchase shares of security *i*. For example, if $\Delta X_i = +.01$ and $\Delta X_j = -.01$, the effect on portfolio expected return would be:

$$
\begin{aligned}
+.01 \times 15 &= +.15 \\
-.01 \times 12 &= \underline{-.12} \\
& +.03
\end{aligned}
$$

and the effect on portfolio variance would be (approximately):

$$+.01 \times 400 = +4$$
$$-.01 \times 400 = \underline{-4}$$
$$0$$

By "swapping" some of security j for security i, the portfolio's expected return could be increased with no change in its risk!

This leads to a major conclusion:

If two securities in a portfolio have the same marginal variance and different expected returns, the portfolio is not optimal.

Put more positively:

If a portfolio is optimal, all securities with a given margin variance (relative to that portfolio) will have the same expected return.

Figure 7-2 provides an illustration. Every security with marginal variance equal to MV_1 must have the same expected return (here, E_1) and plot at point 1. Every security with marginal variance equal to MV_3 must have the same expected return (here, E_3) and plot at point 3.

What about securities with a marginal variance of MV_2, halfway between MV_1 and MV_3? All of them must have the same expected return and plot at one point. But what can be said about the amount of the expected return (i.e., the location of that point)?

Consider a new "security" created by putting a $.50 in a security plotting at point 1 and another $.50 in a security plotting at point 3. The expected return on the $1.00 invested would plot halfway between

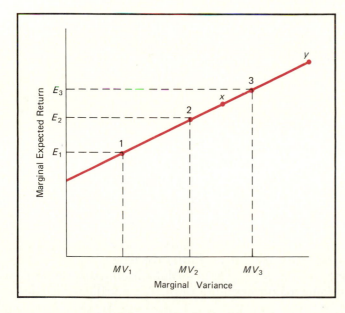

FIGURE 7-2
Portfolio Optimality

E_1 and E_3 (E_2 in the figure). Moreover, the marginal variance of this security would plot halfway between MV_1 and MV_3 (MV_2 in the figure). This follows from the nature of covariance:

$$\text{Cov}(.5R_1 + .5R_3, \ R_p) = .5 \text{ Cov}(R_1, R_p) + .5 \text{ Cov}(R_3, R_p)$$

and the fact that marginal variance is equal to two times the security's covariance with the portfolio.

Clearly, this new "security" will plot at point 2—halfway between points 1 and 3. But if a portfolio is optimal, all securities with a given marginal variance must have identical expected returns. Thus *all* securities with marginal variance equal to MV_2 must have expected returns of E_2.

This exercise can be repeated (ad nauseum). Take any two points (e.g., 2 and 3). A new point can be plotted, halfway between them (e.g., point x in Figure 7-2), indicating the expected return for all securities with the corresponding marginal variance. If this is done many times, a set of points will be plotted that will trace out the straight line between points 1 and 3.

One need not stop at this point. By considering "new securities" made up by selling one security short and purchasing another, points outside the original range can be obtained. For example, by selling security 1 short and purchasing security 3, a "security" plotting at point y can be obtained. Not surprisingly, it will be on the extension of the straight line connecting points 1 and 3.

The conclusion is clear:

If a portfolio is optimal, all securities will plot on a straight line in a diagram with expected return on the vertical axis and marginal variance (relative to the portfolio) on the horizontal axis.

Since investors are assumed to dislike risk and to like expected return, a security that adds more to variance should also add more to expected return. Thus:

If a portfolio is optimal, all securities will plot on an *upward-sloping* straight line in a diagram with expected return on the vertical axis and marginal variance (relative to the portfolio) on the horizontal axis.

This can be termed the *principle of portfolio optimality*.

BETA VALUES

Covariances are expressed in somewhat unfamiliar units. As with many measures, it is useful to express them in *relative* terms.

The covariance of a security with a portfolio is stated in the same units as is the variance of the portfolio itself. A convenient measure of *relative marginal variance* is obtained by dividing the former by the latter. This is called the security's *beta value* relative to the portfolio:

$$\beta_{ip} \equiv \frac{C_{ip}}{V_{ip}}$$

where

β_{ip} = security i's beta value relative to portfolio
C_{ip} = the covariance between the return on security pi and the return on portfolio p
V_p = the variance of portfolio p

The nature of covariances is such that:

$$\beta_{qp} = \sum_{i=1}^{n} X_{iq}\beta_{ip}$$

where

β_{qp} = portfolio q's beta relative to portfolio p
X_{iq} = the proportion of portfolio q invested in security i
β_{ip} = security i's beta value relative to portfolio p

In words: *the beta value of a portfolio is simply a weighted average of the beta values of the component securities, using the proportions invested as weights.*

The covariance of the return on portfolio p with itself is, of course, V_p. Thus:

$$\beta_{pp} = \frac{V_p}{V_p} = 1.0$$

The covariance of a riskless security with a portfolio is zero. Thus:

$$\beta_{ip} = 0 \quad \text{if security } i \text{ is riskless}$$

BETA VALUES AND EXPECTED RETURNS

The marginal variance of security i relative to portfolio p is:

$$2C_{ip}$$

while its beta value relative to the portfolio is:

$$\frac{C_{ip}}{V_p}$$

Thus two securities with the same beta value relative to portfolio p have the same marginal variance relative to the portfolio, and vice versa. The principle of portfolio optimality can therefore be restated in terms of beta values:

> If a portfolio is optimal, all securities will plot on an *upward-sloping* straight line in a diagram with expected return on the vertical axis and beta (relative to the portfolio) on the horizontal axis.

It is important to understand how an investor insures that the relationship described by the principle of portfolio optimality holds. The individual investor takes security prices and prospects as given. Expected returns and security covariances are outside his or her control. The investor is a *price-taker* and *quantity-adjuster*. He or she adjusts security holdings until securities' marginal variances "line up" with their expected returns. The object is to find an optimal portfolio. Marginal variances calculated relative to such a portfolio will give a straight line in a diagram with expected returns on the vertical axis and the relevant marginal variances on the horizontal axis.

THE SECURITY MARKET LINE

In the world of the original Capital Asset Pricing Model the market portfolio is *efficient*. Equivalently:

> The market portfolio is optimal (for someone).

But if it is optimal, the principle of portfolio optimality must hold. Therefore:

> Every security must plot on an upward-sloping straight line in a diagram with expected return on the vertical axis and beta *relative to the market portfolio* on the horizontal axis.

While every beta value must be computed relative to a given portfolio, the most common use is in this context. Thus when one speaks of a security's "beta value," the beta value relative to the market portfolio is meant.

$\beta i = \beta_{im}$ = security i's beta value relative to the market portfolio

Recall that (1) the beta value of a portfolio is a weighted average of the beta values of its component securities and (2) the expected return of a portfolio is a weighted average of the expected returns of its component securities, with relative proportions invested in the securities used as weights in both cases. Thus if every security plots on the security market line, so will every portfolio. More broadly:

> Every security *and portfolio* must plot on an upward-sloping straight line in a diagram with expected return on the vertical axis and beta on the horizontal axis.

Capital Asset Pricing Models

This is illustrated in Figure 7-3. The relationship—termed the *Security Market Line (SML)*—is a key implication of the original Capital Asset Pricing Model.

As shown, the Security Market Line must go through the point representing the market portfolio itself. Its beta value is 1, and its expected return E_m.

In the original Capital Asset Pricing Model, investors are assumed to be able to borrow or lend at the riskless interest rate R_f. Since riskless securities have beta values of zero, the Security Market Line will also go through a point on the vertical axis with an expected return of R_f, as shown in Figure 7-3.

Two points suffice to fix the location of a straight line. Given R_f and E_m, the Security Market Line can be plotted, indicating the "appropriate" expected returns for securities and portfolios with different beta values.

How does the equilibrium relationship shown by the Security Market Line come about? Through the combined effects of investors' adjustments in holdings and the resulting pressures on security prices. Given a set of security prices, investors calculate expected returns and security covariances, then determine desired (optimal) portfolios. If the amount of a security collectively desired differs from the amount available, there will be upward or downward pressure on its price. Given a new set of prices, investors will reassess their desires for various

FIGURE 7-3
The Security Market Line

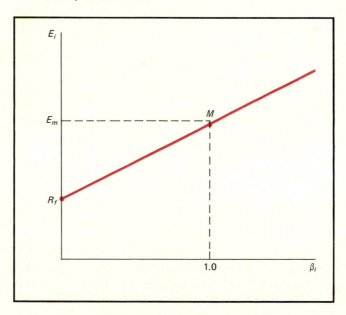

securities. The process will continue until investors' quantity adjustments do not require further marketwide price adjustments.

For the individual investor, security prices and prospects are fixed and quantities held are variable. For the market as a whole, quantities are fixed (at least in the short run) and prices are variable. As in any competitive market, equilibrium requires the adjustment of prices until there is consistency between the amounts desired to be held and the amounts available to be held.

EQUILIBRIUM THEORIES OF SECURITY EXPECTED RETURNS

The Security Market Line represents an *equilibrium theory of security expected returns*. Such a theory asserts a relationship between (1) expected return and (2) one or more *attributes*. The general form is:

$$E_i^e = f(a_{i_1}, a_{i_2}, \ldots) \qquad \text{(7-1)}$$

where:

E_i^e = the equilibrium expected return of security i

$f(\ldots)$ means "is a function of" or "is related to"

a_{i_1} = attribute 1 of security i

a_{i_2} = attribute 2 of security i

The original Capital Asset Pricing Model implies that only one attribute—beta relative to the market portfolio—is relevant:

$$E_i^e = f(\beta_i) \qquad \text{(7-2)}$$

Moreover, the Security Market Line indicates that the function (relationship) is linear:

$$E_i^e = a + b\beta_i \qquad \text{(7-3)}$$

Since the market portfolio and the riskless security plot on the Security Market Line, the coefficients of the relationship can be written in terms of the expected returns on these two investments:

$$E_i^e = R_f + (E_m - R_f)\beta_i \qquad \text{(7-4)}$$

Equation (7-4) is much more specific than equations (7-1), (7-2), and (7-3). The original Capital Asset Pricing Model thus is *powerful*—it makes strong predictions. Powerful theories, if correct, are valuable, since they make strong statements about the world. On the other hand, they are more likely to be incorrect.

ALPHA VALUES

According to the original Capital Asset Pricing Model, asset prices should adjust until every security plots on the Security Market Line. Equivalently: security i's expected return should be given by equation (7-4). If any security or portfolio plots "off the line," the situation is one of *disequilibrium*.

Security analysts and portfolio managers spend a great deal of time searching for securities that appear to be *mispriced*:

A security is *underpriced* if its expected return is greater than it should be.

A security is *overpriced* if its expected return is less than it should be.

To give substance to such statements, a definition is required for the final three words. In general:

A security is *underpriced* if its expected return is greater than the *appropriate* expected return for securities with *comparable relevant attributes*.

A security is *overpriced* if its expected return is less than the *appropriate* expected return for securities with *comparable relevant attributes*.

What attributes are relevant? And what is the appropriate expected return for a given set of attributes? The answer depends on the equilibrium theory of security expected returns that is used. For the original Capital Asset Pricing Model, only one attribute is relevant (beta) and the appropriate expected return is that shown by the Security Market Line (or computed using equation (7-4).

In principle, either security prices and expected returns conform to an equilibrium relationship or they do not. If there is *disequilibrium*, almost any situation may be found. In practice, many investment managers assume that *most* securities are priced to give equilibrium expected returns, but some are overpriced and some are underpriced. The extent to which a security is mispriced is measured by its *alpha value*.

The idea is to determine E_i^e—the *equilibrium expected return* for the security. This is what the expected return "should be" and would be if the security were priced correctly—it is the expected return for correctly priced securities with comparable relevant attributes. For a general equilibrium model:

$$E_i^e = f(a_{i_1}, a_{i_2}, \ldots)$$

and for the original Capital Asset Pricing Model:

$$E_i^e = R_f + (E_m - R_f)\beta_i$$

A security's alpha value is the *difference between its expected return and an appropriate (equilibrium) expected return*:

$$\alpha_i \equiv E_i - E_i^e$$

Figure 7-4 provides an illustration. The expected return on the market portfolio is 15% and the riskless interest rate is 10%, fixing the location of the Security Market Line. Security x has a beta of 1.2 and an expected return of 18%. The Security Market Line indicates that correctly priced securities with betas of 1.2 should have expected returns of 16%. Thus security x offers 2% more in expected return than it should. Its alpha value is +2%.

An opposite situation holds for security y, which has a beta of .8 and an expected return of 13%. The Security Market Line indicates that correctly priced securities with betas of .8 should have expected returns of 14%. Thus security y offers 1% less in expected return than it should. Its alpha value is −1%.

In the original Capital Asset Pricing Model, a security's alpha value is measured by the distance it plots above or below the Security Market Line.

In general:

A security is *underpriced* if its alpha value is positive.

A security is *overpriced* if its alpha value is negative.

FIGURE 7-4
Alpha Values

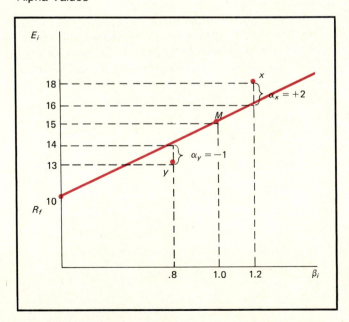

Capital Asset Pricing Models

A security is *correctly priced* if its alpha value is zero.

In equilibrium, all securities are correctly priced, and all alpha values are zero.

Since the expected return of a portfolio is simply a weighted average of the expected returns of its component securities, the alpha value of a portfolio will be a weighted average of the alpha values of the component securities:

$$\alpha_p = \sum_{i=1}^{N} X_{ip}\, \alpha_i$$

where:

α_p = the alpha value of portfolio p

X_{ip} = the proportion of portfolio p invested in security i

α_i = the alpha value of security i

Investment managers who try to "beat the market" hope to construct portfolios with positive alphas. Those who do not try to beat the market expect to construct portfolios with zero alphas. Those who try but make incorrect judgments may erroneously choose portfolios with negative alphas.

ESTIMATING RISK

Table 7-3 shows the ingredients for a calculation of a security's beta value. An analyst has identified ten *scenarios* (possible states of the world). For each one, a return on security i and return on the market portfolio have been estimated. The first three columns at the top of the table show the predictions, as they might be entered in an "electronic spreadsheet" on a microcomputer.

In this case, the analyst considers the scenarios equally probable. Thus the expected return on security i is simply an average of the ten estimates. A similar calculation gives the expected return for the market portfolio. Averages and variances are easily calculated when data are entered in such spreadsheets. The resulting values are shown at the bottom of the associated columns.

Each entry in the third column shows the product of (1) the deviation of security i's return from its expected value times (2) the deviation of the market portfolio's return from its expected value for the scenario in question. Since the scenarios are equally probable, the average of the ten values (shown below the column) is the covariance between the two returns.

The middle panel of the table summarizes the information obtained from these calculations.

TABLE 7-3
Estimating Risk

Event	R_i	R_m	$(R_i - E_i) \times (R_m - E_m)$
a	22	17	136.59
b	−4	4	44.29
c	12	15	38.19
d	14	11	20.79
e	−6	−4	151.29
f	5	8	.39
g	3	0	27.39
h	6	12	−1.11
i	−4	−2	106.09
j	15	22	119.19
Average value:	6.30	8.30	64.31
Variance:	79.01	67.41	

E_i:	6.30
E_m:	8.30
V_i:	79.01
V_m:	67.41
C_{im}:	64.31

Beta:	$.814 = C_{im}/V_m$	
Security variance:		
Market:	44.66	$= \beta_i^2 V_m$
Nonmarket:	34.35	$= V_i - (\beta_i^2 V_m)$
Total:	79.01	$= V_i$
R-squared:	.565	market variance/total variance
Nonmarket risk (std. dev.):	5.86	$\sqrt{\text{nonmarket variance}}$

     The bottom panel of the table derives the value of beta and several additional measures of interest.

Beta

To calculate beta, the covariance (64.31) is divided by the variance of the security (79.01). These predictions imply a beta value of .814.

Market and Nonmarket Risk

Next we calculate an important decomposition of the risk of a security. The total variance (79.01) is divided into the portion *related to market moves* and the portion *not* related to such moves. The former is termed *market risk*; the latter, *nonmarket risk*.
    To calculate market-related risk in *variance* terms, one multiplies

the variance of the market portfolio by the square of the security's beta value. To calculate nonmarket risk in variance terms, one simply subtracts the market risk (44.66) from the total risk (79.01).

R-squared

Since measures expressed in terms of variance are not especially intuitive, a derivative value is commonly used.

R-squared indicates the *proportion* of a security's total variance that is market-related. In this case it is .565 (44.66/79.01). Thus 56.5% of the risk of security i is associated with uncertainty about the return on the market.

Portfolio Risks

All the procedures described here can be applied as easily to the returns on a portfolio as to the returns on a security. As indicated earlier, the beta value for a portfolio will be a weighted average of the beta values of its component securities. However, a comparable relationship does not hold for nonmarket risk and R-squared. In fact, the nonmarket risk of a portfolio may be considerably less than the nonmarket risk of *any* of its component securities, owing to the power of diversification.

A typical value of R-squared for a single stock is about .30. Uncertainty about the overall market thus accounts for only 30% of the uncertainty about the prospects for a typical stock over holding periods from one to a few months. However, the proportion is much higher when highly diversified holdings are considered. The value of R-squared for a large institutional portfolio such as a pension fund is more likely to be well above .90. At the portfolio level, the market component of risk is likely to dominate the nonmarket component by a substantial margin.

Nonmarket Risk in Standard Deviation Units

Nonmarket risk is usually expressed in standard-deviation terms. This is calculated by taking the square root of nonmarket variance (thus 5.86 is the square root of 34.35). Roughly, security i's return would be its expected value plus or minus 5.86%, if the return on the market were known in advance.

The Relevance of Market and Nonmarket Risk

Why break risk into two parts? For the investor, risk is risk—whatever its source. The difference lies in the domain of expected return.

Market risk is related to the risk of the market portfolio and to the beta of the security or portfolio in question. The greater is beta, the greater is market risk. In the world of the Capital Asset Pricing Model, the greater is beta, the greater is expected return. These two relationships together imply that securities or portfolios with greater market risk should have greater expected returns.

Nonmarket risk is not related to beta. Thus there is no reason why securities or portfolios with a greater nonmarket risk should have greater expected returns.

In sum:

According to the Capital Asset Pricing Model, market risk is *rewarded*; nonmarket risk is not.

BETA AS SENSITIVITY TO MARKET MOVES

Figure 7-5(a) plots the values of R_i and R_m for the ten scenarios identified in Table 7-3. There is clearly a tendency for security i to do well in states of the world in which the market portfolio does well, and conversely.

A relationship of this sort may be summarized with a *least-squares regression line*. Such a line provides the best linear approximation of the data, using a standard statistical criterion (to minimize the sum of the squared deviations of the points from the line). As shown in statistics texts, such a line can easily be drawn in a diagram with Y on the vertical axis and X on the horizontal axis, since:

The line must pass through the point at which X equals its average value and Y equals its average value.

The line must have a slope equal to (1) the covariance between Y and X divided by (2) the variance of X.

Figure 7-5(b) shows the regression line that best summarizes the predictions. It is called the security's *characteristic line*.

Not surprisingly, the slope of security i's characteristic line is .814. Since R_i is plotted on the vertical axis and R_m on the horizontal axis, it follows that:

A security's beta value is the slope of its characteristic line.

More directly:

A security's beta value measures the expected change in its return per 1% change in the return on the market portfolio.

Securities with beta values less than 1 (e.g., most utility stocks) are termed *defensive*: in up markets their prices tend to rise at a slower rate than the average security. On the other hand, they tend to fall at a slower rate in down markets. Securities with beta values greater than 1 (e.g., most airline stocks) are termed *aggressive*: in up markets

Capital Asset Pricing Models

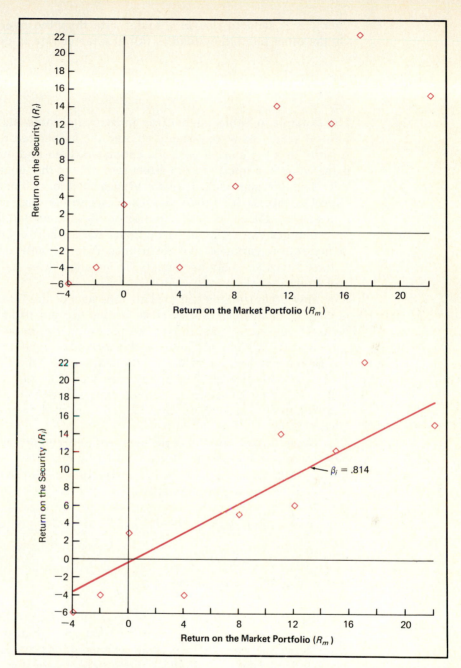

FIGURE 7-5
Security and Market Returns

their prices tend to rise at a faster rate than the average security. On the other hand, they tend to fall at a faster rate in down markets.

ESTIMATING BETA

The example in Table 7-3 involved judgemental forecasts of the future. Several scenarios were considered, and the associated returns for the security and the market portfolio estimated. Beta and other risk measures were then inferred from direct forecasts of the (uncertain) future.

Scenario approaches are sometimes used for estimating risks and expected returns for broad classes of securities (e.g., stocks, bonds, real estate). Cases in which one scenario is considered more likely than another can be handled by using the general definitions of expected return, variance, and covariance. Alternatively, a scenario that is three times as likely can simply be included three times in the list, and so on.

Few organizations use explicit forecasts of the future when estimating beta values for individual securities. Instead, estimates of *future* betas are based, at least in part, on past (historic) betas.

A security's *historic beta* can be derived by examining the return on the security and the return on the market portfolio (or a surrogate for it) for each of a number of time periods. Thus in Figure 7-5, each point might plot the returns in a given month. The slope of a regression line ("historic characteristic line") fitted to such data is the security's historic beta.

Using a security's historic beta without change as an estimate of its (future) beta is equivalent to assuming that the next time period (e.g., month) is equally likely to be like one of the periods used in the calculation (and like none other). This is clearly an extreme assumption. In practice, historic betas are *adjusted* or used in concert with other information when estimates of (future) betas are made.

MARKET VERSUS ECONOMIC RISK

It is important to remember that although the value of beta is usually described in terms of dividends and market price changes over a fairly short period, it really reflects relationships among expectations about the values of fundamental economic variables over a much longer period.

This is most easily seen in the case of a firm financed entirely with equity (stock). The present value of the outstanding stock of such a firm at any time will depend on investors' expectations about the firm's revenues and costs (broadly construed) from that time forward—

in concept, forever. The present value a year later will depend on investors' expectations at that time about the firm's then remaining revenues and costs. The rate of return on the stock between the two dates will equal the difference between these two present values plus the cash paid out in dividends during the period. One source of uncertainty about this return concerns the failure or success of the firm's activities during the period, but in the usual case the more important source is uncertainty concerning investors' expectations at the end of the year about the firm's prospects from that time forward.

The market portfolio is, in essence, the sum of all claims on all capital assets. Its present value at any time will depend on investors' assessments of the prospects from that time forward for all such assets. Since the benefits obtained from capital assets are almost synonymous in many people's minds with the state of "the economy," the relationship can be stated more simply. The current level of the market reflects investors' current feelings about the prospects for the economy. The greater their expectations for the economy, other things equal, the higher will be the level of the market. On the other hand, the greater their uncertainty about the economy, the lower will be the level.

One source of uncertainty regarding the return on the market portfolio over a period will be the uncertainty about what will happen to the economy during the period. More important yet will be uncertainty about investors' feelings at the end of the period about the economy's prospects from that time forward.

What has this to do with beta? A great deal. Beta measures the sensitivity of a security's market return over a fairly short period to changes in the market return on all assets. More fundamentally:

> The beta of a *firm* measures the sensitivity of the underlying assets' prospects (and investors' assessments thereof) to those of the economy as a whole.

For a firm financed wholly by stock, the beta of the *firm* and the beta of its *stock* will be the same. This will, in turn, depend on the basic economics of the firm's activities. Most airlines have high "firm betas," since many of their costs are fixed and their revenues depend heavily on the state of the economy. On the other hand, most utilities have low firm betas, since regulatory authorities control rates in a manner that makes the spread between revenue and cost affected less by swings in economic activity.

Most firms are financed with both debt and equity. Thus the firm's prospects are divided up among various groups of claimants. Both the overall risk and the overall return of such a firm have been apportioned so that debt-holders bear proportionately less risk and expect proportionately less return than do equity-holders. The "stock beta" of a firm financed in this way will exceed the "firm beta," with the difference depending on the amounts and types of debt.

THE EFFECTIVENESS OF DIVERSIFICATION

Diversification typically reduces nonmarket (unrewarded) risk. No reduction in market (rewarded) risk can be expected, since it is related to a portfolio's beta value, which is simply a weighted average of the beta values of the component securities. As more and more securities are included in a portfolio, total risk should fall, reaching the lower limit represented by market risk.

Figure 7-6 shows that these are more than assertions. In Figure 7-6(a) the relationship between the standard deviation of the actual return over time and the number of securities in a portfolio is shown for portfolios of securities chosen randomly from the New York Stock Exchange. In Figure 7-6(b) such values are shown for portfolios chosen from exchanges located in the United States, the United Kingdom, France, Germany, Italy, Belgium, the Netherlands, and Switzerland. In each figure the vertical axis plots the ratio of the standard deviation of portfolio return to that of a typical stock from the group analyzed.

While *ex post* variations in actual return over time are not necessarily the same as risk perceived *ex ante*, it is interesting to note that the historic record is highly consistent with the approach described here. Diversification does reduce risk, and the reduction can be greater, the wider the range of possible investments. But there is a limit: nonmarket risk can be lowered by diversification, but market risk generally remains.

FIGURE 7-6
The Effect of Domestic and International Diversification on Risk

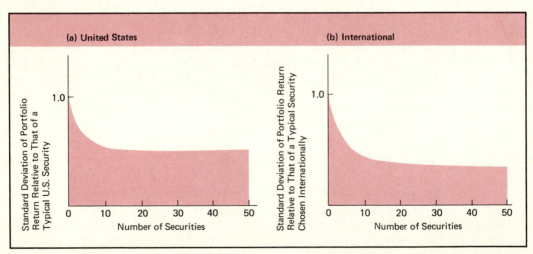

SOURCE: Bruno Solnik, "Why Not Diversify Internationally Rather than Domestically?" *Financial Analysts Journal*, 30, no. 4 (July/August 1974), 48–54.

The relationships in Figure 7-6 are fairly representative. Recall, however, that the values assume diversification in two senses: equal holdings, and no industry or other concentration. Actual portfolios usually have more risk, as managers explicitly or implicitly concentrate their holdings in one way or another, to be in a position to take advantage of "corrections" they anticipate will occur as the market realizes that certain securities are mispriced.

EXTENDED CAPITAL ASSET PRICING MODELS

The original Capital Asset Pricing Model makes strong assumptions and gives strong implications. In the years since it was developed, more complex models have been proposed. Those that begin with assumptions about investor's preferences (i.e., are *utility-based*) are termed *extended Capital Asset Pricing Models*. They are described in general in the remainder of this chapter; specific examples are given in subsequent chapters.

EFFICIENT INVESTMENT POLICIES WHEN BORROWING IS RESTRICTED OR EXPENSIVE

The original Capital Asset Pricing Model assumes that investors can borrow without limit at the riskless rate of interest at which funds can be invested. In fact, of course, such borrowing is likely to be either unavailable or restricted in amount. What impact might this have on investment policy and security prices if the market were (otherwise) efficient?

A useful way to answer the question makes the following working assumptions: (1) investors can lend—that is, purchase assets with a riskless return of R_l or (2) borrow without limit at a higher rate of interest R_b. These values are shown on the vertical axis of Figure 7-7; the shaded area represents risk-return combinations available from investment solely in risky assets.

Were there *no* opportunities to borrow or "lend" (invest in the riskless asset), the efficient frontier would be the curve *WLBZ*, and many combinations of securities would be efficient. However, the availability of a riskless asset returning R_l makes risky portfolios between *W* and *L* uninteresting—combinations of the riskless asset and the portfolio plotting at *L* provide more return for the same risk. Portfolio *L* is thus the optimal mix of risky securities for anyone whose attitude toward risk dictates holding any of the riskless asset (lending). Graphically, point *L* is found by swinging a line out of point R_l until it just touches the original frontier of efficient combinations.

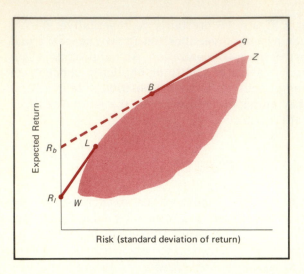

FIGURE 7-7
Efficient Investment Strategies When
Borrowing Costs More than Investing in
Riskless Securities

The ability to borrow money at rate R_b makes another portfolio—
B—of interest. Formerly efficient portfolios between B and Z are now
uninteresting: levered holdings of B dominate them, providing more
return for the same risk. Portfolio B is the optimal mix of risky securities
for anyone whose attitude toward risk dictates any borrowing (e.g.,
margined purchase of stocks). Graphically, point B is found by swinging
a line out of point R_b until it just touches the original frontier of efficient
combinations.

Investors with attitudes toward risk that dictate neither borrowing
nor lending should hold combinations of risky securities plotting along
curve LB. Their holdings should thus be *tailored* to be consistent with
differences in their degrees of aversion to risk.

The capital market line is now two lines and a curve: in Figure
7-7, R_lLBq.

THE "ZERO-BETA" VERSION OF THE SECURITY MARKET LINE

What becomes of the Security Market Line when borrowing rates exceed the riskless rate of interest? The answer depends on whether or
not the market portfolio is in fact one of the efficient combinations
of risky securities along the frontier between L and B in Figure 7-7.[1]
If it is not, little more can be said. If it is, a great deal can be said.

Figures 7-8(a) and (b) show a case in which the market portfolio
(shown by point M) is efficient. The line R_zMy, drawn tangent to the

---

[1] If investors could obtain the proceeds from short sales and there were no restrictions on
such sales, the market portfolio would definitely plot on the efficient frontier between points L
and B.

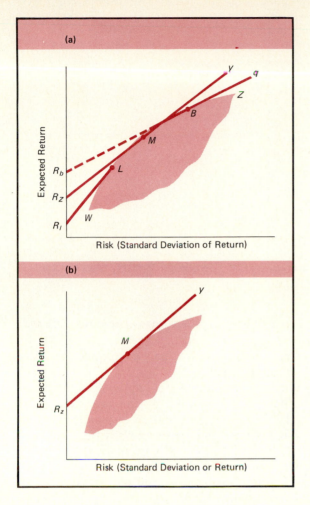

FIGURE 7-8
Risk and Return When the Market Portfolio
Is Efficient

efficient frontier at point M, intercepts the vertical axis at a return of R_z. In Figure 7-8(b) only the new ingredients are shown.

The striking characteristic of Figure 7-7(b) is this: *it is precisely the same picture that would be produced in a market in which investors could borrow and lend without limit at the riskless rate R_z.* Of course, only point M along line R_zMy would be attainable, but security prices would be the same as they would be in a market with borrowing and lending at R_z, and *all securities and portfolios would be priced to plot along a security market line going through point R_z,* as shown in Figure 7-9.

The vertical intercept of a Security Market Line indicates the expected return on a security or portfolio with a zero beta value that can be held in any amount (positive or negative). Since holdings of

Capital Asset Pricing Models

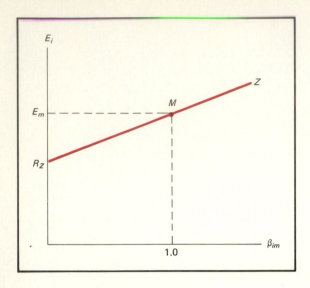

FIGURE 7-9
The "Zero-Beta" Security Market Line

the riskless security are restricted (to nonnegative amounts), it will plot below point R_z.

This approach is termed the *Zero-Beta* or, sometimes, the *Two-Parameter* Capital Asset Pricing Model.

The Zero-Beta Capital Asset Pricing Model implies that the Security Market Line will be flatter than implied by the original theory, since R_z will be above R_l. As a practical matter, it means that the intercept (R_z) must be inferred from the prices of risky securities—it cannot simply be found in the quotations of current returns on, for example, Treasury bills. As described in later chapters, many organizations do estimate such a Security Market Line; and they generally find that it conforms more to the Zero-Beta than to the original Capital Asset Pricing Model.

Cases in which borrowing either is impossible or costs more as one borrows larger amounts lead to only minor modifications in the conclusions. As long as the market portfolio is efficient, all securities will plot along a security market line, but the "zero-beta" return may exceed the riskless rate at which funds can be invested.

OTHER FACTORS: THE SECURITY MARKET HYPERPLANE

The original Capital Asset Pricing Model assumes that investors are concerned only with risk and return. But other factors may matter. Owing to differences in tax status, some investors may prefer return in the form of capital gains to an equal amount in the form of dividends; Chapter 9 considers this aspect. For most investors, real return is what counts: other things equal, securities that provide better hedges against inflation would be preferred over those that do not; Chapter 10 considers this. The prices of certain securities may be affected because they are associated with activities considered immoral by some investors. Potentially, then, a great many factors could be reflected in security prices.

To illustrate this general principle, we will focus on *liquidity*: the cost of selling or buying a security "in a hurry" (its bid-ask spread, potential price impacts, and so on). It is reasonable to assume that in the opinion of most investors, other things equal, the more liquid a portfolio the better. However, investors undoubtedly differ in their attitudes toward liquidity. For some it is very important; for others, fairly important, and for yet others, of little importance.

Under these conditions security prices would adjust until, overall, investors would be content to hold the outstanding securities. Each security can be characterized by three important attributes:

1. Its marginal contribution to the *expected return* of an efficient portfolio.
2. Its marginal contribution to the *risk* of an efficient portfolio.
3. Its marginal contribution to the *liquidity* of an efficient portfolio.

The first two attributes are familiar (marginal expected return and marginal variance or beta, respectively).[2] The third can be denoted L_i.

Note that, other things equal, large values of E_i and L_i are good and large values of β_i are bad. But in an efficient market, other things will not be equal. For example, one would not expect to find two stocks with the same expected returns and beta values but different liquidities, since the stock with the greater liquidity would dominate the other. In an efficient market dominance does not occur—there are no "free lunches."

Figure 7-10 shows the relationship one might expect among E_i, β_i, and L_i in an efficient market. For a given level of contribution to risk (β_i), more liquid securities have lower expected returns (the former is the "good news," and the latter is the "bad news," and, in an efficient market, they always go together). For a given level of liquidity, more risky securities (bad news) have higher expected returns (good news) as in the original Capital Asset Pricing Model. And for a given level of expected return, higher-beta securities (bad news) have higher levels of liquidity (good news).

The Security Market Line has now become a *Security Market Plane.*[3] More aspects could be added, requiring a "diagram" in four or more dimensions. Such a diagram cannot be plotted (an equation

---

[2] As before, we assume that the market portfolio is an efficient combination of securities.

[3] The term "Security Market Plane" is a trademark of Wells Fargo Bank.

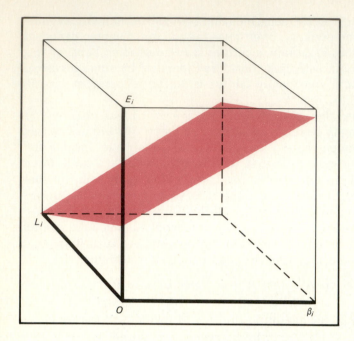

FIGURE 7-10
A Security Market Plane

has to suffice), but the relationship can be given a name: by analogy to the three-dimensional *plane*, it is termed a *hyperplane*.

In an efficient market, all securities will plot on a *Security Market Hyperplane,* the axes of which plot contributions to all attributes of efficient portfolios that matter (on average) to investors.

The relationship of expected return to contributions to the attributes of efficient portfolios depends on the attitudes of investors to the attributes:

If, on average, an attribute is *liked* by investors, securities that contribute more to that attribute will, other things equal, offer *lower* expected returns.

while:

If, on the average, an attribute is *disliked* by investors, securities that contribute more to that attribute will, other things equal, offer *higher* expected returns.

In an efficient market with many relevant attributes, the task of tailoring a portfolio for a specific investor is more complicated:

In a complex efficient market, only an investor with average attitudes and circumstances should hold market proportions of all securities.

In general:

If an investor likes an attribute more (or dislikes it less) than the average investor, he or she should generally hold a portfolio with relatively more of that attribute than is provided by holding securities in proportion to their market values. If an investor likes an attribute less (or dislikes it more) than the average investor, he or she should generally hold a portfolio with relatively less of that attribute than is provided by holding securities in proportion to their market values.

Of course, the right amount of "tilt" away from market proportions will depend on the extent of the difference between the investor's attitudes and those of the average investor and on the added risk involved in such a strategy.

A complex market, even if it is perfectly efficient, requires all the tools of portfolio analysis for managing the money of any investor who is significantly different from the "average investor." On the other hand, in such a world, investment management should be relatively *passive*: after the selection of an initial portfolio, there should be minor and infrequent changes.

Problems

1. Why shouldn't a security having a very large variance of return, but very low beta value, be expected to provide a large excess return?
2. Is the investor who owns any portfolio of risky assets other than the market portfolio exposed to some nonmarket risk?
3. A security analyst forecasts that each of three scenarios for the next year is equally likely: (1) a boom, (2) controlled growth, and (3) a severe recession. Under these three states of the world she projects returns on a specific security, the market portfolio, and Treasury bills as shown in the table below.

STATE OF THE WORLD			
	Optimistic (Boom)	Likely (Controlled Growth)	Pessimistic (Recession)
Probability of state	⅓	⅓	⅓
Return on market portfolio	20%	15%	−5%
Return on security A	25%	20%	−10%
Return on Treasury bills	7%	7%	7%

a. What is the equation for the Capital Market Line?
b. What would be the expected return and variance for a portfolio of which 50% is invested in Treasury bills and 50% in the market portfolio?

c. What is the equation for the Security Market Line?

d. Is the beta for security A such that you would consider the security aggressive or defensive?

e. What is the expected return on security A? What expected return would be appropriate (based on the Security Market Line) for a security with the beta value of security A?

4. Assume that the risk-free rate is 9% and the market portfolio has an expected return of 17%. What expected return would be consistent with the original Capital Asset Pricing Model for a security with a beta value of 0? 0.5? 1.0%? 1.5%?

5. Assume that the risk-free rate is 9% and the market portfolio has an expected return of 17% and a standard deviation of return of 20%. Under equilibrium conditions as described by the original Capital Asset Pricing Model, what would be the expected return for a portfolio having no nonmarket risk and a standard deviation of return of 15%?

6. A neighbor purchased a lottery ticket yesterday but now, owing to an unpredicted crisis, is in desperate need of cash. He offers to sell the ticket to you. You know the payoff and the probability of winning. All of your considerable fortune is invested in a highly diversified portfolio. How would you determine an appropriate price for the ticket?

7. You are trying to choose between two investment strategies. The first involves putting 80% of your funds in a highly diversified portfolio of common stocks and 20% in Treasury bills. The second involves putting all your money in a group of utility stocks, based on the recommendation of your broker, who believes that utilities are currently "out of favor" and represent a "great play." What aspects should you consider before making a decision?

8. If you buy a group of stocks designed to represent the market portfolio, will you have to buy and sell shares every time the relative prices of the stocks you hold change? Why? If not, when would you have to buy and sell?

9. A friend tells you about a gold mining company stock that typically goes down when the stock market rises and goes up when the stock market falls (she estimates its beta value to be $-.2$). Treasury bills currently return 9%, and the consensus opinion is that the stock market is expected to return 16%. If the stock of the mining company is priced efficiently, what return should you expect from it? How would you explain this to someone not familiar with investment theory?

10. If there were no riskless assets and borrowing were impossible, would there be any relationship between risk and return for individual securities? If so, what would it be? On what assumption or assumptions does your answer depend?

11. It has been said that investors care about expected return and risk in real (purchasing-power) terms, not in monetary terms. But in most countries no asset is riskless in real terms. What might this imply about the relationship between risk and return for securities? What changes might be required in the definition and measurement of expected return and beta in this instance?

12. According to some, the Zero-Beta Capital Asset Pricing Model is not as "strong" a theory as the original version (i.e., it makes fewer predictions and is consistent with more possible situations). In what sense is this true? Are the implications of the original version inconsistent with those of the Zero-Beta version?

13. Assume that many investors are revulsed by the antisocial behavior of a certain company. Would you expect its stock to return more than other stocks with comparable relevant attributes? If so, what would be your advice to someone with an average revulsion to the company's behavior? To someone who did not consider the company's actions antisocial at all? To someone who was extremely disturbed by the company's behavior?

14. Should an investor hold only stocks with positive alphas? Should stocks with negative alphas be sold short?

15. Other things equal, what is the likely relationship between the beta value of a stock and:
    a. The sensitivity of the company's sales to overall national income?
    b. The ratio of fixed costs to variable costs in the company's operations?
    c. The ratio of debt to equity in the company's financial structure?

8

Factor Models and the Arbitrage Pricing Theory

FACTORS IN SECURITY RETURNS

Capital Asset Pricing Models make assumptions about investors' *preferences* (utility functions) and derive implications for equilibrium relationships between security expected returns and relevant attributes (beta values, yield, liquidity, and so on). No assumptions are made about the nature of security returns. In particular, the interrelationships (correlations) among security returns can be simple or highly complex.

In practice, it is impossible to make a separate judgmental estimate for the correlation of every security with that of every other security. There are 249,750 potentially different correlation coefficients for a "followed list" of 500 securities. Reliance on historical values is feasible but dangerous. The correlation between two securities in a past period is, at best, a rough estimate of their likely correlation in the future.

Securities move together (or apart) partly by chance and partly in reaction to common forces. When oil prices increase unexpectedly, securities of companies with large oil reserves tend to go up together, while those selling products that use oil (e.g., automobiles) tend to go down together. When expectations for economic recovery turn up, securities of companies highly sensitive to economic activity (e.g., airlines) tend to go up more than those with less cyclical businesses (e.g., regulated utilities).

Within the economy there are major or *pervasive factors* that affect many firms in varying degrees. When investors' expectations about such factors change, the prices of securities of companies sensitive to the factors also change, in relation to their degrees of sensitivity.

A goal of investment analysis is to identify major *factors* in the economy and the *sensitivities* of the values of securities to changes in investors' expectations about future levels of those factors.

A formal statement of such relationships is termed a *factor model of security returns.*

A SINGLE-FACTOR MODEL

Figure 8-1 shows an extremely simple factor model. Each security is assumed to relate to (at most) one *common factor* (such as the consensus expectation about the future course of the economy). The sensitivity of security 1 to changes in the factor is represented by b_1, the sensitivity of security 2 by b_2, the sensitivity of security i by b_i, and so on. Cyclical stocks have high b_i values, noncyclical stocks low ones.

In addition to an estimate of sensitivity to the overall market factor, each stock is characterized by two additional values. The first (a_i) indicates the return that would be expected if the common factor were zero. The second (S_{e_i}) indicates the security's non-factor-related risk, or *security-specific risk*. This indicates the uncertainty attributable to the security's *idiosyncratic* characteristics—for example: changes in value that would result if oil were found under the corporate headquarters building, a new product were to flop, or the research lab were to come up with a new gene.

Two more values complete the picture: E_F is the expected value of the common factor; S_F is the uncertainty about its future value.

FIGURE 8-1
A One-Factor Model

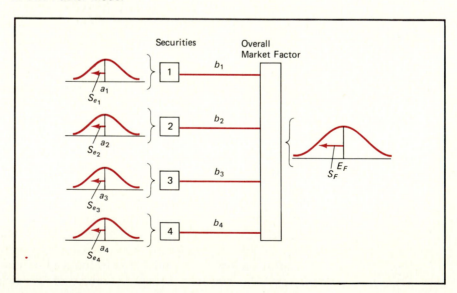

Factor Models and the Arbitrage Pricing Theory

In equation form:

$$\tilde{R}_i = a_i + b_i\tilde{F} + \tilde{e}_i \qquad (8\text{-}1)$$

where:

$\tilde{R}_i$ = the (uncertain) return on security i

a_i, b_i = constants

$\tilde{F}$ = the (uncertain) value of the factor

$\tilde{e}_i$ = the (uncertain) security-specific return

For clarity, values which are not known with certainty before the fact (in Latin: *ex ante*) are often indicated (as here) with *tildes* (squiggly lines). A statistician would say that they are *random variables*. At present we do not know for certain the future value of the common factor, nor security i's security-specific return. As a result, we do not know the precise value of the return on the security.

By convention, the *expected* value of the security-specific component of return is assumed to be zero. This merely requires that a_i include the expected portion of the non-factor-related return. It is also conventional to insure that b_i captures the full sensitivity of the return of the security to changes in the common factor. This implies that the security-specific return (e_i) will be uncorrelated with the factor (F).

Two predictions are required for the common factor:

E_F = the expected value of F

S_F = the standard deviation of F

while three predictions are required for each security:

a_i = non-factor-related return

b_i = sensitivity to the factor

S_{e_i} = standard deviation of the security-specific return

Figure 8-2 provides a graph of the assumed relationship between security i and the common factor.

Given these predictions, the risk and expected return of each security can be calculated. The expected return on security i is:

$$E_i = a_i + b_i E_F \qquad (8\text{-}2)$$

where:

E_i = the expected return on security i

E_F = the expected value of the factor

while the standard deviation can be determined from:

$$S_i^2 = b_i^2 S_F^2 + S_{e_i}^2 \qquad (8\text{-}3)$$

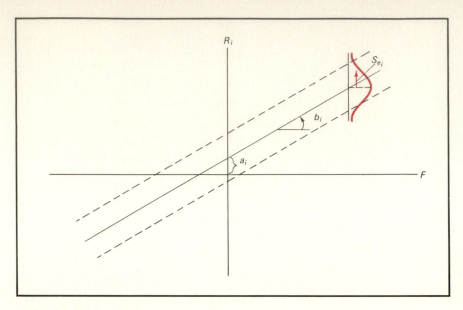

FIGURE 8-2
Security and Factor Returns

where:

S_i = the standard deviation of return on security i

The first term on the right-hand side of the equals sign is the *factor-related risk*, expressed in variance terms. The last term is the *non-factor-related* (security-specific) risk, also expressed in variance terms.

THE EFFECTS OF DIVERSIFICATION

When every *security* is related to a single common factor, as specified in equation (8-1), what can be said about a *portfolio*? If the portion of funds invested in security i is X_i, then:

$$\tilde{R}_p = \sum_{i=1}^{N} X_i \tilde{R}_i \tag{8-4}$$

Combining this with equation (8-1) gives:

$$\tilde{R}_p = \sum_{i=1}^{N} X_i (a_i + b_i \tilde{F} + \tilde{e}_i)$$

$$= \sum_{i=1}^{N} X_i a_i + \left(\sum_{i=1}^{N} X_i b_i \right) \tilde{F} + \sum_{i=1}^{N} X_i \tilde{e}_i \tag{8-5}$$

$$= a_p + b_p \tilde{F} + \tilde{e}_p$$

where:

$$a_p = \sum_{i=1}^{N} X_i a_i$$

$$b_p = \sum_{i=1}^{N} X_i b_i$$

$$\tilde{e}_p = \sum_{i=1}^{N} X_i e_i$$

The portfolio's non-factor-related expected return (a_p) is thus a weighted average of the corresponding values (a_i's) for the securities, using their relative values in the portfolio as weights. Similarly, the portfolio's sensitivity (b_p) to changes in the common factor is a weighted average of the corresponding values (b_i's) for the securities, again using relative values as weights.

The more diversified a portfolio (the larger the number of securities), the smaller will be each value of X_i. This need not cause reductions in factor-related risk. Recall that this component of risk depends on the uncertainty about the factor and on sensitivity to changes in the factor. Since the sensitivity of a portfolio is an *average* of the sensitivities of its securities, the resulting risk will be between that of the least sensitive stock and that of the most sensitive:

Diversification leads to *averaging* of factor-related risk.

This makes sense. When prospects for the economy turn sour, most securities will fall in price. Diversification per se cannot reduce risk due to such pervasive influences.

The situation can be radically different for non-factor-related (security-specific) risk. In a portfolio, some stocks will go up as a result of unexpected good news specific to the issuing company. Others will go down as a result of unexpected company-specific bad news. The net effect on the portfolio may be insignificant. Looking forward, one may anticipate approximately as many companies with good news as with bad news, leading to little net impact on the return of a diversified portfolio.

This can be quantified precisely if security-specific returns are *uncorrelated*. Under such conditions:

$$S_{e_p}^2 = \sum_{i=1}^{N} X_i^2 S_{e_i}^2 \qquad \text{(8-6)}$$

If holdings are equal, each value of X_i will equal $1/N$, and formula (8-6) can be written:

$$S_{e_p}^2 = \sum_{i=1}^{N} \left(\frac{1}{N}\right)^2 S_{e_i}^2$$

$$= \frac{1}{N}\left[\frac{1}{N}\left(S_{e_i}^2 + S_{e_i}^2 + \cdots + S_{e_N}^2\right)\right]$$

The value in the brackets is simply the average security-specific risk (measured by variance) for the component securities. But the portfolio's security-specific risk (measured by variance) is only one-Nth as large as this. The larger the number of securities (N), the smaller will be a portfolio's security-specific risk:

Diversification can substantially reduce security-specific risk.

Factor models generally make the (strong) assumption that all sources of correlation among security returns have been reflected in the identified factors. This makes it plausible to assume that security-specific returns (e_i's) are, in fact, uncorrelated and that *the more diversified the portfolio, the smaller the security-specific (non-factor-related) risk*. For a "highly diversified portfolio" this type of risk is "small enough" to be considered insignificant.

A Two-Factor Model

The health of the economy affects most firms, and thus changes in expectations concerning the future of the economy can be expected to have profound effects on the values of most securities. However, the economy is not a simple, monolithic entity. Several common influences with pervasive effects might be identified. For example:

Expectations about future levels of real gross national product
Expectations about future real interest rates
Expectations about future levels of inflation
Expectations about future oil prices

Instead of a single-factor model, a *multiple-factor model* may be needed.

Figure 8-3 portrays a two-factor model. Potentially, a security may be affected by each of the factors. Four predictions are now required for each security:

a_i = non-factor-related return
b_{i1} = sensitivity to factor 1
b_{i2} = sensitivity to factor 2
S_{e_i} = standard deviation of security-specific return

For each of the factors, two predictions are needed:

E_{F_1} = expected value of factor 1
S_{F_1} = standard deviation of factor 1
E_{F_2} = expected value of factor 2
S_{F_2} = standard deviation of factor 2

In general, the factors may be interrelated. For example, periods characterized by high oil prices are usually also periods of high general infla-

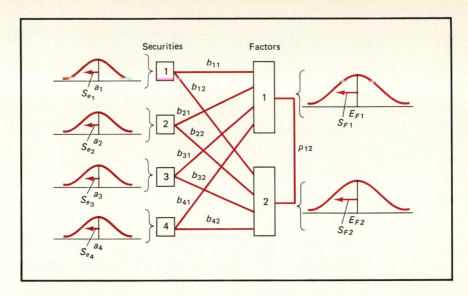

FIGURE 8-3
A Two-Factor Model

tion, so the corresponding factors are positively correlated. In general, an estimate is needed for the correlation of every factor with every other. Here, with only two factors, only one such estimate (ρ_{12}) is required.

In equation form:

$$\tilde{R}_i = a_i + b_{i1}\tilde{F}_1 + b_{i2}\tilde{F}_2 + \tilde{e}_i \tag{8-7}$$

where:

$\tilde{F}_1 = $ the (uncertain) value of factor 1

$\tilde{F}_2 = $ the (uncertain) value of factor 2

As before, security-specific returns are assumed to be uncorrelated with (1) the factors and (2) each other. Everything said earlier about the effects of diversification applies here as well. In particular:

Diversification leads to *averaging* of factor-related risk.

Diversification can substantially *reduce* security-specific risk.

For a "highly diversified portfolio" security-specific risk is "small enough" to be considered insignificant.

As in the previous case, the sensitivity of a portfolio to a factor will be a weighted average of the sensitivities of the securities, using relative values as weights:

$$b_{p1} = \sum_{i=1}^{N} X_i b_{i1}$$

$$b_{p2} = \sum_{i=1}^{N} X_i b_{i2}$$

where:

b_{p1} = sensitivity of the portfolio to factor 1
b_{p2} = sensitivity of the portfolio to factor 2

SECTORS AND FACTORS

Securities in the same industry or economic sector often move together, responding similarly to changes in common prospects. This type of relationship is portrayed in Figure 8-4, which represents a "three-sector" factor model.

FIGURE 8-4
Three-Sector Model

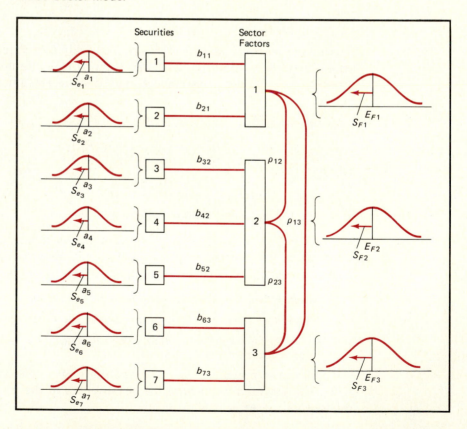

Factor Models and the Arbitrage Pricing Theory

Each security is classified as belonging in one of three economic sectors (e.g., Financial, Utility, and Industrial). Securities in the same sector may move together to a greater or lesser extent. Any comovement between two securities in different sectors is due solely to correlation between the corresponding "sector factors."

Sector models are special cases of the more general type of factor model. The model in Figure 8-4, with three factors, can be written as:

$$\tilde{R}_i = a_i + b_{i1}\tilde{F}_1 + b_{i2}\tilde{F}_2 + b_{i3}\tilde{F}_3 + \tilde{e}_i$$

where:

$\tilde{F}_1 =$ sector factor 1

$\tilde{F}_2 =$ sector factor 2

$\tilde{F}_3 =$ sector factor 3

The special aspect in this situation concerns the sensitivities of the securities to the three factors: each security is sensitive to one (and only one) factor. Thus for a security in sector 1:

$$b_{i1} = 1$$
$$b_{i2} = 0$$
$$b_{i3} = 0$$

For a security in sector 2:

$$b_{i1} = 0$$
$$b_{i2} = 1$$
$$b_{i3} = 0$$

and so on.

GENERAL FACTOR MODELS

In practice, analysts use models with both *common factors* (which affect all securities to a greater or lesser extent) and *sector factors* (which affect only some securities). Often the definitions blur. Moreover, identification and prediction of truly "pervasive" factors is an extremely difficult task. The goal is to focus on *permanent and important* sources of security and portfolio risk and return, not the *transitory and unimportant* phenomena that occur in any given period.

The general form of a factor model can be written as:

$$\tilde{R}_i = a_i + b_{i1}\tilde{F}_1 + b_{i2}\tilde{F}_2 + \cdots + b_{iM}\tilde{F}_M + \tilde{e}_i \qquad \text{(8-8)}$$

where:

$M =$ the number of factors

with the assumptions that:

Factor Models and the Arbitrage Pricing Theory

The expected value of each security-specific return is zero.

Security-specific returns are uncorrelated with factors.

Security-specific returns are uncorrelated with each other.

This is termed an *M-factor model*. For each security, $M + 2$ predictions are needed:

$$a_i$$
$$b_{i1}$$
$$b_{i2}$$
$$.$$
$$.$$
$$.$$
$$b_{iM}$$
$$S_{e_i}$$

For each of the M factors, two predictions are needed:

$$E_F$$
$$S_F$$

Finally, $(M \times (M - 1)/2)$ different estimates are required for the correlations among the factors.

Factor models are sometimes termed *index models*. A number of firms have used single-index (single-factor) models for portfolio management. Increasingly, however, richer multi-index (multifactor) models are employed.

In an important sense, the major tasks of investment analysis are (1) to determine an appropriate factor model (how big is M? what are the M factors?) and (2) to estimate the required values. Neither is easy, and definitive proof that correct answers have been obtained is unlikely to be obtained. Differences of opinion concerning the efficacy of alternative approaches undoubtedly will persist, providing the investor with a wide range of choice.

THE ARBITRAGE PRICING THEORY

A factor model represents relationships among security returns. Selection of an appropriate model is, at base, an empirical issue. Relevant considerations include companies' product lines, types of labor and material used, effects of changes in national income on relative demands and supplies, and so on.

A factor model is not an equilibrium theory. However, when returns are generated by a factor model, equilibrium in the capital markets will result in certain relationships among the *values* of the coefficients of the model.

The *Arbitrage Pricing Theory*, like Capital Asset Pricing Models,

Factor Models and the Arbitrage Pricing Theory

is an equilibrium theory of the relationships between security expected returns and relevant security attributes. Unlike Capital Asset Pricing Models, the APT assumes that returns are generated by an identifiable factor model. It does not, however, make strong assumptions about investor preferences.

FACTOR PORTFOLIOS

Assume that M pervasive factors have been identified and that security returns are related to them as indicated in equation (8-8) (with the ancillary assumptions stated). Moreover, assume that there are "very many" securities and that sensitivities to the factors differ substantially among securities.

In such a world, a number of investment strategies present themselves. Particularly interesting are portfolios that represent *pure factor plays*. Given enough securities with different characteristics, it should be possible to construct a portfolio that is:

Sensitive to factor 1.

Unaffected by every other factor.

So highly diversified that security-specific returns "wash out."

The trick is to combine long and short positions to *hedge out* sensitivities to factors 2, 3, . . . , M and to hold such a large number of securities that approximately as many will experience good security-specific returns as will experience bad ones.

For example, assume that two factors are relevant ($M = 2$) and that securities A and B have the following sensitivities:

Security	b_{i1}	b_{i2}
A	.4	.6
B	.6	.4

If you invest $1 of your own money in security B and sell short $2 worth of security A, investing the proceeds in security B, the proportions (of your money) invested will be:

$$X_A = -2$$
$$X_B = 3$$

The sensitivity of this portfolio to changes in factor 1 will be:

$$b_{p1} = (-2 \times .4) + (3 \times .6) = 1$$

while its sensitivity to changes in factor 2 will be:

$$b_{p2} = (-2 \times .6) + (3 \times .4) = 0$$

If you could invest in a great many securities like B, and sell short a great many securities like A, it would be possible to obtain a portfolio with very little security-specific risk. By choosing the proportions appropriately, you could create a portfolio sensitive only to factor 1:

$$\tilde{R}_p \approx a_p + \tilde{F}_1 \qquad \textbf{(8-9)}$$

This would be a "pure factor 1 play" portfolio. By design, its return moves with the factor on a one-for-one basis (i.e., $b_{p1} = 1$). It is thus a "unit factor 1 play portfolio" or—more simply—a "factor 1 portfolio."

An alternative strategy could provide a factor 2 portfolio. If you were to invest \$1 of your own money in many securities like A and sell short \$2 worth of securities like B, investing the proceeds in the other securities, the sensitivities would be:

$$b_{p1} = (3 \times .4) + (-2 \times .6) = 0$$
$$b_{p2} = (3 \times .6) + (-2 \times .4) = 1$$

giving a portfolio return:

$$\tilde{R}_p \approx a_p + \tilde{F}_2$$

In a market with many securities of diverse characteristics, in which proceeds from short sales may be reinvested, it would be possible to create "pure" factor portfolios (1) sensitive on a one-for-one basis to only one factor and (2) having insignificant security-specific risk. In practice, the required conditions are not met completely, making it necessary to create "impure" factor portfolios (1) sensitive primarily (but not exclusively) to one factor (possibly on other than a one-for-one basis) and (2) having relatively little security-specific risk.

Like most theories, the Arbitrage Pricing Theory assumes purity. As always, the issue is not the relevance of the assumptions, but the validity of the implications.

EXPECTED RETURNS ON FACTOR PORTFOLIOS

The expected return from a pure factor portfolio will depend on the expected value of the relevant factor. It is convenient to break the total into two parts—(1) the riskless rate of interest and (2) the difference between the expected return and the riskless rate. The latter difference is typically indicated by the greek letter *lambda*. It may be regarded as the *expected return premium per unit of sensitivity to the factor*. Thus the expected return on a pure factor 1 portfolio is:

$$R_f + \lambda_1$$

The expected return on a pure factor 2 portfolio is:

$$R_f + \lambda_2$$

and so on.

It is possible that many alternative combinations of securities could be used to construct a "pure factor 1 portfolio." Will each such combination have the same expected return? Yes—unless the capital market is highly inefficient. While factor play *portfolios* may not be unique, their *expected returns* should be.

Imagine a situation in which two factor 1 portfolios had different expected returns. This could be due only to differences in their "*a*-values" [a_p in equation (8-9)]. Now imagine the following investment strategy:

> Sell short $1 worth of the portfolio with the lower expected return.
>
> Use the proceeds to purchase $1 worth of the portfolio with the greater expected return.

For example, if the former had an expected return of 15% and the latter an expected return of 17%, you would stand to make $.02, *no matter what happened to factor 1*. Moreover, you would do so *without investing any of your own money*!

Too good to be true? Undoubtedly. Such opportunities, if present, will cause *arbitrageurs* to spring into action, purchasing the securities in the higher-expected-return portfolio and selling those in the lower-expected-return portfolio. But this will drive up the prices of the former, driving down the expected return of the corresponding portfolio. It will also drive down the prices of the latter, driving up the expected return of the corresponding portfolio. Before long, opportunities to get "something for nothing" will disappear. *Arbitrage* will insure that:

All "factor *j*" portfolios will have the same expected return ($R_f + \lambda_j$).

The presence of a riskless rate of interest is a natural part of the Arbitrage Pricing Theory. With a great many diverse securities it will be possible to find one that has zero sensitivity to *every* factor and is sufficiently diversified to have insignificant security-specific risk. Its expected return, which will be virtually riskless, is the base from which other expected returns are measured.

SECURITY EXPECTED RETURNS

By splitting funds among (1) a riskless portfolio and (2) factor portfolios, it is possible to obtain any of a large number of portfolios with varying sensitivities to the relevant factors. Moreover, such portfolios can be constructed to have insignificant security-specific risks.

Assume that the return on security k is related to factors 1 and 2 as follows:

$$\tilde{R}_k = a_k + .8\tilde{F}_1 + 1.5\tilde{F}_2 + \tilde{e}_k$$

Now, consider a strategy in which $1.30 is borrowed at the riskless rate to supplement an investor's $1. Of the resulting $2.30, $.80 is invested in a factor 1 portfolio and the remaining $1.50 in a factor 2 portfolio. The resulting portfolio will have a sensitivity of .8 to factor 1 and a sensitivity of 1.5 to factor 2. Its expected return will come from three sources:

Riskless security:	$-1.30 \times R_f$	$= -1.30R_f$
Factor 1 portfolio:	$.80 \times (R_f + \lambda_1) =$	$.80R_f + .8\lambda_1$
Factor 2 portfolio:	$1.50 \times (R_f + \lambda_2) =$	$\underline{1.50R_f + \qquad 1.5\lambda_2}$
		$R_f + .8\lambda_1 + 1.5\lambda_2$

Call this strategy portfolio K. Compare it with security k. Each has a sensitivity of .8 to factor 1 and a sensitivity of 1.2 to factor 2. Security k is subject to additional risk due to uncertainty about its security-specific return. Portfolio K has virtually no risk of this type.

What if the expected return from security k were less than that from portfolio K? Clearly, the portfolio would *dominate* the security— the former would provide a greater expected return with less risk than the latter. A clever arbitrageur could sell security k short, using the proceeds to finance purchase of portfolio K, and expect to profit from the difference in their expected returns. The situation would not be totally riskless, since the security-specific return could swamp the difference in expected returns. However, if there were many securities like k, this source of risk could be diversified away.

What if the expected return from security k were more than that from portfolio K? In this case, there is no obvious dominance. However, a clever arbitrageur could sell the portfolio short, using the proceeds to finance purchase of the security, and expect to profit from the difference in expected returns. Here, too, the situation would not be totally riskless, since the security-specific return could swamp the difference in expected returns. However, if there were many securities like k, this source of risk could be diversified away.

The conclusion is thus:

Arbitrage would insure that the expected return on security k would be very close to:

$$E_k = R_f + .8\lambda_1 + 1.5\lambda_2$$

More generally:

$$E_k = R_f + b_{i1}\lambda_1 + b_{i2}\lambda_2$$

When there are M factors:

$$E_k \approx R_f + b_{i1}\lambda_1 + b_{i2}\lambda_2 + \cdots + b_{iM}\lambda_M \qquad \text{(8-10)}$$

Equation (8 10) is the conclusion of the Arbitrage Pricing Theory:

Security expected returns will be related to their sensitivities to pervasive factors. Moreover, the relationship will be *linear*, with a common intercept approximately equal to the *riskless rate of interest*.

If equation (8-10) holds for every security, it must hold for every portfolio. Thus:

Security and portfolio expected returns will be related to their sensitivities to pervasive factors. Moreover, the relationship will be linear, with a common intercept equal to the riskless rate of interest.

While the intercept will equal the riskless rate of interest, the theory is silent about the sizes of the lambda values: they could be large or small; positive, negative, or zero.

Equation (8-10) is sometimes called a *pricing equation*. Like the equations obtained from Capital Asset Pricing Models, it asserts that there is a linear relationship between (1) expected return and (2) various relevant attributes of securities and portfolios. In this case the relevant attributes are sensitivities to major factors in security returns.

ESTIMATING BETA VALUES

When returns are generated by a factor model, it is relatively straightforward to estimate the beta value of a security or portfolio.

Assume that the beta value of security i relative to the market portfolio is needed. If returns are generated by an M-factor model, the return on security i will be:

$$\tilde{R}_i = a_i + b_{i1}\tilde{F}_1 + b_{i2}\tilde{F}_2 + \cdots + b_{iM}\tilde{F}_M + \tilde{e}_i$$

The nature of covariance is such that the covariance of the return on security i with that of the market portfolio will be:

$$\text{Cov}\,(R_i, R_m) = b_{i1}\,\text{Cov}\,(F_1, R_m) + b_{i2}\,\text{Cov}\,(F_2, R_m)$$
$$+ \cdots + b_{iM}\,\text{Cov}\,(F_M, R_m) + \text{Cov}\,(e_i, R_m)$$

The beta of security i relative to the market portfolio is obtained by dividing the covariance by the variance of the market portfolio. Thus:

$$\beta_i = b_{i1}\frac{\text{Cov}\,(F_1, R_m)}{\text{Var}\,(R_m)} + b_{i2}\frac{\text{Cov}\,(F_2, R_m)}{\text{Var}\,(R_m)}$$
$$+ \cdots + b_{iM}\frac{\text{Cov}\,(F_M, R_m)}{\text{Var}\,(R_m)} + \frac{\text{Cov}\,(e_i, R_m)}{\text{Var}\,(R_m)}$$

As a practical matter, the last term will be very small. Little is lost by ignoring it. Each of the other terms involves the ratio of a factor's covariance with the market portfolio to the variance of the market portfolio. But this is simply the *beta value of the factor* relative to the market portfolio. This leads to the conclusion that:

$$\beta_i \approx b_{i1}\beta_{F_1} + b_{i2}\beta_{F_2} + \cdots + b_{iM}\beta_{FM} \qquad \textbf{(8-11)}$$

In words:

> The beta value of a security is a weighted average of the beta values of the relevant factors, with the security's sensitivities to the factors as weights.

Since the beta value of a portfolio is simply a weighted average of the beta values of its component securities, and since this is also the case for its sensitivities to the factors, the same relationship holds for portfolios. Thus:

> The beta value of a security or portfolio is a weighted average of the beta values of the relevant factors, with the security or portfolio's sensitivities to the factors as weights.

The beta values of the factors may be determined from the composition of the market portfolio and the estimated risks and correlations of the factors. Given these values, the beta value of any security or portfolio can be estimated directly, using equation (8-11).

CAPITAL ASSET PRICING MODELS AND THE APT

Capital Asset Pricing Models do not *assume* that returns are generated by a factor model. On the other hand, they are not *inconsistent* with a world in which returns are generated in this manner.

The original Capital Asset Pricing Model implies that security expected returns will be related to their beta values:

$$E_i = R_f + (E_m - R_f)\beta_i \qquad \textbf{(8-12)}$$

If returns are generated by an *M*-factor model, the beta value of security *i* will be related to its sensitivities to the factors and the beta values of the factors, as shown in equation (8-11). Combining this with equation (8-12) gives:

$$E_i = R_f + b_{i1}(E_m - R_f)\beta_{F_1} + b_{i2}(E_m - R_f)\beta_{F_2}$$
$$+ \cdots + b_{iM}(E_m - R_f)\beta_{F_M} \qquad \textbf{(8-13)}$$

Comparing this to the APT equilibrium condition [equation (8-10)] indicates that *if the assumptions of both the APT and the original CAPM hold*:

$$\lambda_1 = (E_m - R_f)\beta_{F_1}$$

$$\lambda_2 = (E_m - R_f)\beta_{F_2}$$

.

.

.

$$\lambda_M = (E_m - R_f)\beta_{F_M}$$

The Arbitrage Pricing Theory says nothing about the sizes or the magnitudes of the factor expected return premiums (λ_j values). By assuming something about investor preferences, the original Capital Asset Pricing Model provides further guidance. It predicts that there will be positive premiums for sensitivity to factors that move with the market and negative premiums for sensitivity to factors that move counter to the market. Moreover, it predicts that the greater the extent to which a factor moves with a market, the greater will be the associated expected return premium.

Extended Capital Asset Pricing Models imply that expected returns may be related to additional security attributes, such as liquidity and taxability. Some of these may, in turn, be related to sensitivities to major factors. If so, the λ_j values would reflect the utility of such attributes for the average investor, in addition to a beta-related expected return premium. Additional sources of utility not related to the factors would lead to additional terms in the equilbrium relationship.

In a factor model setting, Capital Asset Pricing Models *supplement* the Arbitrage Pricing Theory, not *supplant* it. Combined, the two theories are more *powerful* (make stronger predictions) than the Arbitrage Pricing Theory alone. These more detailed predictions can provide considerably more guidance for investment decisions. Ultimately, of course, the value of this added power will depend on the consistency of the predictions with reality.

Problems

1. What dangers are associated with holding only stocks of "small emerging growth companies"?

2. Assume that a major source of uncertainty in the economy concerns the future price of oil. Your investment adviser provides you with a list of stocks. At the top are companies whose profits are most sensitive to oil prices; in the middle, those whose profits are affected less by oil prices; at the bottom, those unaffected by oil prices. Based on this factor alone, what could you say about the expected returns on the companies' stocks? Why? Might other factors make a list based on expected returns look different? Why?

3. Assume that over the last twelve months returns on stocks averaged 18% and the riskless interest rate was 8%. An investment advisory service categorized a list of 1,000 stocks on the basis of "predicted beta" at the beginning of the year. Three groups were identified. Their returns over the subsequent year were:

Low-beta group   20%
Average-beta group   18%
High-beta group   16%

Is this experience consistent with likely expectations, given the overall performance of the market? Does it refute the Capital Asset Pricing Model? Why or why not?

4. Two factors have been identified as pervasive in affecting stock returns. The sensitivities of two securities (A and B) and of a riskless security to each of the factors are shown below, along with the expected return on each:

Security	b_{i1}	b_{i2}	Expected Return
A	.5	.8	16.2%
B	1.5	1.4	21.6%
Riskless	0	0	10.0%

a. Consider a portfolio (C) made up by selling short $.50 of security B and purchasing $1.50 of security A with the proceeds and with your own capital of $1. How sensitive would this portfolio be to each of the factors?

b. Consider a portfolio (D) made up by borrowing $1 and investing the proceeds, along with your own capital of $1 in portfolio C. How sensitive would this portfolio be to each of the factors?

c. Could you achieve the same result as in (b) with the three original securities (A, B, and the riskless security)? How?

d. What is the expected return premium for factor 2?

e. What combination of securities A and B would be insensitive to changes in factor 2?

f. What combination of securities A, B, and the riskless security would move on a one-to-one basis with factor 1 and be insensitive to changes in factor 2?

g. What is the expected return premium for factor 1?

h. An investment banking firm has retained you to estimate the "cost of capital" (appropriate expected return) for a new security. It will have a sensitivity of .8 to factor 1 and a sensitivity of .4 to factor 2. What is your answer? Why?

5. Could a single-factor model have as its factor the return on the market portfolio? Why or why not?

6. When considering international investment, some investment firms structure portfolios by economic sector. For example, securities of financial firms are grouped together, regardless of the country in which the firm is domiciled; securities of industrial firms are also grouped together, and so on. Other investment firms group securities by country. For example, all French stocks are grouped together, all Japanese stocks are grouped together, and so on.

a. How would each of these procedures be described with a factor model?

b. How might you choose between the two procedures if forced to select one or the other?

c. Could you construct a factor model that took differences in both economic sector and country into account? How?

7. Some have argued that the market portfolio can never be measured and that Capital Asset Pricing Models are thus untestable. Others have argued that the Arbitrage Pricing Theory specifies neither the number of factors nor their identity and hence is also untestable. Do you agree? If so, does this mean that the theories are of no value whatever?

8. Assume that oil prices have been identified as a pervasive factor affecting security returns. Should someone expecting to inherit an oilfield hold the market portfolio? If not, how might factor portfolios be used in his or her investment plan?

9

Taxes

INTRODUCTION

A well-worn saying holds that nothing is certain but death and taxes. Unhappily, governments are often responsible for the former, and they are virtually always the source of the latter. Moreover, governmental activities normally play a central role in determining changes in the overall price level of an economy. Upon occasion such changes are in the downward direction—that is, there is deflation. The more common experience, however, is of rising prices, or inflation.

Neither taxation nor inflation should be regarded as an unmitigated evil. Each benefits some at the expense of others. If government policy is responsive to some type of consensus opinion regarding socially desirable actions, the benefits may well outweigh the costs. Whatever the case, both taxes and inflation impact investment results, investment decisions, and the pricing of securities. And they are sufficiently important in present-day societies to warrant considerable discussion. This chapter deals with taxes; the next with inflation.

TAXES IN THE UNITED STATES

Since the United States is the world's largest capital market, we will focus on taxes levied on U.S. citizens and corporations. Many other countries, however, impose taxes similar in kind to those of the United States, so much of the discussion is at least partly relevant for non-U.S. citizens.

Most of the specific tax rates and provisions in this chapter applied in the first half of the 1980s. Changes do occur from year to year, and current regulations should, of course, be consulted when preparing tax returns or considering major investment decisions. However, the material given here can be considered broadly representative of current taxation (primarily federal) in the United States.

By far the most important taxes for investment decision-making are the personal and corporate income taxes, but gift and estate taxes often prove relevant as well. We will describe the essential elements of each, then consider their major influences on the investment market.

THE CORPORATE INCOME TAX

In the United States and most other countries, the corporate form of organization is the most important in terms of the dollar value of assets owned, although many more firms are organized as partnerships or as single proprietorships. Legally, a corporation is regarded as a separate entity, while a proprietorship or partnership is considered an extension of its owner or owners. Income earned by proprietorships and partnerships is taxed primarily through the personal income tax levied on their owners. Income earned by a corporation may be taxed twice— once when it is earned, via the corporate income tax, and again when it is received as dividends by holders of the firm's securities, via the personal income tax.[1]

Double taxation may at first seem inefficient, if not immoral. It also raises questions about the efficiency of the corporate form of organization. Suffice it to say that limited liability and the ability to subdivide ownership and to easily transfer shares of that ownership appear to be of sufficient value to more than offset the disadvantages arising from tax law for the firms that do most of the business in the United States. Moreover, without the corporate income tax, personal tax rates would have to be increased if the level of government expenditures were to remain constant without increasing the national debt. If the burden is properly distributed at present, the overall impact of such a change might be smaller than one might first expect.

CORPORATE TAX RATES

The corporate income tax is relatively simple in one respect. There are usually only a few basic rates. For example, in 1983 there was a tax rate of 15% applicable to the first $25,000 of taxable income each year, a rate of 18% applicable to the next $25,000, a rate of 30% applicable to the next $25,000, a rate of 40% applicable to the next $25,000,

---

[1] Certain corporations with 35 or fewer shareholders may elect to be treated as partnerships for tax purposes. Such firms, often called "Subchapter S corporations" (after the enabling provision of the Internal Revenue Code), constitute an exception to the general rule.

and a rate of 46% applicable to all income over $100,000. The result is shown in Figure 9-1. The top line shows the *marginal* rate—that is, the rate applied to an additional dollar. The bottom line shows the *average* tax rate—that is, the total amount of taxes paid, divided by the total income subject to tax. This ratio is equal to the original rate for incomes below $25,000, but it is below the marginal rate for higher incomes. This is generally the case when marginal rates increase with income. For example, a corporation earning $65,000 would pay:

$$
\begin{array}{rl}
0.15 \times 25{,}000 = & 3{,}750 \\
0.18 \times 25{,}000 = & 4{,}500 \\
0.30 \times 15{,}000 = & \underline{4{,}500} \\
& 12{,}750
\end{array}
$$

or

$$
19.62\% = 100 \times \frac{12{,}750}{65{,}000} \text{ of its total income in taxes}
$$

The average rate measures the overall impact of taxes, but the marginal rate is more relevant for most decisions. For example, if a corporation were considering an investment that would increase its income from $65,000 to $70,000 each year, the increase in income after tax would be $(1 - .30) \times \$5{,}000$, or $3,500, not $(1 - .1962) \times \$5{,}000$.

As shown in Figure 9-1, the larger a corporation's taxable income,

FIGURE 9-1
Marginal and Average Corporate Tax Rates, 1983

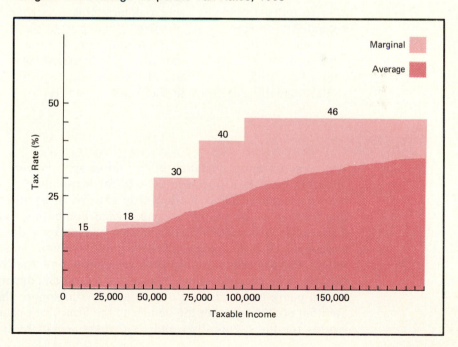

the closer its average tax rate comes to the higher marginal rate. Most corporations with publicly traded shares have sufficiently large incomes to make the distinction between marginal and average rates minor at best. Overall, such corporations pay taxes equal to virtually the largest marginal rate (46%) of the income reported for tax purposes.

DEFINING INCOME

Corporate income is partly a philosophic concept, partly an artifact of legal requirements, partly a result of accounting conventions, partly an indication of the hopes of the firm's management, and sometimes only incidentally related to underlying economic factors.

For tax purposes, corporate income is defined as revenue minus expenses. The problems arise in measuring these two elements. Simply put, the problem is to match cash flows with relevant time periods. If an airplane is sold this year, but payment is to be made in installments over the next five years, when is the sales price to be considered taxable revenue? If a new plant is to be built and paid for this year, but is to be used to produce goods for the next 20 years, when is the outlay to be considered expense? Accountants have a menu of procedures, known as *generally accepted accounting principles*, that can be utilized to handle these and many more subtle cases. However, there is extremely wide latitude within these principles.

The government has thus prescribed certain limits on the methods used to calculate income when determining a corporation's income tax liability. In some cases the firm is required to use the same procedures when reporting to its stockholders; in other cases it can (and often does) use a different set of assumptions, sometimes coming up with a very different estimate of income (although differences of this sort are usually described in the firm's annual report).

DEPRECIATION

The most dramatic instance of the latter sort concerns depreciation of assets used in a business or held for investment. If a corporation buys a computer for $1 million, it is entitled to eventually charge off this cost as a deductible expense when computing taxable income. Each dollar deducted will reduce such income by a dollar, and hence taxes paid by $.46, assuming the corporate income remains in the 46% range. The $1 million outlay thus represents eventual tax savings of $460,000. The *present* value of these tax reductions depends, of course, on the years in which they are obtained. The sooner the cost can be "written off," the greater the benefit to the firm. The best of all possible worlds for the corporation and its owners would be to *expense* the computer—that is, charge the entire cost as a current expense in the year in which it is incurred. Barring this, the firm would like to allocate the cost against income as soon as possible.

Congress, in making tax laws, and the Internal Revenue Service, in administrating them, looks at the situation in a different way. The taxpayer would like to minimize the present value of tax liabilities; other things equal, the tax collector would like to maximize them. Thus the Internal Revenue Service prescribes limits on the manner in which outlays for fixed assets may be charged as costs. For example, the cost of land per se may not be deducted at all, since it is not normally considered to be a depreciating asset, although the cost of improvements to land (e.g., buildings) can generally be deducted over a period of years. The cost of fixed assets regarded as having a limited useful life may be deducted, but not all at once.

THE ACCELERATED COST RECOVERY SYSTEM

For purposes of reporting corporate income to stockholders, a manager might want to allocate the cost of a fixed asset over the period during which it is expected to contribute to revenue. This is usually termed the asset's *estimated useful life*. For tax purposes it is clearly advantageous to underestimate this in order to write the cost off as rapidly as possible. To control this urge, the Internal Revenue Service prescribes a standard set of procedures for allocating the costs of fixed assets to years subsequent to their purchase.

When reporting to shareholders, many firms depreciate the costs of fixed assets using the "straight-line" method, in which the same proportion of the cost is "written off" in each year of the assets' "useful life." However for assets placed in service after 1980 a more advantageous procedure may be used for calculating taxable income. The *accelerated cost recovery system* (*ACRS*) prescribes specific percentages of cost for each of several years. As the name implies, the "recovery" (write-off) of cost is rapid ("accelerated"). While the *total* amount written off will be the same under each method, the *present value* will generally be more (and thus the present value of taxes paid will be less) if the ACRS rules are adopted.

For this purpose, property is grouped into four broad classes. Automobiles, light trucks, and research equipment are considered *three-year property*. Most business equipment is considered *five-year property*. Some public utility property is considered *ten-year property*. The remainder of public utility property and "realty" (buildings, not land) are considered *fifteen-year property*.[2]

---

[2] Except that real property placed in service after March 15, 1984 is considered eighteen-year property.

TABLE 9-1
Accelerated Cost Recovery System Write-offs

Year	3-Year Property	5-Year Property	10-Year Property	15-Year Property
1 (Purchase)	25%	15%	8%	12%
2	38	22	14	10
3	37	21	12	9
4		21	10	8
5		21	10	7
6			10	6
7			9	6
8			9	6
9			9	6
10			9	5
11				5
12				5
13				5
14				5
15				5

The proportions of the cost of each of the four types of property that can be charged as expense in various years are shown in Table 9-1. In the case of fifteen-year realty, the amount charged in the first year depends on the month of purchase (the figures shown assume purchase in January). For all other property, the charges are the same, no matter when the property is purchased within the year.

There are many reasons why corporate income reported to stockholders may differ from that used for tax purposes, but different depreciation assumptions are often the major factor. If the tax paid by a large corporation diverges significantly from 46% of the apparent taxable income, as reported to stockholders, examination of the depreciation procedures may prove illuminating.

INVENTORY VALUATION

Another vexing problem associated with the measurement of corporate income concerns the cost of inventory sold during the year. This arises when prices are changing fairly rapidly and a firm holds inventory for long periods. To take a fairly simple case, imagine a retailer of sailboats. At the start of the year he has 100 in stock, all purchased for $10,000 each. During the year he takes delivery on 100 more, but must pay $11,000 each, ending with 90 in stock. What was his income?

The question, of course, concerns the relevant cost of the 110 boats that were sold and of the 90 that remain. The firm may have sold all the "old" boats first, or all the "new" boats, or a mixture of the two. However, this is rarely taken into account in the calculations. An accountant may assume any of the above combinations, without regard for the actual facts of the situation.

The impact of different assumptions is shown in Table 9-2. In the first column all the old boats are assumed to have been sold first—this is the *first-in-first-out* (FIFO) method. In the second column all the new boats are assumed to have been sold first—this is the *last-in-first-out* (LIFO) method. In the third column equal numbers of both old and new boats are assumed to have been sold—this is an *average-cost* method.

When prices have been rising, the LIFO method will permit a corporation to charge more to cost in the present and less in the future. This will lower taxes in the present and raise them in the future. The net result is a fall in the present value of taxes paid—clearly beneficial to the owners of the firm. Since rising prices are so much a phenomenon of modern society, one would expect firms to adopt LIFO inventory valuation for tax purposes, just as they choose accelerated depreciation in most cases in which it is allowed. However, there is a difference between the two situations. The Internal Revenue Code requires a firm using the LIFO method for tax purposes to use it also for computing income reported to shareholders. The firm can thus either report a high income or pay a small tax. This can be seen in Table 9-2. FIFO accounting gives the largest current income, both before and after tax, but it also requires the payment of the largest tax. Before 1970, many firms used FIFO accounting, suggesting that in times of moderate inflation many managers were willing to sacrifice some real benefits to improve the appearance of their firm's financial statements. However,

TABLE 9-2
The Impact of Different Inventory Valuation Methods

REVENUE: 110 BOATS AT $15,000 = $1,650,000		
Cost by FIFO Method	Cost by LIFO Method	Cost by Average-Cost Method
100 at $10,000 = $1,000,000	100 at $11,000 = $1,110,000	55 at $10,000 = $ 550,000
10 at 11,000 = 110,000	10 at 10,000 = 100,000	55 at 11,000 = 605,000
$1,110,000	$1,210,000	$1,155,000
Income $ 540,000	$ 440,000	$ 495,000
Tax (at 46%) −248,400	−202,400	−227,700
Income after tax $ 291,600	$ 237,600	$ 267,300
Cost of remaining inventory:		45 at $10,000
90 at $11,000 = $ 990,000	90 at $10,000 = $ 900,000	+ 45 at $11,000 = $ 945,000

as the pace of inflation increased, LIFO accounting became much more common.

AMORTIZATION AND DEPLETION

Allocation of the cost of an asset over its estimated useful life is termed depreciation; a comparable procedure applied to a natural resource (e.g., an oil reserve) is called *depletion*, while it is called *amortization* if applied to certain intangible assets. Amortization is often handled via procedures akin to those used for the depreciation of tangible assets. But depletion is another matter.

Depletion is utilized to allocate the cost of finding or purchasing a so-called "wasting asset" to the units of the asset removed and sold. For example, the cost of bringing in an oil well may be divided by the estimated number of barrels of oil that can be pumped out, and the resulting amount written off as an expense for each barrel sold. If the initial estimate proves to have been in error, adjustments can be made so that the entire cost, but no more, is deducted. This is the *cost method* of depletion; it differs only in detail from the procedure used for the depreciation of fixed assets.

More controversial is the *percentage depletion* method. Here the amount charged as cost need bear no relationship to the actual cost. Instead, a stated percentage of the *gross* income from the property (before any costs) may be deducted as expense. An upper limit is generally placed on the amount deducted in this manner—in 1983 it was 50% of the *net* taxable income (after nondepletion deductions) from the property.

The depletion allowance is used to encourage exploitation (and depletion!) of certain natural resources—and, some skeptics argue, to provide political support for certain elected officials. In 1983 percentages ranged from 5% to 22% for various minerals.

DEDUCTIBILITY OF INTEREST PAYMENTS

One of the major attributes of both corporate and personal income taxes in the United States is the deductibility of interest payments. Interest is regarded as an expense and can thus be deducted from revenue when calculating taxable income. For example, consider two firms, each with revenues of $25,000 and noninterest expenses of $15,000. Firm A is financed by both debt and equity and pays $5,000 in interest to its creditors. As shown in Table 9-3, its net income after taxes is $4,250, which is available to be paid as dividends, if desired. Thus a total amount of $9,250 can be paid to those who provided the firm's capital.

TABLE 9-3
The Effect of Deducting Interest Payments

	Firm A	Firm B
Revenue	$25,000	$25,000
Cost of goods sold	15,000	15,000
Revenue minus expense	10,000	10,000
Interest paid	5,000	0
Taxable income	5,000	10,000
Tax (at 15%)	750	1,500
Available for dividends	$ 4,250	$ 8,500

The other part of the table shows the results for firm B, which differs only with respect to financing. All its capital was provided by shareholders. Thus the entire $10,000 of income is subject to tax, leaving only $8,500 for distribution.

The deductibility of interest payments provides an apparent tax advantage for the use of debt over equity funds. For this reason it may seem surprising that firms do not choose to obtain more of their capital via bond issues. Indeed, the dramatic difference in tax treatment raises substantial questions about the definition of debt and interest, on the one hand, and stocks and dividend payments, on the other. The Internal Revenue Service pays considerable attention to exotic arrangements designed to provide the tax characteristics of debt with the financial characteristics of equity. To qualify as debt, there must be a definite obligor, a definite obligee, a definite ascertainable obligation, and a time of maturity. Moreover, corporate debt that greatly exceeds stock may be treated as stock for tax purposes. In general, debt should be represented by an instrument that contains an unconditional promise to pay a certain sum either on demand or on a specific date, with fixed interest.[3] Payments made under any other arrangement are not likely to be deductible for purpose of income taxation.

Obligations of the type required to make payments eligible for deduction are not trivial. Failure to make interest payments, so defined, may have serious consequences for the firm and its management. In many cases bankruptcy results, with mandatory and costly corporate reorganization. The greater the magnitude of nondiscretionary interest payments vis-à-vis discretionary dividend payments, other things equal, the greater the probability of this type of unfortunate event. This provides a brake on excessive use of debt financing, despite its obvious tax advantage.

---

[3] Prentice-Hall, *Federal Tax Handbook 1980* (Englewood Cliffs, N.J.: Prentice-Hall, Inc.), p. 249.

There is another reason why equity financing may be more competitive with debt financing from the viewpoint of a corporation. As discussed in later sections, the *personal* income tax provides preferential treatment for returns taken in the form of capital gains over those taken as interest or dividends. Since some or all of the return on a stock may take the form of capital gains, equity funds may be cheaper on a *before*-corporate-tax basis, and this may offset some or all of their disadvantages in terms of corporate income taxation.

CORPORATE INCOME FROM DIVIDENDS, INTEREST, AND CAPITAL GAINS

To avoid the possibility of taxing dividends time and time again, Congress provided that 85% of most dividends received by a corporation from nonaffiliated domestic corporations can be deducted from income before calculating the firm's income tax liability. The effective tax rate on an additional dollar of dividends received by a corporation with an income in the 46% range is thus $(1 - .85) \times .46 = .069$, or 6.9%.

No deduction is allowed for interest received by a corporation; it is simply added to income and taxed at the regular rates.

Special treatment may, however, be accorded gains from the sale or exchange of certain assets. Such gains must usually be made on assets used in or held for investment by the business (e.g., equipment and securities, respectively) as contrasted with assets held primarily for sale to customers in the ordinary course of the business (e.g., inventory). Moreover, the assets must have been held at least one year. The excess of such gains over certain short-term capital losses may be taxed at a lower rate than that applied to ordinary income.

THE INVESTMENT TAX CREDIT

To stimulate investment, the tax code allows a portion of the amount spent on certain qualified business property during a year to be credited against taxes due. For example, if a new machine costing $100,000 is purchased, the buyer may be allowed to reduce the total taxes paid at year-end by 10% of this amount, or $10,000. In addition, 95% of the total cost may be deducted from revenues during the asset's useful life using the appropriate accelerated cost recovery system table, to determine taxable income.

In 1983 an investment tax credit of 6% was allowed for "three-year property" and a credit of 10% was allowed for five-, ten-, or fifteen-year property. The *basis* for depreciation of property for which a 6% investment tax credit is taken is 97% of cost; for property for which a 10% investment tax credit is taken, the basis for depreciation is 95% of cost.

TAX-EXEMPT ORGANIZATIONS

Many organizations are wholly or partly exempt from federal income taxes. Nonprofit religious, charitable, or educational foundations generally qualify. A small tax (2% in 1983) is levied on the net investment income of such a foundation. In addition, the foundation should pay out all income received by the end of the year following receipt or a minimum percent of its assets (5% in 1983), whichever is higher, since failure to do so can result in a confiscatory tax on the difference.

Investment companies, often called *mutual funds,* may elect to be treated as *regulated investment companies* for tax purposes. This privilege is granted if various conditions are met. For example, funds must be invested primarily in securities, without undue concentration in any one. A regulated investment company pays income tax only on income and capital gains not distributed to shareholders. Such companies thus distribute substantially all income and gains, although the "distribution" is often coincident with an automatic reinvestment in new shares of the fund.

Employee pension, profit-sharing, and stock-bonus plans may also qualify for tax-exempt status. Such plans may entrust their assets to a "fiduciary" (e.g., a bank), which accepts new contributions, makes required payments, and provides investment management. A fiduciary under a "qualified plan," which meets all the requirements of applicable legislation, pays no tax on income or capital gains.

In many cases a fiduciary will serve as a trustee of funds provided for the benefit of one or more individuals by another individual or individuals. Some trusts are created by wills, others by a contract among living persons. Whatever the origin, such a trust, if either long-term or irrevocable, pays tax only on income not distributed to the designated beneficiary or beneficiaries.

Income and capital gains earned by investment companies, pension funds, and personal trusts do not go untaxed forever. Payments made to investment company shareholders (whether automatically reinvested or not), pension fund beneficiaries, and the beneficiaries of personal trust funds are subject to applicable personal income taxation. The exemptions apply only to taxes that might otherwise be levied at the previous stage.

THE PERSONAL INCOME TAX

While the corporate income tax is an important feature of the investment scene, its impact on most individuals is indirect. Not so the personal income tax. Few investors avoid dealing with it in detail, at both an economic and an emotional level. Its provisions have major and direct impacts on behavior in general, and investment behavior in particular.

Personal Tax Rates

Tax must be paid on an individual's income, defined as "all wealth which flows in to the taxpayer other than as a mere return of capital. It includes gains and profits from any source, including gains from the sale or other disposition of capital assets."[4] Certain items are *excluded* from the definition of income; others are *deducted* from it before computing the tax due. Moreover, capital gains and losses are subject to special procedures. The latter are described in a later section. Deductions and exclusions of special importance for investment purposes are described in this and later sections.

Two figures are relevant for tax purposes. The *adjusted gross income* is obtained by subtracting certain allowed deductions (e.g., business expenses, contributions to certain retirement funds) from gross income. This amount less a number of personal expense deductions equals *taxable income,* the figure on which tax liability is based. The amount of tax calculated on this basis must be paid unless the taxpayer is able to claim *tax credits,* which may be subtracted directly from the tax liability to obtain a final amount due the government.

Nothing about the personal income tax in the United States is simple. Four different schedules of tax rates are in effect, the appropriate one depending on the status of the taxable entity. The two most commonly used are those for single taxpayers and married taxpayers filing joint returns.

Table 9-4 shows the rates in effect in 1983 for (1) single and (2) married taxpayers filing joint returns. The values are plotted in Figures 9-2(a) and 9-2(b). The top line in each figure shows the marginal tax rate—that is, the proportion of an additional dollar of income that will be taxed away. This is constant over various ranges of income, but it increases as the taxpayer moves to higher "brackets."

It is important to remember that the total amount of tax paid is generally a smaller proportion of taxable income than indicated by the marginal tax rate. When one's income increases, and with it the marginal rate, only the additional dollars are affected. Thus the often-

---

[4] Prentice-Hall, *Federal Tax Handbook 1980*, p. 120.

TABLE 9-4
Personal Income Tax Rates, 1983

TAXABLE INCOME		SINGLE TAXPAYERS			MARRIED TAXPAYERS FILING JOINT RETURNS		
(1) From ($)	(2) To ($)	Tax ($) on Amount in Column (1)	Marginal Rate (%) on Excess over Amount in Column (1)	Average Rate (%) on Amount in Column (1)	Tax ($) on Amount in Column (1)	Marginal Rate (%) on Excess over Amount in Column (1)	Average Rate (%) on Amount in Column (1)
0	2,300	0	0%	—no tax—	0	0%	—no tax—
2,300	3,400	0	11%	—no tax—	0	0%	—no tax—
3,400	4,400	121	13%	3.56%	0	11%	—no tax—
4,400	5,500	251	15%	5.70%	110	11%	2.50%
5,500	6,500	416	15%	7.56%	231	13%	4.20%
6,500	7,600	566	15%	8.71%	361	13%	5.55%
7,600	8,500	731	15%	9.62%	504	15%	6.63%
8,500	10,800	866	17%	10.19%	639	15%	7.52%
10,800	11,900	1,257	19%	11.64%	984	15%	9.11%
11,900	12,900	1,466	19%	12.32%	1,149	17%	9.66%
12,900	15,000	1,656	21%	12.84%	1,319	17%	10.22%
15,000	16,000	2,097	24%	13.98%	1,676	17%	11.17%
16,000	18,200	2,337	24%	14.61%	1,846	19%	11.54%
18,200	20,200	2,865	28%	15.74%	2,264	19%	12.44%
20,200	23,500	3,425	28%	16.96%	2,644	23%	13.09%
23,500	24,600	4,349	32%	18.51%	3,403	23%	14.48%
24,600	28,800	4,701	32%	19.11%	3,656	26%	14.86%
28,800	29,900	6,045	36%	20.99%	4,748	26%	16.49%
29,900	34,100	6,441	36%	21.54%	5,034	30%	16.84%
34,100	35,200	7,953	40%	23.32%	6,294	30%	18.46%
35,200	41,500	8,393	40%	23.84%	6,624	35%	18.82%
41,500	45,800	10,913	45%	26.30%	8,829	35%	21.27%
45,800	55,300	12,848	45%	28.05%	10,334	40%	22.56%
55,300	60,000	17,123	50%	30.96%	14,134	40%	25.56%
60,000	81,800	19,473	50%	32.46%	16,014	44%	26.69%
81,800	85,600	30,373	50%	37.13%	25,606	44%	31.30%
85,600	109,400	32,273	50%	37.70%	27,278	48%	31.87%
109,400		44,173	50%	40.38%	38,702	50%	35.38%

heard complaint that "by earning more (before tax), I will actually have less (after tax)" is simply incorrect. The lower curves in Figures 9-2(a) and (b) show the *average* tax rate—that is, the ratio of total tax paid to total taxable income. Values for selected taxable incomes are also shown in Table 9-4.

As the figures and Table 9-4 show, a married couple pays less tax than a single person with comparable taxable income. This is often attacked as discriminatory. On the other hand, such a couple may

Taxes

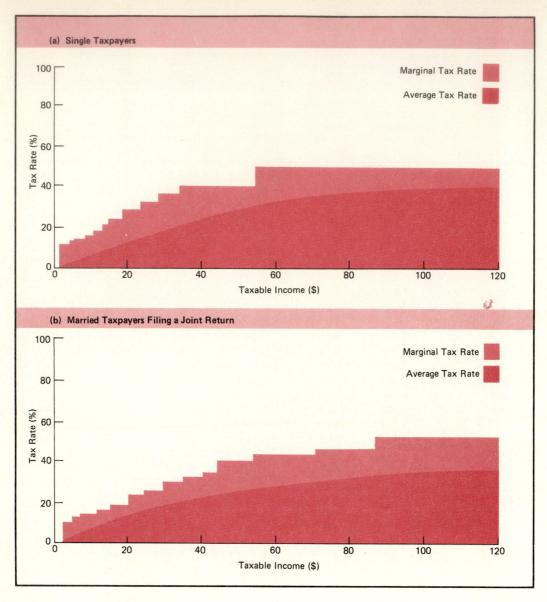

SOURCE: Table 9-4.

FIGURE 9-2
Marginal and Average Tax Rates

pay more tax than two single persons, each with half the couple's taxable income. Owing to the progressive nature of the tax, it may be profitable for tax purposes for two people to marry if their incomes differ substantially. To offset at least part of the "marriage penalty" involved when two people with similar incomes marry, a "two-earner

216   Taxes

married couples deduction" equal to 10% of the income of the spouse with smaller earnings (or $3,000, whichever is smaller) was allowed in 1983.

It is almost a truism that most decisions are made at the margin. Thus the marginal tax rate is likely to be more relevant than the average. For example, a married couple with taxable income of $35,200 are considering an opportunity to increase their income by $3,000. Using the figures in Table 9-4, the impact on taxes will be as follows:

	Before	After	Difference
Taxable income ($)	35,200	38,200	3,000
Tax ($)	6,624	6,624 + (.35 × 3000)	
		= 6,624 + 1,050	1,050
		Effective incremental tax rate:	35.00%

An increase of $3,000 in income before taxes thus results in an increase of $1,050 in taxes, leaving a net increase in spendable income of $3,000 − 1,050, or $1,950. The calculations are simple, because the change left the taxpayer in the same bracket. Thus 35% of the income was taxed away, leaving 65% to be spent. The fact that the average tax rate was well below these figures is virtually irrelevant.

When a decision will move income across brackets, the computations are more complex. For example, assume the opportunity in question would increase income by $20,000. The impact on taxes would then be:

	Before	After	Difference
Taxable income ($)	35,200	55,200	20,000
Tax ($)	6,624	10,334 + (.40 × 9,400)	
		= 14,094	7,470
		Effective incremental tax rate:	37.35%

This result can also be determined by breaking the change into the portions in each bracket, then calculating a weighted average of the marginal rates, using the proportions as weights:

Taxes

(1) Bracket ($)	(2) Amount ($)	(3) = (2)/20,000 Proportion	(4) Marginal Rate (%)	(5) = (3) × (4) Proportion Times Marginal Rate
35,200 to 45,800	10,600	.53	35	18.55
45,800 to 55,200	9,400	.47	40	18.80
		Effective incremental tax rate:		37.35

Both calculations show that the incremental tax liability, 37.35% of the increment to taxable income, is a function of the marginal rates for the brackets over which additional income will be earned.

TAX-EXEMPT BONDS

A major consideration for investors with large taxable incomes is the possibility of obtaining tax-free income. The simplest way to accomplish this exists because the notion of federalism has been interpreted to imply that the federal government should not tax states and municipalities, nor the income produced from their bonds. While the legal basis is complex, the facts are simple. Interest income from most bonds of states, municipalities, and their agencies need not be included in taxable income for federal taxes (and in some cases, for state taxes). The benefits for high-bracket taxpayers are obvious. For example, consider the couple in the previous example. Assume that they can obtain an increment of $20,000 in taxable income each year by investing in corporate bonds or $13,000 per year by purchasing tax-free bonds. As shown earlier, their effective tax rate on an increment of $20,000 in taxable income would be 37.35%, leaving 62.65% or $12,530 to be spent. But $13,000 in tax-free income could all be spent—clearly a preferable situation.

This relationship is no secret. Not surprisingly, tax-exempt bonds offer lower rates of interest than others. Thus they are not attractive for investors with low marginal tax rates.

Figure 9-3 provides evidence on this point. It shows the ratio, over time, of the yield-to-maturity for a group of tax-exempt municipal bonds to that of a group of bonds of public utilities not subject to favorable tax treatment. There is, of course, more to be considered in such a comparison than (promised) yield-to-maturity. On this basis, however, municipal bonds appear to be competitive for those with taxable income subject to marginal tax rates of 20% (when the ratio of before-tax yields is 80%) to 40% (when the ratio is 60%). For those

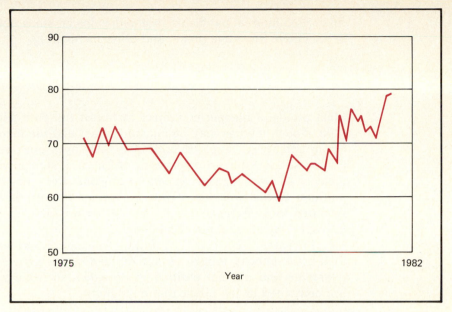

SOURCE: Salomon Brothers, 1982-83 Bond Market: Analysis and Outlook, 1983.

FIGURE 9-3
Ratio of Prime Long-Term Municipal Bond Yield to New Aa Public Utility
Bond Yield, 1976-1982

fortunate enough to be considering investments that provide income in the higher ranges, municipal bonds are well worth investigation. Less fortunate investors are likely to find them unattractive.

ALTERNATIVE MINIMUM TAX

Disturbed by reports that some wealthy individuals were using "tax shelters" to pay only a small percentage of their income in taxes, Congress has added an *alternative minimum tax* (of great complexity) to the Internal Revenue Code.

Taxpayers with substantial "tax preference items" must compute an *alternative minimum taxable income*, which, in effect, involves adding back some of the deductions for such items to the (regular) taxable income. From this, an exemption (of $40,000 for married taxpayers filing joint returns, $30,000 for single taxpayers) is subtracted. The *alternative minimum tax* is 20% of the result. If this is smaller than the "standard" tax liability, no additional taxes must be paid. Otherwise, the alternative minimum tax must be paid (instead of the "standard" tax).

Tax preference items include a portion of accelerated depreciation on real estate, deductions for long-term capital gains, exclusions for certain interest payments received, gains on stock options provided in executive incentive plans, and other exotica.

THE DIVIDEND EXCLUSION

Most dividend income is subject to tax at full rate. However, up to $100 of such income may be excluded from taxable income each year by an unmarried taxpayer and up to $200 by a married couple filing a joint return. Thus an investment of $5,000 in stocks with a dividend yield of 4% would result in tax-free income for a married couple, in addition to the prospect of favorable tax rates on capital gains. As intended by Congress, this provides a considerable incentive to hold at least modest amounts of stocks.

Payments from some institutions (e.g., credit unions, savings and loan associations), though termed dividends, are more akin to interest payments and are not entitled to be excluded from income. Details are contained in the applicable regulations.

DEDUCTIBLE EXPENSES

As with the corporate income tax, interest payments may be deducted from an individual's income to determine taxable income (although the total amount deducted in any year for interest on funds borrowed to finance investments may generally not exceed net investment income plus $10,000). This deduction significantly lowers the effective cost of financing an investment by borrowing. Since property taxes are also deductible, the after-tax cost of home ownership is likely to be considerably lower than the before-tax cost, the magnitude of the difference depending on the relevant marginal tax rates for the taxpayer involved. Since the "income" associated with home ownership is taken in kind, by living in the home, and any capital gains are subject to preferential treatment, such an investment is likely to prove attractive for many taxpayers. This is the intent of Congress, and the high degree of ownership of homes (including condominiums) in the United States is at least partly due to such incentives to own rather than rent.

Many expenses associated with investment may be deducted from income. The test is that they be ordinary and necessary and in line with reasonable expectations of profitable return. Thus, the fees of investment advisers and subscriptions to financial publications may be deducted. Investments that habitually produce financial losses but nonfinancial pleasure may be considered hobbies and some or all of the associated deductions denied by the Internal Revenue Service. This possibility should concern the gentleman racehorse owner, but not the serious investor.

CAPITAL GAINS AND LOSSES

Without question the provisions of the personal income tax laws that have had the greatest impact on investor behavior deal with the treatment of capital gains and losses. Only the basic elements can be described here. Complete understanding of the details requires sufficient effort to keep thousands of lawyers, tax accountants, and investment advisers employed.

Realization

A change in the value of a capital asset is not relevant for tax purposes until it is *realized* by sale or exchange. If a security purchased for $50 appreciates to a value of $100 in a year, no tax is due. But if it is sold for $120 two years after purchase, the difference of $70 must be declared as capital gains realized at the time of sale, and applicable tax paid.

This rule makes the end of the year an interesting time for stockbrokers. Depending on their situations, taxpayers may either be anxious to realize capital gains or losses before a new tax year begins, or reluctant to do so. Investment brokers aid the former by publishing lists pairing similar stocks for those who wish to sell one for tax purposes and buy another with similar characteristics to maintain the essence of their investment position. Such *tax exchanges* are used to accomplish this, because the tax laws preclude a deduction associated with a loss on a *wash sale* in which a security is sold and a "substantially identical" one is bought within 30 days.

End-of-year sales and purchases motivated by tax considerations are fairly common. Volume in securities that experienced substantial price changes during the year tends to be high as holders sell to realize gains or losses. If buyers recognize that the sellers are motivated by knowledge of the tax laws, and not some previously unrecognized news of disastrous developments affecting the companies in question, such "selling pressure" should not seriously depress prices.

There is some evidence that end-of-year buyers are not as aware of tax-motivated selling as one might presume. As discussed in a later chapter, stocks with small market values in December tend to do especially well in the first half of January. This could result from end-of-year tax-motivated selling of securities that have declined in value coupled with beginning-of-year buying by those anxious to take advantage of the resulting bargain prices. There may be other causes of this "January effect," but tax aspects could play a role.

Capital gains and losses are, of course, those realized on capital assets, but the regulations define the latter rather narrowly. Capital assets include all kinds of property except that held in conjunction with the taxpayer's trade or business (e.g., inventories, business property). Gains or losses on property that is an integral part of a taxpayer's business are considered regular income. Gains on the sale of one's personal residence are capital gains, but, owing to special provisions in the tax law, some gains on property held only to rent to others may be considered income. Pro rata appreciation of a fixed-income security issued at a significant discount (e.g., a 90-day Teasury bill) may also be considered income, as it is more like interest than capital gains.

The capital gain or loss realized when an asset is sold or exchanged is the difference between the value received and the asset's *adjusted basis*. For an asset purchased outright, the (initial) basis is equal to the actual outlay (less half the amount of any investment tax credit taken). For an asset received as a gift or inheritance, the recipient's basis may be the donor's adjusted basis or the value at the time of receipt, depending on the relationship between the two and the value at time of eventual sale.

While an asset is held, improvements may be made and their cost added to the basis. On the other hand, any return of capital must be deducted from the basis, as must depreciation. The basis is *adjusted* to account for such changes. The required accounting can become rather complicated. For example, if an investor buys 100 shares at $40 each, then buys another 100 at $50, and later sells 100 shares at $60, what is the realized capital gain? If the lots have been kept separate and only shares priced at the higher amount are sold, the gain is $10 per share. This is the preferred alternative, since it minimizes current tax outlays. If, however, adequate identification of the lots is not possible, regulations require first-in-first-out accounting, which would place the basis at $40 and the gain at $20 per share.

The ability to control the realization of capital gains and losses has a number of obvious advantages. Most important, tax can be paid at the most opportune time. The clearest case involves investment during years of high income (and marginal tax rates) with capital gains realized after retirement, when income and marginal tax rates may be considerably lower.

Short- and Long-Term Gains

The treatment of a capital gain or loss depends critically on the period the asset is held. For assets acquired after June 28, 1984,[5] if the holding period is equal to or less than six months, the gain or loss is *short-*

---

[5] And before January 1, 1988.

term; if more than six months, it is *long-term*.[6] When making the calculations, the day after the asset is acquired is the start of the holding period. The same day on every successive month starts a new month. Taxwise investors keep this rule in mind and watch the calendar with care.

When determining the impact of capital gains and losses on overall tax liability, short- and long-term changes must be considered separately at first. All short-term capital gains and losses must be brought together to obtain the *net short-term capital gain or loss*. Similarly, all long-term gains or losses must be brought together to determine the net long-term capital gain or loss. Finally, all gains and losses can be brought together to obtain the *net capital gain or loss*.

The treatment of capital gains and losses for tax purposes is a logician's nightmare. By and large, if after the above nettings, there are net short-term gains, they are treated as ordinary income; if there are net short-term losses, they are treated as deductions from income. *Net long-term gains* are generally not taxed at full rates. Although such gains are added to taxable income, a deduction equal to 60% of the excess of long-term gains over short-term gains (if any) is allowed. This means that the effective marginal rate on a net long-term gain can be as low as .4 times that on a short-term gain or on ordinary income. *Net long-term capital losses* also require special treatment. They may be used to offset net short-term capital gains (if any) dollar-for-dollar. However, only *half* of any excess of net long-term losses over net short-term gains (or half of the long-term losses if there are no net short-term gains) may be deducted from income.

No more than $3,000 in losses may be deducted from income in any single year, although any excess may be carried forward for use in subsequent tax years. Moreover, losses on personal-use property (except some due to various casualties and theft) are not deductible at all, although gains will be taxed.

Special provisions apply to capital gains realized from the sale of an individual's principal residence. If a new residence is purchased within two years, no tax need be paid if the price of a new home exceeds the proceeds realized from the old one. The untaxed gain on the old home will be added to any gain from the new one if it is sold later, but the upward-mobile individual who would never think of buying a less expensive home can look forward to a life free from the payment of capital gains taxes on increases in property values.

An additional provision softens the blow if cheaper (or rental) housing is desired later in life. A person 55 or older can elect to make a once-in-a-lifetime exclusion of the first $125,000 of realized gain on the sale of a residence if he or she has lived there for three of the preceding five years.

---

[6] For assets acquired before June 28, 1984 the holding period required for long-term treatment is one year.

STATE INCOME TAXES

Most states levy personal income taxes, following a format similar to that of the federal government. Although lower, such taxes are also likely to be progressive. Table 9-5 provides a summary for 1983.

The impact of these taxes is not quite as large as might first appear, for all taxes paid to state governments may be deducted from income before computing federal income tax. For example, consider an investor whose marginal rates for state and federal income taxes are 10% and 50%, respectively. An additional $100 of income will result in $10 of state tax. This leaves $90 subject to federal income tax, which will thus add $45 to total federal income taxes. Overall, then, $55 will be taxed away, giving an effective combined marginal rate of 55%.

As indicated earlier, income from bonds issued by municipalities within a state may be exempt from that state's income tax. Some states extend this exemption to include dividends from certain corporations domiciled within the state or to income taxes paid to the federal government. State income taxes may thus affect one's investment decisions.

THE FEDERAL ESTATE TAX

A person may escape taxes by dying, but his or her estate may not. State governments usually impose "death taxes," and the federal government requires payment of an estate tax. Double taxation is mitigated to an extent, however, as some of the state tax paid may be credited against the federal tax liability.

The estate tax (formally, the federal unified transfer tax at death) is quite progressive, reflecting the idea that egalitarian principles may be met with less adverse impact on incentives via such a tax than perhaps any other, although the effect of the tax appears to have been rather small. Rates in effect in 1983 are shown in Table 9-6.

Not all of an estate is subject to tax. An unlimited *marital deduction* makes it possible for property to be transferred to a surviving spouse without any tax at all. Property transferred to nonprofit organizations that qualify for an income tax charitable deduction may also be deducted. The *taxable estate* is the amount left after all deductions.

The actual tax that must be paid on an estate will equal an amount calculated using Table 9-6 less a *tax credit* ($79,300 in 1983, increasing to $192,800 from 1987 on).

TABLE 9-5
State Government Individual Income Taxes, 1983

[As of September 1. Only basic rates, brackets and exemptions are shown. Taxable income rates and brackets apply to single individuals; other schedules may be used for married taxpayers filing jointly or separately and/or heads of households in California, Georgia, Hawaii, Idaho, Kansas, Maine, New Mexico, Oklahoma, Oregon, Utah, and West Virginia. Alaska, Florida, Nevada, South Dakota, Texas, Washington, and Wyoming have no State income tax]

STATE	TAXABLE INCOME RATES (RANGE IN PERCENT)	TAXABLE INCOME BRACKETS		PERSONAL EXEMPTIONS			SIZE OF STANDARD DEDUCTION[1]			FEDERAL INCOME TAX DEDUCTIBLE[2]
		Lowest: Amount Under	Highest: Amount Over	Single	Married-Joint Return	Dependents	Per-cent	Single	Married-Joint Return	
Ala[3]	2.0-5.0	$500	$3,000	$1,500	$3,000	$300	20	$2,000	$4,000	Yes
Ariz[4]	2.0-8.0	1,017	6,102	1,759	3,518	1,056	17	880	1,759	Yes
Ark	1.0-7.0	2,999	25,000	[5]17.50	[5]35	[5]6	10	1,000	1,000	No
Calif.[4]	1.0-11.0	4,600	25,430	[5]38	576	[5]12	(x)	1,510	3,020	No
Colo.[4]	2.5-8.0	1,415	14,153	1,203	2,406	1,203	(x)	1,415	1,415	Yes
Conn.				Very limited State income tax[6]						
Del.[3]	1.4-13.5	1,000	50,000	600	1,200	600	10	1,000	1,000	Yes[7]
D.C.	2.0-11.0	1,000	25,000	750	1,500	750	10	1,000	1,000	No
Ga.	1.0-6.0	750	7,000	1,500	3,000	1,500	[8]15	[8]2,300	[8]3,000	No
Hawaii	2.25-11.0	800	30,000	1,000	2,000	1,000	(x)	800	1,000	No
Idaho	2.0-7.5	1,000	5,000	Same as Federal						No
Ill.	3.0	Flat Rate		1,000	2,000	1,000	(x)	(x)	(x)	No
Ind.[3]	3.0	Flat Rate		1,000	2,000	500	(x)	(x)	(x)	No
Iowa[3][4]	.5-13.0	[9]1,023	[9]76,725	[5]19	[5]38	[5]14	[8]15	[8]1,200	[8]3,000	Yes
Kans.	2.0-9.0	2,000	25,000	1,000	2,000	1,000	[8]16	[8]2,400	[8]2,800	Yes
Ky.[3]	2.0-6.0	3,000	8,000	[5]20	[5]40	[5]20	(x)	650	650	Yes

225

TABLE 9-5 (continued)

STATE	TAXABLE INCOME RATES (RANGE IN PERCENT)	TAXABLE INCOME BRACKETS		PERSONAL EXEMPTIONS			SIZE OF STANDARD DEDUCTION[1]			FEDERAL INCOME TAX DEDUCTIBLE[2]
		Lowest: Amount Under	Highest: Amount Over	Single	Married-Joint Return	Dependents	Per-cent	Single	Married-Joint Return	
La.	2.0–6.0	10,000	50,000	6,000	12,000	6,000	Same as Federal			Yes
Maine[4]	1.0–10.0	2,044	25,000	1,000	2,000	1,000	16	2,453	2,862	No
Md.[3]	2.0–5.0	1,000	3,000	800	1,600	800	13	1,500	3,000	No
Mass.	[10]5.375	Flat Rate		2,200	([11])	700	(x)	(x)	(x)	No
Mich.[3]	[12]6.35	Flat Rate		1,500	3,000	1,500	(x)	(x)	(x)	No
Minn.[4]	[13][14]1.6–16.0	667	36,632	[5]67	[5]134	[5]67	10	2,250	2,250	Yes
Miss.	3.0–5.0	5,000	10,000	6,000	9,500	1,500	15	2,300	3,400	No
Mo.[3]	1.5–6.0	1,000	9,000	1,200	1,200	400	(x)	2,300	3,400	Yes
Mont.[4]	[13]2.0–11.0	1,200	42,000	960	1,920	960	20	1,800	3,600	Yes
Nebr.	20% of Federal income tax liability for tax year 1983									
N.H.	Very limited State income tax[15]									
N.J.	[16]2.0–3.5	20,000	50,000	1,000	2,000	1,000	(x)	(x)	(x)	No
N. Mex.	.7–7.8	1,000	100,000	Same as Federal						No
N.Y.[3]	[17]2.0–14.0	1,000	23,000	800	1,600	800	17	2,500	2,500	No
N.C.	3.0–7.0	2,000	10,000	1,100	[18]2,200	800	10	550	([19])	No
N. Dak.	[20]2.0–9.0	[20]3,000	[20]50,000	1,000	2,000	1,000	(x)	2,300	3,400	Yes
Ohio[3]	[21].5–5.0	5,000	100,000	1,000	2,000	1,000	(x)	(x)	(x)	No
Okla.	[22].5–6.0	[22]1,000	[22]27,500	1,000	2,000	1,000	[8]15	[8]2,000	[8]2,000	Yes[22]
Oreg.[4]	[23]4.0–10.0	500	5,000	[5]85	[5]170	[5]85	13	1,500	1,500	Yes[24]

TABLE 9-5 (continued)

STATE	TAXABLE INCOME RATES (RANGE IN PERCENT)	TAXABLE INCOME BRACKETS		PERSONAL EXEMPTIONS			SIZE OF STANDARD DEDUCTION[1]			FEDERAL INCOME TAX DEDUCT-IBLE[2]
		Lowest: Amount Under	Highest: Amount Over	Single	Married-Joint Return	Depend-ents	Per-cent	Single	Married-Joint Return	
Pa.[3]	[25]2.45	Flat Rate		(x)	(x)	(x)	(x)	(x)	(x)	No
R.I.	26.75% of Federal income tax liability for tax year 1983									No
S.C.[4]	2.0-7.0	2,000	10,000	800	1,600	800	10	1,000	2,000	Yes[26]
Tenn.	Very limited State income tax[27]									
Utah	2.75-7.75	750	3,750	750	1,500	750	[8]15	[8]2,000	[8]2,000	Yes
Vt.	26% of Federal income tax liability for tax year 1983 (with special allowances)									No
Va.	2.0-5.75	3,000	12,000	600	1,200	600	15	2,000	2,000	No
W. Va.	[28]2.1-13.0	2,000	60,000	700	1,400	700	10	1,000	1,000	No
Wis.[4]	[1]33.4-10.0	3,900	51,600	[5]20	540	520	(x)	2,300	3,400	No

X Not applicable. [1] The lesser of either a) the percentage indicated, multiplied by adjusted gross income or b) the dollar value listed. [2] A State provision that allows the taxpayer to deduct *fully* the Federal income tax payment reduces the effective marginal tax rate for persons in the highest State and Federal tax brackets by approximately one-half the nominal tax rate—the deduction is of a lesser benefit to other taxpayers. [3] States in which one or more local governments levy a local income tax. [4] Indexed by an inflation factor. Colo., Iowa, Oreg., S.C., and Wis. have suspended indexing through *at least* 1983. [5] Tax credit. [6] There is an income tax on interest and dividend income *only*. The rate of this tax ranges from 6% of interest and dividend income for taxpayers with an AGI of $50,000-$59,999 to 13% of such income of taxpayers with an AGI over $100,000. Capital gains are taxed at 7%. [7] Federal income tax deduction limited to $300 ($600 married). [8] A minimum standard deduction exists. In instances where the percentage standard deduction is less than the minimum, the minimum deduction amount should be taken. [9] Tax cannot reduce after-tax income of taxpayer to below $5,000. [10] Rate *includes* a 7.5% surcharge which has been in effect since 1976. 10% (flat rate) imposed on net gains, interest and dividends. Tax cannot reduce after-tax income to below $3,000 ($5,000 married couple). [11] Exemption is the smaller of $4,400 or $3,000 plus the income of the spouse having the smaller earned income. [12] In January 1984 the rate will drop to 6.1%; in January 1985, 5.35%. [13] A 10% surcharge on the liability is additional. [14] Indexing figures are for the 1982 tax year. [15] There is a 5% tax on dividend and interest income (excluding income from savings bank deposits) in excess of $1,200 ($2,400, married). [16] No taxpayer is subject to tax if gross income is $3,000 or less ($1,500 married, filing separately). [17] No tax due from individuals with an adjusted gross income of $2,500 or less, or married head of household, or surviving spouse of $5,000 or less. [18] An additional exemption of $1,100 is allowed the spouse with the smallest income. Joint returns not allowed. [19] An additional $550 is allowed a married woman with separate income. Joint returns are not allowed. [20] Taxpayers have the option of paying a tax of 10.5% of the taxpayers adjusted Federal income tax liability. [21] For tax year 1983, there is an additional 83.3% surcharge on liability. In January 1984, there is a permanent 90% rate increase. [22] These tax rates and brackets apply to single persons not deducting Federal income tax. For individuals deducting Federal income tax, rates range from .5% of the first $1,000 to 7% on income over $49,000. [23] An 8% surcharge on tax liability is additional. [24] Federal tax deduction limited to $7,000 ($3,500 married, filing separately). [25] The tax rate is 2.35% beginning July 1984. [26] Federal tax deduction limited to $500. [27] Interest and dividends taxed at 6%; dividends from Tenn. corporation taxed at 4%. [28] A 12% surcharge on the tax liability for taxpayers with taxable income over $10,000 in effect April 1983-June 1984.

SOURCE: *Statistical Abstract of the United States, 1984* (Washington, D.C.: U.S. Department of Commerce, Bureau of the Census).

TABLE 9-6
Estate Tax Rates, 1983

(A) Taxable Estate More than ($)	(B) Taxable Estate Less than or Equal to ($)	(C) Tax on Amount in Column (A) ($)	(D) Rate of Tax on Excess over Amount in Column (A) (%)
0	10,000	0	18
10,000	20,000	1,800	20
20,000	40,000	3,800	22
40,000	60,000	8,200	24
60,000	80,000	13,000	26
80,000	100,000	18,200	28
100,000	150,000	23,800	30
150,000	250,000	38,800	32
250,000	500,000	70,800	34
500,000	750,000	155,800	37
750,000	1,000,000	248,300	39
1,000,000	1,250,000	345,800	41
1,250,000	1,500,000	448,300	43
1,500,000	2,000,000	555,800	45
2,000,000	2,500,000	780,800	49
2,500,000	3,000,000	1,025,800	53
3,000,000	3,500,000	1,290,800	57
3,500,000	. . .	1,575,800	60

THE FEDERAL GIFT TAX

Partly to foil attempts to evade or reduce estate and income taxes, the federal government levies taxes on large gifts. Any transfer of property without adequate compensation may make the *donor* subject to tax.

A number of provisions make the gift tax of little or no consequence for many people. Up to $10,000 may be given to each individual every year, tax-free. Thus one can give away hundreds of thousands of dollars each year without incurring any gift tax liability, as long as each recipient receives no more than $10,000 per year. Moreover, gifts to nonprofit organizations are exempt. Since such gifts may be made in kind, it is possible for a wealthy person to give appreciated securities to his or her alma mater, escape both capital gains and gifts taxes, and deduct both the original cost and part of the appreciation from current income as a charitable contribution. Small wonder that gifts to nonprofit organizations tend to increase in bull markets.

The federal gift tax is integrated with the estate tax; together they form a unified tax on life and death transfers. Taxable gifts are cumulated over time and considered equivalent to a prepayment on a decedent's estate. No tax is paid until the tax due on the cumulative total (using Table 9-6) exceeds the standard estate tax credit; afterward, taxes are levied as required to bring the total tax paid up to that required for the cumulative total of taxable gifts. Upon death, taxable gifts are added to the donor's estate and the tax liability on the total amount computed. Gift taxes paid are subtracted from this liability to determine the tax actually due. While exceptions and special provisions complicate the calculations, the gift and estate taxes are essentially one.

TAX SHELTERS

Many advertisements implore high-tax-bracket investors to put their money in cattle, oil drilling, certain kinds of real estate, and other investments with purportedly attractive tax characteristics. Such "tax shelters" are devised to take advantage of tax provisions allowing large deductions to create a "tax loss" in the present, followed by a later profit, preferably in the form of a capital gain. Such enterprises are generally formed as limited partnerships. A promoter, or general partner, puts together the operation, with individual investors as limited partners. The hoped-for results are tidy profits for the promoter and the investors, at the expense of the tax collector.

A little thought should call into question the likely permanence of such a situation. The key provisions of the tax law may, of course, be changed. But even if loopholes remain unplugged, economic forces may diminish any opportunities for abnormally high profit.

If large gains can be made, why should the promoter share them to any major extent with the investors? Instead, such investments might be priced to prove only advantageous enough on the basis of risk and return to attract needed capital. Moreover, since the attractiveness is greater, the higher one's marginal tax rate, presumably only those in the highest brackets should find such investments interesting.

But one can go even farther. If large profits remain for promoters, why won't more promoters enter the business? The answer is that they will, potentially until the risk and return available from promoting tax shelters is competitive with that in other occupations. Anomalies in the tax laws are more likely to bring abnormally large amounts of investment into cattle feeding programs, oil drilling, and so on than to provide well-lighted roads to untold riches for high-bracket investors.

This is not to deny that advantages can be gained from the early discovery of some scheme for tax-sheltered investment. But often investors in such deals reduce their taxes, as advertised, but only by taking real and permanent losses. Upon occasion the arrangements appear more like "con games" in which the professional swindler profits at the expense of the amateur swindler, leaving the latter's intended victim (the Internal Revenue Service) unscathed.

DIVIDENDS VERSUS CAPITAL GAINS

Over any holding period, there are two fundamental ways to make money on an investment: (1) by receiving interest or dividend payments and (2) via sale or exchange at an increase in value—that is, capital gains. As the previous sections of this chapter have shown, taxation of returns from these sources differs considerably. Corporations are taxed more heavily on capital gains than on dividends received. Tax-exempt organizations are taxed on neither but may have a preference for one or the other, depending on the nature of their fiduciary relationships with beneficiaries, legal constraints on spending out of capital, and so on. Individuals need pay no tax at all on small amounts of dividend income but are generally taxed at full rates on the remainder and on all interest received. Realization of capital gains may be deferred until a propitious time for tax purposes; gains realized at least six months after purchase will be taxed at lower rates than would dividend and interest income received in the same year. And so on.

Given all these complications, it is very difficult to predict, *ex cathedra*, the overall impact of taxes on likely returns from alternative sources and thus to determine preferred investment policies for those with different tax situations. Instead, one must look at the data to try to see what sorts of relationships appear to obtain among returns from these major sources.

Unfortunately, risk, which is such a key attribute of the investment environment, makes it difficult to obtain precise answers on this score. In the absence of any tax effects, expected returns on securities would differ primarily on the basis of differences in relevant risks. But these very risks make it hard to assess before-the-fact expected returns with any precision, since after-the-fact average returns may diverge considerably from prior expectations.

The entire return from a U.S. Treasury bill is treated as interest for tax purposes. At the other extreme, some stocks are certain to pay no dividends at all in the near future, by explicit policy of the Board of Directors. Any return on such a stock over, say, the next year, must thus come from capital appreciation. Since this type of security is considerably more risky than a government bond, its total expected return should be greater, at least after taxes. But for whom—an individual investor in a high tax bracket? a tax-exempt institution? a corporate investor?

If two investments have comparable risk, but one has a higher dividend yield, the other must offer a larger expected capital gain. But what will be the ratio at which the two types of return will trade? Will "the market" give up a dollar of expected dividends only in exchange for an additional dollar of expected capital appreciation? Or will, say, $.75 of the latter be accepted for a dollar of the former?

To even begin to answer this question we should examine investments with roughly comparable degrees of relevant risk. This suggests the desirability of focusing on common stocks with different dividend yields, rather than comparing, say, bonds and stocks.

Yield can be measured by dividing (1) the dividends paid by (2) the price of the stock. In general, low-yield stocks are expected to increase in value. The market is willing to sacrifice some dividend yield in return for the prospect of capital gains. Potential increases in value are not obtained by magic, of course. Securities expected to increase substantially in value are generally those of companies that retain a large proportion of earnings to "plow back" into the firm.

Table 9-7 shows this relationship. Overall, high-yield stocks tend to be those with high payout ratios and relatively poor prospects for large increases in value per share. At the other extreme, low-yield stocks tend to be those with relatively small payout ratios and relatively good prospects for future growth in value. Of course, reinvesting earnings in a business does not guarantee an increase in value. The result depends on both the amount invested and the return on the investment. but on average, the expected relationship holds.

By and large, stocks with low dividend yields in one year tend to have low yields in the next year. Thus it is not too difficult to create a portfolio likely to have a small yield, another to have a larger yield, another likely to have yet a larger yield, and so on. If each portfolio

TABLE 9-7

Dividend Yield Versus Payout: 1,000 Stocks Grouped by
Yield, 1950-1970

Yield Group	Average Annual Dividend Yield (%)	Average Payout Ratio: Dividends/Earnings
I	5.9	.78
II	5.2	.63
III	4.5	.59
IV	3.8	.55
V	2.4	.43

SOURCE: Fischer Black and Myron Scholes, "The Effects of Dividend Yield and Dividend Policy on Common Stock Prices and Returns," *Journal of Financial Economics*, 1, no. 1 (May 1974), 1-22.

is also constructed to have an estimated beta of approximately 1.0, differences in before-tax return may be attributed to differences in yield. Figure 9-4 shows the results obtained when this approach was applied to data covering the period from 1947 through 1970. Each point plots one portfolio's average annual excess return (roughly, its return minus the return on the market as a whole) and dividend yield. In general, the greater the yield, the greater the before-tax return, although the relationship is far from perfect.

An example shows what this implies. Assume that two stocks—A and B—are similar in risk (beta) but have different dividend yields. Stock A will pay dividends equal to 5% of its current value, while B will pay dividends equal to 6% of its current value. Assume that A is expected to increase 7% in value, for a total return of 12%. The relationship in Figure 9-4 suggests that the total return on B should be greater than 12%, since its yield is greater than that of A. For example:

	Stock A	Stock B	Difference (B − A)
Yield	5.0%	6.0%	+1.0%
Expected capital gain	7.0	6.2	−.8
Total expected return	12.0	12.2	+.2

Stock B offers .2% more expected return than does stock A to compensate for the fact that it provides more return in the form of

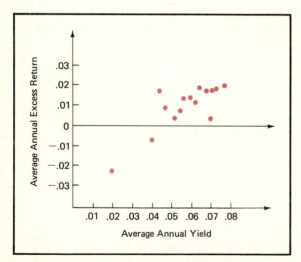

FIGURE 9-4
Average Annual Excess Return and Dividend Yield: Seventeen Portfolios with Estimated Beta = 1.0, 1947-1970.

SOURCE: Bernell K. Stone and Brit J. Bartter, "The Effect of Dividend Yield on Stock Returns: Empirical Evidence on the Relevance of Dividends," Working Paper No. E-76-8, Georgia Institute of Technology, 1979.

yield. As the last column shows, by pricing the two stocks to give these returns, the market allows an investor, by switching between A and B, to "trade" 1% of yield for .8% of gain—or, more generally, to trade $1 of yield for $.80 of expected capital gain.

Stock B offers a higher total expected return *before tax*. But what about expected returns *after tax*? The answer depends, of course, on the investor's tax status.

For a tax-exempt investor, expected return before tax *is* expected return after tax. For such a person, stock B would be more attractive than stock A.

For an investor who pays an effective marginal tax rate of 30% on dividends and 12% on gains,[7] the two investments would be similar on an after-tax basis:

	STOCK A		STOCK B	
	Before Tax	After Tax	Before Tax	After Tax
Yield	5.0%	3.50%	6.0%	4.20%
Expected capital gain	7.0	6.16	6.2	5.46
Total expected return	12.0	9.66	12.2	9.66

For an investor who pays an effective marginal tax rate of 50% on dividends and 20% on gains,[8] stock A would be more desirable on an after-tax basis:

	STOCK A		STOCK B	
	Before Tax	After Tax	Before Tax	After Tax
Yield	5.0%	2.50%	6.0%	3.00%
Expected capital gain	7.0	5.60	6.2	4.96
Total expected return	12.0	8.10	12.2	7.96

For the investor in the 30% bracket, the two securities are equally desirable; diversification considerations suggest that both be held. If securities are generally priced in this manner—that is, so that $1 in dividends can be traded for $.80 in capital gains—such an investor should consider holding market proportions of all securities.

---

[7] For example, if an investor realizes all gains after a year and pays tax on 40% of the gain at a 30% marginal rate, the effective rate on gains is .4 × 30%, or 12%.

[8] That is, .4 × 50%.

Those, such as tax-exempt investors, with less preference for gains vis-à-vis dividends should invest relatively more in security B and relatively less in A. That is, they should *tilt* their portfolios toward higher yields, with the extent of the tilt determined by diversification considerations.

Investors with more preference for gains vis-à-vis dividends should tilt in the direction of lower yields. Thus the investor in the 50% bracket should hold relatively more of security A and relatively less of B.

In general:

The market portfolio will be most appropriate for those whose *willingness* to trade expected capital gains for dividends is equal to the rate at which they are *able* to trade gains for dividends in the market. Investors with greater preferences for gains vis-à-vis dividends should tilt their holdings toward lower yields. Those with smaller (or no) preferences for gains vis-à-vis dividends should tilt their holdings toward higher yields.

How much should one tilt a portfolio? And in what way should a given level of tilt be achieved? A full answer requires assessment of risks and the weighing of risk versus tax-induced changes in after-tax expected return. To do this effectively, one should use all the techniques of portfolio analysis.

A particularly important consideration is the fact that the relationship between yield and before-tax return is by no means always the same. Figures 9-5(a) through (d) show that even when periods of several years are considered, the relationship can differ substantially from expectations. Each portion shows one of the six-year subperiods from 1947 through 1970. While the overall results (shown in Figure 9-4) indicated higher before-tax returns for higher-yield portfolios, the results in intermediate periods varied considerably from this relationship. Thus a "yield tilt" may increase expected after tax return, but it will also increase risk—a fact that must be taken into account when deciding how far to go in such a direction.

EX-DIVIDEND PRICE DECLINES

Another manifestation of the impact of taxes of investors' attitudes towards dividends and capital gains focuses on the behavior of a security's price after it goes "ex-dividend." A security may sell for $50 per share at the close of trading on the last day on which buyers are entitled to receive a dollar of dividends from the stock. Those who purchase the stock the next day will not get the dividend, and it is then said to sell *ex-dividend*. Other things equal, the stock's price should be less.

We can see this most easily by considering an investor who has decided to buy the stock at about the time it is scheduled to go ex-

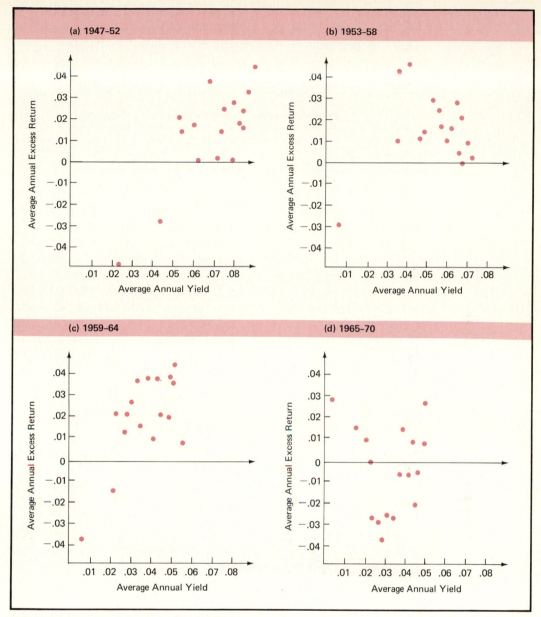

SOURCE: Bernell K. Stone and Brit J. Bartter, "The Effect of Dividend Yield on Stock Returns: Empirical Evidence on the Relevance of Dividends," Working Paper No. E-76-8, Georgia Institute of Technology, 1979.

FIGURE 9-5

Average Annual Excess Return and Dividend Yield, Seventeen Portfolios with Estimated Beta = 1.0

dividend. Assume that he or she expects to sell it in some later year at, say, $60, and can either buy it for $50 "cum (with) dividend" or for $49.25 ex-dividend. The alternatives are thus:

	(1) Buy with Dividend	(2) Buy Ex-Dividend	(2) − (1) Difference
Capital gain ($)	60 − 50 = 10	60 − 49.25 = 10.75	+.75
Dividend income ($)	1	0	−1.00

By purchasing the stock ex-dividend, the investor can give up $1 in dividends in exchange for an additional $.75 in capital gains.

A study of the magnitude of this phenomenon[9] showed that by the end of the day when a stock went ex-dividend, on average the price fell by about this amount. The exact figure was .78.

This result answers one question but raises another. Security brokers and dealers pay the same tax rate on dividends as on capital gains when shares are purchased and sold for "inventory" (as opposed to investment). If these two kinds of dollars (dividends and capital gains) do not trade on a one-for-one basis, why don't market-makers exploit the disparity? And if they do, why does the disparity persist?

THE CLIENTELE EFFECT

Since taxpayers with different marginal tax rates have different attitudes toward dividends vis-à-vis capital gains, high-bracket investors tend to hold relatively more low-yield stocks, and low-bracket and tax-exempt investors tend to hold relatively more high-yield stocks. Different securities thus have somewhat different clienteles. This is reflected in ex-dividend price behavior as well. Figure 9-6 shows the average one-day price fall relative to the dividend involved for each of ten groupings of stocks based on dividend yield. The results are generally consistent with the "clientele hypothesis." Investors attracted to stocks in the highest-yield group appear to be unwilling to give up a dollar of dividends unless they receive at least a dollar in expected capital gain, while those attracted to stocks in the lowest-yield groups appear to be willing to forego a dollar of dividends in return for considerably less than a dollar in capital gain.

Here, too, the lack of effects of dealer activity remains a puzzle.

---

[9] Edwin Elton and Martin Gruber, "Marginal Stockholder Tax Rates and the Clientele Effect," *Review of Economics and Statistics*, 52, no. 1 (February 1970), 68-74.

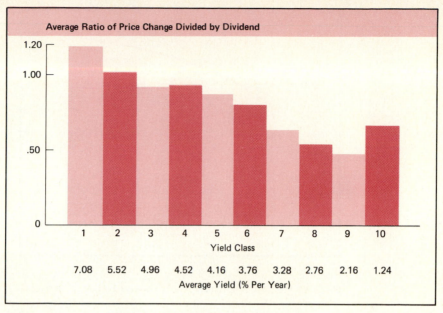

SOURCE: Edwin Elton and Martin Gruber, "Marginal Stockholder Tax Rates and the Clientele Effect," *Review of Economics and Statistics*, 52, no. 1 (February 1970), 68-74.

FIGURE 9-6
Ex-Dividend Price Changes Versus Divided Yield

With price declines of low-yield stocks roughly half as large as the amounts received in dividends, it would appear that juicy returns await the professionals for whom tax treatment of the two types of income is the same and for whom transactions costs are extremely low.

Clientele effects, if they persist, could affect the relationship between expected return and yield. It is possible that large numbers of tax-exempt investors, preferring to concentrate their holdings in high-yield securities, could push down the expected returns at the end of the yield spectrum, while large numbers of high-tax-bracket investors, preferring to concentrate their holdings in low- or zero-yield securities, could push down expected returns at that end of the yield spectrum.

The relationship between expected return and yield could thus be upward-sloping but curved, as shown in Figure 9-7.

It is, of course, difficult to provide definitive and precise statements of the relationship between expected return and various factors, and the magnitudes of such relationships undoubtedly change over time as well. Any estimate of the "yield effect" will, at best, be subject to error. Moreover, the phenomenon may be due at least in part to some other factor that tends to go with yield—that is, high-yield stocks may have more or less of something else that is desirable or undesirable.

Taxes

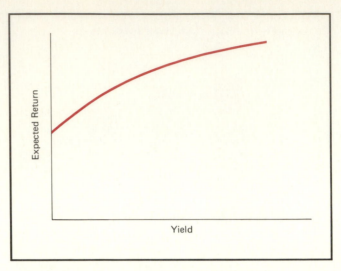

FIGURE 9-7
Possible Relationship Between Expected Return and Yield
with Clienteles.

The existence of a continuing before-tax reward for receiving income in the form of dividends rather than capital gains has been questioned by some on the grounds that clever tax planning may make it possible for investors to turn dividends into capital gains and that, if there were such a strong preference for gains, corporations would pay fewer or no dividends.

All these aspects merit consideration and further study. In any event, it behooves the serious investor to consider whether or not high-yield stocks are likely to do better than low-yield stocks (other things equal) in the future and to carefully weigh the resulting expectations about return against estimates of risk, taking into account his or her particular tax status.

Problems

1. A friend reports that she has just received a raise of 10%. Will her after-tax income go up by 10%? Why? Assume that prices are expected to be 10% higher next year. Will her real (constant-purchasing-power) income after taxes be the same next year as it was this year? Why?
2. At what levels of corporate income is the marginal corporate tax rate precisely equal to the average rate? At what levels are they almost the same?

3. A corporate bond is selling for $950. It matures in a year and a day, at which time the holder will receive $1,000. In addition, the bond will pay $50 in interest during the year. What would be the after-tax return on the bond for an investor in the 50% personal income tax bracket? What if the bond had been a municipal bond?

4. Assume that a particular bond issued by the State of New York is completely default-free, as is a similar bond issued by the State of California. Would you recommend that an investor who is a resident of California hold both bonds? Why? What about a resident of New York? A resident of the State of Washington? What if neither bond were completely riskless?

5. Assume that you are the trustee for a small fund left by a lawyer to support his widow. The provisions of the trust state that all income from dividends and interest payments will go to the widow. On her death the "corpus" of the fund will go to the lawyer's brother or his heirs. The brother is fabulously wealthy and the widow is very poor. What sorts of investments would you select? What if the trust provisions allowed you to "invade capital" for the widow—that is, pay her out of income and/or sell investments and pay her the proceeds?

6 An investor buys 100 shares of a stock selling for $50 per share at the end of 1981. At the beginning of 1983 it is selling for $60 per share. At the beginning of 1984 it is selling for $70 per share. He pays an effective marginal tax rate of 20% on realized capital gains.
   a. How much would he have after taxes if he held the stock until the beginning of 1984, then sold it? (Ignore transactions costs.)
   b. How much would he have after taxes in 1984 if he sold all his shares at the beginning of 1983, then bought back as many shares as possible with the difference between the proceeds and the tax on gains realized in 1983? (Ignore transactions costs.)
   c. What is the cost of realizing capital gains earlier (i.e., in 1983)?

7. You have a house worth $100,000 on today's market. You paid $50,000 for it some years ago and now own it outright. Your neighbor is in precisely the same situation. He suggests to you the following business deal. First, you sell your house to him for $100,000 and he sells his house to you for $100,000. Then you rent your (present) house from him for $200 per month. Neither of you has to move.
   a. What are the tax implications of the deal?
   b. What if each of you had a mortgage with $40,000 outstanding and arranged to have the mortgages transferred with the houses?
   c. What is the main tax advantage of home ownership?

10

Inflation

INTRODUCTION

The story is told of the modern-day Rip Van Winkle, who awoke in the year 2010 and immediately called his broker. (Fortunately, pay phones at the time permitted a call of up to three minutes without charge.) He first asked what had happened to the $10,000 he had instructed the broker to put in short-term Treasury bills, continually reinvesting the proceeds. Owing to high interest rates and the power of compounding, this had grown to over $1 million. Incredulous, Mr. Van Winkle inquired about his stocks, which were also worth about $10,000 when he dozed off. The broker told him that he was in for an even more pleasant surprise: they were now worth $2.5 million. "In short, Mr. Van Winkle," said the broker, "you are a millionaire 3.5 times over." At this point an operator cut in: "Your three minutes are over, please deposit one hundred dollars for an additional three minutes."

While this clearly overstates the case, there is no doubt that inflation is a major concern for investors. By and large, people have come to fear significant, rampant, or even runaway inflation.

INFLATION IN THE UNITED STATES

Figure 10-1 provides some historical perspective. It shows the U.S. Consumer Price Index (CPI) from 1925 through 1982, adjusted so that the value in 1925 equals 100. As an aid to interpretation, the values are plotted on a *logarithmic* or *ratio* scale. This makes a given vertical distance represent a specific percentage change, no matter where it is plotted. Such scales are often used when interest centers on percentage rates of growth or decline. In such a graph, a series of values

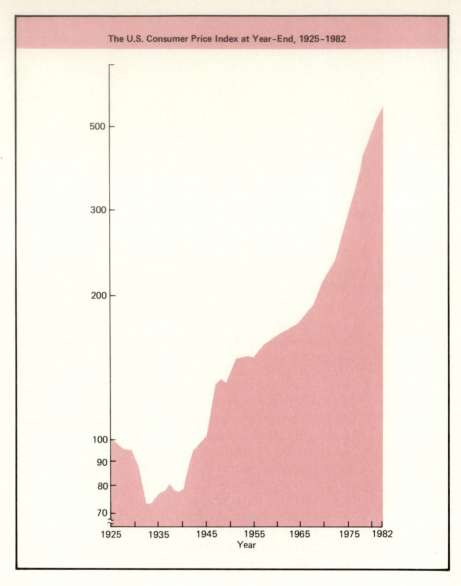

FIGURE 10-1
The U.S. Consumer Price Index at Year-End, 1925-1982

growing at a constant percentage rate plot as a straight line. Such is not the case in Figure 10-1. Following the substantial deflation from 1926 to 1933, prices increased in almost every year, but there were three subperiods with different rates of inflation: fairly rapid from 1934 to 1952, mild from 1953 to 1965, and substantial from 1966 to 1982. Table 10-1 shows the rate of growth of prices for each of these subper-

TABLE 10-1
Growth Rates of the U.S. Consumer Price Index

From	To	Rate of Growth (% per Year)
1926	1933	−3.8
1934	1952	3.8
1953	1965	1.4
1966	1982	6.8

iods, computed by taking the geometric means of the ratio of the ending value to the beginning value. For example, at the end of 1982 the consumer price index was 206% higher than it had been at the end of 1965, seventeen years earlier. A similar result could have been obtained with a constant growth rate of 6.8% per year, since:

$$\sqrt[17]{3.06} = 1.068$$

INFLATION IN OTHER COUNTRIES

Figure 10-2 shows that inflation is by no means solely an American problem. Most industrial countries have experienced the phenomenon, and in some there is a feeling that unless fundamental changes are made, substantial inflation may become a way of life.

PRICE INDICES

As indicated in Chapter 4, no price index can prove totally satisfactory as an indicator of the "cost of living" for all consumers, and most indices are likely to overstate the extent to which the cost of attaining a given level of satisfaction actually increases during any inflationary period, even for the people whose purchases the index was intended to reflect. Although this is fairly well understood, and most governments compute a number of alternative indices to provide a wider choice for analysis, people tend to focus on one index as an indicator of "the" price level. In the United States the Consumer Price Index, computed by the Bureau of Labor Statistics, often fills this role, despite some attempts by government officials to discourage such widespread use.[1] The composition of this index has been changed from time to

---

[1] A number of authorities prefer "deflators" derived from the gross national product figures, such as the one used for the comparative data in Figure 10-2, but such indices have not received the publicity accorded the Consumer Price Index.

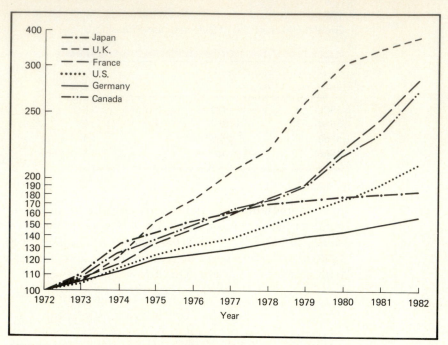

SOURCE: International Monetary Fund, *International Financial Statistics.*

FIGURE 10-2
Gross National Product Price Deflators (1972 = 100)

time to provide a more representative basket of goods and services. The process by which data are gathered and verified has also been improved periodically.

For better or worse, most people consider a given percentage change in the Consumer Price Index to be as good or as bad as a comparable change in the price of every good and service. While this is at best only approximately true, in the remainder of this chapter we will sidestep the issue, simply referring to changes in "the price level" or "prices."

NOMINAL AND REAL RETURNS

As shown in Chapter 4, the real interest rate on a loan will be approximately equal to the nominal or monetary rate less the percentage change in prices during the period in question. This can be generalized to cover any return, certain or uncertain:

$$\tilde{R}^r \approx \tilde{R}^n - \tilde{c} \qquad \textbf{(10-1)}$$

where:

$\tilde{R}^r$ = the return in real terms

$\tilde{R}^n$ = the return in nominal or monetary terms

$\tilde{c}$ = the change in prices

As usual, the tildes indicate the variables not known with certainty in advance.

The simplest view of investors' attitudes toward inflation is that described in Chapter 4: they are concerned with real, not monetary, returns, and a single price index is adequate to characterize the difference.

This makes it imperative to account for the impact of inflation on both the expected value and the risk associated with the real return from a security or portfolio.

The impact on expected return is straightforward: the expected real return equals the expected nominal return less the expected change in prices:

$$E(\tilde{R}^r) = E(\tilde{R}^n) - E(\tilde{c}) \tag{10-2a}$$

where:

$E(\tilde{R}^r)$ = the expected real return on a security or portfolio

$E(\tilde{R}^n)$ = the expected nominal, or monetary, return on a security or portfolio

$E(\tilde{c})$ = the expected rate of change in prices

If a security is to provide a given expected real return, the expected nominal return must be larger by the amount of inflation expected over the relevant holding period.[2] This can be seen by rearranging the equation:

$$E(\tilde{R}^n) = E(\tilde{R}^r) + E(\tilde{c}) \tag{10-2b}$$

If investors are concerned with real returns, all securities will be priced so that expected monetary returns incorporate expected inflation. The expected return on every security should thus account for *expected* inflation (though not necessarily for unanticipated departures of actual inflation from expectations, as we will see shortly).

INTEREST RATES AND INFLATION

Before the fact, nominal interest rates for securities with no risk of default should cover both a requisite expected real return and the

---

[2] This discussion, entirely in terms of before-tax income, ignores the impact of taxation of interest income (described in a later section).

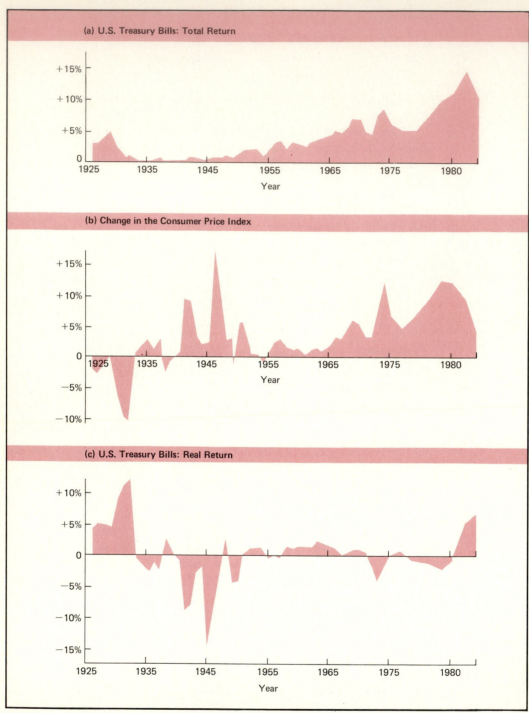

(a) U.S. Treasury Bills: Total Return

(b) Change in the Consumer Price Index

(c) U.S. Treasury Bills: Real Return

SOURCE: Roger G. Ibbotson and Rex A. Sinquefield, *Stocks, Bonds, Bills and Inflation: The Past and the Future, 1982 edition*, The Financial Analysts Research Foundation, 1982.

FIGURE 10-3

Nominal and Real Returns on Short-Term Default-Free Investments, 12-Month Periods Ending December 1926–December 1983 amount of inflation expected over the period in question. After the fact, of course, the real return will be the difference between the nominal return and the amount of inflation actually experienced. Only when actual inflation equals expected inflation will actual real return equal expected real return on such securities.

Figure 10-3(a) shows how short-term interest rates varied over the last 57 years, while Figure 10-3(b) indicates the variation of the annual changes in the Consumer Price Index. The differences between the two, shown in Figure 10-3(c), represent actual real returns.

One cannot help being struck with the fact that those who invested in short-term securities over this period frequently ended up with less purchasing power than they started with: real return was negative in 25 of the 57 years. Perhaps even more surprising, the average real return over the period was close to *zero*!

While *expected* real returns may well vary from year to year, the variation may be relatively small. If so, investors may well have been willing to invest in short-term highly liquid securities even though they expected to earn nothing at all in real terms. If they are willing to do so still, such securities will be priced to give an expected real return of approximately zero.

If this assumption is made, the "market's" predicted rate of inflation over the near future can be estimated by simply looking at the current annual yield on short-term government securities. In a sense, Treasury bill yields represent a *consensus prediction* of inflation—a prediction likely to be more accurate in many cases than the predictions of any single forecaster.

REMOVING THE MONEY VEIL

The overall price level can be considered a unit of measure for expressing relative prices. If agreement were reached to call every dollar one cent, nothing of true economic importance would have to be changed, simply the manner in which accounts were kept. To some extent, money simply acts as a veil, obscuring the real underlying economic forces.

This can be seen most clearly in a prototypically simple agrarian economy in which wheat is invested (planted) this year to obtain wheat next year. In such a situation, the only uncertainty in terms of wheat is productive uncertainty: how much will come up? The real return depends solely on the relationship between the wheat harvested and that planted. In terms of the value-relative:

$$1 + \tilde{R}^r = \frac{\tilde{W}_1}{W_0}$$

where:

$\tilde{W}_1 =$ wheat harvested in year 1
$W_0 =$ wheat planted in year 0
$\tilde{R}^r =$ real return in terms of wheat

What about the nominal, or monetary, return? We can represent the price of wheat at the time of planting by P_0 and the (generally uncertain) price at time of harvest by $\tilde{P}_1$. Then the "cost" of the investment would be $P_0 W_0$ and the value of the harvest would be $\tilde{P}_1 \tilde{W}_1$. The nominal return, expressed as a value-relative, would be:

$$1 + \tilde{R}^n = \frac{\tilde{P}_1 \tilde{W}_1}{P_0 W_0}$$

To convert a nominal return into a real return, one adjusts for price changes. In this case we can simply divide by P_1/P_0, which will give W_1/W_0.

The point illustrated here is simple enough. No matter what happens to prices (e.g., P_1), the real return on the wheat will be unaffected. It may be high or low, but the determining factors do not include the actual level of overall prices.

In the real world much more is uncertain than the results of physical production. But many, if not all, of these influences concern relative prices—for example, the level of the prices of a firm's outputs relative to those of its inputs. The real profits obtained from some capital assets may be affected by the overall level of prices, but when the effects are averaged across all assets, such effects may well balance out. The real return on the overall "market portfolio," which includes all capital assets, may thus be related primarily to overall real output and only secondarily to the level of overall prices.

This suggests that uncertainty about inflation per se may directly add little to the uncertainty about the real return on a widely diversified set of capital assets. It may contribute indirectly, however, through the impact of inflation on real output.

There are limits to the ability of an economy to accommodate substantial rates of inflation, especially those not perfectly anticipated. For example, if the money stock is increased rapidly, it will be very difficult for firms and individuals to merely increase all prices and wages by the appropriate percentage. Some prices and wages are fixed by long-term contracts, others are subject to government control, and so on. This can cause distortions in relative prices and an overall drop in the efficiency with which the economy functions. Resources must be used to convey and obtain information about the latest prices, re-value inventories, and the like. Inflation that differs from expectations can thus cause a decrease in both real output and the overall real return obtained by producers.

INFLATION, BORROWERS, AND LENDERS

While deviations of actual inflation from expected inflation may have relatively little effect on investments as a whole, they may well affect specific investments. In fact, one would expect a direct impact on the real returns associated with investments whose payments are fixed in monetary terms.

A simple example will illustrate the relationship. Assume that in year zero everyone expects inflation to run at an annual rate of 5% per year forever. This is shown by the solid line in Figure 10-4. (Note that the vertical axis is a ratio scale, so that constant percentage changes plot along a straight line.) Now imagine that a lender has agreed to provide funds at a zero real expected return. Thus one can borrow $100 now and pay back $110.25 in two years. If actual inflation

FIGURE 10-4
Actual and Expected Future Price Levels

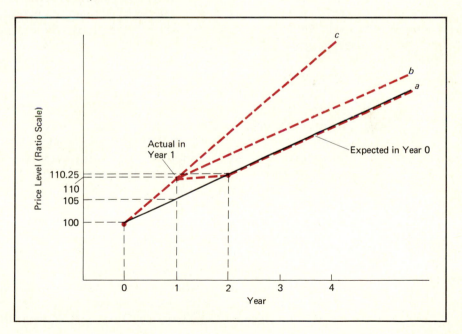

equals expected inflation, a one-year loan would require a payment of $100 in constant (year-zero) dollars a year hence, while a two-year loan would require a payment of $100 in constant (year-zero) dollars two years hence. In each case, the real rate of interest would be zero, as intended.

Now imagine that two individuals take advantage of the lender's offer; one borrows short-term (one year) and the other long-term (two years). How will they be affected if actual inflation differs from expected inflation?

Say that in year 1 prices rise by 10% instead of the expected 5%. This is shown by the dashed line in Figure 10-4. Clearly the short-term borrower gains. He or she now pays back $105, but in terms of year-zero dollars, this is only $105/1.10 = $95.45, giving an actual real rate of interest of −4.55%. When actual inflation exceeds expected inflation, those with commitments to make payments fixed in nominal terms (debtors) gain in real terms at the expense of those to whom payments are to be made (creditors). Conversely, when actual inflation is less than expected inflation, monetary creditors gain and monetary debtors lose.

But what about the person who borrowed long-term? Will he or she gain or lose? If the loan is paid as scheduled, the answer will depend on the actual level of prices in year 2. If it is paid early, on terms agreeable to the lender, the answer will depend on the lender's expectations *in year 1* about prices in year 2. And if the obligation is transferred to someone else at an agreed-upon price, the answer will depend on the other party's expectations in year 1 about prices in year 2.

Figure 10-4 shows three possible patterns of expected future price levels, given the unanticipated increase in year 1. Pattern *a* assumes that investors consider unanticipated deviations to be irrelevant for predicting future price *levels*. Thus after a 10% rise an increase of slightly less than one-fourth of 1% (from 110 to 110.25) is expected. Pattern *b* assumes that investors consider unanticipated deviations to be irrelevant for predicting the *rates* of increases of future prices. Increases of 5% per year will still be anticipated, but from a new, higher base. Pattern *c* assumes that the actual rate is expected to continue in the future. Thus every subsequent year is expected to bring a 10% increase in prices.

The impact of revised expectations on the long-term borrower is substantial. Table 10-2 shows the value of the payment in year-zero dollars for each of the three patterns. With pattern *a* the borrower expects to gain nothing: with pattern *b* he or she expects to pay back the same amount in real terms as the short-term borrower pays; with pattern *c* he or she expects to pay back less in real terms than does the short-term borrower.

Which pattern is most likely? The answer generally depends on

TABLE 10-2
Value of a Payment in Year-Zero Dollars

Pattern	Amount Paid in Year 2 ($)	Expected Price Level in Year 2 ($)	Expected Value of Amount Paid in Year-Zero Dollars
a	110.25	110.25	100.00
b	110.25	115.50	95.45
c	110.25	121.00	91.12

the cause of the unexpected change, but a typical response would probably lie somewhere between patterns *b* and *c*. When actual inflation exceeds expectations, investors are likely to use the current level of prices as a base and also raise their estimates of the future rate of inflation, but not by the full amount of the difference. When actual inflation falls below expectations, investors are likely to lower their expectations of the rate of future inflation, but not by the full amount of the difference.

The implication is that long-term borrowers are likely to gain somewhat more than short-term borrowers when actual inflation exceeds expected inflation and lose somewhat more when actual inflation falls below expectations. Similarly, long-term lenders are likely to lose somewhat more than short-term lenders when actual inflation exceeds expectations and gain somewhat more when actual inflation falls below expectations.

INFLATION AND STOCK PRICES

A company's financial statements can be used to obtain a rough estimate of the impact of a divergence between actual and expected inflation on the value of the firm's common stock. Each item can be classified as either a (1) real, (2) short-term monetary, or (3) long-term monetary asset or liability. In some cases the classification is fairly obvious; in others it is somewhat arbitrary. However, detailed knowledge of a company and careful reading of its reports can often reduce the arbitrariness of such breakdowns.

Two additional monetary assets need to be considered. Both relate to future taxes. The amount of dollar income subject to taxation will undoubtedly depend on the extent of inflation. However, taxable income is reduced by two items: depreciation charges and interest payments. For example, future federal corporate income taxes can be reduced by roughly 46% of the current amount of a firm's undepreciated plant and equipment. The present value of such tax reductions is a long-term monetary asset, since the amounts will not vary with subsequent inflation. This present value will, of course, depend on the timing of the depreciation charges and be smaller than the total (undiscounted) value.

A similar consideration applies to the interest payments on currently outstanding debt. Taxes will be reduced by approximately 46% of this amount; the present value of such reductions thus constitutes another long-term monetary asset.

To carefully estimate a stock's exposure to unanticipated inflation, market values of assets and liabilities should be used if possible. Moreover, the value of future tax reductions should be discounted. Finally, explicit account should be taken of the maturities of the firm's bonds and the likely effects of current surprises on future expectations. However, a crude estimate can be obtained by using book (accounting) values of assets and liabilities, estimating only the total (undiscounted) value of future tax reductions, and making a very rough adjustment for the impact of changing expectations (for example, according long-term assets and liabilities twice the weight of short-term assets and liabilities on the assumption that a dollar of a long-term commitment has twice the overall effect of a dollar of short-term commitment). With such assumptions a firm's *net monetary position* can be estimated. If monetary assets exceed monetary liabilities, the firm is a *net monetary creditor* and its stockholders can be expected to *lose* if inflation is greater than expected and to *gain* if inflation is less than expected. On the other hand, if monetary assets are less than monetary liabilities, the firm is a *net monetary debtor* and its stockholders can be expected to *gain* if inflation is greater than expected and to *lose* if inflation is less than expected.

REPLACEMENT COST ACCOUNTING

One definition of earnings or profit holds that if a firm paid out the entire amount of profit each year, it would neither increase nor decrease in size, measured by the real value of its productive capacity. This notion is often summarized by the term "sustainable earnings." A firm that pays out more than the total amount of such earnings can be expected to decline, while one that pays out less can be expected to grow.

While there may be some objections to this definition on principle, they are overshadowed by the problems associated with its implementation. And these problems are seriously aggravated in an inflationary environment.

Consider a firm that purchases ten units of some semifinished good at the beginning of each year, hires labor to work on it, then sells the finished product at the end of the year. For simplicity assume that labor is paid from the proceeds of sales. In the absence of inflation, the firm's operations might be summarized as follows:

At the beginning of the year:
  Buy 10 units at $100 each: $1,000
At the end of the year:
  Sell 10 units at $200 each: 2,000
  Pay labor   −800
    Net cash received $1,200

The firm thus invests $1,000 to obtain $1,200 a year later, giving a return of 20%. Viewed somewhat differently, after an initial investment of $1,000, profits of $200 can be paid out each year, assuming no inflation. The latter is the magnitude of sustainable earnings or profit.

Now assume that in the course of the year all prices and wages increase 10%. The results are then:

At the beginning of the year:
  Buy 10 units at $100 each: $1,000
At the end of the year:
  Sell 10 units at $220 each: 2,200
  Pay labor   −880
    Net cash received $1,320

An investment of $1,000 thus produces receipts of $1,320 a year later, for a return of 32% and a difference of $320. Is this the amount of sustainable earnings? Clearly not. Assuming no further inflation, $1,100 will be required to replace the inventory at the beginning of the next year. Thus only $220 can be paid out if the firm is to avoid a decline in real productive capacity. Put somewhat differently, the total "profit" of $320 resulted from an increase in the value of the firm's inventory plus normal operations.

To keep these aspects separate, a number of authorities recommend *replacement cost accounting*. In essence, this involves the use of estimated replacement costs instead of historic costs when calculating profit. In this case such a procedure would give:

Receipts from sales		$2,200
Less cost of goods sold		
Wages	$ 880	
Materials, at replacement cost	1,100	1,980
Equals net profit		$ 220

An equivalent procedure subtracts from reported profit an *inventory valuation adjustment*, representing the excess of replacement cost over the amount utilized in the standard accounts:

Reported profit		$320
Less inventory valuation adjustment		
Replacement cost	$1,100	
Reported cost	1,000	
Adjustment		100
Adjusted profit		$220

Even after the adjustment, profit is stated in current dollars. To compare the amount with that of a previous year, the value must be adjusted for price-level changes. In this case the amount in current dollars is $220, while the amount in constant, year-zero dollars is 220/1.10, or $200 (which is the amount that would have been obtained in the absence of inflation).

The magnitude of the appropriate inventory valuation adjustment depends on the length of time inventory is held, the extent of the rise in its replacement cost, and the method used to account for such costs when calculating reported profit. As discussed in Chapter 9, the LIFO method comes closest to replacement costs, while the FIFO method lies at the other end of the spectrum.

A similar situation arises with capital assets. Their historic costs are charged to operations over assumed productive lives, using various depreciation formulas. As discussed in Chapter 9, accelerated depreciation is generally used for tax purposes, but more gradual procedures may be used for reporting profits and earnings to stockholders. However, assets "used up" in the production process are generally valued at historic, not replacement costs. Other things equal, this will cause an understatement of cost and an overstatement of sustainable earnings.

At the beginning of each year a firm will have an "inventory" of capital assets. During the year the replacement costs of these assets may change, resulting in associated gains or losses, although such changes may not be realized at the time. The portion of this inventory of assets used up in production should be valued at replacement cost to estimate sustainable profit from operations. If historic costs are used instead, the resulting amount should be adjusted to account for the difference between replacement and historic costs.

The Financial Accounting Standards Board's *Statement of Financial Accounting Standards No. 33* requires companies with total assets of more than $1 billion or inventories, property, plant, and equipment with a gross value of more than $125 million to provide supplementary inflation-adjusted financial statements. Two methods are to be used: a *constant-dollar* procedure that accounts for general inflation and a *current-cost* method that accounts for specific price changes. The standard also requires that assets and liabilities be classified as monetary or nonmonetary and that an estimate be made of the gain or loss on the net monetary position resulting from general inflation.

The U.S. Department of Commerce shows the estimated portion of aggregate corporate profits attributable to inventory valuation increases in its *Survey of Current Business*. The estimated difference between aggregate depreciation based on historic cost ("capital consumption") and that based on replacement cost ("economic capital consumption") is also reported. Table 10-3 shows how profits are altered in inflationary times when the *inventory valuation adjustment* (*IVA*) and *capital consumption adjustment* are taken into account. Not surprisingly, as a comparison of the last two columns shows, the effect is generally greater, the greater the rate of inflation.

TABLE 10-3
Profits Before and After Inventory Valuation and Capital Consumption Adjustments; U.S. Nonfinancial Corporations, 1976–1982

Year	Profit before Taxes ($ billions)	Profit before Taxes after Adjustments ($ billions)	Percentage Difference	Percentage Change in the Consumer Price Index
76	135.0	107.3	20.5	4.8
77	153.5	126.3	17.7	6.8
78	174.3	137.6	21.1	9.0
79	193.4	136.7	29.3	13.3
80	183.8	123.6	32.8	12.4
81	186.6	145.6	22.0	8.9
82	152.4	143.0	6.2	3.9

SOURCE: U.S. Department of Commerce, *Survey of Current Business*.

A potential beneficiary of inflation in most countries is the government. This result derives from the nature of the tax structure and can arise in several ways.

One source of such a shift of real wealth from the private to the public sector is the taxation of dividends, interest, and capital gains. For example, consider an investment with a real return of 7% held by someone in a 30% marginal tax bracket. In the absence of inflation, the investor would retain .7 × 7% for an after-tax nominal and real return of 4.9%. Now assume that there is inflation at the low rate of 2%, and that the return on the asset rises accordingly to 9%. The investor's after-tax nominal return becomes .7 × 9 = 6.3%, but in real terms this is approximately a 6.3 − 2.0, or 4.3%. The effective tax rate has increased—a larger portion of the real return is being allocated through the public sector. If inflation rises to 4%, and with it the return to 11%, the investor's after-tax return becomes .7 × 11 = 7.7%, but in real terms this is about 7.7 − 4.0, or 3.7%.

Barring a change in the tax structure, the greater the rate of inflation, the greater will be the resulting shift of earnings on capital from the private to the public sector. Moreover, an increase in the anticipated rate of inflation will, under these conditions, lower the present value of capital assets.

For an asset's real after-tax return to be the same with a high inflation rate as with a low rate, its price must fall enough to increase the nominal before-tax return sufficiently to compensate for *both* inflation and the larger effective tax rate. In the previous example the return would have to rise to 9.86% if the rate of inflation were 2% and to 12.72% if it were 4%:

	0%	2%	4%
Rate of inflation			
Before-tax return	7.0	9.86	12.72
Return after tax	4.90	6.90	8.90
(= .7 × return before-tax)			
Real return after tax	4.90	4.90	4.90
(≈ return after tax − inflation rate)			

In this case a 2% increase in the rate of expected inflation would increase the expected return on the asset by 2.86%. In other words, expected return would change by 1.43 times the change in the expected rate of inflation.

This phenomenon could be avoided by levying taxes on *real* returns. Alternatively, tax rates could be changed often enough to give a similar result. If such changes were expected to be made when required, prices of capital assets might not fall when the rate of anticipated inflation increased, and expected returns would change one-for-one with changes in the expected rate of inflation.

SECURITIES AS HEDGES AGAINST INFLATION

Presumably, investors are concerned more with real returns than with nominal returns. This implies that securities that provide a hedge against inflation should be considered more attractive, other things equal, than those that do not. Of course in an efficient capital market other things would not be equal, and the former would be priced to be inferior in some other dimension—for example, expected return.

But what does it mean to say that a security is a "hedge" against inflation? And what does empirical research suggest about the abilities of various classes of assets to act as such hedges?

For a tax-exempt investor a security would provide a perfect hedge against inflation if its return moved one-for-one with changes in inflation, for then its real return would be the same no matter what the rate of inflation. For an investor paying taxes the relationship might have to be more than one-for-one. And, of course, most security returns are subject to additional uncertainty because of factors unrelated to inflation. The ability of a security to hedge against inflation could be summed up in a number (h_i) in an equation of the form:

$$\bar{R}_i = a_i + h_i \tilde{c} + \tilde{e}_i \tag{10-3}$$

where:

a_i = a constant
h_i = the security's sensitivity to inflation
$\tilde{c}$ = the rate of inflation
$\tilde{e}_i$ = the uncertain portion of the return of the security not related to inflation

Formula (10-3) has one drawback—it fails to differentiate between *expected* and *unexpected* inflation. For instance, all securities might serve as hedges against expected inflation, but only certain ones might hedge against unexpected changes in the rate of inflation. It is thus preferable to treat the two aspects separately:

$$\bar{R}_i = a_i + h_i^e \tilde{c}_e + h_i^u \tilde{c}_u + \tilde{e}_i \tag{10-4}$$

where:

a_i = a constant
h_i^e = the security's sensitivity to expected inflation

Inflation

c_e = the expected rate of inflation

h_i^u = the security's sensitivity to unexpected inflation

$\tilde{c}_u$ = the unexpected inflation (i.e., the difference between the actual rate of inflation and the rate that was expected)

$\tilde{e}_i$ = the uncertain portion of the return of the security not related to inflation

Before the fact, both $\tilde{c}_u$ and $\tilde{e}_i$ are uncertain, and roughly as likely to be positive as negative.

As indicated earlier, a rough estimate of short-term expected inflation is provided by the return on short-term Treasury bills. Thus, if investors are willing to settle for an expected real return of zero on six-month Treasury bills, the return on such a bill will indicate a consensus estimate of inflation over the forthcoming six months. The difference between the actual rate of inflation during a period and the Treasury bill rate at the beginning of the period can thus be considered the amount of unexpected inflation (c_u).

This relationship makes it possible to estimate for any short period both expected and unexpected inflation. By comparing returns on various securities with these estimates of expected and unexpected inflation over a number of periods, we can measure *ex post* sensitivities to the two aspects.[3]

Table 10-4 provides estimates derived in this manner for several types of investments. Since the values are based on after-the-fact relationships rather than before-the-fact expectations about such relationships, little attention should be paid to minor differences in magnitudes. However, the major differences warrant attention.

The evidence shows that the interest rate on a six-month Treasury bill is a relatively unbiased estimate of the rate of inflation expected over the next six months. It thus hedges one-for-one against expected inflation. This suggests that investors either are unaware of tax consequences or assume that rates will be revised as needed to avoid changes in effective rates as inflation changes.

Of course a six-month Treasury bill cannot provide a hedge against unanticipated inflation over its life. If inflation is expected to be 5% per six months, such a bill might be priced to return 5% over six months. If inflation actually turns out to be 6% over the period, the return on the bill will still be 5%. Thus the value of h_i^u is zero.

Longer-term U.S. government bonds appear to have provided hedges against expected inflation on roughly a one-for-one basis. However, all failed to serve as hedges against unexpected inflation. In fact, all had *negative* sensitivities, with the value of h_i^u more negative, the longer the term of the bond. This relationship is not especially surprising

---

[3] The procedure involves the use of multiple regression to estimate the coefficients in formula (10-4).

TABLE 10-4

Sensitivities of Assets to Expected and Unexpected Inflation, Six-Month Holding Periods, July 1959–July 1971

Asset	Sensitivity to Expected Inflation (h_i^e)	Sensitivity to Unexpected Inflation (h_i^u)
6-month U.S. Treasury bills*	1.0	0
1-2 year U.S. government bonds	1.08	−1.15
2-3 year U.S. government bonds	1.03	−1.75
3-4 year U.S. government bonds	.88	−2.37
4-5 year U.S. government bonds	.79	−2.75
Private residential real estate	1.27	1.14
Common stocks†	−4.26	−2.09

* Values are assumed.

† Value-weighted average of all stocks listed on New York Stock Exchange.

SOURCE: Eugene F. Fama and G. William Schwert, "Asset Returns and Inflation," *Journal of Financial Economics*, November 1977, pp. 115-146. By permission of North-Holland Publishing Co., Amsterdam.

in light of the way investors revise expectations based on recent experience.

Assume that inflation is expected to run at the rate of 5% per six months throughout the year. At the beginning of the year a one-year government bond is priced to return 5% per six months. Now assume that during the first half of the year inflation runs at the rate of 6% (per six months). Investors will likely revise upward their estimate of inflation for the second half of the year—say from 5% to 5.5%. But if the bond is to return 5.5% over the second half of the year, its price at midyear must be lower than it would have been otherwise. Investors who held it during the first half of the year thus would not obtain a return of 5%, but less. Higher-than-anticipated inflation caused them to obtain a lower-than-anticipated return. There were thus two sources of *bad* news: (1) inflation was greater than expected and (2) their investments did worse than expected. Of course, had inflation been less than expected, the situation would have been reversed and there would have been two sources of *good* news.

The longer the remaining life of a bond, the longer the period over which revised expectations of inflation are relevant. Thus it is not surprising that prices of longer-term bonds are affected more by unexpected changes in inflation than are the prices of shorter-term bonds.

Residential real estate provides a bright spot in an otherwise somewhat gloomy record. Of the investments studied, it alone served as a hedge against both expected and unexpected inflation. To some extent the reason is that the Consumer Price Index includes the cost of such real estate, but there is undoubtedly more to it.

The record of common stocks is depressing, to say the least. They did not serve as hedges against either expected or unexpected inflation during this period. Quite the contrary—stock returns tended to be lower, the greater the rate of expected or unexpected inflation.

Rudimentary notions of market efficiency suggest that all assets should be priced to take expected inflation into account. The fact that stocks tended to do worse when inflation was expected to be large is thus puzzling. The fact that they did worse when inflation was greater than expected is perhaps less surprising. It could reflect the impact of larger effective corporate tax rates in periods of high inflation, the costs of accommodating to rapid inflation, and so on. While the results in Table 10-4 might simply be due to the chance arrival of news about inflation concurrent with news about the *real* aspects of the economy, they do call into question the assertion that common stocks are hedges against inflation. However, they do not imply that stocks cannot provide returns greater than inflation. There is every reason to expect stocks to provide positive *real* returns. But they may provide greater real returns in periods of low inflation than in periods of high inflation.

INFLATION HEDGING AND EXPECTED RETURN

The original Capital Asset Pricing Model deals with nominal returns. If the rate of inflation is reasonably predictable, this causes no problem, for inflation will add little to the uncertainty concerning the return of any asset. But if there is considerable uncertainty about the rate of inflation, the situation is different. The real return of a default-free investment such as a U.S. Treasury bill will not be certain; the risk associated with the real return of the market portfolio may differ considerably from the risk associated with its nominal return; and the beta of a security relative to the market portfolio may change when both returns are expressed in real terms instead of nominal terms.

If investors think in terms of real returns, the relationship between risk and return may look like that shown in Figure 10-5. The shaded area in Figure 10-5(a) indicates the available risk-return combinations in terms of *real* returns (note that there is no riskless alternative). Point M represents the market portfolio, which is assumed to be an efficient investment. The situation is thus formally equivalent to the "zero-beta" model. As Figure 10-5(a) shows, securities will be priced as if it were possible to borrow or lend without limit at a riskless rate of Z^r. Thus all securities and portfolios will plot along a straight line such as that shown in Figure 10-5(b), relating expected real return to "real beta." The equation of this "real" Security Market Line is:

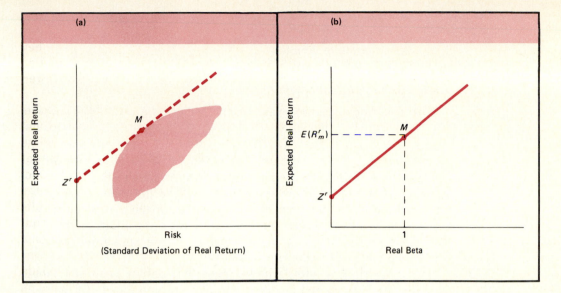

FIGURE 10-5
A Capital Asset Pricing Model in Real Terms

$$E(R_i^r) = Z^r + \beta_i^r[E(R_m^r) - Z^r] \qquad \textbf{(10-5)}$$

where:

$E(R_i^r) =$ the expected real return on security i

$E(R_m^r) =$ the expected real return on the market portfolio

$Z^r =$ the expected real return of a security or portfolio with a zero real beta

$\beta_i^r =$ security i's real beta $[= \text{cov}\,(R_i^r, R_m^r)/\text{var}\,(R_m^r)]$

Equation (10-5) provides a succinct statement of the effect of uncertain inflation on security expected returns. But what does it imply about the relationship among expected nominal returns, traditional beta values, and sensitivities of nominal returns to inflation? As shown in Appendix 10A, in such a world, securities will also plot on a *Security Market Plane* with these three attributes on the axes. The equation of such a plane is:

$$E(R_i) = Z_1 + Z_2\beta_i - Z_3 h_i^u \qquad \textbf{(10-6)}$$

where:

$E(R_i) =$ the expected nominal return on security i

$Z_1 =$ the expected nominal return on a security or portfolio with both β_i and h_i^u equal to zero

$\beta_i =$ security i's (traditional) beta value $[= \text{cov}\,(R_i, R_m)/\text{var}\,(R_m)]$

Inflation

h_i^u = security i's sensitivity to unexpected changes in inflation
$[= \text{cov}(R_i, c)/\text{var}(c)]$
Z_2 = a positive constant
Z_3 = a positive constant

As the third term indicates:

> In a world of uncertain inflation: securities will be priced to give lower expected returns, other things equal, the greater their ability to hedge against unexpected changes in inflation.

The value of Z_3 indicates the reduction in expected return per unit increase in inflation sensitivity. Not surprisingly, the greater the uncertainty about inflation, the greater will be the magnitude of this trade-off. However, since uncertainty concerning the market portfolio's return is typically much greater than that concerning inflation, the effect of differences in β_i on $E(R_i)$—indicated by the magnitude of Z_2—will generally be considerably greater.

Stocks of firms with large net monetary debtor positions should be better hedges against unexpected inflation than those of firms with large net monetary creditor positions. However, differences in inflation sensitivities among stocks may be relatively small and difficult to predict in advance. If so, the inclusion of inflation sensitivity in a Security Market Plane or Hyperplane may add only slightly to the explanation of differences in expected returns under normal circumstances. But when uncertainty about inflation is considerable, differences in hedging abilities—especially among different classes of assets—are likely to be accompanied by substantial differences in expected returns.

As is typical in an efficient market, bad news tends to accompany good news. For example, the good news might be that real estate is a good hedge against inflation and the bad news that its expected return is less than that of assets that entail similar risk in other regards but are poorer hedges against inflation.

INDEXATION

In a world of uncertain inflation, even default-free bonds are subject to *purchasing power risk*. Contractual interest rates can cover expected inflation, but the actual real return from any investment with payments fixed in nominal terms will depend on the actual amount of inflation. As long as the two may differ, real return will be uncertain.

While one can invest in some consumption goods directly (by storing canned goods in the basement) or indirectly (via commodity futures contracts), for other goods and services such alternatives are either costly or unavailable. For example: barbers' services cannot be stored and there is no organized futures market.

If a specified price index can adequately measure purchasing power, there is no reason why a contract cannot be written with specified *real* but not nominal payments. Thus if the index stands at P_0 in year 0, and will be $\tilde{P}_1$ in year 1, $\tilde{P}_2$ in year 2, and so on, a borrower might promise to pay $\$10\tilde{P}_1$ in year 1, $\$10\tilde{P}_2$ in year 2, . . . , and $\$100\tilde{P}_{10}$ in year 10, in return for a loan of $100P_0$ dollars in year zero. To convert these amounts to constant real dollars, we simply divide each value by the price level:

Year	Amount	Price Level	Amount in Constant Dollars
0	$-100P_0$	P_0	-100
1	$10\tilde{P}_1$	$\tilde{P}_1$	10
2	$10\tilde{P}_2$	$\tilde{P}_2$	10
.			
.			
.			
10	$100\tilde{P}_{10}$	$\tilde{P}_{10}$	100

The real value of each payment will be the amount shown in the final column, no matter what happens to prices (e.g., no matter what the actual values of P_1, P_2, and so on may be). Moreover, the real rate of interest on the loan is certain as long as there is no risk of default. The loan is completely *indexed*; that is, all amounts are tied to a stated price index on a one-for-one basis.

In some countries a great many contracts are tied to standard price indices (two notable cases are Israel and Brazil). Government bonds, returns on savings accounts, wage contracts, pension plans, insurance contracts—all can be indexed and have been at various times and places. In the United States, social security payments are indexed, as are the wages and pension plans of many employees. Some of these are fully indexed: for example, the payment is increased by 10% when the price index increases by 10%. Others incorporate only partial indexation: for example, the payment might be increased by 7% when the price index increases by 10%.

The key advantage of indexation is its role in reducing or eliminating purchasing power risk. Typically, higher expected inflation is accompanied by increased uncertainty about the actual rate of inflation. Thus pressures for indexation increase when countries move into periods of seemingly unchecked inflation. If an index of general enough relevance can be computed, indexed contracts should dominate nonindexed contracts. When uncertainty about inflation is substantial, one would thus expect indexation to become widespread. However, government action is usually required to enable truly effective indexation, especially on debt instruments. Laws regulating interest rates preclude completely indexed debt, since they usually limit the nominal rate of interest, not the real rate. This leads to predictable inefficiencies when expected inflation increases: the effective limit placed on the expected real rate of interest falls, requiring rationing of the types of credit subject to such limits. A notable example occurred in the 1970s in the United States, as limits placed on interest rates paid by Savings and Loan Companies, coupled with increased inflationary expectations (and thus higher unregulated interest rates), caused a substantial diminution in funds flowing to such companies and a corresponding reduction in the money made available by them for home mortgages.

INFLATION AND DEBT TERMS

Since inflation is generally harder to predict, the longer the period over which the prediction is made, uncertainty about inflation often leads to a reduction in the length of time over which fixed-payment agreements are made. Thus the average maturity of fixed-coupon debt issued in periods of great inflationary uncertainty is usually less than in more stable times. Alternatively, debt with long maturity can be written with *variable-rate* (also known as *floating-rate*) interest. Such instruments provide long-term debt at short-term rates. Interest payments are allowed to vary, with each one determined by adding a fixed differential (e.g., 1%) to a specified base, such as the "prime rate" or the yield on a 90-day U.S. Treasury bill in the prior period. If short-term interest rates anticipate inflation reasonably well, such a security is at least a partial substitute for a fully indexed bond.

Inflation, if allowed to run rampant, with great uncertainty about the actual level, can threaten the entire structure of a monetary economy, and with it the whole financial sector. On the other hand, it can be controlled within limits, and financial instruments can be designed to avoid some of its serious side-effects.

Problems

1. An investor is considering purchase of a stock with risk characteristics that make an expected real rate of return of 5% appropriate. He expects the rate of inflation to continue at about 7% per year, believes that the stock will pay no dividends during the coming year, and thinks that it will sell for approximately $40 at the end of the year. How much should he be willing to pay for the stock if he intends to hold it for one year?

2. Why are the effects on borrowers and lenders likely to be different when actual inflation deviates from expected inflation?
3. Why might inflation (without indexation) lead to a shift of real wealth from the private to the public sector?
4. In 19X5 a U.S. Government bond due in 19X9 sold at a price that made its yield-to-maturity equal 10.5%. Does this imply that in 19X5 investors were predicting that inflation over the next four years would average 10.5% per year, more, or less? Why?
5. If net monetary debtors gain when inflation exceeds expectations, why doesn't everyone become a net monetary debtor?
6. Will someone who finances a home with a conventional fixed-rate mortgage gain if inflation is less than expected? What about someone who finances with a floating-rate (variable-rate) mortgage?
7. If the expected return on common stocks is 12% when no inflation is expected, and the figures in Table 10-4 represent sensitivities to changes in inflation in the future, what would be the expected return on stocks if inflation were expected to run at a rate of 10%? Is this consistent with market efficiency?
8. Commodity futures allow one to purchase a good such as wheat several months in advance of delivery. The values of contracts of this sort tend to rise with increases in the general level of prices. Given this, why doesn't everyone invest in commodity futures instead of common stocks, since stock prices have tended to fall with increases in the general level of prices? Should the average investor hold commodity futures, common stocks, or both?
9. Assume that the consensus expectation is that inflation over the coming year will run at a rate of 10% but you are convinced that it will be 8%. Assuming that the figures in Table 10-4 represent likely sensitivities to changes in inflation, what investments would be particularly attractive to you?
10. An investor has estimated that the current relationship among expected returns, beta values, and inflation sensitivities is:

$$E(R_i) = 6.0 + 4.0\beta_i - .2h_i^u$$

Stock A has a beta of 1.0 and provides no hedge against inflation. What should its expected return be? Stock B has a beta of 1.1; how sensitive to inflation would its return have to be to make its appropriate expected return equal to that of stock A?

APPENDIX 10-A

Expected Returns, Beta Values, and Inflation Hedging

In a world of uncertain inflation where investors are concerned with real returns, security prices could adjust until all securities and portfolios plotted on the "real Security Market Line" given in formula (10-5). To see how this relates to more traditional concepts, we make use of the approximation for converting nominal returns to real returns:

$$R_i^r \approx R_i - c \qquad \text{(10A-1)}$$
$$R_m^r \approx R_m - c \qquad \text{(10A-2)}$$

where:

R_i = the nominal return on security i
R_i^r = the real return on security i
c = the rate of inflation
R_m = the nominal return on the market portfolio
R_m^r = the real return on the market portfolio

We also use the following relationships (which come from the definition and construction of covariances and variances):

$$\text{cov}\,[(a - b), (c - d)] = \text{cov}\,(a, c) - \text{cov}\,(a, d)$$
$$- \text{cov}\,(b, c) + \text{cov}\,(b, d) \qquad \text{(10A-3)}$$
$$\text{var}\,(a - b) = \text{var}\,(a) - 2\,\text{cov}\,(a, b) + \text{var}\,(b) \qquad \text{(10A-4)}$$

From (10A-1) and (10A-2):

$$E(R_i^r) = E(R_i) - E(c)$$
$$E(R_m^r) = E(R_m) - E(c)$$

Substituting in (10-5):

$$E(R_i) - E(c) = Z^r + \beta_i^r[E(R_m) - E(c) - Z^r] \qquad \textbf{(10A-5)}$$

By definition:

$$\beta_i^r = \frac{\operatorname{cov}(R_i^r, R_m^r)}{\operatorname{var}(R_m^r)}$$

Using (10A-1) and (10A-2), we can write this as:

$$\beta_i^r = \frac{\operatorname{cov}[(R_i - c), (R_m - c)]}{\operatorname{var}(R_m^r)}$$

which can be converted, using (10A-3) and (10A-4), to:

$$\beta_i^r = \frac{\operatorname{cov}(R_i, R_m)}{\operatorname{var}(R_m^r)} - \frac{\operatorname{cov}(R_i, c)}{\operatorname{var}(R_m^r)} - \frac{\operatorname{cov}(R_m, c)}{\operatorname{var}(R_m^r)} + \frac{\operatorname{var}(c)}{\operatorname{var}(R_m^r)}$$

or

$$\beta_i^r = \frac{\operatorname{cov}(R_i, R_m)}{\operatorname{var}(R_m)} \cdot \frac{\operatorname{var}(R_m)}{\operatorname{var}(R_m^r)}$$
$$- \frac{\operatorname{cov}(R_i, c)}{\operatorname{var}(c)} \cdot \frac{\operatorname{var}(c)}{\operatorname{var}(R_m^r)}$$
$$+ \frac{\operatorname{var}(c) - \operatorname{cov}(R_m, c)}{\operatorname{var}(R_m^r)}$$

Substituting the definitions of β_i and h_i^u

$$\beta_i^r = \beta_i \frac{\operatorname{var}(R_m)}{\operatorname{var}(R_m^r)} - h_i^u \frac{\operatorname{var}(c)}{\operatorname{var}(R_m^r)}$$
$$+ \frac{\operatorname{var}(c) - \operatorname{cov}(R_m, c)}{\operatorname{var}(R_m^r)}$$

Substituting in (10A-5) and simplifying:

$$E(R_i) = \left\{ E(c) + Z^r \right.$$
$$+ [E(R_m) - E(c) - Z^r] \left[\frac{\operatorname{var}(c) - \operatorname{cov}(R_m, c)}{\operatorname{var}(R_m^r)} \right] \right\}$$
$$+ \left\{ [E(R_m) - E(c) - Z^r] \left[\frac{\operatorname{var}(R_m)}{\operatorname{var}(R_m^r)} \right] \right\} \beta_i$$
$$- \left\{ [E(R_m) - E(c) - Z^r] \left[\frac{\operatorname{var}(c)}{\operatorname{var}(R_m^r)} \right] \right\} h_i^u$$

Or, using the notation in (10-6):

$$E(R_i) = Z_i + Z_2\beta_i - Z_3 h_i^u$$

Note that:

$$\frac{Z_2}{Z_3} = \frac{\text{var } (R_m)}{\text{var } (c)}$$

and, since the variance of R_m is large (e.g., $400 = 20^2$) relative to that of c (e.g., $16 = 4^2$), Z_2 [the effect of β_i on $E(R_i)$] is likely to be considerably greater than Z_3 [the effect of h_i^y on $E(R_i)$].

Note also that if var $(c) = 0$, the formula simplifies to the zero-beta version of the traditional Capital Asset Pricing Model.

11

Fixed-Income Securities

INTRODUCTION

This chapter begins the analysis of particular kinds of securities. The goal is to survey the major types, with emphasis on those currently popular in the United States. Such a survey cannot be exhaustive. A security is, after all, a representation of rights to future prospects. The prospects of organizations differ, and with them the prospects represented by their securities. A firm may divide up its prospects among two or more groups of people by issuing more than one type of security. An organization may even be created solely to acquire some securities and issue others, thus rearranging prospects into related but different packages. The number of securities that can be created is thus great indeed. Which ones will be created? The answer depends on tastes, relevant risks, and government policies (among other things). Mere classification is difficult, enumeration of every possibility virtually out of the question.

FIXED-INCOME SECURITIES

The term "fixed-income" commonly used to cover the types of securities discussed in this chapter is a bit misleading. They have in common stated amounts to be paid and times of payment. Many have specified termination dates. However, all the terms are *promised*, not necessarily *realized*, or even *expected* (in the formal sense in which each possible outcome is weighted by its probability of occurrence). In many cases there is at least some risk that a promised payment will not be made in full and on time. In such instances the income is not fixed, only its upper limit.

SAVINGS DEPOSITS

Perhaps the most familiar type of fixed-income investment is the personal savings account at a bank, savings and loan company, or credit union. Such an account provides substantial or complete safety of principal, low probability of failure to receive interest, substantial liquidity, and (inevitably) relatively low return.

Commercial Banks

Almost everyone maintains a checking account in a commercial bank. Formally, these are termed *demand deposits*, since the depositor can remove his or her money on demand. Such an account has two quite different aspects. The bookkeeping required to support check-writing, deposits, and so on is costly. On the other hand, the balance in such an account is available to support interest-earning loans made by the bank. Within bounds set by regulations, banks offer terms for checking accounts that reflect these aspects. Customers with small balances who write many checks pay the bank; those with large balances who write few checks are paid by the bank. Often the two elements are identified separately, with *service charges* assessed for check-writing, and so on and *interest* paid on average balances. In some cases the amount of interest paid changes substantially if a minimum balance is maintained.

An alternative to a checking account is a standard *savings account*. Although a written request for a withdrawal may be required up to 30 days in advance, in practice requests for withdrawals are almost always honored on demand. Almost any amount may be invested in a savings account. No security is issued; instead, the current balance plus interest earned is posted to the bank's records and (if desired) to the depositor's "passbook."

Most banks also offer *negotiable order of withdrawal* (NOW) accounts, which pay interest and on which checks may be written. Credit unions offer services similar to NOW accounts, via *share draft accounts*, and many investment companies (described in Chapter 18) provide at least limited check-writing services.

The standard ("passbook") savings account is only one of many types of time deposits. A *single-maturity deposit* may be withdrawn at a stated maturity date (e.g., one year after the initial deposit). A *multiple-maturity deposit* may be withdrawn at a stated date or left for one or more periods of equal length (thus a 90-day multiple-maturity deposit can be withdrawn three, six, nine, . . . months after the deposit). In practice, both single- and multiple-maturity deposits can usually be withdrawn at any time, but at the cost of recomputing the interest earned, using a lower rate, and deducting the difference plus an additional penalty from the account balance.

Some types of time deposits may be made in almost any amount, while others may be made only in units of, say, $10,000 each. The latter may be represented by *certificates of deposit*, which clearly qualify to be called securities. Large-denomination certificates of deposit may be *negotiable*—i.e., the original depositor may sell the certificate to someone else before maturity. In most cases the certificate is equivalent to a transferable discount bond, since all interest is paid, along with the principal, at maturity.

Most bank accounts in the United States are insured by the *Federal Deposit Insurance Corporation*, a government agency that guarantees the payment of principal on any account up to a stated limit ($100,000 in 1984) if the bank is closed and liquidated. The FDIC, created in 1933, levies insurance premiums on its member banks and is authorized to borrow funds from the U.S. Treasury, if needed, although it has never done so. By opening certain kinds of multiple accounts, each with less than the limit, an investor can usually insure a considerable amount.

Savings and Loan Companies and Mutual Savings Bank

Savings and loan companies and mutual savings banks accept relatively short-term deposits, then use the money to make relatively long-term loans, primarily for home mortgages. All mutual savings banks, and many savings and loan companies, are nominally owned by their members, while other savings and loan companies (like commercial banks) are owned by stockholders who may or may not deposit funds or obtain loans there.

Savings and loan companies and mutual savings banks pay "dividends" instead of "interest." The distinction is more semantic than real, however. The Internal Revenue Service treats such payments as interest for tax purposes.

In the United States most accounts in savings companies are insured by a government agency—either the Federal Deposit Insurance Corporation or the Federal Savings and Loan Insurance Corporation (FSLIC). The principal of each account is insured up to the limit used for bank accounts, but here, too, judicious use of multiple accounts makes it possible to insure even more.

The terms offered by institutions of this type are similar to those offered by commercial banks.

Credit Unions

A credit union accepts deposits from employees of an organization and then loans these funds to other (or the same) employees of the organization. Typically, loans are relatively small and for relatively short terms (e.g., to finance the purchase of an automobile). Excess funds are invested in highly liquid short-term assets.

Each credit union is owned by its members, who elect a board of directors. Deposits are generally similar to passbook accounts in a bank or savings and loan company and also earn "dividends" instead of interest.

Deposits in all federally chartered credit unions are insured by the National Credit Union Administration (NCUA), a U.S. government agency that serves the same function as the Federal Deposit Insurance Corporation and the Federal Savings and Loan Insurance Corporation. The insurance coverage provided by all these agencies is identical in both amount and provisions.

Other Types of Personal Savings Accounts

A number of institutions similar to those described above can be found. For example, there are companies chartered to accept deposits and use the proceeds to make consumer loans. In some countries the government post office accepts savings deposits. Certain kinds of life insurance policies include a savings component, since payments often exceed the amount strictly required to cover the insurance involved. The "cash value" of such a policy may be obtained by cancellation; alternatively, some or all of it may be "borrowed" without canceling the policy. The implicit rate of return on the cash value of an insurance policy is typically quite low, reflecting the extremely low risk to the policyholder and the length of the insurance company's commitment.

DEREGULATION OF DEPOSITARY INSTITUTIONS

Until 1980, institutions accepting demand and time deposits in the United States were highly regulated. The Board of Governors of the Federal Reserve System, under "Regulation Q," established maximum limits on the amount of interest paid on various types of deposits, and nondepositary institutions were constrained from competing directly with banks, savings and loan companies, and the like for the savings of small investors.

The passage of the Depositary Institutions Deregulation and Monetary Control Act of 1980 began a series of changes designed to permanently alter such institutions. The intent is to make a formerly highly regulated industry highly competitive. While the transition has caused profound changes for certain institutions, the net effect in the long run should be a more efficient industry.

When deregulation began, it was widely feared that interest rates charged borrowers by depositary institutions would rise as competition brought increases in the "cost of funds." However, both theoretical and empirical arguments suggest that the fear was unjustified.

Under Regulation Q, interest paid on "small" deposits (e.g., up to $100,000) was limited (to, say, 5%), while that paid on large deposits was typically determined by competitive forces. Figures 11-1 show the effects of such constraints on the supply of deposits under the assumption that small savers have no available alternatives for the investment

FIGURE 11-1
Effects of Deregulation on Interest Rates

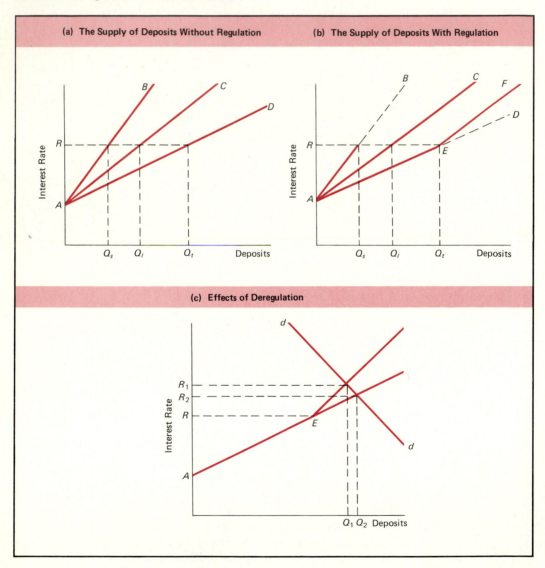

of such funds. In Figure 11-1a curve AB shows the amount of funds supplied by small savers at various interest rates, while curve AC shows the amounts supplied by large savers. For example, at rate of interest R, small savers will deposit Q_s and large savers will deposit Q_l dollars. Curve AD shows the total amount deposited for each interest rate. For example, at interest rate R, the total amount is Q_t, which equals $Q_s + Q_l$. In the absence of regulation, as shown in Figure 11-1(a) curve AD is the *supply curve* of funds for depositary institutions.

Now assume that interest paid small savers is limited to $R\%$. At lower interest rates, nothing is changed. But if more than Q_t funds are wanted, depositary institutions must raise rates paid to large savers. The supply curve is thus AEF in Figure 11-1(b), not AED (as before).

Figure 11-1(c) shows the impact of deregulation under such conditions. Curve dd shows the demand for funds, which reflects returns on loans and investments available to depositary institutions. Initially, Q_1 funds are deposited, with small investors paid R (the regulatory maximum) and large institutions paid R_1. Borrowers are charged R_1—the *marginal* cost of funds. After deregulation, the rate paid large investors falls to R_2 and the rate paid small investors rises (also to R_2) the new marginal cost of funds, with the total amount deposited increasing to Q_2.

Figure 11-2 shows that rates charged borrowers did indeed reflect the marginal cost of funds. The dotted curve plots the rates paid on large (generally unregulated) certificates of deposit, while the lower solid curve shows the "passbook" rates paid on small (regulated) deposits. The upper solid curve shows the "prime rate" on which most commercial loans were based. Here, as elsewhere, prices were set "at the margin."

In practice, the effect of deregulation on rates charged borrowers was relatively small because, prior to 1980, small savers were not precluded entirely from placing funds in depositary institutions at high interest rates. Investment companies known as *money market funds* accepted funds from small investors and used the proceeds to buy large certificates of deposit from banks. Such investment companies, many operated by brokerage firms, provided a convenient means for circumventing the spirit (but not the letter) of the regulatory restrictions. Some even offered check-writing privileges, seriously threatening to turn banks into wholesale rather than retail depositary institutions.

Regulation could limit interest rates paid small savers to levels somewhat below free-market rates, but when the gap increased as interest rates rose in response to increased inflation, the system broke down. Officers of many banks and savings and loan companies decided that regulated savings rates were hurting rather than helping them. The political process responded, and small savers can now avoid the bother and added expense of using an intermediary institution to obtain an appropriate rate of interest on their deposits.

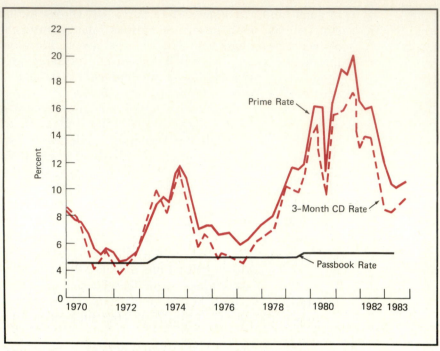

SOURCE: *Federal Reserve Bank of San Francisco Weekly Letter,* January 13, 1984.

FIGURE 11-2
Interest Rates and Costs of Funds

MONEY MARKET INSTRUMENTS

Certain types of short-term, highly marketable loans play a major role in the investment and borrowing activities of operating corporations and financial intermediaries. Individual investors with substantial funds may invest in such instruments directly, but most do so indirectly via accounts at banks or savings and loans, or money market funds.

Some money market instruments are negotiable and are traded in active secondary markets; others are not. Some may be purchased by anyone with adequate funds, others only by particular types of institutions. Many are sold on a discount basis—e.g., a $100,000 90-day note might be sold for $98,000, the difference representing interest payable at maturity. Interest rates are usually reported on a bank discount basis. Such a note might be described as having a discount of 2% per quarter, or 8% per year. Of course, the true interest rate on the funds involved is higher—in this case, 2,000/98,000 or 2.04% per quarter, equivalent to 8.41% per year with quarterly compounding.

Short-term obligations of the U.S. government and its agencies are also considered money market instruments; they will be described in the next section.

Bankers' Acceptances

Historically, bankers' acceptances were created to finance goods in transit. In such a transaction the buyer of the goods promises to pay a given sum within a short period of time (e.g., 180 days or less). A bank then "accepts" this promise, obligating itself to pay the amount of the note if requested, and obtaining in return a claim on the goods as security. The note representing the loan becomes a liability of both the bank and the buyer of the goods and is thus subject to very low risk of default.

Some bankers' acceptances are created as a by-product of short-term loans by banks to corporations for working capital, with no underlying goods as security. Others are used to create dollar exchange for international trade. All represent joint obligations of the original borrower and the accepting bank. An indication of the low risk involved is provided by the promised interest rates on such instruments: they are usually only 1% or 2% higher than those of U.S. Treasury instruments of equal duration (e.g., 9%, compared to 8%).

Negotiable Certificates of Deposits

These are certificates representing time deposits at commercial banks or savings and loan associations. Issued in denominations of $100,000 or more, with a specified maturity, such "CD's" are highly marketable and compare in risk and return with bankers' acceptances. Such certificates are insured, but only for the maximum amount ($100,000 in 1984).

Commercial Paper

This term refers to unsecured short-term promissory notes issued by corporations, finance companies, or banks. Many notes of this type are issued by large firms with open lines of bank credit, making it highly likely that the loan will be paid off when it becomes due. Interest rates reflect this: rates of "prime commercial paper" are normally close to those of CD's and bankers' acceptances.

Commercial paper is usually issued in denominations of $100,000 or more, with maturities of up to 270 days (the maximum allowed by the Securities and Exchange Commission without registration). Such paper is generally not negotiable, but the issuer may be willing to prepay the note (perhaps by issuing another) if necessary.

Federal Funds

Banks that belong to the Federal Reserve System must maintain specified reserves in Federal Reserve Banks. However, no interest is paid on any excess. As a result, much activity is devoted to overnight "loans" from banks with excess reserves to those with deficiencies. The interest rate on such loans is termed the *Federal Funds rate*. While it cannot diverge substantially or for long from rates available to the general public, the fact that it applies to very short-term loans within a limited community leads to a certain amount of seemingly erratic behavior.

Brokers' Call Loans

When an individual buys securities "on margin," he or she borrows money from a broker to finance part of the purchase. The broker, in turn, borrows money from a bank, using the securities as collateral and promising to repay the loan "on call" at any time the bank requests it (although such an occurrence is rare). The rate charged on such loans is 1% to 2% greater than short-term rates on U.S. Treasury bills; the broker adds a small amount to determine the interest charged the customer for the margin loan.

Eurodollars

In the rarefied atmosphere of international finance, large short-term loans on deposits are often made in dollars to or through banks outside the United States. The demand and supply conditions for such loans may differ from those for other U.S. money market instruments, owing to restrictions imposed (or likely to be imposed) by the United States and other governments. However, enough commonality exists to keep interest rates from diverging too much from those available on domestic alternatives.

Analysts refer to transactions of this sort in a number of ways. Popular terms include the "Eurodollar," "Asian Dollar," and "Petrodollar" markets, although none is very well defined.

U.S. GOVERNMENT SECURITIES

It should come as no surprise that the U.S. government relies heavily on debt financing. Revenues seldom cover expenses, and the difference is financed primarily by issuing debt instruments. Moreover, old debt issues come due and new ones must be sold to obtain needed funds. Some refunding is done in kind, with holders of maturing or other issues exchanging them directly for new issues, and often receiving beneficial treatment for tax purposes for doing so. One way or another, the U.S. Treasury is omnipresent in the capital market.

Some idea of the magnitude and the ownership of this debt can be gained from Table 11-1. The government itself is a large holder, as is the Federal Reserve System. However, a large amount is held by nongovernment organizations and individuals. These securities are a major factor in the portfolios of commercial banks and other financial institutions. Operating corporations also use them, primarily as outlets for relatively short-term excess working capital. The amount held by individuals is also substantial, with over half the total being invested in savings bonds and notes.

Over two-thirds of the public debt is marketable—i.e., represented by securities that can be sold by the original purchaser. The major nonmarketable issues are held by government agencies, foreign governments, and individuals (the latter in the form of U.S. Savings Bonds). Marketable issues include Treasury bills, notes, and bonds. Table 11-2 shows the amounts in each category in 1982.

The maturity structure of the debt is influenced by a number of factors. As time passes, of course, the time to maturity of an outstanding issue will decrease. Moreover, the Treasury has considerable latitude in selecting maturities for new issues and can also engage in refunding operations. From time to time, legislative limits on amounts issued or

TABLE 11-1
Ownership of Outstanding U.S. Public Debt, December 1982

Held By	Amount ($ Billions)	
U.S. government accounts		209.4
Federal Reserve banks		139.3
Private investors:		
Commercial banks	131.4	
Money market funds	42.6	
Insurance companies	39.1	
Corporations	24.5	
State and local governments	113.4	
Individuals	116.5	
Foreign and international	149.5	
Other investors (including government-sponsored agencies, savings and loan associations, corporate pension funds, etc.)	231.4	
		848.4
		1,197.1

SOURCE: *U.S. Treasury Bulletin*, Winter Issue, First Quarter 1984.

TABLE 11-2
Interest-Bearing Public Debt, December 1982

Category	Amount ($ Billions)	
Nonmarketable:		
Government account series	205.4	
U.S. Savings Bonds	67.7	
Foreign series	14.7	
Other	26.2	
		314.0
Marketable:		
Bills	311.8	
Notes	465.0	
Bonds	104.6	
		881.5
		1,195.5

SOURCE: *U.S. Treasury Bulletin*, Winter Issue, First Quarter 1984.

interest paid on certain types of instruments may force reliance on other types. Debt operations may also be employed as a conscious instrument of policy in an attempt to influence the term structure of interest rates.

Table 11-3 shows the maturity structure of marketable interest-bearing debt in 1982. The average maturity was three years and ten months.

A great many types of debt have been issued by the federal government and by government agencies and organizations sponsored by the federal government. Figure 11-3 shows a typical list of price quota-

TABLE 11-3
Maturity Distribution of Marketable
Interest-Bearing U.S. Public Debt Held by
Private Investors, December 1982

Maturity	Amount ($ Billions)
Within 1 year	346.3
1-5 years	239.3
5-10 years	77.6
10-20 years	35.7
20 years and over	37.3

SOURCE: *U.S. Treasury Bulletin*, Winter Issue, First Quarter 1984.

Fixed-Income Securities

Treasury Issues/*Bonds, Notes & Bills*

Friday, May 25, 1984

Mid-afternoon Over-the-Counter quotations; sources on request.

Decimals in bid-and-asked and bid changes represent 32nds; 101.1 means 101 1/32. a-Plus 1/64. b-Yield to call date. d-Minus 1/64. n-Treasury notes.

Treasury Bonds and Notes

Rate	Mat.	Date	Bid	Asked	Bid Chg.	Yld.
13¾s,	1984	May n	100	100.4	– .2	0.00
8⅞s,	1984	Jun n	99.25	99.29	....	9.63
14⅜s,	1984	Jun n	100.8	100.12	– .1	9.38
13⅛s,	1984	Jul n	100.13	100.17	– .1	9.54
6⅜s,	1984	Aug	99.1	99.17	....	8.47
7¼s,	1984	Aug n	99.7	99.11	– .1	10.21
11⅝s,	1984	Aug n	100.4	100.8	....	10.31
13¼s,	1984	Aug n	100.14	100.18	– .2	10.14
12⅛s,	1984	Sep n	100.8	100.12	....	10.75
9¾s,	1984	Oct n	99.10	99.14	....	11.07
9⅞s,	1984	Nov n	99.7	99.11	....	11.25
14⅜s,	1984	Nov n	101.9	101.13	– .1	11.09
16s,	1984	Nov n	102.1	102.5	– .1	11.00
9⅜s,	1984	Dec n	98.24	98.28	....	11.41
14s,	1984	Dec n	101.11	101.15	– .1	11.35
9¼s,	1985	Jan n	98.13	98.17	– .1	11.58
8s,	1985	Feb n	97.16	97.20	– .2	11.56
9⅝s,	1985	Feb n	98.13	98.17	– .2	11.71
14⅝s,	1985	Feb n	101.25	101.29	– .1	11:77
9⅝s,	1985	Mar	98.5	98.9	– .2	11.84
13⅜s,	1985	Mar n	101.4	101.8	– .3	11.77
9½s,	1985	Apr n	97.28	98	– .3	11.86
3¼s,	1985	May	94.5	95.5	+ .1	8.61
4¼s,	1975-85	May	94.4	95.4	– .1	9.69
9⅞s,	1985	May n	97.28	98	– .3	12.05
10⅜s,	1985	May n	98.21	98.25	– .2	11.75
14⅛s,	1985	May n	101.23	101.27	– .2	12.03
14⅜s,	1985	May n	101.31	102.3	– .3	12.00
14s,	1985	Jun n	101.24	101.28	– .3	12.11
10s,	1985	Jun n	97.25	97.29	– .3	12.11
10⅝s,	1985	Jul n	98.7	98.11	– .3	12.18
8¼s,	1985	Aug n	96.5	96.9	+ .1	11.62
9⅝s,	1985	Aug n	97.3	97.7	– .3	12.16
10⅝s	1985	Aug n	97.31	98.3	[illegible]	12.31
13⅛s,	1985	Aug n	100.24	100.28	– .4	12.33
10⅞s,	1985	Sep n	98.8	98.12	– .3	12.23
15⅞s,	1985	Sep n	104.7	104.11	– .4	12.26
10½s,	1985	Oct n	97.20	97.24	– .4	12.27
9¾s,	1985	Nov n	96.19	96.23	– .3	12.27
10½s,	1985	Nov n	97.11	97.15	– .3	12.40
11¾s,	1985	Nov n	99.10	99.14	– .3	12.18
10⅞s,	1985	Dec n	97.21	97.25	– .2	12.45
14⅛s,	1985	Dec n	102.4	102.8	– .1	12.52
10⅝s,	1986	Jan n	97.6	97.10	– .3	12.45
10⅞s,	1986	Feb n	97.12	97.14	– .3	12.55
13½s,	1986	Feb n	101.9	101.13	– .2	12.56
9⅞s,	1986	Feb n	95.26	95.30	– .2	12.58
14s,	1986	Mar n	102.4	102.8	– .2	12.59
11½s,	1986	Mar n	98.3	98.5	– .2	12.65
11¾s,	1986	Apr n	98.13	98.15	– .1	12.67
7⅞s,	1986	May n	91.30	92.2	....	12.57
9⅜s,	1986	May n	94.9	94.13	....	12.69
12⅝s,	1986	May n	99.24	99.26	....	12.73
13¾s,	1986	May n	101.24	101.28	– .1	12.64
14⅞s,	1986	Jun n	103.25	103.29	– .1	12.68
8s,	1986	Aug n	91.3	91.7	– .1	12.67
11⅜s,	1986	Aug n	97.9	97.13	– .1	12.75
12¼s,	1986	Sep n	98.29	99.1	– .2	12.74
6⅛s,	1986	Nov	89.2	90.2	+ .2	10.83
11s,	1986	Nov n	96.7	96.11	– .1	12.78
13⅞s,	1986	Nov n	102	102.4	– .2	12.84
16⅛s,	1986	Nov n	106.16	106.24	– .4	12.84
10s,	1986	Dec n	93.25	93.29	– .2	12.84
9s,	1987	Feb n	91.5	91.9	– .1	12.90
10⅞s,	1987	Feb n	95.8	95.12	– .2	12.95
12¾s,	1987	Feb n	99.14	99.18	– .2	12.94
10¼s,	1987	Mar n	93.17	93.21	– .2	13.00
12s,	1987	May n	97.27	97.31	– .2	12.85
12½s,	1987	May n	98.22	98.24	– .2	13.02
14s,	1987	May n	102.4	102.8	– .3	13.06
10½s,	1987	Jun n	93.14	93.18	– .3	13.10
13¾s,	1987	Aug n	101.15	101.19	– .3	13.13
11⅛s,	1987	Sep n	94.26	94.30	– .3	13.04
7⅝s,	1987	Nov n	85.29	86.5	– .2	12.69
12⅝s,	1987	Nov n	98.19	98.23	– .2	13.10
11¼s,	1987	Dec n	94.20	94.24	– .2	13.14
12⅜s,	1988	Jan n	97.22	97.26	– .2	13.15
10⅛s,	1988	Feb n	90.31	91.3	– .3	13.24
12s,	1988	Mar n	96.7	96.9	– .5	13.27
13¼s,	1988	Apr n	100.1	100.5	– .4	13.20
8¼s,	1988	May n	85.2	85.10	– .3	13.12
9⅞s,	1988	May n	89.19	89.22	– .3	13.31
14s,	1988	Jul n	102.3	102.11	– .3	13.24
10½s,	1988	Aug n	90.27	90.31	– .4	13.37
15⅜s,	1988	Oct n	106.21	106.29	– .6	13.25
8¾s,	1988	Nov n	85.6	85.14	– .5	13.17
11¾s,	1988	Nov n	94.18	94.22	– .3	13.37
14⅝s,	1989	Jan n	103.25	103.29	– .7	13.46
11⅜s,	1989	Feb n	92.24	92.28	– .7	13.46
14⅜s,	1989	Apr n	102.29	103.1	– .9	13.51
9¼s,	1989	May n	85.10	85.18	– .5	13.32
11¾s,	1989	May n	93.26	93.30	– .6	13.47
14½s,	1989	Jul n	103.13	103.17	– .3	13.53
11⅞s,	1989	Oct n	93.29	94.5	– .5	13.43
10¾s,	1989	Nov n	89.13	89.17	– .5	13.52
10½s,	1990	Jan n	88.2	88.10	– .5	13.53
3½s,	1990	Feb	89.12	90.12	– .4	5.49
10½s,	1990	Apr n	87.23	87.31	– .5	13.53
8¼s,	1990	May	79.6	79.22	– .5	13.29
10¾s,	1990	Jul n	88.7	88.11	– .5	13.62
10¾s,	1990	Aug n	88.7	88.15	– .5	13.56
11½s,	1990	Oct n	91.6	91.10	– .5	13.58
13s,	1990	Nov n	97.18	97.22	– .5	13.56
11¾s,	1991	Jan n	91.27	91.31	– .9	13.63
12⅜s,	1991	Apr	94.13	94.17	– .6	13.63
14½s,	1991	May n	103.17	103.25	– .8	13.64
14⅞s,	1991	Aug n	105.9	105.17	– .8	13.65
14¼s,	1991	Nov n	102.13	102.21	– .10	13.67
14⅝s,	1992	Feb n	104.1	104.9	– .6	13.71
13¾s,	1992	May n	100.1	100.9	– .6	13.69
4¼s,	1987-92	Aug	89.14	90.14	+ .5	5.73
7¼s,	1992	Aug	69.18	70.2	+ .1	13.37
10½s,	1992	Nov n	84.4	84.8	– .7	13.70
4s,	1988-93	Feb	89.21	90.21	+ .2	5.36
6¾s,	1993	Feb	66.18	67.2	– .1	13.23
7⅞s,	1993	Feb	70.22	70.30	– .7	13.69
10⅞s,	1993	Feb n	85.22	85.26	– .4	13.71
10⅛s,	1993	May n	81.23	81.27	– .4	13.71
7½s,	1988-93	Aug	68.6	68.22	– .8	13.55
8⅝s,	1993	Aug	73.28	74.4	– .3	13.64
11⅞s,	1993	Aug n	90.12	90.16	– .6	13.72
8⅝s,	1993	Nov	73.9	73.17	– .8	13.70
11¾s,	1993	Nov	89.20	89.24	– .8	13.72
13⅛s,	1994	May	96.22	96.24	– .6	13.73
9s,	1994	Feb	74.27	75.3	.7	13.72
4⅛s,	1989-94	May	89.12	90.12	– .1	5.39
8¾s,	1994	Aug	73	73.8	– .7	13.68
10⅛s,	1994	Nov	80.8	80.16	– .6	13.68
3s,	1995	Feb	89.12	90.12	+ .1	4.12
10½s,	1995	Feb	82.5	82.13	– 1.7	13.67
10⅜s,	1995	May	81.8	81.16	– .6	13.69
12⅝s,	1995	May	93.25	94.1	– .9	13.69
11½s,	1995	Nov	87.10	87.18	– .2	13.68
7s,	1993-98	May	59.16	60	– .16	13.41
3½s,	1998	Nov	89.10	90.10	+ .1	4.41
8½s,	1994-99	May	66.30	67.14	– .8	13.67
7⅞s,	1995-00	Feb	62.20	62.28	– .9	13.69
8⅜s,	1995-00	Aug	65.18	65.26	– .6	13.67
11¾s,	2001	Feb	86.24	87	– .9	13.75
13⅛s,	2001	May	96.2	96.10	– .7	13.68
8s,	1996-01	Aug	62.11	62.19	– .13	13.71
13⅜s,	2001	Aug	97.14	97.22	– .13	13.73
15¾s,	2001	Nov	116.7	116.15	– .12	13.30
14¼s,	2002	Feb	103.8	103.16	– .6	13.72
11⅝s,	2002	Nov	85.22	85.30	– 1.8	13.74
10¾s,	2003	Feb	79.23	79.31	– .5	13.75
10¾s,	2003	May	79.24	80	– .5	13.74
11⅛s,	2003	Aug	82.2	82.10	– .9	13.76
11⅞s,	2003	Nov	87.16	87.24	– .8	13.69
12⅜s,	2004	May	90.20	90.28	– .8	13.73
8¼s,	2000-05	May	62.21	62.29	– .7	13.65
7⅝s,	2002-07	Feb	58.31	59.7	+ .2	13.38
7⅞s,	2002-07	Nov	60.1	60.9	– .7	13.50
8⅜s,	2003-08	Aug	63.7	63.15	– .2	13.53
8¾s,	2003-08	Nov	65.14	65.22	– .1	13.61
9⅛s,	2004-09	May	67.27	68.3	– .1	13.65
10⅜s,	2004-09	Nov	76.13	76.21	– .3	13.68
11¾s,	2005-10	Feb	86.5	86.13	– .4	13.67
10s,	2005-10	May	73.22	73.30	– .4	13.69
12¾s,	2005-10	Nov	93.4	93.12	– .4	13.68
13⅞s,	2006-11	May	101.5	101.13	– .7	13.67
14s,	2006-11	Nov	102.3	102.11	– .8	13.66
10⅜s,	2007-12	Nov	76.10	76.18	– .3	13.65
12s,	2008-13	Aug	87.27	87.31	+ .2	13.68
13¼s,	2014	May	96.21	96.25	+ .2	13.70

U.S. Treas. Bills

Mat. date	Bid (Discount)	Asked (Discount)	Yield
1984-			
5-31	2.00	1.00	1.01
6- 7	7.92	7.74	7.86
6-14	8.75	8.67	8.82
6-21	8.71	8.63	8.80
6-28	8.18	8.10	8.27
7- 5	9.13	9.05	9.26
7-12	9.17	9.09	9.32
7-19	9.12	9.06	9.30
7-26	9.26	9.20	9.47
8- 2	9.52	9.46	9.76
8- 9	9.67	9.61	9.93
8-16	9.66	9.60	9.94
8-23	9.58	9.54	9.90
8-30	9.74	9.66	10.04
9- 6	9.82	9.74	10.15
9-13	9.88	9.82	10.25
9-20	9.95	9.87	10.33
9-27	9.97	9.91	10.39
10- 4	10.07	10.01	10.52
10-11	10.12	10.06	10.60
10-18	10.21	10.15	10.72
10-25	10.24	10.18	10.77
11- 1	10.36	[illegible]	[illegible]
11- 8	10.41	10.31	10.96
11-15	10.39	10.31	10.99
11-24	10.40	10.36	11.07
11-29	10.48	10.42	11.15
12-27	10.38	10.32	11.05
1985-			
1-24	10.32	10.26	11.02
2-21	10.64	10.60	10.46
3-21	10.72	10.66	10.59
4-18	10.75	10.69	10.69
5-16	10.78	10.76	11.85

FIGURE 11-3
Price Quotations for U.S. Treasury Securities

tions for such securities. Each type will be discussed in the sections that follow.

U.S. Treasury Bills

Treasury bills are issued on a discount basis, with maturities of up to one year. Offerings of three-month and six-month bills are usually made once each week; twelve-month bills are usually offered at the end of each month. All are sold by auction. Bids may be entered on either a *competitive* or *noncompetitive* basis. For example, a buyer may enter a bid for a stated number of three-month bills at a price of 98.512. If the bid is accepted, he or she will pay $985.12 for each $1,000 of par value—i.e., an investment of $985.12 will generate a receipt of $1,000 if held to maturity three months later.

The Treasury accepts a number of competitive bids at every auction, filling each one in whole or in part at the price entered on the bid. A quantity-weighted average is also computed, and all noncompetitive bids are filled in whole or in part at this price. The yield obtained by the purchaser is, of course, a function of the price paid. Reported yields on Treasury bills are usually stated on a bank discount basis.

Treasury bills are generally issued in denominations of $10,000 or more, although at times denominations as small as $1,000 have been offered. All are issued in *book-entry form*—the buyer receives a receipt at time of purchase and the face value at maturity.

Individuals may purchase new issues of Treasury bills directly from one of the Federal Reserve banks or indirectly via a bank or broker. Government security dealers maintain an active secondary market in bills, and it is a simple matter to buy or sell one prior to maturity (especially if the original purchase was through a bank or broker). Terms offered by government security dealers are reported daily in the financial press, stated on a discount basis. For example, a bill with 120 days left to maturity might be listed as "7.48% bid, 7.19% ask." To determine the relevant prices, one need only "undo" the bank discount computation. For example, the bid discount of 7.48% was obtained by dividing the actual discount by 120/360 (the portion of a 360-day year involved). To find the actual discount, merely multiply:

$$7.48 \times \frac{120}{360} = 2.493$$

The dealer is bidding $100 - 2.493 = \$97.507$ per $100 of par values; this is the price he or she will pay to buy such a bill. On the other hand, the dealer is offering to sell such a bill at $97.603 per $100 of par value, as can be seen by repeating the calculation using 7.19%. The difference between the prices—the dealer's spread—is compensation for carrying inventories of bills, taking associated risks, and bearing the clerical and other costs associated with market-making.

In addition to the bid and asked discounts, the *Wall Street Journal* provides an equivalent yield. As shown in Figure 11-1, the quotations on May 25, 1984, for a bill maturing on September 27. 1984 were:

Bid Discount	Asked	Yield
9.97	9.91	10.39

indicating that the equivalent annual yield was 10.39%.

Although Treasury bills are sold at discount, their yield is treated as interest for tax purposes.

U.S. Treasury Notes

Treasury notes are issued with maturities from one to ten years and generally pay interest semiannually. Some, issued prior to 1983, are in *bearer* form, with interest coupons attached; the owner simply submits each coupon on its specified date to receive the interest due. Beginning in 1983, the Treasury ceased the issuance of bearer notes and bonds. All new issues are now in *registered* form; the current owner is registered with the Treasury, which sends him or her each interest payment when due and the principal value at maturity. When a registered note is sold, the new owner's name and address are substituted for that of the old owner on the Treasury's books.

Treasury notes are issued in denominations of $1,000 or more. Coupon rates are set so the notes will initially sell close to par value. In most cases an auction is held, with both competitive and noncompetitive bids.

Treasury notes are traded in an active secondary market made by dealers in U.S. government securities. For example, as shown in Figure 11-1, the *Wall Street Journal* carried the following quotation in May 1984:

Rate	Mat. Date	Bid	Asked	Bid Chg.	Yld.
8s	1986 August n	91.3	91.7	−.1	12.67

This indicated that a note (n) maturing in August 1986 could be sold to a dealer for $91\frac{3}{32}$ (i.e., $91.09375) per $100 of par value; alternatively, such a note could be purchased from a dealer for 91$\frac{7}{32}$ (i.e., $91.21875) per $100 of par value. (The custom of expressing the fractional part in terms of $\frac{1}{32}$'s has outlived its usefulness but lingers on nonetheless.) On the day in question the bid price was $\frac{1}{32}$ less than it had been on the previous trading day. The note in question entitles its owner to receive $8 per $100 of par value each year, in semiannual payments of $4 each. The effective yield-to-maturity at the time was, of course, greater. Based on the asked price, it came to approximately 12.67% per year.

In practice, the situation is a little more complicated. The buyer is generally expected to pay the seller not only the stated price, but also any *accrued interest*. For example, if four months has elapsed since the last interest payment, an amount equal to four-sixths of the semiannual payment is added to the stated purchase price to determine the total amount required. This procedure is commonly followed with both government and corporate bonds.

U.S. Treasury Bonds

Treasury bonds have maturities greater than ten years at time of issue. Those issued prior to 1983 may be in either bearer or registered form; more recent issues will be in registered form. Denominations range from $1,000 upward. Unlike Treasury notes, some Treasury bond issues are *callable* during a specified period (usually five to ten years prior to maturity); during this period the Treasury has the right to force redemption at par value at any scheduled interest-payment date. Callable issues are identified by stating the range of years during which the call can be exercised instead of a single maturity date. Thus the 7½'s of 1988-93 mature in 1993 but may be called beginning in 1988. For callable issues, yield-to-maturity is calculated on the assumption that the bond is called at the earliest allowed date.

Dealers' bid and asked quotations for Treasury bonds in the secondary market are stated in the same form used for Treasury notes.

Some bonds, initially issued in times of low interest rates, have been designated as acceptable *at par* for payment of federal estate taxes under certain conditions. Since they would otherwise sell at considerable discounts in times of high interest rates, such bonds represent attractive investments for wealthy individuals in danger of an early demise. Known in the trade as *flower bonds*, such issues are priced to reflect their unique advantage, and they constitute a relatively unattractive investment for one who enjoys good health or lacks a substantial estate. Relatively few of these bonds remain outstanding, and no new issues provide this curious feature.

U.S. Savings Bonds

These nonmarketable bonds are offered only to individuals and selected organizations. No more than a specified amount (e.g., $15,000 of issue price) may be purchased by any person in a single year. Two types are available. Series EE bonds are essentially discount bonds; no interest is paid prior to maturity. The time to maturity is changed from time to time; for bonds issued in 1984 it was ten years. Series HH bonds mature in ten years and pay interest semiannually. Both types are registered. Series EE bonds are available in small denominations (beginning at $50 par value) and may be purchased from commercial banks and many other institutions or obtained via payroll savings plans. Series HH bonds are available only in exchange for eligible Series EE (or the earlier Series E) bonds and must be obtained from the Treasury Department or Federal Reserve banks.

Series EE bonds issued in 1984 utilize a *floating rate* with a *minimum floor*. For bonds held more than five years, interest is paid at a rate equal to (1) 85% of the average market return on Treasury bonds and notes with five years remaining to maturity or (2) 7.5% per year, whichever is larger. The applicable rate is computed and compounded every six months. Series HH bonds issued in 1984 provide a fixed annual rate of 7.5%.

The terms on which savings bonds are offered have been revised from time to time. In some cases improved terms have been offered to holders of outstanding bonds. Terms have often been inferior to those available on less well-known or less accessible instruments with similar characteristics. At such times the Treasury Department sells savings bonds by appealing more to patriotism than to the desire for high return.

FEDERAL AGENCY SECURITIES

There is nothing simple about the government of the United States. While much of its activity is supported directly, via taxes and debt issued by the Treasury Department, much is financed in other ways. Some government departments issue securities to support their own activities. Others provide explicit or implicit support for the securities of quasi-governmental agencies. Some of these arrangements are so convoluted that cynics suggest that the original legislative intent was to obscure the nature and extent of governmental support. In any event, a wide range of bonds with different degrees of government backing has been created in this manner, many considered second in safety only to the debt obligations of the U.S. government itself.

Table 11-4 lists several major securities of this type and the

TABLE 11-4
Interest-Bearing Securities Issued by Government Agencies and Government-Sponsored Institutions Outstanding in December 1982

Interest-Bearing Securities of Government Agencies	Amount Outstanding ($ Millions)
Defense Department: Family Housing and Homeowner's Assistance	354
Federal Housing Administration	288
Government National Mortgage Association	2,165
Export-Import Bank of the U.S.	41
Postal Service	250
Tennessee Valley Authority	1,725
Other	1
	4,824

Interest-Bearing Securities of Nongovernment Agencies	
Farm Credit Banks	65,014
Banks for Cooperatives	220
Federal Home Loan Banks	104,188
Federal Intermediate Credit Banks	926
Federal Land Banks	6,813
Federal National Mortgage Association	84,502
Student Loan Marketing Association	1,591
	263,254

SOURCE: *U.S. Treasury Bulletin*, Winter Issue, First Quarter 1984.

amounts outstanding in 1982. A typical list of price quotations is shown in Figure 11-4.

Bonds of Government Agencies

Bonds issued by government agencies provide funds for support of housing (either through direct loans or the purchase of existing mortgages), export and import activities (via loans, credit guarantees, and insurance), the postal service, and the activities of the Tennessee Valley Authority. Many issues are guaranteed by the full faith and credit of the U.S. government, but some (e.g., those of the Tennessee Valley Authority) are not.

Bonds of Government-Sponsored Agencies

Government-sponsored agencies that issue securities have been established to support the granting of credit to farmers, homeowners, and the like. A common procedure involves the creation of a series of banks

Government, Agency and Miscellaneous Securities

Friday, May 25, 1984

Representative mid-afternoon Over-the-Counter quotations supplied by the Federal Reserve Bank of New York City, based on transactions of $1 million or more.

Decimals in bid-and-asked and bid changes represent 32nds; 101.1 means 101 1/32. a-Plus 1/64. b-Yield to call date. d-Minus 1/64. n-Treasury notes.

FNMA Issues

Rate	Mat	Bid	Asked	Yld
6.25	6-84	99.26	99.30	7.90
9.25	6-84	99.28	100	8.87
8.20	7-84	99.22	99.26	9.56
9.05	7-84	99.23	99.27	10.09
11.10	8-84	99.30	100.2	10.43
7.95	9-84	99.3	99.7	10.63
9.75	9-84	99.17	99.21	10.78
10.05	9-84	99.19	99.23	10.84
11.70	10-84	100	100.4	11.16
14.90	10-84	101.2	101.6	11.27
17.20	11-84	102.13	102.17	11.23
6.90	12-84	97.30	98.2	10.74
7.55	12-84	98	98.4	11.28
15.05	12-84	101.19	101.23	11.59
9.90	1-85	98.29	99.1	11.54
17.00	2-85	103.10	103.14	11.66
7.65	3-85	97.1	97.5	11.51
14.25	3-85	101.22	101.26	11.69
13.75	4-85	101.13	101.15	11.86
11.30	5-85	99.6	99.8	12.14
15.25	5-85	102.17	102.21	12.17
8.60	6-85	96.20	96.24	12.04
9.95	6-85	97.30	98.2	12.00
7.25	7-85	94.26	95.2	12.10
15.65	7-85	103.14	103.16	12.16
14.10	8-85	101.22	101.26	12.38
15.00	9-85	102.27	102.31	12.37
7.90	10-85	94.19	94.23	12.20
8.80	10-85	95.22	95.26	12.20
10.15	10-85	97.12	97.16	12.17
13.00	11-85	100.20	100.24	12.41
14.90	12-85	103.3	103.7	12.51
13.00	1-86	100.13	100.21	12.51
11.70	2-86	98.14	98.22	12.55
8.20	3-86	92.25	93.1	12.67
9.50	3-86	94.25	95.1	12.68
10.95	4-86	97.1	97.5	12.69
9.20	4-86	94.1	94.9	12.73
11.00	5-86	96.24	97	12.78
14.63	6-86	102.21	102.29	12.94
7.95	7-86	90.19	90.27	13.03
14.30	7-86	102.8	102.16	12.89
13.90	8-86	101.12	101.20	13.00
7.90	9-86	89.29	90.1	13.08
13.25	9-86	100.10	100.18	12.93
10.10	10-86	94.5	94.13	12.90
10.95	11-86	95.26	96.2	12.87
7.30	12-86	87.21	87.29	13.06
10.13	12-86	93.25	94.1	12.96
11.05	12-86	95.30	96.6	12.86
10.70	1-87	94.11	94.19	13.19
11.15	1-87	95.14	95.18	13.19
9.90	2-87	92.16	92.24	13.16
11.05	2-87	95.4	95.8	13.18
7.75	3-87	87.20	87.28	13.08
11.25	3-87	95.19	95.23	13.11
11.55	3-87	96.5	96.13	13.11
14.30	4-87	102.9	102.17	13.19
12.25	4-87	97.18	97.22	13.23
11.15	5-87	94.30	95.6	13.16
7.65	6-87	86.12	86.20	13.14
11.20	6-87	94.26	95.2	13.23
9.10	7-87	89.13	89.21	13.25
15.25	7-87	104.19	104.27	13.28

Federal Land Bank

Rate	Mat	Bid	Asked	Yld
8.10	7-85	95.22	95.26	12.09
7.95	10-85	94.17	94.21	12.22
8.80	10-85	95.21	95.25	12.16
7.60	4-87	87.9	87.13	12.95
7.25	7-87	84.28	85	13.23
7.85	1-88	85.17	85.25	12.85
8.20	1-90	78.14	78.30	13.66
7.95	4-91	74.24	75	13.65
7.95	10-96	65.8	65.24	13.79
7.35	1-97	61.20	61.28	13.80

Fed. Home Loan Bank

Rate	Mat	Bid	Asked	Yld
9.60	6-84	99.28	100	9.22
14.00	6-84	100.6	100.10	9.10
15.55	7-84	100.20	100.24	10.11
7.85	8-84	99.8	99.12	10.27
16.00	8-84	101.1	101.5	10.71
13.85	9-84	100.21	100.25	11.07
16.40	9-84	101.17	101.21	10.77
14.45	10-84	101.5	101.9	11.00
7.38	11-84	98.5	98.9	11.05
12.25	12-84	100.8	100.12	11.52
13.55	1-85	101.1	101.5	11.60
7.38	2-85	97.1	97.5	11.46
10.80	3-85	99.6	99.10	11.66
14.55	4-85	102.4	102.8	11.82
8.13	5-85	96.10	96.14	12.02
12.00	5-85	99.29	99.31	12.03
12.20	6-85	100.2	100.6	11.99
15.00	6-85	102.26	102.30	11.97
12.80	7-85	100.13	100.17	12.25
13.90	7-85	101.18	101.22	12.25
9.35	8-85	96.20	96.24	12.22
14.15	9-85	101.31	102.3	12.34
8.10	11-85	94.11	94.15	12.28
14.70	12-85	102.29	103.1	12.50
13.85	1-86	101.22	101.30	12.49
9.55	2-86	95.3	95.11	12.59
15.30	2-86	103.30	104.6	12.51
15.75	3-86	104.23	104.31	12.58
10.25	4-86	95.22	95.30	12.70
11.70	4-86	98.6	98.10	12.71
15.50	5-86	104.7	104.15	12.89
15.35	7-86	104.5	104.13	12.92
14.60	8-86	102.26	103.2	12.95
16.40	9-86	106.19	106.27	12.87
10.80	10-86	95.17	95.21	12.94
11.30	11-86	96.18	96.26	12.83
10.45	2-87	93.28	94.4	13.05
11.05	2-87	95.16	95.20	12.98
11.10	3-87	95.5	95.13	13.08
11.25	3-87	95.15	95.23	13.10
7.65	5-87	86.25	87.1	13.02
13.00	5-87	99.20	99.22	13.13
10.30	6-87	92.26	93.2	13.11
11.35	7-87	95.11	95.19	13.08
7.60	8-87	85.11	85.19	13.20
12.15	10-87	97.9	97.13	13.11
10.65	11-87	92.18	92.26	13.29
11.30	11-87	94.9	94.17	13.31
10.20	3-88	90.14	90.22	13.38
11.90	3-88	95.18	95.22	13.36
10.15	4-88	90.8	90.16	13.34
11.40	10-88	93.4	93.12	13.43
14.20	11-88	102.5	102.13	13.47
11.38	1-89	92.22	92.26	13.49
15.10	2-89	104.30	105.6	13.56
14.25	4-89	102.4	102.12	13.56
14.13	7-89	101.18	101.26	13.61
14.55	9-89	103	103.8	13.66
11.55	11-89	91.30	92.6	13.61
13.70	11-90	100.2	100.6	13.65
12.50	9-90	94.26	95.2	13.68
10.90	12-90	87.18	87.26	13.77
11.88	2-91	91.18	91.26	13.77
11.10	8-91	87.14	87.22	13.84
11.75	9-91	90.10	90.18	13.83
11.70	4-92	89.14	89.22	13.88
10.85	10-92	84.24	85	13.93
11.10	11-92	85.28	86.4	13.94
10.70	1-93	83.22	83.30	13.94
10.75	5-93	83.18	83.26	13.97
11.70	7-93	88.10	88.18	13.94
11.95	8-93	89.18	89.26	13.93
7.38	11-93	66.4	66.20	13.78
12.15	12-93	90.16	90.24	13.92
12.00	2-94	89.20	89.28	13.92
7.88	2-97	64.16	64.24	13.83

World Bank Bonds

Rate	Mat	Bid	Asked	Yld
11.72	9-84	99.28	100.6	10.90
8.15	1-85	97.8	98.4	11.35
5.00	2-85	95.8	95.24	10.80
9.92	3-85	96.28	97.12	11.60
8.60	7-85	95.24	96.8	12.15
8.85	12-85	94.20	95.4	12.35
8.38	7-86	91.28	92.12	12.60
16.38	11-86	106.12	106.28	13.00
7.80	12-86	90.12	90.28	12.00
14.63	12-86	103.24	104.8	12.65
7.65	5-87	87.12	87.28	12.70
7.75	8-87	86.24	87.8	12.70
14.63	8-87	104.4	104.20	12.80
13.45	9-87	101.4	101.20	12.80
10.38	3-88	91.16	92	13.00
10.00	5-88	90.12	90.28	13.00
15.00	12-88	105.12	105.28	13.25
11.00	10-89	91.24	92.8	13.05
4.50	2-90	66.24	67.24	12.60
5.38	7-91	65.12	66.12	12.70
16.63	11-91	113.12	113.28	13.60
15.13	12-91	106.16	107	13.60
5.38	4-92	63	63.16	12.90
14.75	6-92	105.16	106	13.50
13.63	9-92	100.8	100.24	13.45
10.90	3-93	87	87.16	13.35
10.38	5-93	83.8	83.24	13.55
5.88	9-93	61.24	62.8	13.00
6.50	3-94	63.4	64.4	13.10

Inter-Amer. Devel. Bk.

Rate	Mat	Bid	Asked	Yld
4.50	11-84	96.20	97.4	11.15
8.25	1-85	97.12	97.22	11.55
8.00	3-85	96.24	97.8	11.65
8.38	2-86	93.8	93.24	11.50
14.00	12-86	102	102.16	12.80
10.75	8-87	94.12	94.28	12.75
15.00	4-89	106.12	106.28	13.05
5.20	1-92	64.20	65.20	12.25
14.63	8-92	104.20	105.4	13.55
6.50	11-92	70.12	71.12	11.95
6.63	11-93	69.12	70.12	11.95
8.63	10-95	78	78.16	12.15
9.00	2-01	68.28	69.12	13.70
8.75	7-01	67	67.16	13.70
8.38	6-02	64.8	64.24	13.70
9.63	1-04	71.28	72.12	13.70

Asian Development Bank

Rate	Mat	Bid	Asked	Yld
8.63	8-86	92.24	93.8	12.15
	7-92	35.20	36.4	12.90
7.75	4-96	67.12	67.28	13.15
11.13	5-98	85	85.16	13.45

Bank for Co-ops

Rate	Mat	Bid	Asked	Yld
7.75	1-86	93.5	93.13	12.43

Federal Farm Credit

Rate	Mat	Bid	Asked	Yld
9.45	6-84	99.31	100.1	3.65
10.30	6-84	99.31	100.1	4.34
9.70	6-84	99.31	100.1	7.11
9.63	7-84	99.28	100	9.05
9.75	7-84	99.28	100	9.38
14.80	7-84	100.18	100.22	10.06
15.25	7-84	100.16	100.20	10.05
9.55	8-84	99.23	99.27	10.16
9.63	8-84	99.22	99.26	10.17
9.63	9-84	99.16	99.20	10.59
9.95	9-84	99.20	99.24	10.67
11.75	9-84	100.2	100.6	10.72
9.90	10-84	99.16	99.18	10.80
10.60	10-84	99.23	99.27	10.89
12.85	10-84	100.14	100.18	11.22
14.35	10-84	101.3	101.7	11.08
9.70	11-84	99.4	99.8	11.20
10.50	11-84	99.18	99.22	11.18
9.55	12-84	98.31	99.3	11.42
10.10	12-84	99.4	99.8	11.38
10.65	12-84	99.16	99.20	11.42
10.75	1-85	99.11	99.15	11.51
10.90	1-85	99.15	99.19	11.52
14.35	1-85	101.17	101.21	11.54
10.70	2-85	99.7	99.11	11.66
13.20	3-85	100.29	101.1	11.68
13.25	4-85	101	101.2	11.93
14.80	4-85	102.9	102.11	11.93
9.20	6-85	97.9	97.13	12.00
11.60	7-85	99.11	99.15	12.08
10.00	7-85	97.20	97.24	12.13
12.75	9-85	100:9	100.13	12.35
14.90	9-85	102.23	102.27	12.35
14.30	12-85	102.9	102.13	12.50
17.00	12-85	105.31	106.3	12.44
10.90	1-86	97.12	97.20	12.52
15.80	1-86	104.15	104.23	12.50
13.95	3-86	101.28	102.4	12.53
10.85	4-86	96.24	96.28	12.74
14.00	4-86	101.20	102.4	12.68
15.10	6-86	103.17	103.25	12.90
15.15	7-86	103.25	104.1	12.91
11.63	7-86	97.27	97.31	12.65
13.35	9-86	100.15	100.23	12.95
14.50	9-86	102.19	102.27	12.98
9.95	10-86	93.25	94.1	12.92
10.75	10-86	95.14	95.22	12.89
10.00	12-86	93.22	93.30	12.91
9.90	1-87	92.23	92.31	13.12
14.63	1-87	103	103.8	13.11
11.45	3-87	96.3	96.7	13.11
12.40	3-87	98.6	98.14	13.07
14.38	4-87	102.18	102.26	13.16
14.40	4-87	102.18	102.26	13.18
10.63	7-87	93.10	93.18	13.18
10.55	6-87	93.15	93.23	13.15
10.13	9-87	91.30	92.6	13.14

FIC Bank Debs.

Rate	Mat	Bid	Asked	Yld
7.95	4-86	92.5	92.13	12.69
6.95	1-87	86.24	86.30	13.02

GNMA Issues

Rate	Mat	Bid	Asked	Yld
8.00		66.24	67	13.91
9.00		70.31	71.7	14.21
9.50		73.18	73.26	14.21
10.00		76.7	76.15	14.21
11.00		82.1	82.9	14.01
11.50		84.26	85.2	14.11
12.00		87.26	87.28	14.10
12.50		90.11	90.19	14.11
13.00		93.6	93.14	14.12
13.50		95.29	96.5	14.12
14.00		98.16	98.24	14.21
15.00		101.21	101.29	14.60

SOURCE: Reprinted with permission of the *Wall Street Journal*,

FIGURE 11-4
Price Quotations for U.S. Government, Agency and Miscellaneous Securities

to buy securities representing loans of this type from private organizations that grant them in the first instance. Some or all the initial capital for these banks may be provided by the government, but subsequent amounts typically come from bond issues and contributions from those who utilize their services.

While the debts of agencies of this type are usually not guaranteed by the federal government, governmental control is designed to insure that each issue is backed by extremely safe assets (e.g., mortgages insured by another quasi-governmental agency). Moreover, it is generally presumed that governmental assistance of one sort or another would be provided, were there any danger of default on such a bond.

Farm Credit Banks provide credit to farmers, ranchers, and rural homeowners. *Banks for Cooperatives* support loans made to farmers' cooperative associations. *Federal Home Loan Banks* make loans to thrift institutions (primarily savings and loans associations). *Federal Intermediate Credit Banks* support loans made to agricultural credit corporations and similar organizations. *Federal Land Banks* provide funds for first mortgages on rural real estate. The *Federal National Mortgage Association* (known in the trade as "Fannie Mae") purchases and sells real estate mortgages—primarily those insured by the Federal Housing Administration or guaranteed by the Veterans Administration. The *Student Loan Marketing Association* ("Sallie Mae") purchases federally guaranteed loans made to students by other lenders (e.g. banks) and may make direct student loans under special circumstances.

Participation Certificates

To support credit for export and import operations and encourage the use of home mortgages, the government has authorized the issuance of *participation certificates*. A group of assets (e.g., mortgages) is placed in a pool, and certificates representing interests in those assets are issued to pay for them. The holders of certificates receive the interest and principal payments, minus a small service charge. The most important certificates of this type are those issued by the *Government National Mortgage Association*. Such "Ginnie Mae pass-throughs" are guaranteed by the Association and backed by the full faith and credit of the U.S. government. Unlike regular bonds, they are self-extinguishing, like the mortgages they represent. The holder receives monthly payments, each of which includes interest and a return of principal. A similar instrument, issued in denominations of $100,000 or more, is the "guaranteed mortgage certificate" sold by the *Federal Home Loan Mortgage Corporation*. A number of banks have offered similar pass-through mortgage certificates backed by private insurance companies.

BONDS OF INTERNATIONAL AGENCIES

Certain international organizations also receive support from the U.S. government. The *International Bank for Reconstruction and Development* (the "World Bank") raises funds via the issuance of bonds in various currencies to finance development loans in a number of countries. The *Inter-American Development Bank* and *Asian Development Bank* perform similar functions for the countries of North and South America and Asia.

GOVERNMENT-GUARANTEED BONDS

To encourage urban development, the U.S. merchant marine, and other activities deemed worthy of support, the full faith and credit of the United States has been pledged to guarantee both principal and interest on bonds issued by private organizations. Thus some bonds issued by, e.g., property developers and shipping companies are comparable in risk and return to similar instruments issued by the government itself.

ZERO-COUPON TREASURY SECURITY RECEIPTS

A noncallable Treasury note or bond is, in effect, a portfolio of *zero-coupon bonds*—one issue for each coupon payment and one for the principal. In 1982, a number of brokerage firms began separating these components, using a process known as *coupon stripping*.

Treasury bonds of a given issue are purchased and placed in trust with a custodian (e.g., a bank). Sets of *receipts* are then issued, one set for each coupon date. For example, an August 15, 1991, receipt might entitle its holder to receive $3,000 on that date (and nothing on any other date). The amount required to meet the payments on all the August 15, 1991, receipts would just equal the total amount received in coupon payments from the Treasury securities held in the trust account. A final set of receipts would allow the holders to share in the principal payment (if the underlying Treasury security was callable, the final set of receipts would cover all payments received after the date of first call).

Three early examples were Lehman Brothers' *Lehman Investment Opportunity Notes* (LIONs), Merrill Lynch's *Treasury Investment Growth Receipts* (TIGRs), and Salomon Brothers' *Certificates of Accrual on Treasury Securities* (CATs). Not surprisingly, such securities are known in the trade as "animals."

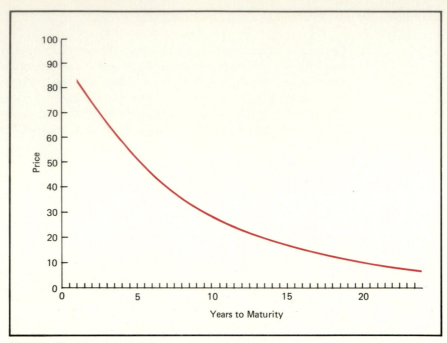

SOURCE: Merrill Lynch Capital Markets' Offering Prices, Zero-Coupon Treasury Investment Growth Receipts, Series 7.

FIGURE 11-5
Prices of Zero-Coupon TIGRs, December 1, 1983

The Internal Revenue Service requires that tax be paid on the interest earned on such securities as it accrues. Thus they are attractive primarily for tax-exempt investors and as investments in the names of children with low taxable incomes.

Figure 11-5 shows the prices of a series of such securities. In effect, it shows the *discount function* at the time.

STATE AND MUNICIPAL GOVERNMENT SECURITIES

The 1982 Census of Governments showed that there were 82,340 governmental units in the United States, in addition to the federal government itself:[1]

    50 states

   3,041 counties

 19,076 municipalities

 16,734 townships

---

[1] *Statistical Abstract of the United States,* 1984.

    Fixed-Income Securities

28,588 special districts

14,851 school districts

A great many of these units borrow money, and, as discussed in Chapter 9, the interest (but not any capital gain) is exempt from federal income taxes. For this reason, securities of this type are often called *tax-exempts*. More often they are all termed *municipals* ("muni's" for short), with only the securities of the U.S. government being referred to as "governments."

Whatever they are called, municipal securities are important. Table 11-5 provides estimates of the amounts of various types of fixed-income securities outstanding at the end of 1983. With approximately $475 billion in value, municipals clearly warrant attention.

TABLE 11-5
Estimated Amounts of Various
Fixed-Income Securities Outstanding,
December 1983

Type of Security	Amount ($ Billions)
Privately held federal debt	1,504.2
Corporate and foreign	617.5
Tax-exempt notes and bonds	474.7

SOURCE: Salomon Brothers, *1984 Prospects for Financial Markets*.

Issuing Agencies

Table 11-6 shows the dollar values of municipal bonds issued in 1983 by various issuing agencies.

States issue debt to finance capital expenditures (primarily for highways and education); in principle, the revenue generated by the resulting facilities can be used to make the required debt payments. In some cases the link is direct (e.g., tolls may be used to pay for a bridge), in other cases somewhat indirect (e.g., gasoline taxes may be used to pay for highway construction) or very indirect (e.g., state sales or income taxes may be used to pay for the construction of new government buildings). In some cases no capital expenditure is involved (e.g., for the payment of a veterans' bonus).

States may not be sued without their consent. Thus the bondholder may have no legal recourse in the event of default. However, bonds backed by the full faith and credit of a state government are considered

TABLE 11-6
New Security Issues of State and Local Governments, 1983,
Classified by Issuer

Issuer	Amount ($ Billions)
States	7.1
Municipalities, counties, townships, and school districts	27.3
Special districts and statutory authorities	50.6
	85.0

SOURCE: *Federal Reserve Bulletin*, April 1984.

quite safe. Bonds issued by states but dependent on particular revenues may, of course, involve considerable risk.

Local governments may be sued against their will, making it possible for bondholders to force officials to collect whatever revenues may be available to meet required debt payments. In many cases only revenues from specific projects may be used (e.g., the tolls collected on a particular throughway). In other cases collections from a particular tax may be used, although possibly only up to some statutory limit.

Some local governments (e.g., Cleveland in 1978-79) have defaulted on their debts and others (e.g., New York City in 1975) have "restructured" debt, giving holders new certificates offering lower or deferred interest and longer maturities in exchange for old holdings.

Counties and municipalities are familiar to most people, but other local governments exist, most notably school and other districts and authorities created by statute to finance and operate ports, airports, and the like. All are created by state charter and may be granted monopoly powers as well as rights to collect certain types of taxes. Often limits are placed on the amount of taxes collected, the tax rate charged, and the amount or type of debt issued. The primary source of tax revenue for such agencies is the property tax. Since a given property may be liable to taxes levied by several agencies (e.g., a city, a country, a school district, a port authority, a sewer district), the risk of the bonds of an issuer may depend on both the value of property subject to its taxes and the amount of other debt dependent on the same property.

Purposes for Which Debt Is Issued

Much of the debt issued each year by state and local government is short-term, designed to cover outlays prior to the receipt of taxes. Such obligations are often called *tax-anticipation notes* or (misleadingly) *warrants:* the taxes due but not yet paid serve as security.

TABLE 11-7

New Security Issues of State and Local Governments, 1983, Classified by Purpose

Purpose of Bonds	Amount ($ Billions)
Education	8.2
Transportation	4.4
Utilities and conservation	13.5
Social welfare	26.4
Industrial aid	7.1
Other purposes	11.6

SOURCE: *Federal Reserve Bulletin*, April 1984.

Table 11-7 shows the purposes for which municipal bonds were issued in 1983.

Types of Municipal Bonds

In 1983 new municipal bonds with a par value of $85.1 billion were issued: $21.5 billion of *general obligation bonds* ("G.O.'s") and $63.6 billion of *revenue bonds*.

General obligation bonds ("G.O.s") are backed by the full faith and credit (and thus the taxing power) of the issuing agency. Most are issued by agencies with unlimited taxing power, although in a minority of cases the issuer is subject to limits on the amount of taxes and/or the tax rate.

Revenue bonds are backed by revenues from a designated project, authority, or agency or by the proceeds from a specific tax. In many cases such bonds are issued by agencies that hope to sell their services, pay the required expenses, and have enough left over to at least meet required payments on outstanding debt. Except for the possible grant of monopoly powers, the authorizing state and local government may provide no further assistance. In such a case the bonds are as good as the enterprise in question, but no better.

Many revenue bonds are issued to finance capital expenditures for publicly owned utilities (e.g., water, sewer, electricity, and/or gas). Others are issued to finance quasi-utility operations (e.g., public transportation). Some are financed by *special assessments* levied on properties benefiting from the original expenditure (e.g., those connected to a new sewer system). *Industrial development bonds* are used to finance the purchase and/or construction of industrial facilities to be rented or leased to firms on a favorable basis. Such bonds in effect provide tax-exempt loans to businesses choosing to locate in the area in question.

Other Tax-Exempt Issues

The avoidance of federal income tax on interest earned on a bond makes such a security attractive to wealthy individual investors and corporate investors as well. Accordingly, such issues can be sold to yield a considerably lower rate of interest than that required from taxable securities. This lowers the cost of financing to the issuer and provides a federal subsidy to any agency allowed to issue bonds of this type.

Over the years this subsidy has been used to support activities deemed worthy of encouragement (albeit somewhat hidden encouragement). Private universities may issue tax-exempt bonds to finance certain types of improvements, and private firms may do so to finance certain pollution-reducing activities. Such instruments are generally backed only by the resources of the issuer, with government involvement limited to the granting of favorable tax treatment.

Ownership of State and Local Government Securities

Since interest on municipal securities is exempt from both personal and corporate income taxes, and since the rate on the latter is substantial, such securities are particularly attractive to corporate investors

TABLE 11-8
Estimated Ownership of State and Local Securities, December 1983

	($ Billions)	Percent
Mutual savings banks	2.2	.5
Savings and loan associations	.1	.0
Life insurance companies	11.3	2.4
Property liability companies	89.3	18.8
State and local retirement funds	2.5	.5
Municipal bond funds	86.8	18.3
Security brokers and dealers	1.6	.3
Commercial banks	163.8	34.5
Nonfinancial corporations	4.6	1.0
Households direct	112.5	23.7
	474.7	100.0

SOURCE: Salomon Brothers, *1984 Prospects for Financial Markets*.

and especially to financial institutions. This is shown in Table 11-8, which provides estimates of the ownership of state and local securities at the end of 1983.

The Market for Municipal Bonds

Municipal bonds are usually issued in *serial* form. One group matures a year after issue, another two years after issue, another three years after, and so on. The overall package is generally offered by the issuer on a competitive basis to various *underwriters*. The winning bidder then *reoffers* the individual bonds, either publicly or via a *private placement*. An offering may include both serial and *term bonds* (i.e., bonds that mature on a given date in the fairly distant future). Some issues consist entirely of term (i.e., normal) bonds.

Municipal bonds may be callable at specified dates and prices. Occasionally the issuing authority is obligated to make designated payments into a *sinking fund*, which is used to buy either its own or similar bonds.

A secondary market in municipal bonds is made by various dealers. However, the relatively small amounts of particular issues and maturities outstanding limit the size of the market. Many individuals who invest in municipals simply buy new issues and hold them to maturity.

Municipal Bond Insurance

An investor concerned about possible default of a municipal bond can purchase an insurance policy to cover losses incurred if interest or principal is not paid in full and on time.

Some issues are insured at the time of offering. Alternatively, an investor can contract with a company to have a specific portfolio insured. Premiums depend on the bonds included and their ratings.

FOREIGN BONDS

A number of foreign governments, agencies, and corporations have issued "dollar bonds": the security is initially sold for dollars, and both principal and interest are paid in dollars. The issuers of such bonds can default on required payments, and an assessment of the risk involved requires both economic and political analysis.

EUROBONDS

Owing in part to government restrictions on investment in foreign securities, a number of borrowers have found it advantageous to sell securities in other countries. The term *Eurobond* is loosely applied to bonds that are offered outside the country of the borrower and usually outside the country in whose currency the securities are denominated.

In 1983, Eurobonds with a value of $48.5 billion were issued; of the total, $34.9 billion were "Eurodollar" issues.[2] Since the Eurobond market is neither regulated nor taxed, it offers substantial advantages for many issuers and buyers of bonds. For example, a foreign subsidiary of a U.S. corporation may issue a Eurobond in "bearer" form. No tax will be withheld by the corporation, and the tax paid by the purchaser (if any) will depend on his or her country of residence.

Because tax statuses differ, interest rates on Eurobonds tend to be somewhat less than those of domestic bonds denominated in the same currency. Such rates do, however, tend to move in concert, although not perfectly, since movement of capital between domestic and foreign markets is difficult or costly for some issuers and/or purchasers.

CORPORATE BONDS

In some respects corporate bonds are similar to those issued by state and local governments. They promise to make specified payments at specified times, legal remedies being provided in the event of default. Restrictions often are placed on the activities of the issuing corporation to provide additional protection for bondholders. Interest received by the owner of such a bond is not tax-exempt, of course, and typically only the issuing corporation is obligated to make the required payments. A great many variations on the general theme exist, but the essential idea is both simple and familiar.

Debt Versus Equity Financing

From the viewpoint of the issuing corporation, debt differs from equity in two crucial respects. First, principal and interest payments are obligatory. Failure to make any payment in full and on time can expose the firm to expensive, time-consuming, and potentially disruptive legal actions. In return for this drawback, interest payments are considered expenses and hence can be deducted from profit before calculating the corporation's income tax liability. A dollar paid in interest reduces profit before tax by a dollar. As a result, taxes are also reduced (by

---

[2] *Wall Street Journal*, May 29, 1984.

46 cents, for a firm in the 46% marginal tax bracket), leading to less than a dollar decline in profit after tax (for example, of 54 cents). A dollar paid in dividends reduces profit after tax by a dollar. Other things equal, debt financing is cheaper.

Of course, other things are not equal. Interest received by individuals is taxed as income, while a portion of the return to stockholders is typically provided as capital gains, which are taxed only when realized and at lower rates. Thus the before-tax cost of equity capital to a corporation may be less than the cost of debt capital. In equilibrium, the risk-adjusted after-tax costs of debt and equity capital could, in fact, be the same, as argued by Miller.[3]

Extensive use of debt in a firm's capital structure increases the likelihood of bankruptcy, with its associated costs. Thus, in the United States, the highest leverage (i.e., the ratio of the amount of debt to the total value of the firm) is found in the utility industry, where stability of earnings reduces the dangers associated with substantial interest payments.

The Indenture

An issue of bonds is generally covered by a *trust indenture*, in which the issuing corporation promises a specified *trustee* that it will comply with a number of stated provisions. Chief among these is, of course, the payment of required interest and principal on the issue. But terms are often included to control the sale of pledged property, the issue of other bonds, and the like.

The trustee for a bond issue, usually a bank or trust company, acts for the bondholders either automatically as required by the indenture, voluntarily, or in response to a request from the holders of some specified portion of the issue.

If the corporation defaults on an interest payment, after a relatively short period of grace (e.g., one to six months) the entire principal (par value) typically becomes due and payable—a procedure designed to enhance the holders' status in bankruptcy or related legal proceedings.

Types of Bonds

An exhaustive list of the names used to describe bonds would be intolerably long. Different names are often used for the same type of bond, and occasionally the same name will be used for two quite different bonds. A few major types do predominate, however, with relatively standard nomenclature.

---

[3] Merton Miller, "Debt and Taxes," *Journal of Finance*, 32, no. 2 (May 1977), pp. 261-75.

Mortgage Bonds.   Bonds of this type represent debt that is secured by the pledge of specific property. In the event of default, the bondholders are entitled to obtain the property in question and sell it to satisfy their claims on the firm. In addition to the property itself, the holders of mortgage bonds have an unsecured claim on the corporation.

Mortgage bondholders are usually protected by a number of terms included in the bond indenture. The corporation may be constrained from pledging property for other bonds (or such bonds, if issued, must be "junior" or "second" mortgages, with a claim on the property only after the first mortgage is satisfied). Certain property acquired after the issue may also be pledged to support the bonds.

Collateral Trust Bonds.   These bonds are backed by other securities, usually held by a trustee. A common situation of this sort arises when the securities of a subsidiary firm are pledged as collateral by the parent firm.

Equipment Obligations.   Known also as *equipment trust certificates*, these securities are backed by specific pieces of equipment—railroad rolling stock, commercial aircraft, and the like. The equipment is usually readily salable and can be delivered inexpensively to a new owner. The legal arrangements used to facilitate the issuance of such bonds can be very complex. The most popular procedure uses the "Philadelphia plan," in which a trustee holds the equipment, issues obligations, and leases the equipment to the using corporation. Money received from the corporation is used to make interest and principal payments to the holders of the obligations; if all payments are made on schedule, the corporation takes title to the equipment.

Debenture Bonds.   These are general obligations of the issuing corporation and thus represent *unsecured* credit. To protect the holders of such bonds, the indenture will usually limit the issuance of secured debt as well as additional unsecured debt and possibly other operations of the firm that might be inimical to the welfare of the holders.

Subordinated Debentures.   When more than one issue of debentures is outstanding, a hierarchy may be specified. For example, subordinated debentures are junior to unsubordinated debentures; in the event of insolvency, junior claims are intended to be considered only if senior claims can be fully satisfied.

Other Types of Bonds.   *Income bonds* are more like preferred stock (described in a later section) than bonds. Payment of interest in full and on schedule is not absolutely required, and failure to do so need not send the corporation to court. Interest on such bonds may or may not qualify as a deductible expense for corporate income taxes. The type is rarely used, except in reorganizaitons of insolvent railroads.

Guaranteed bonds are issued by one corporation but backed in some way by another (e.g., a parent firm). *Participating bonds* require stated interest payments but provide additional amounts if earnings permit. *Voting bonds*, unlike regular bonds, give the holders some voice in management. *Serial bonds*, with different portions of the issue maturing at different dates, are sometimes used by corporations, primarily for equipment financing.

Convertible bonds may, at the holder's option, be exchanged for other securities, often common stock. Such bonds, which have become very popular in recent years, are discussed in detail in Chapter 16.

Call Provisions

Corporate management would prefer to have the right to pay off any bond at par at any time prior to maturity. This provides desirable flexibility, since debt can be reduced, its maturity can be altered via refunding, and, most important, expensive debt issued in times of high interest rates can be replaced with cheaper debt if rates decline.

Not surprisingly, investors hold quite different opinions on the matter. The issuer's ability to redeem an issue at par at any time virtually precludes a rise in price over par and robs the holder of potential gains associated with declining interest rates; moreover, it introduces a new form of uncertainty. A bond with such a feature will almost certainly sell for less when issued and afterward than one without it.

Despite the cost of obtaining this sort of flexibility, many corporations include *call provisions* in their bond indentures. The corporation retains the option to "call" some or all of the bonds from their holders at stated prices during specified periods. In a sense, the firm sells a bond and simultaneously buys an option contract: the net price of the bond is thus the difference between the two values.

Investors are usually given some *call protection*: during the first few years an issue may not be callable. In addition, a *premium* may be paid when a bond is called; often this amount is smaller, the closer the date of call to the scheduled maturity of the issue.

An entire issue may be called, or only specific bonds (drawn by lot by the trustee). In either case, *a notice of redemption* will appear in advance in the financial press.

When a convertible bond can be exchanged for securities worth more than the bond's call price, the issuer may notify remaining holders of an intent to call the bond to force conversion.

Sinking Funds

Often a bond indenture will require the issuing corporation to make annual payments into a sinking fund. The idea is to pay part of the principal of the debt as well as the interest and thus to reduce the amount outstanding at maturity.

The corporation may transmit cash to the trustee for the issue, who can then purchase bonds in the open market. Alternatively, the corporation may obtain the bonds itself, by either purchase or call, and deposit them with the trustee. Call prices for sinking fund purchases may differ from those specified for optional redemptions.

Required contributions to a sinking fund may or may not be the same each year. In some cases the required amount may depend on earnings, output, and so on; in others the goal is to make the total paid for interest and principal the same each year.

Private Placements

Bonds intended for eventual public sale are usually issued in denominations of $1,000 each. Both *coupon* and *registered* forms may be utilized. Often, however, a single purchaser or a small group of purchasers will buy an entire issue. Such private placements are typically purchased by large institutional investors.

A related instrument is the *term loan*. Running for several years, it is a corporate loan made by a commercial bank. Payments on principal may or may not be required prior to maturity. Credit of this type is generally unsecured, but restrictions may be imposed on the corporation as a condition for the granting of the loan.

Bankruptcy

When a corporation fails to make a scheduled payment of either interest or principal on a bond, the firm is said to be in *default* on that obligation. If the payment is not made within a relatively short period, some sort of litigation almost inevitably follows.

A corporation unable to meet its obligatory debt payments is said to be *technically insolvent* or *insolvent in the equity sense*. If the value of the firm's assets falls below its liabilities, it is said to be *insolvent*, or *insolvent in the bankruptcy sense*.

Behind these definitions lie much legislation, many court cases, and varied legal opinions. While the details differ, the usual situation begins with a default of one or more required payments. If voluntary agreements with creditors cannot be obtained, this usually leads to a filing of bankruptcy—usually "voluntary"—by the corporation itself. Subsequent developments involve courts, court-appointed officials, representatives of the firm's creditors, and the management of the firm, among others.

A question that arises in most cases is whether the firm's assets should be *liquidated* and the proceeds divided among the creditors. Such an action is taken only if the court feels the resulting value would exceed that likely to be obtained if the firm continued in operation (perhaps after substantial reorganization).

If the firm's assets are liquidated in a "straight bankruptcy," secured creditors receive the property pledged for their loans or the proceeds from its sale. If this falls short of their claims, the difference is considered an unsecured debt of the firm; on the other hand, any excess is made available for other creditors. Next, assets are used to pay the claims of *priority* creditors to the extent possible. These include claims for such items as administrative expenses, wages (up to a stated limit per person), uninsured pension claims, taxes, and rents. Anything left over is used to pay unsecured creditors in proportion to their claims on the firm.

Reorganization.

If the value of a firm's assets when employed as part of a "going concern" appears to exceed the value in liquidation, a reorganization of the firm and its liabilities may be undertaken. Such proceedings, conducted under the provisions of Chapter X of the Federal Bankruptcy Act, may be *voluntary* (initiated by the firm) or *involuntary* (initiated by three or more creditors). A number of parties must concur in the proposed reorganization, including the holders of two-thirds of the value in each general class of creditor affected by the reorganization.

Typically, creditors are given new claims on the reorganized firm, intended to be at least equal in value to the amounts that would have been received in liquidation. For example, holders of debentures might receive bonds of longer maturity, holders of subordinated debentures might become stockholders, and stockholders might be left without any interest in the firm.

Among the goals of reorganization are "fair and equitable" treatment of various classes of securities and the elimination of "burdensome" debt obligations. Neither concept is founded on a very secure base of financial theory. Presumably, a fair and equitable plan is one that investors expected to apply in the circumstances in question. A debt obligation that can be covered by assets need not be burdensome if the firm is prepared to alter its activities sufficiently, and so on.

Arrangements.

A third procedure is available to financially embarrassed corporations. Chapter XI of the Federal Bankruptcy Act authorizes *arrangements*, in which debts may be extended (to longer maturities) and/or *composed* (reduced). Under the Bankruptcy Reform Act of 1978, the initiation of Chapter XI proceedings may be either voluntary or involuntary. While Chapter XI proceedings are going on, the corporation is protected by the court from creditor lawsuits. Eventually, a plan for handling debts will be proposed; if a majority of creditors (who are due over two-thirds of the value) approve, the changes can be made and the firm returned, at least temporarily, to the ranks of the solvent.

Some Financial Aspects of Bankruptcy.   While the subject is far too complex for detailed treatment here, two aspects of bankruptcy deserve some discussion.

First, the choice between continuation of a firm and liquidation of its assets should be unrelated to considerations of bankruptcy. If an asset can be sold for more than the present value of its future earnings, it should be. Management may have to be taken to court to be forced to do this, but the issue is not really one of solvency or lack thereof.

Second, the definition of insolvency is rather vague. Assume, for the sake of argument, that assets can be adequately valued at the larger of liquidating or going-concern value. A firm is said to be insolvent if this value is less than that of the firm's liabilities. But how should the latter be valued? Their current market value will inevitably be less than the value of the assets as long as stockholders can expect to receive something under at least some circumstances.

An alternative procedure could value liabilities using the current discount function for default-free zero-coupon bonds. If assets cover liabilities calculated in this manner, the firm could meet its obligations by selling assets (perhaps to another firm) and purchasing bonds with appropriate payments. Or it could simply buy its own bonds in the open market. Thus, the possibility of a technically but not "really" insolvent firm would not arise.

Neither of these procedures is very satisfactory. One might argue that the goal is to value the liabilities as if the firm had not gone bankrupt. But this involves circular reasoning.

Rightly or wrongly, par value is typically utilized to compute liabilities for this purpose, although it can lead to anomalies, such as the award of a greater value to a claimant than the present value of a government bond with equal terms.

Ownership of Corporate Bonds

At the end of 1983, $617.5 billion of corporate bonds was estimated to be held in the United States. Such securities were owned by both institutional and individual investors, as shown in Table 11-9.

TABLE 11-9
Estimated Ownership of Corporate and Foreign Bonds, December 1983

	Amount ($ Billions)	Percent
Mutual savings banks	21.5	3.5
Life insurance companies	226.3	36.6
Property liability companies	25.8	4.2
Private noninsured pension funds	68.6	11.1
State and local retirement funds	118.6	19.2
Endowments	15.6	2.5
Stock mutual funds	12.0	1.9
Security brokers and dealers	4.3	0.7
Commercial banks	11.3	1.8
Foreign	37.8	6.1
Households direct	75.7	12.3
	617.5	100.0

SOURCE: Salomon Brothers, *1984 Prospects for Financial Markets.*

Prices of Corporate Bonds

Some corporate bonds are traded on the New York Stock Exchange, and the prices at which such trades are made can be found in the financial press. Figure 11-6 provides an example. Thus, the entry:

Bonds	Current Yield	Volume	High	Low	Close	Net Change
ATT 7⅛s03	13.	182	54½	54⅛	54¼	−⅜

indicates that American Telephone and Telegraph Company's bonds carrying a 7⅛% coupon and maturing in 2003 traded at prices ranging from 54½ to 54⅛ inclusive, with the last trade of the day at 54¼. The *current yield*[4] was approximately 13.0%. In all, 182 bonds, worth $1,000 each, traded hands on the exchange during the day, and the closing price was ⅜ below that of the previous day.

In a sense, the New York Stock Exchange is the "odd-lot" market

---

[4] This is not shown for convertible bonds; "cv" is listed instead.

New York Exchange Bonds

Friday, May 25, 1984

CORPORATION BONDS
Volume, $22,930,000

Bonds	Cur Yld	Vol	High	Low	Close	Net Chg.
Advst 9s08	cv	21	76½	76	76	−1
AetnLf 8⅛s07	13.	3	62	62	62	−1
AirPr 12¾94	14.	48	93½	93½	93½	− ⅞
AlaP 8½s01	14.	5	59⅞	59⅞	59⅞	−1⅛
AlaP 7¾s02	14.	5	57	57	57	+1
AlaP 8⅞s03	15.	13	62¼	61⅛	61⅛	− ½
AlaP 8¼s03	14.	5	58½	58½	58½	− ⅛
AlaP 9¾s04	14.	9	68¾	67	68¾	+1¾
AlaP 10⅞s05	15.	5	74	74	74	.....
AlaP 10½05	15.	5	71⅞	71⅞	71⅞	− ⅛
AlaP 8¾07	15.	4	59¾	59¾	59¾	−1¼
AlaP 12⅝10	15.	3	85	85	85	+2
AlaP 15¼10	15.	24	101¾	100½	100½	.....
AlaP ·17⅜11	16.	40	106¼	105½	106	− ¼
AlaP 18¼89	16.	1	112	112	112	.....
AlskH 18⅜01	17.	16	109	107	107⅛	+ ⅛
AlskH 15s92	14.	3	103⅝	103⅝	103⅝	.....
AlldC zr87	..	40	67¼	66	67¼	+2¼
AlldC zr2000s	..	2	14¾	14¾	14¾	+ ⅞
AlldC d6s88	8.2	21	73⅛	72¾	72¾	+ ½
AlldC d6s90	9.4	11	64	64	64	− ½
AlsCha 12s90	14.	145	85½	85	85	− ¾
AlsCha 16s91	16.	3	100¾	100¾	100¾	+1¼
Alcoa 9s95	12.	2	76	76	76	.....
Alcoa 9.45s00	14.	5	69	69	69	+ ⅝
AluCa 9½95	12.	5	77⅞	77¾	77¾	+ ⅜
AMAX 8s86	8.7	2	91½	91½	91½	.....
Amax 14¼90	15.	10	96⅜	96⅜	96⅜	−3½
AFoP 4.8s87	6.0	5	79½	79½	79½	+ ¼
AForP 5s30	13.	17	38¾	38½	38⅝	− ⅛
ABrnd 5⅞s92	9.6	25	61	61	61	.....
ABrnd 8⅛s85	8.4	22	96 13-16	96¾	96 13-16	+1-16
ABrnd 11⅛s89	12.	38	90½	90¼	90¼	− ¼
ACan 6s97	11.	18	52¾	52⅝	52⅝	+1
ACan 13¼93	14.	10	93	92½	93	+1
ACeM 6¾91	cv	10	74	74	74	.....
AExC 8½s85	9.0	1	94	94	94	.....
AExC 14¾92	15.	5	100¼	100¼	100¼	−3¼
AmGn 11s07	cv	1	122¾	122¾	122¾	+ ¾
AmGn 11s08	cv	6	122	121¾	121¾	+ ¾
AmMed 9½01	cv	6	113¼	112¼	113¼	+ ¼
AmMed 8¼08	cv	10	86	85	86	+ ½
AmMot 6s88	cv	7	79	78½	78½	−1
ASmel 4⅝s88	6.2	1	74¼	74¼	74¼	.....
ATT 3¼s84	3.3	26	97 29-32	97 29-32	97 29-32	
ATT 4⅜s85	4.6	60	94 15-16	94⅝	94⅝	−1-16
ATT 2⅝s86	3.0	25	86¾	86¾	86¾	+ ¼
ATT 2⅞s87	3.5	31	82	82	82	.....
ATT 3⅞s90	5.5	128	70⅝	70¼	70¼	− ⅛
ATT 8¾00	13.	94	67⅛	66¼	66¼	− ⅜
ATT 7s01	13.	98	55⅛	54¾	54⅞	.....
ATT 7⅛s03	13.	182	54½	54⅛	54¼	− ⅜
ATT 8.80s05	14.	225	64⅞	64½	64⅞	+ ⅛
ATT 8⅝s07	14.	109	63¼	63⅛	63¼	− ⅜
ATT 10⅜90	12.	84	89	87	87½	+ ⅛
ATT 13¼91	14.	537	97⅝	97	97¼	− ¼
Ancp 13⅞02f	cv	32	42	41	42	−1
Anchr 8⅝06	14.	20	60½	60½	60½	−5
Anxtr 8¼03	cv	25	88½	88	88	−1
ArizP 10⅝00	15.	2	72½	72½	72½	.....
ArizP 12⅛09	15.	17	79⅞	79⅞	79⅞	+ ⅝
AshO 8.8s00	13.	6	66½	66½	66½	+1⅛
AshO 11.1s04	15.	2	76	76	76	.....
AsCp 11s87	12.	14	93¾	93¾	93¾	+1¼
ARich 7.7s00	12.	16	62	61	62	+ ¾
ARich 7⅝03	13.	15	60½	60½	60½	.....
ARich 13⅝11	14.	60	97	97	97	+ ½
ARch d7s91	10.	10	68⅞	68⅞	68⅞	− ¼
AvcoC 5½93	cv	32	66	65½	65½	.....
AvcoC 12s90	13.	25	90	90	90	−1⅛
AvcoF 11s90	12.	6	92⅜	92⅜	92⅜	−1⅞
Avnet 8s13	cv	13	90	90	90	+1
BakInt 7.55s87	8.9	10	85	85	85	−1⅝
BldwU 10s09f	47.	13	22	21	21¼	− ¾
Bally 6s98	cv	5	79	78¼	78¼	−1¾
Bally 10s06	cv	34	85¾	85⅝	85¾	+ ¼
B O 4¼95	8.5	1	50¼	50¼	50¼	.....
BalGE 8⅜06	14.	34	61	59	59½	−2½
BalGE 8¼07	13.	15	61½	61½	61½	−2
BalGE 16¾91	15.	15	111	111	111	.....
BalGE 14¾92	14.	15	104	104	104	−1
BangP 11½98	15.	2	79¼	79¼	79¼	− ⅛
BkBos 10.65s87	11.	25	93	93	93	− ⅜
BkCal 6½96	cv	5	168¾	168¾	168¾	+ ¼
BkNY 12s06	cv	14	122	120½	122	.....
Banka 7⅞03	14.	13	56¾	55⅜	55⅜	− ⅞
Banka 8⅞05	14.	26	62½	61¾	61¾	−1¼
Bkam zr87A	..	5	64½	64½	64½	− ¼
Bkam zr90s	..	20	44⅜	42	42	−2⅛
Bkam zr92s	..	110	33⅛	32½	32¾	+ ¼
Bkam zr87D	..	47	61½	61¼	61¼	+ ¼
Bkam zr91s	..	12	40	40	40	+ ½
Bkam zr93s	..	272	32⅛	30½	30½	− ⅞
BnkTr 8⅛99	14.	7	58¼	58¼	58¼	−1¾
BarcA 9¾86	10.	10	95¼	95¼	95¼	+ ½
BarcA zr90s	..	6	42⅛	40⅛	40⅛	−2
Barnet 12¼06	cv	10	124	124	124	−1
BeatF 10⅞10	14.	1	78⅛	78⅛	78⅛	.....
BecD 4⅛s88	cv	5	88⅛	88⅛	88⅛	.....
BecD 5s89	cv	5	77	77	77	+1
Beker 15⅞03	17.	5	95¾	95¾	95¾	+ ¾
BellCn 14½91	14.	1	102¾	102¾	102¾	−2¼
BellPa 8⅝06	14.	5	62⅝	62⅝	62⅝	− ⅛
BellPa 7⅛12	14.	22	52⅝	52⅝	52⅝	− ¼
BellPa 7½13	14.	2	54⅜	54⅜	54⅜	+ ⅜
BellPa 9⅝14	14.	15	68	66¾	67½	+ ⅞
BenCp 8s01	8.4	22	95¾	95⅝	95¾	+ ¾
BenCp 8.4s08	9.4	40	89	89	89	− ½
BenCp 10¼87†	11.	10	96½	96½	96½	− ½
BethSt 4½90	7.0	1	64¼	64¼	64¼	+ ⅛
BethSt 9s00	15.	8	62	62	62	− ⅛
BethSt 8.45s05	15.	38	56½	56½	56½	− ¼
BethSt 8⅜01	15.	5	57	57	57	−1
Beverly 15s02	16.	10	95⅜	95⅜	95⅜	+ ¼
BigT 8½06	cv	14	78	77	77	−1½
Boeing 8⅞06	cv	27	108¼	107⅜	108¼	+ ¼
BorW 8⅜86	9.1	25	91¾	91¾	91¾	−1
BrkUn 9⅛95	13.	1	70⅞	70⅞	70⅞	+ ⅛
BrkUn 9¾85	10.	5	96½	96½	96½	+ ½
BurlInd 8¾08	cv	15	79	79	79	.....
Burro 13½91	14.	8	98½	98½	98½	− ½
Butte 10¼97	17.	35	63½	61⅞	61⅞	−1⅝

FIGURE 11-6
Price Quotations for Corporate Bonds

for bonds. Major trades are negotiated elsewhere by dealers and institutional investors, either directly or through brokers. Thus, reported prices may be poor guides to values associated with large transactions.

REAL ESTATE MORTGAGES

While many people purchase fixed-income securities, even more issue them. Almost any loan can be regarded as such a security, and anyone who borrows money can be considered to have issued one.

The most important type of personal loan in the United States is the home mortgage. As the name implies, this is secured debt, similar to the mortgage bonds issued by corporations. The loan represents a general obligation of the borrower, with the home in question pledged as security. In the event of default, the lender can sell the property; any excess received over the debt outstanding is returned to the borrower, while any deficiency constitutes a remaining debt.

Some home mortgages in the United States are written for a *long term*, with *fixed interest*, and are *fully amortized*. This differs from traditional corporate mortgage bonds, which only require the issuer to make interest payments prior to maturity, with the entire principal due at maturity. A fully amortized loan requires the issuer to make payments for both principal and interest during the life of the loan, so by maturity the debt is completely repaid via the periodic payments.

In the usual case equal monthly payments are required. For example, a 30-year mortgage of $120,000 at 9% per year (more precisely, $\frac{9}{12}$ of 1% per month) would involve 360 montly payments of $965.55 each. Not surprisingly, the present value of $965.55 per month for 360 months at $\frac{9}{12}$ of 1% per month is $120,000. In fact, the monthly payment is determined by finding the amount that will have the required present value. This can be done with a computer, a business calculator, a book of tables, or a standard formula.

The present value (PV) of a payment of $\$P$ per period for N periods at a discount rate of r (stated as a decimal) per period is:

$$PV = P \left[\frac{1 - \dfrac{1}{(1 + r)^N}}{r} \right] \tag{11-1}$$

In this case:

$$120,000 = 965.55 \left[\frac{1 - \dfrac{1}{(1 + .0075)^{360}}}{.0075} \right]$$

To find the periodic payment $\$P$ with a specified present value, one can rearrange formula (11-1) to give:

$$P = \cfrac{PV}{\left[\cfrac{1 - \cfrac{1}{(1+r)^N}}{r} \right]}$$

In this case:

$$965.55 = \cfrac{120{,}000}{\left[\cfrac{1 - \cfrac{1}{(1+.0075)^{360}}}{.0075} \right]}$$

A fully amortized loan is similar to an issue of serial bonds or a regular bond issue with a sinking fund. In each case the amount owed decreases during the life of the loan. Since the value of the property pledged as security may also decrease over time, amortization (or an equivalent procedure) reduces the probability that the value of the property will fall below the amount of debt outstanding prior to maturity.

Many home mortgages in the Unites States include a *prepayment option*, which is in effect a call option. Typically the borrower may repay the principal amount at any time, although often a "prepayment penalty" (call premium) is assessed if the option is exercised during the first few years after the loan is written.

Some mortgage loans are only partially amortized: each payment exceeds the amount of interest due at the time, but unpaid principal remains at maturity. Second mortgages, often written by the seller of a home, are usually of this type. For example, a ten-year $10,000 mortgage at 12% per year (more precisely, 1% per month) might require monthly payments of $130 and a "balloon" payment of $3,098.83 at maturity. This is equivalent to two loans, one fully amortized and one with no payments prior to maturity. Formula (11-1) shows that the present value of the 120 monthly payments is:

$$130 \left[\cfrac{1 - \cfrac{1}{(1.01)^{120}}}{.01} \right] = 9{,}061.07$$

The remaining amount borrowed, $938.93 (= 10,000 − 9,061.07), must be paid with interest at maturity. The future value 120 months hence is thus:

$$938.93 \times (1.01)^{120} = 3{,}098.83$$

Partially amortized mortgages at fixed interest rates for fairly short terms are often used to avoid long-term commitments at fixed interest rates. The borrower need not pay the remaining principal in full at

TABLE 11-10
Estimated Real Estate Mortgages Outstanding, December 1983

Type	Amount ($ Billions)	Percent
One- to four-family	1,234.7	68.1
Multifamily	145.0	8.0
Commercial	320.7	17.7
Farm	111.4	6.1
	1,811.9	100.0

SOURCE: Salomon Brothers, *1984 Prospects for Financial Markets*.

maturity; instead, the amount may be refinanced in whole or in part via another mortgage at the then-prevailing rate of interest.

An alternative mechanism for avoiding a long-term commitment at a fixed interest rate is the long-term *variable-rate* mortgage. A borrower agrees to pay a stated amount each month until his or her loan is repaid, with each month's interest rate dependent on, for example, the average cost of capital for savings and loan companies in a particular area. The interest required on the current principal is deducted from the payment each month and the balance applied to reduce the principal. The number of payments required to pay off the loan depends on the interest charged. Alternative procedures involve variation in the amount paid each period as interest rates fluctuate.

Mortgages are written on many types of real estate, including commercial property and farms. Table 11-10 shows the estimated amounts outstanding in various categories at the end of 1983. The total amount is substantial—for example, almost three times the amount of corporate bonds outstanding.

The most important sources of mortgage loans are savings companies, life insurance companies, and commercial banks, as Table 11-11 shows.

CONSUMER LOANS

Secured consumer loans are usually of the fixed-interest, fully amortized type, with relatively short maturities. For example, a loan for which an automobile is pledged as security might be written for four years. Other types of *installment loans*, such as those for which appliances and home improvements are pledged, can run up to ten years. The length of the term is usually keyed to the rate at which the value of the pledged asset is likely to decline.

TABLE 11-11
Estimated Ownership of Real Estate Mortgages Outstanding, December 1983

Owner	Amount ($ Billions)	Percent
Mutual savings banks	98.5	7.5
Savings and loan associations	531.0	40.2
Credit unions	6.1	0.5
Life insurance companies	150.8	11.4
Private noninsured pension funds	5.1	0.4
State and local retirement funds	15.9	1.2
Endowments	1.6	0.1
Real estate investment trusts	2.2	0.2
Mortgage corporations	18.0	1.4
Commercial banks	333.3	25.3
Household direct	156.7	11.9
	1,319.5	100.0

SOURCE: Salomon Brothers, *1984 Prospects for Financial Markets*.

Some consumer loans are unsecured. A major type is the "revolving charge account." Purchases are added to the current balance of the account; if the customer pays this amount in full when billed, no interest is charged. Otherwise, interest is added (often at the rate of 1½% per month). In most cases a stated minimum payment exceeding the interest due must be made each month.

Table 11-12 shows the ownership of consumer loans outstanding at the end of 1983. Relatively few of these loans are sold by the original lender to another firm. Thus, department stores, finance companies,

TABLE 11-12
Estimated Ownership of Consumer Loans Outstanding, December 1983

Owner	Amount ($ Billions)	Percent
Mutual savings banks	5.5	1.2
Savings and loan associations	25.8	5.4
Credit unions	52.3	11.0
Commercial banks	212.0	44.4
Finance companies	121.2	25.4
Nonfinancial corporations	60.8	12.7
	477.6	100.0

SOURCE: Salomon Brothers, *1984 Prospects for Financial Markets*.

Fixed-Income Securities

credit unions, and commercial banks provide the bulk of such financing, as anyone who has charged a purchase or signed an automobile loan might suspect.

PREFERRED STOCK

In some respects preferred stock is like a perpetual bond. A given amount is to be paid each year. This may be stated as a percent of the stock's par value (e.g., 8% of $100, or $8 per year) or directly as a dollar figure. Since the security is a stock, such payments are *dividends* instead of interest and hence do not qualify as an expense for purposes of computing the issuing corporation's income tax. On the other hand, failure to make such a payment does not constitute grounds for bankruptcy proceedings.

A recent innovation is the *adjustable-rate preferred stock* (ARPS). The dividend is specified in terms of an *applicable rate*. For example, the annualized percent of par might be set at 1.25% below the specified rate. Differentials may be negative (e.g., −1.25% in the previous case), zero, or positive. The applicable rate for major ARPS issues in 1983 was the largest of the rates on (1) three-month Treasury bills (2) ten-year Treasury bonds, and (3) 20-year Treasury bonds. Rates are generally recomputed and dividends paid quarterly.

Preferred stock is generally *preferred as to dividends*. Specified payments must be made on the preferred stock before any dividends may be paid to holders of the firm's common stock. Failure to pay a preferred dividend in full does not constitute default, but unpaid dividends are usually *cumulative*: all must be paid (but seldom with interest) before a dividend may be declared on the common stock.

No indenture is provided with a preferred stock issue, but protective provisions against potentially harmful actions (e.g., issue of new senior securities) may be written into the corporation's charter. Preferred stockholders may or may not be given voting rights (in some cases such rights are granted only when dividends are in arrears).

Many issues of preferred stock are *callable*, often at a premium; such stock is sometimes said to be *redeemable* at a stated *redemption price*. *Participating* preferred stock entitles the holder to receive extra dividends when earnings permit. *Convertible* preferred stock may, at the option of the holder, be converted into another security (usually the firm's common stock) on stated terms. Some firms issue more than one class of preferred stock, with preference accorded the various classes in a specified order.

In the event of a dissolution of the firm, preferred stock is often *preferred as to assets*. For example, holders might be entitled to receive the stock's par value before any payment is made to common stock holders.

Since preferred stock has many features of a bond without the substantial tax advantage the latter gives to the issuer, it is used less than debt. In 1983, $8.2 billion of such stock was issued, compared with $44.8 billion of publicly offered corporate debt.[5]

As indicated in Chapter 9, interest income from bonds held by a corporation is subject to the corporate income tax, but 85% of any dividend income received may be deducted before the tax liability is determined. This makes the effective tax rate on dividends from preferred stock held by a corporation approximately 6.9% ($.46 \times .15$), compared to a full 46% for interest received from other fixed-income securities. For this reason, preferred stocks tend to sell at prices that give lower before-tax yields than long-term bonds, even though the latter may be considerably lower in risk. Thus, preferred stocks are generally unattractive holdings for noncorporate investors.

Many preferred stocks are traded on major exchanges. Prices at which trades are completed are reported in the financial press in the same format used for common stocks.

Problems

1. Explain the differences in interpreting quotations for U.S. Treasury bills and U.S. Treasury notes.
2. Many bond indentures include call provisions. What are the potential effects of such provisions on the corporation and its bondholders?
3. What are the differences in the following three yield figures: current yield, yield-to-maturity, and coupon yield?
4. When is a bond's current yield greater than its coupon rate?
5. Figure 11-3 shows the following bid and asked prices for 7¼% U.S. Treasury bonds maturing August 1992:

Bid	Asked
69.18	70.2

What is the dollar spread between bid and asked prices for this bond?

[5] Drexel Burnham Lambert, *Public Offerings of Corporate Securities*, *1983*.

Fixed-Income Securities

6. Consider a 7.5% 25-year Treasury bond having a 15-year deferred call provision that has just been sold for $1,002. If the current yield-to-maturity on fully callable Treasury bonds is 8%, what dollar value are investors placing on the deferred call provision? Assume interest payments are made annually.

7. Suppose on January 1, 1984, you purchased a U.S. Treasury bill that matures in 360 days. Your purchase price was $9,300.
   a. What was the interest rate reported in the *Wall Street Journal* for the bill you purchased?
   b. Is it possible that you could receive a realized yield greater than that calculated in (a) if you were to sell the bill before its maturity? Explain fully.

8. An investor has $20,000 in cash. She will need the cash in six months, but not before. Compare the relative advantages to her of investing her money in (a) a six-month U.S. Treasury bill, (b) a bank passbook savings account, and (c) a savings and loan six-month account paying a competitive interest rate.

9. Some lenders offer mortgages with monthly payments that increase from year to year. How can you be sure that the scheduled set of payments is correct, given the stated rate of interest? How does the decline of principal on such a mortgage compare with that on a conventional mortgage with equal payments every month?

12

Bond Prices, Yields, and Returns

INTRODUCTION

Five attributes of a bond greatly influence its price: (1) maturity, (2) coupon rate, (3) call provisions, (4) tax status, and (5) "agency rating" (an estimate of the likelihood of default). At any time the structure of prices for bonds differing in these dimensions can be examined and used to estimate the prices of other bonds (whether already issued or not). The underlying relationships usually are described in terms of equivalent yields, the overall pattern being called the *yield structure*. Often attention is confined to differences along a single dimension, holding the other attributes constant. Thus the set of yields of bonds of different maturities constitutes the *term structure*, the set of yields of bonds of different risk the *risk structure*, and so on.

The return on a bond over any given holding period depends to a major extent on its price at the beginning of the period and its price at the end of the period. Thus the return on a bond over, say, a one-year period will depend on the yield structure at the beginning of the year and at the end of the year. To analyze possible bond returns one must thus analyze possible changes in the yield structure. Indeed, this is the essential element in bond analysis. While the characteristics of the issuer are relevant for estimating default risk, well-known agencies regularly analyze such factors for major issues and assign standard ratings. Though many may disagree with a bond's rating, its market price will tend to follow the prices of bonds with similar terms and ratings.

FORWARD AND SPOT INTEREST RATES

Chapter 4 introduced the idea of a forward interest rate. The *forward interest rate* for a commitment made today to loan money in year t_1, to be repaid (with interest) in year t_2, can be described by:

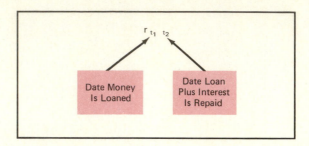

The only risk associated with a forward contract arises when there is some possibility that one of the parties might fail to meet its terms. Although the commitments are made now, no money need change hands until time t_1.

A *spot interest rate* is one in which money is borrowed now, to be repaid at some later date. At any time there can be a one-year spot rate, a two-year spot rate, and so on. There can also be a forward rate for a one-year loan beginning in one year, another beginning in two years, and so forth, as well as a forward rate for a two-year loan beginning in one year, another for one beginning in two years, and so on.

Some structure of spot and forward rates will apply to default-free commitments. The promised terms in such cases will equal the actual results, and there will be no divergence between actual and expected values. However, in cases in which there is some possibility of default, promised terms will be higher, to compensate for the potential shortfall. Expected results will, in such cases, be below the promised amounts.

Most analysts consider the interest rates for default-free bonds to form "the" yield structure; "risk differentials" are then added to obtain the relevant yields for bonds of lower quality. While subject to some criticism, this procedure makes it possible to think about a complicated set of relationships sequentially.

Differentials between yields of related instruments are usually termed *yield spreads* and measured in *basis points*. One basis point equals .01%. If the yield-to-maturity for one bond is 7.50% and that of another is 7.90%, the spread is 40 basis points.

THE DISCOUNT FUNCTION AND FORWARD INTEREST RATES

Arbitrage is the act of buying something at one price and selling it or something equivalent at a higher price, virtually concurrently. The advantages associated with this sort of activity make arbitrage situations well worth discovering and exploiting. This insures that any disparity will be quickly discovered; when arbitrageurs exploit such a disparity, prices will tend to move back into line as buying pressure drives up the price of one investment and selling pressure drives down the price of the other. Arbitrageurs can make money, but not much and not for long from any one situation. With small and temporary exceptions, equivalent things will not sell at two different prices.

This means that the entire structure of prices for default-free bonds could (in the absence of taxes) be described by a set of discount factors:

$d_1 =$ the present value of $1 received with certainty one period hence

$d_2 =$ the present value of $1 received with certainty two periods hence

and so on. The set of such factors constitutes the current *market discount function*.

While the U.S. government does not issue zero-coupon bonds with a wide range of maturity dates, the zero-coupon securities issued by brokerage firms and backed by government bonds act as surrogates for such securities. For example, if a $1,000 par three-year zero-coupon bond sells for $830:

$$d_3 = .83$$

The structure of prices for zero-coupon default-free bonds of different maturities is the discount function.

The relationship between forward rates and the discount function is relatively straightforward. One dollar grows to $(1+ r_{01})$ dollars in one year. It grows to $(1 + r_{01})(1 + r_{12})$ dollars in two years, and so on. Thus:

$$d_1 = \frac{1}{1 + r_{01}} \tag{12-1a}$$

$$d_2 = \frac{1}{(1 + r_{01})(1 + r_{12})} \tag{12-1b}$$

$$d_3 = \frac{1}{(1 + r_{01})(1 + r_{12})(1 + r_{23})} \tag{12-1c}$$

Dividing (12-1b) by (12-1c) gives:

$$\frac{d_2}{d_3} = 1 + r_{23}$$

In general:

$$\frac{d_{t_1}}{d_{t_2}} = 1 + r_{t_1,t_2}$$

where the forward interest rate is expressed in terms of the length of time between t_1 and t_2.

ESTIMATING THE DISCOUNT FUNCTION

Prices of all zero-coupon Treasury security-backed bonds are not readily available to all investors, and secondary markets for some of them are not sufficiently active at times to provide direct estimates of some current discount factors. For historic studies, prices of such bonds cannot be used prior to the 1980s, since none existed. Fortunately, it is possible to *infer* the discount function from the prices of regular (coupon-bearing) bonds.

A simple procedure uses statistical analysis (multiple regression). Bonds with different coupons and maturities are analyzed. As discussed earlier, the price of each bond should be related to the amounts paid each period, with the relationship depending on the current set of discount factors. If the relationship were perfect, the price of every bond could be completely "explained" in this way. However, owing to the use of prices from trades that occurred at different times, the effects of call provisions, differences in tax treatment, and so on, there will be "unexplained" portions of some prices.

The relationships to be analyzed are:

$$P_i = d_1 P_{i1} + d_2 P_{i2} + \cdots + U_i$$
$$P_j = d_1 P_{j1} + d_2 P_{j2} + \cdots + U_j$$
$$\cdot$$
$$\cdot$$
$$\cdot$$

where:

$$P_i = \text{the price of bond } i$$
$$P_{i1}, P_{i2}, \ldots = \text{the amounts paid by bond } i \text{ in periods 1, 2, } \ldots$$
$$d_1, d_2, \ldots = \text{the discount factors for periods 1, 2, } \ldots$$
$$U_i = \text{the unexplained part of } P_i$$
$$P_j = \text{the price of bond } j$$
$$P_{j1}, P_{j2}, \ldots = \text{the amounts paid by bond } j \text{ in periods 1, 2, } \ldots$$
$$U_j = \text{the unexplained part of } P_j$$

In regression parlance, each bond is an *observation*. Bond prices are the *dependent variables*, and their payments are the *independent varia-*

bles. Regression analysis provides estimates of the *coefficients*, which are the desired discount factors. It also determines a *residual* for each bond, which is the difference between its price and the value attributed to its discounted payments.

This type of analysis is used by some organizations solely to estimate a discount function, with no use being made of the residuals, which are assumed to be due solely to factors not taken into account in the analysis. Other organizations do use the residuals, choosing to further investigate the prices and characteristics of bonds with large (positive or negative) residual values on the grounds that those with large positive residuals might be overpriced and those with large negative residuals might be underpriced.

Many organizations that estimate the discount function from prices of coupon bonds use considerably more sophisticated procedures. Periods of differing length may be chosen, with payments within a period being "moved" to the middle of the period, based on (for example) the bond's yield-to-maturity. Added factors may be employed to represent call provisions, differential pricing of, e.g., Federal agency issues, and the like. Procedures may be incorporated to take differences in tax treatment into account. And so on.

THE TERM STRUCTURE OF INTEREST RATES

To determine appropriate prices for default-free bonds one needs to know the relevant discount factors—i.e., the current market prices of $1 one period hence, two periods hence, and so on. Alternatively, one needs to know the current set of forward interest rates, for from them the discount factors can be computed. A set of interest rates for different time periods is called a *term structure*.

What factors influence the term structure? To address the question, it is useful to consider two aspects: (1) the determination of spot interest rates and (2) the relationship between forward rates and expected future spot rates.

The first aspect was discussed at some length in earlier chapters. Supply and demand for credit are the direct determinants of spot interest rates. But the fundamental forces are productive opportunities, preferences for present versus future consumption, and expected inflation. The first two factors determine the expected real rate of interest; when expected inflation is added, the result approximates the nominal rate of interest.

The second aspect is more difficult. Several theories have been advanced to explain the term structure. One, the *expectations theory*, holds that every forward rate represents a consensus opinion of the expected spot rate for the period in question. This leads to the notion of a fairly stable long-run rate of interest involving a "normal" real rate and "normal" inflation. When current conditions make short-term rates abnormally high (owing, say, to excessive rates of inflation), the term structure will be downward-sloping. When current conditions make short-term rates abnormally low (owing, say, to temporary recession and deflation), the term structure will be upward-sloping.

This approach is reasonably consistent with experience. But it suggests that the term structure is likely to be downward-sloping as often as it is upward-sloping. However, upward-sloping structures tend to be more common.

To explain this, the notion of *liquidity preference* has been advanced. If investors are concerned with relatively short holding periods, short-term instruments will be considered less risky than long-term ones (since any subsequent change in interest rates will affect the year-end value of a long-term instrument, and hence its one-year return). To hold a long-term instrument, investors may thus require a risk premium in the form of greater expected return. Moreover, governments and corporations may be willing to pay such a premium. There are two possible reasons why issuers might prefer long-term borrowing, even at higher interest rates. First, frequent refinancing may be costly in terms of registration, advertising, paperwork, and so on. Second, issuers may be concerned with longer holding periods. If so, long-term bonds will be less risky than short-term bonds in their view, and they will be willing to pay (via higher expected interest costs) to reduce risk.

This theory implies that each forward rate will equal the expected spot rate for the period in question plus a liquidity premium, and that the latter will be larger, the farther in the future is the period.

Figure 12-1 shows possible effects of such premiums on forward rates. In Figure 12-1(a) spot rates are expected to remain constant. Liquidity premiums are presumed to increase, but at a decreasing rate, leading to an upward-sloping forward-rate curve. In Figure 12-1(b) liquidity premiums are similar, but spot rates are expected to increase from presently low levels to more normal values. Both elements contribute to make the term structure upward-sloping. In Figure 12-1(c) current spot rates are considered abnormally high. A combination of decreasing expected spot rates and increasing liquidity premiums may lead to forward rates that either decrease or else increase and then decrease, giving a "humped" pattern such as that shown in the figure.

A third explanation for the determination of the term structure rests on the assumption that there is *market segmentation*: various holders and issuers are asserted to be restricted by law, preference, or custom to *preferred habitats* in terms of maturity. This implies that only major disparities in rates for securities of different maturities may lead to substantial changes in the buying, selling, and issuance of bonds.

Empirical evidence provides some insight into the determinants

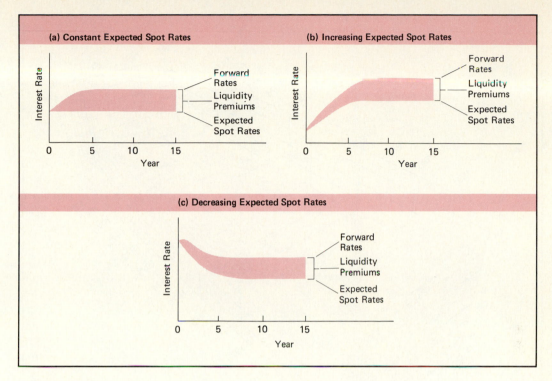

FIGURE 12-1
Effects of Liquidity Premiums on Forward Interest Rates

of the term structure, but it is difficult to assess the relative importance of these three factors with any precision.

The market-segmentation hypothesis receives relatively slight empirical validation. While there is some lack of flexibility on the part of bond buyers, sellers, and issuers, it apparently does not cause substantial and persistent anomalies in the term structure.

The liquidity-premium hypothesis receives some support from empirical evidence. In the majority of years over the last four decades long-term bond yields have exceeded short-term interest rates. If a bond's yield-to-maturity is expected to be the same at the end of a year, the expected holding-period return for the year will also equal its yield-to-maturity. Under these conditions an upward-sloping pattern of liquidity premiums thus implies that expected one-year returns will be greater for long-term than for short-term bonds. This is reasonable enough, as the uncertainty associated with one-year returns is also greater for long-term bonds. The prices of long-term bonds (and hence their short-term returns) are more sensitive to changes in the yield curve than are those of short-term bonds; the former thus have more

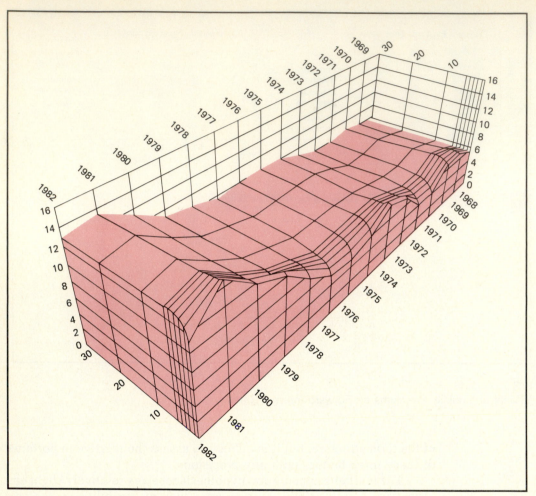

SOURCE: Salomon Brothers, *1982-83 Bond Market Analysis and Outlook*.

FIGURE 12-2
The Government Yield Curve, 1968-1982

"interest-rate risk." This type of risk is reduced but not eliminated when a highly diversified market portfolio, including both bonds and stocks, is held.

On average, the one-year holding-period return from a long-term bond has been slightly higher than that from a short-term investment. For example, from 1926 to 1982 the difference between the return on an index of long-term government bonds and that on U.S. Treasury bills averaged .05% per month (approximately .56% per year).[1] A reason-

[1] Based on data in Roger C. Ibbotson and Rex A. Sinquefield, *Stocks, Bonds, Bills and Inflation: The Past and the Future*, 1982 edition, The Financial Analysts Research Foundation, 1982, as updated by the authors.

able conclusion might hold that liquidity premiums range from zero for one-year commitments to 1% for long-term ones.[2]

Figure 12-2 shows the term structure of interest rates on U.S. government coupon-bearing bonds from 1968 through 1982. In general, the structure was upward-sloping (long-term yields higher than short-term yields) in periods of lower interest rates and downward-sloping (long-term rates less than short-term rates) in periods of higher interest rates.

THE EFFECT OF COUPON RATE ON YIELD-TO-MATURITY

As indicated earlier, one of the attributes of a bond considered relevant for price determination is its coupon rate. In part, this is due to the differential tax treatment of interest income and capital gains. But there is another factor: the influence of the coupon rate on the effective maturity of a bond.

To illustrate the point, consider two default-free noncallable bonds, each with ten years remaining until maturity; one has a 3% coupon rate, the other a 10% rate. Assume further that taxes need not be considered. Table 12-1 shows the forward rates for each year, the associated present-value (discount) factors, the payments for each of the bonds, and the present values of the payments.

The price of each bond is simply the sum of the present values of its payments. Thus the low-coupon bond will sell at a discount ($71.39), while the high-coupon bond will sell at a premium ($121.98). Although priced appropriately, the bonds do not provide the same yield-to-maturity: that of the low-coupon bond exceeds that of the high-coupon bond by 20 basis points.

The reason is not hard to see. Relatively more of the low-coupon bond's value is provided at maturity. Thus the payment at maturity represents 72% of the value of the low-coupon bond (51.20/71.39 ≈ .72). But it represents only 45% of the value of the high-coupon bond (54.68/121.98 ≅ .45). A low-coupon bond is, in effect, a "longer" bond than a high-coupon bond of similar maturity. And when the term structure is upward-sloping, longer bonds offer higher yields.

The yield spread between low- and high-coupon bonds of the same maturity clearly depends on the disparity in their coupons. It also depends on the structure of interest rates. In the absence of tax effects, with an upward-sloping term structure high-coupon bonds would offer lower yields than low-coupon bonds (as in the example in Table 12-1); with a flat term structure coupon rates would not affect yields; and with a downward-sloping term structure high-coupon bonds would offer higher yields than low-coupon bonds. This is illustrated

---

[2] The estimated standard error of the mean value suggested that the odds were two out of three that the "true" value lay between (.56 − .92)% and (.56 + .92)% per year.

TABLE 12-1
Prices and Yields of Low- and High-coupon Bonds

Year (t)	Forward Rate (%)	Present Value of $1 ($d_t$)	LOW-COUPON BOND		HIGH-COUPON BOND	
			Payment ($)	Present Value of Payment ($)	Payment ($)	Present Value of Payment ($)
1	5.0	.9524	3.00	2.8572	10.00	9.524
2	5.5	.9027	3.00	2.7081	10.00	9.027
3	6.0	.8516	3.00	2.5548	10.00	8.516
4	6.5	.7997	3.00	2.3991	10.00	7.997
5	7.0	.7473	3.00	2.2419	10.00	7.473
6	7.5	.6952	3.00	2.0856	10.00	6.952
7	8.0	.6437	3.00	1.9311	10.00	6.437
8	8.5	.5933	3.00	1.7799	10.00	5.933
9	9.0	.5443	3.00	1.6329	10.00	5.443
10	9.5	.4971	103.00	51.2013	110.00	54.681
				71.3919		121.983
			Yield-to-maturity:	7.09%		6.89%

in Figures 12-3(a), (b), and (c), which show curves for forward rates, the yields-to-maturity for zero-coupon bonds, and the yields-to-maturity for regular (positive) coupon bonds.

The yield-to-maturity on a zero-coupon bond is, in effect, an average of all the forward rates up to the maturity date.[3] Thus when forward rates increase (decrease) with maturity, the yield-to-maturity on a zero-coupon bonds will be less (more) than the forward rate for the bond's maturity date. The yield-to-maturity on a positive-coupon bond is a more complicated kind of average that places even more weight on earlier years' forward rates; thus it will be smaller (larger) than the yield-to-maturity on a zero-coupon bond when forward rates increase (decrease) with maturity.

DURATION AND CHANGES IN THE TERM STRUCTURE

When interest rates change, most bond prices change also, but some react more than others. To predict the magnitude of the effect of a shift in interest rates on a given bond's price, we must know more

---

[3] If y_T represents the yield-to-maturity on a zero-coupon bond maturing in year T:

$$1 + y_T = \sqrt[T]{(1 + r_{01})(1 + r_{12}) \cdots (1 + r_{T-1,T})}$$

and $(1 + y_T)$ is the geometric mean of $(1 + r_{01})$ through $(1 + r_{T-1,T})$.

Bond Prices, Yields, and Returns

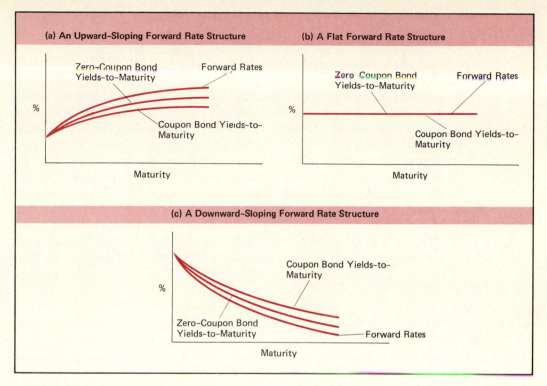

FIGURE 12-3
Possible Term Structures

about the shift. We will consider, first, a situation in which every yield changes in the same way, then realistic cases in which shorter-term yields change more than longer ones.

Let y_t represent the yield-to-maturity on a t-year zero-coupon bond, expressed as a decimal. For example, if the yield on a three-year bond of this type is 7%, $y_3 = .07$ and $(1 + y_3) = 1.07$. Now assume that each value of $(1 + y_t)$ changes by the same percentage; then the change in a bond's present value can be estimated by:

$$\% \text{ change in } PV \approx - \left[\sum_{t=1}^{T} \left(\frac{t \cdot PV(P_t)}{PV} \right) \right] \times \% \text{ change in each } (1 + y_t)$$

where:

$T =$ the period in which the bond matures
$PV(P_t) =$ the present value of P_t, the payment in period t
$PV =$ the current present value of the bond

The bracketed expression is the bond's *duration*. As discussed earlier, this is a weighted average of the times when payments are made,

Bond Prices, Yields, and Returns

each being weighted by the proportion of present value contributed by the payment made at the time.

In Chapter 4 we said that bonds of similar duration tend to react similarly to changes in interest rates. The formula shows that when all yields change in the manner assumed here, prices of bonds of equal duration change by approximately equal percentages. However, rarely do yields on long-term bonds move as much as those on short-term ones. For example, a common cause of a shift in the yields on default-free bonds is a change in expectations regarding inflation. If the likely degree of near-term inflation increases, short-term yields will rise. So will long-term yields, but unless expectations for long-term inflation are revised upward to the same extent, long-term yields will rise by a smaller amount. Figure 12-4 shows the relationship between monthly changes in yield-to-maturity for bonds of various maturities and changes in yield-to-maturity of one-year bonds from 1930 through 1979. For every 1% change in the yield-to-maturity on a one-year bond, two-

FIGURE 12-4
Sensitivities of Changes in Yield-to-Maturity for Bonds of Various Maturities to Changes in Yield-to-Maturity on One-Year Bonds, 1930-1979

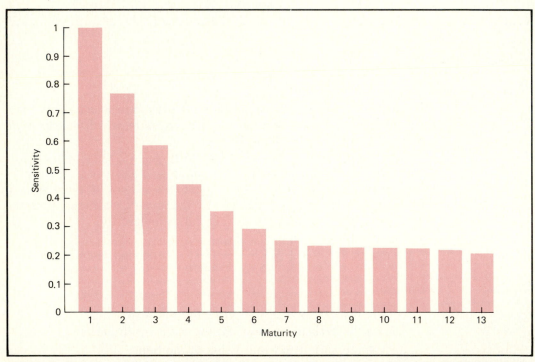

SOURCE: Jeffrey Nelson and Stephen Schaefer, "The Dynamics of the Term Structure and Alternative Portfolio Immunization Strategies," in George G. Kaufman, G. O. Bierwag, and Alden Toevs, *Innovations in Bond Portfolio Management*: *Duration Analysis and Immunization* (JAI Press, Inc., 1983), p. 75.

year bond yields changed only .767% on average, while thirteen-year bond yields changed only .208%, with intermediate maturities falling between these values.

If long-term rates did change as much as short-term rates when the term structure shifted, duration would provide a good estimate of the sensitivity of a bond's price to changes in interest rates. When the price of a bond with a duration of one year changed by 1%, the price of a bond with a duration of five years would change by 5%. Over time, the standard deviation of the holding-period returns of the five-year-duration bond would be five times as large as that of the one-year-duration bond. Figure 12-5 shows that this has not been the case. From 1950 through 1979, the return on a portfolio of bonds with a duration of five years varied less than twice as much as that of a portfolio of bonds with a duration of one year.

FIGURE 12-5
Relative Standard Deviations of Rates of Return on Bonds
with Different Durations, 1950–1979

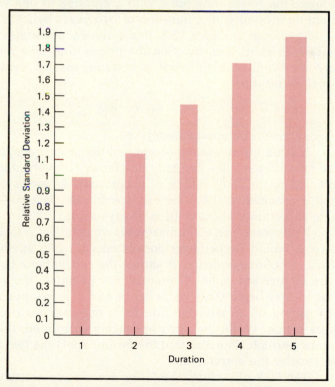

SOURCE: Jonathan E. Ingersoll, Jr., "Is Immunization Feasible? Evidence from the CRSP Data," in George G. Kaufman, G. O. Bierwag, and Alden Toevs, *Innovations in Bond Portfolio Management*: *Duration Analysis and Immunization* (JAI Press, Inc., 1983), p. 175.

Since long-term rates tend to move less than short-term rates, duration will generally *overstate* the magnitude of the reaction of a bond's price to changes in short-term rates. However, it can still serve as a useful measure, since bonds with similar durations will still react in relatively similar ways to typical shifts in the term structure.

FACTOR MODELS OF BOND RETURNS

Duration is sometimes advocated as the key element in a one-factor model of bond returns. For example:

$$\tilde{R}_i = a_i + b_{i1}\tilde{F}_1 + \tilde{e}_i \tag{12-2}$$

where:

$b_{i1} = -D_i$ (the duration of bond i)

$F_1 = $ the one-year interest rate

In this model, a 1% increase in the one-year interest rate is expected to lower the return on a bond with a duration of one year by 1%, the return on a bond with a duration of two years by 2%, and so on.

As shown in Figure 12-5, this seriously overstates the impact of changes in short-term rates on the prices (and thus returns) of long-duration bonds. A better approach would specify a response *proportional* to duration:

$$b_{i1} = -kD_i$$

where k might be approximately .5.

A strict interpretation of some of the procedures used with duration measures implies that only one factor is involved in bond returns and that is the *only* source of uncertainty. In terms of formula (12-2), it is assumed that the security-specific risk is zero—i.e., that there is no uncertainty about e_i (it is always zero).

If this were true, all interest rates would move in lock step: changes in rates would be perfectly correlated with one another. Table 12-2 provides counterevidence. It shows the correlations between various pairs of forward rates of interest. For example, the rate for a one-year loan to begin three years hence had a correlation over the 1950–1979 period of .86 with the rate for a one-year loan to begin twenty years hence. While the rates are highly correlated, the relationships are not perfect. Note also that the farther apart the two rates involved, the smaller the correlation.

The lack of perfect correlation among interest rates suggests the presence of more than one pervasive factor in the determination of changes in bond prices (and thus bond returns). Since long-term interest rates are not perfectly correlated with short-term rates, the inclusion

TABLE 12-2
Correlations of Forward Interest Rates, 1950-1979

Maturity	1	3	5	7	10	15	20
1	1.00	.96	.94	.88	.92	.83	.80
3		1.00	.95	.94	.96	.87	.86
5			1.00	.94	.92	.87	.87
7				1.00	.91	.83	.87
10					1.00	.87	.85
15						1.00	.95
20							1.00

SOURCE: Jonathan E. Ingersoll, Jr., "Is Immunization Feasible? Evidence from the CRSP Data," in George G. Kaufman, G. O. Bierwag, and Alden Toevs, *Innovations in Bond Portfolio Management: Duration Analysis and Immunization* (JAI Press, Inc., 1983), p. 175.

of *both* as factors can help explain the returns of not only short- and long-term bonds, but also those with intermediate maturities.

A direct approach might specify a model of the form:

$$\tilde{R} = a_i + b_{i1}\tilde{F}_1 + b_{i2}\tilde{F}_2 + \tilde{e}_i \qquad (12\text{-}3)$$

where:

F_1 = a short-term interest rate
F_2 = a long-term interest rate $\qquad$ (12-3a)

For some purposes it is preferable to focus instead on (1) a long-term interest rate and (2) the *spread* between long-term and short-term interest rates[4] —that is:

F_1 = the difference between the long-term interest rate and the short-term interest rate $\qquad$ (12-3b)
F_2 = the long-term interest rate

In this case, the first factor measures the *slope* of the term structure. It is positive when the structure is upward-sloping, zero when it is flat, and negative when it is downward-sloping. One study[5] found the spread averaged about 1% from 1930 to 1979 and tended to be *mean-reverting*—moving back toward its average after diverging from it. The speed of reversion appeared to be moderate, with about 5% of the gap being closed (on average) in one month.

Over the 1930–1979 period, the long-term interest rate did not

---

[4] This approach was first proposed in H. R. Ayres, and J. Y. Barry, "The Equilibrium Yield Curve for Government Securities," *Financial Analysts Journal*, May/June, 1979, pp. 310–39.

[5] See Jeffrey Nelson and Stephen Schaefer, "The Dynamics of the Term Structure and Alternative Portfolio Immunization Strategies," in George G. Kaufman, G. O. Bierwag, and Alden Toevs, *Innovations in Bond Portfolio Management: Duration Analysis and Immunization* (JAI Press, Inc., 1983).

appear to be mean-reverting. Instead, it moved more or less randomly from month to month (i.e. followed a *random walk*). Moreover, movements in the long-term rate were uncorrelated with changes in the spread between long-term and short-term rates.[6] Such information can be used to better estimate the expected values of the factors in a model such as that given in formula (12-3b) as well as their risks.

There remains the problem of estimating the sensitivities (b_{i1}, b_{i2}) of a given bond to such factors. Historic relationships cannot be used directly, for the remaining life of a bond grows shorter each year, changing its maturity. Instead, a bond can be broken into its component parts and the sensitivities of each component estimated.

Let:

b_{t1} = the sensitivity of the return on a t-year zero-coupon bond to factor 1

b_{t2} = the sensitivity of the return on a t-year zero-coupon bond to factor 2

Such sensitivities can be estimated by analyzing the relationships between changes in discount factors and changes in interest rates.

Bond i can be considered a portfolio of zero-coupon bonds, each of which has a set of sensitivities to the two factors. Given the present discount function, the present value of each of these zero-coupon bonds can be determined. For a default-free bond, the sum will equal the bond's present price (i.e., the value of the portfolio). The ratio of each present value to the sum indicates the portion of the portfolio with the related maturity.

The sensitivity of a portfolio to a factor is a weighted average of the sensitivities of its component securities to that factor, using relative market values as weights. In this case:

$$b_{i1} = \sum_t \frac{PV(P_{it})}{P_i} \, b_{t1}$$

$$b_{i2} = \sum_t \frac{PV(P_{it})}{P_i} \, b_{t2}$$

where:

P_{it} = the amount paid by bond i in period t

P_i = the price of bond i

which provides the needed estimates of the sensitivities of the return of the bond to the two factors.

To accommodate corporate bonds as well as government bonds, additional factors may be employed. For example, a "corporate-government bond differential" factor might be included, with corporate bonds

---

[6] *Ibid.*

assigned a sensitivity of 1.0 to it, and the government bonds assigned a sensitivity of 0.0. Better yet, sufficient factors to explain the major determinants of bond *and* stock prices could be included, with appropriate sensitivities of each bond (or stock) to each of the factors selected. The ultimate goal is one factor model, including all the pervasive factors that affect security prices.

IMMUNIZATION

Many organizations face a set of liabilities requiring payments at various times in the future. To help make such payments, assets are invested in the interim. The closer the "match" of assets with liabilities, the smaller the risk of the difference (i.e., net worth).

Financial intermediaries (banks, savings and loan companies, insurance companies, and so on) provide clear examples. So do corporate pension funds, in which a set of assets (the *pension fund*) is invested on behalf of pension-plan *beneficiaries*, who have *accrued* benefits to be paid routinely following their retirement. In the case of a pension fund, the difference between liabilities and assets is termed the *unfunded liability*; it is, in effect, the negative of net worth.

The process of minimizing the variance in net worth of such an investor can be accomplished by *immunizing* the liabilities.

The simplest case involves *cash-flow matching*. For example, zero-coupon bonds might be purchased with appropriate amounts and maturities so that the cash paid each year was precisely the amount needed to make the required cash payment. In this way, the liabilities are *completely immunized* and there is no uncertainty about net worth. Alternatively, coupon-bearing bonds might be combined in such a way that the cash received each period sufficed to make the required payments. To find the appropriate mix of such bonds often requires sophisticated analysis, using, for example, the techniques of linear or quadratic programming.

If it is infeasible to match cash flows, the sensitivities of the assets to key factors can be chosen to be as close as possible to the corresponding sensitivities of the liabilities. If a set of assets is selected that has an overall duration equal to that of the liabilities, more or less "parallel" shifts in the term structure of interest rates will have little if any effect on net worth, since both asset and liability values will respond by the same amount. A number of portfolio managers employ this type of *duration matching* for the portion of a pension fund designated to back the benefits of employees already in retirement.

A better procedure would attempt to match sensitivities to both long-term interest rates and the spread between long-term and short-term rates [i.e., b_{i1} and b_{i2} in formula (12-3b)]. Even in this case, however, only *partial immunization* would be achieved, since some risk would remain, owing to the security-specific risks of the assets and liabilities.

Immunization can reduce the risk associated with net worth. But this does not necessarily make it desirable. Reducing risk may or may not reduce expected future net worth. A broader view would consider the effects of different kinds of assets on *both* the risk and the expected value of future net worth. Inefficient investment strategies (which provide a given expected return with unnecessarily large risks) should be rejected. Of those remaining, the optimal one will depend, as always, on the risk tolerance of the person(s) or organization(s) that will ultimately be affected by changes in the net worth.

TAXES AND BOND YIELDS

We have already seen the impact of differential tax treatment on the yields of tax-free municipal bonds vis-à-vis those of otherwise similar taxable bonds. As shown in Chapter 9, the former have yields-to-maturity 20% to 40% lower than those of the latter.

Taxation affects bond prices and yields in other ways. For example, any low-coupon bond selling at a discount provides return in two forms: coupon payments and capital gains. In the United States the former are taxable as ordinary income, while the latter may qualify for the more favorable treatment accorded capital gains. This suggests that low-coupon ("deep discount") bonds might be priced to give lower before-tax yields than high-coupon bonds, other things equal.

There may be at least three separate though related sets of discount factors (and associated forward interest rates) for default-free bonds: one for fully taxable returns, another for price changes taxed as capital gains and losses, and a third for the return of principal and tax-exempt interest. Given a large enough set of bonds of different types, it is possible to estimate all three sets of rates concurrently. However, this is generally not done. Instead, a yield curve or discount function for bonds of one type is estimated. Yields or discount factors for bonds with other tax attributes are either analyzed separately or compared with those of the first type and "normal" yield or discount factor spreads estimated.

YIELDS ON CALLABLE BONDS

Callable bonds issued at times of high yields appear to offer more than they are likely to deliver. A 12% ten-year bond issued at par ($100) might be callable five years later at $100. At that time, if yields on similar five-year bonds were substantially less than 12%, the bond would probably be called. For example, if yields on similar five-year bonds were 8%, an investor who had planned to hold the original bond for ten years might end up with an 8% five-year bond with the proceeds obtained when the first bond was called. If the second bond were not subsequently called, the apparent and actual results would be as shown below. This suggests that the higher the yield-to-maturity of a callable bond, the greater is the likely divergence between actual and apparent yields.

		COUPONS RECEIVED IN YEAR											
Investment		1	2	3	4	5	6	7	8	9	10	Principal Received in Year 10	Yield-to-Maturity
Apparent	$100	$12	$12	$12	$12	$12	$12	$12	$12	$12	$12	$100	12.0%
Actual	$100	12	12	12	12	12	8	8	8	8	8	100	10.5%

This is borne out by experience. Figure 12-6 plots the coupon rate at time of issue (horizontal axis) and actual yield obtained up to

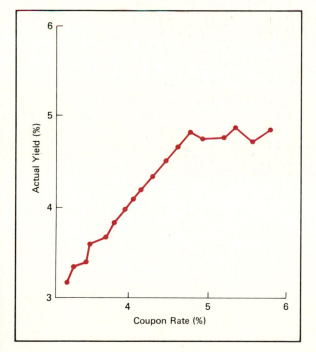

FIGURE 12-6
Promised and Actual Yields of Callable Aa Utility Bonds, 1956-1964

SOURCE: Frank C. Jen and James E. Wert, "The Effect of Call Risk on Corporate Bond Yields," *The Journal of Finance*, XXII (December 1967), 646.

the original maturity date by an investor (vertical axis), assuming that payments obtained in the event of a call were reinvested in noncallable bonds with appropriate maturities. The curve is based on experience for a group of callable bonds issued by utility companies during a period of fluctuating interest rates.

BOND RATINGS

In 1909 John Moody began to rate bonds; now both Moody's and Standard and Poor's provide ratings for thousands of corporate and municipal bonds. Figure 12-7 provides details on the ratings assigned by Standard and Poor's. Classifications used by Moody's are shown in Figure 12-8.

A broader set of categories is often employed, with bonds being classified as of either *investment grade* or *speculative grade*. At times certain regulated financial institutions (banks, savings and loans, insurance companies) have been precluded from purchasing bonds that were not of "investment grade," with this term defined to include bonds assigned one of the four top ratings (e.g., AAA through BBB from Standard and Poor's).

Investment-grade bonds are sometimes thought to command "superpremium" prices, and hence disproportionately low yields, since an important group of buyers is encouraged or forced to purchase them. However, such a disparity in yields could attract a great many issuers who would increase the supply of such bonds, causing their prices to fall and their yields to rise. For a significant superpremium to persist, rather substantial market segmentation on both the buying and the selling side would be required. There is no clear evidence that the differences in yields between investment-grade bonds and others are more than commensurate with the differences in risk.

According to Moody's, ratings are designed to provide "investors with a simple system of gradation by which the relative investment qualities of bonds may be noted."[7] Moreover:

> Since ratings involve a judgment about the future, on the one hand, and since they are used by investors as a means of protection, on the other, the effort is made when assigning ratings to look at "worst" potentialities in the "visible" future rather than solely at the past record and the status of the present. Investors using the ratings should not, therefore, expect to find in them a reflection of statistical factors alone, since they are an appraisal of long-term risks including the recognition of many nonstatistical factors.[8]

---

[7] *Moody's Industrial Manual*, 1979.
[8] *Ibid*.

A Standard & Poor's corporate or municipal debt rating is a current assessment of the creditworthiness of an obligor with respect to a specific obligation. This assessment may take into consideration obligors such as guarantors, insurers, or lessees.

The debt rating is not a recommendation to purchase, sell, or hold a security, inasmuch as it does not comment as to market price or suitability for a particular investor.

The ratings are based, in varying degrees, on the following considerations:

1. Likelihood of default—capacity and willingness of the obligor as to the timely payment of interest and repayment of principal in accordance with the terms of the obligation;

2. Nature of and provisions of the obligation;

3. Protection afforded by, and relative position of, the obligation in the event of bankruptcy, reorganization, or other arrangement under the laws of bankruptcy and other laws affecting creditor's rights.

AAA   Debt rated 'AAA' has the highest rating assigned by Standard & Poor's. Capacity to pay interest and repay principal is extremely strong.

AA   Debt rated 'AA' has a very strong capacity to pay interest and repay principal and differs from the highest rated issues only in small degree.

A   Debt rated 'A' has a strong capacity to pay interest and repay principal although it is somewhat more susceptible to the adverse effects of changes in circumstances and economic conditions than debt in higher rated categories.

BBB   Debt rated 'BBB' is regarded as having an adequate capacity to pay interest and repay principal. Whereas it normally exhibits adequate protection parameters, adverse economic conditions or changing circumstances are more likely to lead to a weakened capacity to pay interest and repay principal for debt in this category than in higher rated categories.

BB
B
CCC
CC   Debt rated 'BB', 'B', 'CCC', or 'CC' is regarded, on balance, as predominantly speculative with respect to capacity to pay interest and repay principal in accordance with the terms of the obligation. 'BB' indicates the lowest degree of speculation and 'CC' the highest degree of speculation. While such debt is likely to have some quality and protective characteristics, these are outweighed by large uncertainties or major risk exposures to adverse conditions.

C   This rating is reserved for income bonds on which no interest is being paid.

D   Debt rated 'D' is in default, and payment of interest and/or repayment of principal is in arrears.

Plus (+) or Minus (—): The ratings from 'AA' to 'B' may be modified by the addition of a plus or minus sign to show relative standing within the major rating categories.

SOURCE: *Standard and Poor's Credit Overview*, 1982, pp. 87, 88.

FIGURE 12-7
Standard and Poor's Debt Rating Definitions

Aaa

Bonds which are rated Aaa are judged to be of the best quality. They carry the smallest degree of investment risk and are generally referred to as "gilt edge." Interest payments are protected by a large or by an exceptionally stable margin and principal is secure. While the various protective elements are likely to change, such changes as can be visualized are most unlikely to impair the fundamentally strong position of such issues.

Aa

Bonds which are rated Aa are judged to be of high quality by all standards. Together with the Aaa group they comprise what are generally known as high grade bonds. They are rated lower than the best bonds because margins of protection may not be as large as in Aaa securities or fluctuation of protective elements may be of greater amplitude or there may be other elements present which make the long term risks appear somewhat larger than in Aaa securities.

A

Bonds which are rated A possess many favorable investment attributes and are to be considered as upper medium grade obligations. Factors giving security to principal and interest are considered adequate but elements may be present which suggest a susceptibility to impairment sometime in the future.

Baa

Bonds which are rated Baa are considered as medium grade obligations, *i.e.*, they are neither highly protected nor poorly secured. Interest payments and principal security appear adequate for the present but certain protective elements may be lacking or may be characteristically unreliable over any great length of time. Such bonds lack outstanding investment characteristics and in fact have speculative characteristics as well.

Ba

Bonds which are rated Ba are judged to have speculative elements; their future cannot be considered as well assured. Often the protection of interest and principal payments may be very moderate and thereby not well safeguarded during both good and bad times over the future. Uncertainty of position characterizes bonds in this class.

B

Bonds which are rated B generally lack characteristics of the desirable investment. Assurance of interest and principal payments or of maintenance of other terms of the contract over any long period of time may be small.

Caa

Bonds which are rated Caa are of poor standing. Such issues may be in default or there may be present elements of danger with respect to principal or interest.

Ca

Bonds which are rated Ca represent obligations which are speculative in a high degree. Such issues are often in default or have other marked shortcomings.

C

Bonds which are rated C are the lowest rated class of bonds and issues so rated can be regarded as having extremely poor prospects of ever attaining any real investment standing.

SOURCE: *Moody's Industrial Manual*, 1983.

FIGURE 12-8
Moody's Corporate Bond Ratings

Despite this disclaimer, the influence of "statistical factors" on the raters is apparently not insignificant. Several studies[9] have investigated the relationship between historical measures of a firm's performance and the ratings assigned its bonds. Many of the differences in the ratings accorded various bonds can in fact be attributed to differences in the issuers' situations, measured in traditional ways. For corporate bonds, better ratings are generally associated with lower leverage (debt-to-total assets), smaller past variation in earnings over time, larger asset base (firm size), more profitable operations, and lack of subordination to other debt issues.

[9] For examples, see: Thomas F. Pogue and Robert M. Soldofsky, "What's in a Bond Rating?" *Journal of Financial and Quantitative Analysis*, 4, no. 2 (June 1969), 201-28; George E. Pinches and Kent A. Mingo, "A Multivariate Analysis of Industrial Bond Ratings," *The Journal of Finance*, XXVII (March 1973), 1-18; and Robert S. Kaplan and Gabriel Urwitz, "Statistical Models of Bond Ratings: A Methodological Inquiry," *Journal of Business*, 52, no. 2 (1979).

DEFAULT AND RISK PREMIUMS

Stocks make no promises: thus they are not subject to default. To assess the prospects for such securities, one might consider all possible outcomes, estimate the probability of each, and summarize the situation (among other ways) in terms of an expected holding-period return, with each possible return weighted by its probability.

A similar procedure can be employed with bonds. Most commonly, the analysis focuses on yield-to-maturity. Formally, every possible value is considered, along with its probability, and a weighted average computed to determine an expected yield-to-maturity.[10] As long as there is any possibility of default or late payment, the expected value will fall below the promised (maximum) value. In general, the greater the risk of default and the greater the amount of loss in the event of default, the greater will be this disparity.

This is illustrated in Figure 12-9 for a hypothetical bond. Its promised yield-to-maturity is 12%, but, owing to a high default risk, the expected yield is only 9%. The difference (300 basis points) is the *default premium*: the difference between promised and expected return. Any bond that could default should offer such a premium, and it should be greater, the greater the risk of default.

As discussed in previous chapters, it is useful to compare the expected return of a security with the certain return on a default-free instrument. In an efficient market the difference will be related to the relevant risk of the security. For stocks the expected holding-period

FIGURE 12-9
Yield-to-Maturity for a Risky Bond

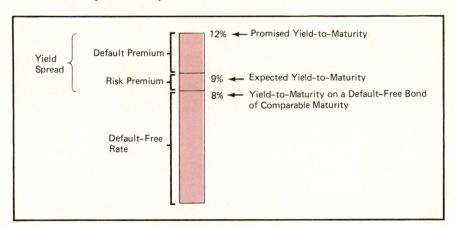

---

[10] Chapter 4 showed that yield-to-maturity is subject to a number of criticisms; these hold, *a fortiori*, for values obtained by averaging many different yields-to-maturity. The present discussion follows common practice in focusing on this measure despite its obvious flaws. Fortunately, the basic relationships described here apply rather generally.

return over a period of a year or less is commonly compared with the yield of a Treasury bill of the appropriate maturity.

The traditional approach with bonds contrasts expected yield-to-maturity with that of a default-free bond of roughly comparable maturity. Any difference is the bond's *risk premium*.

In the case shown in Figure 12-9 default-free bonds of similar maturity offer a certain 8% yield-to-maturity, 1% (100 basis points) below the bond's expected 9% yield-to-maturity. The difference is the bond's risk premium.

The Default Premium

How large should a bond's promised yield-to-maturity be to allow for possible default? The answer depends, of course, on both the probability of default and the likely loss in the event of default.

Imagine a bond equally likely to default in every year (if it has not already defaulted), with the probability that it will default in any given year represented by p_d. Assume that if the bond does default, a payment equal to $(1 - \lambda)$ times its price a year earlier will be received. Pye[11] has shown that a bond of this type will be priced to promise a yield-to-maturity of:

$$y = \frac{r + \lambda p_d}{1 - p_d}$$

where

$y =$ promised yield to maturity
$r =$ the bond's expected return each year while in a nondefault status

The difference between a bond's yield-to-maturity and its expected return can be used as a measure of its default premium:

$$d = y - r = \left(\frac{r + \lambda p_d}{1 - p_d}\right) - r$$

From 1920 to 1939, 2.3% of all outstanding medium-grade bonds defaulted per year on average, and the holder of a defaulted bond lost about half its par value,[12] If a bond with these characteristics is to have an expected return of, say, 9%, it must be priced so that:

$$d = \left[\frac{.09 + (.5 \times .023)}{1 - .023}\right] - .09 = .0139$$

Its default premium would thus be about 139 basis points.

---

[11] Gordon Pye, "Gauging the Default Premium," *Financial Analysts Journal*, 30, no. 1 (January–February 1974), 49-52.

[12] *Ibid*.

Bond Prices, Yields, and Returns

The Risk Structure of Interest Rates

The greater a bond's risk of default, the greater its default premium. This alone will cause riskier bonds to offer higher promised yields-to-maturity. If risk premiums also increase with risk, the relationship will be even more pronounced. In any event, bonds given lower agency ratings should offer higher yields-to-maturity if such ratings really do indicate relative risk of default.

Figure 12-10 shows that this is indeed the case. Each of the curves

FIGURE 12-10

Industrial Bond Yields by Ratings

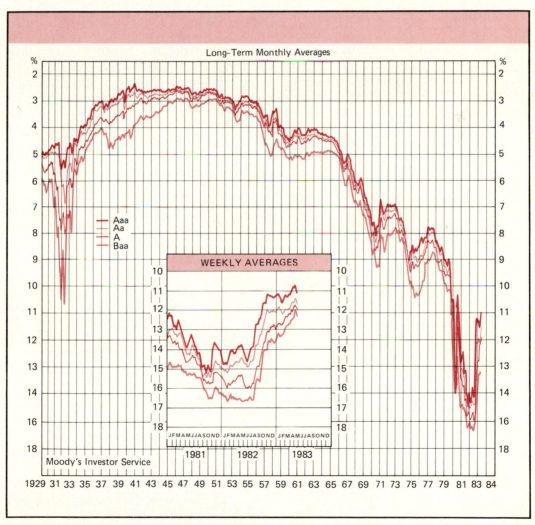

SOURCE: *Moody's Industrial Manual*, 1983.

plots the yield-to-maturity of a group of corporate bonds assigned the same ratings by Moody's. Note that the scale is "upside down," so that higher yields plot at lower positions on the diagram. This procedure is often employed. For a previously issued bond, low yields correspond to high prices, and high yields to low prices. A fall in yields plots as an upward movement on the diagram, and a rise in yields as a downward movement. Since the value of a corresponding portfolio of previously purchased bonds will move in the same direction, such a diagram captures the feelings of anyone holding such bonds; falling yields are good news, and rising yields are bad news.

As Figure 12-10 shows, bonds are priced so that higher promised yields go with lower ratings. However, the spreads vary considerably over time.

This suggests that agency ratings do not indicate *absolute* levels of risk. It would be convenient if each classification were associated with a particular range of probabilities of default. As overall uncertainty about the economy increased, bonds could then be reclassified as necessary. If this were done, yield spreads among classes might change relatively little. However, rating agencies prefer to avoid wholesale changes. Instead, the classes are used more to indicate *relative* risk. Overall increases in economic uncertainty result in only minor reclassifications and are manifested to a greater extent in increased yield spreads among classes of corporate bonds and an increased spread between corporate and government bond yields.

If the spread between the yields of bonds of different rating classes moves with changes in the degree of uncertainty about the economy, the former may be used as a surrogate for the latter. Some factor models have exploited this relationship by incorporating a factor representing the spread between *yields* on, say, bonds rated AAA and those rated BBB by Standard and Poor's. Others utilize differences in the *returns* on portfolios of bonds with different ratings. Such factors may represent changes in economic risk, the premium in expected return required by investors to bear a given amount of such risk, or both.

DETERMINANTS OF YIELD SPREADS

The spread between a corporate bond's promised yield-to-maturity and that of a government bond of the same maturity and coupon rate is the sum of its default and risk premiums. The greater the risk of default, the greater should be this difference. Moreover, bonds that can be bought or sold more readily and/or cheaply might command an additional "marketability" premium in price (and hence offer a lower yield-to-maturity). Given a large enough sample of bonds, and surrogate measures for risk and marketability, it should be possible to see if these relationships really do exist.

In a study of corporate bond prices, Fisher[13] did just this. Three measures were used to assess the probability of default:

1. The extent to which the firm's net income had varied over the preceding nine years (measured by the coefficient of variation—the ratio of standard deviation of earnings to the average value).

2. The length of time that the firm had operated without forcing any of its creditors to take a loss.

3. The ratio of the market value of the firm's equity to the par value of its debt.

The fourth measure provided an indication of marketability:

4. The market value of the firm's outstanding debt.

For each of 366 bond values, Fisher computed the yield spread and each of the four measures. He then took the logarithm of every value and used multiple regression to obtain the relationship that best fit all the data. It was:

$$
\begin{aligned}
\log \text{(yield spread)} = &\ .987 \\
&+ .307 \log \text{(earnings variability)} \\
&- .253 \log \text{(time without default)} \\
&- .537 \log \text{(equity/debt ratio)} \\
&- .275 \log \text{(market value of debt)}
\end{aligned}
$$

This relationship accounted for roughly 75% of the variation in the bonds' yield spreads.

The advantage of an equation such as this is that the coefficients may be easily interpreted. Since all values have been converted to logarithms, the effect is similar to that of using ratio scales on all axes of a diagram. Thus a 1% increase in earnings variability can be expected to bring about an increase of about $\frac{3}{10}$ of 1% in yield spread (.307%), other things equal. A 1% increase in the time without default can be expected to cause a decrease of approximately ¼ of 1% (.253%) in yield spread, and so on. Each coefficient is an *elasticity*, indicating the percentage change in yield spread likely to accompany a 1% change in the associated value. Note that every factor operates in the expected direction, providing substantial support for the hypothesized relationships.

A subsequent study[14] showed that this relationship can be used to predict agency ratings with a reasonable degree of accuracy. This is not surprising. Agencies attempt to measure risk of default, and their estimates impact yield spreads. If historical measures provide

---

[13] Lawrence Fisher, "Determinants of Risk Premiums on Corporate Bonds," *Journal of Political Economy*, 67, no. 3 (June 1959), 217-37. © 1959 by the University of Chicago. All Rights Reserved.

[14] R. R. West, "An Alternate Approach to Predicting Corporate Bond Ratings," *Journal of Accounting Research*, 8, no. 1 (Spring 1970), 118-25.

information on the likelihood of future default, all three elements will be related.

RISK PREMIUMS

Every bond that might default should offer a default premium. But the risk premium is another matter. A security's expected return should be related only to its contribution to portfolio risk; its total risk is not directly relevant. For example, if a group of companies all faced the possibility of bankruptcy, but from totally unrelated causes, a portfolio including all their bonds would provide a yield very close to its expected value. There would be little reason for this expected yield to differ significantly from that of a default-free bond, and the bonds should be priced to offer little or no premium for risk (but substantial premiums for default).

However, the risks associated with bonds are not unrelated. Figure 12-11 shows, for each year from 1900 to 1965, the ratio of the (par) value of bonds defaulting during the year to the (par) value outstanding at the beginning of the year. Not surprisingly, the peaks coincide with periods of economic distress. When business is bad, most firms are affected. The value of a firm's equity will decline when a downturn is anticipated; if the likelihood of default on its debt also increases, the value of outstanding bonds will follow suit. Thus, the holding-period return on a bond may be correlated with the returns of other bonds and with those of stocks. Most important, a risky bond's holding-period return is likely to be correlated, to at least some extent, with the return

FIGURE 12-11
Default Rates 1900-1965

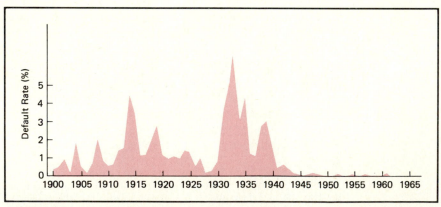

SOURCE: Thomas R. Atkinson and Elizabeth T. Simpson, *Trends in Corporate Bond Quality* (Columbia University Press, 1967).

Bond Prices, Yields, and Returns

on a widely diversified "market portfolio" (which includes both corporate bonds and stocks, in proportion to outstanding values). This part of the risk of a bond should command a risk premium in the form of greater expected return.

The riskier a bond is, the greater its likelihood of default and thus its potential sensitivity to market declines representing lowered assessments of prospects for the economy as a whole. This is illustrated in Table 12-3, which analyzes the performance of the three bond funds in the Keystone group over a twenty-year period. All values are based on annual returns. As one might anticipate, the riskier bonds outperformed the more conservative ones on average, but year-to-year returns on the former were much more variable. To estimate sensitivity to changes in stock prices the returns were compared with those of Standard and Poor's 500-stock index. The beta values indicate the sensitivity of each fund to stock market swings; they indicate that riskier bonds also move more with stocks and thus should have higher returns on average. The final row in the table shows the proportion of the year-to-year variation in returns associated with stock market swings; as indicated, relatively more of a risky portfolio's total risk is associated with the stock market than is the case with a less risky bond. For conservative bonds, interest-rate risk is by far the more important factor, and even the relatively small correlation of the returns of such bonds with stock returns may be due to the impact of interest rates on both bonds and stocks.

While the sensitivity of a bond to stock market swings should have a major influence on its expected return, it may not be the only relevant factor. A better-than-average return on a stock is typically as likely to be followed by another better-than-average return as is a worse-than-average return. Stock returns exhibit almost no *serial correlation*: the particular value of return in the last period provides little if any help in predicting the likelihood of various possible returns in the next period.

TABLE 12-3
Risk and Return, Keystone Bond Funds, 1963-1982

	FUND B1	FUND B2	FUND B4
	Conservative Bonds	Investment Grade Bonds	Discount Bonds
Average return (% per year)	5.64	6.70	9.08
Standard deviation of return (% per year)	8.99	10.57	11.57
Beta value, relative to S&P 500-stock index	.19	.36	.50
Proportion of variance explained by S&P index	.08	.29	.50

Not so with bonds. An obvious case arises when a default-free bond has two years remaining before maturity. Consider a 10% bond currently priced at 100. If its price rises to 102, it will return 12% this year. But it will then return about 8% next year $[(100 + 10 - 102)/102 = .0784]$. Conversely a return of 8% this year, via a price decline to 98, will be followed by a return of about 12% next year $[(100 + 10 - 98)/98 = .1224]$. Bond returns thus tend to be *negatively serially correlated*: above-average returns are more likely to be followed by below-average returns, and conversely.

An investment adviser might tell a bondholder, "There is good news and bad news: the good news is that you can now get more on your money (interest rates have risen), the bad news is that your portfolio is worth less as a result." There is thus a relationship between bond returns and future investment opportunities—a relationship that may be absent for stocks. However, the relationship is concerned more with *nominal* than with *real* returns. When interest rates rise solely to offset increases in expected inflation, *real* investment opportunities are no better than before (and there is no good news after all). Real returns on bonds need not be serially correlated. Since investors are presumably more concerned with real than with nominal returns, the negative serial correlation of nominal returns may thus be of little if any relevance in their valuation.

PROMISED VERSUS REALIZED YIELDS

What sort of experience might the long-run bond investor anticipate? And how is it likely to be related to the risk of the bonds held?

In a massive study of all large bond issues and a sample of small bond issues, Hickman attempted to answer this question. He analyzed investor experience for each bond from 1900 through 1943 to determine the actual yield to the date on which the bond matured, defaulted, or was called—whichever came first. He then compared this with the promised yield-to-maturity based on the price at time of issue. Every bond was also classified according to the ratings assigned at time of issue. Table 12-4(a) shows the major results.

As one would expect, riskier bonds promised higher yields at time of issue. Moreover, a higher percentage of such bonds defaulted, in whole or in part, before maturity.

What about actual yield-to-maturity? As the table shows, in four out of five classifications it exceeded the promised amount, on average. Why? Because during the period studied, a substantial drop in interest rates made it attractive for issuers to call old bonds at premiums.

To see what might have happened had this not been the case, Fraine and Mills reanalyzed the data for large investment-grade issues. Their results are shown in Table 12-4(b). The initial columns differ

TABLE 12-4
Actual and Realized Bond Yields-to-Maturity, 1900-1943

(a) ALL LARGE AND A SAMPLE OF SMALL ISSUES				
Composite Rating	Comparable Moody's Rating	Promised Yield-to-Maturity at Issue (%)	Percent Defaulting Prior to Maturity	Actual-Yield-to-Maturity (%)
I	Aaa	4.5	5.9	5.1
II	Aa	4.6	6.0	5.0
III	A	4.9	13.4	5.0
IV	Baa	5.4	19.1	5.7
V-IX	below Baa	9.5	42.4	8.6

(b) ALL LARGE ISSUES				
Composite Rating	Comparable Moody's Rating	Promised Yield-to-Maturity (%)	Actual Yield-to-Maturity (%)	Modified Actual Yield-to-Maturity (%)
I	Aaa	4.5	5.1	4.3
II	Aa	4.5	5.1	4.3
III	A	4.9	5.0	4.3
IV	Baa	5.4	5.8	4.3

SOURCE: (a) W. Braddock Hickman, *Corporate Bond Quality and Investor Experience* (Princeton, N.J.: Princeton University Press, 1958). (b) Harold G. Fraine and Robert H. Mills, "The Effect of Defaults and Credit Deterioration on Yields of Corporate Bonds," *The Journal of Finance*, XVI, no. 3 (September 1961), 433.

from those of Table 12-4(a) only because smaller issues are excluded. The major difference appears in the final column. It was obtained by substituting promised yield for realized yield whenever the latter was larger, thus removing the effects of most calls.

Both sets of results suggest that within the highest grades there was little if any difference in realized returns. Such bonds are all quite low in market risk and thus should carry similar (and small) risk premiums. Medium-grade (Baa) bonds performed somewhat better, which is consistent with a premium for their somewhat larger market risk. Low-grade bonds seem to have done even better on average, which is not surprising, given their substantial sensitivity to changes in anticipations about the economic climate.

BONDS VERSUS STOCKS

Bonds and stocks are different kinds of securities with quite different characteristics. Choice between them cannot easily be based on a simple one-dimensional comparison. In many cases, optimal investment policy will involve the choice of *both* bonds and stocks.

While historic relationships may not adequately predict future relationships, it is instructive to examine the average values, standard deviations, and correlations of bond and stock returns in the past. Figures 12-12 do this for 60-month (five-year) "windows." The leftmost points in the diagrams are based on the returns from January 1926 through December 1932; the next points are based on the returns from February 1926 through January 1933, and so on. The rightmost points are based on the returns from January 1979 through December 1983.

Figure 12-12(a) shows the five-year (arithmetic) annualized returns. On this basis, stocks appear to have virtually dominated bonds, providing more return in almost every five-year period and only slightly less in most of the remaining periods. Major exceptions occurred in the Great Depression of the 1930s and the severe market collapse in

FIGURE 12-12
Average Values, Standard Deviations, and Correlations of S&P 500 and Long-Term Government Bond Returns

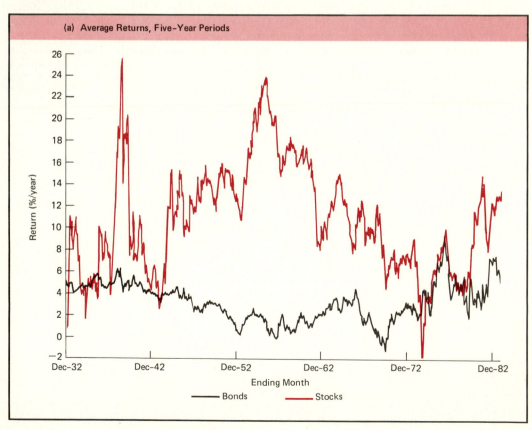

Bond Prices, Yields, and Returns

the early 1970s. For the investor with a reasonably long horizon, stocks appear to have substantial advantages.

There is good reason to believe that the average returns on long-term bonds are not representative of investor's *ex ante* expectations. The figures show the results obtained by purchasing a government bond with roughly twenty years remaining before maturity, holding it for a period of time, then replacing it with another with (again) roughly twenty years remaining before maturity. The total returns include both income and capital gains or losses. During this period, bond price changes were negative more often than positive, averaging slightly over −1% per year. A better estimate might be obtained by assuming that investors' expected price would be as likely to increase as decrease. *Expected* returns on bonds might thus have been 1% greater than shown in Figure 12-12(a).

Moreover, for an investor concerned with month-to-month variation (i.e., one with a possible need for liquidity and/or a known short horizon), the situation might be reversed. Figure 12-12(b) shows the

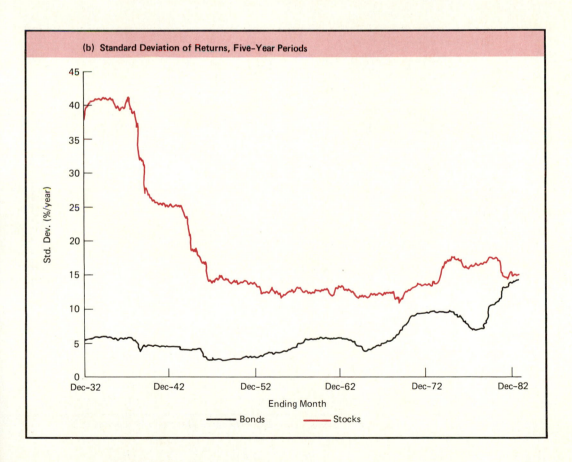

(b) Standard Deviation of Returns, Five-Year Periods

annualized standard deviation of returns within each five-year period. In this sense, stocks were riskier than bonds throughout the period. Note that the increased uncertainty concerning the rate of inflation has greatly increased the variability of bond returns. In the five years from 1979 through 1983, bond returns varied almost as much as did stock returns.

Figure 12-2(c) shows the correlation between stock and bond returns. During the 1950s and 1960s the values were actually negative, indicating that portfolios combining both types of instruments could benefit considerably from the resulting diversification. More recently, however, correlations have been positive (and substantially so), owing in part to common reactions to changes in inflationary expectations. The more highly correlated are two returns, of course, the smaller the benefits to be obtained from diversification.

Are bonds bad investments? It seems unlikely. They may be priced for their ability to hedge long-term liabilities. Perhaps more important,

FIGURE 12-12 (Cont.)

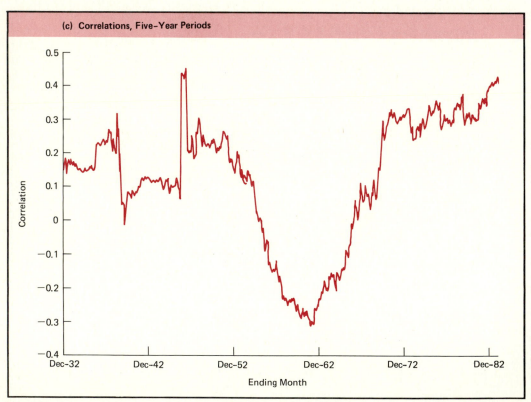

SOURCE: Based on data from Roger G. Ibbotson, *Stocks, Bonds, Bills and Inflation 1984 Yearbook* (Chicago: R. G. Ibbotson Associates, Inc., February 1984).

they may be priced to reflect their relative resistance to deep recessions and depressions and thus they pale in comparison to stocks over any period, no matter how long, in which such events do not occur.

FINANCIAL RATIOS AS PREDICTORS OF DEFAULT

For years analysts have used ratios of accounting values to indicate the probability that a firm will fail to meet its financial obligations. Specific procedures have been developed to predict default with such ratios. *Univariate* analysis attempts to find the best single predictor for the purpose, while *multivariate* analysis searches for combinations of two or more predictors.

Univariate Methods

Cash inflows and outflows can be considered variable contributions to and drains from the firm's cash balance. When the balance falls to zero, default is likely to occur. The smaller the balance, the smaller the average net cash inflow before payments to creditors and stockholders, and the more variable the cash flows, the greater the probability of default.

In an examination of various measures used to assess these factors, Beaver found that the ratio of cash flow (income before depreciation, depletion, and amortization charges) to total debt was particularly useful. Figure 12-13(a) shows the mean value of this ratio for a group of firms that defaulted on a scheduled payment and for a companion group that did not. As early as five years before default the two groups' ratios diverged, and the spread widened as the year of default approached.

This suggests that the probability of default may not be constant through time. Instead, warning signals may indicate an increase in the probability, which will in turn cause a fall in the price of the firm's bonds (and hence a rise in their promised yield-to-maturity) along with a fall in the price of its stock. Figure 12-13(b) shows that such signals are recognized by the market. The median value of stock in the firms that did not default went up, while that of the other firms went down as the date of default approached.

Multivariate Methods

Altman[15] considered combinations of ratios as predictors of default. His analysis suggested the use of a *Z-score*, computed as follows:

---

[15] Edward I. Altman, "Financial Ratios, Discriminant Analysis and the Prediction of Corporate Bankruptcy," *Journal of Finance*, September 1968, pp. 589-609.

$$Z = 1.2X_1 + 1.4X_2 + 3.3X_3 + .6X_4 + .99X_5$$

where:

$X_1 =$ (current assets − current liabilities)/total assets

$X_2 =$ retained earnings/total assets

$X_3 =$ earnings before interest and taxes/total assets

$X_4 =$ market value of equity/book value of total debt

$X_5 =$ sales/total assets

FIGURE 12-13
Financial Ratios and Market Prices for Firms that Defaulted and Those that Did Not

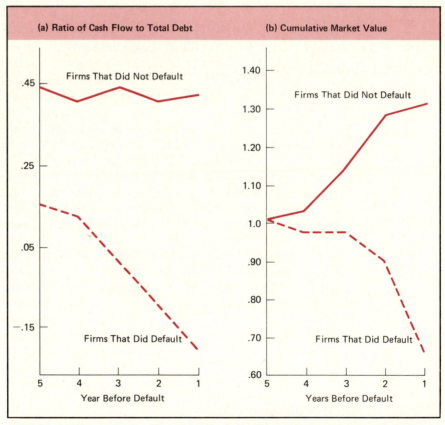

SOURCE: (a) William H. Beaver, "Financial Ratios as Predictors of Failure," *Empirical Research in Accounting, Selected Studies*, The Institute of Professional Accounting, Graduate School of Business, University of Chicago (1966), pp. 71-127. (b) Based on median values of annual returns in William H. Beaver, "Market Prices, Financial Ratios and the Prediction of Failure," *Journal of Accounting Research*, 6, no. 2 (Autumn 1968), 1979-92.

Any firm with a Z-score below 1.8 is considered a likely candidate for bankruptcy, and the lower the score, the greater the likelihood.[16]

Investment Implications

Does this mean that securities of firms whose cash-flow-to-total-debt ratio and/or Z-score has fallen should be avoided, since further declines in such measures, and hence in market prices, can be anticipated? Hardly. For example, the firms represented by the dashed lines in Figure 12-13 were chosen because they did eventually default. Had all firms with declining ratios been selected, recent decreases in price would undoubtedly have been observed, reflecting the increased probability of future default. But only some of them would have continued down to disaster while the others recovered, and the gains on the latter might well have offset the losses on the former.

HORIZON ANALYSIS

It may or may not be possible to identify transitory shifts in yield structures. In any event, the analyst who believes he or she has found a situation of this sort will want to translate belief into action.

To fully analyze the impacts of future yields on alternative bond portfolios is an almost impossible task. First, all possible future yield structures would have to be identified and the likelihood of each combination assessed. Then the optimal initial portfolio and every appropriate revision to it would have to be determined. Even with an unlimited computer budget this would be a formidable task indeed. In practice, much simpler approaches are taken. *Horizon analysis*, advocated by Martin L. Leibowitz of Salomon Brothers, provides a good example. A single holding period is selected for analysis, and possible yield structures at the end of the period (i.e., at the "horizon") are considered. The possible returns for two bonds—one currently held and one candidate to replace it—are then analyzed. Both are assumed to be free of default risk up to the horizon date. In the process of the analysis, the sensitivities of the returns to changes in key assumptions regarding yields are estimated, allowing at least a rough assessment of some of the relevant risks.

Figure 12-14 represents a page from a standard yield book for bonds with a 4% coupon. As indicated, a 4% bond with ten years remaining to maturity priced at $67.48 has a 9% yield-to-maturity. In the future, such a bond's time-to-maturity will decrease and the relevant yield-

---

[16] Subsequent refinements to incorporate effects of leases and so on have been incorporated, leading to a revised procedure known as "zeta analysis."

Yield to Maturity (%)	YEARS TO MATURITY						
	10 Yrs	9 Yrs	. . .	5 Yrs	. . .	1 Yrs	0 Yrs
7.00	78.68	80.22		87.53		97.15	100.00
7.50	75.68	77.39		85.63		96.69	100.00
y_H ⟨8.00⟩	72.82	74.68		⟨83.78⟩ ← P_H		96.23	100.00
8.50	70.09	72.09		81.98		95.77	100.00
y_0 ⟨9.00⟩ P_0	⟨67.48⟩	69.60		⟨80.22⟩ → P_A		95.32	100.00
9.50	64.99	67.22		78.51		94.87	100.00
10.00	62.61	64.92	. . .	76.83	. . .	94.42	100.00
10.50	60.34	62.74		75.21		93.98	100.00
11.00	58.17	60.64		73.62		93.54	100.00

Actual Price Pattern Over Time

Yield Change Effect

Time Effect

SOURCE: Martin L. Leibowitz, "Horizon Analysis for Managed Bond Portfolios," *Journal of Portfolio Management*, 1, no. 3 (Spring 1975), 26.

FIGURE 12-14
The Effect of Time and Yield Change on a 4% Coupon Bond

to-maturity will also probably change. The bond might thus follow a path through the table such as that shown by the dashed line. If so, it would end up at a price of $83.78 at the *horizon* (five years hence) with an 8% yield-to-maturity.

Over any holding period a bond's return will typically be affected by both the passage of time and a change in yields. Horizon analysis breaks this into two parts: one due solely to the passage of time, with no change in yields; the other due solely to a change in yields, with no passage of time. This is illustrated in Figure 12-14. The total change from $67.48 to $83.78 is broken into a change from $67.48 to $80.22, followed by an instantaneous change from $80.22 to $83.78. The intermediate value is the price the bond would command at the horizon if its yield-to-maturity had remained unchanged at its initial level. The actual price is that which it commands at its actual yield-to-maturity.

The total price change can be broken into two parts, representing the two effects:

price change = yield change effect + time effect

Thus far no account has been taken of the coupon payments to be received before the horizon date. In principle one should consider all possible uses of such flows or at least analyze possible alternative yield patterns during the period to determine likely reinvestment opportunities. In practice this is rarely done. Instead a single reinvestment rate is assumed and the future value of all coupon payments at the horizon date is determined by compounding each one forward using this rate. This takes care of both interest (coupons) and "interest on interest"—i.e., interest received by investing coupon payments. For example, if $2 is received each six months for five years and every payment is reinvested at 4.25% per six months, the value at the end of five years will be approximately $25.32. Of this amount, $20 can be considered interest (coupon payments) and $5.32 "interest on interest."

For relatively short horizons this treatment of coupon payments may be acceptable. But for longer horizons the importance of interest on interest is likely to be greater than that of any changes in capital value, and alternative possible future reinvestment rates may have to be considered. There are thus two components: the total amount of coupons and the interest on interest, with only the former completely predictable in advance.

A bond's overall return can thus be broken into four components. In the example:

$$= \left(\frac{83.78 - 80.22}{67.48}\right) + \left(\frac{80.22 - 67.48}{67.48}\right) + \left(\frac{20.00}{67.48}\right) + \left(\frac{5.32}{67.48}\right)$$
$$= .0528 + .1888 + .2964 + .0788$$

The first term is the uncertain return due to yield change, the second the (assumed certain) return due to the passage of time, the third the (certain) coupon return, and the fourth the (uncertain) return due to interest on interest.

Since the first term is uncertain, it is important to analyze it further. Moreover, as Leibowitz points out, it is helpful to relate the market yield movements that a bond manager *follows* to the resulting price changes that he or she *feels*.

In the example, a change in yield from 9.0% to 8.0% at the horizon will change price from $80.22 to $83.78. By substituting an expected value for the yield at the horizon, one can compute an expected holding-period return. By using different values with their probabilities, one can estimate the probabilities of different values of the holding-period return and thus the bond's risk.

Bond analysts devote a great deal of attention to predictions of future yields. This is often done by considering a *hierarchy* of yields. Figure 12-15 provides an example. A bond's yield at any time is assumed to be related to that of a *sector* of the bond market, the average yield for which is related to that of all bonds of like *maturity*, the average yields of which are related, via the term structure, to that of all bonds in the *market*. At the horizon, or end of the "workout period," any

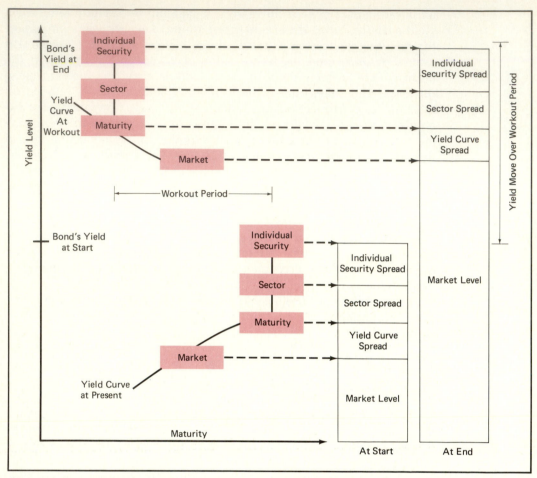

SOURCE: Martin L. Leibowitz, "An Analytic Approach to the Bond Market," *Financial Analysts' Handbook* (Homewood, Ill.: Dow Jones-Irwin, Inc., 1975), p. 262.

FIGURE 12-15
The Structure of a Bond's Yields at the Start and the End of a Workout Period

or all of the relationships can change, and of course the bond will have moved leftward on the maturity axis. The total yield move may thus be decomposed into the changes due to the various components, each of which may be estimated separately.

BOND SWAPS

Given a set of predictions about future bond yields, one can estimate holding-period returns over one or more horizons (workout periods) for one or more bonds. The goal of *bond swapping* is to actively manage a portfolio, switching bonds to take advantage of any superior ability to predict such yields.

Bond swaps are made for many reasons. Four idealized categories have been described by Homer and Leibowitz:

> The *Substitution Swap* is ideally an exchange of a bond for a perfect substitute or "twin" bond. The motivation here is temporary price advantage, presumably resulting from a monetary imbalance in the relative supply/demand conditions in the marketplace.

> The *Intermarket Spread Swap* is a more general movement out of one market component and into another with the intention of exploiting a currently advantageous yield relationship. The idea here is to trade off of these changing relationships between the two market components. Short-term Workout Periods are usually anticipated. While such swaps will almost always have some sensitivity to the direction of the overall market, the idealized focus of this type of swap is the spread relationship itself.

> On the other hand, the *Rate Anticipation Swap* is frankly geared towards profiting from an anticipated movement in overall market rates.

> The *Pure Yield Pickup Swap* is oriented toward yield improvements over the long term with little heed being paid to interim price movements in either the respective market components or the market as a whole.[17]

Problems

1. Why may it be inappropriate to mix yields of "flower bonds" with those of other Treasury bonds when plotting yield curves?
2. Empirical evidence indicates that the cash-flow/total-debt ratio is, to some extent, a valid indicator of the probability that a bond issuer will default. Does this evidence, therefore, lead to the contention that a trading mechanism exists for obtaining a yield greater than that justified by the commensurate risk?
3. Would an observed downward-sloping yield curve be inconsistent with the notion of liquidity preference?
4. Would you expect the yield-to-maturity of a fully callable bond to be higher than that of a bond with a deferred call provision?
5. Assume that the current structure of forward interest rates is upward sloping (going from left to right). Which will have a lower yield-to-maturity:
   a. A fifteen-year zero-coupon bond or a ten-year zero-coupon bond?
   b. A ten-year 5% coupon bond or a ten-year 6% coupon bond?
6. What would be your answers to Problem 5 if the forward interest-rate structure were downward-sloping (going from left to right)?

---

[17] Martin L. Leibowitz, "Horizon Analysis for Managed Bond Portfolios," *Journal of Portfolio Management* 1, no. 3 (Spring 1975), 32, 33.

7. Assume the currently available one-year rate is 6% per year, and the forward one-year rates for one year hence and two years hence, are, respectively:

$$r_{12} = 7\%, \; r_{23} = 8\%$$

What would be the current price of a $1,000, 6% coupon bond redeemable at the end of three years? The first interest payment is one year from today.

8. Assume that the spread between the yield-to-maturity on BBB bonds and that on AAA bonds has recently widened considerably. What might this indicate?

9. Assume that you are advising an investor whose tax bracket makes holding municipal bonds attractive. What would you say about a corporate bond selling at a substantial discount from par value? A corporate bond selling at a premium (i.e., at a price above par value)?

10. The government of a nearby country has issued three bonds that pay in dollars. The first, which pays $1,000 in one year, is now selling for $909.09. The second, which pays $100 at the end of this year and $1,100 at the end of next year, is selling for $991.81. The third, which pays $100 at the end of this year, $100 at the end of next year, and $1,100 at the end of the following year, is selling for $977.18.

    a. What are the current discount factors for money one, two, and three years hence?
    b. What are the forward interest rates?
    c. A friend offers to pay you $500 at the end of this year, $600 at the end of next year, and $700 at the end of the following year if you loan him some money today. How much should you loan him?

11. You estimate that a company has a probability of .10 of defaulting on its bonds each year and that, if default occurs, bondholders will receive an amount equivalent to half the value of the bonds in the prior year. You believe that the bonds, if fairly priced, should offer an expected return of 10%. What yield-to-maturity would you consider appropriate?

13

Common Stocks

CHARACTERISTICS OF COMMON STOCK

Common stocks are easier to describe than fixed-income securities, but they are harder to analyze. Fixed-income securities almost always have a limited life and an upper limit on cash payments. Common stocks have neither. Although the basic principles of valuation apply to both, the role of uncertainty is larger for common stocks, so much so that it often dominates all other elements in their valuation.

Common stock represents *equity*, or an *ownership* position in a corporation. It is a *residual* claim, in the sense that creditors and preferred stockholders must be paid as scheduled before common stockholders can receive any payments. In bankruptcy, equity holders are in principle entitled only to any value remaining after all prior claimants have been satisfied (although in practice courts sometimes violate this principle).

The great advantage of the corporate form of organization is the *limited liability* of its owners. Common stock is generally "full-paid and nonassessable." Stockholders may lose their investment, but no more. They are not further liable for any failure on the part of the corporation to meet its obligations. This limits the ability of the corporation to obtain credit at low rates of interest, of course. But it makes possible the impersonality of corporate ownership and the simple transfer of the certificates representing that ownership.

The Charter

A corporation exists only when it has been granted a *charter* or *certificate of incorporation* by a state. This document specifies the rights and obligations of stockholders. It may be amended, with the approval of some specified proportion of the stock (in some states a majority, in others two-thirds, and so on). Both the initial terms and the terms of any amendment must be approved by the state in which the corporation is chartered. Because it is particularly hospitable in this respect and in levying corporate taxes, Delaware has captured a disproportionate share of corporate charters.

Stock Certificates

In the United States an investor's holding of a firm's stock has typically been represented by a single certificate, with the number of shares filled in. Such a stock certificate can be registered, with the name and the holdings of the investor included on the corporation's books. Payments, voting material, reports, and so on are then mailed directly, taking into account the size of the investor's holdings.

Stock holdings may be transferred to a new owner in whole or in part via endorsement and presentations to either the issuing corporation or (more commonly) its designated *transfer agent* and/or *registrar*—usually a bank or trust company.

Many stockholders have chosen to avoid these rather cumbersome procedures. Instead, clearing arrangements are used to substitute computerized records for embossed certificates. Shares are issued to a *clearing corporation*, which *immobilizes* them, leaving transfers of ownership to be dealt with by the computers of brokers, banks, and (in some cases) individual investors.

Voting

Since the holder of common stock is an owner of the corporation, he or she is entitled to vote for its directors and to vote on matters brought before the annual meeting. Any owner may attend and vote in person, but most choose instead to vote by *proxy*. Typically, the incumbent directors solicit every stockholder. The recipient is asked to sign a "proxy statement," which is a power of attorney authorizing the designated party to cast all the investor's votes on any matter brought before the meeting. Occasionally, desired positions on specific issues may be solicited on the proxy statement. Most votes are perfunctory. The majority of votes is held by the incumbent management via proxy statements, and there is little if any controversy or excitement.

Once in a while, however, a *proxy fight* develops. Insurgents or aggressors from outside the corporation solicit proxies to vote against current management, often in order to effect a merger of some sort. Stockholders are deluged with literature and appeals. The incumbents often win, but the possibility of a loss in such a skirmish tends to curb activities clearly not in the stockholders' interest.

In the United States the number of votes given an investor equals the number of shares held. Each director is typically elected by a simple majority of all votes cast. Thus a majority of shares voting can elect an entire board. This is the ordinary or *statutory* voting procedure.

Some corporations use *cumulative* voting, in which the number of votes given an investor equals the number of shares held times the number of directors to be elected, and directors are appointed in order of total votes received. With this procedure, votes may be allocated to candidates in any manner desired. Thus investors holding less than 50% of a corporation's shares can, by concentrating their votes, elect some members to the board.

Tender Offers

Periodically, a firm or wealthy individual, convinced that the management of a corporation is not exploiting its opportunities, will attempt a *takeover*. First, a substantial number of shares must be acquired. This is usually attempted via a *tender offer*. Advertisements are placed in the financial press and/or material mailed to the stockholders. The raiding party offers to buy, at a stated price, some or all shares tendered by present stockholders. The offer is usually contingent on the tender of a minimum number of shares by a fixed date and may include other restrictions as well. When the offer is first made, the tender price is generally set considerably above the current market price, although the offer itself usually leads to a subsequent price increase.

Attempted takeovers provide spice in a stockholder's otherwise routine relationship with a corporation. Management usually counters with advertisements, mailings, and the like. Takeovers often fail, but every now and then one succeeds.

Occasionally a corporation will issue a tender offer to buy back some of its own stock. Such an offer may provide a signal that the corporation considers its shares underpriced; if so, the stock price is likely to rise. However, if the corporation has simply chosen to pay out cash in the form of capital gains rather than dividends, no increase in price may result.

Ownership versus Control

Much has been written about the effects of the separation of ownership and control of the modern corporation. While it is true that over a wide range, incumbent management can exercise its discretion with little if any effective control from its nominal owners, the potential of a proxy fight or tender offer takeover provides at least some check on excesses. Moreover, management typically owns stock in the corporation and thus has strong incentives to increase the value of the stock whenever possible.

Common Stocks

To align the interests of management and stockholders, many corporations offer *stock options* to officers of the firm. A specified number of shares may be purchased at a stated price (often below the market price). However, as the corporation's shares become more and more important in a manager's portfolio, adding to his or her already large investment of human capital in the firm, a new problem emerges. The manager's holdings may be more concentrated than those of many of the corporation's other owners. While the latter are concerned primarily or exclusively with *factor-related risks*, the manager may also worry about *security-specific risk*, resulting in a divergence of interests when, for example, a new project is considered. The most appropriate level of ownership for a corporation's managers thus requires a balance between *incentive* and *concentration* effects.

Par Value

When a corporation is first chartered, it is *authorized* to issue up to a stated number of shares of common stock, each of which will often carry a specified *par value*. Historically, this was considered the amount of capital invested by owners for the protection of creditors. Legally, a corporation may be precluded from making payments to common stockholders if doing so would reduce the stated value of the equity below the amount represented by the par value of outstanding stock. For this reason the stated par value is typically low relative to the price for which the stock is initially sold. A par value of $1 is now used frequently. Some corporations issue *no-par* stock, but state and local taxes tend to make *low-par* issues more advantageous.

As long as stock is initially sold by the corporation for more than its par value, it is "full-paid and nonassessable." Otherwise, the stock could be considered "watered" (a reference to early fraudulent sales of Florida land, much of which was under water), and stockholders might be liable for the difference between the par value and the amount paid for the stock.

When stock is sold for more than its par value, the difference may be carried separately on the corporation's books (e.g., with an entry for "capital in excess of par value").

Book Value

As a corporation's life proceeds, it generates income, much of which is paid out to creditors (for interest and principal) and stockholders (as dividends). Any remainder is added to the amount shown as cumulative *retained earnings* on the corporation's books. The sum is the *book value* of the equity. The *book value per share* is obtained by dividing this figure by the number of shares outstanding.

Reserved and Treasury Stock

Typically a corporation will issue only part of its authorized stock. Some of the remainder may be specifically *reserved* for outstanding options, convertible securities, and so on.

When a corporation buys its own stock, either in the open market or via a tender offer, the stock may be "held in the treasury." It is not entitled to vote or receive dividends and is equivalent economically (though not legally) to unissued stock.

If a corporation wishes to issue new stock in excess of its original authorization, the charter must be amended, requiring approval by both the state and a given proportion of the voting stock.

Classified Stock

Some corporations issue two or more classes of common stock. For example, Class A stock might have a preferred position vis-à-vis dividends but no voting rights, and Class B a lower claim on dividends but full voting rights. Often this is equivalent to an issue of preferred stock with no maturity date, along with a "normal" type of common.

Letter or Restricted Stock

In the United States, securities regulation requires that most stock be *registered* before it may be sold in a public offering. Under some conditions *unregistered* stock may be sold directly to a purchaser, but its subsequent sale is *restricted*, usually by a letter from the buyer stating that the stock is to be held as an investment. Such *letter stock* must be held at least two years and cannot be sold even then unless ample information on the company is available and the amount sold is a relatively small percentage of the total amount outstanding.

Dividends

Payments to stockholders made in cash are termed *dividends*. These are typically declared quarterly and paid to *stockholders of record* at a specified date. Since transfer of ownership requires some time, major stock exchanges specify an *ex-dividend date* several days prior to the date of record. Shares purchased before an ex-dividend date are entitled to receive the dividend in question. Those purchased afterward do not receive it.

A corporation's board of directors may declare a dividend of almost any amount or none at all, subject only to restrictions contained in the charter, bond indentures, state laws, and so on. Dividends may even exceed earnings, although the reverse is more common.

Stock Dividends and Stock Splits

Occasionally a corporation's management decides to forego a cash dividend but "pay" a *stock dividend* instead. For example, if a 5% stock dividend is declared, the owner of 500 shares receives 25 additional shares, issued for the occasion. Par value is not changed, but since more shares are outstanding, the stated value of common stock on the corporation's balance sheet will increase; to keep the total book value of equity the same, the surplus account is simply decreased by a corresponding amount.

A *stock split* is similar but differs in both magnitude and accounting treatment. In this case par value is adjusted appropriately and the surplus account left unchanged. For example, if a $1-par stock is split "2-for-1," the holder of 500 old shares will receive 1,000 new $.50-par shares.

A *reverse split* reduces the number of shares and increases the par value per share. For example, in a reverse 2-for-1 split, the holder of 500 $1-par shares would exchange them for 250 $2-par shares.

Stock dividends and splits must be taken into account when following the fortunes of a company's shares. For example, a fall in price per share may be due solely to a large stock dividend. To reduce confusion, most financial services provide data *adjusted* for at least some of these changes. Thus, if a stock split 2-for-1 on January 30, 1984, prices prior to that date might be divided by two to facilitate comparison.

Why do corporations issue stock dividends and split their stocks? Nothing of importance would appear to be changed, only the size of the units in which ownership may be bought and sold. Moreover, the process involves administrative effort and cost.

It is sometimes argued that shareholders respond positively to "tangible" evidence of the growth of their corporation. Another view holds that splits and stock dividends, by decreasing the price per share, may bring a stock into a more desirable trading range and hence increase the total value of the amount outstanding.

Figure 13-1 summarizes the results of 219 stock splits (including some cases involving stock dividends of 25% or more) that occurred between 1945 and 1965. For each case the stock's "normal" performance was determined by relating monthly returns to the returns on the overall stock market, and "abnormal" performance was then computed for the 54 months prior to the split and the 54 months following it. These values were averaged across the cases and then cumulated.

As the figure shows, prior to splitting, the stocks tended to increase in value relative to normal market moves by a substantial amount (about 30% in 54 months). Was this due to anticipation of the coming split? Not necessarily. The causal relationship could well be just the reverse: stocks split after unusual price increases; unexpected positive

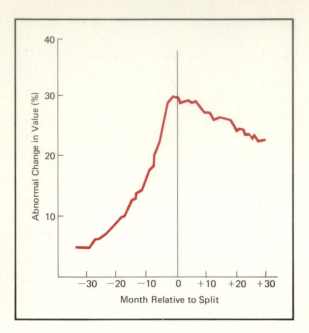

FIGURE 13-1
Abnormal Changes in Value Before and
After Stock Splits

SOURCE: Sasson Bar-Yosef and Lawrence D. Brown, "A Re-examination of Stock Splits Using Moving Betas," *Journal of Finance* (September 1977).

developments increased the value of these firms, then management decided to split the stock. The behavior of (adjusted) postsplit prices indicates that after the split, investors did not continue to gain. In the study shown in Figure 13-1 they actually lost some ground. Other studies, using different stocks and time periods, found postsplit patterns that were either horizontal or slightly upward-sloping.[1]

The evidence also suggests that rather than *decreasing* transactions costs, stock splits actually *increased* them.[2] A study of pre- and postsplit behavior showed that after splits, trading volume rose less than proportionately, and both commission costs and bid-ask spreads, expressed as a percent of value, increased—hardly the reactions claimed by proponents of stock splits.

Preemptive Rights

Under common law (and most state laws) a stockholder has an inherent right to maintain a proportionate share of the corporation. When new shares are to be sold, old stockholders may be given the right of first refusal. A certificate is issued to each person indicating the number

---

[1] See Eugene Fama, Lawrence Fisher, Michael Jensen, and Richard Roll, "The Adjustment of Stock Prices to New Information," *International Economic Review* (February 1969), and Guy Charest, "Split Information, Stock Returns and Market Efficiency—I," *Journal of Financial Economics* (June/September 1978).

[2] Thomas E. Copeland, "Liquidity Changes Following Stock Splits," *Journal of Finance*, March 1979.

of new shares for which subscription is authorized (this will be proportional to the number of old shares held). Usually the new shares will be priced below the current market value, making such *rights* valuable. The stockholder can *exercise* the rights by purchasing additional stock and maintaining his or her proportional ownership in the firm, but at the cost of providing additional capital. Alternatively, the rights can be sold or simply allowed to expire, causing the person's share in the corporation to decline as others are given ownership in the expanded firm in return for the provision of new capital.

STOCK PRICE AND VOLUME QUOTATIONS

Figures 13-2 and 13-3 provide examples of quotations summarizing a day's trading in stocks traded over-the-counter (i.e., through dealers) and on the major stock exchanges.

Active stocks traded with the aid of the National Association of Securities Dealers' Quotation system (NASDAQ) are summarized in the forms shown in Figures 13-2(a), (b), and (c). Transactions in securities designated *National Market Issues* are summarized in detail, as shown in Figure 13-2(a). The highest and lowest price recorded in the prior 365 days are shown first, followed by the security name and dividend rate (letters refer to footnotes giving further details). Amounts traded during the day are indicated (in hundreds of shares), followed by the highest, lowest, and last price recorded. The final column shows the net change from the last price on the previous trading day.

Information on stocks with somewhat less activity is shown in the form illustrated in Figure 13-2(b). Volume traded through NASDAQ during the day is shown (in hundreds of shares) along with the highest price *bid* and lowest price *asked* by market-makers (dealers) as of 4 P.M. Eastern time and the net change in the former from the previous day's quote. Investors pay the asked price to purchase shares and receive the bid price when shares are sold. In addition, markdowns or markups and commissions may be added by the investor's retail broker.

Information on over-the-counter stocks with relatively little activity is shown in the form illustrated in Figure 13-2(c). Only bid and asked price quotations (as of 4 P.M. Eastern time) are given.

Activity in stocks traded on major exchanges is summarized in the form shown in Figures 13-3(a) and (b). Stocks listed on the New York Stock Exchange are shown in one section, those listed on the American Stock Exchange in another. Figure 13-3(a) provides an illustration of the former; Figure 13-3(b) the latter.

High and low prices for the preceding 52 weeks are shown, along with an annual dividend rate (in dollars) based on the latest declared

(a) National Market Issues

365-Day High	365-Day Low	Stock & Div	Sales (hds)	High	Low	Last	Net Chg
		--A A--					
19½	14	Aaron Rents	14	16½	16	16	– ¼
18⅛	8⅝	Acadmyln .20	254	9¼	9	9	– ⅛
13¼	3¼	Accelratn .05b	101	11¼	10¾	10¾	+ ¼
26¾	14⅛	AccurayCp .16	104	15⅝	15¼	15¼	– ⅜
22	(L)	Adac Labs	619	5⅜	5⅛	5⅜	+ ⅛
28⅛	8¾	Adage Inc	140	9½	8¾	9	– ¼
9⅛	1 13-16	Advnc Circuit	53	7⅝	7⅜	7⅜	– ⅛
19⅞	11½	AffilBnksh .80	x22	17⅞	17⅝	17⅝	– ⅜
24⅜	14½	A F G Indust	15	15⅞	15¼	15¼	– ¾
32¼	15	AGS Computr	19	17	16¾	16¾	...
14	2½	A I A Indust	98	2¾	2½	2¾	+ ⅛
14⅜	10¼	Aircal Inc	43	10½	10¼	10¼	– ¼
20	9⅛	AirWiscSv 10i	62	9¾	9½	9½	– ¼
19¼	17½	AlaskPcB .25f	35	18	17½	18	+ ¼
29¾	25¼	AlexBld s1.20	478	27	26¾	26¾	...
17	10½	Alfin Fragrnc	10	11¾	11¼	11¾	+ ¼
35	19	Algorex Corp	75	25¼	24⅝	25	+ ¼
19	13½	Allegh Bev .40	141	14	13½	14	+ ½
14⅝	10¾	AllghWstn En	10	12½	12⅜	12⅜	– ⅜
25¾	20¾	AlliedBcsh .80	x833	22¼	21¾	22¼	– ⅛
7⅛	3½	AllnetCm Svc	54	4	3⅞	3⅞	– ⅛
18½	11¾	Alpha Micrsys	89	12¼	11¾	12	...
20½	7¼	Altos Comptr	344	9⅝	9¼	9½	+ ⅛
23¾	21¾	AmCstInd s.40	164	23¼	23	23	...
15¾	7⅜	Am Adventure	115	11	10¼	10½	– ½
15¾	9⅜	ABkrs Ins .50g	216	11	10¾	10⅞	– ⅜
16⅝	(L)	Am Carrier s	135	9	8½	8¾	– ¼
11¾	(L)	Amer Cont'l	122	7	6¼	7	– ¼
20	7¼	AmFed SL .60	323	11¾	11	11½	– ¼
33½	19¾	AmFletch 1.48	119	28¼	27¾	28¼	+ ⅜
29¼	21½	AmGreetg .50	1077	24¼	24	24¼	+ ⅛
16½	10	AmIncLf .20d	144	11⅛	10¾	11	– ⅛
76¼	50⅞	AmIntlGrp .44	x1950	56½	55	56¼	+ ¾
26	11¾	AmerMgt Sys	1	14¼	14¼	14¼	+ ¼
27¾	18	AmNatlIns .96	68	23⅞	23½	23⅜	– ½
9⅛	5⅜	Am Physician	36	7⅝	7½	7½	– ⅛
10½	4	Am Quasr Pet	56	4⅝	4½	4½	– ⅛
31¼	12¾	Am Software	37	13½	13	13	...
32½	4¼	AmSolar King	198	5⅝	5⅜	5½	...
19⅛	1¾	Am Surgery	866	2⅝	2⅜	2½	...
12½	7½	AmWest Airl	880	8	7½	7½	– ½
48½	41	Ameritrst 2.88	x67	42	41½	41½	– ¼
18	4⅝	Amgen	142	5⅝	5⅜	5⅝	...
20⅜	16⅜	AmskgBk .18d	51	17⅛	16⅞	17⅛	+ ⅛
14¾	(L)	AnaditeInc .10	12	8	7⅞	8	...
31⅜	13¾	Analogic Corp	297	15	14⅛	15	+ ½
16½	4	Analysts Intl	63	5¼	4¾	4¾	– ¼
15½	7½	Anaren Micrw	36	9½	9⅜	9½	+ ⅛
44½	28½	Andrew Corp	4	30	30	30	...
10	6	Andros Anlyz	13	6½	6	6	...
14¾	8¼	ApogeeEnt .12	9	9	8¾	9	...
24⅜	17	ApolloCmptr s	1534	20¼	19½	20	+ ¼
63¼	17¼	Apple Comptr	5362	29⅞	29⅛	29½	+ ⅛
21½	16½	Appld Biosyst	81	19¾	19¼	19¼	...
18½	8½	Applied Comu	442	10¾	10½	10¾	+ ½
48¾	25¾	Applied Matrl	361	28	26¾	27¼	– ¼
16⅜	10⅜	Applied Solar	60	10⅝	10½	10⅝	+ ¼
4½	2¼	AppldSolar wt	50	2⅜	2⅜	2⅜	– ⅜
28¼	14	ArgoSyst Inc	29	15½	15	15½	+ ¼
20¼	15⅞	ArizBncw .80g	34	17⅞	17⅝	17⅝	– ⅛
14	6⅝	Artel Commn	12	8¾	8¼	8¼	– ¼
21¼	11¼	AskCmptr Sys	88	14¼	14	14¼	+ ¾
18¾	5⅞	Assoc Host .12	661	12⅜	12	12⅜	+ ⅛
12¼	6½	Astrosystms	47	7⅜	7⅛	7¼	...
26⅜	15¼	AtlantcBcp .80	90	24⅝	24¼	24¼	– ⅛
11⅛	8⅞	AtlantcFed SL	565	9⅛	8⅞	9	...
12	8¼	AtlantFin Fed	360	10	9½	10	+ ¼
43	22½	Atl Research	96	28	27	28	+ 1
14⅝	7⅝	AtlSoest Airl	22	10⅛	10	10	– ⅛
25	16¼	Atwood Ocncs	2	18½	18½	18½	– ¼
6¾	3½	Austron Inc	3	4⅜	4⅜	4⅜	...
27¼	(L)	Automatix Inc	231	10½	10	10½	+ ¼
29¼	12½	AutoTrol Tech	45	15	14½	14¾	– ⅛
18¾	8¼	Auxton Cmptr	125	11¼	10¾	11¼	– ¼
28¾	15¼	Avant Garde	161	18½	18	18½	...
33¼	16½	Avantek Inc	173	18⅝	18⅛	18⅝	+ ¼
16½	13	Avatar Holdg	20	15½	14¾	14¾	– ¼
10¼	7¾	Aztec Mfg .20	15	8¼	7¾	7¾	– ½
6⅜	2⅝	AztechIntl 10k	59	3⅛	3	3⅛	...

(b) Other Active Issues

Stock & Div	Sales 100s	Bid	Asked	Net Chg.
AA Importing	52	4¼	4¾	...
A&MFood Svc	30	5⅝	5⅞	+ ⅛
Acapulco Rest	22	3⅞	4	...
AcetoChem 4i	3	18¼	19¼	...
AcmeGen .20a	1	9½	10¼	...
Acro Energy	2	5¾	6½	...
AcroEnrgy ut	25	6	6¾	– ¼
Activision Inc	103	1⅝	1¾	+ ⅛
ActMedia Inc	5	18	18¾	...
AddWesley .60	x36	21¼	21¾	...
Advance Ross	9	5½	5¾	...
AdvGenetc Sci	2	4	4½	...
AdvTobPrd ut	480	6⅛	6⅜	– ⅛
AEC Inc .08d	5	13¼	14	...
AEL Indust A	76	25	26	– ½
Aero Services	9	1⅞	2⅛	...
Aero Syst Inc	119	2⅞	3	...
Aerosonic Cp	121	2 5-16	2⅜	...
AffilBankCp 1	1	21½	23	...
AFP Imaging	16	3½	3¾	...
Agnico Eagle	291	12⅞	13	+ ⅝
AirMidwst Inc	3	10	10½	...
Air One Inc	276	2⅞	3⅛	...
AlamoSvgs .60	14	20	21	– ½
Alanco Ltd	511	9-16	⅝	+ ⅛
Alaska Bncrp	6	5⅞	6¼	...
AlMutlBcp 10i	166	13¾	14¼	+ 1¼
AlaTennR 2.20	378	40	40¾	...
Alexndr Enrg	30	3½	3¾	...
Alico Inc .30	10	56	61	...
Allen Org .48g	x11	45	46½	+ ⅛
AlliedCaptl 1a	18	18½	19¼	...
Allied Resrch	98	3⅛	3¼	+ ⅛
All Seasons	17	11¾	12½	– ½
Ally Gargano	10	6½	7	...
AM Cable TV	10	3¼	3⅜	...
AMC Ent .06d	48	11½	12	+ ¼
Amerford .07b	2	5¾	6¾	– ¼
Ameribnc 1.32	6	23½	25	...
AmAggregat 1	11	22¾	24¼	...
AmApraisl .48	z35	14¾	15¾	...
AmCellrTel A	19	4	4½	...
Amer Ecology	370	4	4¼	...
AmEquit 1.38b	9	20¾	22¼	...
Am Filtrn 1.16	8	20½	21¼	...
AFncl pfF 1.80	10	12	12½	+ ⅛
AmerFirst 5i	3	6⅝	7¼	...
Am Fructose	37	6⅝	7	– ⅛
Amer Furn .28	10	7¾	8⅛	...
AGuarnF .05e	40	1¼	1½	– ⅛
AmIndem 1.12	12	16	16½	– ¼
Am Integrity	10	7¾	8¼	...
AmItIG pf5.85	17	100	105	...
AmInvsLf .20g	109	7⅜	7⅝	+ ⅜
Am Land Cr	3	6	6½	...
AmLeisure B	50	2⅛	2¼	...
AmLeisure A	722	1	1 1-32	+ 1-32
AmLeisure ut	21	2⅜	2 7-16	...
Am Magnetics	13	8½	9	...
AmMedS .15g	5	7¼	8	– ½
Am Monitor	57	4¼	4⅜	...
ANtlHld 1.08a	13	18	18½	...
AmNatl Petro	8	¾	⅞	...
AmPacific Cp	13	3⅞	4⅛	+ ⅛
ARecreatn .16	25	9	9½	...
Am Restaurnt	64	4½	4¾	+ ¼
Am Secur 1.01	93	26	26¾	– ½
Ameriwest Fn	88	15¾	16	– ⅝
Amistar Corp	33	7	7¼	+ ¼

(c) Less Active Issues

	Bid	Asked
ABM Computer	2⅛	2⅜
ACS Entrprise	1¾	2
ADI Electrnics	4⅛	4¼
ADI Electrn wt	1½	1⅝
AdvCellulr Tech	5-32	3-16
AdvCommun ut	6	6⅜
AdvMonitring p	1⅞	1 15-16
AdvnNMR Syst	2	2¼
AdvNMRSyst ut	7	7½
AIM Telephone	1⅝	1¾
AIN Leasing ut	3¾	4
AlaskaAp GldM	1½	1⅝
Alcide Corp	1⅜	1 9-16
Alcide Corp ut	6½	7
Alfacell Corp	2⅞	3¼
Allied Nursing	1½	1⅝
AloScherer Hlth	12	13
Alpine Geophys	2½	2⅝
Alpine Intl Corp	15-32	17-32
Amarco Resour	15-32	½
Ambassadr Grp	⅜	⅝
Amber Resourc	⅜	7-16
Ambra Oil Gas	1 5-16	1 7-16
Ambulatory Md	3	3¼
AmCell Netwrk	2¾	3
AmCellNwrk ut	3½	3¾
Am Comm Tel	3-16	7-32
Am Comm Serv	1⅞	2
Am Cytogenics	1	1½
Am Diagnostics	5¼	5½
AmEducatn Cm	13¾	14¼
AFamlyPzza ut	4	4¼
AmFiber Optics	3½	5¼
AmerFuel Tech	1 9-16	1⅝
Am Genetics Itl	5-16	11-32
AmerHome Ind	5-16	7-16
Am Hm Patient	4⅜	4⅞
AmHome Schld	3⅜	3⅝
AmerMed Alert	2	2¼
AmMedAlert ut	3	3¼
Amer MediDent	1⅜	1 7-16
AmNtl Entrprs	1½	1⅝
Am Nuclear Cp	2¼	2½
Am Nucleonics	15-16	1⅛
Am Pacific Intl	1⅛	1 3-16
AmPhnmet clA	2⅞	3⅛
AmPyramid Rs	1 1-16	1⅛
AmSoftware Tc	3-32	5-32
AmSport Advisr	½	⅝
Amerihealth	3-16	¼
Amicor Inc	½	19-32
Ampower Tech	15-16	1 1-16
Amtech Resrce	¼	11-32
AnCon Genetics	1 5-16	1 7-16
Annandale Corp	1⅜	1⅝
AntaresOil Corp	7-16	9-16
Apache Energy	⅛	5-32
Apollo Industrs	1⅞	2⅛
Applied MedDv	3-16	¼
AppldMedDV ut	7-32	9-32
Aquaculture Pr	1-32	1-16
Aquanautics Cp	2	2¼
Aqua Sol Inc ut	2½	2⅝
Aracca Petrolm	¼	7-16
Arapaho Petrol	1¼	1½
Argonaut Enrgy	1 11-16	1⅞
Ariz Silver Corp	2¾	3
Arrays Inc	5¼	5¾
Assoc Comm A	9½	10¼
Assoc Comm B	9½	10
Astrdyne Cmptr	1¼	1½
Astrocom Corpn	2¾	3
Astrosystem wt	2⅜	2½
AthenFed SvBk	8½	9
AutoMedcl Labs	2⅝	2¾
AvinoMn Resr	1⅞	2 1-16
AW Comptr Sys	8	8½

SOURCE: Reprinted with permission of the *Wall Street Journal*. © Dow Jones & Company, Inc. (May 29, 1984). All Rights Reserved.

FIGURE 13-2
Summary of Active Stocks Traded with the Aid of the NASDAQ System, May 25, 1984

amount (letters refer to footnotes providing details concerning extra or special dividends and yields). This amount is divided by the price to obtain the figure shown for yield. The ratio of the current price to the last twelve months' earnings is given next. The remaining entries summarize the day's transactions in the major markets in which the stock is traded. Sales, in hundreds of shares, are indicated, followed

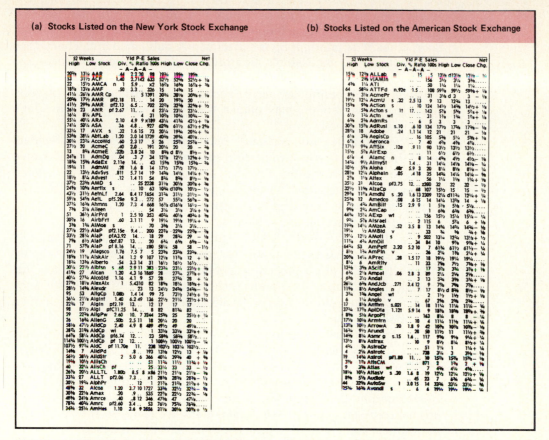

(a) Stocks Listed on the New York Stock Exchange

(b) Stocks Listed on the American Stock Exchange

FIGURE 13-3
Summary of Activity in Stocks Traded on Major Exchanges, May 25, 1984

by the highest and lowest prices at which trades were completed during the day. The next entry is the *closing price*—the price at which the last trade of the day was made (this is also used to compute yield and the price-earnings ratio). The final entry shows the difference between the day's closing price and that of the preceding day.

INSIDER TRADING

The United States Securities and Exchange Acts of 1933 and 1934 require the officers and directors of a corporation whose securities are traded on an organized exchange and anyone who owns more than

Common Stocks

10% of the outstanding amount of such a security to report their transactions in it within ten days following the month in which the transaction takes place. The information is subsequently published in the Securities and Exchange Commission's monthly *Official Summary of Securities Transactions and Holdings*. For example, the summary of trades made in January (and reported by early February) is published early in March. Thus up to two months may elapse before knowledge of an insider's trade is widespread.

The Securities and Exchange Acts also require corporate insiders to return all short-term profits from security transactions in their own stocks to the corporation. For this purpose, "short-term" is defined as less than six months. As one might expect, few insiders are sufficiently devoted to their firm to realize such profits; most prefer to wait until the six-month period is over.

In the United States it is illegal for anyone to make a security transaction that takes advantage of "inside" corporate information unavailable to the other person or persons involved in the trade. This proscription includes corporate insiders and also those whom such insiders give secret information (the recipient of such a "tip" is termed the "tipee").

Legally, there are two types of nonpublic information: that which is "private" (i.e., legal) and that which is "inside" (i.e., possibly illegal). The law-abiding but dedicated security analyst must try to obtain as much of the former as possible, while completely avoiding the latter. Unfortunately, the distinction between the two types is highly ambiguous, guaranteeing continuing employment for lawyers specializing in the subject and continuing problems for security analysts.

Legal issues aside, two questions of relevance to outside investors may be posed: (1) do insiders make unusual profits on transactions in their own stocks, and (2) if they do, can others profit by following their example as soon as it becomes public knowledge?

Insiders trade their stock for many reasons. Some purchases result from the exercise of options, some sales from the need for cash, and so on. Moreover, it is not unusual to find some insiders purchasing a stock during a month in which others are selling it. However, when a major piece of inside information suggests that a stock's value differs significantly from its present price, and insiders find it difficult to resist the temptation to profit from this knowledge, one would expect a preponderance of insider trades on one side of the market (i.e., either purchases or sales).

One way to search for such situations is to examine the *Official Summary* and count the number of days during a month each insider traded his or her stock (excluding the exercise of options). If the days on which purchases were made exceeds those on which sales were made, the individual can be counted as a net purchaser during that month; and if the converse holds, as a net seller. Next, the number

TABLE 13-1

Abnormal Performance Associated with Insider Trading

SAMPLE			AVERAGE ABNORMAL RETURN (%) OVER EIGHT MONTHS FOLLOWING:	
Cut-off (No. of Net Purchasers or Sellers)	No. of Cases	Period	Month of Transaction	Month Information Became Publicly Available
1	362	1960s	1.36	.70
3	861	1960s	5.07	4.94
4	293	1950s	5.14	4.12
5	157	1950s	4.48	4.08

SOURCE: Jeffrey F. Jaffe, "Special Information and Insider Trading," *The Journal of Business*, 47, no. 3 (July 1974), 410-29. © 1974 by the University of Chicago. All Rights Reserved.

of purchasers and sellers for the stock can be considered. If there were at least, say, three more purchasers than sellers, one might infer that positive inside information motivated at least some insider trades during the month. In the opposite case, one might infer that negative insider information played a role.

Different cut-off levels could be used in this process to reflect the intensity of insider trading. A cut-off of 1 would require more trades of one type than the other, a cut-off of 5, substantial balance on one side of the market, and so on.

Such a procedure was used in a detailed study of insider transactions during the 1950s and 1960s.[3] Table 13-1 summarizes the key results. Each figure indicates the "abnormal" return above that expected, given market moves, over an eight-month period for trades of the same type as the predominant insider transaction. For example, during the 1960s, if one purchased every stock in the sample for which there were three or more net purchasers and sold every stock for which there were three or more net sellers during a month, more or less coincident with the transactions of the insiders themselves, an average abnormal return of 5.07% could have been earned over the subsequent eight months. If the transactions had been made instead at roughly the time the information was published in the *Official Summary*, an average abnormal return of 4.94% could have been earned over the next eight months.

As the first row in the table shows, a bare majority of insider trades does not appear to isolate possible effects of insider information. But a majority of three, four, or five does seem to do so. The figures shown are gross of any transactions costs, but even so one might well

---

[3] Jeffrey F. Jaffe, "Special Information and Insider Trading," *The Journal of Business*, 47, no. 3 (July 1974), 410-29. © 1974 by the University of Chicago. All Rights Reserved.

conclude that insiders can and do make money from special knowledge of their companies. This is not surprising. If insiders do not know the value of their firms, who does? Profits of 4% or 5% per eight months are hardly large enough to arouse the suspicion of regulatory authorities, let alone provide adequate evidence for punitive action.

On the other hand, the abnormal returns associated with transactions that could have been made by outsiders, using only publicly available information on insider trading, *are* surprising. Moreover, those associated with cut-offs of three, four, or five pass statistical tests designed to see if they might be simply due to chance. After transactions costs, trades designed to capitalize on such information would not prove wildly profitable, but the argument that "if you can't beat them, join them" (even two months later) does seem to have some merit.

In the 1970s the *Value Line Investment Survey*[4] began to include an "index of insider decisions" for each stock covered in its weekly service. In essence, this is a cumulative index of the net number of purchasers including those who exercise options (counted as plus values) and sellers (counted as negative values). The increasingly public nature of such information should make it less valuable as more and more investors attempt to profit by it. It might thus be unwise to expect to obtain abnormal returns as large as those shown in Table 13-1 now.

EX ANTE AND EX POST VALUES

Equilibrium theories such as Capital Asset Pricing Models and the Arbitrage Pricing Theory imply that in the consensus of well-informed analysts, stocks with certain attributes will, other things equal, have large expected returns, while those with other attributes will have small expected returns. Such concepts are based on opinions held *before the fact* (in Latin: *ex ante*) about possible outcomes and their relative probabilities. After the fact (in Latin: *ex post*) only one outcome will be recorded for each stock. Analysts will then form new and possibly different opinions, another set of stock returns will subsequently be recorded, and so on.

This makes it extremely difficult to tell whether security attributes and expected returns do in fact go together in the manner implied by various equilibrium theories. Moreover, such theories are relatively silent concerning simple ways in which a security's *future* attributes and expected return might be estimated by processing *historic* data on its past performance.

To bridge this gap, a number of investigators have used past outcomes of security returns as surrogates for *ex ante* expectations. This requires an assumption that relevant predictions do not change from

---

[4] Published by Arnold Bernhard and Co., Inc., New York.

period to period and that sufficient information will eventually be available to determine what such expectations actually were. Thus actual *average* returns are used as estimates of *expected* returns, slopes of regression lines relating *actual* security returns to surrogates for factors are used as estimates of predicted sensitivities to such factors, and so on. Two obvious objections may be made. First, expectations almost certainly change from time to time: nothing in valuation theory suggests otherwise. Second, even if expectations did not change over time, an extremely long historic record might be required to obtain reasonable estimates of their magnitudes.

Despite these and other problems, historic data are worth examining.

HISTORIC AND FUTURE BETA VALUES

For purposes of portfolio management, the relevant risk of a security concerns its impact on the risk of a reasonable portfolio. In the world of the original Capital Asset Pricing Model, reasonable portfolios will be well diversified and subject primarily to market risk. This suggests the importance of a security's sensitivity to likely future market moves. To estimate this, one should in principle consider possible sources of such moves in the future, project the security's reactions to all such sources, and estimate the probabilities of each. In the process, the economics of the relevant industry and firm, the impact of both operating and financial leverage on the firm, and other fundamental factors can and should be taken into account.

But what about simply investigating the extent to which a security's price moved with the market in the past? Such an approach ignores a myriad of possible differences between past and future. However, it is simple, and it does have some merit.

As shown in Chapter 7, a security's beta value can be regarded as the slope of the characteristic line that best fits the relationship between its return and that of the market. If such a relationship were constant from period to period, one could estimate the value of beta for a stock by fitting a characteristic line to points representing the stock's return and the return on an index chosen to serve as a surrogate for the market portfolio. A simpler procedure would use only the period-by-period percentage changes in the price of the stock and percentage changes in the level of the index. Happily for those who must calculate such numbers, the estimates obtained using the two procedures are very similar. One study showed that well over 99% of the differences in the estimated beta values of 1572 securities obtained via the complex procedure were associated with the differences among the estimates obtained in the simpler manner.[5]

---

[5] William F. Sharpe and Guy M. Cooper, "Risk-Return Classes of New York Stock Exchange Common Stocks, 1931-1967," *Financial Analysts Journal,* 28, no. 2 (March/April 1972), 46-54.

FIGURE 13-4

Sample Page from: Merrill Lynch, Pierce, Fenner & Smith, Inc., Market Sensitivity Report for November 1979

TKR Symb	Security Name	10/79 Close Price	Beta	Alpha	R-Sqr	Resid Std Dev-n	Std.Err. of Beta	Std.Err. of Alpha	Adjusted Beta	Number of Observ
THRS	THREASHOLD TECKNOLOG	9.750	.85	1.92	.06	12.99	.40	1.69	.90	60
FXN	THREE D DEPTS	4.375	1.71	4.54	.18	17.07	.45	2.21	1.47	60
TDMC	THREE DIMENTIONAL CI	.562	-.63	8.65	.02	41.62	1.46	5.78	-.08	52
TFTA	THRIFTIMART INC A	21.375	.80	1.21	.13	8.49	.26	1.11	.87	60
THRF	THRIFTWAY LEASING CO	.000	1.02	3.84	.02	26.06	.66	3.38	1.01	60
TFD	THRIFTY CORP	11.625	1.92	.87	.46	8.80	.27	1.15	1.61	60
TEXT	TI-CARO	20.500	.94	1.58	.23	7.17	.22	.93	.96	60
TIM	TIDEWATER INC	25.750	.86	.39	.19	7.30	.22	.95	.91	60
TDW	TIDWELL INDS INC	5.750	5.11	4.85	.17	46.73	1.42	6.10	3.73	60
FLY	TIGER INTL INC	19.750	1.63	1.55	.33	9.87	.30	1.29	1.42	60
TI	TIME INC	43.250	1.24	1.39	.36	6.87	.21	.90	1.16	60
TPLX	TIMEPLEX INC	9.125	2.38	5.23	.11	26.83	.82	3.50	1.91	60
PWII	TIMBERLAND INDUSTRIES	6.250	.78	3.18	.06	13.68	.35	1.77	.85	60
TMC	TIMES MIRROR CO	32.500	1.60	1.19	.61	5.41	.16	.71	1.39	60
TKR	TIMKEN CO	51.000	1.13	.65	.40	5.82	.18	.76	1.09	60
TNSL	TINSLEY LABS INC	6.000	.84	1.60	.03	17.49	.48	2.27	.90	60
TLK	TIPPERARY CORP	11.250	.95	2.12	.08	12.86	.39	1.68	.97	60
TIN	TITAN GROUP	1.500	1.53	-1.81	.04	24.91	.85	3.22	1.35	60
TICT	TLL INDUS	3.000	1.61	-.23	.12	17.29	.53	2.26	1.40	60
AIKZ	TOBIAS KOIZIN CO	5.000	1.18	2.44	.07	16.98	.52	2.22	1.12	60
TBN	TOBIN PACKING INC	3.625	1.10	-.41	.09	13.89	.42	1.81	1.06	60
TOCM	TOCOM INC	10.500	1.72	2.98	.19	14.69	.45	1.92	1.48	60
TOD	TODD SHIPYARDS CORP	23.750	.31	3.12	.01	16.88	.51	2.20	.54	60
TOK	TOKHEIM CORP	15.875	2.39	2.46	.39	12.72	.39	1.66	1.92	60
TKM	TOKIO MARINE INS ADR	129.500	.32	1.43	.01	7.57	.23	.99	.55	60
TED	TOLEDO EDISON CO	18.125	.79	-.28	.34	4.60	.14	.60	.86	60
NOHO	TOLEDO TRUSTCORP	27.500	.35	.91	.09	4.35	.13	.57	.57	60
TILLY	TOLLEY INTL CORP	1.000	.21	-2.34	.01	19.46	.59	2.54	.48	60
TLOC	TOMLINSON OIL INC	10.500	1.28	3.68	.07	17.49	.53	2.28	1.19	60
TKA	TONKA CORP	10.875	1.77	.47	.33	10.60	.32	1.38	1.51	60

BASED ON S&P 500 INDEX, USING STRAIGHT REGRESSION

Estimates Derived from Historic Data

Figure 13-4 shows a page from a report prepared by Merrill Lynch, Pierce, Fenner and Smith, Inc. Price changes for each of up to 60 months are compared with changes in Standard and Poor's 500-stock index via regression analysis. Five of the resulting values are of interest. The figure shown for *beta* indicates the slope of the best-fit line for each stock. For example, during the period covered, the stock of the Timken Company exhibited slightly aggressive behavior, moving roughly 13% more than the index in a typical market move. The value of *R-squared* shows the proportion of total variance in the security's monthly price changes accounted for by market moves. Forty percent of the variation in Timken's price could be attributed to the market over the period studied. The *residual standard deviation* is the standard deviation of the distances of the points from the line; it provides ex post evidence of nonmarket risk. In roughly two months out of three, Timken's price change equaled that expected, given its beta value and the behavior of the market at the time, plus or minus 5.82% (e.g., 582 basis points).

If a security's "true" beta remained the same forever, its historic beta, obtained in the manner illustrated in Figure 13-4, would still change from time to time because of sampling error. If a nonmarket factor caused a large price increase in a month when the market rose, beta would probably be overestimated. If the good news came when the market was falling, beta would probably be underestimated. Since nonmarket factors affect the typical stock more than does the market itself, the likelihood of such a situation is quite high.

The *standard error of beta* attempts to indicate the extent of such errors. For example, given a number of necessary assumptions (e.g., stability of beta), the chances are roughly two out of three that the true value of Timken's beta is within .18 of the estimated value.

Adjusting Beta Values

But more needs to be said. Absent *any* information at all, one would presume a stock's beta relative to a representative index of all stocks to be 1.0. Given a chance to see how the stock moved relative to the market over some period, a modification of this *prior* estimate would seem appropriate. But a sensible *posterior* estimate would undoubtedly lie between the two values.

Formal procedures for making such estimates have been adopted by most producers of beta values. The specific adjustments made typically differ from time to time and, in some cases, from stock to stock. In Figure 13-4 the *adjusted beta* values were obtained by giving approximately 66% weight to the measured beta and approximately 34% weight to the prior value of 1.0 for each stock. Thus for Timken:

$$\text{adjusted beta} = (.34 \times 1.0) + (.66 \times 1.13)$$
$$= 1.09$$

Table 13-2 shows the extent to which such procedures anticipate differences between past and future betas. The first column lists the unadjusted betas for eight portfolios of 100 securities each, based on monthly price changes from July 1947 through June 1954 (the portfolios were designed to have significantly different betas during this period). The second column of the table shows the values obtained when an adjustment of the type used by the Merrill Lynch service was applied. The betas in the third column are based on price changes over the subsequent seven years. For many of the portfolios, the ex post value was even closer to 1.0 than the adjusted ex ante figure. The final column shows the values obtained using the data for the following seven years. By and large, continued reversion to the mean of 1.0 is evident.

TABLE 13-2
Ex Ante and Ex Post Beta Values for Portfolios of 100 Securities Each

| Portfolio | July 1947-June 1954 | | July 1954-June 1961 | July 1961-June 1968 |
	Unadjusted	Adjusted		
1	.36	.48	.57	.72
2	.61	.68	.71	.79
3	.78	.82	.88	.88
4	.91	.93	.96	.92
5	1.01	1.01	1.03	1.04
6	1.13	1.10	1.13	1.02
7	1.26	1.21	1.24	1.08
8	1.47	1.39	1.32	1.15

SOURCE: Marshall E. Blume, "Betas and Their Regression Tendencies," *The Journal of Finance*, XXX, no. 3 (June 1975), 785-96.

Apparently "true" betas not only vary over time but have a tendency to move back toward average levels. This is plausible enough, for extreme postures are likely to be moderated over time. A firm whose operations or financing make the risk of its equity considerably different from that of other firms is more likely to move back toward the average than away from it. Such changes in beta values are due to real economic phenomena, not simply an artifact of overly simple statistical procedures. There is, however, no reason to expect every stock's true beta to move in the same way, to the same average, and at the same speed. In this regard, a little fundamental security analysis may prove more useful than the adoption of more sophisticated statistical methods for processing past price changes.

Changes in Stock Beta Values

Table 13-2 shows that *at the portfolio level* historic data can provide substantial information on future beta values, although the precise adjustment required to estimate the numeric magnitudes may be difficult to determine. However, as the standard errors of beta in Figure 13-4 suggest, estimates of beta for *individual securities* are subject to great error and should be treated accordingly. Nonetheless, a security's historic beta value provides some indication of its future beta.

Figure 13-5 shows that the predictive ability of historic beta improves as more diversified portfolios are considered. The vertical axis plots the percent of the differences in (measured) portfolio betas (based on weekly price changes) in one year that can be attributed to differences in their (measured) betas in the prior year. The horizontal axis indicates the number of securities in each portfolio. Data from other countries give similar results.

Table 13-3 provides another view. Every stock listed on the New York Stock Exchange was assigned to one of ten classes in each year from 1931 through 1967, based on its beta value over the preceding five years. The stocks in the top 10% of each January's "beta book" were assigned to class 10, the next 10% to class 9, and so on. The table shows the percent of the stocks in each class five years later. Also shown are the entries that would be expected if there were *no* relationship between such past and future beta classes.

Although both true beta values and, *a fortiori*, measured beta values of individual stocks do change, a security's past sensitivity to

FIGURE 13-5

Percent of Differences in Beta Values Attributable to Differences in Prior Year's Betas

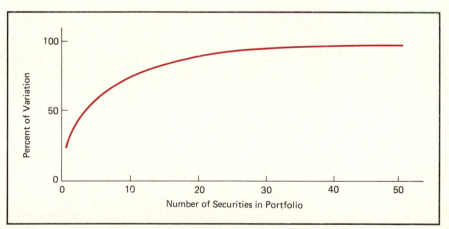

SOURCE: Robert A. Levy, "On the Short-term Stationarity of Beta Coefficients," *Financial Analysts Journal*, 27, no. 6 (November/December 1971), 55-62.

TABLE 13-3
Movement of Stocks Among Beta Classes

RISK CLASS	PERCENT OF STOCKS IN THE SAME BETA CLASS FIVE YEARS LATER		PERCENT OF STOCKS IN THE SAME BETA CLASS OR WITHIN ONE RISK CLASS FIVE YEARS LATER	
	Actual	Expected if There Were No Relationship	Actual	Expected if There Were No Relationship
10 (highest beta values)	32.2	10	69.3	20
9	18.4	10	53.7	30
8	16.4	10	45.3	30
7	13.3	10	40.9	30
6	13.9	10	39.3	30
5	13.6	10	41.7	30
4	13.2	10	40.2	30
3	15.9	10	44.6	30
2	21.5	10	60.9	30
1 (lowest beta values)	40.5	10	62.3	20

SOURCE: William F. Sharpe and Guy M. Cooper, "Risk-Return Classes of New York Stock Exchange Common Stocks, 1931-1967," *Financial Analysts Journal*, 28, no. 2 (March/April 1972), 46-54.

market moves is still worth examining. This is especially so since, even when a number of rather inaccurate (but unbiased) estimates of security beta values are used, quite an accurate estimate of a diversified portfolio's beta value may be obtained. And portfolio risk is, after all, more relevant than security risk.

Industry Beta Values

The future beta value for a *firm* depends on the sensitivity of the demand for its products or services and of its costs to the economic factors about which there is the greatest uncertainty. The beta value of a firm's *stock* depends on the beta of the firm and its degree of financial leverage.

One might expect firms in industries characterized by highly cyclical demand and/or large fixed costs to have higher betas than those in industries with more stable demand and/or greater freedom to vary costs. Differences in financial leverage could wholly offset such factors, leaving few if any differences among the beta values of the common stocks of firms in different industries. However, this does not seem to be the case. Stocks of firms in certain industries do tend to have higher beta values than those in other industries, and by and large the classifications accord with prior expectations.

Table 13-4 shows the average values of beta for stocks in various

TABLE 13-4
Average Values of Beta for Stocks in Selected Industries, 1966-1974

Industry	Beta Value	Industry	Beta Value
Air transport	1.80	Chemicals	1.22
Real property	1.70	Energy, raw materials	1.22
Travel, outdoor recreation	1.66	Tires, rubber goods	1.21
Electronics	1.60	Railroads, shipping	1.19
Miscellaneous finance	1.60	Forest products, paper	1.16
Nondurables, entertainment	1.47	Miscellaneous, conglomerate	1.14
Consumer durables	1.44	Drugs, medicine	1.14
Business machines	1.43	Domestic oil	1.12
Retail, general	1.43	Soaps, cosmetics	1.09
Media	1.39	Steel	1.02
Insurance	1.34	Containers	1.01
Trucking, freight	1.31	Nonferrous metals	.99
Producer goods	1.30	Agriculture, food	.99
Aerospace	1.30	Liquor	.89
Business services	1.28	International oil	.85
Apparel	1.27	Banks	.81
Construction	1.27	Tobacco	.80
Motor vehicles	1.27	Telephone	.75
Photographic, optical	1.24	Energy, utilities	.60
		Gold	.36

SOURCE: Barr Rosenberg and James Guy, "Prediction of Beta from Investment Fundamentals," *Financial Analysts Journal*, 32, no. 4 (July/August 1976), 62-70.

industry classifications. Stocks of firms whose products are termed "necessities" tend to respond less than most stocks when expectations about the future health of the economy are revised, while the stocks of firms that manufacture consumer and producer durables and products considered "luxuries" tend to respond more than most. However, there are significant exceptions.

Information of the type shown in Table 13-4 can be used to "adjust" historic beta values. For example, the knowledge that a corporation is in the air transport industry suggests that a reasonable estimate of the beta value of its stock is greater than 1.0. It thus makes more sense to adjust a historic beta value toward a value above 1.0 than to the average for all stocks.

Beta Prediction Equations

The procedure used to "adjust" historic betas involves an implicit *prediction equation* for future beta. Writing formula (13-1) in a more general way:

$$\text{future beta} = a + b \cdot \text{historic beta} \qquad \textbf{(13-2)}$$

But a stock's historic beta value is only one of several pieces of information that can be used to predict its future beta value. For example, firms in the airline industry tend to have higher betas than those in the utility industry. This can be incorporated by including industry effects in the equation:[6]

$$\begin{aligned}
\text{future beta} = \ &a \\
&+ b \cdot \text{historic beta} \\
&+ c_1 \cdot \text{percent of earnings in the airline industry} \qquad \textbf{(13-3)} \\
&+ c_2 \cdot \text{percent of earnings in the utility industry} \\
&+ \cdots
\end{aligned}$$

Other attributes can also be used. For example, stocks with high dividend yields might have lower betas because more of their value is associated with near-term than with far-term dividends. The equation could thus be augmented to:

$$\begin{aligned}
\text{future beta} = \ &a \\
&+ b \cdot \text{historic beta} \\
&+ c_1 \cdot \text{percent of earnings in industry 1} \\
&+ c_2 \cdot \text{percent of earnings in industry 2} \qquad \textbf{(13-4)} \\
&+ \cdots \\
&+ c_n \cdot \text{percent of earnings in industry } n \\
&+ d \cdot \text{yield}
\end{aligned}$$

As indicated in Chapter 8, implicit in any factor model of security returns is an equation for predicting the beta of a security relative to any desired index or portfolio. A complex equation for predicting beta values is thus best derived as a by-product (albeit possibly the most important one) of a more general factor model.

Table 13-5 shows a beta prediction equation derived in this manner, using historic data from 1928 through 1982. To estimate the beta of a security[7] using it, one starts with a constant based on the sector in which the security is classified. For example, for the stock of a firm in a "basic industry," the base value is .455. To this is added the security's historic beta times .576 [note that this is similar to the "adjustment for historic beta in equation (13-1)]. From this is subtracted the security's dividend yield[8] times .019 and its size[9] times .105.

---

[6] For stocks with all earnings in one industry this is equivalent to adjusting historic betas toward an industry average.

[7] In this model, both historic and predicted betas are calculated relative to a value-weighted index of the returns on all stocks listed on the New York Stock Exchange. All attributes were calculated using data available a full month prior to the beginning of the month in which return is measured. This avoids statistical problems and provides results that can be used for actual portfolio management.

[8] Measured in percent per year (e.g., 4 for 4% per year).

[9] Calculated by taking the logarithm (to the base 10) of the total market value outstanding (price per share times shares outstanding), where the latter is expressed in billions of dollars.

TABLE 13-5
A Beta Prediction Equation Derived
from a Factor Model

CONSTANT TERM	
Sector	Value
Basic industry	.455
Capital goods	.425
Consumer staple	.307
Consumer cyclical	.443
Credit cyclical	.429
Energy	.394
Finance	.398
Transportation	.255
Utilities	.340
VARIABLE TERMS	
Attribute	Coefficient
Beta	.576
Yield	−.019
Size	−.105

SOURCE: Blake Grossman and William F.
Sharpe, "Factors in Security Returns," paper presented at the Center for the Study of Banking
and Financial Markets, University of Washington,
March 1984.

In this formula, securities with higher yields are predicted to have
lower beta values, as are those with large market values of equity
outstanding. Other things (historic beta, yield, and size) equal, stocks
of firms in basic industries, cyclical sectors, and capital goods are
expected to have high future betas, while stocks of firms in the transportation, utility, and consumer staple sectors are expected to have low
future betas. And so on.

Such prediction equations, based on multifactor models, fit historic
data considerably better than those that use only historic betas. One
analysis,[10] focusing on beta values, reported an improvement of 86%
over the more simple "adjusted beta" approach. Of course, such figures
describe the extent to which the equations fit a given set of data. Since
the true test of a prediction equation is its ability to *predict*, only
extensive experience with such approaches can, in the final analysis,
determine how well various factor models can predict beta values.

---

[10] Barr Rosenberg and Vinay Marathe, "The Prediction of Investment Risk: Systematic and
Residual Risk," *Proceedings of the Seminar on the Analysis of Security Prices*, University of Chicago,
November 1975.

Beta Services

Services providing betas on a regular basis in published form or for direct use in computer systems are available in several countries. Many use only past price changes to form estimates, but some are derived from more general factor models. Procedures differ. One service uses weekly data for two years; another, monthly data for five years. One estimates beta values for U.S. securities relative to Standard and Poor's 500-stock index; another, relative to the New York Stock Exchange Composite Index; and so on. In each case, estimates for individual securities are subject to error. It is thus hardly surprising that measured values for a given security obtained by different services using different procedures are not the same. This does not indicate that some are useless, only that they should be used appropriately.

FACTOR MODELS OF STOCK RETURNS

To operate successfully in the stock market one needs a good model of the relationships among stock returns. Theory provides little guidance concerning the best level of detail for such a model and the specific aspects to be included. The task is thus primarily empirical. Procedures employed for estimating stock factor models typically combine *judgments* concerning important factors with *statistical analysis* of historic data. Both art and science are involved.

A One-Factor Model

Figure 13-6 provides a (hypothetical) example of the relationship between stock returns in a given time period and one attribute. Each point represents one stock, showing its return during the month of January 19XX (on the vertical axis) and its dividend yield (on the horizontal axis). In this case, securities with higher yields tended to do better (have higher returns) than those with lower yields. To quantify the relationship, a straight line has been fitted to the data points using (simple) regression analysis. Since the points represent different securities and one time period, this is a *cross-section analysis*.

The equation of the line in Figure 13-6 is:

$$\text{return} = 4.0 + .5 \cdot \text{yield}$$

This can be written somewhat more generally as:

$$\text{return} = f_0 + f_1 \cdot \text{yield}$$

where:

$f_0 = $ the "zero factor"
$f_1 = $ factor 1

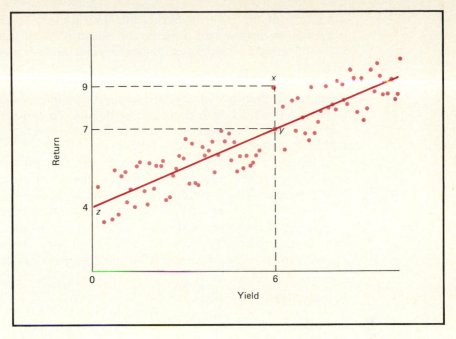

FIGURE 13-6
A One-Factor Model

The intercept (the point where the line crosses the vertical axis) indicates the return on a typical stock with zero yield. Thus it is termed the *zero factor*. In Figure 13-6, it is 4%. The slope indicates the additional return per unit increase in yield. Since yield is the first (and only) *attribute* in this example, the slope is termed *factor 1*. In Figure 13-6, the yield factor is 0.5 ($= (7 - 4)/6$).

The return on any given security may lie above or below the line. A complete description of the relationship can be written as:

$$R_{it} = f_{ot} + b_{i1t}f_{1t} + d_{it}$$

where:

R_{it} = the return on security i in period t
b_{i1t} = security i's sensitivity to factor 1 in period t
f_{ot} = the "zero factor" in period t
f_{1t} = factor 1 in period t
d_{it} = security i's *nonfactor return* in period t

Each symbol has been assigned a time-subscript (t) to indicate the particular time period (here, January 19XX). The yield *attribute* has been denoted in the conventional manner, since it is assumed to indicate *sensitivity* to the *yield factor*. The final term indicates the *nonfac-*

Common Stocks

tor return of the security during the time period. In Figure 13-6, for example, security *x* had a nonfactor return of +2%, since it returned 9% while the typical stock with the same yield (such as stock *y*) returned only 7%.

Empirically determined factors are closely related to the more fundamental factors of a standard factor model but may differ in certain respects. Appendix 13-A provides the details. To emphasize the difference between "empirical factors" and "fundamental factors" the former will be denoted by lower-case letters.

In months such as that shown in Figure 13-6, high-yield securities tend to outperform low-yield securities: the yield factor is *positive*. In other months, high-yield securities tend to underperform low-yield securities. The regression line in the corresponding diagram is downward-sloping and the yield factor is *negative*. In still other months there is no relationship between yield and return. The regression line in the corresponding diagram is flat and the yield factor is *zero*.

A Two-Factor Model

In some months small stocks tend to outperform large stocks. In other months the converse is true. To measure this, one can analyze the relationship between security returns and size. For this purpose, many models use a "size attribute" computed by taking the logarithm of the total market value of equity outstanding (where the latter is computed by multiplying a security's price per share times the number of shares outstanding). Thus a stock with $1 million of value might be assigned a size attribute of 0, a stock with $10 million a size attribute of 1, a stock with $100 million a size attribute of 2, and so on. This convention is based on the empirical observation that the impact of the "size factor" on a security with a large total value is likely to be twice as great as that on a security with one-tenth the total value. More succinctly: the effect appears to be roughly "linear in the logarithms."

To estimate the "size factor" in a given month, the procedure used in Figure 13-6 to estimate the "yield factor" could be employed. The size attributes of securities could be plotted on the horizontal axis and their returns plotted (as before) on the vertical axis. The slope of the resultant line would provide an estimate of the size factor for the month.

This procedure has drawbacks, however. Large stocks tend to have high yields. Thus differences in returns between large and small stocks might be due to some extent to differences in yield, not size. The estimated "size factor" might be, in part, a reflection of a true yield factor. The problem is, of course, symmetrical. A "yield factor" estimated as in Figure 13-6 might be, in part, a reflection of a true size factor.

To mitigate this problem, returns can be compared with *both* size and yield attributes, using *multiple* regression. Figure 13-7 provides an illustration. Each security is represented by a point in a three-dimensional graph, with return during the month shown on the vertical axis, its yield attribute shown on one of the bottom axes, and its size attribute shown on the other. Cross-sectional multiple regression analysis is then used to fit a *plane* to the data.

The relationship in Figure 13-7 can be written as:

$$R_{it} = f_{0t} + b_{i1t}f_{1t} + b_{i2t}f_{2t} + d_{it}$$

In this case, the "zero factor" indicates the return on a typical stock with zero yield *and* a zero size attribute (e.g., a market value of $1 million). Factor 1 is the yield factor—i.e., the slope of the plane in the "yield direction." It indicates the additional return per unit of yield *holding other attributes (here, size) constant*. Factor 2 is the size factor: the slope of the plane in the "size direction." It indicates the additional return per unit of size, *holding other attributes (here, yield) constant*. The nonfactor return for a security indicates the difference between its return and that typical of securities with the same attributes (here, securities with the same yield and size).

FIGURE 13-7
A Two-Factor Model

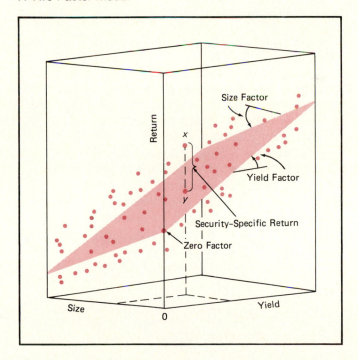

Multifactor Models

The inclusion of both yield and size, and the use of multiple regression analysis, can help "sort out" the effects of differences in yield and size on differences in security returns. It cannot deal adequately with influences that are not represented at all, nor can it guarantee that the included attributes are not simply serving as "proxies" for other, more fundamental attributes. Statistical tests can indicate the ability of the variables included in the analysis to explain or predict *past* security returns. But judgment and luck are required to identify variables that can help predict *future* security expected returns, risks, and correlations.

Most factor models of stock returns employ more than two factors (and some use a great many more than two). With M attributes, diagrams must be forsaken, since $M + 1$ dimensions would be required. Cross-section multiple regression analysis can be used, however, to obtain a relationship of the form:

$$R_{it} = f_{0t} + b_{i1t}f_{1t} + b_{i2t}f_{2t} + \cdots + b_{iMt}f_{Mt} + d_{it} \qquad \textbf{(13-5)}$$

If a diagram could be drawn, this would plot as a *hyperplane* (the generalization of a plane). In the regression analysis, each security provides one observation, with the return for the month serving as the dependent variable and the selected attributes as the independent variables. The intercept and the slope coefficients from the regression are the desired factor values, and the residuals' values are the securities' nonfactor returns.

Zero-One Attributes

Attributes such as a security's historic beta, dividend yield, or size are measured with numbers such as .95 or 1.03. But some attributes are represented more simply, with either 0 or 1. For example, consider a "basic industry attribute." Securities of firms in such industries could be assigned an attribute of 1 (indicating that all their activities are classified in this sector), while securities of firms in other industries could be assigned a basic industry attribute of 0 (indicating that none of their activities is classified in this sector). While a more sophisticated analysis might allow firms to be classified in two or more industries, using values between 0 and 1, most factor models have at least some "zero-one attributes" of this type.

An extreme model uses only such attributes. M sectors are identified, with:

$$b_{ijt} = \begin{cases} 1, & \text{if security } i \text{ is in sector } j \\ 0, & \text{if security } i \text{ is not in sector } j \end{cases}$$

$$f_{jt} = \text{the "sector } j \text{ factor" for period } t$$

Note that when each security is classified as belonging in one (and only one) sector, no "zero factor" is used.

A more common approach uses some attributes that are of the zero-one type and some that are not. The factor model used to obtain the beta prediction equation in Table 13-5 was of this type.

ESTIMATING RISKS AND CORRELATIONS

After fitting a factor model using data for January 19XX, it is a simple matter to fit the same model using data for February 19XX. February returns are used as the dependent variable and security attributes calculated prior to February as independent variables. The resulting coefficients are the February factor values and the residual values are the securities' nonfactor returns for the month.

After five years of this sort of activity, 60 sets of factor values will have been obtained. *If the future is expected to be like the past*, these results can be used to estimate likely factor values for next month. For example, the *average* value of factor 1 over the last 60 months could be taken as an estimate of the *expected* value of the factor for next month. The *actual* standard deviation of factor 2 over the past five years could be taken as an estimate of the *uncertainty* concerning its value next month. The *actual* correlation between two factors over the last 60 months could be taken as an estimate of the relevant correlation estimate for next month's values. And so on.

A similar procedure could be applied to the nonfactor returns. After five years, 60 such values will have been obtained for every security. *If the future is expected to be like the past*, the average nonfactor return for security 1 over the last 60 months could be taken as an estimate of its expected value for next month, and the standard deviation of the values could be taken as an estimate of the uncertainty regarding next month's value (i.e., the security's *nonfactor risk*). While historic nonfactor returns of some securities may have been correlated with those of other securities or factor values, if the model is "well specified," such correlations should be relatively small and could be assumed to be zero in the future.

Analysis of the behavior of factor values and nonmarket returns from period to period constitutes a final phase when estimating a factor model. After many (e.g. 60) cross-sectional analyses, a *time-series analysis* is performed. This may be simple (e.g. computing averages, standard deviations, and correlations) or complex (searching for time-dependent patterns in the data, and so on). The goal is to find some way to use *historic* data to make predictions about *future* returns and factor values.

Just as historic data are often used to provide simple estimates of future beta values, so, too, historic factor model results are often used to provide estimates of future *risks* (standard deviations, beta values, and so on) and *correlations*. Empirical evidence suggests that historic data are less valuable for predicting *expected* returns. These are usually estimated more directly, using procedures of the type described in Chapter 14.

ESTIMATING SENSITIVITIES TO FACTORS

In some factor models, security attributes that serve as sensitivities to factors are selected on "fundamental" grounds. Zero-one variables are based on standard classifications of securities by industry; historic betas are calculated utilizing a selected number of months of prior data; dividend yields, market values of equity outstanding, and other values are computed in standard ways, and so on.

Statistical tests may be used to assess the relevance of such preselected attributes and factors. But such tests cannot measure the usefulness of factors not considered at all.

Some factor models are estimated with a *multiple-phase* approach. In the first phase, historic data are analyzed to obtain promising security attributes. In the second phase, these attributes are used to estimate factor values for various periods. In the final (third) phase, results from the cross-section regressions are analyzed (using time-series methods) to estimate risks, correlations, and so on. Statistical procedures can be used to indicate the extent to which the resulting model "fits the data." More relevant are *out-of-sample tests* which measure the ability of the model to predict risks, returns, correlations, and so on in periods subsequent to those from which the historic data were taken. Such tests can (and should) be the fourth phase of the analysis.

Homogeneous Security Groups

Most stocks move together to some extent when expectations of the future of the economy change and "the market" moves accordingly. But *nonmarket* returns of various securities also move together. A *homogeneous group* is composed of securities that tend to move together, even when there is little or no change in the overall level of the stock market.

Some idea of the ways in which such groups can be identified can be gained from the results of two typical studies.

The first study investigated the influence of industrywide factors. A major problem in this connection involves the very concept of an industry. Classification of stocks by industries, always a difficult task, has become even more arbitrary with the rise of conglomerate firms producing many diverse products and services. Nonetheless, the U.S. Securities and Exchange Commission publishes lists in which corporations are assigned *Standard Industrial Codes*,[11] Standard and Poor's Corporation classifies a number of stocks by industry,[12] and Value Line[13] assigns the stocks covered in its service to industry groups. If industry effects are pronounced, one would expect the prices of stocks classified as belonging in the same industry to display at least some resulting comovement.

To see whether this was the case, a sample of 63 stocks in six different industries (based on Standard Industrial Classification codes) was selected. Monthly prices from 1927 through 1960 were examined, and the market's average effect on each stock estimated using standard regression analysis. Price changes of each stock in each month were then broken into two components—that due to market behavior, and the remainder, due to all nonmarket factors.

The key part of the study involved a step-by-step analysis of the correlations among the nonmarket returns. A computer was told to search for the two stocks for which this was the largest. They were then grouped together to form a new "pseudostock." The analysis was then repeated, using the 61 stocks plus the new pseudostock. The highest correlation was again determined, and the two items combined, leaving 60 remaining. The process was repeated, again and again, clustering together stocks with similar price behavior. Figure 13-8 shows the results. Each column represents a stage in the analysis, while each type of bar indicates a different group of stocks.

As the figure shows, stocks in the same industry tended to group together. This happened even though the grouping procedure was based entirely on comovement of prices—i.e., the computer did not know which stocks were from which industries. There is little doubt that during the period covered, industry factors accounted for significant amounts of nonmarket risk. How much? For the typical stock, approximately 50% of total price variance from 1927 through 1960 could be attributed to market effects. Roughly an additional 10% could be attributed to industrywide factors. The first figure declined through the period, reaching approximately 30% for the typical stock in the latter part, while the second figure changed little.

A second study was designed to find possible comovement due to neither market nor industry effects. One hundred stocks were selected to cover many different industries in the hope of thwarting any attempt by the computer to group along industry lines. Monthly price changes from 1961 through 1969 were analyzed using procedures similar to those of the previous study (i.e., *cluster analysis*).

---

[11] Securities and Exchange Commission, "Directory of Companies Filing Annual Reports with the Securities and Exchange Commission."

[12] Standard and Poor's Corporation, "Trade and Security Statistics."

[13] Published by Arnold Bernhard and Co., Inc., New York.

FIGURE 13-8
Grouping Stocks by Nonmarket Risk: Industry Effects

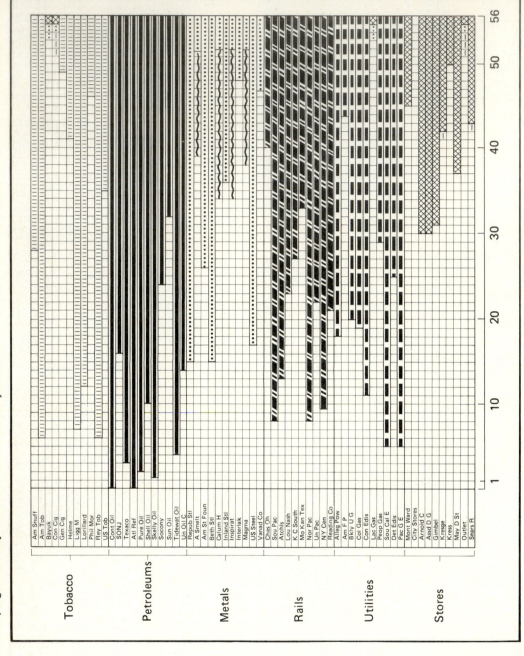

SOURCE: Benjamin F. King, "Market and Industry Factors in Stock Price Behavior," *The Journal of Business*, 39, no. 1 (January 1966), 139–40. © by the University of Chicago. All Rights Reserved.

In this case the computer was instructed to stop grouping stocks together when four major clusters remained. With relatively few exceptions, stocks in the first cluster were those considered by most analysts to be *growth stocks*: "companies expected to show an above average rate of secular expansion."[14] The second cluster contained mostly *cyclical stocks*: "those of companies that have an above average exposure to the vagaries of the economic environment."[15] The third group included predominantly *stable stocks*: "those of companies whose earning power is less affected than the average firm by the economic cycle."[16] The final group showed that at least one industry had sufficient homogeneity to stand out despite the attempt to ignore industry effects: during the period studied, the eight oil companies' prices moved together in a manner sufficiently unique to cause the computer to group them in a completely separate cluster.

How much variation in prices could be attributed to these factors? Table 13-6 shows the average values for the stocks in each of the four clusters. Also shown is the size of the market effect (roughly 30%). The results, combined with those of the earlier study, suggest that sector comovement can be as important as industry comovement.

Table 13-7 provides a dramatic indication of the possible results from concentration in market sectors. The relative proportions in the four sectors are shown for the portfolio represented by Standard and Poor's 500-stock index and for two mutual funds. The two funds had similar market exposures, as indicated by their estimated beta values. During the nineteen-month period from December 31, 1972, through July 31, 1974, the "market" fell 29%, suggesting that one might have

TABLE 13-6
Influence of Market and Sector Factors on Security Returns

AVERAGE PERCENT OF VARIATION IN MONTHLY RETURN FROM 1961 THROUGH 1969 DUE TO:		
Sector	The Market Factor	The Sector Factor
Growth stocks	31	15
Stable stocks	29	12
Cyclical stocks	33	9
Oil stocks	31	31

SOURCE: James L. Farrell, Jr., "Analyzing Covariation of Returns to Determine Homogeneous Stock Groupings," *The Journal of Business 47*, no. 2 (April 1974), 186-207. © 1974 by the University of Chicago. All Rights Reserved.

---

[14] James L. Farrell, Jr., "Homogeneous Stock Groupings: Implications for Portfolio Management," *Financial Analysts Journal*, 31, no. 3 (May/June 1975), 50.

[15] *Ibid.*

[16] *Ibid.*

TABLE 13-7
Sector Concentration and Portfolio Return

	PERCENT INVESTED		
Sector	Standard and Poor's 500-Stock Index	Affiliated Fund	T. Rowe Price Fund
Growth	39.8	10.5	80.2
Cyclical	24.0	57.5	8.7
Stable	20.0	18.0	4.1
Oil	16.2	14.0	7.0
Estimated beta	1.00	1.09	1.11
Performance	−29%	−16%	−42%

SOURCE: James L. Farrell, Jr., "Homogeneous Stock Groupings: Implications for Portfolio Management," *Financial Analysts Journal*, 31, no. 3 (May/June 1975), 58.

expected the two funds to fall by roughly 32% (since 1.1 × 29% = 31.9%).

In fact, one fund's shares fell much less than the market, and the other's shares fell much more. The portfolio composition figures show why. This was a period when growth stocks did especially poorly. The first fund was well positioned, concentrating more money in cyclical stocks and less in growth stocks than did the market as a whole. The second was poorly positioned, with a heavy concentration in growth stocks, to its investors' detriment. The results could be reversed in a period in which growth stocks do especially well. The point is not that one fund or investment strategy is better than another—rather, that neither fund was in fact as well diversified, as a simple check of the number of stocks might suggest.

Group Factors

Once homogeneous groups have been identified via cluster analysis or some other method, they may be incorporated into a factor model. The simplest procedure is to assign each security entirely to the group with which it "clusters." The corresponding factor model could include a "market sensitivity" attribute (based, e.g., on historic beta) and one zero-one attribute for each of the homogeneous groups. The factors from the cross-section analyses would then represent "the market" and the nonmarket returns of each of the homogeneous groups.

An alternative procedure includes an intermediate step. The non-market returns of each security over time are compared with those of the homogeneous groups. For each security a time-series regression is performed, and the sensitivities of the security to each of the groups are estimated. These are used as the corresponding attributes in the final phase, instead of zero-one variables.

TABLE 13-8
Nonmarket Factors in the Boston Company
Model

Growth
Utility
Oil and related
Basic industries
Consumer cyclical

SOURCE: Robert D. Arnott, "Cluster Analysis and Stock Price Comovement," *Financial Analysts Journal*, November/December 1980, pp. 56-62.

In a model based on this approach using data from 1968 through 1978 for over 500 stocks, the Boston Company obtained five nonmarket factors, characterized as shown in Table 13-8.

Composite Attributes

Many models use values such as historic betas, yields, and measures of size as attributes. Each can be considered a *simple attribute*, since it is related to either a single aspect of the security or a ratio of two such aspects.

Some models go farther, combining several aspects of a security into one *composite attribute*, several other aspects into a second composite attribute, and so on. Choices of aspects and formulas for combining them are usually based on econometric analyses of historic data. Table 13-9 shows the fundamental attributes used to compute each of six composite attributes in one widely used model.

Scenario Approaches

A more fundamental approach is employed by Salomon Brothers—a major institutional brokerage firm:

> The idea . . . is simple. We build a simple model of corporate profits, specified in terms of a few revenue variables and a few cost variables. One of these simple models is constructed for each company in our data base (about 1500 companies). These are linked to a macro model of the economy. Then the macro model is estimated in several scenarios, a "base case" and a number of alternatives. Each of the alternatives is constructed by altering a single one of the major governing variables that determine the character of the base case. For each scenario, profit models are built for each of about 400 lines of business, a set that includes all the major businesses pursued by the companies in our data base.
>
> Finally, the growth rate of profits of each company is modeled in each of the cases, by putting together the appropriate lines of business in

TABLE 13-9
Attributes in the BARRA E1 Factor Model

1. Index of market variability

   Historical beta estimate
   Historical sigma estimate
   Share turnover, quarterly
   Share turnover, 12 months
   Share turnover, five years
   Trading volume/variance
   Common stock price (ln)
   Historical alpha estimate
   Cumulative range, one year

2. Index of earnings variability

   Variance of earnings
   Extraordinary items
   Variance of cash flow
   Earnings covariability
   Earnings/price covariability

3. Index of low valuation and unsuccess

   Growth in earnings/share
   Recent earnings change
   Relative strength
   Indicator of small earnings/price ratio
   Book/price ratio
   Tax/earnings, five years
   Dividend cuts, five years
   Return on equity, five years

4. Index of immaturity and smallness

   Total assets (log)
   Market capitalization (log)

   Market capitalization
   Net plant/gross plant
   Net plant/common equity
   Inflation adjusted plant/equity
   Trading recency
   Indicator of earnings history

5. Index of growth orientation

   Payout, last five years
   Current yield
   Yield, last five years
   Indicator of zero yield
   Growth in total assets
   Capital structure change
   Earnings/price ratio
   Earnings/price, normalized
   Typical earnings/price ratio, five years

6. Index of financial risk

   Leverage at book
   Leverage at market
   Debt/assets
   Uncovered fixed charges
   Cash flow/current liabilities
   Liquid assets/current liabilities
   Potential dilution
   Price-deflated earnings adjustment
   Tax-adjusted monetary debt

SOURCE: Andrew Rudd and Henry K. Clasing, Jr., *Modern Portfolio Theory: The Principles of Investment Management* (Homewood, Ill.: Dow Jones-Irwin 1982), p. 114.

the appropriate proportions. From the data thus obtained, we can estimate the sensitivity of the growth rate of a company's expected profits to each of the variables that was used to determine an alternative scenario. These sensitivities are the essential ingredients in the Fundamental Factor Model.[17]

Table 13-10 shows the factors used in the model. For each security, the procedure provides five attributes, representing the sensitivities of the corporation's profits over the next five years to changes in the corresponding variables.

---

[17] Source: Tony Estep, Nick Hanson, Michelle Clayman, Cal Johnson, and Jonathan Singer, "The Fundamental Factor Model of Risk and Return in Common Stocks," Salomon Brothers, July 1981.

TABLE 13-10
Factors in the Salomon Brothers Model

Inflation
Real economic growth
Oil prices
Defense spending
Real interest rates

SOURCE: Tony Estep, Nick Hanson, and Cal Johnson, "Sources of Value and Risk in Common Stocks," *Journal of Portfolio Management*. Summer 1983, p. 10

Figure 13-9 shows the relative performance of five "factor play portfolios" over seventeen months. Each was constructed to be sensitive to one of the five factors and relatively insensitive to the other four. Changes in the values of such portfolios can be interpreted as representing changes in *expectations* concerning the associated fundamental economic factors.

Sensitivities to Macroeconomic Variables

The Salomon Brothers approach uses forward-looking projections of a relatively detailed type to estimate the sensitivities of corporate profits to changes in fundamental economic variables. A simpler approach, based on the assumption that history can provide adequate guidance concerning the future, compares changes in security values with estimates of changes in expectations concerning macroeconomic variables.

In such an analysis, it is important that only changes in *expectations* of such variables be used, since security prices change significantly only in response to *unanticipated* changes in prospects for future profits. Unfortunately, it is often difficult to estimate changes in expectations about future values of key economic variables.

In a study using this approach,[18] four variables were found to be useful: (1) the growth rate in U.S. industrial production, (2) unanticipated changes in risk premia, measured by the difference between the return on a portfolio of "under Baa bonds" and that of a portfolio of Aaa bonds, (3) twists in the yield curve, measured by the difference between the return on a portfolio of long-term government bonds and that of Treasury bills, and (4) unanticipated inflation, measured by the difference between actual inflation and a prediction derived from Treasury bill rates.

Once values for such unanticipated changes in expectations con-

---

[18] Nai-fu Chen, Richard Roll, and Stephen A. Ross, "Economic Forces and the Stock Market: Testing the APT and Alternative Asset Pricing Theories," unpublished (December 1983).

cerning macrovariables have been obtained, the desired sensitivities of security returns can be estimated. For each security a time-series regression is performed, with each time period providing one observation. In the regression, the security's return is the dependent variable, and the changes in expectations of the macrovariables are the independent variables. The resulting coefficients are estimates of the sensitivi-

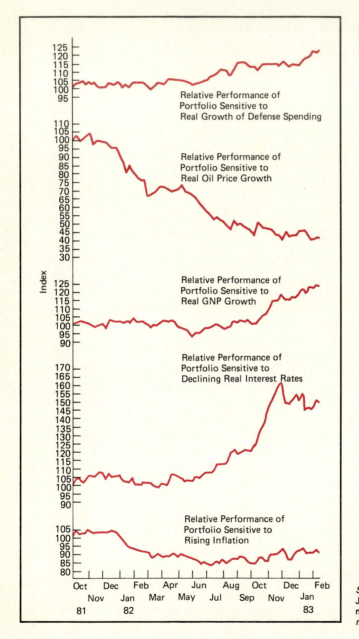

SOURCE: Tony Estep, Nick Hanson, and Cal Johnson, "Sources of Value and Risk in Common Stocks," *Journal of Portfolio Management*, Summer 1983, p. 11.

FIGURE 13-9
Relative Performance of Economic Factor Portfolios

ties of the security to each of the economic factors. These are then used as the security's attributes when estimating the factor model.

Factor Analysis

Cluster analysis can be used to estimate zero-one security attributes from historic returns. These attributes can then be used in cross-section analyses to derive factor values. The resulting factors may be recognizable as, for example, changes in fundamental economic factors, or they may appear to be simply statistical artifacts. With such a mechanical approach, it may be difficult or impossible to incorporate additional (fundamental) information.

This type of procedure assumes that historic returns contain all the information needed to produce useful estimates of future risks and correlations.

Factor analysis, a more complex procedure,[19] is similar in spirit. Given returns for many securities over many time periods, a computer is used to (1) determine a reasonable number of attributes, (2) compute the corresponding attributes for each security, and (3) derive the corresponding factors for each time period. An early study[20] employing factor analysis suggested that five factors might suffice to represent the "pervasive" underlying determinants of correlation among security returns. Other studies have found more "significant" factors.

There is more information about securities than that reflected in past returns alone, and it is undoubtedly desirable to take it into account when estimating factor models. Factor analysis can provide useful guidance concerning the appropriate number of factors, useful variables, and so on but should not be used as a "black box" into which returns are placed and out of which come purely mechanical estimates of future prospects, to be used "as is."

TESTING EQUILIBRIUM THEORIES

Equilibrium theories such as the Arbitrage Pricing Theory and Capital Asset Pricing Models make assertions about relationships between security *expected* returns and the *future* values of various security attributes. *Actual* values from the *past* may or may not serve as useful surrogates. *If* expected returns, beta values, sensitivities to factors, and so on remain the same from month to month over an extended period *and* if actual returns over the period conform to these predic-

---

[19] The term *factor analysis* denotes a general approach; there are, in fact, many alternative statistical procedures for performing such an analysis.

[20] Richard Roll and Stephen A. Ross, "An Empirical Investigation of the Arbitrage Pricing Theory," *Journal of Finance*, (December 1980), pp. 1073-1103.

tions, then historic data may prove useful for testing equilibrium theories. Otherwise the effort may be wasted.

Any test of an equilibrium theory based on historic data is a *joint* test of (1) assumptions concerning stability of predictions, conformance of realized results with predicted results, the appropriate factor model of security returns, and so on and (2) a particular theory of equilibrium. If such a test fails, it may indicate that the equilibrium theory is in error. Alternatively, one or more of the other assumptions may be inappropriate. As a practical matter, such procedures cannot *reject* an equilibrium theory. They can, however, provide suggestive evidence.

Tests of the Arbitrage Pricing Theory

Since the Arbitrage Pricing Theory *assumes* a factor model of security returns, any test of its predictions must incorporate such a factor model and be, in effect, a joint test of the equilibrium theory and the appropriateness of the selected factor model. Moreover, the APT makes relatively weak predictions. It does imply that when all pervasive factors are taken into account, the remaining portion of return on a typical security should be expected to equal the riskless interest rate. Testing this implication is possible in principle, but difficult in practice. For example, when a model such as that shown in equation (13-5) is fitted to data for stock returns, the "zero factor" will include elements of a "stock factor." Analyses using both bonds and stocks can include corresponding factors explicitly, reducing the possibility that the "zero factor" does, in fact, include elements of pervasive sources of risk. However, it may never be possible to find a set of securities so diverse that consistency of the zero factor with riskless interest rates can be used as a test of the Arbitrage Pricing Theory.

A more promising test concerns the prediction that security expected returns will be related only to sensitivities to "pervasive factors." In particular, there should be no relationship between expected returns and securities' nonfactor risks. Since the total risk of a security includes nonfactor risk as well as risk related to factors, its inclusion in an analysis of expected returns should not help explain differences in expected returns.

In a study using returns from 1962 through 1972, Roll and Ross[21] computed average returns, sensitivities to each of five factors (obtained via factor analysis), and the total standard deviation of returns for 1,260 securities. Given the computational demands of the factor-analysis method utilized, much of the analysis had to be performed on groups of 30 stocks rather than on the full set of securities. For each of the resulting 42 groups, a regression analysis was performed with average

---

[21] *Ibid.*

return as the dependent variable and sensitivities to the five factors and total standard deviation as independent variables. In the majority of groups there was a statistically significant relationship between average return and sensitivity to at least one factor. On the other hand, in the majority of groups there was no statistically significant relationship between average return and total standard deviation. The results, while not definitive, are broadly consistent with the theory.

Tests of Capital Asset Pricing Models

Both the original and extended versions of the Capital Asset Pricing Model suggest that, other things equal, securities with large future beta values should have large expected returns. This does not mean that they will necessarily have large actual returns. If the market goes up substantially, one expects actual returns to be higher for high-beta stocks; on the other hand, if the market goes down, one expects high-beta stocks to go down the most. But even these are expectations. A stock's future beta is based on a composite of possible sources of market moves. Ex post, only some of those sources will have contributed in the expected direction to the market move, and some factors not even considered in advance may also have played a role. For all these reasons, actual returns over even reasonably long periods may bear little if any relationship to expectations and hence to predicted beta values.

An additional problem concerns the measurement of beta. The relevant figure measures a security's sensitivity to a widely diversified market portfolio including all types of stocks, bonds, real estate, and so on. Many empirical studies have instead used a broad-based index of widely traded stocks, since adequate data on other securities have been difficult or impossible to obtain. Clearly, a security's beta relative to, say, the New York Stock Exchange "market portfolio" could differ significantly from that measured relative to the full United States market portfolio, let alone an international market portfolio.

Despite all these problems it is instructive to see how well common stocks with different historic beta values have done over time.

Risk-Return Groups. The development of a computerized file of monthly returns for all stocks listed on the New York Stock Exchange from 1926 to the present[22] has facilitated extensive investigation of risk and return for such securities. Using these data, the relationship between risk and return can be examined by measuring each security's beta relative an index of the returns on all the stocks over some historic period (e.g., five years), then forming portfolios designed to include

---

[22] Performed at the Center for Research in Security Prices at the University of Chicago, and sponsored by Merrill Lynch, Pierce, Fenner and Smith, Inc.

many stocks but also to differ as much as possible in this respect. For example, on January 1, 1931, equal dollar amounts of the top 10% of all securities listed by historic beta might be placed in one portfolio, equal dollar amounts of the top 20% in another portfolio, and so on. On January 1, 1932, the process might be repeated, rebalancing each portfolio to again contain equal dollar proportions of the stocks in the appropriate part of the then-current "beta-book."

This approach defines several *risk-return groups* of stocks with similar historic betas and thus, hopefully, similar future betas and expected returns.

Table 13-11 shows the stocks included in ten groups used in one such study, and Figure 13-10 shows some of the results. In Figure 13-10(a), each bar indicates the arithmetic average annual return from 1931 through 1967 for a risk-return group. Figure 13-10(b) shows the ex post beta values, and Figure 13-10(c) provides a cross-plot of the average returns and ex post beta values for all ten groups along with the best-fit regression line. Despite the potential problems with such analyses, the results are substantially consistent with the theoretical relationship between expected returns and beta values.

Figure 13-11 shows the results from a study concerned with longer holding periods. In this case the eight five-year nonoverlapping periods from mid-1928 through mid-1968 were analyzed and the percentage change in value determined for an account that remained fully invested during each period (all dividends received during the five years were

TABLE 13-11
Composition of Risk-Return Groups

Risk-Return Group	Stocks from Beta Book Included
10 (highest)	top 10%
9	top 30%
8	top 50%
7	top 70%
6	top 90%
5	bottom 90%
4	bottom 70%
3	bottom 50%
2	bottom 30%
1 (lowest)	bottom 10%

SOURCE: Data used for study reported in William F. Sharpe and Guy M. Cooper, "Risk-Return Classes of New York Stock Exchange Common Stocks, 1931-1967," *Financial Analysts Journal*, 28, no. 2 (March/April 1972), 46-54.

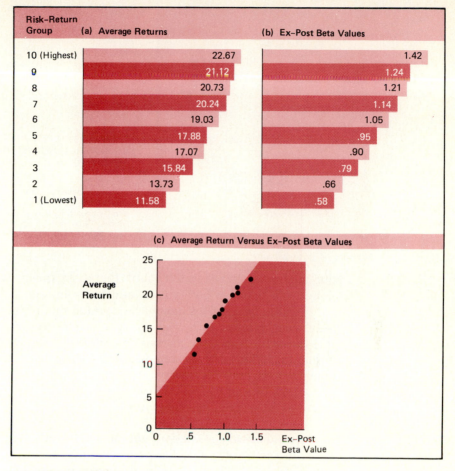

FIGURE 13-10(a)(b)(c)
Performance of Ten Risk-Return Groups for One-Year Holding Periods, 1931-1967

reinvested).[23] The results are roughly consistent with a positive relationship between beta values and medium-term returns.

What about return over very long holding periods? Figure 13-10(d) shows the performances of the risk-return groups used in the first study over the 37-year period from 1931 through 1967. Each bar indicates the geometric mean return for one of the ten groups. This equals the constant annual return that would have given the same terminal value as the actual strategy, assuming a fully invested position throughout the period, with no withdrawals. The picture is less clear than those

---

[23] Portfolios were rebalanced monthly, and each portfolio contained the 10% of the stocks with historic betas in the same decile.

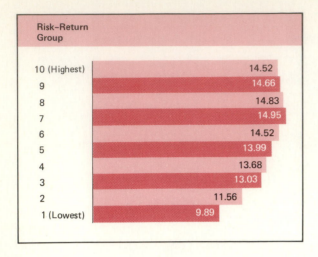

Risk–Return Group	
10 (Highest)	14.52
9	14.66
8	14.83
7	14.95
6	14.52
5	13.99
4	13.68
3	13.03
2	11.56
1 (Lowest)	9.89

FIGURE 13-10(d)
Equivalent Constant Annual Returns, 1931-1967

SOURCE: Based on data used in the study reported in William F. Sharpe and Guy M. Cooper, "Risk-Return Classes of New York Stock Exchange Common Stocks, 1931-1967," *Financial Analysts Journal*, 28, no. 2 (March/April 1972), 46-54.

obtained earlier, but overall it shows that there appears to be a positive relationship between beta values and long-run returns.

Historic beta values cannot be counted on to predict returns precisely, even relative to market moves, over every period. Figures 13-12(a) through (d) plot the average monthly returns over four different 105-month periods for ten risk-return classes based on historic beta values. In each case the market return (indicated by a square) exceeded the riskless rate of interest. Three of the lines of best fit are upward-sloping as expected, but one is not.

Historic Beta Factors. Many factor models include a security's historic beta value as an attribute. The corresponding *historic beta factor* provides a measure of the difference in returns between high-historic-beta

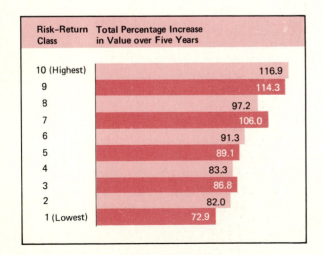

Risk–Return Class	Total Percentage Increase in Value over Five Years
10 (Highest)	116.9
9	114.3
8	97.2
7	106.0
6	91.3
5	89.1
4	83.3
3	86.8
2	82.0
1 (Lowest)	72.9

FIGURE 13-11
Average Performance of Ten Risk-Return Classes over Eight Five-Year Holding Periods, 1928-1968

SOURCE: Marshall E. Blume and Irwin Friend, "Risk, Investment Strategy, and the Long-run Rates of Return," *Review of Economics and Statistics*, LVI, no. 3 (August 1974), 259-69.

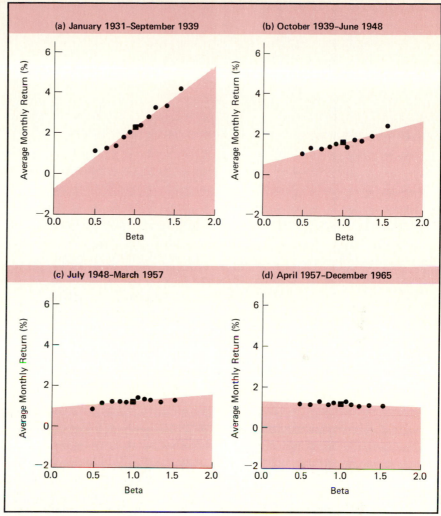

SOURCE: Fischer Black, Michael C. Jensen, and Myron Scholes, "The Capital Asset Pricing Model: Some Empirical Tests," in Michael C. Jensen (ed.), *Studies in the Theory of Capital Markets* (New York: Praeger Publishers, Inc. 1972).

FIGURE 13-12
Performance of Ten Risk-Return Classes, Four 105-Month Periods, 1931-1965

and low-historic-beta stocks, other attributes equal. If historic betas are useful for predicting future betas, the beta factor should be *positive* in most periods when the return on stocks exceeds the riskless rate of interest and *negative* in most periods when the return on stocks is less than the riskless rate.

Figure 13-13 shows that this has in fact been the case. In months in which the excess return on the New York Stock Exchange (i.e., the

Common Stocks

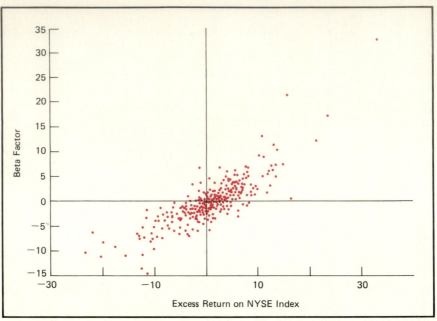

SOURCE: Blake Grossman and William F. Sharpe, "Factors in Security Returns," paper presented at the Center for the Study of Banking and Financial Markets, University of Washington, March 1984.

FIGURE 13-13
Beta Factor Values and NYSE Returns, 1928-1982

return minus the Treasury Bill rate) was positive, the beta factor was generally positive—i.e., stocks with high historic betas tended to outperform those with low historic betas. In months in which the excess return on stocks was negative, the beta factor was generally negative—i.e., stocks with high historic betas tended to underperform those with low historic betas. The relationship is highly significant statistically,[24] indicating that historic beta can provide useful predictions of future beta. By combining it with other information from a factor model (as in Table 13-5), even better estimates can be obtained.

While most of the points in Figure 13-13 are in the upper-right and lower-left quadrants, some are not. In such cases the actual relationship between return and beta differed from that one might expect, given the performance of the market.

Tests of the Zero-Beta CAPM.   In a detailed test of the original and Zero-beta Capital Asset Pricing Models, Fama and MacBeth[25] used portfolio groups to examine the relationship between average returns

---

[24] The *t*-statistic was 41.7.

[25] Eugene F. Fama and James D. MacBeth, "Risk, Return and Equilibrium: Empirical Tests," *Journal of Political Economy*, (May/June 1983), pp. 607-36.

and historic beta values. They also tested (and rejected) the possibilities that average returns were related in a nonlinear manner to beta values and that average returns were related to nonmarket risks.

Figure 13-14 contrasts the actual relationship for the period from 1938 through mid-1968 with that consistent with the original Capital Asset Pricing Model. The vertical intercept, which corresponds to the zero-beta return, is .61% per month (equivalent to approximately 7.32% per year), while the average Treasury bill return, which corresponds to the riskless rate of interest, was only .13% per month (equivalent to approximately 1.56% per year). The difference was substantial and statistically significant. Assuming that beta values measured relative to a stock index are adequate surrogates for "true" betas measured relative to the overall market portfolio, such results provide more support for the zero-beta version of the CAPM than for the original version.

Similar tests have been performed using returns from securities in other countries, with mixed but not dissimilar results.[26]

FIGURE 13-14
Average Return and Beta

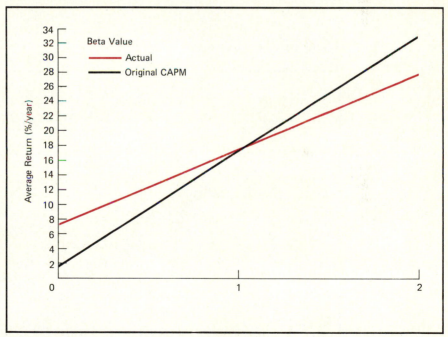

[26] For a comprehensive summary of studies using European data, see Gabriel Hawawini, "European Equity Markets: A Review of the Evidence on Price Behavior and Efficiency," in *European Equity Markets: Risk, Return and Efficiency* (Garland Publishing, Company, 1984).

THE SMALL-STOCK EFFECT

In some months stocks with large market values outstanding tend to do better than those with small values outstanding. In other months the situation is reversed. Since large stocks tend to have lower beta values than small stocks, they might be expected to do somewhat worse on average. However, the evidence suggests that large stocks underperform small stocks by substantial amounts much of the time. Small stocks seem to do better "than they should."

Figure 13-15 shows the pattern of this relationship over time. The vertical axis plots the *cumulative value* of the size factor from a multifactor model. Periods when the curve goes up are those in which large stocks outperformed small stocks with similar attributes. Periods when the curve goes down are those in which large stocks underperformed small stocks with similar attributes. Clearly, the latter were more frequent.

The magnitudes involved are substantial. The average size factor was −.345% per month (equivalent to approximately −4.14% per year). In principle, by trading the securities in a portfolio for others ten times

FIGURE 13-15
The Size Factor, 1928-1982

SOURCE: Blake Grossman and William F. Sharpe, "Factors in Security Returns," paper presented at the Center for the Study of Banking and Financial Markets, University of Washington, March 1984.

Common Stocks

as large but with otherwise similar attributes (here, historic beta, yield, and sector composition), one might have reduced portfolio return by 4.14% per year on average. Adjusting for the accompanying decrease in future beta, the difference would still have been large (3.38% per year) and highly significant.[27]

Factor returns are useful for estimating expected returns but may be impossible to realize in practice, since costless short selling is not feasible, and there may not be a wide enough range of securities to obtain a "pure factor play" with little residual risk. To determine the possibility of actual returns, a reasonably realistic *investment strategy* should be analyzed.

A simple strategy for exploiting the small-stock effect has been studied by Ibbotson and Sinquefield.[28] All stocks on the New York Stock Exchange were ranked by market value outstanding on December 31, 1925. A portfolio was then formed using the stocks in the bottom quintile (the smallest 20%). Within the portfolio, stocks were purchased in accordance with market values outstanding (i.e., the portfolio was value-weighted). This portfolio was "held" for five years. On December 31, 1930, all the stocks on the NYSE were again ranked on size and a new value-weighted portfolio formed from the smallest quintile. This portfolio was "held" for the next five years. And so on.

Returns from this strategy have been calculated for every month from 1926 through 1981. In 1981 Dimensional Fund Advisors established a "Small Company Fund," which follows a similar approach. For assessing the strategy from 1982 onward, actual returns on this fund can be used, providing even more realistic values.

Table 13-12 contrasts the performance of the "small-stock portfolio" with that of Standard and Poor's 500-stock index from 1926 through 1983. Since the latter includes primarily stocks with large market capitalizations, this can be viewed as a comparison of small stocks with large ones.

On average, the small-stock portfolio outperformed the SP500 by 0.48% per month, or approximately 5.79% per year. Although the small-stock portfolio outperformed the SP500 only 51.7% of the time, the average difference was positive, and significantly so.[29]

This does not imply that a "pure" small-stock strategy dominates investment in the SP500. The small-stock portfolio's returns varied much more: its standard deviation was 32.35%, while that of the SP500 was 20.62%. But one need not choose small *or* large stocks. The goal is to

---

[27] The *t*-statistic was −10.2.

[28] Roger G. Ibbotson and Rex A. Sinquefield, *Stocks, Bonds, Bills and Inflation: The Past and the Future* (Financial Analysts' Research Foundation, 1982).

[29] The *t*-statistic was 2.40.

TABLE 13-12
Small- and Large-Stock Performance, 1926-1983

	Small Stocks	SP500	Small Stocks − SP500
Average (%/year)	17.05%	11.26%	5.79%
Standard deviation (%/year)	32.35%	20.62%	18.34%
Number of months with positive values	406	408	360
Percent of months with positive values	58.3%	58.6%	51.7%

SOURCE: Based on data in Roger G. Ibbotson, *Stocks, Bonds, Bills and Inflation 1984 Yearbook* (Chicago: R. G. Ibbotson Associates, Inc., 1984).

select an appropriate mix of small *and* large stocks. To make the choice, estimates of expected returns, risks, and correlations are needed (as always). Both Figure 13-15 and Table 13-12 suggest that small stocks may offer superior expected returns relative to their risks and correlations—an aspect that one may wish to incorporate when making such estimates for the future.

These results are consistent with an extended Capital Asset Pricing Model in which the average investor prizes liquidity enough to sacrifice some expected return to obtain the low transactions costs associated with large stocks (i.e., those with large outstanding market values).

The phenomenon is not limited to the United States. Similar results have been found in other countries.[30]

SEASONALITY IN STOCK RETURNS

Individuals' desires for liquidity change from day to day and from month to month. Moreover, due to weekends, summer vacations, Christmas holidays, and so on the "average individual's" desires may change in a predictable manner. There may thus be *seasonality* in stock returns.

One might presume that such patterns would be relatively unimportant. However, the evidence suggests that at least two are significant: the "January effect" and the "weekend effect."

---

[30] See, for example, Takeo Nakamura and Noboru Terada, "The Size Effect and Seasonality in Japanese Stock Returns," paper presented at the Institute for Quantitative Research in Finance, May 7, 1984.

The January Effect

Are stock returns typically higher in some months than in others? In the United States, the answer appears to differ for small and large stocks.

Figure 13-16(a) shows the average return of Standard and Poor's 500-stock index in each of the 57 Januaries from 1926 through 1983, the average return in each of the 57 Februaries from 1926 through 1983, and so on. No obvious pattern is apparent. This is confirmed by an analysis of the variations in returns from year to year.[31]

Figure 13-16(b) provides comparable data for the small-stock portfolio analyzed earlier. In this case there is an obvious pattern: small stocks had significantly higher returns in January than in other months.[32]

Figure 13-16(c) summarizes the *difference* between the returns on small and large stocks by month. In January, the small-stock portfolio outperformed the SP500 by 5.86% on average. As indicated in Table 13-12, the comparable figure for the *entire year* was 5.79%. This suggests that the small-stock effect occurs entirely in January!

Figure 13-17 provides confirmation. It shows the average magnitude of the size factor shown in Figure 13-15 for each month. The large negative value in January represents underperformance by large stocks—i.e., superior performance by small stocks.[33]

Daily returns indicate that the "small-stock effect" is large and statistically significant on the last trading day of December and the first four days of January, then declines in importance during the rest of the month.[34]

Why do small stocks outperform large stocks at the turn of the year? Could it reflect a desire for liquidity prior to Christmas and the investment of "mad money" in small stocks afterward? Or might it have something to do with the end of the tax year?

One possible explanation concerns the realization of capital losses for tax purposes. A group of "small stocks" will include a disproportionate number with prices that have fallen over the prior twelve months. At the end of the tax year, many investors may wish to sell such stocks to realize losses. This could exert "selling pressure," temporarily depressing prices. When this pressure is removed (so the story goes), prices will rise to the appropriate levels, bringing corresponding large returns.

---

[31] Only the September returns were significantly different from those of the other eleven months (the *t*-statistic was −2.42; all other months had *t*-statistics with absolute values of less than 2.0). The fact that the *t*-statistic for one month was slightly greater than 2.0 is not surprising, given the fact that twelve different months were analyzed.

[32] The *t*-statistic was 4.82; the absolute values of *t*-statistics for all other months were below 2.0.

[33] The *t*-statistic for the difference between the January size factor and that of the other eleven months was −8.87.

[34] Richard Roll, "Vas ist Das?," *Journal of Portfolio Management*, Winter 1983.

FIGURE 13-16
Average Returns by Month, 1926-1983

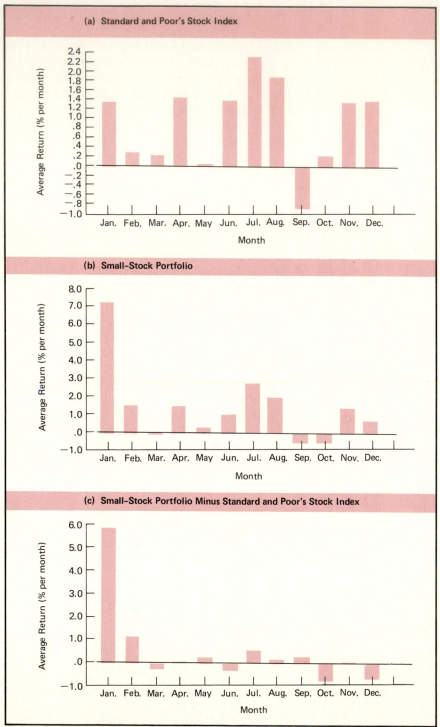

SOURCE: Based on data in Roger G. Ibbotson, *Stocks, Bonds, Bills and Inflation 1984 Yearbook* (Chicago: R. G. Ibbotson Associates, Inc., 1984).

406

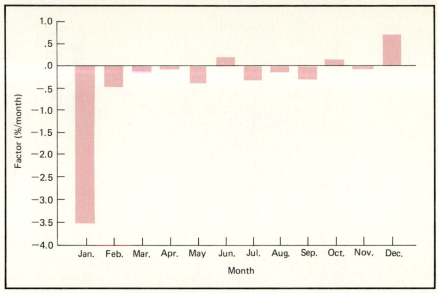

SOURCE: Blake Grossman and William F. Sharpe, "Factors in Security Returns," paper presented at the Center for the Study of Banking and Financial Markets, University of Washington, March 1984.

FIGURE 13-17
Size Factor by Month, 1928-1982

There is evidence that the story has some merit: stocks with low returns during the year tend to have higher returns at the "turn of the year."[35] However, this is at best only a partial explanation.

The January effect is often termed an *anomaly*, since it is difficult to reconcile it with standard theories of equilibrium in efficient markets. If there is tax-loss selling pressure, clever investors should step in to exploit it, thereby minimizing the impact. If some investors wish more liquidity, others should be prepared to provide it at a relatively low price in resulting returns.

More complex equilibrium theories such as expanded Capital Asset Pricing Models and the Arbitrage Pricing Theory can accommodate the January effect. But this is not the important point. The ultimate question concerns the future. Should one expect returns to behave in similar ways and in similar magnitudes in *future* Januaries?

The Weekend Effect

For most people the weekend differs from weekdays in many ways. Mondays differ from Fridays in many places. Why not in the stock market?

---

[35] *Ibid.*

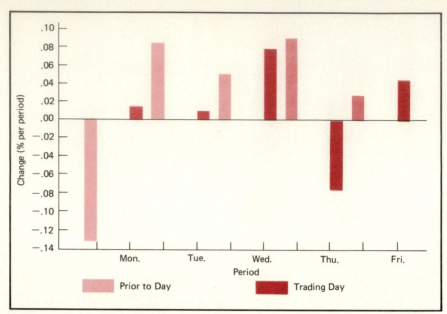

SOURCE: Richard J. Rogalski, "New Findings Regarding Day of the Week Returns over Trading and Non-trading Periods," The Amos Tuck School of Business Administration, Dartmouth College, June 1984.

FIGURE 13-18

Changes in the Standard and Poor's 500-Stock Indexes, January 2, 1979-April 30, 1984

Figure 13-18 shows the average percentage changes in Standard and Poor's 500-stock index from January 2, 1979, through April 30, 1984, for each day of the week and for the periods prior to each day of the week during which the Exchange was closed. Only two values were negative, and only one was significantly so. On the average, the market fell over the weekend, and by an amount greater (in absolute value) than its rise on any trading day but Wednesday.

These magnitudes are too small to exploit by selling stocks at the close of the market on Friday, then buying them back at lower prices when the market opens on Monday. However, if this anomaly is expected to continue, one might at least avoid buying stocks on Friday afternoons or selling them early on Monday mornings.

Problems

1. Three dates are involved in most stock splits: (1) the date when the management proposes a split, (2) the date when the stockholders approve the split, and (3) the date when the split actually becomes effective. Figure 13-1 is concerned with only the third date. In an efficient market what would you expect to be the average behavior of nonfactor stock returns before and after each of the other two dates? If the evidence were not consistent with market efficiency, how might you exploit it?

2. What might account for the differences in the bid/ask spreads in Figure 13-2(c)? Why are bid and ask values not shown in Figure 13-2(a)?

3. Some have advocated that insider trading be allowed, even if the insider involved has information not known to those outside the firm, on the grounds that this will bring the information to the marketplace in an efficient and timely manner. Yet public policy places severe limits on this action on the grounds of equity. What considerations are involved in this issue? What form of public policy would you advocate?

4. State public utility commissions are charged with the task of setting rates for telephone, electricity, and gas companies that will provide a "reasonable return on capital." Many of the hearings involve testimony as to the implications of equilibrium models and the relevant values of security attributes for the firms involved. What issues are important for such decisions in terms of (1) models of expected returns and (2) estimation of security attributes?

5. Assume that every stock is classified so that its earnings come completely from one industry. Show that an equation such as (13-3) is equivalent to adjusting each stock's beta value back toward an "average beta" for its industry.

6. Empirical evidence shows that, other things equal, stocks with low prices per share tend to have higher beta values than those with high prices per share. Why might this be the case? Under what conditions should it definitely *not* be the case that a lower price would indicate a higher beta value?

7. Empirical evidence indicates that, other things equal, stocks with large market values of equity outstanding tend to move together while those with small amounts of equity outstanding also tend to move together, but not always in the same direction as large stocks. What sorts of changes in future prospects might have differential effects on large versus small stocks?

8. Stocks with above-average beta values tend to have below-average yields. If both yield and beta are relevant for expected return, why might an analysis in which average return is compared with beta values be likely to understate the true relationship between expected return and beta per se?

9. a. A friend tells you that he selects his portfolio by throwing 100 darts at a page of *The Wall Street Journal*, then purchasing the 100 "selected" stocks. Is it important that he obtain good estimates of the resulting portfolio's attributes? Why?

   b. Another friend likes to make "industry plays." She feels that she cannot identify superior and inferior stocks within industries but can determine situations in which the stocks in one industry are overvalued while those in another are undervalued. Accordingly, she concentrates her holdings by industry but holds many stocks from each of the selected industries. What types of attributes are particularly important to her?

c. A third friend is a "stock picker." He likes to identify a few "undervalued" stocks and "plunge." What sorts of attributes are especially relevant for him?

10. What time of the year would you recommend for bringing stocks of young firms to market via initial public offerings? Why?

APPENDIX 13-A

Empirical and Fundamental Factors

As indicated in the text, factors determined empirically may differ from fundamental factors. This will be the case even if the relevant attributes are selected and measured without error.

Assume that the underlying factor model is:

$$\tilde{R}_i = a_i + b_{i1}\tilde{F}_1 + \cdots + b_{iM}\tilde{F}_M + e_i$$

From the assumption that the final term has an expected value of zero:

$$E_i = a_i + b_{i1}\bar{F}_1 + \cdots + b_{iM}\bar{F}_M$$

where:

$$E_i = \text{the expected return on security } i$$
$$\bar{F}_1, \ldots, \bar{F}_M = \text{the expected values of factors } 1, \ldots, M$$

The Arbitrage Pricing Theory implies that:

$$E_i = R_f + b_{i1}\lambda_1 + \cdots + b_{iM}\lambda_M$$

where:

$$R_f = \text{the riskless rate of interest}$$
$$\lambda_1, \ldots, \lambda_M = \text{the expected return premia for factors } 1, \ldots, M$$

Since both equations indicate the expected return on the security, the two right-hand sides must equal. This imples that:

$$a_i = R_f + b_{i1}(\lambda_1 - \bar{F}_1) + \cdots + b_{iM}(\lambda_M - \bar{F}_M)$$

Common Stocks

Substituting this value into the equation of the underlying factor model gives:

$$\tilde{R}_i = R_f + b_{i1}(\lambda_1 + \tilde{F}_1 - \overline{F}_1) + \cdots + b_{iM}(\lambda_m + \tilde{F}_m - \overline{F}_M) + \tilde{e}_i$$

When security returns are regressed on the relevant attributes, the "empirical factors" obtained will equal the parenthesized expressions. Using the notation from the chapter:

$$\tilde{f}_1 = \lambda_1 + (\tilde{F}_1 - \overline{F}_1)$$
$$\vdots$$
$$\tilde{f}_M = \lambda_M + (\tilde{F}_M - \overline{F}_M)$$

where:

$$\tilde{f}_1, \ldots, \tilde{f}_M = \text{empirical factors } 1, \ldots, M$$

Thus each empirical factor will equal the expected return premium for the corresponding fundamental factor plus the deviation of the fundamental factor from its expected value.

If all relevant attributes are included, the intercept in the cross-section regression should equal the riskless rate of interest. And if historic results are adequate proxies for unchanging expectations, the average values of the empirical factors should equal the expected return premia. As indicated in the chapter, these are stringent requirements, unlikely to be totally fulfilled in practice.

14

The Valuation of Common Stocks

VALUATION BASED ON EXPECTED DIVIDENDS

The value of a noncallable default-free bond can be determined in a relatively straightforward manner. Each cash flow to be received by its owner can be discounted, using current discount factors and the sum of all such values computed; this is the present value of the bond.

If there is some chance that a bond will default, two changes can be made. First, *expected* cash payments can be estimated for each period. Second, these can be discounted using interest rates appropriate for the relevant risk involved.

The valuation of a common stock can proceed along similar lines. One obvious modification is required: while bonds mature, stocks typically do not and can, in principle, provide cash flows forever. Taking this into account, we can write the basic formula for the valuation of a common stock as:

$$v_0 = \frac{\bar{d}}{1 + r_1} + \frac{\bar{d}}{(1 + r_1)(1 + r_2)}$$

$$+ \frac{\bar{d}}{(1 + r_1)(1 + r_2)(1 + r_3)} + \cdots$$

(14-1)

where

$\bar{d}_1, \bar{d}_2, \bar{d}_3, \ldots =$ the expected dividends per share (plus the value of any other distributions) in years 1, 2, 3, . . .

$r_1, r_2, r_3, \ldots =$ the appropriate discount rates for the relevant risk involved

$v_0 =$ the present value of the stock at time zero

The dots indicate that the terms continue on—i.e., that this is an *infinite series*.

It should be emphasized that only itmes of value *received* by the stockholder are relevant in the valuation process. Generally these take the form of cash dividends. Other distributions (e.g., stock dividends) can be treated by adding the expected proceeds from their sale. Alternatively, the assumption can be made that the resulting shares are held, and their dividends can be included in subsequent cash flows.

It might seem that this formula could imply an infinite value. This is mathematically, but not economically, possible. The present value of a dollar will be less, the farther in the future its receipt. Unless dividend payments grow faster than the rate of discount, the present values of more and more distant dividends will eventually become smaller and smaller, and the series will converge to a finite value.

VALUATION BASED ON HOLDING-PERIOD RETURN

Formula (14-1) is relevant for an investor who plans to hold a stock forever. But what about someone who plans to sell in a year? Clearly, the relevant value in such a case will depend on the price for which the stock can be sold at year-end. The valuation formula is thus:

$$v_0 = \frac{\bar{d}_1}{1 + r_1} + \frac{\bar{P}_1}{1 + r_1} \qquad \text{(14-2a)}$$

where $\bar{P}_1$ is the expected price of the stock at the end of year 1.

It may seem easier to estimate near-term dividends and future price than to estimate dividends over the infinite future. However, the former procedure does not really obviate the latter. To estimate future price, one must predict the valuation procedure that will be used by a purchaser and the ingredients that will go into it at the time.

The simplest approach assumes that the purchaser will offer a price based on the then-remaining expected dividends, and that the best estimate (at present) is that next year neither expected dividends nor the appropriate discount rates will have changed. The expected price is thus:

$$\bar{P}_1 = v_1 = \frac{\bar{d}_2}{1 + r_2} + \frac{\bar{d}_3}{(1 + r_2)(1 + r_3)} + \cdots \qquad \text{(14-2b)}$$

Substituting this into (14-2a) gives:

$$v_0 = \frac{\bar{d}_1}{1 + r_1} + \frac{1}{1 + r_1}\left[\frac{\bar{d}_2}{1 + r_2} + \frac{\bar{d}}{(1 + r_2)(1 + r_3)} + \cdots\right]$$

$$= \frac{\bar{d}_1}{1 + r_1} + \frac{\bar{d}_2}{(1 + r_1)(1 + r_2)} + \frac{\bar{d}_3}{(1 + r_1)(1 + r_2)(1 + r_3)} + \cdots$$

which is exactly the same as formula (14-1).

A similar process can be used to show that no matter how long the desired holding period, under these conditions the present value will be the same.

Most stocks are held by a long series of investors, each of whom is interested only in the price paid, the price received when the stock is sold, and the dividends received while it is held. But every selling price is someone else's buying price. Intermediate prices thus wash out, leaving dividends as the essential elements of value.

THE STRUCTURE OF DISCOUNT RATES

When bonds are analyzed, a term structure of interest rates is generally considered. The relative precision with which receipts can be estimated warrants attention to such details. Practice is quite different, however, when stocks are considered. The difficulty involved in projecting dividends years into the future makes attention to a detailed structure of different interest rates seem misplaced in the eyes of most analysts. Even though dividends might be considered more risky the farther in the future their date of payment, a single discount rate is typically used for all dividends of stocks with similar relevant attributes (e.g., sensitivities to pervasive factors), and no attempt is made to identify any sort of term structure.

The resulting valuation equation is thus:

$$v_0 = \frac{\bar{d}_1}{1+r} + \frac{\bar{d}_2}{(1+r)^2} + \frac{\bar{d}_3}{(1+r)^3} + \cdots \qquad \textbf{(14-3)}$$

where:

$$r = \text{the appropriate discount rate}$$

VALUATION BASED ON EARNINGS

A recurrent but somewhat pointless controversy concerns the relevance of dividends versus earnings as a source of value. Earnings are important, but only because they can provide dividends. One cannot eat earnings. But there is a sense in which they can be considered a source of value.

In the course of a year, a firm produces revenue and incurs costs. With *cash accounting* the difference would be termed "cash flow." With *accrual accounting,* used by almost all firms, both revenues and costs are likely to include estimates made by accountants of the values of noncash items. Depreciation charges, taxes, interest payments, and so on are deducted from cash flow to obtain *earnings*. Moreover, each year some amount is invested in the business. Of the total (*gross*) investment, a portion will be equal in value to the estimated depreciation of capital; the rest is *net* (new) investment.

The amount of new investment each year should be a function of investment opportunities, not of earnings, cash flow, and the like. Any investment project with an expected return in excess of that available in the market from comparable investments should be undertaken. Desirable projects may be financed via depreciation, retained earnings, and/or new capital, but this is a separate issue.

The investment decisions of a firm can and should be relatively independent of its financial decisions. The future prospects of the firm can thus be described by a series of expected total earnings (E_1, E_2, . . .) and the expected total (net) investment required to produce such earnings (I_1, I_2, . . .), all predicated on the firm's expected investment decisions.

Figure 14-1(a) shows the usual disposition of earnings. Some of the total is used to make dividend payments for the year (D_t); the remainder is *retained* by the firm and used to finance the next year's investment (I_t).

In Figure 14-1(a), total dividends are equal to earnings minus new investment ($E_t - I_t$). This need not be the case, however. In the situation shown in Figure 14-1(b) more is paid out and new capital is obtained to complete the financing of planned investment. In Figure 14-1(c) the situation is reversed. Here dividends and investment do not exhaust total earnings, and the remainder is used to reduce outstanding capital—for example, by purchasing outstanding shares of common stock.

What will be the total value of a corporation if any of the strategies illustrated in Figure 14-1 can be adopted? The simplest way to answer this is to consider an investor presently holding 1% of the total stock of the firm. If markets are efficient, the value of such a holding should be the same whether the owner intends to sell some or all of it and/

FIGURE 14-1
Earnings, Dividends, and Investment

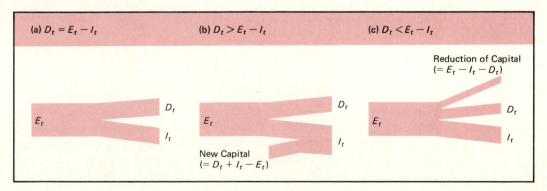

or buy additional shares in the future. Imagine then that our investor is determined to maintain ownership of 1% of the firm. When earnings are used as shown in Figure 14-1(a), no problem arises; his or her dividends will equal $.01D_t$ or $.01(E_t - I_t)$ and can be spent at will.

When the distribution is similar to that shown in Figure 14-1(b), however, the investor must put up additional capital to avoid a diminished proportional ownership of the firm. How much is needed? One percent of the total, or $.01(D_t + I_t - E_t)$. The net amount available to be spent is thus:

$$.01D_t - .01(D_t + I_t - E_t) = .01(E_t - I_t)$$

In a case similar to that shown in Figure 14-1(c), when the firm reduces capital by purchasing shares, our investor must sell back some of his or her holdings to maintain ownership of 1% of the firm. This will generate additional income, bringing the total to:

$$.01D_t + .01(E_t - I_t - D_t) = .01(E_t - I_t)$$

Thus no matter what the firm's financing policy, an investor choosing to maintain a constant proportional ownership will be able to spend a proportional share in the firm's earnings net of investment $(E_t - I_t)$ each year. Discounting the expected values by a (constant) interest rate, the value of 1% of the current shares outstanding will be:

$$\frac{.01(\overline{E}_1 - \overline{I}_1)}{1 + r} + \frac{.01(\overline{E}_2 - \overline{I}_2)}{(1 + r)^2} + \frac{.01(\overline{E}_3 - \overline{I}_3)}{(1 + r)^3} + \cdots$$

And the value of all shares outstanding—i.e., the total value of the firm's equity—will be:

$$V_0 = \frac{\overline{E}_1 - \overline{I}_1}{1 + r} + \frac{\overline{E}_2 - \overline{I}_2}{(1 + r)^2} + \frac{\overline{E}_3 - \overline{I}_3}{(1 + r)^3} + \cdots \qquad \textbf{(14-4a)}$$

or:

$$V_0 = \left[\frac{\overline{E}_1}{1 + r} + \frac{\overline{E}_2}{(1 + r)^2} + \frac{\overline{E}_3}{(1 + r)^3} + \cdots \right]$$
$$- \left[\frac{\overline{I}_1}{1 + r} + \frac{\overline{I}_2}{(1 + r)^2} + \frac{\overline{I}_3}{(1 + r)^3} + \cdots \right] \qquad \textbf{(14-4b)}$$

Formula (14-4a) shows that the value of equity is the present value of expected earnings net of required investment; the second version, formula (14-4b), shows that it equals the present value of expected earnings (the first bracketed series) less the present value of the expected investment required (the second bracketed expression).

DETERMINANTS OF DIVIDENDS

Both interviews with corporate executives and empirical analyses of financial data indicate that most firms have a *target payout ratio* that changes relatively little from year to year. Such a value represents a desired ratio of dividends to earnings over some relatively long period. Alternatively, it may be thought of as a target ratio of dividends to long-run or sustainable earnings.

Few firms attempt to maintain a constant ratio of dividends to *current* earnings, since at least some of the variation in earnings from year to year is likely to be transitory. Moreover, since many corporate executives appear to dislike cutting dividends, regular payments are often increased only when management believes it will be relatively easy to maintain the new, higher level in the future (sometimes "special" or "extra" dividends are declared, usually at year-end, to indicate that the increase may not be maintained). Nonetheless, larger earnings are likely to be accompanied by some sort of increase in dividends, as Table 14-1 shows.

Although dividend payments are increased more often than they are decreased, reductions do take place. Moreover, a decline in earnings is more likely to be accompanied by a decline in dividends than is an increase in earnings. During the period covered in Table 14-1, almost half the firms experiencing two successive years of declining earnings reduced dividends.

A formal representation of the kind of behavior implied by a constant long-run target payout ratio was suggested by Lintner.[1] As-

TABLE 14-1

Dividend and Earnings Changes for 392 Major Industrial Firms, 1946-1964

EARNINGS CHANGES		PERCENT OF CASES IN WHICH FIRMS			
Current Year	Previous Year	Percent of Cases	Increased Dividends	Did Not Change Dividends	Decreased Dividends
+		59.3	65.8	13.9	20.3
−		40.7	42.8	17.9	39.5
+	+	33.4	74.8	11.4	13.8
−	−	16.0	31.8	19.4	48.8

SOURCE: Eugene F. Fama and Harvey Babiak, "Dividend Policy: An Empirical Analysis," *American Statistical Association Journal*, 63, no. 324 (December 1968), 1132-61.

---

[1] John Lintner, "Distribution of Incomes of Corporations Among Dividends, Retained Earnings, and Taxes," *American Economic Review*, XLVI, no. 2 (May 1956), 97-113.

sume that the goal is to pay out k^* (e.g., .6) of long-run earnings. If this target ratio were maintained every year, total dividends paid in year t would be:

$$D_t^* = k^* E_t$$

where

D_t^* = target for total dividends paid in year t
k^* = target payout ratio
E_t = total earnings in year t

The difference between target dividends in year t and the previous year's actual dividends would be:

$$D_t^* - D_{t-1} = k^* E_t - D_{t-1}$$

Few if any firms would adjust dividends by this amount. Instead, actual dividends change by some proportion of the difference:

$$D_t - D_{t-1} = p(D_t^* - D_{t-1}) \qquad \textbf{(14-5a)}$$

where p is a "speed of adjustment" coefficient (less than 1.0). Rearranging formula (14-5a):

$$D_t = pk^* E_t + (1-p)D_{t-1} \qquad \textbf{(14-5b)}$$

Statistical analysis can be used to estimate a firm's target payout ratio (k^*) and speed of adjustment (p). Table 14-2 summarizes some of the values obtained in one such study. The typical firm had a target payout ratio of about 60% (.591) and adjusted dividends on average about

TABLE 14-2
Target Payout Ratios and Speed of Dividend Adjustment Factors for 298 Firms, 1946-1968

SPEED OF ADJUSTMENT COEFFICIENT		TARGET PAYOUT RATIO		PERCENT OF VARIANCE EXPLAINED	
Value	Percent of Firms with Smaller Value	Value	Percent of Firms with Smaller Value	Value (%)	Percent of Firms with Smaller Value
.104	10	.401	10	11	10
.182	30	.525	30	32	30
.251	50	.584	50	42	50
.339	70	.660	70	54	70
.470	90	.779	90	72	90
average .269		average .591		average 42	

SOURCE: Eugene F. Fama, "The Empirical Relationship Between the Dividend and Investment Decisions of Firms," *American Economic Review*, LXIV, no. 3 (June 1974), 304-18.

one-fourth (.269) of the way toward its target per year. However, most firms' dividends varied substantially from the pattern implied by their targets and adjustment factors. Somewhat less than half (42%) of the annual variance in the typical firm's dividends could be explained in this manner.

THE INFORMATION CONTENT OF DIVIDENDS

Given an estimate of a firm's target payout ratio and speed of dividend adjustment, it is possible to estimate "normal" dividends for a year. If a lower or higher amount is announced, it seems reasonable to interpret the action as conveying information about management's assessment of the prospects for future earnings. For example, a higher dividend than normally associated with an increase in earnings might indicate that management expects the increase to be more permanent than usual. A lower-than-normal dividend increase under such circumstances might suggest that management considers the increase more transitory than usual. And so on.

One test of this procedure yielded fairly disappointing results. Statistical analysis was used to estimate each firm's target payout ratio and speed of adjustment and then to classify dividends as unexpectedly larger or smaller than normal. Earnings were also categorized as unexpectedly larger or smaller than "normal" (i.e., relative to an average trend-line annual increase). Table 14-3 shows the results obtained when dividend changes were compared with earnings changes in the subsequent year. While unexpectedly high dividends were more likely to signal unexpectedly high earnings in the next year than were unexpectedly low dividends, the information content of dividends measured in this manner was rather low. Similar tests to see if dividends, when

TABLE 14-3
Unexpected Dividend Changes versus Unexpected Earnings Changes in the Subsequent Year, 310 Firms, 1945-1968

Unexpected Change in Dividends	NUMBER OF CASES IN WHICH THE UNEXPECTED CHANGE IN EARNINGS IN THE SUBSEQUENT YEAR WAS		Total Number of Cases
	Positive	Negative	
Positive	1,667	1,457	3,124
Negative	1,507	1,569	3,076
	3,174	3,026	

SOURCE: Ross Watts, "The Information Content of Dividends," *The Journal of Business*, 46, no. 2 (April 1973), 191-211. © 1973 by the University of Chicago. All Rights Reserved.

analyzed in this way, provide information about earnings more than one year hence reached roughly similar conclusions.

These results may indicate that even managers of corporations find it difficult to predict their future earnings. Alternatively, the results may simply reflect the crude methods used to categorize dividends as unexpectedly large or small. An "outside" analyst familiar with a company might be able to better classify dividends and thus capture more of their information content concerning future earnings.

Another way to assess the information content of dividends is to see how the market reacts when a fairly long-standing dividend pattern is broken. One study,[2] which examined changes of 10 cents a share or more after two years of a stable dividend pattern, obtained somewhat surprising results. Figure 14-2(a) plots the cumulative "abnormal" performance of the 913 stocks that increased their dividends in this manner; the performance is shown from 24 months before the announcement of the change until 24 months afterward. Figure 14-2(b) plots the results for the 397 stocks that decreased their dividends. In each case the "normal" return was taken to be that of stocks with beta values similar to that of the stock in question, and "abnormal" return to be the difference between the stock's return and this normal value.

In both Figures 14-2(a) and (b) the behavior of stock returns *up to* the date of the dividend announcement can be easily explained. The news could have been anticipated before the actual announcement, causing abnormal changes in price. If so, the dividend changes were the *cause* and the price changes the *effect*. Alternatively, the *causes* of the price changes may have concerned the prospects of the firms, with *both* the dividend changes and the price changes representing effects of these more fundamental aspects.

Whatever the explanation for price changes *in advance* of dividend-change announcements, the evidence is not inconsistent with market efficiency. But the patterns *after* the announcements suggest the possibility of some inefficiency. In the two years after a significant increase in dividends, the stocks provided returns 4% greater than normal, on average. In the two years after a significant decrease, the stocks provided returns 8% smaller than normal, on average.

To some extent this may be due to tax effects: stocks with increased dividends are likely to provide more of their return in the form of yield and may thus be priced to give higher before-tax total returns. Conversely, stocks with decreased dividends may provide less of their return in the form of yield and be priced to give smaller before-tax returns. But there is probably more to it than this.

While the magnitudes of the "abnormal" returns are not large

---

[2] Guy Charest, "Dividend Information, Stock Returns and Market Efficiency—II," *Journal of Financial Economics*, June/September 1978.

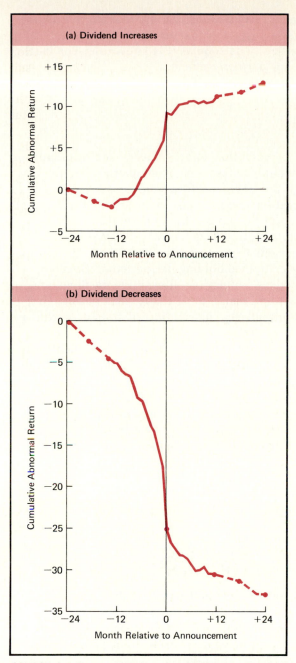

FIGURE 14-2
Abnormal Returns Before and After
Substantial Dividend Changes

(a) Dividend Increases

Cumulative Abnormal Return

+15

+10

+5

0

−5

−24   −12   0   +12   +24

Month Relative to Announcement

(b) Dividend Decreases

Cumulative Abnormal Return

0

−5

−10

−15

−20

−25

−30

−35

−24   −12   0   +12   +24

Month Relative to Announcement

SOURCE: Guy Charest, "Dividend Information, Stock Returns and
Market Efficiency—II," *Journal of Financial Economics*, June/Sep-
tember 1978. By permission of North-Holland Publishing Company.

and there is no guarantee that any single stock will react in this manner, this evidence does create a suspicion that the market may not "fully reflect" all information virtually as soon as it is knowable. The market may thus be *highly* but not *perfectly* efficient.

PRICE-EARNINGS RATIOS

Despite the credentials of valuation approaches based explicitly on dividends, many security analysts use a much simpler procedure. First, a stock's future *earnings per share* (EPS) a year or so hence will be estimated; then the analyst (or someone else) will estimate a "normal" *price-earnings ratio* (P/E) for the stock. The product of these two numbers gives the estimated future price. Together with estimated dividends to be paid during the period (e.g., over the next year) and current price, this determines the estimated holding-period return. Some organizations expand the procedure, estimating alternative earnings and/or price-earnings ratios (e.g., optimistic, most likely, and pessimistic) to produce a rudimentary probability distribution of holding-period returns.

How can such procedures be related to the determinants of value? And what characteristics will cause a stock to sell at a high or low price relative to earnings?

Such questions can be answered by rearranging equation (14-3) and introducing some new variables. As indicated earlier, a firm's (actual) *payout ratio* is simply the ratio of dividends to earnings in a year. This can be written using per-share values:

$$k_t = \frac{d_t}{e_t}$$

Thus $d_t = k_t e_t$ and $\bar{k}_t \bar{e}_t$ can be substituted for $\bar{d}_t$ in the valuation formula:[3]

$$v_0 = \frac{\bar{k}_1 \bar{e}_1}{1+r} + \frac{\bar{k}_2 \bar{e}_2}{(1+r)^2} + \frac{\bar{k}_3 \bar{e}_3}{(1+r)^3} + \cdots$$

where $\bar{k}_1, \bar{k}_2, \bar{k}_3, \ldots$ are the expected payout ratios in years 1, 2, 3, ...

Expected earnings in any year can be expressed as a function of expected earnings in the prior year. Thus we can define *expected earnings growth rates* ($\bar{g}_1, \bar{g}_2, \ldots$) so that:

---

[3] The product of two expected values will not equal the expected value of the product unless the two variables are uncorrelated. This subtlety is ignored here and in the subsequent formulas.

$$\bar{e}_1 = (1 + \bar{g}_1)e_0$$
$$\bar{e}_2 = (1 + \bar{g}_2)e_1 = (1 + \bar{g}_1)(1 + \bar{g}_2)e_0$$
$$\bar{e}_3 = (1 + \bar{g}_3)e_2 = (1 + \bar{g}_1)(1 + \bar{g}_2)(1 + \bar{g}_3)e_0$$

.

.

.

where e_0 is earnings per share in the current year.

A "normal" price-earnings ratio results when a stock sells for its "intrinsic value"—i.e., $P_0 = v_0$. Making this substitution, along with those relating expected future earnings to present earnings, the valuation formula becomes:

$$P_0 = \frac{\bar{k}_1(1 + \bar{g}_1)e_0}{1 + r} + \frac{\bar{k}_2(1 + \bar{g}_1)(1 + \bar{g}_2)e_0}{(1 + r)^2}$$
$$+ \frac{\bar{k}_3(1 + \bar{g}_1)(1 + \bar{g}_2)(1 + \bar{g}_3)e_0}{(1 + r)^3} + \cdots$$

Rearranging:

$$\frac{P_0}{e_0} = \frac{\bar{k}_1(1 + \bar{g}_1)}{1 + r} + \frac{\bar{k}_2(1 + \bar{g}_1)(1 + \bar{g}_2)}{(1 + r)^2}$$

(14-6)

$$+ \frac{\bar{k}_3(1 + \bar{g}_1)(1 + \bar{g}_2)(1 + \bar{g}_3)}{(1 + r)^3} + \cdots$$

This shows the determinants of a stock's normal price-earnings ratio (P_0/e_0). Other things equal, it will be *higher*:

the *greater* the expected payout ratios $(\bar{k}_1, \bar{k}_2, \ldots)$
the *greater* the expected earnings growth rates $(\bar{g}_1, \bar{g}_2, \ldots)$
the *smaller* the appropriate discount rate (r)

The qualifying phrase "other things equal" should not be overlooked. For example, a firm cannot increase the value of its shares by simply planning greater payouts. This will increase $\bar{k}_1, \bar{k}_2, \ldots$ but decrease expected growth in earnings per share $(\bar{g}_1, \bar{g}_2, \ldots)$. As shown previously, if the firm's investment policy is not altered, the effects of the reduced growth in earnings per share will just offset the effects of the increased payouts, leaving value per share unchanged. Another example involves an increase in the appropriate discount rate. If this reflects an increase in expected inflation, projected growth rates in *nominal* earnings per share should be adjusted upward as well. Unless the firm can be expected to gain or lose from inflation, the two effects should offset each other, leaving value per share unchanged.

CONSTANT-GROWTH MODELS

Little in life grows forever at a constant rate, and stocks are no exception. However, many analysts use a simplified valuation model that assumes that they do.

The key idea is to replace $\bar{g}_1, \bar{g}_2, \ldots$ with a single expected rate, $\bar{g}$, at which earnings per share are assumed to grow forever. Clearly, it must be less than the appropriate discount rate, or the value of the stock would be infinite. To further simplify the problem, a constant payout ratio is assumed, and $\bar{k}$ replaces $\bar{k}_1, \bar{k}_2, \ldots$ Formula (14-6) thus becomes:

$$\frac{P_0}{e_0} = \frac{\bar{k}(1+\bar{g})}{1+r} + \frac{\bar{k}(1+\bar{g})^2}{(1+r)^2} + \frac{\bar{k}(1+\bar{g})^3}{(1+r)^3} + \cdots$$

Happily there is a formula for the value of an infinite series of this type, which applies as long as $\bar{g}$ is less than r. It provides the *constant-growth valuation model*:[4]

$$\frac{P_0}{e_1} = \frac{\bar{k}}{r - \bar{g}} \tag{14-7a}$$

or:

$$P_0 = \frac{\bar{k}e_1}{r - \bar{g}} = \frac{d_1}{r - \bar{g}} \tag{14-7b}$$

Some insight into the model can be gained by rearranging (14-7b) to obtain:

$$r = \frac{d_1}{P_0} + \bar{g} \tag{14-7c}$$

Thus the expected return equals yield (d_1/P_0) plus expected growth $(\bar{g})$. In the constant-growth model everything grows at the same rate. Since the payout ratio is constant, dividends will grow at the same rate as earnings. And since the price-earnings ratio is constant [as formula (14-7a) shows], price will also grow at this rate.

Formula (14-7c) holds, no matter what, if $\bar{g}$ is interpreted as the expected growth in *price* over the coming year, for expected total return *must* equal the expected value of yield plus expected capital gain. The difference here is that both price and earnings are assumed to grow at the same rate each year, and that this rate is to be the same from year to year.

---

[4] Note that these formulas use e_1 and d_1 instead of e_0 and d_0. Some analysts replace e_1 and d_1 with $e_0(1 + \bar{g})$ and $d_0(1 + \bar{g})$, respectively. Others simply replace them with e_0 and d_0, on the grounds that the resulting errors will be small. The latter changes can be shown to be exactly correct under the somewhat unrealistic assumptions that earnings and dividends grow continuously at the rate g, and that dividends are paid out and discounted continuously at the interest rate r.

A variation of the constant-growth model makes further assumptions concerning the sources of earnings growth. Assuming that no new capital is obtained and no shares repurchased, the portion of earnings not paid out will constitute the net investment each year:

$$I_t = (1 - k_t)E_t$$

If this investment produces a proportional return of ρ per year, it will add ρI_t to earnings in year $t + 1$ (and every year thereafter). If every previous investment also produces perpetual earnings at a constant rate of return, next year's earnings will equal this year's plus the new earnings resulting from this year's incremental investment:

$$
\begin{aligned}
E_{t+1} &= E_t + \rho I_t \\
&= E_t + \rho(1 - k_t)E_t \\
&= E_t[1 + \rho(1 - k_t)]
\end{aligned}
$$

Growth rate in earnings per share is defined by:

$$E_{t+1} = E_t(1 + g_t)$$

and thus:

$$g_t = \rho(1 - k_t)$$

If expected growth is to be constant, $\bar{\rho}$, the *expected (average) return on incremental investment*, must also be the same in every year. The constant-growth valuation formula thus becomes:

$$\frac{P_0}{e_1} = \frac{\bar{k}}{r - \bar{\rho}(1 - \bar{k})} \tag{14-8a}$$

or:

$$P_0 = \frac{\bar{k}e_1}{r - \bar{\rho}(1 - \bar{k})} = \frac{d_1}{r - \bar{\rho}(1 - \bar{k})} \tag{14-8b}$$

Under these assumptions, a stock's price-earnings ratio will be greater, the greater its expected return on incremental investment, other things equal. Earnings growth depends on how much is kept $(1 - \bar{k})$ and what it earns $(\bar{\rho})$. And the greater earnings growth (other things equal), the greater a stock's value.

Many analysts assume that after some date a firm will find that none of its available investment opportunities offers an abnormally high return. At this point the firm is usually said to have reached *maturity*. The price-earnings ratio for such a firm can be found simply. As long as management does not choose to invest in projects with inferior returns, $\bar{\rho}$ (the average return on incremental investment) will equal r (the appropriate discount rate), and formula (14-8a) can be simplified to:

$$\frac{P_0}{e_1} = \frac{\bar{k}_1}{r - r(1 - \bar{k})} = \frac{1}{r} \qquad \textbf{(14-8c)}$$

Thus *the appropriate price-earnings ratio for a mature firm is one over the discount rate,* or equivalently, *the appropriate earnings-price ratio is the discount rate.*

THE MERRILL LYNCH APPROACH

Between the generality of formula (14-6) and the extreme simplifications incorporated in constant-growth models lie countless possibilities for simplified models of earnings growth. Many of these have been proposed and a number of them implemented. Most are characterized by the assumption that at some estimated future date, growth will stabilize and henceforth forever remain constant, with the stock in question priced accordingly. At this point the stock's price can be estimated by applying an "appropriate" price-earnings multiple to its earnings, or by applying the constant-growth model directly. In either case, given estimates of earnings growth rates and payout ratios prior to "maturity," and given estimates of the relevant characteristics for the (infinitely long) mature period, it is possible either (1) to estimate present value, for an appropriate assumed discount rate, or (2) to calculate a discount rate associated with the current price of the stock.

The Dividend Discount Model

Security analysts at Merrill Lynch, Pierce, Fenner and Smith Inc.—a major financial services firm—routinely provide inputs for a *dividend discount model* (DDM) designed to compute an *implied return* for each of over 900 securities. The underlying model breaks the growth of a company into three stages:

> *Growth stage.* The growth stage is characterized by a rapidly expanding market, high profit margins, and abnormally high growth in earnings per share. New-product introduction and technological advances give rise to unusual opportunities. Because the profitability of investment opportunities is high, the payout ratio generally is low. Theoretically, the shareholders' best interest is served if retention rates remain high, as long as the rate of return on reinvested funds is higher than investors could earn elsewhere on investments of equivalent risk. The unusual return potential enjoyed in this stage presumably attracts competitors, and although growth in the first-to-market company may remain above average, it gradually declines.
>
> *Transition stage.* In the later years of an industry's life, fewer technological advances and increased product saturation begin to reduce the growth rate for all companies, and profit margins come under pressure. As investment opportunities begin to mature, capital requirements de-

cline, and the company begins to pay out a larger percentage of earnings. This results from the fact that management will find a declining number of projects that offer unusual return potential.

Mature stage. Eventually, the company reaches an equilibrium—none of the available investment opportunities offer *abnormally* high returns. At that time, earnings growth, payout ratio, and return on equity stabilize at levels where they remain for the life of the company. The DDM model calls this the steady-state stage.[5]

Figure 14-3 portrays the stages. Note that the vertical scale is logarithmic, so that a straight line represents a constant rate of growth.

For each security, a Merrill Lynch analyst furnishes the following estimates:[6]

Five years of expected earnings and dividends or a growth rate of earnings from the base year to the level of earnings in the fifth year. (Because those estimates generally account for one-third of value, these estimates are critical.)

Growth rate in earnings and the payout ratio for the start of the transitional state.

The duration of the transition stage—i.e., the number of years until the company reaches maturity or steady-state. With that information, the analyst places the company on the growth curve.

FIGURE 14-3
The Three Stages of the Merrill Lynch Dividend Discount Model

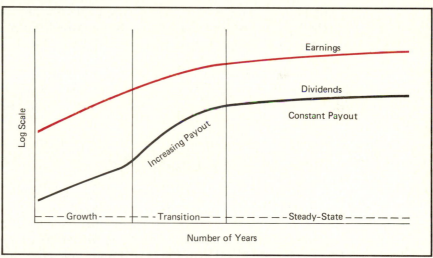

SOURCE: Carmine J. Grigoli, "Demystifying Dividend Discount Models," Merrill Lynch Quantitative Research, April 1982.

---

[5] Carmine J. Grigoli, "Demystifying Dividend Discount Models," Merrill Lynch Quantitative Research, April 1982.

[6] *Ibid.*

Growth patterns for the transitional stage. Analysts have five choices of decay rates. By selecting an appropriate combination of decay rate and years to steady-state, the analysts directly control the length of the growth period.

Combination of earnings growth and payout ratio that produces the desired return on equity for the steady-state period. The ROE is allowed to vary within a few percentage points of the mean of all companies. The ROE is the primary source of value in the steady-state period.

The use of slightly different estimates for return on equity (ROE) for the steady-state period reflects an assumption that true "maturity" may not be reached for 40 or 50 years, while most analysts limit the time required for the first two stages to 18 to 25 years.

Convergence of Profitability and Growth

Multistage dividend discount models assume that, ultimately, economic forces will force convergence of the profitability and growth rates of different firms. Figures 14-4 provide support. Adequate data were available to analyze 679 firms covered by Merrill Lynch analysts. The firms were grouped into quintiles based on average return on equity in the five years ending in 1966. The average ROE of the 20% of the firms in the top quintile was 1.74 times the universe average in 1966. In 1980, fourteen years later, the five-year average ROE of the same set of firms had fallen to 1.24 times the universe average.

Figure 14-4(a) shows the changes in ROE over time for both the top and bottom quintiles. Figure 14-4(b) shows the payout ratios (dividends/earnings) and Figure 14-4(c) the growth rates in dividends per share for the same sets of firms. As in Figure 14-4(a), values are shown relative to the universe average.

In all three respects, convergence toward an overall mean is apparent. While the results may not be fully representative, owing to the selection of the securities after-the-fact (e.g., in 1981), the phenomenon is undoubtedly real.

The Security Market Line

Given the estimates provided by an analyst, it is relatively straightforward to determine a company's predicted dividends for each year prior to the steady-state period and the predicted (constant) growth rate for dividends thereafter. From these values the present value of the predicted dividend pattern associated with any given discount rate can be calculated. Using computerized trial-and-error, it is also possible to determine the discount rate that equates the value of a stock's projected dividends with its current price. This is the *long-run internal rate of return* for the security implied by the analyst's estimates. Merrill Lynch terms this the security's *implied return*.

FIGURE 14-4
Convergence of Profitability, Payout, and Growth

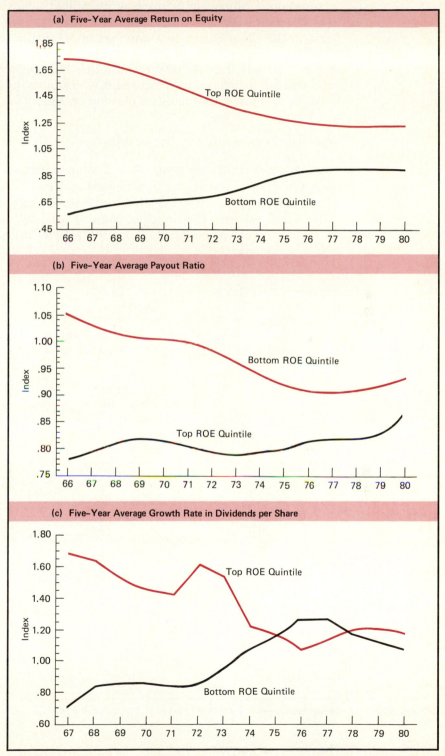

SOURCE: Carmine J. Grigoli, "Demystifying Dividend Discount Models," Merrill Lynch Quantitative Research, April 1982.

After an implied return has been estimated for each stock, the information is plotted on a graph with implied return on the vertical axis and estimated beta values on the horizontal axis. A line is then fitted to the data. Figure 14-5 provides an example. In this case the added premium in higher implied return for an increase in beta is small. In other periods the "security market lines" obtained in this manner were steeper, as reflected in Figure 14-6, which plots the implied returns for high- and low-beta securities plotting on such lines.

Implied Return on the Stock Market

Another product of this analysis is a value-weighted implied return for a portfolio of the stocks in Standard and Poor's 500-stock index. This is compared with bond yields to estimate the current risk premium in the stock market. The resulting value is used by Merrill Lynch as an input for recommendations concerning *asset allocation* between bonds and stocks.

Required Returns

Given implied returns on Standard and Poor's 500-stock index and bond yields, a *required return* is determined for each level of beta. In the Merrill Lynch system this is based on a security market line

FIGURE 14-5
A Security Market Line

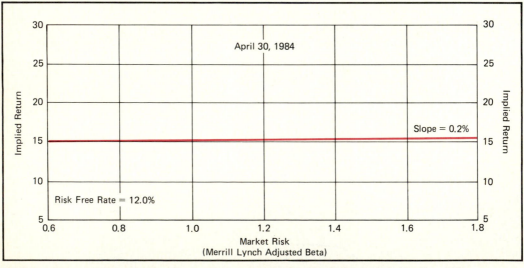

SOURCE: Carmine J. Grigoli, "Common Stock Valuation," Merrill Lynch Quantitative Analysis, May/June 1984.

FIGURE 14-6
Implied Returns on High- and Low-Beta Stocks

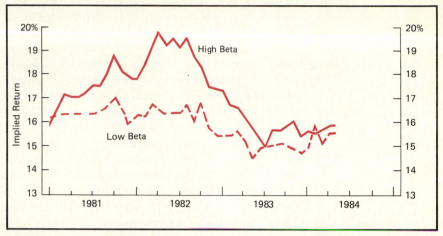

SOURCE: Carmine J. Grigoli, "Common Stock Valuation," Merrill Lynch Quantitative Analysis, May/ June 1984.

derived using the assumptions of the original Capital Asset Pricing Model (i.e., a line drawn through the "stock" and "bond" points). An alternative approach, based on the Zero-Beta Capital Asset Pricing Model, could use an empirically determined line such as the one shown in Figure 14-5.

Alpha Values

The difference between a stock's *implied* return (from the dividend discount model) and an appropriate *required* return is termed its *alpha*. This is considered "the degree to which a stock is mispriced. Positive alphas indicate undervalued securities and negative alphas indicate overvalued securities."[7]

DIVIDEND DISCOUNT MODELS AND EXPECTED RETURNS

The procedures used by Merrill Lynch are similar to those employed by many brokerage firms and investment managers. Discount rates obtained from a dividend discount model using long-term dividend projections are treated as *expected holding-period returns*. Procedures based on equilibrium models (e.g., Capital Asset Pricing Models) are

---

[7] Carmine J. Grigoli, "Common Stock Valuation," Merrill Lynch Quantitative Analysis, May/ June 1984. A subsequent procedure divides the alpha value by "residual risk" (nonmarket risk) to obtain a *standardized alpha,* then classifies the security into one of ten "standardized alpha deciles."

then utilized to determine "expected returns" on stocks, "risk premia," "alpha values," and so on.

A DDM-based discount rate is similar to the yield-to-maturity of a bond: it is a "yield-to-perpetuity." Just as the return on a bond over a short period may differ considerably from its yield-to-maturity, so, too, the return on a stock over a short period may differ from its DDM-based discount rate. Not only can the *actual* holding-period return differ from the discount rate, but the *expected* return can also.

A simple set of examples will indicate the major aspects involved. Assume that the consensus opinion of "the market" (most investors) is that a stock will pay a dividend of $1 per year forever. On the other hand, a security analyst predicts that the dividend will equal $1.10 per year forever. This is a *deviant* or *nonconsensus* prediction.

Assume that both the analyst and other investors agree that the appropriate expected rate of return for a stock of this type is 10%. The constant-growth formula [equation (14-7b)] can be adapted to indicate the present value of a stock expected to pay d per year forever, with a discount rate of r. Since the growth rate in dividend per year is assumed to be zero:

$$P_0 = \frac{d}{r}$$

In this case:

$$P_0 = \frac{d}{.10} = 10\,d$$

—i.e., the stock should sell for ten times its expected dividend.

Column A in Table 14-4 summarizes the situation. Since other investors expect to receive $1 per year, the stock will sell for $10 at present. Assume that the analyst plans to sell it at the end of the year. What rate of return might he or she expect?

The answer depends on (1) the *accuracy of the prediction* and (2) the rate of *convergence* of investors' predictions.

The case shown in Column A assumes that the prediction is correct—at year-end the stock does in fact pay the predicted dividend of $1.10. Despite this, other investors regard the higher dividend as a fluke and steadfastly refuse to alter their projections of subsequent dividends from their initial estimates of $1. As a result, the security's price remains at $10 (= $1/.10) at year-end.

In this case the analyst's total return equals 11%, all obtained from dividend yield. This equals the (equilibrium) required return of 10% plus an "actual alpha" of 1% from the portion of the dividend unanticipated by other investors.

If the situation shown in Column A were to continue in subsequent years, with dividends of $1.10 paid each year and other investors contin-

TABLE 14-4
Predictive Accuracy and Convergence of Predictions

	A	B	C	D	E
Now:					
Dividend predictions:					
Consensus	1.00	1.00	1.00	1.00	1.00
Analyst	1.10	1.10	1.10	1.10	1.10
Required return	10%	10%	10%	10%	10%
Stock price	10.00	10.00	10.00	10.00	10.00
Implied return	11%	11%	11%	11%	11%
Predicted alpha	1%	1%	1%	1%	1%
At Year-end:					
Actual dividend	1.10	1.10	1.10	1.05	1.05
Dividend predictions:					
Consensus	1.00	1.10	1.05	1.00	1.05
Analyst	1.10	1.10	1.10	1.05	1.05
Stock Price	10.00	11.00	10.50	10.00	10.50
Performance:					
Dividend yield	11%	11%	11%	10.5%	10.5%
Capital gain	0%	10%	5%	0%	5.0%
Total return	11%	21%	16%	10.5%	15.5%
Actual alpha	1%	11%	6%	0.5%	5.5%

uing to regard the situation as unlikely to be repeated, the analyst could receive an "extra" 1% per year (alpha) forever by continuing to hold the stock. Each year's holding-period return would equal the initially calculated implied return (discount rate) of 11%. If the analyst were to sell the stock after a year, the total return would equal the discount rate (11%), but the alpha of 1% would be earned only once.

In this case the analyst's prediction was perfect. Despite this, the consensus prediction did not change at all: there was no *convergence* of predictions. The net result was an actual alpha just equal to the predicted alpha.

Column B shows a very different situation. Here, too, the prediction is perfect, but in this case other investors see the errors of their ways and completely revise their predictions. At year-end they, too, predict future dividends will equal $1.10 per year; thus the stock sells for $11 (= $1.10/.10). Under these conditions the analyst can achieve a holding-period return of 21% by selling the stock at the end of the year, obtaining 11% in dividend yield and 10% in capital gains. The capital gains result directly from the *repricing* of the security due to the convergence of predictions.

In this case, the fruits of the superior prediction are all obtained in one year. Instead of 1% "extra" per year forever, the analyst obtains 1% in extra yield this year plus 10% in (extra) capital gains. By continuing to hold the stock in subsequent years, he or she would earn only the normal required (equilibrium) return of 10% per year.

Column C shows an intermediate case. Here the predictions of other investors only converge halfway (from $1 to $1.05 instead of $1.10). Total return in the first year is 16%: 11% in yield plus 5% in capital gains. To obtain the remainder of the "extra return," the stock would have to be held longer.

In the cases in columns B and C, return in the first year is *larger* than the discount rate of 11%, and the actual "alpha" (total return minus required return) is larger than the expected alpha of 1%, as shown in the bottom row of the table.

The cases in columns A through C assume that the prediction is perfect. Columns D and E do not. In these cases, actual dividends exceed the consensus forecast ($1) by only $.05, instead of the originality predicted amount of $.10.

In the case shown in Column D, other investors regard the first year's dividend of $1.05 as a fluke and refuse to alter their predictions for subsequent years. The stock price remains at $10, limiting total return to 10.5%. Owing to an overly optimistic deviant prediction, the actual alpha (0.5%) is *less* than the predicted amount (1%).

The case in Column E assumes that at year-end both the analyst and other investors regard the actual dividend of $1.05 as permanent and revise their predictions for subsequent dividends accordingly. Here the two effects operate in different directions. Owing to the overly optimistic prediction, dividend yield is 10.5%—less than the predicted 11%. But since the prediction was in the right *direction*, capital gains are realized, as other investors revise their predictions in conformance with actual results. In this case the capital gains more than offset the less-than-expected yield, bringing total return well above the implied return (discount rate) of 11%. Actual alpha is 5.5%—greater than predicted (1%).

In other cases of this sort, total return could be more or less than the predicted discount rate and the actual alpha could be greater or less than predicted.

Other things equal, *holding-period return will be larger, the greater is predictive accuracy, and the faster the rate of convergence of predictions*.

Many investors who use dividend discount models use the implied discount rate as a surrogate for a relatively short-term (e.g., one-year) expected holding-period return. This could reflect an assumption of perfect predictive accuracy and no convergence of predictions. More likely, it reflects beliefs that (1) deviant predictions are less than perfectly accurate, but contain some information, and (2) other investors will revise their predictions in the corresponding direction by a large enough amount to provide capital gains which will offset any shortfall from predicted dividend yield.

An alternative approach does not simply use outputs from a dividend discount model "as is," but *adjusts* them, based on relationships between previous predictions and actual outcomes. Figures 14-7(a) and (b) provide examples.

Each point in Figure 14-7(a) plots a *predicted* return on the stock market (on the horizontal axis) and the *actual* return in a period subsequent to the prediction (on the vertical axis). The line fitted through the points indicates the general relationship between prediction and outcome. If the current prediction is 15%, history suggests that an estimate of 14% would be superior.

Each point in Figure 14-7(b) plots a predicted alpha value for a security (on the horizontal axis) and the corresponding "abnormal return" in a period subsequent to the prediction (on the vertical axis).

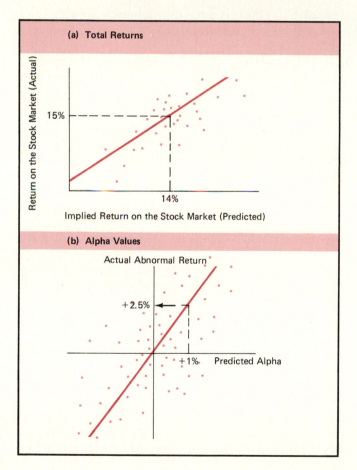

FIGURE 14-7
Adjusting Predictions

Such a diagram can be very full: if an organization has made predictions for 100 securities in each of the last 60 months, there can be 6,000 points in Figure 14-7(b) [but only 60 in Figure 14-7(a)]. Again, a line can be fitted through the points. In this case, if the current prediction of a security's alpha value is +1%, this relationship suggests that an "adjusted" estimate of +2.5% would be superior.

An important by-product of analyses of this type is the measure of *correlation* between predicted and actual outcomes (which indicates the nearness of the points to the line). This can serve as a measure of *predictive accuracy*. If the correlation is too small to be significantly different from zero in a statistical sense, the value of the predictions is subject to considerable question.

DISCOUNT RATES AND EQUILIBRIUM MODELS

Equilibrium models assert that there is a relationship between expected returns and specific attributes of securities, where all such measures are *forward-looking predictions*.

Dividend discount models can provide predictions of expected returns, given assumptions about predictive accuracy and convergence of predictions. Such expected returns may then be compared with predicted beta values, measures of size, sensitivities to macreconomic variables, and so on to estimate parameters of equilibrium models.

The procedure followed by Merrill Lynch provides an example. As shown in Figure 14-5, expected returns are related to beta values, giving an empirical estimate of the Security Market Line of the Zero-Beta Capital Asset Pricing Model. Deviations from a relationship based on the original Capital Asset Pricing Model are then used as estimated alpha values.

Other organizations use DDM outputs for estimating relationships from other equilibrium models.

When a regression analysis is conducted with expected return as the dependent variable and beta and yield as independent variables, the results locate the current position of a Security Market Plane from an extended Capital Asset Pricing Model. Deviations from the resulting plane serve as alpha values for the securities. Each indicates the difference between a security's expected return and an appropriate expected return, given its beta and yield.

A similar type of analysis can be used to estimate the Arbitrage Pricing Theory's expected return premia associated with sensitivities to pervasive factors. Expected returns derived from a dividend discount model are regressed on estimates of sensitivities fo factors. The coefficients obtained from the regression serve as forward-looking estimates of the corresponding premia (i.e., the desired lambda values). Deviations from the resulting hyperplane can be used as alpha values, if desired.

PREDICTING RETURNS

Fitting a Security Market Line, Security Market Plane, or Arbitrage Pricing Theory equation using expected returns obtained from a dividend discount model can be considered the estimation of a *cross-sectional valuation equation*. The use of deviations of individual securities' expected returns from such an equation to identify potential opportunities for profit assumes that deviant predictions have some accuracy. Unfortunately, deviations often tend to persist, indicating that they may be due more to errors in dividend projections or to relevant factors ignored in the valuation equation than to temporary mispricing. Perhaps more vexing, both the equilibrium relationship (e.g., Security Market Plane, APT equation) and the relevant attributes for a security are likely to change as well, giving a new intrinsic value. Analysts must thus attempt to shoot at a moving target.

The solution for these problems is as straightforward conceptually as it is difficult to achieve. Say that one-year holding-period returns are to be predicted. First, the equilibrium relationship *one year hence* should be estimated. Then the values of dividends for the coming year and the relevant consensus expectations to be held by analysts one year hence should be predicted. Applying the predicted equilibrium relationship to these estimates, one can predict the stock's intrinsic value a year later. Estimating the likely reduction in deviations per year, the amount expected to remain after a year can be added to or subtracted from this to estimate the ending price. Comparing this to the present price, and adding dividends expected to be paid during the year, one can obtain the desired prediction of return.

In the best of all possible worlds, one would try to accurately predict future equilibrium relationships and all the required ingredients. However, to gain abnormal profits, only a better-than-average ability to predict *some* element is required. A capacity to foresee deviations from the market's consensus predictions of *any* aspect could prove profitable. Not surprisingly, few organizations forecast all the required ingredients.

This does not imply that *bottom-up* analyses of the type described here are useless. Quite the contrary. They provide estimates of the manner in which the market currently values securities, and this is essential information. Even if the *deviations* of individual securities from this relationship reflect only predictive errors and are thus of no significance whatever, the *equilibrium equation* itself could be a good estimate of the current relationship between expected returns and relevant security attributes, amply justifying the entire effort. And if the deviations indicate likely mispricing rather than errors in security analysis, the procedure can be even more valuable.

Problems

1. Why is the assumption that $\bar{g}$ is less than r necessary for the constant-growth valuation model?

2. Suppose that the dividend yield on IBM stock is 2½% lower than the interest rate on U. S. government bonds. Does this mean that IBM can raise equity capital more cheaply than the U. S. government can borrow in the bond market?

3. The stock of the Mississippi Bubble Corporation currently pays a yearly dividend of $3 per share. The dividend is expected to grow at 4% per year forever. Stocks with similar characteristics are currently priced to give an expected return of 12%. What is an appropriate price for MBC?

4. Assume you are convinced that at the end of this year a Security Market Line of the type shown in Figure 14-5 will be steeper than it is at present. What does this suggest about the relative performance between now and the end of the year of high-beta stocks versus that of low-beta stocks?

5. Analysts typically classify a security as a *growth stock* if earnings per share are expected to grow rapidly. It is often said that growth stocks should have higher price-earnings multiples than other stocks to reflect the relatively greater earnings they will produce in the future. Others say that the multiple of a growth stock should depend on the source of the growth—i.e., whether it is from highly profitable investment opportunities or simply a substantial plow-back of earnings into the business. In what sense should a stock's price-earnings multiple be related to future growth? to the source of that growth?

6. In what sense should value be related to dividends? to earnings? Under what conditions is double-counting involved if all dividends and all earnings are taken into account in determining value? Are there reasonable valuation methods that take *some* dividends and *some* earnings into account?

7. According to the text, the patterns in Figures 14-2(a) and (b) before the announcement of dividend changes are not inconsistent with market efficiency, while those after the announcement are inconsistent. Why might one be able to make abnormal returns after the announcement but not before?

8. Silicon Valley Electronics is expected to pay out 40% of its earnings and to earn an average return of 15% per year on its incremental reinvested earnings forever. Stocks with similar characteristics are currently priced to return 12% to investors. By what percentage can SVE's earnings per share be expected to grow each year? What is an appropriate price-earnings multiple for the stock? What portion of SVE's total return is likely to come from capital gains? from dividend yield?

9. Feathered Feast, a fast-food enterprise that sells barbequed chicken, currently pays a dividend of $1 per share. Its earnings are $3 per share. You expect the dividend to grow at a rate of 20% per year for the next ten years. At that time

the firm will be mature and you assume that it will be priced accordingly. Stocks with similar characteristics return 10% per year. What price is appropriate for FF?

10. A venture-capital firm currently is paying a dividend of $2 per share on earnings of $4 per share. Its stock is selling for $200 per share. Stocks of comparable risk and yield are currently priced to return 15% per year. What kind of return on incremental investment could explain investors willingness to pay a price equal to 50 times earnings on this stock?

11. The Security Market Line shown in Figure 14-5 is very flat. At the time it was estimated, the difference between the expected return on stocks and that on bonds was over 2%. Merrill Lynch bases its "required returns" on (1) beta values and (2) the difference between expected returns on stocks and bonds. Alpha values are computed by subtracting this required return from the implied return obtained from the dividend discount model. Would you expect a randomly chosen group of low-beta stocks to have positive or negative alphas on average? What about a randomly chosen group of high-beta stocks? What is the relationship between this situation and the difference between the original Capital Asset Pricing Model and the Zero-Beta Capital Asset Pricing Model?

12. What explanation can you offer for the fact that the Security Market Line in Figure 14-5 is so flat?

15

Earnings

ACCOUNTING VERSUS ECONOMIC EARNINGS

The prediction of earnings plays a central role in security analysis and investment research. This makes essential a review of what is known about earnings and the relationship between earnings and prices. More fundamental is a consideration of the concept itself. Just what is meant by "earnings" to those who product the figures, and how does this affect the valuation process?

A firm's accountant, in cooperation with management, operating under constraints and guidelines imposed by regulatory authorities and professional organizations, produces a figure each quarter for the firm's "earnings." In a broad sense, such earnings represent the difference between revenues and costs, including the costs associated with non-equity sources of funds. This difference, the *total earnings* "available for common stock," is divided by the number of shares outstanding to calculate *earnings per share* (EPS). It may also be divided by a measure of the value of the equity to calculate the *return on equity* (ROE).

Earnings are related to cash flows, which are the ultimate source of value. However, value is related to potential *future* cash flows, while reported (accounting) earnings represent a combination of past, current, and estimated future cash flows.

A basic principle of accounting makes the "book" value of a firm's equity at the end of a year equal to (1) its value at the end of the previous year plus (2) any retained earnings (assuming no change in stock outstanding, and so on):

$$B_t = B_{t-1} + E_t - D_t \qquad \textbf{(15-1)}$$

where:

B_t = the book value of equity at the end of year t

E_t = accounting earnings in year t

D_t = dividends paid in year t

Accounting earnings can thus be considered the change in book value plus dividends paid:

$$E_t = (B_t - B_{t-1}) + D_t \qquad \text{(15-2)}$$

Economic earnings may be defined as the amount that would be obtained if each year's book value equaled economic value:

$$E_t^e = (V_t - V_{t-1}) + D_t \qquad \text{(15-3)}$$

where:

V_t = the economic value of the firm's equity at the end of year t

E_t^e = the economic earnings in year t

The *accounting return on equity* relates accounting earnings to book value:

$$R_t = \frac{E_t}{B_{t-1}} = \frac{B_t - B_{t-1} + D_t}{B_{t-1}} \qquad \text{(15-4)}$$

where

R_t = the accounting return on equity in year t

The *economic return on equity* relates economic earnings to economic value:

$$R_t^e = \frac{E_t^e}{V_{t-1}} = \frac{V_t - V_{t-1} + D_t}{V_{t-1}} \qquad \text{(15-5)}$$

where:

R_t^e = the economic return on equity in year t

Investors' estimates of the economic value of a firm's equity are reflected in the market value of its outstanding shares. The economic return on equity thus equals the market return on the firm's stock. No new principles are required to understand the behavior of *economic* earnings, only the application of what is known concerning the behavior of stock returns.

A firm's *expected* economic return on equity should be related to relevant attributes, in conformance with an equilibrium model of security expected returns. Its *actual* economic return on equity in any given year will often diverge from this amount, but the divergence will generally be unpredictable and unrelated to that of the previous year. In other words, a firm's annual economic returns on equity are not likely to be serially correlated (positively or negatively).

Table 15-1 provides an illustration of the way in which variations in return on equity can impact economic value (V_t) and economic earnings (E_t^e). The firm in question begins with an economic value of $1,000 and earns 10% on its equity on average, but occasionally earns more (e.g., 15% in year 3) or less (e.g., 5% in year 6). Each year 40% of economic earnings is paid out in dividends. As usual, the economic value at the end of the year equals the beginning value plus earnings, minus dividends.

As the table shows, relatively modest fluctuations in return on equity can cause substantial changes in economic earnings. Better-than-average years are likely to cause large transitory increases in earnings (e.g., a +59% change from year 2 to year 3), but such increases are likely to be followed by substantial decreases (e.g., a −27% change

TABLE 15-1
Economic Earnings for a Firm

Year (t)	Beginning Economic Value ($) (V_{t-1})	Economic Return on Equity (%) (R_t^e)	Economic Earnings ($) $(E_t^e) = R_t^e \times V_{t-1}$
1	1,000.00	10	100.00
2	1,060.00	10	106.00
3	1,123.60	15	168.54
4	1,224.72	10	122.47
5	1,298.20	10	129.82
6	1,376.09	5	68.80
7	1,417.37	10	141.74
8	1,502.41	10	150.24
9	1,592.55		

Year	Dividends $(= .4E_t^e)$ ($) (D_t)	Ending Economic Value ($) $(V_t = V_{t-1} + E_t - D_t)$	Growth in Economic Earnings (%) $= 100 \times (E_t^e - E_{t-1}^e)/E_{t-1}^e$
1	40.00	1,060.00	
2	42.40	1,123.60	+6
3	67.42	1,224.72	+59
4	48.99	1,298.20	−27
5	51.93	1,376.09	+6
6	27.52	1,417.37	−47
7	56.70	1,502.41	+106
8	60.10	1,592.55	+6

Earnings

from year 3 to year 4). As year 6 illustrates, worse-than-average years can have the opposite effects.

Growth rates in a firm's total economic earnings or economic earnings per share over successive years will generally be negatively related, as these are. Following a major increase in earnings, the best estimate of next year's earnings will be *smaller* than the most recent value. Following a major decrease, the best estimate will be larger than the most recent value. Simply increasing current economic earnings by a fixed percentage to obtain an estimate of next year's economic earnings would give very poor results following a major change (such as that in year 3 or year 6).

To predict economic earnings, one should multiply the appropriate expected return on equity by the current economic value of equity. The expected return will change little if at all from year to year, but the economic value of equity will, owing to both unanticipated changes in future prospects and additional investment (including that obtained via retained earnings). Economic earnings—the product of these two factors—will thus change from year to year in partly predictable and partly unpredictable ways.

If accountants attempted to report economic earnings, annual earnings fluctuations of the sort shown in Table 15-1 would be common, and any attempt to value securities by applying a standard "multiple" to current earnings would give bizarre results. However, if economic earnings *were* reported, valuation would be simple, since the accountant would have already done the job. The economic value of a stock would be its book value, and there would be no reason to even consider earnings per se.

Little evidence is required to show that investors often consider stocks to be worth considerably more or less than reported book values. Figure 15-1 shows the ratio of (1) the year-end market price per share for Standard and Poor's Industrial Stock Index, to (2) the year-end book value per share. The ratio is typically greater than 1.0 and has fluctuated considerably from year to year.

Figure 15-2 plots book values (horizontal axis) and market values (vertical axis) for stocks in the Dow-Jones Industrial Average at the end of 1982.[1] As the extensive scatter of the points indicates, investors feel that economic values differ from book values by different amounts for different stocks. Clearly, accounting earnings also differ from investors' estimates of economic earnings.

Additional evidence is provided by the behavior of accounting earnings over time. As shown in the next section, reported earnings are much less erratic than the economic earnings implicit in market values. This is due in part to the accountant's greater reliance on *real-*

---

[1] Only 29 stocks are plotted. The book value of International Harvester was nil at the time, although its price was positive.

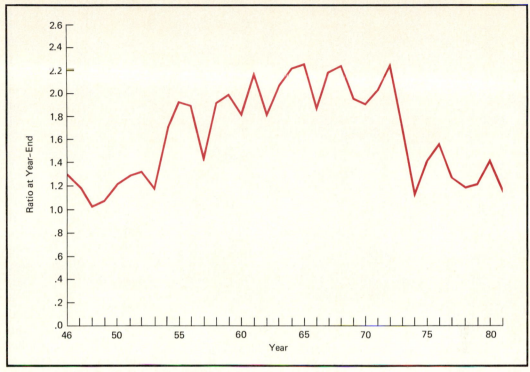

SOURCE: Standard and Poor's *Statistical Service*.

FIGURE 15-1
Ratio of Price to Book Value: Standard and Poor's Industrial Stock Index, 1946-1981

ized and *objective* figures than on *predicted* and *subjective* estimates of future events and their implications for current values.

A rather old-fashioned view holds that the accountant's task is strictly to communicate facts about *past* events, leaving the task of estimating the *future* prospects of a firm (and thus its *present* value) to the security analyst. As a former editor of the *Financial Analysts Journal* put it, the accountant's function is to *measure* and *report*, while that of the security analyst is to *judge* and *value*, but this is not the case in practice.[2] Accountants estimate the present value of future prospects in many ways, although often implicitly. For example the manner in which a capital asset is depreciated is an implicit decision about its economic life. Such decisions affect current earnings, from which analysts estimate value.

The trouble with earnings is accountants' awareness that investors consider current and recent earnings when estimating the value

[2] See Jack L. Treynor, "The Trouble with Earnings," *Financial Analysts Journal*, 28, no. 5 (September/October 1972), 41-43.

Earnings

447

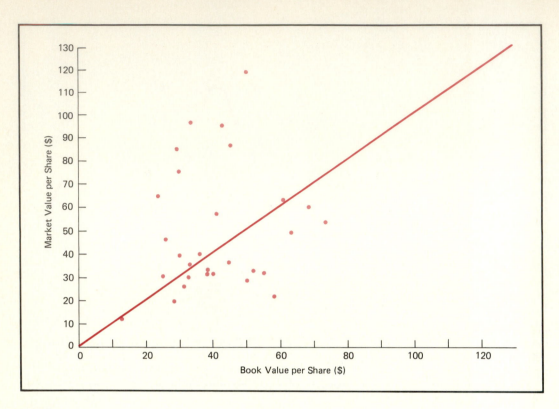

FIGURE 15-2
Market and Book Values, Stocks in Dow-Jones Industrial Average, Year-end, 1982

of a security. This leads to the temptation to try to "manage" earnings to make a firm appear more valuable than it is, thus fooling investors, at least temporarily. Management may pressure accountants to maximize the level of reported earnings, to maintain a high growth rate of reported earnings, and/or to reduce the year-to-year variability of earnings around a growth rate. Some of these activities can be continued only for a limited number of years; others can go on indefinitely.

To obtain a truly independent estimate of value, an analyst must dissect reported earnings. Anyone who estimates value by applying a formula (no matter how complex) to reported earnings is not producing a completely independent estimate.

This is not to say that such figures are irrelevant for security valuation. However, reported earnings are best viewed as a *source of information about the future prospects of a firm*. Since the present value of a firm's equity is related to its future prospects, there should be a *correlation* between reported earnings and price. But since reported earnings generally differ from economic earnings, this correlation will be less than perfect. Accounting earnings are thus an important source of information about value, but neither a perfect source nor the only relevant one.

PRICE-EARNINGS RATIOS

Figure 15-3 provides some evidence on the behavior of overall earnings, prices, and price-earnings ratios for common stocks, as represented by Standard and Poor's Composite Index.

Figure 15-3(a) shows year-end price-earnings ratios. The variation is considerable, indicating that investors do not simply apply a standard multiple to earnings in order to determine an appropriate value.

The curves in Figure 15-3(b) show the *logarithm* of earnings per share (the lower curve) and the logarithm of the price index (the upper curve). Plotting logarithms is equivalent to plotting the original values on a *ratio scale*. In this type of diagram, a given vertical distance

FIGURE 15-3
Price, Earnings, and P/E Ratios, Standard and Poor's Composite Stock Index, Year-end, 1951-1983

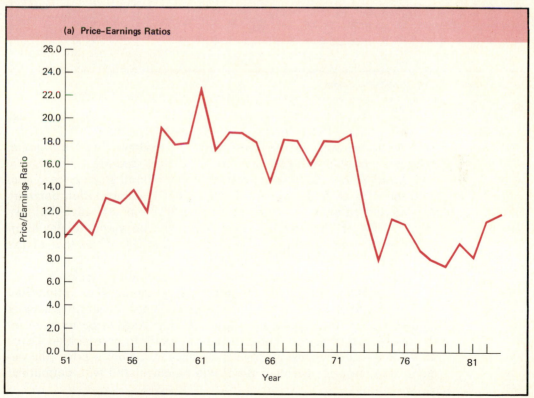

Earnings

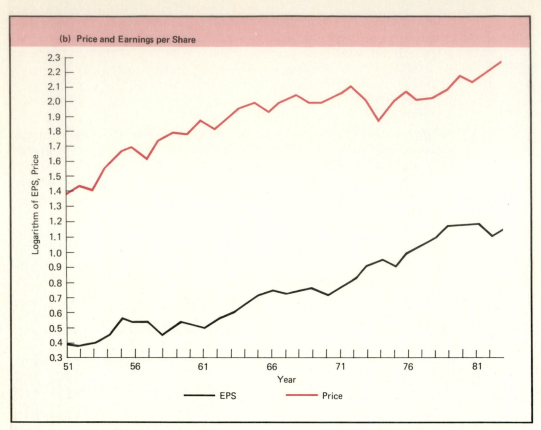

SOURCE: Standard and Poor's *Statistical Service*.

FIGURE 15-3 (*continued*)

represents the same *percentage* change, no matter where it appears, making it possible to compare *relative* changes directly.

Both Figures 15-3(a) and (b) suggest that overall stock prices move with reported earnings, but not in lock step. The correlation between the two sets of values shown in Figure 15-3(b) was .84—high, but less than 1.0. Prices changed less than earnings: the standard deviation of the values on the higher (Price) curve was .21, while that of the values on the lower (EPS) curve was .25.

A similar relationship is found when individual stocks are analyzed, suggesting that some differences in price-earnings ratios may be due to *temporary* differences in earnings. Reported earnings usually include both *permanent* components that are likely to be repeated in the future and *transitory* components not likely to be repeated. Since value depends on future prospects, changes in a stock's price (the numerator in the price-earnings ratio) will be correlated with permanent changes in its earnings (the denominator in the ratio) but not with transitory changes. Transitory changes in earnings will thus change the denominator but not the numerator, causing the price-earnings ratio to change less than in proportion to the total change in earnings.

If this were the only relevant factor, differences in price-earnings ratios would themselves be transitory. But they are not. Figure 15-4 shows the behavior over time of such ratios for two groups of stocks; one includes stocks with high price-earnings ratios at the beginning of the period; the other includes stocks with low price-earnings ratios at the beginning of the period. Over time, the price-earnings ratios tend to *revert to the mean* ratio for the market as a whole. The changes are substantial in the first two years, owing undoubtedly to the influence of transitory components of earnings. But differences persist for many years—indicating that there is more to the phenomenon.

FIGURE 15-4
Price-Earnings Ratios Over Time for Two Groups of Stocks

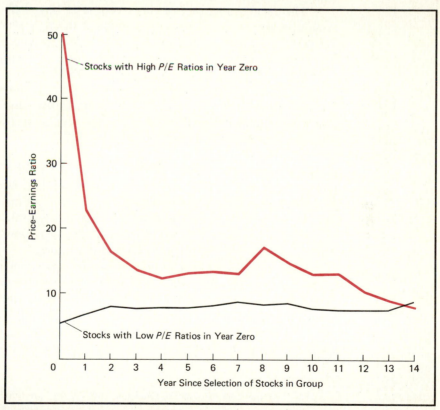

SOURCE: William Beaver and Dale Morse, "What Determines Price-Earnings Ratios?" *Financial Analysts Journal,* July/August 1978.

Earnings

Two explanations can be offered for persistent differences in price-earnings ratios among stocks. First, appropriate discount rates (expected returns) differ because of differences in security attributes. Second, there may be permanent differences between economic and reported earnings due to the use of different accounting methods. There is evidence that the market sees though such differences in reported earnings.[3] Thus it is not surprising that the price-earnings ratios of stocks differ and that some of the differences are long-lasting.

RELATIVE GROWTH RATES OF FIRMS' EARNINGS

Since the average change in earnings for firms as a whole varies considerably from year to year, and in a rather unpredictable way, it is not surprising that the earnings of a given firm do so, too. But the very idea of a "growth stock" suggests that growth in *some* firms' earnings will exceed the average growth of all firms' earnings in most years, while others grow less than the average.

The results of a test of this hypothesis based on a study of 610 industrial companies' earnings from 1950 through 1964 are shown in Table 15-2. In every year, each firm's earnings were compared with the previous year's and the percentage change computed; this was counted as "good" if it was in the top half of such figures for the year and "bad" otherwise. If some firms tend to consistently experience above- or below-average earnings growth, fairly long *runs* of consistently good years should occur for some stocks and fairly long runs of consistently bad years for others.

The first two columns of Table 15-2 indicate the actual number of runs of various lengths. The final column shows the number that would be expected if for every firm a fair coin had been flipped each year, with earnings classified as "good" if the coin came up heads and "bad" if it came up tails. The three columns are remarkably similar. Better-than-average earnings growth in the past does not appear to presage better-than-average growth in the future.

A study[4] using longer time periods for measuring growth reached generally similar conclusions. For each of 323 companies with positive earnings in each year from 1946 through 1965, average growth rates were computed for (1) the period from 1946 through 1955 and (2) the period from 1956 through 1965. Differences among firms' earnings growth rates in the first period accounted for less than 1% of the varia-

[3] See William H. Beaver, *Financial Reporting: An Accounting Revolution* (Englewood Cliffs, N.J.: Prentice-Hall, Inc. 1981) for more information on this and many other aspects of earnings.

[4] John Lintner and Robert Glauber, "Higgledy Piggledy Growth in America," in James Lorie and Richard Brealey, eds., *Modern Developments in Investment Management* (New York: Praeger Publishers, Inc., 1972).

TABLE 15-2
Earnings Growth, 610 Firms, 1950-1964

Length of Run	Actual Number of Runs of Good Years	Actual Number of Runs of Bad Years	Number of Runs of Good or Bad Years Expected if the Odds Each Year Were 50-50, Regardless of Past Performance
1	1,152	1,102	1,068
2	562	590	534
3	266	300	267
4	114	120	133
5	55	63	67
6	24	20	33
7	23	12	17
8	5	6	8
9	3	3	4
10	6	0	2
11	2	0	1
12	1	0	1
13	0	0	0
14	0	1	0

SOURCE: Reprinted from *An Introduction to Risk and Return from Common Stocks* by Richard Brealey by permission of The M.I.T. Press, Cambridge, Massachusetts. Copyright ©1969.

tion in the differences among their earnings growth rates in the second period. However, when adjustments were made for changes in economic activity and only firms with fairly steady earnings growth in the past were considered, slightly more consistency was found: differences in past rates accounted for approximately 16% of the differences in future growth rates.

COMOVEMENT OF FIRMS' EARNINGS

Past changes in security prices are of limited value for the prediction of future changes. And past changes in the overall level of the market are of limited help in the prediction of future market moves. Yet security price changes are related to *concurrent* market (and often industry and/or economic sector) changes, the strengths of the relationships differ among securities, and historic data can generally be utilized to help estimate the relative future strengths of the relationships for different securities. To the extent that accounting earnings are correlated with economic earnings, relationships among the former values for firms may be similar to those among the changes in the latter.

Earnings

TABLE 15-3
The Proportion of the Variance of a Firm's Earnings Attributable to Economywide and Industry Earnings Changes

Industry	PROPORTION ATTRIBUTABLE TO:	
	Economywide Earnings Changes (%)	Additional Influence of Changes in Industry Earnings (%)
Aircraft	11	5
Autos	48	11
Beer	11	7
Cement	6	32
Chemicals	41	8
Cosmetics	5	6
Department stores	30	37
Drugs	14	7
Electricals	24	8
Food	10	10
Machinery	19	16
Nonferrous metals	26	25
Office machinery	14	6
Oil	13	49
Paper	27	28
Rubber	26	48
Steel	32	21
Supermarkets	6	33
Textiles and clothing	25	29
Tobacco	8	19
All firms	21	21

SOURCE: Reprinted from *An Introduction to Risk and Return from Common Stocks* by Richard Brealey by permission of The M.I.T. Press, Cambridge, Massachusetts. Copyright © 1969.

Table 15-3 shows that this is the case, at least to some extent. Earnings reported by 217 corporations from 1948 through 1966 were compared first with the earnings for Standard and Poor's 425-stock index (which served as a surrogate for economywide earnings) and then with the average earnings of all firms in the same industry. The proportion of each firm's earnings variations that could be attributed to each of these factors was determined, and the results were averaged across all the firms in each industry. The results are shown in the table.

Some of the differences among industries may be statistical artifacts of the period analyzed, but some undoubtedly reflect continuing economic relationships—for example, the substantial extent to which the earnings of automobile manufacturers depend on the health of the economy and thus the earnings of all firms.

The final row of Table 15-3 shows the values obtained by averaging over all 217 corporations. Changes in economywide earnings accounted for 21% of the variation in the earnings of the typical firm, and changes in the earnings of firms in its industry accounted for another 21%. Anyone attempting to predict the earnings of a firm should undoubtedly (1) try to estimate the relationship between its earnings and those of the economy as a whole and/or firms in its industry or sector, (2) make predictions of the latter, and then (3) use all these elements in the process of predicting the firm's future earnings.

ACCOUNTING BETAS

Security prices are related to expected future earnings, and the level of the market as a whole is related to expected future economywide earnings. When estimates of the future health of the economy change, the level of the market follows suit. And when estimates of the future level of a firm's earnings change, the price of its stock generally moves as well. Figure 15-5 shows these relationships diagrammatically. As expectations about the future change, causing changes in the price of a stock and the level of the market, we obtain information that can be used to estimate the stock's regular or *market beta*. Its magnitude will depend on the extent to which expectations of the firm's economic

FIGURE 15-5
Earnings, Prices, and Beta Values

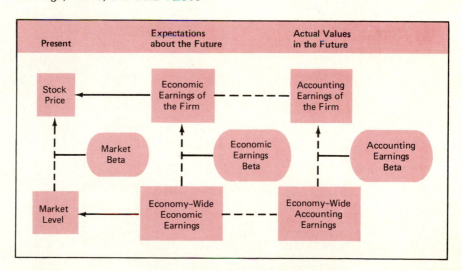

earnings are related to the expectations of economywide economic earnings—a relationship indicated in the figure as the firm's *economic earnings beta*. Clearly, market betas are closely related to such earnings betas.

Unfortunately, direct measures of changes in expected economic earnings are difficult to obtain. In their place analysts generally use changes in *actual* (instead of *expected*) *accounting* (instead of *economic*) earnings. Changes in such earnings can be used (along with book values of equity) to compute an *accounting earnings beta* (or, more simply, an *accounting beta*). While not likely to be as helpful as the directly relevant economic earnings betas, accounting betas

FIGURE 15-6
Accounting and Market Betas, 254 Firms, 1951-1969

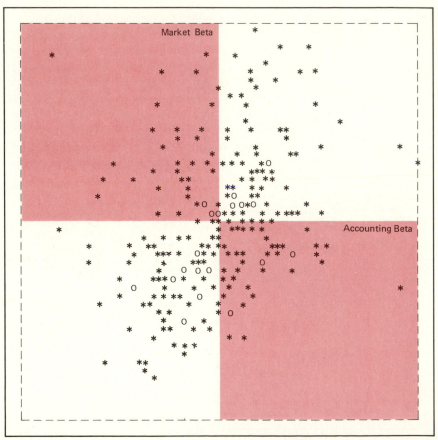

Note: "*" represents one firm, "o" represents more than one firm.

SOURCE: William Beaver and James Manegold, "The Association between Market-determined and Accounting-determined Measures of Systematic Risk: Some Further Evidence," *Journal of Financial and Quantitative Analysis*, X, no. 2 (June 1975), 259.

should nevertheless shed some light on differences in firms' market betas.

Figure 15-6 shows that they do. Each point plots an accounting beta (horizontal axis) and market beta (vertical axis) for one of 254 firms, estimated using data from 1951 through 1969.[5] To compute the accounting betas, each earnings figure was used to compute an (accounting) return on equity by dividing the annual earnings by the beginning book value of assets.[6] Averaging such figures across all firms gave a comparable value for the "market" for each year. A firm's accounting beta over a period of years was then computed by comparing the annual values of its accounting return on equity to those of the market, using standard regression analysis. Market betas were computed in the usual manner, using (in effect) economic returns on equity.

While the two measures obviously differ for most firms, there is a positive relationship, as Figure 15-6 shows. When portfolios were analyzed, instead of individual stocks, the similarities were considerably greater.

EARNINGS SURPRISES AND PRICE CHANGES

A number of studies have shown substantial price changes for stocks of companies reporting earnings differing substantially from consensus expectations. Figure 15-7 shows the median values for (1) forecasted change in earnings per share, (2) actual change in earnings per share, and (3) actual change in stock price during 1970 for three groups of stocks. The first group includes the 50 stocks listed on the New York Stock Exchange that experienced the greatest price increases during 1970, the second is made up of 50 stocks chosen randomly from the Exchange, while the third includes the 50 stocks that experienced the greatest price declines during 1970. Analysts' predictions[7] hardly suggested the differences that occurred. In fact, the median stock in the "bottom 50" was expected to increase earnings by more than that in the "top 50" (+15.3%, compared with +7.7%). Unfortunately, this prediction was disastrously wrong. In the bottom group the median firm's earnings declined 83.0%, while that of the top group increased 21.4%. And, as Figure 15-7 shows, prices very definitely followed suit. Unexpected changes in earnings do indeed affect prices.

[5] William Beaver and James Manegold, "The Association between Market-determined and Accounting-determined Measures of Systematic Risk: Some Further Evidence," *Journal of Financial and Quantitative Analysis*, X, no. 2 (June 1975), 231-84.

[6] Beaver and Manegold (*op. cit.*) used several measures for their study. The values shown in Figure 15-6 were obtained using the ratio of net income before nonrecurring items to the book value of total assets.

[7] The predictions were taken from Standard and Poor's *Earnings Forecaster*, which reports estimates made by a number of investment research organizations.

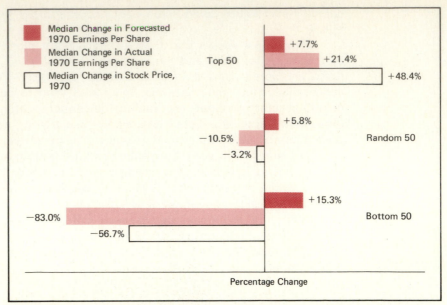

SOURCE: Victor Niederhoffer and Patrick J. Regan, "Earnings Changes, Analysts' Forecasts, and Stock Prices," *Financial Analysts Journal*, 28, no. 3 (May/June 1972), 67.

FIGURE 15-7

Earnings and Price Changes: Selected Stocks Listed on the New York Stock Exchange 1970

But do earnings surprises affect prices before or after their announcement? In a completely efficient market, such information would be reflected in prices as soon as it had been disseminated to a few major market participants. Afterward, only other (new) information would cause substantial price changes.

Deviations from Time-Series Models of Earnings

A comprehensive study involving 2,053 companies from 1974 through 1981[8] provides evidence concerning the speed of response of security prices to earnings announcements. For each company an *expected* earnings figure was computed for each quarter, using the following model of the *time-series behavior* of earnings:

$$E\left(Q_{i,t}\right) = Q_{i,t-4} + a_i\left(Q_{i,t-1} - Q_{i,t-5}\right) + d_i$$

---

[8] George Foster, Chris Olsen, and Terry Shevlin, "Earnings Releases, Anomalies and the Behavior of Security Returns," *The Accounting Review,* October 1984.

where:

$E(Q_{i,t})$ = expected earnings for firm i in quarter t

$Q_{i,t-4}$ = earnings for firm i in quarter $t-4$

$Q_{i,t-1}$ = earnings for firm i in quarter $t-1$

$Q_{i,t,-5}$ = earnings for firm i in quarter $t-5$

a_i = the "adjustment factor" for firm i

d_i = the "drift factor" for firm i

For example, the earnings expected for firm i in the second quarter of 1980 would equal (1) the firm's earnings in the second quarter of 1979 plus (2) a_i times the change in earnings from the first quarter of 1979 to the first quarter of 1980, plus (3) d_i. The values of a_i and d_i would be determined by analysis of the behavior of earnings prior to the second quarter of 1980.

Given actual earnings and an estimate of expected earnings, a *forecast error* can be computed:

$$FE_{i,t} = Q_{i,t} - E(Q_{i,t})$$

where:

$FE_{i,t}$ = the forecast error for the earnings of firm i in quarter t

The forecast error for a quarter is the difference between actual earnings and the amount expected, based on past relationships.

The forecast error provides a measure of "surprise," but it fails to differentiate between stocks for which large earnings fluctuations are routine and those for which they are unusual. The important surprises are those associated with forecast errors that are large by historic standards.

To account for this, a forecast error can be related to previous values to obtain a measure of *standardized unexpected earnings* (*SUE*):

$$SUE_{i,t} = \frac{FE_{i,t}}{\sigma_{i,t}(FE)}$$

where:

$SUE_{i,t}$ = The standardized unexpected earnings for firm i in quarter t

$\sigma_{i,t}(FE)$ = The standardized deviation of forecast errors for the earnings of firm i in quarters *prior* to t

In this case, each earnings announcement was assigned to one of ten SUE deciles. Group 1 included cases with the largest positive SUEs, and group 10 those with the most negative SUEs. Figure 15-8 shows *cumulative abnormal returns* for the ten groups for the period

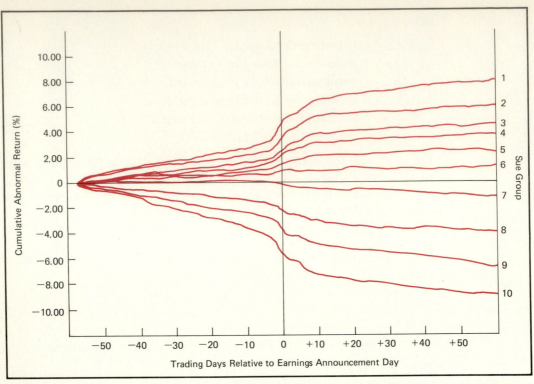

SOURCE: George Foster, Chris Olsen, and Terry Shevlin, "Earnings Releases, Anomalies and the Behavior of Security Returns," *The Accounting Review*, October 1984.

FIGURE 15-8

Cumulative Abnormal Returns for Ten Standardized Unexpected Earnings Groups

from 60 trading days prior to the earnings announcement date to 60 trading days after the date.

Prices of firms that announced unexpectedly high earnings tended to increase prior to the announcement (date 0), suggesting that information not taken into account in this prediction process was becoming available to the market. Prices of firms that announced unexpectedly low earnings tended to decrease prior to the announcement, undoubtedly for the same reason. These changes could not have been exploited by an investor without preknowledge of the actual announcements. Thus the patterns prior to the announcement date do not indicate market inefficiency.

The changes after the announcement dates are more remarkable. Prices of stocks of firms announcing unexpectedly *high* earnings tended to *increase* for many days *after* the announcements, while those of firms announcing unexpectedly *low* earnings tended to *decrease* for many days after the announcements.

These relationships were quite consistent over time. Figure 15-9(a) shows quarter-by-quarter average cumulative abnormal returns from day +1 to day +60 for stocks with very large SUEs. The average value was +3.23%. Cumulative abnormal returns for stocks with large negative SUEs are shown in Figure 15-9(b). The average value was −3.08%. Almost all the values in Figure 15-9(a) were significantly positive, while almost all those in Figure 15-9(b) were significantly negative.

Analysts' Estimates of Future Earnings

How well can analysts forecast earnings? And do their forecasts incorporate information other than that contained in past earnings? Table 15-4 provides some answers to these questions. Two sets of forecasts were examined for the earnings of 50 firms over the period from 1971 through 1975. The first set was obtained by applying sophisticated mechanical models[9] to the firms' previous earnings history. The second set was obtained from published earnings forecasts of security analysts.[10] The latter clearly outperformed the former. For example, 63.5% of the analysts' forecasts were within 25% of the actual earnings values, while only 54.5% of the forecasts made via mechanical means came as close. Analysts appear to base their forecasts on both past earnings and other information; and the latter appears to help.

Revisions in Analysts' Forecasts

When "new news" about a company becomes available, professional security analysts revise their forecasts of firms' earnings. As investors respond to such revisions, security prices adjust to the news.

Will this process be rapid or somewhat slow? Is the information that analysts have recently revised their earnings estimates for a firm valuable only to those who get it early? Should one favor stocks for which earnings estimates have been revised upward in the last month or so and disdain those for which estimates have been revised downward?

Many institutional brokerage firms estimates annual earnings for one or two years in the future. Summaries of forecasts for 2,400 companies from 50 U.S. brokerage firms are routinely collected and disseminated to individual investors in the Zachs Investment Research *Corporate Earnings Estimator* data base. Forecasts for 2,700 companies from over 80 brokerage firms are provided to institutional investors by Lynch, Jones and Ryan through their *Institutional Brokers Estimate System* (*IBES*) data base. Both services may be accessed over telephone lines with computers or computer terminals.

---

[9] That is, Box-Jenkins techniques.

[10] That is, the forecasts published in the *Value Line Investment Survey*.

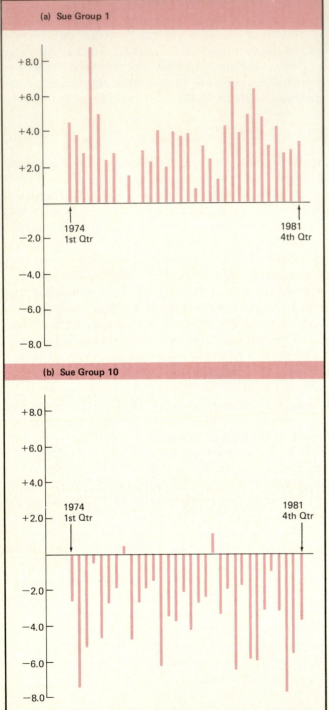

SOURCE: George Foster, Chris Olsen, and Terry Shevlin, "Earnings Releases, Anomalies and the Behavior of Security Returns," *The Accounting Review*, October 1984.

FIGURE 15-9

Cumulative Abnormal Returns for 60 Days after Earnings Announcements

TABLE 15-4

Accuracy of Mechanical and Judgmental Earnings Forecasts

EARNINGS FORECAST ERROR AS A PERCENT OF ACTUAL EARNINGS	PERCENT OF FORECASTS WITH A SMALLER ERROR	
	Mechanical Model	Analysts' Forecasts
5%	15.0%	18.0%
10	26.5	32.0
25	54.5	63.5
50	81.0	86.5
75	87.5	90.5
100	89.5	92.0

SOURCE: Lawrence D. Brown and Michael S. Rozeff, "The Superiority of Analyst Forecasts as Measures of Expectations: Evidence from Earnings," *Journal of Finance*, March 1978.

To calculate a consensus forecast for a firm's earnings in a particular year, the mean of the forecasts from different brokerage firms can be used. In one study[11] the IBES data base was used to classify firms into those for which consensus earnings forecasts (1) increased, (2) stayed the same, or (3) decreased. Returns for securities in each category over the period starting up to one month *after* the forecast date and continuing for eleven more months were determined and averaged.

Table 15-5 shows some of the results. Stocks for which forecasts for earnings one year ahead were increased did not experience signifi-

TABLE 15-5

Forecast Revisions and Abnormal Returns, 1976-1980

REVISION OF CONSENSUS FORECAST FOR:		
One Year Ahead	Two Years Ahead	Average Cumulative Abnormal Return for Months +1 through +12
Increased		+ .04
Decreased		−3.80
Increased	Increased	+ .60
Decreased	Decreased	−4.57

SOURCE: Philip Brown, George Foster, and Eric Noreen, "Security Analyst Multi-year Earnings Forecasts and the Capital Market," unpublished (1984), Table 5.12.

---

[11] Philip Brown, George Foster, and Eric Noreen, "Security Analyst Multi-year Earnings Forecasts and the Capital Market," unpublished (1984).

cantly abnormal returns—the cumulative value over the eleven-month period was +.04%. On the other hand, stocks for which such forecasts were decreased experienced abnormal returns of −3.80%—significantly different from those of other stocks.[12]

Stocks for which forecasts for *both* earnings one year ahead and earnings two years ahead changed in the same direction experienced even greater abnormal returns, as Table 15-5 shows.

Value Line Rankings

Further evidence on the usefulness of quarterly earnings surprises as an ingredient in stock selection is provided by the performance of stocks assigned different rankings for performance over the succeeding twelve months by the *Value Line Investment Survey*.[13] Each week, every one of approximately 1,700 stocks is assigned one of five ranks. By design the categories include the same number of stocks each week, as follows:

Rank	Number of Stocks
1 (highest)	100
2 (above average)	300
3 (average)	900
4 (below average)	300
5 (lowest)	100

Many factors go into the ranking procedure. Not surprisingly, exact details are not made public. However, the key elements[14] are:

1. The last year's earnings and average price relative to the comparable values for the previous ten years (all adjusted for changes in the prices and earnings of the market as a whole), and the stock's average price over the preceding ten weeks relative to that of the preceding 52 weeks (also after adjustment for corresponding changes in the market as a whole). These factors are combined to determine a composite score, using an equation obtained empirically via cross-sectional analysis.

2. The stock's current price-earnings ratio relative to that of the

---

[12] The *t*-statistic was −13.84.

[13] Published by Arnold Bernhard and Co., Inc., New York.

[14] For details see Arnold Bernhard, "Investing in Common Stocks with the Aid of the Value Line Rankings and Other Criteria of Stock Value," Arnold Bernhard and Co., Inc., 1975.

market, compared with the average of the corresponding figures over the last five years.

3. "Earnings momentum": the most recent quarter's earnings are compared with the amount reported four quarters earlier; the stocks for which this ratio is within the top third of the values are assigned a high score, those within the middle third a medium score, and the remainder a low score.

4. "Earnings surprise": the most recent quarter's earnings are also compared with the amount estimated in advance by Value Line's security analysts. Five categories are used, as follows:

Deviation between Actual and Value Line's Estimated Quarterly Earnings

+30% or more (highest)
+15 to +29% (above average)
−14 to +14% (average)
−15 to −29% (below average)
−30% or worse (lowest)

A test[15] of the resulting rankings showed them to be of some value. Beginning in April 1965, five portfolios were formed (on paper). The first included all stocks ranked "1" at the beginning of the month, in equal dollar values; the second included all stocks ranked "2," and so on. At the beginning of the next month each portfolio was altered as necessary to again include equal dollar values of all stocks with the appropriate ranks at the time. The procedure was continued until the end of 1970. Then each portfolio's performance was compared with that of the market (represented by the full set of stocks covered by the Survey). After adjustment for market sensitivity (beta values), the portfolio of top-ranked stocks "beat the market" by about 10% per year, while that of bottom-ranked stocks was beaten by the market by about 10% per year. Both figures were significantly different from zero in a statistical sense.

This does not provide a guaranteed formula for outstanding portfolio performance. No transactions costs were charged in the calculations, and turnover exceeded 130% per year. But the results do suggest that in choosing among stocks, Value Line rankings may prove useful.

One might conjecture that if Value Line rankings "work," it may be due primarily to the use of quarterly earnings (both "momentum"—

---

[15] Fischer Black, "Yes Virginia, There Is Hope: Tests of the Value Line Ranking System," *Financial Analysts Journal,* 29, no. 5 (September/October 1973), 10–14.

which is a form of surprise—and the "surprise" factor itself). Even so, the persistence of such a phenomenon might be a sign of market inefficiency. The Value Line Survey is available to everyone willing to pay the price (approximately $300 per year) and can be found in some libraries and brokerage offices. Value Line rankings can also be obtained from "computer utilities" in machine-readable form as soon as released. The rankings are thus quite public.

Unexpected Earnings and Abnormal Returns

One plausible explanation for these results concerns the cost of information transfer. "New news" must reach a large number of investors before the appropriate new equilibrium price can be completely established. While large institutional investors can obtain news quickly, it may take some time before it reaches smaller institutional investors and individuals. During the period when this is taking place, small abnormal returns may occur on average, but not in every instance.

Alternatively, firms with high SUEs or upward revisions in earnings forecasts may have different exposures to one or more "pervasive factors" than firms with low SUEs or downward revisions in earnings forecasts. If so, subsequent differences in returns may simply reflect different sensitivities to factors. A more complete measure of "normal return" would take this into account, leaving no significant "abnormal" return.

There appear to be considerable ex post differences in returns for firms with different SUEs and revisions in earnings forecasts—differences in returns that cannot be wholly explained by different levels of beta. While the magnitudes may be too small to warrant extensive trading, they do suggest the consideration of SUE values when money must be invested or a portion of an existing portfolio liquidated.

EARNINGS ESTIMATES AND STOCK SELECTION

One way to attempt to identify a mispriced security involves the estimation of all relevant data (e.g., future earnings and/or dividends, the relevant risk class and discount rate) and the insertion of such figures in a valuation equation to estimate the stock's intrinsic value. If a relevant equation is utilized, the resulting value will equal the stock's price if the analyst's estimates agree with the consensus of market opinion. If the analyst disagrees with this consensus, the two values will generally differ. If the difference of opinion concerns only one element, the direction of the implied divergence of price from intrinsic value is easy to predict, and it will be greater the greater the difference between the analyst's estimate and the market consensus.

As a practical matter, many analysts do not utilize detailed valuation procedures. Instead, they search for situations in which their opinion of the future differs from that of the market as a whole. Stocks likely to be most affected positively if and when the correctness of the analyst's opinion becomes obvious are recommended for purchase. Those likely to be most affected negatively are recommended for sale.

The test of any procedure for identifying potentially mispriced stocks is, of course, its record of performance. Figure 15–10 shows how this might be analyzed when an analyst concentrates on predicting earnings. Each prediction is represented by one point. The horizontal axis plots the difference between the analyst's estimate of the stock's future earnings and the consensus estimate at the time, with the difference expressed as a percent of, say, the firm's book value per share of stock. The vertical axis plots a relevant measure of the abnormal portion of the stock's return over the relevant period after the earnings projection was made. If the analyst's estimates are worth considering, there should be some positive relationship between the two values; regression analysis can be used to estimate it and a line such as that shown in Figure 15–10 obtained. Henceforth, the analyst's predictions can be checked against the consensus, the result (e.g., E^*) located on the horizontal axis, and the associated expected abnormal return (e.g., a^*) estimated. This can be used directly by the portfolio manager, with no explicit use of a valuation model at any stage in the process.

Analysts do concentrate on the prediction of relatively near-term earnings and recommend stocks accordingly. This by no means implies that the principles of security valuation do not hold. As always, it is not the form but the substance that counts.

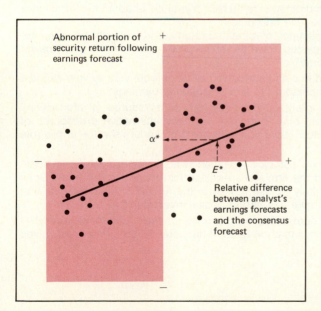

Abnormal portion of security return following earnings forecast

α^*

E^*

Relative difference between analyst's earnings forecasts and the consensus forecast

FIGURE 15-10

Comparing Abnormal Returns with the Difference between an Analyst's Earnings Forecasts and Those of the Consensus of Analysts.

Earnings

Problems

1. Do deviations from expected earnings represent a valid leading indicator of stock price changes? If so, what implications does this have for investment management?

2. Value Line's top-coded stocks appear to have "beaten the market" by about 10% per year. Should investors hold only stocks given such a code by Value Line? Why or why not?

3. Evidence shows that: (1) there is a statistically significant correlation between analysts' estimates of earnings changes and the subsequent actual changes and (2) there is also a significant statistical correlation between earnings changes and stock price changes. Does it then follow that (3) analysts' earnings forecasts must be useful in predicting price changes?

4. Should a security analyst buy stocks for which he or she forecasts large earnings increases and sell stocks for which he or she forecasts small increases, no increases, or decreases? Why or why not?

5. Why might the price of a stock react only partially to an "earnings surprise" on the first day or two after the earnings announcement?

6. Assume that you want to manage portfolios by trading off risk and return with a computerized "optimizer" (e.g., a quadratic programming routine). You have estimates of risk and have access to a "security market plane" estimated by one organization and the "security rankings" estimated by Value Line. You are convinced that all these estimates are valuable.
   a. How could you use the "security market plane" and your risk estimates to obtain estimates of "normal" (efficient market) expected returns for stocks?
   b. How could you use the Value Line rankings (1, . . . , 5) to obtain estimates of expected returns that incorporate both normal and "abnormal" elements?
   c. In what sense would your answer to (b) reflect your belief about the "predictive accuracy" of the Value Line rankings?
   d. When you use your estimates of expected returns and risk with the computer program, a set of suggested holdings will be produced. How will your answer to (b) affect the outcome?

7. Why might a steady trend in a firm's reported earnings from year to year suggest that the figures do not represent the firm's *economic* earnings?

8. If reported earnings are intended to simply provide a "source of information" about the value of a firm, may there not be many alternative procedures of equal use to investors? How might you evaluate a procedure's value in this role after many years of use?

9. The price per share of a firm's stock is less than its book value. Does this indicate that those who now hold the firm's shares have lost money in the past? Does it indicate that they are likely to lose money in the future? Does it indicate that the firm should not undertake any further capital investment?

10. Analysts often evaluate companies on the basis of their "return on equity"— the ratio of reported earnings to book value. What potential problems are involved in this procedure?

16

Options

INTRODUCTION

Option contracts are hardly new. In biblical times, Jacob bought an option to marry Rachel from her father Laban for seven years' labor.[1] But, since provisions against fraud were not enforced by regulatory authorities, Laban was able to switch daughters at the time of delivery, and Jacob found himself married to Leah, the elder daughter. Undeterred, he agreed to work another seven years to obtain Rachel as well. The three did not live happily ever after, but that is another story.

Webster's New Collegiate Dictionary defines an *option* in the financial sense as "a contract conveying a right to buy or sell designated securities or commodities at a specified price during a stipulated period.[2] More precisely, it is an agreement between two parties in which one grants the other the *right*, but not the *obligation*, to buy an asset from or sell it to him or her under stated conditions. The party retaining the option (i.e., having a choice to make) is usually termed the *option buyer*, since he or she must pay for the privilege involved. The party with no subsequent choice is termed the *option seller* or in some cases the *writer* or *maker* of the option.

TYPES OF OPTIONS CONTRACTS

The variety of contracts containing an option feature is bewildering. Even within the domain of publicly traded securities many types can

---

[1] For further details, see the book of *Genesis*, Ch. 29. This slightly forced analogy with modern options comes from Julie Connelly, "How Institutions Are Playing the Options Game," *Institutional Investor*, VIII, no. 2 (February 1974), 45-49, 109-10.

[2] By permission. From *Webster's New Collegiate Dictionary* © 1980 by G. & C. Merriam Co., Publishers of the Merriam-Webster Dictionaries.

be found. Traditionally, only certain instruments are termed options per se; the others, though similar in nature, are designated in other ways.

Call Options

The most prominent type is the *call option*. It gives the buyer the right to "call away" a specified number of shares of a given *underlying security* from the option seller (writer) at a specified price, up to some indicated date. A *European* call option allows the security to be called away only on the specified date. An *American* call option allows it to be called away at any time up to and including the specified date. If and when the security is called away, the option is said to have been *exercised*. The final date on which exercise is allowed is termed the *expiration date*. The price at which the option can be exercised is termed the *exercise price* or, since it is in theory "struck" when the buyer and seller negotiate the terms of the option, the *striking price*.

Call options, usually termed just *calls*, are traded on exchanges in the United States. Each exchange facilitates transactions in calls for a given list of securities for specific expiration dates and exercise prices.

Exchange-traded (or *listed*) options are considerably more important than the *over-the-counter* (OTC) or negotiated options created through the auspices of brokers and dealers. Prior to 1973, put and call dealers and brokers brought would-be-buyers and sellers together, arranged terms, helped with the paperwork, and charged the substantial fees required for the work involved. There was little standardization, low volume, and virtually no *secondary market*. A buyer wishing to close out a position prior to expiration could exercise an option, but it was usually too expensive to try to find another buyer. A seller would usually wait until the expiration date or the day the buyer chose to exercise an option, but it was usually too expensive to try to find another buyer. A seller would usually wait until the expiration date or the day the buyer chose to exercise an option, rather than incur the expense involved in finding someone to take over the obligation.

The advent of listed options changed this. Existing options can now be bought or sold on the exchanges as easily as new ones, and either a buyer or a seller can close out a position at any time.

The buyer of a call option must, of course, pay the seller for the privilege involved. The amount paid is called the *premium*, although "option price" is a more appropriate term.

The *Options Clearing Corporation* greatly facilitates trading in listed options, since such options exist only in the storage of a series of computers located at the Corporation and in the offices of its member firms. Each position in each option contract is recorded. The mechanics for keeping track of all of them are rather complex, but the principles are simple enough. As soon as a buyer and a seller decide to trade a particular option contract and the former pays the latter the agreed-upon premium, the Clearing Corporation steps in, becoming the effective seller to the buyer and the effective buyer from the seller: all direct links between original buyer and seller are severed. If a buyer chooses to exercise an option, the Clearing Corporation will randomly choose a seller who has not closed his or her position in it and *assign* the exercise notice accordingly. The Corporation also *guarantees* delivery of stock if the seller defaults.

The mechanism of a Clearing Corporation makes it possible for a buyer to "sell out" a position and a seller to "buy in" a position at any time. In effect, when offsetting positions in a specific contract are found in the same account, a computer simply wipes out both entries. Thus if an investor buys an "October 20 on Telephone" on Monday and sells another on Tuesday, his or her net position will be zero, and both records can be removed. The second trade is a *closing sale*, since it serves to close out the position created by the first trade. Closing sales transactions thus allow buyers to sell options rather than exercise them. A similar procedure allows a seller to pay to be relieved of the obligation to deliver stock on call. An investor who sells an October 20 on Telephone on Tuesday can buy one on Wednesday. The latter is a *closing purchase* and serves to close out the position entirely.[3]

Call options may be *protected* against stock splits, stock dividends, and even cash dividends on the underlying stock. Since any of these events will cause the stock's price to fall below what it otherwise would have been, they work to the disadvantage of the holder (buyer) of a call option. Virtually all option contracts specify that the exercise price and number of shares will be adjusted to account for splits and stock dividends on the underlying stock. For example, if a firm declares a 50% stock dividend, an outstanding option would be adjusted to cover one-and-a-half as many shares at two-thirds of the original exercise price per share. Over-the-counter options contain provisions for reducing the exercise price by the amounts of any cash dividends paid on the underlying stock, but such protection is not included in listed option contracts, except in the unusual case in which a dividend is formally designated a return of capital.

Put Options

A *put* is an option to sell an underlying stock to the option seller at a specified price, up to a given expiration date. As with calls, there are both American and European puts. The former provide the buyer

---

[3] A more extensive discussion of this clearing process, in the context of the commodity futures market, where it originated, can be found in Chapter 17.

the option of putting the stock at any time before the expiration date; the latter can be exercised only on one date.

The exercise price and the number of shares in both listed and over-the-counter put contracts are automatically adjusted to account for splits and stock dividends on the underlying stock. Over-the-counter puts also provide for reductions in exercise price equal to the amounts of any cash dividends paid on the underlying security.

OPTION TRADING

Exchanges open trading in a new set of options periodically. When established, each option has roughly nine months remaining before expiration with a standardized exercise price equal to the price of the underlying stock, rounded, for example, to the nearest multiple of $5. Subsequently, as the stock price varies, new options may be declared eligible for trading. Once on the list, an option remains until expiration. Options on common stocks generally expire on the Saturday after the third Friday of the specified month; those on other instruments may expire on different days.

In 1984 options on stocks and stock indices were traded on the Chicago Board Options Exchange and the American, Pacific, Philadelphia, and New York Stock Exchanges. Options on futures contracts were traded at the Chicago Board of Trade, Comex, Chicago Mercantile Exchange, and the New York Futures Exchange.

Prior to any adjustment for stock splits and so on, options are traded in contracts, each of which covers 100 shares of stock. Figure 16-1 shows an example of a report on a day's trades in one set of such contracts. Call prices are shown first, followed by prices for puts. The first entry for GM (General Motors) refers to options written with an exercise price of 60. The first call contract shown entitled the holder to call away 100 shares of General Motors at $60 per share any time up to and including the third Friday of June. The last trade of the day was made at a price of $4 per one-share option, or $400 per contract. The price at which General Motors last traded during the day on the New York Stock Exchange is also shown—in this case, it was $63¼ per share.

Figure 16-1 shows that the "June 60 puts" on GM sold for 5/16. Thus a purchaser paid $5/16 per one-share option, or $31.25 per contract for the right to "put" 100 shares of General Motors to the seller (writer) at a price of $60 per share any time up to the third Friday of June.

Some options are not traded during a day—these are indicated by the letter "r" in Figure 16-1. Others, though included because of the format of the report, have not been introduced and are thus unavailable for trading; they are indicated by the letter "s".

At the bottom of the listings for an exchange are shown the total

Listed Options Quotations

Friday, May 25, 1984

Closing prices of all options. Sales unit usually is 100 shares. Security description includes exercise price. Stock close is New York or American exchange final price.

Chicago Board

Option & NY Close	Strike Price	Calls—Last			Puts—Last		
		Jun	Sep	Dec	Jun	Sep	Dec
Apache	..10	3 3/8	r	r	r	r	r
13 5/8	...15	1/8	1/2	r	1 3/4	r	r
BrisMy	..40	4 3/4	6	r	1/8	5/8	7/8
44 1/2	...45	3/4	2 1/2	r	1 1/8	2	2 5/8
44 1/2	...50	1-16	3/4	1 1/2	r	r	r
Bruns	.27 1/2	1/8	s	s	r	s	s
24 3/4	...20	4 7/8	5 3/8	r	r	1/4	r
24 3/4	...25	3/4	2	3	1 1-16	1 7/8	2 5/8
24 3/4	...30	1-16	3/4	r	r	r	r
Celan	65	r	r	r	1/8	r	r
69 1/4	...70	1 1/4	3 5/8	r	1 7-16	r	r
69 1/4	...75	1/4	r	r	5 1/2	r	r
Chamin	.20	3/4	1 9-16	2 3/8	3/4	1 5-16	1 1/2
19 3/4	...25	r	5-16	r	r	r	r
CompSc	.15	1-16	9-16	1 1/8	r	2 1/2	r
Dow Ch	.25	r	5 1/4	r	r	r	r
29 3/8	...30	9-16	1 7/8	2 3/8	1	1 1/2	2
29 3/8	...35	1-16	7-16	7/8	r	r	r
Esmark	.40	18 5/8	r	19	r	1-16	r
58 5/8	...45	13 3/4	13 1/2	13 5/8	r	r	3/8
58 5/8	...50	8 3/4	9	r	1-16	1/8	r
58 5/8	...55	s	4 3/8	r	s	5-16	r
58 5/8	...60	s	3-16	3/8	s	1 1/2	r
FBost	...35	2	r	r	1/2	1 1/2	r
36 1/4	...40	1/4	r	2	r	r	4 1/2
36 1/4	...45	1-16	r	r	r	r	r
Ford o	.36 5/8	1 1/8	s	s	1	s	s
36 5/8	...40	3/8	s	s	3 1/4	s	s
Ford	30	6 3/4	7 3/4	8 3/4	1-16	3/8	7/8
36 5/8	...35	2 3-16	3 7/8	5	3/8	1 1/2	2 1/4
36 5/8	...40	3/8	1 5/8	2 3/4	3 3/8	4 1/2	5
36 5/8	...45	1-16	5/8	1 3/8	r	r	r
36 5/8	...50	r	1/4	s	r	r	s
Gen El	..45	7 3/8	7 3/4	s	1-16	5-16	s
52 3/8	...50	2 1/2	4	5	7-16	1 1/2	2
52 3/8	...55	5-16	1 3/4	3	3 5/8	4	r
52 3/8	...60	1-16	9-16	1 3/8	r	r	r
G M	60	4	6	7 1/4	5-16	1 3-16	2 1/8
63 1/4	...65	3/4	2 13-16	4 1/4	2 1/8	3 1/2	4 5/8
63 1/4	...70	1-16	1 1-16	2 1/4	6 1/2	6 1/2	r
63 1/4	...75	1-16	1/2	1 1/8	r	r	r
63 1/4	...80	r	3-16	s	16 1/2	r	s
Glf Wn	..25	r	6 1/2	r	r	r	r
31 1/8	...30	1 3/4	3	4	5/8	1 1/4	2
31 1/8	...35	1/4	1 1/8	2	4 1/4	r	r
31 1/8	...40	r	3/8	1	r	9	r
HughTl	..15	2	2 3/4	3 1/8	1/8	3/8	9-16
16 7/8	...20	1/8	11-16	1	3 1/4	3 1/4	3 5/8
16 7/8	...25	r	1-16	r	r	r	r
I T T	...30	s	r	5 3/4	s	r	r
34 1/8	...35	1/2	1 1/2	2 1/4	1 1/8	1 3/4	2 1/2
34 1/8	...40	1/8	1/2	7/8	r	6 1/4	r
34 1/8	...45	r	r	3/8	r	r	r
34 1/8	...50	1-16	r	s	r	r	s
K mart	..25	3	4	r	1-16	3/8	15-16
28	30	5-16	1 1/4	2 1/8	2 1/4	2 9-16	r
28	35	r	3/8	3/4	r	r	r
Litton	...55	r	r	r	1-16	r	r
66 3/4	...60	7	9	10 1/2	1/8	15-16	r
66 3/4	...65	3	5 1/2	7	3/4	2 1/4	3 1/4
66 3/4	...70	5/8	2 7/8	r	3 5/8	5	r
66 3/4	...75	1/8	1 1/4	r	r	r	r
MaryK	..15	1-16	5/8	r	2 3/4	2 7/8	r
Mc Don	.60	3 1/4	r	r	1/2	1 1/4	1 3/8
62 1/2	...65	5/8	2 3/4	r	2 3/4	3 3/8	3 3/8
62 1/2	...70	1-16	1 1/8	r	7 1/4	7	r
62 1/2	...75	r	1/2	s	12	r	s
Mid SU	..10	r	2 3/4	r	r	3-16	3/8
12 5/8	...15	r	1/8	1/8	r	r	r
N C R	.23 3/4	r	r	r	3-16	7/8	1 3/8
25 5/8	.27 1/2	5-16	1 7-16	2 1/2	2 7-16	2 3/4	r
25 5/8	.32 1/2	r	3/8	s	r	r	s
25 5/8	...25	1 1/4	2 1/2	3 1/4	5/8	1 7-16	2
25 5/8	...30	1-16	3/4	1 1/2	r	5	r

FIGURE 16-1
Listed Options Quotations.

volume (number of contracts traded) and open interest (number of contracts purchased but neither liquidated in the secondary market, expired, nor exercised) for calls and puts.

Quotations for all options are reported in the format shown in Figure 16-1. Additional information is provided for the "most active" options on each of several exchanges every day. Figure 16-2 provides an example. Both the change from the prior trading day's "last price" and the sales (in numbers of contracts) are shown.

Trading in options is far from continuous. In the financial press it is not unusual to find prices for various options that appear to be

Most Active Options

Philadelphia Exchange

	Sales	Last	Chg.	N.Y. Close
CALLS				
DomRs Jul20	7065	$2\frac{5}{8}$	$-\frac{1}{4}$	$22\frac{5}{8}$
E D S Jun40	3802	$2\frac{5}{8}$	$+\frac{1}{2}$	$38\frac{1}{4}$
Cty In Jul45	1884	9-16	+ 3-16	40
E D S Jun35	1818	$5\frac{1}{8}$	+ 1	$38\frac{1}{4}$
E D S Jun45	1724	1	+ 1-16	$38\frac{1}{4}$
PUTS				
Cty In Jul40	1945	$2\frac{1}{8}$	$+\frac{5}{8}$	40
Cmdrln Aug30	1314	$4\frac{1}{2}$	$+1\frac{3}{4}$	$27\frac{1}{4}$
Cmdrln Aug25	1107	$1\frac{5}{8}$	$+\frac{3}{4}$	$27\frac{1}{4}$
E D S Jun35	780	$1\frac{7}{8}$	$-\frac{5}{8}$	$38\frac{1}{4}$
Coleco Jul15	712	$1\frac{3}{8}$	− 5-16	$15\frac{1}{8}$

SOURCE: Reprinted with permission of *The Wall Street Journal*. © Dow Jones and Company, Inc., May 29, 1984. All Rights Reserved.

FIGURE 16-2
"Most Active Options" Quotations

"out of line" with one another or with the price of the underlying stock. It is well to remember that each listed price is that of the last trade of the day, and that the trades may have taken place at different times. Apparent price disparities may simply reflect trades that occurred before and after major news, rather than concurrent values at which obviously profitable trades could have been made.

Margin

The buyer of an option desires some assurance that the seller can deliver as required if the option is exercised. In the case of a call, stock is to be delivered in return for the exercise price. In the case of a put, money is to be delivered in return for stock. In either case, the net cost to the option seller will be the absolute difference between the exercise price and the stock's market value at the time of exercise. For listed options, the Clearing Corporation guarantees the buyer that this liability will be met. For over-the-counter options, a similar guarantee is provided by a brokerage firm via *endorsement* of the option contract. In each case the seller is also required to provide some sort of *margin* or backing to guarantee fulfillment of his or her obligation.

Nonstock Options

Not all options are written on individual issues of common stock. In recent years, many new and somewhat exotic options have been listed on existing exchanges and new exchanges opened to specialize in such instruments.

Index Options

A call option on General Motors stock is relatively simple to implement. Upon exercise, the buyer literally calls away 100 shares of GM stock.

The call writer is expected to physically deliver the shares. In practice, both may find it advantageous to close their positions to avoid the costs associated with physical transfer of shares. In this event, the buyer may expect a gain (and the seller a loss) approximately equal to the difference between the current market price of the security and the option exercise price.

It would be entirely feasible to specify that upon expiration no stock would change hands at all. Instead, the writer could be required to pay the buyer an amount equal to the difference between the current price of the security and the exercise price of the call option.

In the event of exercise of a put, the writer could be expected to pay the buyer an amount equal to the difference between the exercise price of the option and the current market price.

While listed options on individual securities retain the obligation to "deliver," the realization that "cash settlement" can serve as a substitute has allowed the creation of a major set of financial markets.

An *index option* is based on the level of an *index of stock prices*. Some indices are designed to reflect movements in the stock market, broadly construed. Other "specialized" indices are intended to capture changes in the fortunes of particular industries or sectors.

Table 16-1 shows major indices on which options were offered in 1984. Some are highly specialized, including only a few stocks. Others are broadly representative of major portions of the stock market. The AMEX Market Value Index covers all the stocks on the American Stock Exchange, while the NYSE Composite Index covers all the stocks on the New York Stock Exchange. Standard and Poor's 500 Stock Index

TABLE 16-1
Major Stock Index Options, 1984

Exchange on Which Options Are Traded	Index	Approximate Number of Stocks
American	AMEX Computer Technical	30
American	AMEX Major Market Value	20
American	AMEX Market Value	800
American	AMEX Oil and Gas	30
Chicago Board	Standard and Poor's 100	100
Chicago Board	Standard and Poor's 500	500
Chicago Board	Standard and Poor's Transportation	20
New York	NYSE Composite	1500
New York	NYSE Telephone	8
Pacific	Pacific Technical	100
Philadelphia	Phil. Gaming Hotel	9

covers 500 large stocks traded on the New York and American Stock Exchanges and over-the-counter.

Most of the indices on which options are written are *value-weighted*—computed by multiplying each stock's price by the number of shares outstanding, then adding the results. A few of the indices are *equal-weighted*—computed by simply adding up the prices of the stocks. Most notable of the equal-weighted indices is the AMEX Major Market Value Index. Inclusion of many stocks from the Dow Jones Industrial Average, and a similar type of computation, lead to a high correlation between it and the DJIA.

Figure 16-3 shows quotations for index options. Contracts are not stated in terms of numbers of shares. Instead, the size of a contract is determined by multiplying the level of the index by a *multiplier* specified by the exchange on which the option is traded. The premium (price) of an option traded on the American or Chicago Board Options Exchange times the applicable multiplier indicates the total amount paid. Premiums for index options traded on the New York Stock Exchange are always multiplied by 100 to determine the total amount paid. At exercise, the difference between the quoted exercise price and the value of the index is multiplied by the applicable multiplier to determine the amount of cash that must be paid to the option buyer by the writer.

Foreign Currency Options

Figure 16-4 shows quotations for *options on foreign currencies*. These are similar to stock options—on exercise the underlying security must be delivered. Since each option involves units of a "foreign" (non-United States) currency, delivery is made in a bank account abroad (in the country of origin of the currency in question).

Interest-Rate Options

Options are also traded on *debt instruments* such as U.S. Treasury securities (bills, bonds, and notes), certificates of deposit, and Government National Mortgage Association pass-through certificates. Options on Treasury bonds and notes are based on specific issues, which must be delivered on exercise. Options on Treasury bills require delivery of a *current bill*—i.e., one newly issued in the week in which settlement is made. Options on other instruments may allow a choice of alternatives for delivery, with the exercise price adjusted according to formula.

Futures Options

Chapter 17 discusses *futures contracts*—agreements to deliver a commodity or security at some date in the future for a previously agreed-

Index Options

Chicago Board

S&P 100 INDEX

Strike Price	Calls–Last June	July	Aug	Puts–Last June	July	Aug
140	....	....	....	1/16	....	....
145	6⅛	7¾	9	⅜	1⅛	1 9/16
150	2 7/16	4⅜	5½	1¾	2⅞	3½
155	11/16	2 1/16	3	5⅛	5¾	6¼
160	⅛	13/16	1⅜	9⅞	10	10⅛
165	1/16	¼	⅝	14¾	14¾	....
170	1/16	1/16	¼	....	....	....
175	....	....	⅛	....	....	....

Total call volume 81,134 Total call open int. 395,762
Total put volume 106,657 Total put open int. 296,350
The index: High 150.76; Low 149.34; Close 150.25, +0.51

S&P 500 INDEX

Strike Price	Calls–Last June	Sept	Puts–Last June	Sept
150	....	....	¾	....
155	....	....	3½	5

Total call volume 0 Total call open int. 339
Total put volume 25 Total put open int. 281
The index: High 152.02; Low 150.85; Close 151.62, +0.39

American Exchange

MAJOR MARKET INDEX

Strike Price	Calls–Last June	July	Aug	Puts–Last June	July	Aug
105	4¼	5⅜	....	5/16	¾	1
110	1	2⅛	3¼	2 1/16	2 11/16	2 13/16
115	⅛	11/16	1 7/16	6⅜	6½	....
120	1/16	3/16	⅜	11	11½	....

Total call volume 7218 Total call open int. 27,256
Total put volume 6216 Total put open int. 26,219
The index: High 109.11; Low 108.09; Close 108.61, +0.20

AMEX MARKET VALUE INDEX

Strike Price	Calls–Last June	July	Aug	Puts–Last June	July	Aug
200	1¾	3¾	5½	3½	4¾	5⅝
205	7/16	2	....	7¼	....	....
210	¼	11/16	....	12	11¾	....
215	⅛	....	....	16½	....	....
220	....	....	....	21½	....	....

Total call volume 234 Total call open int. 1839
Total put volume 454 Total put open int. 1730
The index: High 198.35; Low 197.79; Close 198.35, +0.39

COMPUTER TECHNOLOGY INDEX

Strike Price	Calls–Last June	July	Aug	Puts–Last June	July	Aug
85	2½	4	5½	1⅜	2½	....
90	9/16	....	2⅞	4⅝	....	....
95	⅛	¾	....	10	....	....

Total call volume 743 Total call open int. 7641
Total put volume 1076 Total put open int. 4635
The index: High 86.07; Low 85.06; Close 85.41, +0.22

OIL & GAS INDEX

Strike Price	Calls–Last June	July	Aug	Puts–Last June	July	Aug
105	....	....	....	1/16	....	....
110	....	....	....	¼	....	....
115	2⅝	....	3¾	15/16	1½	....
120	11/16	1⅝	2	....	....	....
125	⅛	....	....	....	....	....

Total call volume 158 Total call open int. 922
Total put volume 45 Total put open int. 360
The index: High 116.69; Low 115.56; Close 116.66, +.79

N.Y. Stock Exchange

NYSE OPTIONS INDEX

Strike Price	Calls–Last June	July	Aug	Puts–Last June	July	Aug
85	2 9/16	3¾	3⅞	⅜	⅞	1 3/16
90	5/6	1	1⅝	3	3¼	3⅝
95	1/16	3/16	⅜	8	7⅞	....
100	....	....	8	....	....	....

Total call volume 6346. Total call open int. 60,883.
Total put volume 6572. Total put open int. 41,188.
The index: High 87.31; Low 86.72; Close 87.12, +0.17

Philadelphia Exchange

GAMING/HOTEL INDEX

Strike Price	Calls–Last June	July	Aug	Puts–Last June	July	Aug

(No Trades)

Total call volume 0 Total call open int. 104
Total put volume 0 Total put open int. 19
The index: High 77.39; Low 76.60; Close 76.92, +0.02

GOLD/SILVER INDEX

Strike Price	Calls–Last June	July	Aug	Puts–Last June	July	Aug
105	9½	....	11½	⅜	1¼	....
110	5⅜	5⅞	....	1¼	2⅞	3⅝
115	2½	4	5⅞	3⅝	5¼	....
120	1⅜	2⅝	....	7⅛	8⅜	....
125	½	1¼	....	....	13½	....
130	1/16	....	....	....	....	....
135	....	....	....	23	....	....

Total call volume 622 Total call open int. 1848
Total put volume 200 Total put open int. 955
The index: High 114.04; Low 108.59; Close 113.36, +4.82

Pacific Exchange

TECHNOLOGY INDEX

Strike Price	Calls–Last June	July	Aug	Puts–Last June	July	Aug
95	....	....	....	13/16	....	....
100	2½	....	....	2½	3½	4¼
105	⅜	2	....	6	....	....
110	3/16	⅝	1¾	....	....	....

Total call volume 104 Total call open int. 947
Total put volume 116 Total put open int. 978
The index: High 99.72; Low 98.88; Close 99.20, -unch-

FIGURE 16-3
Index Options Quotations.

SOURCE: Reprinted with permission of *The Wall Street Journal*. © Dow Jones and Company, Inc., May 29, 1984. All Rights Reserved.

```
Foreign Currency Options

Philadelphia Exchange
                    Friday, May 25, 1984
Option &      Strike
Underlying     Price    Calls-Last        Puts-Last
                     Jun  Sep  Dec    Jun  Sep  Dec

12,500 British Pounds-cents per unit.
BPound      135      r   5.70    r      r   1.20  1.90
138.32     .140    0.60  2.85    r      r   3.50    r
138.32     .145    0.05  1.05  2.05     r     r   6.80
138.32     .150      r   0.40    r      r     r     r
50,000 Canadian Dollars-cents per unit.
CDollar     .80      r     r     r      r   2.65    r
62,500 West German Marks-cents per unit.
DMark        35      r     r     s    0.04    r     s
36.72      ..36    0.98  1.75  2.33   0.11  0.39  0.49
36.72      ..37    0.33    s     r    0.50  0.80    r
36.72      ..38    0.11  0.72  1.25   1.23  1.40    r
36.72      ..39    0.02  0.40  0.76     r     r     r
36.72      ..40    0.01  0.22  0.55     r     r     r
6,250,000 Japanese Yen-100ths of a cent per unit.
JYen       ...41     r   2.90    s      r     r     s
42.13      ..42      r     r   2.75   0.03    r     r
43.13      ..43    0.43  1.34    r      r   0.46    r
43.13      ..44    0.13  0.78  1.40     r   0.84    r
43.13      ..45    0.04  0.39  0.94     r     r     r
43.13      ..46      r   0.20    r      r   2.89    r
62,500 Swiss Francs-cents per unit.
SFranc     ...43     s     r   3.64     s     r     r
44.59      ..44    0.91  1.94    r    0.18  0.30    r
44.59      ..45    0.29  1.26    r    0.58    r     r
44.59      ..46    0.08  0.78    r    1.42    r     r
44.59      ..47    0.03  0.43  1.12     r     r     r
44.59      ..48    0.01  0.25  0.66     r     r     r
44.59      ..49      r   0.11    s   14.08    r     s
Total call vol.    4,885      Call open int.    57,540
Total put vol.     1,219      Put open int.     23,254
r-Not traded.  s-No option offered.  o-Old.
Last is premium (purchase price).
```

FIGURE 16-4
Foreign Currency Options Quotations

upon price. Traditional futures contracts cover commodities, but newer ones call for delivery of securities, foreign currencies, and so on. A major recent innovation is a futures contract for "delivery" of a stock index. Not surprisingly, the index is not actually delivered—instead, cash settlement is used.

Figure 16-5 shows quotations for *options on futures contracts*. In each case delivery is required on exercise. However, the underlying security, currency, or index is not delivered. Instead, the buyer has an option to call (or put) a specified *futures contract* for the underlying security, currency, or index. When such an option is exercised, the writer also pays the option buyer an amount equal to the difference between the current price of the futures contract and the exercise price of the option to "mark the future to market."

OPTION COMBINATIONS

Race tracks offer bettors exotic combinations via the "daily double" and "exacta" races. Options buyers and sellers can put together strips, straps, straddles, and even more exotic combinations of options.

A *straddle* is a package involving one put and one call, on the same stock, at the same striking (exercise) price, and with the same

Futures Options

Friday, May 25, 1984

Chicago Board of Trade

TREASURY BONDS—$100,000; points and 64ths of 100%

Strike Price	Calls—Last Sep	Dec	Mar	Puts—Last Sep	Dec	Mar
54	....	....	....	0-08	....	0-54
58	2-52	....	....	0-52	1-36	....
60	1-44	2-05	2-30	1-36	2-31	....
62	0-60	1-20	1-50	2-49	3-42	....
64	0-28	0-52	1-10	4-17	5-01	....
66	0-12	0-29	0-50	5-62	6-43	....
68	0-04	0-15	....	7-62	8-29	....
70	0-02	0-08	....	9-62	....	....
72	0-01	0-05	....	11-62	....	....
74	0-01	0-03	....	13-62	14-27	....
76	0-01	0-01	....	....	....	....
78	0-01	0-01	....	....	....	....
80	0-01	....	....	....	....	....

Est. total vol. 30,000
Calls: Thurs. vol. 33,305; open int. 140,121
Puts: Thurs. vol. 15,516; open int. 46,345

Comex, New York

GOLD—100 troy ounces; dollars per troy ounce.

Strike Price	Calls—Last Aug	Oct	Dec	Puts—Last Aug	Oct	Dec
340	....	64.50	....	.10	.50	....
360	38.00	44.50	53.00	.70	1.70	1.80
380	20.00	28.00	35.00	3.10	4.30	4.50
400	8.00	14.40	22.30	10.80	10.00	9.00
420	3.20	7.10	12.80	25.00	21.50	19.00
440	1.10	3.20	7.80	44.00	36.00	31.00
460	.50	....	3.80	63.50	....	47.00
480	.20	....	1.90	....	....	....
500	.10	....	....	....	....	....
530	.10	....	....	....	....	....

Est. total vol. 14,000
Calls: Thurs. vol. 5,625; open int. 40,714
Puts: Thurs. vol. 2,472; open int. 21,498

Chicago Mercantile Exchange

S&P 500 STOCK INDEX—Price = $500 times premium.

Strike Price	Calls—Settle Jun	Sep	Dec	Puts—Settle Jun	Sep	Dec
145	....	....	....	0.20	1.05	....
150	2.90	....	....	1.05	2.40	3.00
155	0.70	3.85	....	3.85	4.45	5.00
160	0.10	2.00	....	8.25	7.50	7.40
165	0.05	1.00	2.90	13.20	11.45	10.35
170	.002	0.40	....	18.15	....	....
175	.002	0.20	....	....	....	....
180	.002	0.10	....	....	....	....
185	.002	....	....	....	....	....

Estimated total vol. 2003
Calls: Thurs. vol. 2584; open int. 16,050
Puts: Thurs. vol. 1673; open int. 14,384

W. GERMAN MARK—125,000 marks, cents per mark

Strike Price	Calls—Settle June	Sept	Puts—Settle June	Sept
34	....	....	0.01	....
35	1.83	2.47	0.02	0.18
36	0.89	1.71	0.08	0.35
37	0.26	1.09	0.44	0.72
38	0.07	0.64	1.26	1.24
39	0.03	0.38	2.22	1.95
40	0.01	0.20	3.20	2.70
41	0.01	0.09	....	3.67
42	0.01	0.03	....	....

Estimated total vol. 3,792.
Calls: Thurs vol. 2,672; open int. 28,409.
Puts: Thurs vol. 870; open int. 10,825.

N.Y. Futures Exchange

NYSE Composite Index—Price = $500 times premium.

Strike Price	Calls—Settle Jun	Sep	Dec	Puts—Settle Jun	Sep	Dec
84	3.75	5.70	....	.25	.95	....
86	2.20	4.25	5.80	.70	1.50	1.80
88	1.05	2.95	4.45	1.55	2.20	2.45
90	.50	2.05	3.40	3.00	3.30	3.40
92	.15	1.35	2.50	4.65	4.60	4.50
94	.05	.85	1.85	6.50	6.40	5.85
96	.05	.50	1.30	8.50	7.75	7.30
98	.05	.30	.90	10.50	9.55	8.90
100	.05	.20	.65	12.50	11.45	10.65

Estimated total vol. 844
Calls: Thurs vol. 1,979; open int. 7,845
Puts: Thurs vol. 347; open int. 2,752

FIGURE 16-5
Futures Options Quotations.

expiration date. A *strip* is similar, but in this case two puts are combined with one call. A *strap* combines two calls and one put.

OTHER INSTRUMENTS WITH OPTION FEATURES

Many securities are "optionlike." In some cases the option is explicit; others involve more subtle relationships.

Executive Compensation Options

Many corporations give their executives options to purchase stock as an incentive device or to help the executive better manage tax liabilities. Such options typically do not expire while the individual remains with the firm and cannot be freely traded. Formally, the executive is the buyer and the corporation the seller; the premium is usually paid in hard work, increased devotion to the firm, and/or a lower salary.

Bond Call Provisions

As discussed in Chapter 11, many firms issue bonds with call provisions. This amounts to the sale of a straight bond and the concurrent purchase by the corporation of a call option sold by the purchaser of the bond. The premium is paid by the corporation in the form of a lower price for the bond than for one lacking the call provision. The seller of the call is the bond purchaser.

Bond call provisions usually can be exercised only after some specified date (e.g., five years after issue) and prior to another (the bonds' maturity date). Moreover, the exercise price may be different for different exercise dates. The implicit call option is thus both longer-lived and more complex than those traded on the listed options markets.

Warrants

A *stock purchase warrant* or, more simply, a *warrant* is a call option issued by the firm whose stock serves as the underlying security. There are some exceptions: for example, occasionally a firm will issue warrants for some other security that it owns (e.g., that of a subsidiary).

At the time of issue, a warrant usually has a longer time to expiration (e.g., five or more years) than a typical call option. Some *perpetual warrants*, with no expiration date, have also been issued.

Most warrants are protected against stock splits and stock dividends, but few provide protection against cash dividends. Exercise prices may be fixed, or the amount may be programmed to change during the life of the warrant, usually increasing in steps. The initial exercise price is typically set to exceed the price of the underlying security at the time the warrant is issued, often by a substantial amount.

Generally, warrants may be exercised before expiration—i.e., they are American call options—but some require an initial waiting period.

At time of issue, one warrant typically entitles the holder to purchase one share of stock for the appropriate exercise price. However, adjustments for stock splits and so on can alter the ratio, leading to many cases in which one warrant can be used to purchase more or less than one share of stock.

Warrants are often issued along with other securities to "sweeten" an offering. For example, a bond with warrants attached may be sold as a package. In some cases the warrants are *nondetachable*, except upon exercise or possibly the maturity of the bond. In other cases the warrants are *detachable* and may be traded separately.

Warrants may be distributed to stockholders in lieu of a stock or cash dividend or sold directly as a new security issue.

Terms associated with a warrant are contained in a *warrant agreement*, which serves the same function as an indenture for a bond issue. The scope of the warrant holder's protection is defined (for example, the treatment of warrants in the event of merger, reorganization, and so on), along with any relevant restrictions on corporate behavior.

Some warrants issued with bonds have an additional attribute. Although they may be detached and exercised in the normal way, with cash, an alternative is provided. Bonds from the initial issue may be used in lieu of cash to pay the exercise price, and the bonds will be valued *at par* for this purpose. This tends to prop up the price of such a *usable bond* and to maintain a closer relationship between the two securities than in the more common case in which detachable warrants must be exercised with cash.

One difference between warrants and options is the limitation on the amount of the former outstanding. A specific number of warrants of a particular type will be issued; the total cannot easily be increased and typically will be reduced as the warrants are exercised. An option can be created whenever two parties wish to create one: the number outstanding is thus not fixed. Exercise of an option on its stock has no more effect on a corporation than a transaction in the stock on the secondary market. But exercise of a warrant does. It leaves the corporation with more cash, fewer warrants outstanding, and more stock outstanding. Old stockholders find themselves with a smaller proportion of a larger firm.

Warrants are traded on major stock exchanges and on the over-the-counter market. Quotations for those with active markets are provided in the financial press in the sections devoted primarily to stocks.

Rights

Subscription warrants are issued to give stockholders their *preemptive right* to subscribe to a new issue before the general public. Each share of stock receives a *right*. A stated number of rights plus a specified subscription price are required to obtain one new share. To insure sale of the new stock, the subscription price is usually set below reasonable expectations of its market value. This does not mean that new subscribers get a bargain, since they must pay old stockholders for the required rights, which become valuable as a result.

Rights are generally short-lived (from two to ten weeks) and may be freely traded prior to exercise. Up to a specified date, old shares of the stock trade *cum rights*—the buyer is entitled to receive the rights when issued. Afterward, the stock trades *ex rights* at a correspondingly lower price. Rights for popular issues of stock are sometimes traded on exchanges; others are available in the over-the-counter market. Often trading begins prior to actual availability, with the rights sold for delivery on a *when-issued* basis.

A right is, in effect, a warrant, although one with a rather short time before expiration. It also differs with regard to exercise price, which is typically set above the current stock price for a warrant and below it for a right. Because of their short lives, rights need not be protected against stock splits and dividends. Otherwise, they have all the attributes of a warrant and should be valued accordingly.

Convertible Securities

A particularly popular financial instrument is a security that can be converted into a different security of the same firm under stated conditions. The typical case involves a bond or preferred stock convertible into shares of the firm's common stock, with a stated number of shares received for each bond. Usually no cash is involved: the old security is simply traded in, and the appropriate number of new securities issued in return. *Convertible preferred stocks* are issued from time to time, but tax effects make them, like other preferred stock, attractive primarily for corporate investment. For other investors many issues of *convertible bonds* are available.

If a $1,000 par bond can be converted into 20 shares of common stock, the *conversion ratio* is 20.0. Alternatively, the *conversion price* may be said to be $50 ($1,000/20), since $50 of the bond's *par* value must be given up to obtain one common share. Neither the conversion ratio nor the conversion price is affected by changes in a bond's market value.

A convertible bond's *conversion value*, obtained by multiplying the conversion ratio by the stock's current price, is the value that would be obtained by conversion; it is the bond's current "value as stock." The *conversion premium* is the amount by which the bond's current price exceeds its conversion value, expressed as a percent of the latter. A related amount is the *investment value*: an estimate, based on its maturity, coupon, and rating, of the amount for which the bond might sell if it were not convertible. This is the convertible's "value as bond."

Conversion ratios are typically set so that conversion will not prove attractive unless and until the stock price increases substantially from its value at the time the convertible security was first issued. This is similar to the general practice used in setting exercise prices for warrants.

Convertible securities of great complexity can be found. Some may be converted only after an initial waiting period. Some may be converted up to the bond's maturity date, others only for a stated, shorter period. Some have different conversion ratios for different years. A few can be converted into packages of two or more different securities; others require the additional payment of cash upon conversion, and so on.

Convertible bonds are usually protected against splits and stock dividends via adjustment in the conversion ratio. For example, a bond with an initial conversion ratio of 20.0 could be adjusted to have a ratio of 22.0 following a 10% stock dividend. Protection against cash dividends is not generally provided, but some indentures require that the holders of convertible bonds be notified prior to payment of cash dividends so they may convert before the resultant fall in the stock's price, if desired.

Convertible securities often contain a call provision, which may be used by the corporation to *force conversion* when the stock price is sufficiently high to make the value of the stock obtained on conversion exceed the call price of the bond. Corporations can also encourage conversion by providing stockholders with large cash dividends, valuable subscription rights, and the like.

A convertible bond is, for practical purposes, a bond with nondetachable warrants plus the restriction that *only* the bond is usable (at par) to pay the exercise price. If the bond were not callable, the value of this package of one bond and several *latent warrants* would equal the value of a straight noncallable bond (i.e., the estimated investment value) plus that of the warrants. However, most convertible bonds are callable and thus involve a double option: the holder has an option to convert the bond to stock, and the issuing corporation has an option to buy the bond (typically, only after a stated number of years from issuance). To further complicate the situation, the value of a risky bond is greater, the smaller the risk of default—and, other things equal, the greater a corporation's stock price, the lower the risk that it will default on outstanding bonds.

When a convertible bond is exchanged for common stock, the firm's earnings per share typically will change. Interest costs will fall, increasing total earnings, but the larger amount must be divided among more shares of stock. Most corporations are now required to provide estimates of the value of earnings per share if all securities convertible into common stock were converted. Table 16-2 provides an example. Convertible bonds with a par value of $500,000 are outstanding, with an annual interest cost of $50,000. Each bond is convertible into 20 shares of stock; if all were converted, interest payments would fall by $50,000 and the number of shares would increase by 10,000. Earnings per share would fall from $4.50 to $4.32, as indicated in the table. The latter figure, known as the *fully diluted earnings per share*, can be found in the annual reports of firms with outstanding convertible securities. When warrants with an exercise price below the current

TABLE 16-2
The Calculation of Fully Diluted Earnings Per Share

	Item	Earnings as Reported ($)	Earnings Assuming Conversion ($)
	Earnings before interest and taxes	1,000,000	1,000,000
(less)	Interest payments	100,000	50,000
(equals)	Earnings before taxes	900,000	950,000
(less)	Tax (at 50%)	450,000	475,000
(equals)	Earnings after taxes	450,000	475,000
(divided by)	Number of common shares	100,000	110,000
(equals)	Earnings per share	4.50	4.32

market value of the stock are outstanding, earnings may also be adjusted by assuming the exercise of all warrants and the use of the proceeds to buy back some of the additional shares issued.

The calculation of fully diluted earnings provides recognition of the value of outstanding call options that the stockholders of a firm have issued to the holders of convertible securities. While the desirability of this particular method for reflecting the associated liability may be debated, the need to consider it is not subject to question.

Equity as an Option

The common stock of any levered corporation can be viewed as an option. If payments are made on schedule to creditors, stockholders can keep a corporation's assets. Otherwise, the assets are forfeited. Economically, if not legally, shareholders hold a call option on the firm, an option sold initially by the creditors. The exercise price is the set of payments promised the creditors, and the expiration date is the maturity date of the debt. The creditors have, in a sense, invested their money plus the premium received from the stockholders (i.e., the proceeds from stock issue plus retained earnings) in the firm's assets. In the event of bankruptcy, the creditors retain the assets (minus payments to lawyers). Otherwise, they receive the promised payments (i.e., the exercise price) and have the assets called away from them.

Bankruptcy can be viewed as a decision by stockholders not to exercise their call option, on the grounds that the firm is worth less than the exercise price (required payments to the creditors). The ability to declare bankruptcy, which derives in turn from the limited liability of corporate stock ownership, thus gives common share the attributes of call options.

The importance of the "option attribute" of a stock will depend on the extent to which a firm is levered and the probability of bankruptcy. Firms with substantial leverage typically have many kinds of debt with different maturities, payment schedules, associated restrictions, and so on. The option implicit in common stock is thus likely to be exceedingly complex. However, the fact that many common stocks are themselves options underlines the importance of understanding the basic principles of option valuation.

Underlying Securities

Clearly, an option may be related to any of a number of types of securities. To be perfectly general, we would have to refer to the "underlying security with which an option is associated." To avoid this, the term "stock" will often be used instead, with the understanding that the relationships discussed apply in other cases as well.

TAXATION OF OPTION PROFITS AND LOSSES

There is nothing simple about United States income tax regulations, and the treatment of profits and losses from option transactions is no exception. Complicated cases require legal opinion, but the general approach is reasonably easy to understand.

When a call option is exercised, the buyer is considered to have bought stock for a total cost equal to the exercise price plus the premium paid for the option itself plus any commissions or other costs involved in the option purchase and its exercise. The seller of a call option that is exercised is considered to have sold the stock for a total value equal to the exercise price plus the premium received for the option, minus any commissions or other costs involved in the sale of the option and its exercise. The period between the initial sale of the option and its exercise is irrelevant for tax purposes; all profits and losses are attributed to the holding of the security itself, which begins on the exercise date for the option buyer and ends on that date for the option seller. Exercise of a put option is treated in an analogous manner.

If an investor purchases an option, then sells it, the difference between the prices is considered a *capital* gain or loss, short- or long-term, depending on the holding period.

Treatment of the results obtained by an option seller (writer) who closes out a position is not similar. The difference between the sale price initially received and the price paid for the subsequent closing purchase is always considered a *short-term capital* gain or loss.[4]

---

[4] Unless the option is written in the ordinary course of the taxpayer's business, in which case the result is treated as an ordinary gain or loss.

When a call expires unexercised, the buyer's loss is a *capital* loss, short- or long-term, depending on the length of the period from purchase to expiration. However, the seller's gain is always considered a *short-term capital* gain.

These and other rules give rise to a number of strategies that take tax consequences into account. For example, in the event of exercise, the results from an option transaction are incorporated into a stock purchase or sale for both the buyer and the seller, producing capital gains and losses for tax purposes. Moreover, timing of an exercise or closing transaction may make the difference between a short- and a long-term gain or loss. The decision on whether or not to close a position and, if so, whether to do it via exercise or a transaction in the secondary market thus requires analysis of tax aspects as well as the basic economics of the situation.

Taxes may affect option prices, explaining otherwise anomalous differences between actual prices and those expected in a tax-free environment. Before purchasing or selling any option, an investor should consider the possibility that its current price makes such a transaction better suited for those with a different relationship with the tax collector.

VALUE OF AN OPTION AT EXPIRATION

The value of an option is related to that of its underlying security, but the relationship is not strictly linear. This is particularly obvious just prior to expiration (which we will call "at expiration" to save verbiage). Figure 16-6(a) relates the expiration value of a call option with an exercise price of $100 to the price of the underlying stock. If the stock price is below $100, the option will expire worthless. If it is above $100, the option can be exercised for $100 to obtain a security with a greater value; the net gain will equal the difference between the security's actual price and the exercise. Of course, there is no need to actually exercise the option. Instead, the option seller can simply pay the buyer the difference between the security price and the exercise price, avoiding the bother of exercise for both parties. This is commonly done for listed options, although a minority of investors choose to exercise their options, possibly for tax purposes.

Figure 16-6(b) shows the value of a put option with an exercise price of $100 at expiration. The holder of such an option will find it profitable to exercise it if the stock price is below the exercise price. In such a situation, the security can be sold for the difference between the two amounts. As with a call option, neither party need actually deal in the stock. The seller of *any* option worth exercising at expiration can simply buy off the associated obligation by paying the holder of

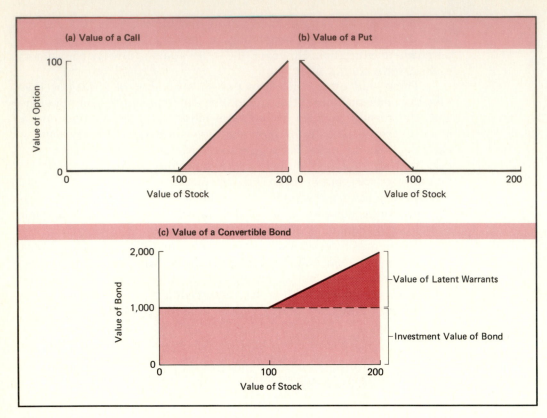

FIGURE 16-6
Values of Options at Expiration.

the option the difference between the stock price and the exercise price.

Figure 16-6(c) shows the value at expiration of a noncallable convertible bond with a conversion ratio of 10.0, on the assumptions that the bond matures when its latent warrants expire and that its investment value at the time is $1,000. If the stock price is below the effective exercise price of $100. (= $1,000/10) at the time, it will not pay to convert; the bond should be allowed to mature and its par value received. But if the stock price exceeds the exercise price, conversion will be profitable. For example, if the stock price is $110, conversion will give ten shares worth $110 each, for a total value of $1,100, as shown in the figure. Comparison of Figures 16-6(a) and 16-6(c) highlights the fact that a noncallable convertible bond is equivalent to a straight bond (which would be represented in this type of diagram by a flat line at $1,000) plus a call option.

Figure 16-6 shows the values of various options at expiration. To determine profits and losses we must also take premiums into account.[5]

Figure 16-7 shows the profits and losses associated with a number of strategies. Each involves a purchase and/or sale at an initial time when the stock under study sells for $100, plus one or more closing transactions at a subsequent time just prior to the expiration of all the options being considered. Outcomes are shown for investors choosing the two sides of each of six positions. Since the profit obtained by a buyer is the seller's loss, and vice versa, each diagram in the figure has a corresponding mirror image.

Figures 16-7(a) and (c) include the value of the initial premium along with the amounts shown in Figures 16-6(a) and (b). Figures 16-7(b) and (d) show the results obtained by the other party in each case. Figure 16-7(e) is obtained by adding the amounts shown in Figures 16-7(a) and (c) to obtain the net profit or loss from buying a straddle. Figure 16-7(f) is the mirror image of Figure 16-7(e), and it also shows the sum of the amounts given by Figures 16-7(b) and (c).

Figure 16-7(g) shows the profit or loss made by an investor who avoids options entirely, but buys a share of the stock (at $100) when others purchase or sell options, and sells the stock when the options expire. If no dividends are paid in the interim, the relationship is that shown by the dashed line. Otherwise the dividends received[6] must be taken into account, giving a relationship like that shown by the solid line. Figure 16-7(h) shows the outcome obtained by an investor who sells stock at the initial date, then buys it back at the terminal date. The initial sale might involve stock previously held, or it could be a "short sale" of stock borrowed for the interim.

Figure 16-7(i) plots the results obtained by an investor who buys one share of stock and simultaneously writes (sells) a call on it. The person involved is said to have written a *fully covered option*, since it is guaranteed by the holding of the required amount of stock. In contrast, the writer whose situation is depicted in Figure 16-7(b) must rely on cash or other assets to make good the associated obligation. An option seller who does not hold the underlying stock is said to have written a *naked option*.

Figure 16-7(j) shows the results obtained by a investor who sells one share of stock and simultaneously buys a call option. While the investor in Figure 16-7(i) faces limited gains and potentially larger

---

[5] For comparability, the actual premium paid when an option is purchased can be converted to an equivalent value at time of expiration, using an appropriate rate of interest: if the premium (i.e., the price of the option) is p, an equivalent value at the time of expiration is $p(1 + r)^t$, where r is an appropriate rate of interest and t is the time between purchase and expiration.

[6] Expressed as an equivalent value at the terminal date.

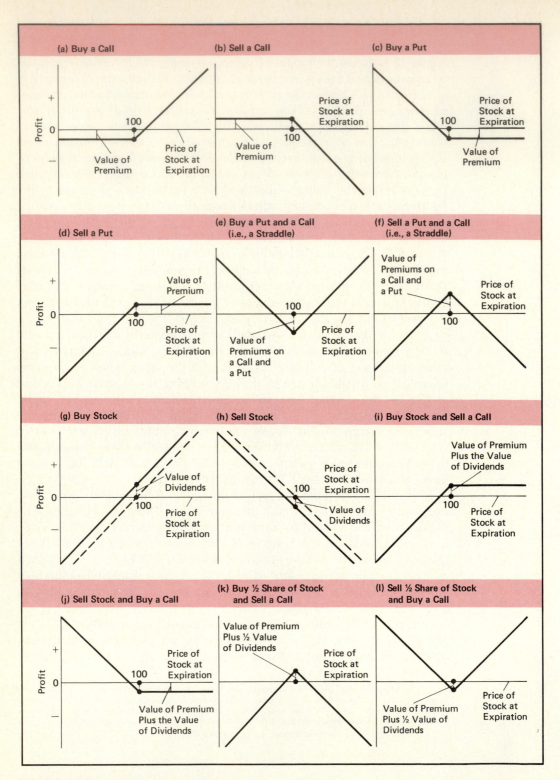

FIGURE 16-7
Profits and Losses from Various Strategies.

losses, the investor in Figure 16-7(j) faces limited losses and potentially larger gains.

Figure 16-7(k) portrays the situation faced by an investor who buys one-half a share of the stock and sells one call (i.e., writes a *partially covered* option). A substantial price move in either direction can cause a loss. A large price increase will result in a call: additional stock will have to be obtained and given up at a loss. On the other hand, a large price decrease will cause a loss on the investor's stock holding. Figure 16-7(1) shows the results obtained by an investor who takes the opposite position, selling one-half a share of the stock and buying one call.

Comparison of the diagrams in Figure 16-7 suggests that similar results can be obtained via alternative strategies. Figures 16-7(f) and (k) are similar, as are (l) and (e), (j) and (c), and (i) and (b). Neither the premiums involved nor the initial investments required need be equal in every case. Nonetheless, the similarity of the results obtained with different "packages" of securities dictates that the total market values of the packages be similar as well.

OPTION VALUATION

Expressing Values as Percentages of the Exercise Price

Figures 16-6 and 16-7 plotted option values and profits and losses from option positions for various levels of the price of the underlying stock. All values were expressed in dollars, on the assumption that options were written with an exercise price of $100. To avoid circumlocution we will continue to discuss cases with this characteristic. However, the results are quite general. The horizontal axes in such diagrams can be interpreted as plotting the stock price expressed as a *percent* of the actual exercise price. Similarly, the vertical axes can be interpreted as plotting option values and/or position profits and losses expressed as percentages of the option exercise price. Thus a reference to a stock price of $92 can be interpreted as a price equal to 92.0% of the exercise price, and a reference to an option value of $2.50 as an amount equal to 2.5% of the exercise price. If the actual exercise price of an option were $40, the corresponding values would then be $36.80 (= .92 × $40) and $1 (= .025 × $40), respectively.

Limits on the Value of a Call Option

Throughout, this book has emphasized the importance of comparing securities or combinations thereof with others of similar characteristics. Nowhere is this more important than in the valuation of options. In this section comparisons will be used to determine *limits* on the value of a call option. The sections that follow will use additional comparisons to develop specific estimates of option values within these limits.

Consider three investments. One is a call option, not protected against cash dividends, with an exercise price (E) of $100; the second is the stock on which the option is written; and the third is a riskless investment. For simplicity, assume that funds can be invested in a bank at any time during the life of the option at a fixed rate of r per period.

What is the *most* one should pay for an option of this type? Since a call can be converted to a share of stock only upon payment of the exercise price, it clearly is less desirable than a share of the stock itself and should never sell at a higher price. This provides an upper limit on its value:

$$P_o \leq P_s \tag{16-1a}$$

where

P_o = the current price of the call option

P_s = the current price of the underlying stock

What is the *least* one should pay for such an option? Consider the following package:

one option, current price = P_o
plus a bank account, current value = $PV(E) + PV(d)$

where

$PV(E)$ = the present value of the option's exercise price ($100) if the latter were paid at expiration

$PV(d)$ = the present value of all dividends to be paid on the stock (more precisely, for which the stock will go ex-dividend) prior to the option's expiration. For simplicity, all dividends and ex-dividend dates are assumed to be known with certainty.

Compare this package with one share of the stock itself. The bank account can be used to provide payments equal to the dividends received from the stock. At the expiration of the option, the account can also be used to exercise the option *if desired*, providing a share at that time. This will deplete the account but require no further investment. Thus the package can duplicate the benefits provided by a share of the stock. Moreover, in the event that exercise proves undesirable, the package will be better than the stock: if the stock price is less than the exercise price at expiration, a share can be purchased on the open market, leaving money in the bank account. Clearly, the package is as good as or better than a share of the stock and should sell for as much or more:

$$P_o + PV(E) + PV(d) \geq P_s$$

Rearranging:

$$P_o \geq P_s - PV(E) - PV(d) \qquad \textbf{(16-1b)}$$

While this argument has considered exercise only at expiration, and thus applies most directly to a European option, an American option will always be at least as valuable, for it provides all the same options and more besides. Thus it is worth at least as much, and formula (16-1b) holds, *a fortiori*, for an American option.

Since a holder is never forced to exercise an option, it cannot be so unattractive that people must be paid to take it. This provides a third limit—the price of an option can never be negative:

$$P_o \geq 0 \qquad \textbf{(16-1c)}$$

Formulas 16-1(a), (b), and (c) provide bounds on the value of a call option. If the price were to move outside these limits, there would be opportunities for profit via arbitrage. While transactions costs and taxes might make it unprofitable for some investors to take advantage of such situations, a substantial departure would certainly lead others to attempt to profit thereby, setting in motion forces that would quickly bring the option price back within bounds.

Figure 16-8 shows the way in which the limits on a call option's price change as expiration nears. For simplicity it has been assumed that the underlying stock is not expected to pay any dividends in the interim. Note that the region gets larger as expiration approaches and the present value of the exercise price rises. The exact relationship at expiration lies along the lower edge of the area, as shown in Figure 16-8(c). Earlier, this is not generally the case. To determine the likely location at some time prior to expiration requires more detailed comparisons, to which we now turn.

Valuation with Simple Price Changes

To make concrete some further principles of option valuation it will prove helpful to deal with a rather simple kind of stock. Figure 16-9(a) shows the general nature of its behavior. In any given period its price will either jump up to some higher value $(P_{s,t+1}^+)$ or down to some lower value $(P_{s,t+1}^-)$. Looking forward from time t to time $t + 1$, there are thus two possible states of the world—up ($+$) and down ($-$). Associated with each state is a known stock price; the probabilities of the two states (p^+ and p^-) have also been estimated.

For every time and stock value there will be some corresponding value for a call option on the stock. These amounts are also indicated in Figure 16-9(a).

The final item in Figure 16-9(a) represents the results obtained

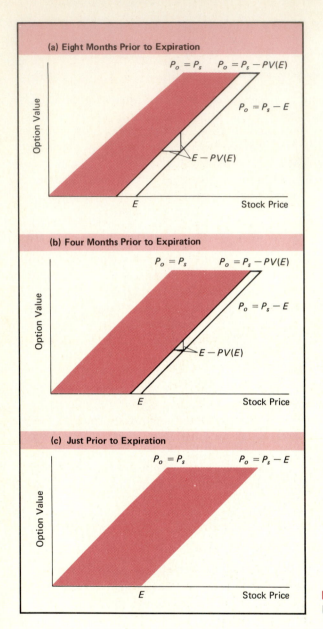

(a) Eight Months Prior to Expiration

$P_o = P_s$ $P_o = P_s - PV(E)$

$P_o = P_s - E$

$E - PV(E)$

Option Value

E Stock Price

(b) Four Months Prior to Expiration

$P_o = P_s$ $P_o = P_s - PV(E)$

$P_o = P_s - E$

$E - PV(E)$

Option Value

E Stock Price

(c) Just Prior to Expiration

$P_o = P_s$ $P_o = P_s - E$

Option Value

E Stock Price

FIGURE 16-8
Limits on the Value of a Call Option.

by investing some amount of money, X, in the bank. It will grow to $(1 + r)$ times its initial value by the end of the period, and this return is certain.

All assumptions used previously will be retained. The option under study has an exercise price of $100, the stock pays no dividends prior to expiration, and the riskless rate of interest is fixed at r per period.

494   Options

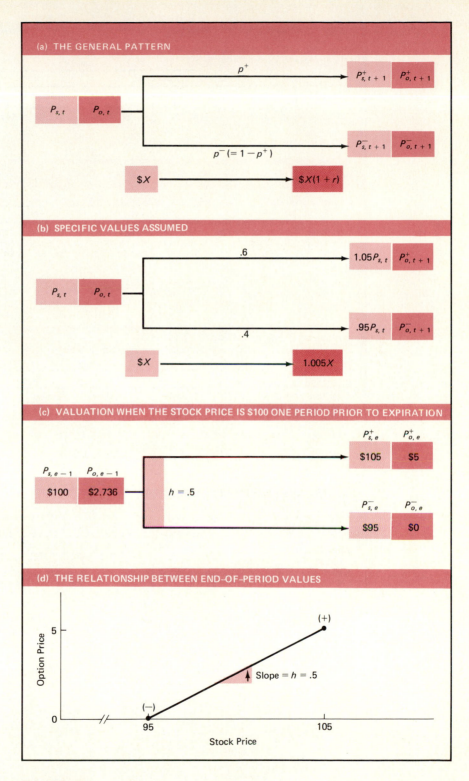

FIGURE 16-9
Stock and Option Prices.

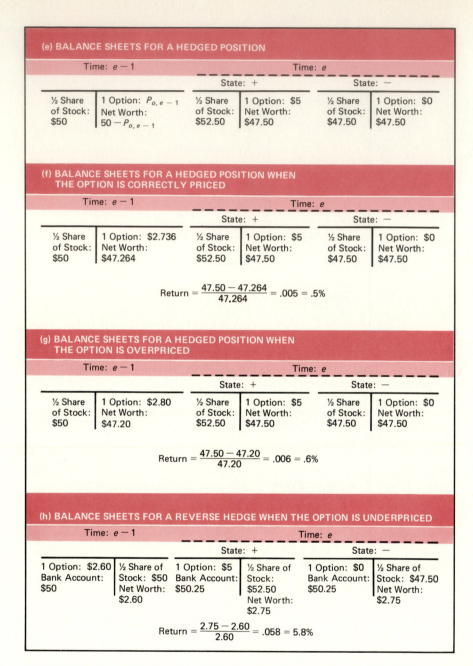

FIGURE 16-9 (*continued*)

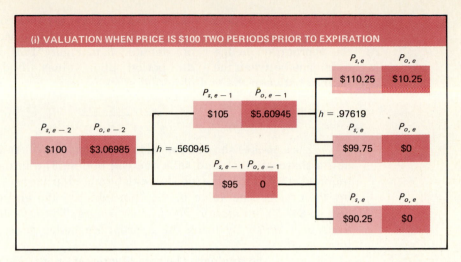

FIGURE 16-9 (*continued*)

Figure 16-9(b) shows specific numeric values that will be used henceforth. The stock price is assumed to have a 60% chance of increasing 5% each period and a 40% chance of decreasing 5%; its expected return thus equals $(.6 \times + 5) + (.4 \times - 5)$, or 1% per period. The riskless interest rate is half this, .5% per period (i.e., $r = .005$).

Figure 16-9(c) fills in some more values. It covers the situation when the stock price is $100 one period prior to expiration. The time of expiration is denoted e, one period prior to expiration $e - 1$, two periods prior $e - 2$, and so on.

There is a good reason for starting with the period prior to expiration. At expiration, the option value associated with every possible stock price is known: it is $(P_{s,e} - E)$ or zero, whichever is larger. In the situation shown in Figure 16-9(c), the end-of-period option value will be either $5 or $0.

What does this imply for the price of the option at the beginning of the period—i.e., how was the box for $P_{o,e-1}$ in Figure 16-9(c) filled in? Not surprisingly, by analogy, as we will see.

Figure 16-9(d) plots the end-of-period values for the stock and the option. Since there are only two possibilities, all (two) of the points lie on a straight line. The securities' returns are perfectly positively correlated. Whenever this is the case, it is possible to *hedge* one against the other and eliminate all risk.

The difference between the stock prices in the two states is $10; the difference between the option prices is $5. It is possible to hold stock and write a call option and to arrange the proportions so that the differences in payoffs in the two positions are exactly equal. The investor's end-of-period net worth will then be the same in either event.

Options

In this case, the appropriate *hedge ratio* is .5%; for every option written (sold), one-half a share of stock should be purchased. More generally, the appropriate hedge ratio, denoted h in Figure 16-9, is simply the difference between the end-of-period option values, divided by the difference between the end-of-period stock values:

$$h = \frac{P_{o,t+1}^{+} - P_{o,t+1}^{-}}{P_{s,t+1}^{+} - P_{s,t+1}^{-}} \qquad (16\text{–}2)$$

Figure 16-9(e) shows how this can be employed. An investor buys half a share of stock and sells one call option. The initial investment required is $50 minus the (yet-to-be-determined) price received for writing the option. The value of the "portfolio" at the end of the period will be $47.50, *no matter which state occurs*. The investor has set up a *riskless hedge* by using the appropriate hedge ratio indicated by formula (16-2).

Now for the analogy. The rate of interest on a riskless investment also returns .5% per period. Since the ending value will be $47.50, the required option value is that which satisfies:

$$(50 - P_{o,e-1})\ 1.005 = \$47.50$$

The solution is:

$$P_{o,e-1} = \$2,736$$

Figure 16-9(f) shows that the hedging strategy will in fact give a certain return equal to the riskless rate if the option price equals $2.736. Figure 16-9(g) shows that if the option were overpriced, at $2.80, the hedging strategy could give a certain return greater than the riskless rate. Such a situation would attract attention, bringing out would-be option sellers whose activities would shortly drive the price back down.

What if the option were underpriced, say at $2.60? Then clever investors could *reverse hedge*, buying options and selling stock. Figure 16-9(h) shows a case in which the stock is sold short and the proceeds placed in an interest-earnings bank account.[7] A certain 5.8% per period is returned on invested funds. Such a situation would attract would-be option buyers, driving the price back up.

Figure 16-9(f) thus portrays the likely situation, and we have an option pricing formula. The option price at time t must satisfy:

$$(hP_{s,t} - P_{o,t})(1 + r) = \begin{cases} [hP_{s,t+1}^{+} - P_{o,t+1}^{+}] \\ [hP_{s,t+1}^{-} - P_{s,t+1}^{-}] \end{cases} \qquad (16\text{-}3)$$

where h is the hedge ratio required to give a riskless return. The first parenthesized expression on the left represents the funds invested at

---

[7] This is generally not possible in practice, lowering or eliminating the profit from such a hedge and raising the possibility that the option could sell at any price within a band limited by the prices at which hedging or reverse hedging would become profitable.

the beginning of the period. The brackets on the right indicate that either of the two included expressions can be used, for they are both equal to the certain end-of-period value. The formula simply requires the option to be priced so that a portfolio hedged to remove all risk will return the riskless rate on the funds invested.

Having established the principles summarized in formulas (16-2) and (16-3), it is possible to determine the option value for any time and stock price. Figure 16-9(i) does this for the case in which the stock price is $100 two periods prior to expiration. The option price boxes are filled in from right to left. Option values at expiration are simply $(P_s - 100)$ or zero, whichever is larger. This takes care of the option values at time e.

Turning to time $e - 1$, note that if a situation will lead to a worthless option no matter what, the option is already worthless. Thus if the stock price is $95 one period prior to expiration, the option will definitely expire worthless, and the option value is zero. This takes care of another box.

Turning to the situation in which the stock price is $105 one period prior to expiration, formula (16-2) is used to determine the hedge ratio (.97619) and then formula (16-3) applied to determine the option price ($5.60945).

To find the remaining hedge ratio (.560945) and option price ($3.06985), we again apply formulas (16-2) and (16-3), using the relevant stock values ($105 and $95) and the previously computed associated option values ($5.60945 and $0).

Figure 16-10 shows some values obtained with this kind of *recursive* calculation. Each curve plots option values associated with various stock prices at a specific time prior to expiration.

One characteristic of the curves in Figure 16-10 is quite general:

If two call options are otherwise identical but one has a longer time remaining before expiration, the latter will be worth at least as much as the former and generally will be worth more.

This is obviously true of American call options, for the one with a longer time to expiration can be used to do anything possible with the other, and more besides. Except in pathological cases caused by large dividend payments, the statement also applies to European call options.

The Black-Scholes Formula

In a world not bothered by taxes and transactions costs, one could adjust hedge positions almost constantly. The effective length of a "period" would thus be very small. And the smaller the length of each period, the closer the value of a call option calculated in the manner described in the previous section would be to that given by an option

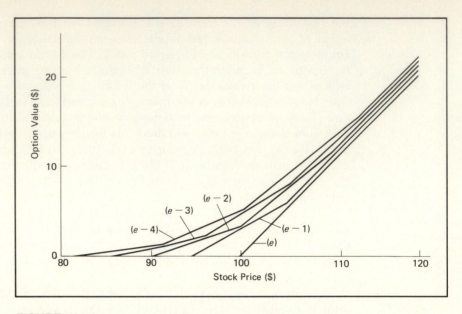

FIGURE 16-10
Option Values at Various Times Prior to Expiration (based on the numeric example in Figure 16-9).

valuation formula developed by Black and Scholes.[8] It is widely used by those who deal with options to search for situations in which price appears to differ from value. The formula is:

$$P_o = P_s N(d_1) - -\frac{E}{e^{rt}} N(d_2) \qquad \textbf{(16-4a)}$$

where

$$d_1 = \frac{\ln (P_s/E) + (r + \frac{1}{2}\sigma^2)t}{\sigma\sqrt{t}} \qquad \textbf{(16-4b)}$$

$$d_2 = \frac{\ln (P_s/E) + (r - \frac{1}{2}\sigma^2)t}{\sigma\sqrt{t}} \qquad \textbf{(16-4c)}$$

and where

P_o = the current value of the option
P_s = the current price of the stock
E = the exercise price of the option
e = 2.71828

---

[8] Fischer Black and Myron Scholes, "The Pricing of Options and Corporate Liabilities," *Journal of Political Economy*, 81, no. 3 (May/June 1973), 637-54. © 1973 by the University of Chicago. All Rights Reserved. For a discussion of the conditions under which the process described in the previous section converges to the Black-Scholes formula, see John C. Cox, Stephen A. Ross, and Mark Rubenstein, "Options Pricing: A Simplified Approach," *Journal of Financial Economics*, September 1979.

$t =$ the time remaining before expiration (in years)

$r =$ the continuously compounded riskless rate of interest

$\sigma =$ the standard deviation of the continuously compounded annual rate of return on the stock.[9]

$\ln (P_s/E) =$ the natural logarithm of (P_s/E)

$N(d) =$ the probability that a deviation less than d will occur in a normal distribution with a mean of zero and a standard deviation of one

The Black-Scholes option valuation formula can be applied directly to value a call option on a stock that pays no dividends prior to expiration. Modifications designed to account for dividends will be discussed later. First, however, the general use of the formula will be illustrated.

Using the Black-Scholes Formula

Table 16-3 provides values of $N(d)$ for various levels of d.[10] This and a table of logarithms suffice for the calculations required by the option valuation formula. For example, consider the following values:

$P_s = \$36$

$E = \$40$

$t = .25$ (i.e., one-fourth of a year, or three months)

$r = .05$ (i.e., 5% per year, continuously compounded)

$\sigma = .50$ (i.e., the standard deviation of the continuously compounded annual return is 50%)

Formulas (16-4b and 16-4c) give the values of d_1 and d_2:

$$d_1 = \frac{\ln (36/40) + [.05 + \tfrac{1}{2}(.50^2)].25}{.50\sqrt{.25}} \approx -.25$$

$$d_2 = \frac{\ln (36/40) + [.05 - \tfrac{1}{2}(.50^2).25}{.50\sqrt{.25}} \approx -.50$$

Table 16-3 can be used to find the corresponding values of $N(d_1)$ and $N(d_2)$:

$$N(d_2) = N(-.25) = .4013$$

$$N(d_2) = N(-.50) = .3085$$

$$P_o = (36 \times .4013) - \left(\frac{40}{e^{.05 \times .25}} \times .3085\right) \approx \$2.26$$

---

[9] The Black-Scholes formula assumes that the standard deviation is constant throughout the life of the option. Formulas based on other assumptions have also been derived. For examples see John Cox and Stephen Ross, "The Valuation of Options for Alternative Stochastic Processes," *Journal of Financial Economics*, no. 3, 1976.

[10] Table 16-2 is an abbreviated version of a standard cumulative normal distribution table. More detailed versions can be found in most statistics textbooks.

TABLE 16-3
Values of $N(d)$ for Selected Values of d

d	N(d)	d	N(d)	d	N(d)
		−1.00	.1587	1.00	.8413
−2.95	.0016	−.95	.1711	1.05	.8531
−2.90	.0019	−.90	.1841	1.10	.8643
−2.85	.0022	−.85	.1977	1.15	.8749
−2.80	.0026	−.80	.2119	1.20	.8849
−2.75	.0030	−.75	.2266	1.25	.8944
−2.70	.0035	−.70	.2420	1.30	.9032
−2.65	.0040	−.65	.2578	1.35	.9115
−2.60	.0047	−.60	.2743	1.40	.9192
−2.55	.0054	−.55	.2912	1.45	.9265
−2.50	.0062	−.50	.3085	1.50	.9332
−2.45	.0071	−.45	.3264	1.55	.9394
−2.40	.0082	−.40	.3446	1.60	.9452
−2.35	.0094	−.35	.3632	1.65	.9505
−2.30	.0107	−.30	.3821	1.70	.9554
−2.25	.0122	−.25	.4013	1.75	.9599
−2.20	.0139	−.20	.4207	1.80	.9641
−2.15	.0158	−.15	.4404	1.85	.9678
−2.10	.0179	−.10	.4602	1.90	.9713
−2.05	.0202	−.05	.4801	1.95	.9744
−2.00	.0228	.00	.5000	2.00	.9773
−1.95	.0256	.05	.5199	2.05	.9798
−1.90	.0287	.10	.5398	2.10	.9821
−1.85	.0322	.15	.5596	2.15	.9842
−1.80	.0359	.20	.5793	2.20	.9861
−1.75	.0401	.25	.5987	2.25	.9878
−1.70	.0446	.30	.6179	2.30	.9893
−1.65	.0495	.35	.6368	2.35	.9906
−1.60	.0548	.40	.6554	2.40	.9918
−1.55	.0606	.45	.6736	2.45	.9929
−1.50	.0668	.50	.6915	2.50	.9938
−1.45	.0735	.55	.7088	2.55	.9946
−1.40	.0808	.60	.7257	2.60	.9953
−1.35	.0885	.65	.7422	2.65	.9960
−1.30	.0968	.70	.7580	2.70	.9965
−1.25	.1057	.75	.7734	2.75	.9970
−1.20	.1151	.80	.7881	2.80	.9974
−1.15	.1251	.85	.8023	2.85	.9978
−1.10	.1357	.90	.8159	2.90	.9981
−1.05	.1469	.95	.8289	2.95	.9984

Only a hand calculator is needed to estimate the value of an option using the Black-Scholes formula. Programmable calculators or computers can be "taught" the needed calculations, allowing the entire job to be done automatically as soon as the key values are input.

Analysis of formulas (16-4) (or experimentation with alternative numeric examples) shows that, other things equal, a call option is generally *more* valuable:

the *higher* the current stock price relative to the exercise price,

the *longer* the time remaining before expiration,

the *higher* the riskless rate of interest, and

the *greater* the risk of the underlying stock.

Only the last of these factors requires estimation, but it is of crucial importance.

Estimating Stock Risk

Since the risk of the underlying stock greatly influences the value of an option, it is important to give it due consideration. Note that for *option valuation* the *total risk* of a stock is relevant, since a "portfolio" involving another security (the option) highly correlated with it is being analyzed. On the other hand, for *security valuation* only *factor-related risks* are relevant. Option valuation fixes the value of an option *relative* to that of its underlying security. Security valuation is required to fix the value of both the security and options written on it.

To estimate the total risk of a security, historic data can be analyzed, subjective estimates of various future possibilities made, or the two combined. For any estimate of future uncertainty, historic data are more likely to prove helpful than definitive. And since recent history may prove more helpful than ancient history, some analysts study daily price changes over the most recent six to twelve months, sometimes giving more weight to later days than to earlier ones. Others take into account the price histories of related stocks and the possibility that a stock whose price has recently decreased may be more risky in the future than it was in the past. Still others make explicit subjective estimates of the future, taking into account changes in uncertainty concerning the economy in general, specific industries, sectors, and/or stocks. In some cases an analyst's estimate of a stock's risk over the next three months may differ from that for the following three months, leading to the use of different inputs for options on the same stock, but with different times to expiration.

The Market Consensus of a Stock's Risk

One way to estimate a stock's total risk is to let "the market" do it. Given the observable characteristics of a stock and an option on the stock, and given an estimate of the stock's risk, one can find the appropriate value for the option. If investors value options in accordance with their own estimates of stock risk, the procedure can be *reversed* to obtain a market consensus option of that risk. For example, assume that the riskless interest rate is 6%, and that a six-month option with an exercise price of $40 sells for $4 when the price of the underlying stock is $36. Different estimates of risk can be "plugged into" formula (16-4) until an implied value of $36 is obtained. In this case the current situation is consistent with an estimated annual standard deviation of .40 for the underlying stock over the next six months.

The procedure can be used to estimate a stock's risk over any given horizon by averaging values obtained from options with different exercise prices.

A similar procedure can be employed with the prices of index options to estimate the market consensus of the risks of the associated indices. Options on broad-based market indices (such as Standard and Poor's 500-stock index and the New York Stock Exchange Composite Index) can provide estimates of the current risk of the stock market as a whole. Options on specialized indices (such as oil and gas, computer stocks, and so on) can provide estimates of the current risks of praticular sectors.

Prices of options on financial instruments can be used to estimate the current risk of the underlying securities and, by inference, *interest-rate risk*.

Hedge Ratios

Figure 16-11 plots the values of a call option with an exercise price of $100 when nine months remain before expiration. An interest rate of 5% and annual stock price standard deviation of .50 (50%) are as-

FIGURE 16-11
Option Values at Various Times Prior to Expiration.

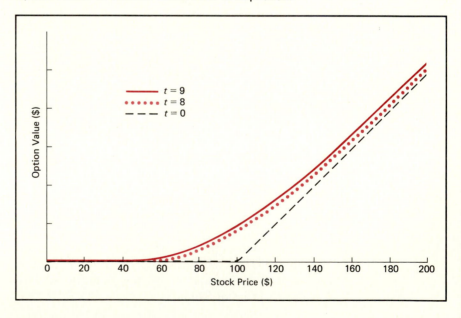

sumed. The figure also shows the values of such an option eight months before expiration and at expiration.

The *slope* of the option value curve at any point represents the expected change in option price per dollar change in the stock price. This amount is the *hedge ratio* that will neutralize the effects of small stock price changes on an investor's portfolio in a manner similar to that of the simple case shown in Figure 16–9. In general:

An option's *hedge ratio* is the estimated change in the price of the option associated with a $1 change in the price of the underlying security.

The Black-Scholes formula provides a direct estimate of the hedge ratio: it equals $N(d_1)$ in formula (16-4).

An option's hedge ratio never exceeds 1.0 and is usually less. Thus a $1 change in the stock price will typically move an option's price by less than $1. However, the price of the option will generally change by a greater *percentage* than will that of the stock. It is this relationship that leads people to say that options offer *high leverage*.

If a stock is hedged against an option, or vice versa, with the relative proportions equal to the appropriate hedge ratio, the effect on the investor's net worth of a change in the price of the stock will be roughly the same, whether the price goes up or down. Moreover, a small change in stock price will have little effect on net worth. Stock price risk is not eliminated; to do this the hedge ratio would have to be adjusted continuously as the stock price changed. But the risk is reduced.

Adjustments for Dividends

Thus far the issue of dividend payments on the underlying stock during the life of an option has been avoided. Other things equal, the greater the dividends to be paid during the life of a call option, the smaller its value. Moreover, it may pay to exercise an American call option just prior to an ex-dividend date. This possibility will be considered shortly. First we describe a way to deal with dividends on the assumptions that they can be predicted with certainty and that the option will not be exercised prior to expiration.

The procedure is straightforward. One simply assumes that all relevant dividends have already been announced and that the stock has already gone ex-dividend for all of them. The current stock price is reduced by an amount equal to the expected dividends (or their present value), and the option valuation formula or tables are used with this "dividend-adjusted" price instead of the actual value.

In the absence of dividends an American call option would be worth at least as much "alive" (not exercised) as "dead" (exercised), up to its expiration date. When dividends are involved, however, the situation may be different. This is shown in Figure 16-12. The option's

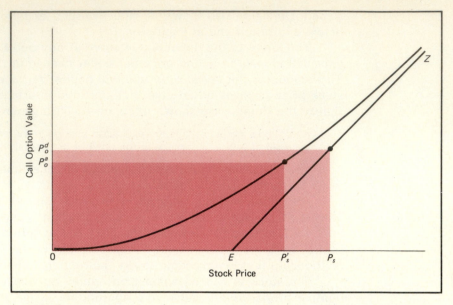

FIGURE 16-12
Option Values Before and After an Ex-Dividend Date.

value if exercised immediately lies along the border OEZ. If allowed to live, the option's value will lie along a higher curve, such as that shown in the figure. Imagine that the stock is currently priced at P_s and is about to go ex-dividend for the last time prior to the option's expiration. Afterward, it can be expected to sell for a lower price, P'_s. The Black-Scholes formula can be used to find the option's value if it remains "alive." In Figure 16-12 it is P^a_o. If instead the option is exercised while the stock price is still P_s, a value of P^d_o will be obtained. If this is greater, the option should be exercised early; if not, it should not.

To take this possibility into account when computing the value of an option at an earlier date, two estimates can be made. The first assumes holding until expiration and subtracts the present value of all dividends from the current stock price before applying the usual procedure. The second assumes holding until just before the final ex-dividend date and subtracts the present value of all dividends but the last from the current stock price before applying the procedure. The current value of the option can be assumed to equal the larger of these two values. While not exact,[11] this procedure is probably sufficient for many listed options.

---

[11] For an exact method, see Richard Roll, "An Analytic Valuation Formula for Unprotected American Call Options on Stocks with Known Dividends," *Journal of Financial Economics*, vol. 5 (1977). For a practical method that can come as close as desired to the exact value, see Cox, Ross, and Rubenstein, "Options Pricing: A Simplified Approach."

The Valuation of Put Options

If similar results can be obtained in different ways, then unless certain relationships hold among prices of related instruments there will be possibilities for arbitrage. When such opportunities arise, investors will rapidly take advantage of them, causing prices to return quickly to more appropriate values.

An example is provided by European puts and calls. Assume that a call with an exercise price of E sells for P_c and that a put on the same stock with the same exercise price and expiration date sells for P_p. Assume also that it is possible to obtain a loan of $PV(E)$ dollars today in return for a promise to pay back E dollars on the day that the options expire. Finally, assume that the stock in question is not expected to pay any dividends prior to the option's expiration date.

Figure 16-13(a) shows the position on the day of expiration of an investor who buys a share of the stock, borrows $PV(E)$ dollars today, and then sells the stock and pays back the loan on the options' expiration date. Figure 16-13(b) shows the position of an investor who buys the call and sells the put. The pictures are exactly the same; thus the two strategies should have the same cost. If P_s is the current price of the stock, the net outlay required for the first strategy is:

$$P_s - PV(E)$$

while that required for the second strategy is:

$$P_c - P_p$$

And the prices should be such that:

$$P_c - P_p = P_s - PV(E) \tag{16-5}$$

This is the *put-call parity theorem*. Given the prices of any two of these securities, the "appropriate" price of the third can be found using formula (16-5).

Since the Black-Scholes formula provides an estimate of the appropriate value for a European call option, the appropriate value of a European put can be determined using the Black-Scholes formula and formula (16-5):

$$P_p = P_c - P_s + PV(E) \tag{16-6}$$

where:

P_c = the value of a European call, using the Black-Scholes formula
P_p = the appropriate value of a European put

While formula (16-6) applies to European options on stocks that will not pay dividends prior to the options' expiration, simple modifications can give reasonable approximations for the values of options

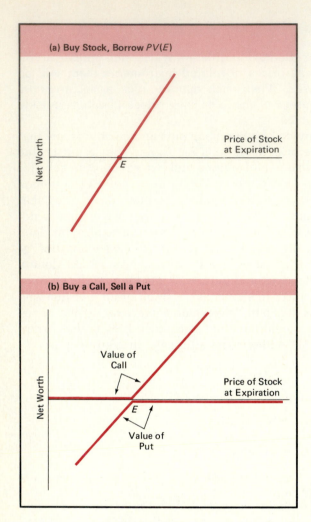

FIGURE 16-13
The Put-Call Parity Theorem.

on stocks paying dividends.[12] A more serious problem arises when American options are to be valued. To obtain exact values for the appropriate price for an American put option, extensive computer calculations may be required.[13] However, some of the errors involved in applying (16-6) are offsetting, so this formula provides a reasonable starting point for evaluating the current price of an American put option.

---

[12] If the dividends are known with certainty, an amount—$PV(D)$—equal to the present value of the dividends to be paid to holders of record prior to expiration can be borrowed as part of the first strategy, with the loan repaid with the dividends received. The right-hand side of (16-5) would thus be: $P_s - PV(E) - PV(D)$, and (16-5) would become:

$$P_p = P_c - P_s + PV(E) + PV(D)$$

[13] For alternative procedures see Michael J. Brennan and Eduardo S. Schwartz, "The Valuation of American Put Options," *Journal of Finance*, May 1977, and Cox, Ross, and Rubenstein, "Options Pricing: A Simplified Approach."

PORTFOLIO INSURANCE

Consider an investor who holds a highly diversified portfolio. He or she is delighted to participate in the "upside potential" of the stock market but would like very much to avoid the "downside risk." There are, in principle, at least three ways this might be accomplished.

Purchasing an Insurance Policy

One alternative would be to contract with an insurance company. For example, assume that the portfolio is currently worth $100,000. The insurance company might agree to cover any loss in value over some specified period, e.g., a year. At the end of a year, if the portfolio value were $95,000, the insurance company would pay $5,000. On the other hand, if the value were $105,000, the insurance company would pay nothing.

Figure 16-14(a) portrays the situation. The horizontal axis plots the value of the portfolio at year-end. The 45-degree line *OBC* shows the value of the "uninsured" portfolio. Curve *ABC* shows the value of the portfolio plus any insurance payment. It is the "payoff function" for an *insured portfolio*.

Purchasing a Protective Put

Unfortunately, insurance companies rarely write policies on portfolios. However, this is not the only alternative.

Assume that a listed put is available on an index that is, for practical purposes, virtually perfectly correlated with the portfolio. Curve *ADE* in Figure 16-14(b) shows the payoffs to a *buyer* of such a put with an exercise price of 100 and one year remaining before expiration. Curve *OBC* is the payoff function for the holder of the portfolio.

What would happen to an investor who (1) held the portfolio and (2) purchased a put? Figure 16-14(c) shows the answer. The payoff function (*ABC*) is simply the combination of the payoffs shown in Figure 16-14(b). Not surprisingly, it is precisely the same as curve *ABC* in Figure 16-14(a).

In this case, the purchase of a put provides protection against declines in portfolio value. In this role it is termed a *protective put*.

In practice, stock indices may be considerably less than perfectly correlated with desired portfolios. Purchase of a stock index option may thus provide imperfect insurance. In a graph such as that shown in Figure 16-14(c), the resulting curve would be somewhat fuzzy, owing to the risk of divergence of values of the portfolio and index.

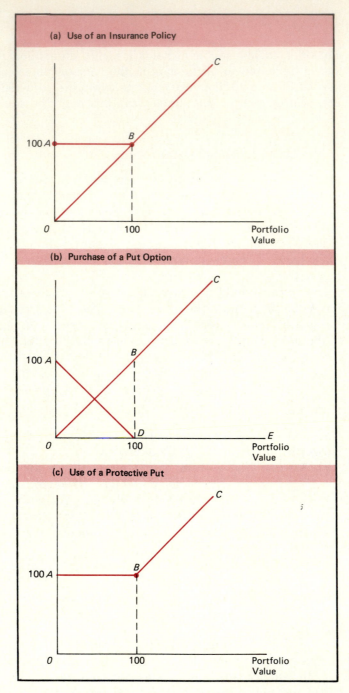

FIGURE 16-14
Portfolio Insurance

Dynamic Asset Allocation

What if neither explicit insurance nor an appropriate put were available? Can something still be done? Yes, if the allocation of funds between the portfolio and a riskless security can be altered frequently enough (and at reasonable cost).

Figure 16-15(a) provides a simple example. Assume that the portfolio value may increase from $100,000 to $120,000 or fall to $80,000 in six months. In the former case, it may end up worth $140,000 or $100,000 after another six months. In the latter case, the possible ending values are $100,000 and $60,000. In the figure, each of the possible *states of the world* is indicated by a letter.

Figure 16-15(a) shows two sets of terminal values. The first gives the values of an uninsured portfolio. The second shows the desired values—i.e., those of an insured portfolio.

Now, imagine that six months have passed and that state of the

FIGURE 16-15
Dynamic Asset Allocation.

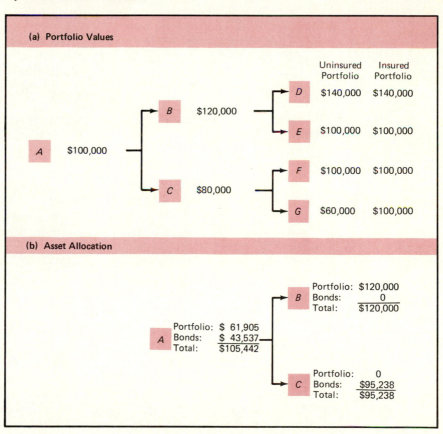

world B has occurred. In this situation, how might one be certain to have $140,000 if the final state is D and $100,000 if the state is E? The answer is simple—invest $120,000 *in the portfolio*. Thus an *initial* strategy is required that will provide $120,000 if the state of the world is B, so there will be adequate funds at that point.

Now, imagine that after the first six months, state of the world C has occurred. In this situation, how might one be certain to have $100,000 if the final state is F and $100,000 if the state is G? Assume that riskless bonds return 5% per six months. Clearly, the desired situation requires the investment of $95,238 (= $100,000/1.05) *in bonds*. Thus an *initial* strategy is required that will provide $95,238 if the state of the world is C.

Figure 16-15(b) shows the investments and the amounts required in situations B and C. It remains only to determine an appropriate initial set of investments (at point A).

An amount of $1 invested in the portfolio will grow to $1.20 if the state of the world is B, and P invested in the portfolio will grow to $1.2P$. Similarly, B invested in bonds will grow to $1.05B$. We require investments that will provide $120,000 in this situation. Thus:

$$1.2P + 1.05B = 120,000$$

If the state of the world is C, P invested in the portfolio will end up worth $.8P$, while B invested in bonds will be worth $1.05B$. We require investments that will provide $95,238 in this situation. Thus:

$$.8P + 1.05B = 95,238$$

Since *both* conditions must be met, we must find values for P and B that satisfy both equations. This is straightforward, since there are two equations and two unknowns. The solution is shown in Figure 16-15. A total amount of $105,442 must be invested, with $61,905 in the portfolio and $43,537 in bonds.

Note that this is equivalent to purchasing the portfolio for $100,000 and buying a protective put option (or an insurance policy) for $5,442. Indeed, this analysis could be used to determine the appropriate price for such an option or insurance policy.

By design, this investment can provide precisely the desired ending values, but only if the "mix" is altered as values change. The goal is achieved not by adopting a *static* mix of investments, but rather by using a *dynamic strategy* in which investments are bought and sold at intermediate points, depending on the performance of the underlying assets.

In this example, *more* money is invested in stocks when the portfolio *rises* in value. When the portfolio *falls* in value, stocks are sold. In this (extreme) case, the percentage invested in stocks goes from 41.86% to either 100% (if stocks go up) or 0% (if stocks go down).

More realistic situations involve many time periods, with smaller "jumps" in each period and smaller reactions to changes in value. However, the essential nature of the strategy is the same:

When stock prices rise, buy more stocks.

When stock prices fall, sell some stocks.

If there are only two states of the world in each "period," and reallocation is possible after every period, the payoffs associated with any desired "insured portfolio" can be replicated exactly with a dynamic allocation strategy. In practice, however, the results are likely to be only approximately equal. First, transactions costs associated with buying and selling securities will require more investment (or provide lower returns) for the dynamic strategy. Second, it may be impossible to act in time to "cover" a major change. If a period is defined as a length of time over which only two alternative states of the world may occur, the actual time required for a "period" may vary considerably. Many such "periods" might occur in such a short time that reallocation was impossible until they were over. This is equivalent to price movements that are "orderly" most of the time but take big "jumps" at other times.

Despite these potential drawbacks, dynamic allocation strategies remain attractive in many instances in which insurance and appropriate listed options are not available. In practice, heuristic rules are applied to avoid "churning" or "whipsawing," and estimates are made of the extent to which the desired insurance is likely to be achieved.

Who Should Insure?

If some investors insure their portfolios, others must "write the insurance." When dynamic allocation strategies are used, the former buy more stocks when prices rise, and sell some when prices fall. The "insurance writers" are the investors who sell them the stocks when prices rise and buy the stocks back when prices fall.

Figure 16-16 shows the situations of three investors. Curve OBC indicates the payoffs for an investor who simply holds a portfolio at all times. Curve ADE shows the payoffs for an investor who insures the portfolio by purchasing a protective put. In this case the investor is assumed to have borrowed money to pay for the put (e.g., $5,442 in the previous example), and the payoffs are *net* of the cost of repaying the loan.

Curve FGH shows the payoffs for an investor who holds riskless securities and sells the put. He or she is assumed to have also invested the proceeds from the sale of the put in riskless securities, and the payoffs include the proceeds of this added investment.

If dynamic asset allocation strategies were used instead of explicit sale and purchase of a put option, the curves would differ only by the inclusion of transactions costs.

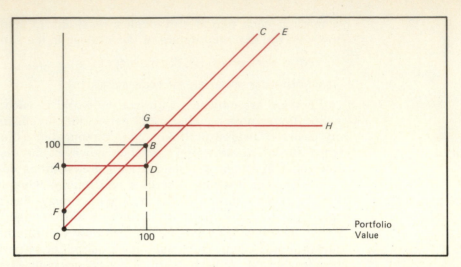

FIGURE 16-16
Buying and Selling Portfolio Insurance.

At a global level, it is useful to consider the "portfolio" involved to be the market portfolio of bonds and stocks. Here, too, the three curves can be considered representative of those who insure (curve *ADE*), those who neither insure nor write insurance (curve *OBC*), and those who write insurance (curve *FGH*).

In an efficient market, investors with "average" attitudes toward risk should neither insure nor write insurance. Those who are especially averse to "downside risk" (relative to "upside potential") may find it useful to buy insurance from those who are less averse than average to such risk. Key is the nature of investors' *utility functions*. Those whose tolerance for risk decreases most rapidly as they become poorer should buy insurance from those whose tolerance decreases least rapidly. Those who are average in this respect should neither buy nor sell insurance.

Our examples have considered only extreme insurance policies: the resulting payoff functions were composed of two straight lines and a clear "kink." Many other alternatives are possible, including many "kinks" and smoother curves. Clever use of dynamic asset allocation strategies can provide almost any desired payoff function (but at a cost).

OPTION TERMINOLOGY

Those who deal in listed options have invented a number of new terms to spice up conversations that would otherwise be devoted almost wholly to numbers. Figure 16-17 shows some of them, using a call

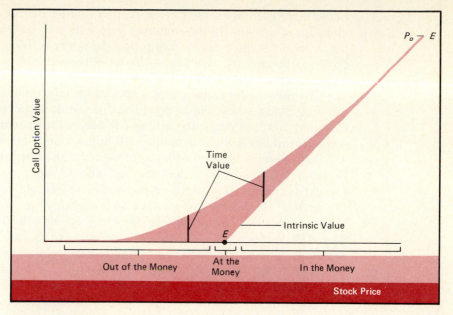

FIGURE 16-17
Option Terminology.

option for illustration. Options with exercise prices near the current price are said to be *at the money*. Those with exercise prices well above the current stock price are *out of the money*, while those with exercise prices well below the current stock price are *in the money*. Occasionally finer gradations are invoked, and one hears of "near-the-money," "deep-in-the-money," "far-out-of-the-money," and so on.

The amount an option would command if it were exercised immediately is termed its *intrinsic value*. The excess of its price over this amount is the option's *time value*, which is due to its attributes and the time remaining before expiration. As illustrated in Figure 16-17, the time value of an option near the money is larger than that of one that is far out of the money or far in the money.

OPTION SPREADS

If one can find overpriced options and underpriced options on the same stock, why not try to profit from the redress of this presumably transitory imbalance and avoid the stock itself entirely? Such is the reasoning behind the creation of an *option spread*.

A *price spread* involves the purchase of one option and the sale of another written on the same security with the same expiration date but with a different exercise price. A *time spread* involves the purchase and sale of options on the same security with the same exercise price but with different times to expiration. In a *butterfly spread* one call option is bought and two sold—one on either side (in time or money), or vice versa.

To reduce the exposure of a spread to movement in the price of the underlying stock, the hedge ratios of the options can be utilized. Consider a stock currently selling for $40, with an annual standard deviation of .50. Two nine-month call options on it are available: one with an exercise price of $50, the other with an exercise price of $40. Formula (16-4) indicates that the first should sell for $3.40 and the second for $7.49. It also gives the hedge ratios: .42 for the "out-of-the-money" option and .62 for the "at-the-money" option.

Assume that the actual option prices are not $3.40 and $7.49 but $4 and $7, respectively. An investor attempting to profit from this apparent aberration would want to buy the underpriced option and sell the overpriced one. However, equal amounts of the two options would leave the portfolio highly exposed to stock price movements, since a $1 change in stock price may be expected to change the out-of-money options' price by $.42 and the other option's price by $.62. The solution is to utilize only .68 (= .42/.62) times as many of the latter options as the former.

VALUING CONVERTIBLE BONDS

Valuation of a noncallable convertible bond is difficult enough. Valuation of a callable convertible is even worse. And most convertible bonds are callable. No simple formula is available for the purpose.[14] But the relevant relationships can be indicated; they are illustrated in Figure 16-18.

Figure 16-18(a) shows, for various prices of the corporation's stock, the value such a security would have were it a nonconvertible, noncallable (but risky) bond. The greater the value of the corporation's stock, the smaller the risk of default and the closer the convertible's "value as a bond" comes to that of an otherwise equivalent default-free noncallable, nonconvertible bond.

Figure 16-18(b) shows a likely pattern for the value of the latent warrants implicit in the conversion privilege. Were the bond not callable, the sum of the values shown in Figures 16-18(a) and (b) would equal the total value of the bond, giving a pattern such as that shown in Figure 16-18(c). But the presence of a call provision restricts a bond's

---

[14] For a discussion of numerical procedures that can be used, see M. J. Brennan and E. S. Schwartz, "Convertible Bonds: Valuation and Optimal Strategies for Call and Conversion," *Journal of Finance*, December 1977.

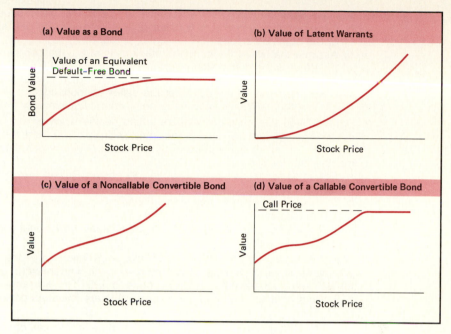

FIGURE 16-18
Components of Value for a Convertible Bond.

value: once the deferral period has passed, the price is not likely to rise significantly above the call price (if it did, the corporation would undoubtedly call the bond). The overall relationship is thus likely to be more like that shown in Figure 16-18(d).

Almost all options and securities with option characteristics are difficult to value. This undoubtedly accounts for much of their fascination. When the value of a security is especially difficult to estimate with precision, an investor may hope that mispricing will occur and that he or she will be able to detect it and profit thereby. However, such a profit is likely to be someone else's loss. In a relatively efficient market, one is not likely to be able to make this kind of gain repeatedly.

Problems

1. The Jay Gould Corporation has an issue of 5% convertible debentures outstanding which will mature in ten years. The present conversion price is $40; the call price is $110. Nonconvertible bonds of similar quality are selling to yield 5%. Dividends on the common stock of Jay Gould are $2 per share.

a. If the common stock sells at 30, what will be the minimum price of the bond?
b. If the bond is quoted at 120 (bond points), what can be said about the price of the common stock?
c. Assume that when the common stock sells at 60, the bond sells at 170.
  (1) What is the conversion premium?
  (2) If the bonds are called, with the common at 60, what will be the price of the bond on the day after the call is announced?
  (3) Will the call be likely to force conversion? Explain your answer fully.

2. Russell Sage has only a few hours left to decide whether to exercise his call option on Levi Strauss. Levi is currently selling at $60, and the call option in question has an exercise price of $54. Russell originally purchased the call six months ago for $400.
  a. For what range of stock price on LVI should Russell exercise the call on the last day of the call life?
  b. For what range of stock price on LVI would Russell realize a net loss (including the original market price of the call)?
  c. If Russell had purchased a put instead of a call, how would you answer parts (a) through (c)?

3. Warrants issued by the Dutch East India Corporation allow the holder to buy six shares of Dutch East India common for each warrant held. The stock sells for $25 per share and the exercise price is $20. The warrants are selling for $40. What premium over the conversion value are investors paying for this warrant?

4. Given the information below, calculate the three-month call option price that is consistent with the Black-Scholes model.

$$P_s = \$47, \ E = \$45, \ r = .05, \ \sigma = .40$$

5. If the risk of a stock increases, what is likely to happen to the prices of call options on the stock? To the prices of put options? Why?

6. Some assert that if one writes call options on stocks held in a portfolio, it is possible to increase return *and* reduce risk. Do you agree with both assertions, one, or neither? Why?

7. If the average premium on call options has recently declined, does this indicate that such options are better buys than they were previously? Why or why not?

8. On Thursday, February 7, 1980, three call options on Monsanto stock, all expiring in July 1980, sold for the following prices:

Exercise Price	Option Price
$50	$7½
60	3
70	1½

Consider a "butterfly spread" with the following positions:

buy 1 call at $50
sell (write) 2 calls at $60
buy 1 call at $70

What would be the values at expiration of such a spread for various prices of Monsanto at the time? What investment would be required to establish the spread? Given information about the prices of the $50 and $70 options, what could you predict about the price of the $60 option?

9. A six-month call option with an exercise price of $40 is selling for $5. The current price of the stock is $41.25. According to the Black-Scholes formula, if the price of the stock changes by $1, the price of the option will change by $.65.

    a. What *percentage* change in the option price is likely to accompany a 1 *percent* change in the stock price?

    b. If the stock's beta is 1.10, what is the beta of the option?

    c. Assume that securities are currently priced in accordance with a Zero-Beta Capital Asset Pricing Model in which zero-beta stocks have an expected return on 8% and stocks with a beta of 1.0 have an expected return of 15%. What should be the expected return on the option?

    d. Let P_o be the price of a call option, h its hedge ratio, P_s the price of the stock, and β_s the beta of the stock. Write a formula relating β_o, the beta of the option, to P_o, h, P_s, and β_s.

10. In early February 1980 a September call at $55 on Corning Glass Works sold for $4.375 and a September put at $55 sold for $6. At the time Treasury bills coming due in September were priced to give an annual yield of 12.6% and Corning stock was selling for $53.

    a. What value would formula (16-6) suggest was appropriate for the Corning put?

    b. Corning was expected to make three dividend payments between February and September. Could that account for the discrepancy between your answer to (a) and the actual price of the put? Why?

    c. If Corning stock were to fall to a very low value before September, might it pay the owner of the put to exercise it? Why?

17

Futures Contracts

INTRODUCTION

There is nothing unusual about contracts made in advance of delivery. Whenever something is ordered instead of purchased on the spot, a *forward* or *future* contract is involved. The price is decided at the time the order is placed, but cash is exchanged for merchandise later. For some items the lag may be a few days; for others, such as houses, several months. In either case the buyer may be requested to earmark some money to guarantee fulfillment of the obligation. This need not equal the full value of the purchase, only enough to cover the seller's loss in the event that another buyer must be found.

Futures contracts (*futures* for short), provide a standardized means of engaging in such transactions for agricultural and other commodities and for financial instruments and stock indices. One person may want to deliver wheat nine months hence but not know anyone who wishes to receive it, while someone else may want wheat for delivery at that time and not know a seller. An exchange that establishes a standard futures contract for a specified amount and type of wheat makes it possible for such traders to execute their transaction on the floor of the exchange without personal contact. For example, a contract might specify that the seller will deliver 5,000 bushels of a particular grade of wheat to the buyer nine months hence. The exchange of cash for wheat will occur on the delivery date, but each party is required to provide some sort of guarantee that his or her obligation can be met. The amount does not have to equal the full value involved, only the likely loss to the other party in the event that a new partner must be found.

THE FUTURES CONTRACT

The essence of a futures contract is standardization. For example, the Chicago Board of Trade specifies the following requirements for its July wheat contract:

1. The seller agrees to deliver 5,000 bushels of either:
   —No. 2 soft red wheat
   —No. 2 hard red winter wheat
   —No. 2 dark northern spring wheat
   —No. 1 northern spring wheat

   at the agreed-upon price. Alternatively, a number of other grades can be delivered at specified premiums or discounts from the agreed-upon price. In any case the seller is allowed to decide which grade shall be delivered.

2. The grain will be delivered by registered warehouse receipts issued by approved warehouses in Chicago or in Toledo, Ohio (deliveries from Toledo are discounted $.02 per bushel).

3. Delivery will take place during the month of July, with the seller allowed to decide the actual date.

4. Upon delivery of the warehouse receipt from the seller to the buyer, the latter will pay the former the agreed-upon price in cash.

A commodity exchange sets all the terms of a futures contract but the price, then authorizes trading in it. Buyers and sellers or their agents meet on the floor of the exchange, usually in a "pit" provided for the purpose, and try to agree on a trade. If they succeed, one or more contracts will be created, with all the standard terms plus an additional, individual, one—the price involved.

Legally, the seller of a wheat futures contract is obliged to deliver wheat and the buyer to accept delivery. However, as we will see, few contracts are held open until the specified delivery date. The specter of a hapless buyer's front lawn covered with unwanted wheat is part of the folklore of the futures market, not the reality.

Prices are normally stated on a per-unit basis. Thus if a buyer and seller agree to a price of $4.40 per bushel for a contract of 5,000 bushels of wheat, the amount of money involved is $22,000.

Figure 17-1 shows a set of quotations giving the prices at which some commodity futures contracts were traded on one day and the total volume of sales for each type of contract. Such listings, published daily in the financial press, indicate the active futures markets, the number of units per contract, and the terms on which prices are stated. Details of contracts made during the day are given for each type of contract. The *open* price is that at which the first transaction was made; the *high* and *low* represent the highest and lowest prices during

FIGURE 17-1

Quotations for Commodity Futures Prices.

Futures Contracts

523

the day, and the *settlement* is a representative price (e.g., the average of the high and low prices) during the "closing period" designated by the exchange in question (e.g., the last two minutes of trading). After the change from the previous day's settlement price, the highest and lowest prices recorded during the lifetime of the contract involved are indicated. Also shown is the *open interest* (the number of outstanding contracts) on the previous day. For each futures contract, summary figures are given for the total volume (number of contracts) traded on the day in question and on the previous trading day as well as the total open interest in such contracts and change in open interest from the previous day.

Several contracts are usually available for trading in a specific commodity on a single exchange. They differ only with respect to delivery month. Thus Figure 17-1 shows that in May 1984 the Chicago Board of Trade offered contracts in wheat for delivery in May, July, September, and December of 1984 and March, May, and July of 1985.

THE CLEARING HOUSE

Each futures exchange has an associated clearing house, which becomes the "seller's buyer" and the "buyer's seller" as soon as the transaction is concluded. The procedure is similar to that used for options. This is not surprising, since the first market in listed options was set up by people associated with the Chicago Board of Trade. The essential procedures were given in Chapter 16; a detailed description in the context of futures contracts follows.

Figure 17-2 shows how the clearing house operates in this market. When trading in July wheat is first allowed, A agrees to buy 5,000 bushels (one contract) from B at $4.40 per bushel, as shown in Figure 17-2(a). The clearing house immediately steps in and breaks the transactions apart, as shown in Figure 17-2(b). Now it is the obligation of the clearing house to deliver the wheat to A and to accept delivery from B. There is now an *open interest* of 5,000 bushels in July wheat, since a contract exists to deliver that much and, of course, to buy it.

Assume that on the next day, A finds that C will buy July wheat for $4.50 per bushel. This represents a chance for a sure profit of $.10 per bushel, since A has already arranged to buy wheat in July for $4.40 per bushel and could simply wait until July, accept delivery, then turn around and sell the wheat to C for $4.50. As shown in Figure 17-2(c), A makes a *reversing trade* with C, although C neither knows nor cares about A's reasons. Again, the clearing house steps in, as shown in Figure 17-2(d).

Now the benefits of a clearing house, with its ability to break traders apart and depersonalize agreements, become apparent. Figure 17-2(e) shows the current positions of all parties. A's situation can

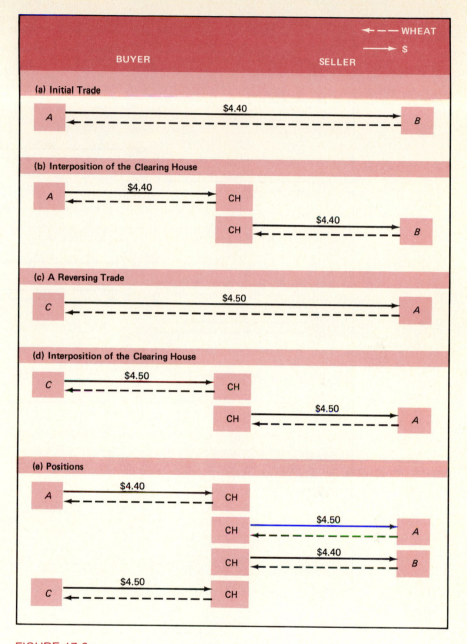

FIGURE 17-2
The Clearing Process.

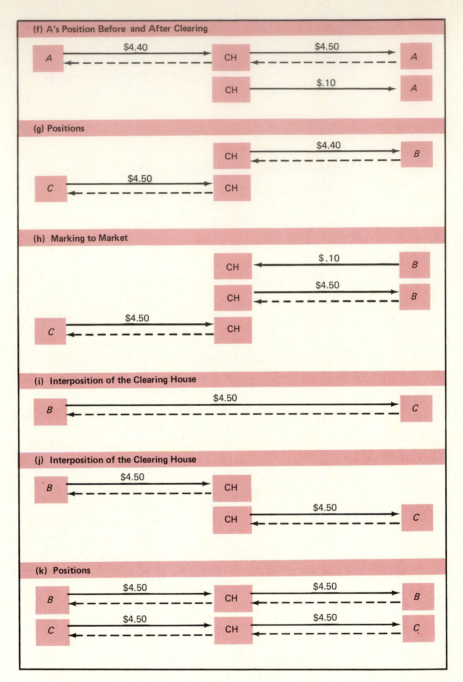

FIGURE 17-2 (*continued*)

clearly be simplified. Figure 17-2(f) shows how it is done. Nominally, A is obligated to deliver 5,000 bushels of wheat to the clearing house in July, which is in turn obligated to deliver it back to A. In addition, A must deliver $4.40 per bushel, or $22,000, to the clearing house, which must in turn deliver $4.50 per bushel, or $22,500, to A. To save expense, the clearing house could just deliver $.10 per bushel, or $500, to A in July and forget the wheat entirely. In fact, the clearing house will deliver the money immediately.

Figure 17-2(g) shows the situation after A is dispatched, profit in hand. B is obligated to deliver wheat to the clearing house in July, which could then deliver it to C (in fact, the clearing house would *assign* the delivery of B's wheat to C). At that time, C could pay the clearing house $4.50 per bushel ($22,500) and the clearing house could pay B $4.40 per bushel ($22,000), keeping the difference. Although B and C did not trade with one another initially, they can be paired by the clearing house in this manner, if desired.

In fact, the procedure is simplified by the rule that every position is *marked to market* at the end of each day.

At the end of the second day the settlement price is $4.50—up $.10 from the previous day's value. At the end of the previous day, B held a contract to deliver wheat in July at $4.40 per bushel. In effect, this is *replaced* with a new contract to deliver wheat in July at $4.50 per bushel. Since this is a better price for B, he must pay the difference ($.10 per bushel) to the clearing house *now*. This amount—$500—is exactly equal to the money paid to A by the clearing house.

If the settlement price had fallen to $4.30 rather than risen to $4.50, B would have been *paid* $500 by the clearing house, to compensate him for replacing a contract to deliver wheat in July at $4.40 with one to deliver wheat at $4.30.

In effect, a futures contract is a forward contract that is settled every day and replaced with a new contract, with a delivery price equal to the previous day's settlement price. This daily settlement process insures that the clearing house is even at all times.

Figure 17-2(h) shows the process of marking all outstanding contracts to market.

In most cases the process is even more complex. Only brokers belong to a clearing house, and it is *their* accounts that are settled by the clearing house at the end of every day. Each brokerage firm acts in turn as a clearing house for its own clients.

What if B and C want to avoid delivery of actual wheat? Imagine that on the third day they trade with each other at a price of $4.50, as shown in Figure 17-2(i). The clearing house comes in again, as shown in Figure 17-2(j), giving the net positions shown in Figure 17-2(k). The positions are then closed out, reducing open interest by 5,000 bushels.

These rather complex arrangements make it possible for futures traders to think in very simple terms. In the example, A bought a contract of July wheat at $4.40 and sold it on the next day for $4.50, making a profit of $.10 per bushel. B sold a contract of July wheat for $4.40 and later bought it back for $4.50, suffering a loss of $.10 per bushel, and C bought a contract at $4.50 and sold it for $4.50, realizing neither a profit nor a loss.

FUTURES POSITIONS

Consider a speculator who buys a contract of July wheat. He or she now has a *long position* and is said to be *long* one contract (5,000 bushels) of July wheat.

An open position created by the *sale* of a commodity future is termed a *short position*, and the account holder is said to be *short* the contract.

The process of marking contracts to market every day means that changes in the settlement price are *realized* as soon as they occur. When the settlement price *rises*, those with long positions realize *profits* equal to the change and those who are short realize *losses*. When the settlement price *falls*, those with long positions realize *losses*, while those with short positions realize *profits*. In either event, total profits always equal total losses.

MARGINS

Strictly speaking, the purchase or sale of a futures contract is not an investment. The buyer of July wheat does not own wheat, only the obligation to exchange a specified amount of money for wheat in July. Similarly, the seller is obligated solely to deliver wheat in July at that price. Prior to July, money will change hands as a result of the daily marking to market, but such amounts may be positive or negative, depending on the course of prices.

There is, however, a requirement for the posting of *margins*— security deposits intended to guarantee that people with positions in futures will in fact be able to fulfill their obligations.

Calculations of gains and losses are made routinely by brokerage firms handling customers' *commodity accounts*. Each account of this type must be kept separately from other, noncommodity accounts.

A commodity account can include cash, interest-earning default-free assets (e.g., Treasury bills), and open commodity positions. The key figure is the net *equity* in the account, defined as follows:

equity = cash and/or cash-equivalents
 (e.g., U.S. Treasury bills)
 plus gains on open positions
 less losses on open positions

Margin requirements are designed to insure that a commodity account has a sufficiently large equity, relative to the size of all open positions, to make the probability of reaching a negative equity position in a day very small.

Each exchange sets minimum margin requirements for its contracts; brokers often require additional amounts. Practice varies, but the *initial margin*, assessed when a position is first opened, is usually 5% to 10% of the total value of the contract. If the equity in an account falls below this amount, the customer may be required to add cash to the account to increase the equity. The *maintenance margin*, below which equity is not allowed to fall without remedial action, is usually 75% to 80% as large as the initial margin. The initial margin and the maintenance margin are typically stated as fixed dollar amounts per contract. In general, the greater the value of a contract and the variability of its price, the larger will be the required margins.

When the equity in an account falls below the maintenance margin, the customer receives a *margin call*. If additional cash is not obtained, the broker may close out one or more positions to reduce the required margin until it conforms to the current value of the equity in the account. When the equity exceeds that required for margin, cash may be removed, in some cases up to the point at which the margin requirements are just met.

Some brokers require a minimum dollar value of equity in a commodity account. Some allow only cash to be used and pay no interest on it. Others allow the use of interest-earning cash equivalents (usually U.S. Treasury bills), at least for accounts with equity greater than a specified minimum.

If interest-earning securities can be posted to meet margin requirements, it is clear that no investment is involved in an open commodity position. The individual's funds are invested, but in Treasury bills. Open commodity positions can be regarded as bets that have yet to be settled. On the other hand, if only cash is allowed, the required margin may be considered the investment needed to support the open commodity positions. This will be small relative to the values of such positions and even relative to the possible gains and losses from them. This has led many to argue that commodity futures are "highly levered" and extremely risky investments. Taking the margin required as an investment base, they certainly are, but there is no more need for an investor to maintain such high leverage than there is to purchase stocks using the maximum allowable amount of margin.

FUTURES CONTRACTS VERSUS CALL OPTIONS

People occasionally make the mistake of considering a futures contract an option. It is not. While the seller is allowed some alternatives concerning the delivery date and grade, both parties are obligated to complete the transaction, either by a reversing trade or actual delivery.

Figure 17-3 contrasts the situations faced by (a) the buyer and seller of a call option and (b) the buyer and seller of a commodity futures contract. In each case, it is assumed that positions are taken one day prior to the last possible moment—the expiration date for the option, and the delivery month for the futures contract.

As shown in Figure 17-3(a), no matter what the price of the underlying stock, at expiration an option buyer cannot lose and an option seller cannot gain. Option buyers compensate sellers for putting themselves in this position by paying them a premium when the agreement is first concluded. The exercise price is set more or less arbitrarily, and the premium negotiated. In a broader sense, the *premium* is the equilibrating factor, bringing quantity demanded and quantity supplied together in the options market.

The situation is quite different with a futures contract. As shown in Figure 17-3(b), the buyer may gain or lose, depending on the commodity price in the delivery month, and so may the seller. The higher the original contract price, the greater the likelihood that the buyer will lose and the seller will gain. The lower the original contract price, the greater the likelihood that the seller will lose and the buyer will gain. If the contract price were set arbitrarily, some sort of payment from one party to the other would undoubtedly be required to obtain agreement. However, this is not done. Instead, the contract price is negotiated in an attempt to find a value that will lead both parties to consider the resulting prospects worth their while.

In the futures market, the *contract price* is the equilibrating factor, bringing together the quantity demanded and the quantity supplied. No money is paid by either party to the other.

FIGURE 17-3
Values of Positions.

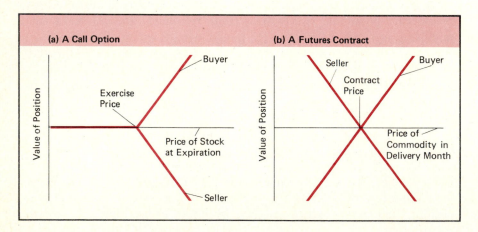

Futures Contracts

RETURNS ON COMMODITY FUTURES

During the period from 1950 through 1976 a portfolio made up of unlevered positions in 23 different commodity futures contracts provided results similar to those that could have been obtained with a diversified portfolio of common stocks:[1]

	Average Return (% per year)	Standard Deviation of Return (% per year)
23 commodity futures	13.83	22.43
Standard and Poor's 500-stock index	13.05	18.95

Historically, commodity futures have been similar to common stocks in terms of risk, when evaluated on a comparable basis. They have also provided similar returns. Given a choice of one type of investment or the other, an investor might consider the two alternatives equally desirable. But during the period covered, each was dominated by a combination of the two. The returns of these portfolios were *negatively* correlated, so the return on a diversified futures/stock portfolio would have varied considerably less. The correlation coefficient was −.24, and the standard deviations of return for portfolios with different proportions were as follows:[2]

Percent in Stock	Percent in Futures	Standard Deviation
0	100	22.43
20	80	17.43
40	60	13.77
60	40	12.68
80	20	14.74
100	0	18.95

Not surprisingly, commodity futures have served as at least a partial hedge against inflation. During the 1950–1976 period the returns

---

[1] Source: Zvi Bodie and Victor Rosansky, "Risk and Return in Commodity Futures," *Financial Analysts Journal*, May/June 1980.

[2] *Ibid.*

on the portfolio of 23 commodity futures were positively correlated with changes in the consumer price index.[3] As a result, the variation in real returns was less than that of nominal returns. This contrasts with the results for common stocks, where the results were just the opposite:[4]

STANDARD DEVIATION OF TOTAL RETURN (% PER YEAR)		
	Nominal Return	Real Return
23 commodity futures	22.43	19.44
Standard and Poor's 500-stock index	18.95	19.65

OPEN INTEREST

When trading is first allowed in a contract, there is no open interest; it grows as people begin to make transactions. At any time, open interest equals the amount that those with short positions are currently obligated to deliver. It also equals the amount that those with long positions are obligated to accept and pay for.

Open interest figures are shown with futures prices. For example, Figure 17-1 indicates that on May 24, 1984, a total of 27,431 contracts in July 1984 wheat were outstanding on the Chicago Board of Trade. Note the substantial differences in the open interest figures for the other wheat contracts on the Chicago Board of Trade on that day. This is quite typical. Figure 17-4 shows why. Open interest in a December wheat contract is shown for every month from the preceding January until the contract expired at the end of the delivery month. From January until the end of September, more trades were generally made to open new positions than to close out old ones, and open interest continued to increase. As the delivery month came closer, reversing trades began to outnumber those intended to open new positions, and open interest began to decline. The amount remaining at the beginning of December was the maximum number of bushels of wheat that could have been delivered against futures contracts, but most of these contracts were also settled by reversing trades instead of delivery.

Relatively few commodity futures positions—less than 3% of the

---

[3] The correlation coefficient was .58.

[4] The correlation coefficient between stock returns and changes in the consumer price index was −.43.

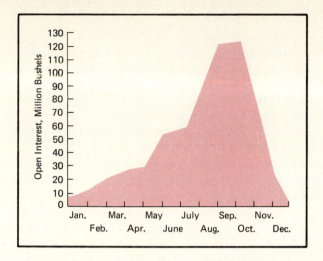

FIGURE 17-4
Open Interest December 1978
Chicago Board of Trade Wheat
Contract: January 3, 1978 through
December 28, 1978.

total[5] —end in actual delivery of the commodity involved, but the fact that delivery is a possibility makes a contract's value in the delivery month differ only slightly, if at all, from the price of the actual commodity. No more is needed, as an analogy from the insurance industry will illustrate.

Policies that insure against loss from fire or theft generally guarantee replacement with an equivalent item. In fact, settlement is often made in cash, which the insured party can use to purchase an equivalent item (or not, as desired). As long as the cash involved bears a close relationship to the value of the designated item, there is no need for actual "delivery." The commodities futures market, which provides a kind of insurance, can also function effectively with a few if any deliveries. The potential for delivery insures that in the final month the futures price will bear a close relationship to the commodity's spot price. Few buyers wish to have the specific commodity offered by the futures contract: most prefer to settle in cash and acquire the type of asset they want at the location they want.

Most futures contracts on financial instruments require delivery of the corresponding security. However, stock index futures do not require delivery of the set of stocks comprising the corresponding index. Instead, an amount equal to the difference between the level of the index and the contract price is paid *in cash*. As in other futures markets, most positions are closed out with reversing trades prior to the date at which delivery (in kind or in cash) is required.

---

[5] Merrill Lynch, Pierce, Fenner and Smith, Inc., *Speculating on Inflation: Futures Trading in Interest Rates, Foreign Currencies and Precious Metals*, July 1979.

PRICE LIMITS

It is said that a farmer, tired of violent fluctuations in temperature, had his thermometer altered so it could not move more than 5 degrees in either direction from the previous day's reading. The story is undoubtedly apocryphal but it is instructive.

The U.S. Commodity Futures Trading Commission, which regulates trading on U.S. commodity exchanges, places limits on the extent to which futures prices are allowed to vary from day to day. For example, if July wheat closed at $4.40 on the previous day, contracts at prices outside the range from $4.20 to $4.60 might be forbidden. If a major piece of news during the day led traders to consider $4.65 a reasonable value for the contract, they would have to: (1) trade privately, foregoing the advantages offered by the exchange, (2) trade on the exchange at the *limit price* of $4.60, or (3) wait until the next day, when prices from $4.60 to $4.80 would be allowed, based on the current day's closing price of $4.60 (a "limit move"), even though the latter price might simply represent an unfulfilled bid.

The placing of limits on price fluctuations derives from a feeling that traders may overreact to major news and should be "protected" from voluntarily entering into agreements under such conditions. However questionable the position, it is firmly held and of long standing.

TAXATION OF FUTURES PROFITS AND LOSSES

A *speculator* in a futures market is considered to have a *capital asset* for tax purposes, whether he or she is long or short. When the position is closed out, the resultant profit or loss is treated as a *capital* gain or loss. If the holding period is less than six months, the gain or loss is *short-term*; otherwise it is *long-term* for tax purposes.

Hedgers' positions in the futures market are considered part of their commercial activities. Their profits and losses are thus generally treated as *ordinary* income or loss for tax purposes.

HEDGING

When two horse race enthusiasts bet with each other, the activity is termed *gambling*. This has an antisocial connotation, as it involves the creation of a new risk where there was none before. However, when the owner of one of the horses in a race makes a bet on one or more of the other horses, the situation is different (and generally illegal). The other party involved may be a gambler, but the owner is "hedging his bets" and can be termed a *hedger*. If the owner's horse wins, there will be good news and bad news: the good news is winning the prize money, the bad news is losing the bets. Conversely, if the horse loses, the prize money will be lost, but not all the bets. Astute betting may even allow the initial risk to be *completely hedged*, so the owner's income will be unaffected by the outcome of the race. In this case all the original risk has been *transferred* from the owner to the gambler. If the risk were only partially hedged, of course, there would be only a partial transfer.[6]

If two disinterested parties make a bet on whether or not your house will burn down, they are gambling—creating risk. But if you make a bet that it will burn down, you are hedging. This is usually done by purchasing fire insurance, and the "gambler" involved is an insurance company. The result is usually considered socially desirable. The insurance company, able to pool risks, is willing to take on a homeowner's risk at a price that he or she is willing to pay to reduce exposure to a single, uncertain event.

The same situation occurs in the futures market. Farmers, dealers, processors, and others heavily exposed to possible fluctuations in, say, commodity prices are willing to pay others to take over some or all of the associated risk. Outsiders who act as the insurance companies are called *speculators*.

The view of a futures market as a place in which everyone "in the trade" completely hedges all risk by dealing with speculators who make themselves available to serve as bearers of such risk is both too simple and too idealistic. First, many people in the trade choose to bear some risk—either the risk due to general fluctuations in the price of an asset or that due to fluctuations in the differences between the prices of different assets, the same asset in different locations, and so on: partial hedging is far more common than complete hedging. Second, many hedgers trade with one another. Finally, speculators also trade with one another. Both gambling and insurance can be found in most futures markets.

The usual characterization of a commodity hedger is that of someone forced to hold a large inventory of a commodity that for some reason cannot be sold until a later date. To "fix the price" such a person can sell a corresponding futures contract. This is termed *short hedging*, since the hedger is long (owns) the actual commodity and *short* (has sold) a futures contract. As long as the value of the actual inventory moves in concert with the commodity futures price, this will provide a hedge: when the actual commodity is sold, the hedge can be "lifted" via a reversing trade. Any gain on the commodity will be offset by a comparable loss on the futures contract, while any loss

---

[6] An owner who bets on his own horse, thereby increasing risk instead of transferring and reducing it, is said to have taken a "Texas hedge" (Merrill Lynch, Pierce, Fenner and Smith, Inc., *The Hedger's Handbook*, 1971).

on the commodity will be offset by a comparable gain on the futures contract.

The opposite situation can also occur. A manufacturer or dealer may have contracted for delivery of a commodity or a product that uses it as input at some later date. Purchase of the commodity at present may be undesirable for reasons such as space limitations. To fix the price, a *long* position in an appropriate commodity futures contract can be opened; this is termed *long hedging*. Assuming that the futures price moves with that of the commodity, the implicit short position in the actual good can be offset by the position in the futures market. When the commodity is purchased, the hedge can be lifted via a reversing trade. Any gain on the commodity due to a fall in price prior to purchase will be offset by a loss on the commodity futures contract; any loss due to a rise in price prior to purchase will be offset by a gain on the futures contract.

In some cases a short hedger will literally deliver his or her commodity inventory to the buyer of a contract. In others a long hedger will actually take delivery. But such instances are rare, for they are likely to involve the "wrong" grade, place, or time.

The availability of futures contracts on financial instruments makes it possible for financial institutions to hedge some of the risks associated with their business. Savings and loan companies can take positions in mortgage futures to offset much of the interest-rate risk associated with their loan portfolio. Holders of stock portfolios can take positions in stock index futures to offset much of the "market-related" risk of their portfolios. And so on.

BASIS

An investor with both long and short positions has, in effect, invested in the difference between them, since this is what determines his or her net worth. For a hedger with a position in the actual commodity or financial instrument and an opposite position of equal magnitude in a futures contract, the difference between the futures price and the price of the corresponding asset for immediate delivery is crucial. The latter is termed the *spot* price. The difference is the *basis*:

$$\text{basis} = \text{futures price} - \text{spot price}$$

A person with a long position in a futures contract and a short position in the actual asset will profit if the basis widens and lose if it narrows. One with a short position in a futures contract and a long position in the actual asset will suffer a loss if the basis widens and gain if it narrows.

Anyone who has "completely" hedged on asset position has exchanged price risk for basis risk. Only uncertainty about the difference between the value of the specific asset and that of the futures contract remains. The individual can thus be said to be *speculating on the basis*. For commodities this will depend on differences in the prices of different grades, geographic locations, and so on. For bonds it will depend on differences in maturities, investment quality, and so on. For stock portfolios and stock indices, it will depend on differences in sensitivities to various factors and nonfactor returns.

With such an approach, success requires knowledge of local conditions that affect price *differences*, not global conditions that affect price *levels*. For example, a "stock picker" might feel that he or she has no expertise in predicting the course of the stock market as a whole but can select stocks that will perform *relatively* well. By purchasing such stocks and taking a short position in a futures contract on a diversified index of stocks, he or she can hedge out market risk. The net outcome will then depend on the *nonmarket return* of the portfolio, as desired.

SPREADS

It is quite possible to take a long position in a futures contract and a short position in another contract in the same commodity, but with a different delivery date. The person who does this is speculating on changes in the difference between the prices of the two contracts, a difference that constitutes the "basis" for this particular hedge.

Others attempt to profit from temporary imbalances among the prices of futures contracts on different but related commodities. For example, one might take a position in soybeans with offsetting positions in the items produced from them: soybean oil and soybean meal. Another possibility involves a position in wheat with an offsetting position in corn, which serves as a substitute for wheat in many applications.

Like a hedger, a *spreader* reduces or eliminates the risk associated with general price moves, taking on instead the risk associated with changes in price *differences*. Superior knowledge and ability are required to attain a profit from such changes, and spreaders believe they have what is required to handle such a risk.

SPOT PRICES

Most commodity futures exchanges provide areas in which buyers and sellers can negotiate cash (or spot) sales. No attempt is made to standardize such agreements; everything, including grade, location, and delivery, is negotiable. For this reason there is no such thing as a standardized spot price. Instead, the nearest futures price is often used as a surrogate for one. In fact, deals in the spot market may even be made in terms of the price of the nearest futures contract—for example, two parties might agree to trade at 2 cents per bushel more than the relevant futures price. In essence, trades are conducted in terms of the basis.

The price of any commodity is determined by demand and supply. It is in the realm of supply that wheat differs from, say, automobiles. Wheat is a *seasonal* commodity, generally harvested in the United States from late May through September (although in other countries harvests occur at other times). Seasonality has important implications for price determination.

Key is the concept of *carrying costs*. These include all costs associated with holding an inventory of the commodity. The major components are foregone *interest* on the money invested in the inventory and the cost of *storage* for the inventory.

If everyone knew that the price of a commodity was certain to rise by an amount *exceeding* its carrying cost, arbitrageurs would purchase the entire supply in order to make a profit from selling it at a later date. As a result, its present price would rise, until the predicted future price change was in line with carrying costs.

In practice there is considerable uncertainty about the future price of any commodity. However, the costs associated with storing inventories lead to a typical pattern in which prices of seasonal commodities tend to increase after the main harvest season, and fall as each new harvest comes in. Figure 17-5 shows a possible pattern for three harvest seasons, on the assumption that all three harvests are of equal size. Figure 17-6 shows actual prices. Some traces of a "normal" seasonal pattern can be seen, but new information frequently moved the entire pattern up or down. Uncertainty brings relatively random price changes, and prices of seasonal commodities are no exception to the general rule.

For commodities such as copper, gold, and silver there is no "harvest season." This is true, *a fortiori*, for financial instruments such

FIGURE 17-5
Spot Prices for a Seasonal Commodity.

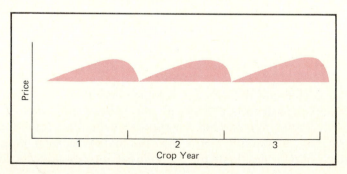

Futures Contracts

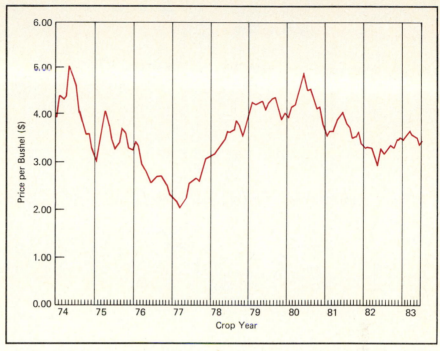

SOURCE: Chicago Board of Trade, *1983 Statistical Annual: Cash and Futures Data, Grains, Forest Products.*

FIGURE 17-6
Wheat: Average Monthly Cash Prices, No. 2 Red Winter, Chicago.

as foreign currencies, bonds, and stock indices. In such cases, there is no reason to expect a strong seasonal pattern in spot prices.

FUTURES PRICES

If all spot prices could be predicted with certainty, there would be little reason to make a contract for future delivery; however, nothing would preclude people from doing so. If they did, each futures price would simply equal the (perfectly predictable) spot price on the relevant delivery date.

Figure 17-7(a) shows this relationship for a seasonal commodity harvested in June. Three futures contracts are assumed to be traded at any time, offering delivery on the last day of March, July, and September, respectively. Each contract is traded during the 364 days prior to the specified delivery date. Since no uncertainty is involved, no margin need be posted by either party. With no investment and no

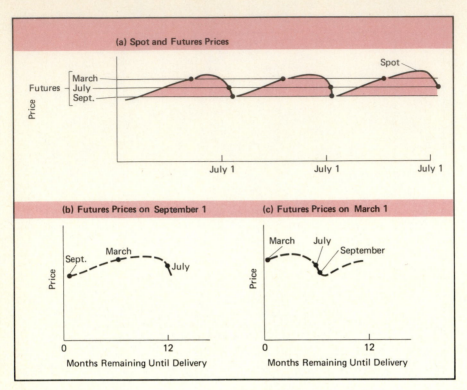

FIGURE 17-7
Commodity Prices in a World of Certainty.

uncertainty, it is hardly surprising that the price of a futures contract would not change during its life.

Note that during the life of any contract the spot price is sometimes above and sometimes below the futures price. Note also that at some times "distant" futures contracts sell for more than "near" ones, and at other times the situation is reversed. This is shown in Figures 17-7(b) and 17-7(c), which plot the prices of various contracts versus their remaining lives at two times of the year. In this case, if contracts were available for every possible delivery date, their prices would plot along the dashed curves, which reflect the (known) future pattern of spot rates.

In fact, there is considerable uncertainty about the spot prices of most assets. This makes it difficult to make definitive statements about futures prices.

It is easier to say what futures prices will *not* be than what they *will* be. Assume, for example, that wheat currently sells for $4 per bushel, the riskless rate of interest is .5% per month, and carrying costs are 2.5 cents per bushel per month. What can be said about the current price for a 12-month futures contract? If it were, say, $4.60, a *certain* profit could be made in the following manner:

Now

borrow $4
use the loan to buy wheat at $4 per bushel
sell (short) a 12-month contract at $4.60 per bushel

12 Months from Now

pay back loan for $4 × (1.005¹²)	= $4.25 per bushel
pay carrying costs (12 months at $.025 per bushel)	= $ .30 per bushel
	$4.55 per bushel
deliver wheat to purchaser of futures contract: receive:	$4.60 per bushel
net profit:	$ .05 per bushel

Opportunities for a certain profit are rare indeed. In all likelihood the futures contract in question would sell for less than $4.55.

This can be stated more generally:

$$P_t^f \le P^s(1 + r)^t + kt \tag{17-1}$$

where:

P_t^f = the current price of a futures contract for delivery in t months
P^s = the current spot price
r = the riskless rate of interest per month
k = the cost of storage per month (insurance can be included in k or, if dependent on price, in r)

Similar reasoning can be used to place limits on the relationship between the prices of futures contracts for delivery in two different months:[7]

$$P_{t_2}^f \le P_{t_1}^f(1 + r)^{(t_2 - t_1)} + k(t_2 - t_1) \tag{17-2}$$

where:

$P_{t_2}^f$ = the current price of a futures contract for delivery in t_2 months
$P_{t_1}^f$ = the current price of a futures contract for delivery in t_1 months (where $t_1 < t_2$)

If formula (17-2) did not hold, one could take a long position in the contract for delivery at time t_1 and a short position in the contract

---

[7] Formula (17-1) can be considered a special case of formula (17-2) with $t_1 = 0$.

for delivery at time t_2. By taking delivery at t_1 for $P^f_{t_1}$, storing the commodity, then delivering at t_2 for $P^f_{t_2}$, a certain profit could be obtained. Since this is literally too good to be true, the relationship in formula (17-2) is almost never violated.

While this places limits on the relative values of various futures prices, it does not imply that they must move in lockstep with each other. Nevertheless, the linkages are very close, as shown in Figure 17-8, which plots the daily prices of three different futures contracts over a seven-month period. Each price is related to expectations of the future pattern of spot prices, although the contracts are tied to three different points on that pattern. When new information shifts the expected pattern upward, all three prices rise; when it shifts the expected pattern downward, all three prices fall. Unless the pattern of expected future spot prices is altered substantially, in addition to being shifted, prices of all futures contracts for a commodity are likely to change by roughly similar amounts.

Although lack of standardization makes it difficult to analyze the relationship between movements in futures prices and the current spot price for a commodity, the price of an expiring futures contract can be used as a surrogate for the spot price. Not surprisingly, spot and futures prices are also highly correlated, as Figure 17-8 suggests.

FIGURE 17-8
Daily Closing Prices, Three Futures Contracts for Wheat on the Chicago Board of Trade, May 1 to November 30, 1967.

The interrelationship of spot and futures prices makes hedging both possible and effective. This is fortunate, since exposure to the fluctuations of commodity prices may entail substantial risk, as Figures 17-6 and 17-8 amply indicate.

Futures Prices and Expected Spot Prices

It is good to know something about the way in which futures prices are related to each other, but a more important question remains: exactly how are futures prices related to expected spot prices?

The simplest answer is that given by the *expectations hypothesis*: the current price of a futures contract equals the market consensus expectation of the spot price on the delivery date. In symbols:

$$P^f = \exp(\tilde{P}^s)$$

where:

$P^f =$ the current price of a futures contract

$\tilde{P}^s =$ the spot price at the delivery date of the futures contract

$\exp(\tilde{P}^s) =$ the current expectation of $\tilde{P}^s$

If this hypothesis is correct, a speculator can expect neither to win nor to lose from a position in the futures market, be it long or short. Neglecting margin requirements, a speculator who takes a long position at P^f must pay P^f at the delivery date for a commodity worth $\tilde{P}^s$ at the time. His or her profit (which is uncertain in advance) will be:

$$\tilde{P}^s - P^f \qquad \text{(17-3a)}$$

while the expected profit will be:

$$\exp(\tilde{P}^s) - P^f \qquad \text{(17-3b)}$$

which will equal zero if the expectations hypothesis holds.

A speculator with a short position will have to pay P^f for a commodity worth $\tilde{P}^s$ on the delivery date, giving a profit of:

$$P^f - \tilde{P}^s \qquad \text{(17-4a)}$$

and an expected profit of:

$$P^f - \exp(\tilde{P}^s) \qquad \text{(17-4b)}$$

which will also be zero if the expectations hypothesis holds.

Another way to look at the situation is to imagine a speculator who posts 100% margin—i.e., P^f—in the form of interest-earning assets. If a long futures position is initiated at time zero and closed out just prior to the delivery date at time t, the following results will be obtained:

at time zero:
invest P^f (as interest-earning margin)

at time t:

value of margin $= (1 + r)P^f$

proceeds from closing out the futures position $= (\tilde{P}^s - P^f)$

actual return:

$$1 + \tilde{r}_a = \frac{(1 + r)P^f + (\tilde{P}^s - P^f)}{P^f}$$

(17-5a)

$$= (1 + r) + \left(\frac{\tilde{P}^s - P^f}{P^f}\right)$$

where:

$\tilde{r}_a =$ the actual holding-period return on the position from time zero to time t

If the spot price turns out to exceed the futures price, a speculator with such a position will obtain a return greater than that obtained from riskless assets. If the futures price equals the *expected* spot price, a speculator will *expect* to earn only the riskless rate.

The situation faced by a speculator with a short position can be approached in the same manner:

at time zero:

invest P^f (as interest-earning margin)

at time t:

value of margin $= (1 + r)P^f$

proceeds from closing out the futures position $= (P^f - \tilde{P}^s)$

actual return:

$$1 + \tilde{r}_a = \frac{(1 + r)P^f + (P^f - \tilde{P}^s)}{P^f}$$

(17-5b)

$$= (1 + r) + \left(\frac{P^f - \tilde{P}^s}{P^f}\right)$$

In this case actual return will exceed the riskless rate if the spot price turns out to be below the futures price. If the futures price equals the *expected* spot price, a short speculator (like a long speculator) can *expect* to earn only the riskless rate of interest.

The expectations hypothesis is often defended on the grounds that speculators are indifferent to risk and are thus happy to accommodate hedgers without any compensation in the form of a risk premium. This seems unlikely. However, the impact of a specific commodity position on the risk of a diversified portfolio that includes many types of assets may be very small. Diversified investors may thus be willing to take over some risk from hedgers with little if any compensation in the form of expected return over and above the riskless interest

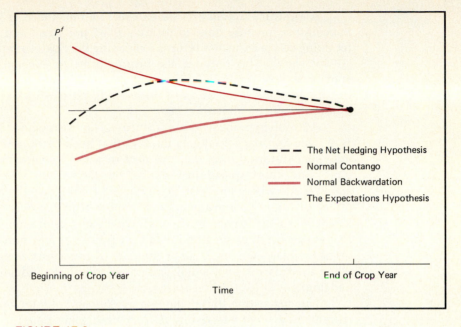

FIGURE 17-9
Price of a Futures Contract for Delivery at the End of the Crop Year When the Spot Price Expected at the Time of Delivery Does Not Change.

rate. This is the strongest argument in favor of the expectations hypothesis.

Figure 17-9 shows the pattern of futures prices implied by the expectations hypothesis, when the expected spot price does not change during the life of the contract.

John Maynard Keynes,[8] no stranger to speculative markets, felt that the expectations hypothesis did not correctly explain futures prices. He argued that hedgers wish to transfer risk to speculators, and that, on net, hedgers will be short the commodity futures and speculators will have to be long. To entice speculators to take such risks (i.e., to provide desired insurance), he suggested, the expected return from a *long* position would have to exceed the riskless rate. As formula (17-5a) shows, this requires the futures price to be less than the expected spot price. Such a relationship, termed *normal backwardation*, implies that the price of any futures contract can be expected to *rise* during its life, as shown in Figure 17-9.[9]

---

[8] J. M. Keynes, *Treatise on Money*, 2 (London: Macmillan, 1930), 142-44. By permission of Macmillan, London and Basingstoke, and the International Economic Association.

[9] If expected spot prices for different delivery dates are the same, normal backwardation also implies that prices of futures with early delivery dates will exceed those with later delivery dates. In fact, to describe the relationship, Keynes adapted the term "backwardation," which characterizes a situation in which futures prices are below spot prices.

A contrary hypothesis holds that, on net, there is long hedging. Speculators must be enticed to take *short* positions and be rewarded for doing so via expected returns exceeding the riskless rate. As formula (17-5b) shows, this requires the futures price to exceed the expected spot price. Such a relationship, which might be termed *normal contango*, implies that the price of any futures contract can be expected to *fall* during its life, as shown in Figure 17-9.[10]

A fourth hypothesis is that portrayed by the dashed curve in Figure 17-9. This approach[11] reflects the fact that hedgers may wish to attract long speculators during the first part of a crop year when stocks are large, and short speculators during the latter part when stocks are small. If speculators have to be rewarded for bearing the risk involved, prices of futures contracts may be expected to rise when hedgers are short and speculators long, then fall when hedgers are long and speculators short. Another version holds that futures prices may be expected to rise when there is a large amount of net short hedging and fall when there is *either* a small amount of net short hedging *or* net long hedging.

The suggestion that hedgers may choose to be long on the futures market may seem surprising. At any time some people (e.g., farmers, grain elevator operators) with too much inventory for their comfort will wish to *short hedge*, while others (e.g., processors) with commitments in excess of inventories will wish to *long hedge*. When total stocks are large, the former may outnumber the latter, and there will be *net short hedging*, requiring speculators to make up the gap with long positions. As inventories fall, the balance may begin to shift, leading eventually to net long hedging, requiring speculators to make up the gap with short positions.

FINANCIAL FUTURES

Futures contracts were limited to those on agricultural products, metals, and so on until the 1970s. No longer. In fact, *financial futures*, based on foreign currencies, fixed-income securities, and stock indices, are now more important than traditional contracts.

Currency Futures

Anyone who has crossed a national border knows that there is an active market for foreign exchange, and that the rate at which one

---

[10] If expected spot prices for different delivery dates are the same, normal contango will result in lower prices for futures with early delivery dates than for those with later delivery dates. The term is derived from "contango," which describes a situation in which futures prices are above spot prices.

[11] See Paul H. Cootner, "Speculation and Hedging," Stanford University, *Food Research Institute Studies*, Supplement, 1967.

currency can be exchanged for another varies frequently. At any particular time, however, all such rates must be in conformance, or else a riskless arbitrage situation would arise. For example, it is usually possible to exchange U.S. dollars for British pounds, then exchange the British pounds for French francs, and finally to exchange the French francs for dollars. If the three exchange rates were not in line, one might end up with more dollars at the end of this chain of transactions than at the beginning. Such an opportunity would attract large amounts of money, placing pressure on exchange rates and rapidly restoring balance. On the other hand, if a profit could be made by completing the circle in the opposite direction (dollars to francs to pounds to dollars), heavy pressure would soon move exchange rates accordingly, again restoring the balance.

Transactions costs and exchange restrictions limit the ability of arbitrageurs to exploit imbalances among exchange rates. But the limits are still quite narrow.

The familiar market in foreign exchange, operated by banks, travel agents, and so on, is in effect a *spot market*, since both the agreement on terms and the exchange of currencies occur at the same time. There are also markets for agreements involving future delivery of foreign exchange.

The largest such market is operated by banks and specialized brokers, maintaining close communications with each other throughout the world. Corporations, institutions, and some individuals deal in this market via large banks. Substantial amounts of money are involved, and every agreement is negotiated separately. Typical rates are quoted in the financial press.

This network of large institutions is generally termed the market for *forward exchange*, since standardized contracts are not used, and there is no organized secondary market.

The other market deals in futures contracts for foreign exchange. Procedures are similar to those used for commodity futures. For example, one of the *currency futures* contracts traded on the International Monetary Market of the Chicago Mercantile Exchange requires the seller to deliver 25,000 British pounds sterling to the buyer on a specified date for a number of U.S. dollars agreed upon in advance. Only the price of the transaction (expressed in dollars per British pound) is negotiated by the parties involved; all other terms are standard. Clearing procedures allow positions to be covered by reverse transactions, and few if any contracts result in the actual delivery of foreign currency. Price and volumes for such contracts are quoted with those for commodity futures in the financial press. Figure 17-10(a) provides examples.

Markets for foreign exchange futures attract both hedgers and speculators. The former wish to reduce or possibly eliminate risk associated with planned future transfers of funds from one country to another. The latter hope to profit from a difference between the current rate

(a) Currency Futures

```
BRITISH POUND (IMM) 25,000 pounds; $ per pound
June   1.3855 1.3895 1.3840 1.3845 + .0020 1.5520 1.3730 13,740
Sept   1.3925 1.3970 1.3905 1.3915 + .0010 1.5240 1.3810  3,606
Dec    1.4015 1.4050 1.4005 1.3995 .....  1.5100 1.3910    322
Mar85  1.4100 1.4150 1.4100 1.4085 .....  1.5170 1.3990    107
   Est vol 3,498; vol Thur 8,436; open int 17,775, −728.

CANADIAN DOLLAR (IMM) 100,000 dlrs.; $ per Can $
June    .7724 .7740 .7720 .7727 + .0005 .8168 .7701 6,936
Sept    .7732 .7745 .7726 .7731 + .0006 .8147 .7702   941
Dec                 .7733 + .0004 .8048 .7708 1,688
Mar85   .7730 .7730 .7730 .7735 + .0003 .8050 .7711 1,481
June                .7737 + .0003 .7835 .7715     9
   Est vol 955; vol Thur 1,018; open int 11,055, −93.

JAPANESE YEN (IMM) 12.5 million yen; $ per yen (.00)
June    .4333 .4351 .4320 .4322 − .0021 .4565 .4180 21,024
Sept    .4395 .4412 .4378 .4382 − .0022 .4615 .4348  5,357
Dec     .4467 .4477 .4455 .4460 − .0017 .4663 .4395  1,061
Mar85   .4533 .4540 .4530 .4530 − .0013 .4695 .4487     28
   Est vol 12,621; vol Thur 16,590; open int 27,470, +184.

SWISS FRANC (IMM) 125,000 francs; $ per franc
June    .4459 .4484 .4457 .4478 + .0014 .5045 .4382 20,618
Sept    .4550 .4573 .4546 .4568 + .0015 .5020 .4474  3,377
Dec     .4654 .4662 .4645 .4650 + .0014 .5000 .4558    292
Mar85   .4740 .4745 .4740 .4735 + .0035 .5035 .4640     33
June                .4820       .4900 .4734      8
   Est vol 19,463; vol Thur 24,447; open int 24,328, −1,272.

W. GERMAN MARK (IMM) 125,000 marks; $ per mark
June    .3681 .3710 .3673 .3681 − .0010 .4002 .3568 28,211
Sept    .3742 .3765 .3732 .3736 − .0014 .4037 .3602  4,485
Dec     .3818 .3818 .3795 .3796 − .0012 .4080 .3640    655
Mar85   .3868 .3868 .3860 .3858 − .0010 .4110 .3699    219
   Est vol 28,723; vol Thur 28,882; open int 33,570, +907
```

(b) Interest–Rate Futures

```
EURODOLLAR (IMM) −$1 million; pts of 100%
                                    Yield              Open
       Open  High  Low  Settle Chg  Settle Chg      Interest
June  87.95 88.09 87.93 87.99 + .08 12.01 − .08     27,426
Sept  86.65 86.78 86.56 86.65 + .10 13.35 − .10     34,895
Dec   86.00 86.14 85.89 85.93 .....  14.07 .....    15,768
Mar85 85.55 85.68 85.41 85.51 − .04 14.49 + .02      5,851
June  85.22 85.28 85.15 85.19 − .01 14.81 + .01      2,970
Sept  84.94 84.94 84.85 84.89 − .02 15.11 + .04      1,686
   Est vol 23,837; vol Thur 32,383; open int 88,596, +1,370.

EURODOLLAR (LIFFE) −$1 million; pts of 100%
June  88.19 88.35 88.16 88.26 + .06 90.63 87.77 4,532
Sept  86.73 87.11 86.78 86.99 + .09 89.63 86.78 6,505
Dec   86.14 86.49 86.14 86.30 − .01 89.36 86.31 2,595
Mar85 85.88 85.93 85.88 85.88 − .04 88.85 85.88   568
June  85.67 85.67 85.66 85.63 + .07 88.13 85.66    73
   Est vol 9,778; vol Thur 8,910; open int 14,273, −294.

STERLING DEPOSIT (LIFFE) −£250,000; pts of 100%
June  90.33 90.35 90.27 90.31 − .17 91.28 89.06 2,096
Sept  89.50 89.50 89.30 89.36 − .21 91.06 89.26 4,356
Dec   88.80 89.00 88.33 88.86 − .24 90.91 88.77 1,866
Mar85 88.48 88.48 88.48 88.42 − .13 90.86 88.48   261
June  88.10 88.10 88.10 88.10 − .14 90.60 88.10    32
   Est vol 1,177; vol Thur 2,184; open int 8,611, +113.

GNMA 8% (CBT) −$100,000 prncpl; pts. 32nds. of 100%
June  65-22 65-23 64-27 64-31 − 14 14.334 + .108 14,555
Sept  64-10 64-12 63-18 63-22 − 13 14.659 + .104 13,779
Dec   63-05 63-05 62-16 62-22 −  9 14.919 + .074  4,192
Mar85 62-09 62-09 61-24 61-27 −  8 15.143 + .067  1,293
June              61-04        −  5 15.338 + .068    260
Sept  60-22 60-22 60-14 60-19 −  7 15.484 + .060    107
Dec   60-09 60-09 60-03 60-06 −  7 15.598 + .061    295
Mar86 60-11 60-11 59-27 59-28 −  7 15.685 + .061    455
   Est vol 6,500; vol Thur 10,279; open int 34,936, +1,123.

TREASURY BONDS (CBT) −$100,000; pts. 32nds of 100%
June  61-04 61-06 60-11 60-27 +  1 13.809 − .007 96,546
Sept  60-12 60-16 59-20 60-03 +  1 13.980 − .007 78,053
Dec   59-28 59-28 59-04 59-19 +  1 14.095 − .007 10,512
Mar85 59-16 59-18 58-26 59-08 +  1 14.176 − .007  5,640
June  59-07 59-07 58-24 58-31 ...  14.242 .....   4,078
Sept  59-05 59-05 58-18 58-24 −  1 14.294 + .007  1,823
Dec   58-19 58-24 58-13 58-24 −  2 14.339 + .015  1,502
Mar86 58-22 58-22 58-11 58-13 −  3 14.377 + .023  1,748
June  58-16 58-16 58-04 58-06 −  3 14.407 + .023  2,995
Sept  58-15 58-18 58-04 58-06 −  3 14.430 + .023    888
Dec   58-12 58-12 58-02 58-04 −  3 14.445 + .023     64
   Est vol 150,000; vol Thur 223,934; op int 203,849, +6,229.

TREASURY NOTES (CBT) −$100,000; pts. 32nds of 100%
June  72-05 72-06 71-17 71-24 − 3 13.160 + .035 14,027
Sept  71-13 71-15 70-27 71-00 − 5 13.334 + .036 15,074
Dec   70-13 70-18 70-08 70-13 − 4 13.473 + .029    157
Mar85             69-28        − 4 13.599 + .030      1
   Est vol 8,000; vol Thur 11,899; open int 29,260, +1,278.

TREASURY BILLS (IMM) −$1 mil.; pts. of 100%
                                   Discount           Open
       Open  High  Low  Settle Chg  Settle Chg      Interest
June  90.14 90.36 89.96 90.18 + .14  9.82 − .14     16,165
Sept  88.69 88.70 88.53 88.63 + .08 11.37 − .08     30,881
Dec   88.14 88.15 87.97 88.04 + .05 11.96 − .05      5,797
Mar85 87.78 87.79 87.60 87.71 + .06 12.29 − .06      3,610
June  87.56 87.56 87.36 87.46 + .05 12.54 − .05        881
Sept  87.21 87.28 87.21 87.27 + .02 12.73 − .02        487
Dec   87.05 87.10 87.02 87.10 + .01 12.90 − .01        308
Mar86             86.96        + .01 13.04 − .01        118
   Est vol 38,150; vol Thur 36,330; open int 58,247, −2,349.

BANK CDs (IMM) −$1 million; pts. of 100%
June  88.36 88.52 88.33 88.42 + .10 11.58 − .10 8,089
Sept  87.07 87.22 87.01 87.12 + .12 12.88 − .12 15,436
Dec   86.40 86.57 86.33 86.40 + .02 13.60 − .02 6,131
Mar85 86.02 86.12 85.90 86.00 ...  14.00 .....  2,309
June  85.67 85.75 85.58 85.67 + .02 14.33 − .02 2,103
Sept              85.37        − .01 14.63 + .01 1,231
```

(c) Stock Index Futures

```
S&P 500 FUTURES INDEX (CME) 500 Times Index
June  151.75 152.55 151.20 151.85 + .10 177.10 151.20 24,530
Sept  154.20 154.95 153.70 154.35 + .15 178.15 153.70  5,893
Dec   156.25 157.45 156.20 156.75 + .15 179.20 156.15    406
Mar85 159.70 159.70 158.65 159.05 + .10 180.25 158.60     47
June                     161.65 + .20 180.70 161.75     21
Sept                     164.35 + .15 173.40 165.70     12
   Est vol 41,442; vol Thur 52,716; open int 30,909, +578.

S&P 500 STOCK INDEX (Prelim)
      151.43 152.02 150.85 151.62 + .38

S&P 100 FUTURES INDEX (CME) 200 Times Index
June  150.20 151.55 149.85 150.60 + .45 177.80 149.80 2,310
Sept  152.60 153.60 152.35 153.00 + .40 168.30 152.35    36
   Est vol 599; vol Thur 769; open int 2,346, +70.

S&P 100 STOCK INDEX (Prelim)
      150.16 150.76 149.34 150.24 + .50

NYSE COMPOSITE FUTURES (NYFE) 500 Times Index
June  87.20 87.90 87.15 87.50 + .10 103.00 82.30 6,328
Sept  88.45 89.20 88.30 88.75 + .10 103.10 88.30 1,791
Dec   89.70 90.35 89.70 90.00 + .10 103.55 89.70   557
Mar85 91.50 91.55 91.50 91.25 + .10 103.80 91.10   151
June  92.35 92.35 92.35 92.50 + .10 105.00 92.35    97
Sept  93.65 93.65 93.65 93.75 + .10  99.75 93.65    77
   Est vol 8,707; vol Thur 15,013; open int 9,001, −263.

NYSE COMPOSITE STOCK INDEX
      86.90 87.31 86.72 87.12 + .17

KC VALUE LINE FUTURES (KC) 500 Times Index
June  168.85 170.10 168.50 169.50 + .30 212.00 168.50 3,697
Sept  170.70 172.30 170.70 171.70 + .50 213.50 170.70   296
Dec   173.80 174.05 173.70 174.00 + .65 210.00 173.35    15
   Est vol 3,569; vol Thur 4,090; open int 4,008, +301.

KC VALUE LINE COMPOSITE STOCK INDEX
      169.78 169.90 169.36 169.79 + .05
```

SOURCE: Reprinted with permission from *The Wall Street Journal*. © Dow Jones and Company, Inc., May 29, 1984. All Rights Reserved.

FIGURE 17-10
Quotations for Financial Futures Prices.

for future exchange and the actual spot rate in the future. Contrary to popular opinion, many institutions take speculative positions, besides engaging in hedging operations for themselves and/or their customers.

Interest-Rate Parity   Using U.S. dollars and British (U.K.) pounds, Figure 17-11 illustrates the relationship among (1) the spot exchange rate, (2) the interest rate in the U.S., (3) the interest rate in the U.K., and (4) the forward exchange rate. All four links are two-way. Thus it is possible to trade D_s dollars now for 1 pound now, or vice versa. It is also possible to contract now to trade D_f dollars for 1 pound "later." On

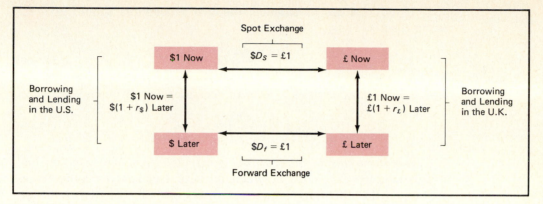

FIGURE 17-11
Relationships Among Interest and Exchange Rates.

the U.S. domestic market for loans, a dollar now can be traded for $(1 + r_\$)$ dollars later, or vice versa, while on the U.K. domestic market a pound now can be traded for $(1 + r_£)$ pounds later, or vice versa.

This circle of possible transactions allows one to trade any of the four items for any other in either of two ways—clockwise or counter-clockwise in Figure 17-11. For example, if 1 pound later is desired, with payment in dollars later, a contract can be made directly on the forward exchange or currency futures market to:

$$\text{pay } D_f \text{ dollars later and receive 1 pound later}$$

Alternatively, the other three links can be used:

Now:
(1) borrow $D_s/(1 + r_£)$ dollars in the U.S.,
(2) exchange these dollars for $1/(1 + r_£)$ pounds, and
(3) lend these pounds in the U.K.

Later:
(1) receive the proceeds of the loan in the U.K.

$$= (1 + r_£)\left(\frac{1}{1 + r_£}\right) = 1 \text{ pound}$$

(2) pay off the loan in the U.S.

$$= (1 + r_\$)\left(\frac{D_s}{1 + r_£}\right) \text{ dollars}$$

Since only other people's money is used in the initial period, the net effect is to:

$$\text{pay } \left(\frac{1 + r_\$}{1 + r_£}D_s\right) \text{ dollars later and receive 1 pound later}$$

Futures Contracts

If markets are in balance, the two procedures should give the same results. Thus:

$$\left(\frac{1+r_\$}{1+r_\pounds}\right) D_s = D_f \tag{17-6a}$$

Rearranging and omitting a term of secondary importance:

$$\left(\frac{D_f - D_s}{D_s}\right) = r_\$ - r_\pounds \tag{17-6b}$$

This is known as the *interest-rate parity theorem*, which holds that the percentage difference between forward and spot exchange rates will equal the difference between interest rates in the two countries.

If interest-rate parity did not hold, and if there were no transactions costs, exchange restrictions, or transfer risk (i.e., possibility of future exchange restrictions), it would be possible to make money with no risk by running the circle in the appropriate direction. Of course, such ideal conditions are not found in the real world. Thus interest-rate parity holds only approximately.

During February 1980 *The Wall Street Journal* quoted the following rates for British pounds:

spot:	$2.3005
180-day futures:	$2.2737

Applying formula (17-6b):

$$\left(\frac{2.2737 - 2.3005}{2.3005}\right) = -.012 = r_\$ - r_\pounds$$

At the same time, rates for West German deutsche marks were:

spot:	$.5749
180-day futures:	$.5935

which implied:

$$r_\$ - r_{DM} = .032$$

To a major extent, differences in interest rates can be attributed to differences in expected rates of inflation. In 1980 the expected rate of inflation for the U.K. could well have exceeded that for the U.S. by 1.2% per 180 days, or approximately 2.4% per year. And the expected rate of inflation in the U.S. could have exceeded that for West Germany by 3.2% per 180 days, or approximately 6.4% per year. It is not surprising that at the time people expected exchange rates to move against the pound and in favor of the deutsche mark.

While arbitrage maintains a close relationship among exchange rates and interest rates, none is in any sense determined by the others. Instead, all are determined jointly by present and future levels of international trade, the demand and supply for loans, and estimates of future rates of inflation. Anyone who believes he or she has superior ability to predict such factors can attempt to profit by speculating, using either one of the markets for currency futures or the spot market plus the loan markets in the two countries. Transactions costs, margin and collateral requirements, and so on will determine the relative advantages of the various alternatives for any particular speculator or hedger.

INTEREST-RATE FUTURES

Chapter 4 discussed the concept of the forward interest rate: the terms of a loan to be made at some future date and repaid subsequently, but with the rate of interest negotiated now. Forward loans can be made implicitly by issuing short-term instruments and using the proceeds to purchase longer-term instruments. But such procedures may be cumbersome. Instead, an explicit forward or futures interest market may be utilized.

A good example is provided by the futures markets for 90-day U.S. Treasury bills. As Figure 17-10(b) indicates, in May 1984 someone purchased a contract calling for delivery in September 1984 of $1,000,000 face value of 90-day Treasury bills (maturing in December of 1984) for a "price" of 88.63. More precisely, the seller of the contract was obligated to deliver the bills in September 1984 for an amount that would make the return, stated on a discount basis, equal to 11.37% per year, as shown in Figure 17-10(b).

As with commodity futures, neither the buyer nor the seller of such a contract must hold a position until the delivery date. Reversing trades can be made at any time, and relatively few contracts result in actual delivery.

As Figure 17-10(b) shows, in May 1984 the structure of three-month forward rates[12] was upward-sloping, with discounts ranging from 9.82% for June 1984 delivery to 13.04% for March 1986 delivery. If the expectations hypothesis characterizes this market, such rates can be considered unbiased estimates of future spot rates. If forward rates include a liquid-

---

[12] Strictly speaking, the rates in Figure 17-10(b) are *futures* rates, not *forward* rates.

ity premium, forward rates will exceed expected future spot rates. In either event, it seems likely that at the time the consensus opinion of investors held that three-month rates could be expected to increase over the next two years.

Figure 17-10(b) provides information on "interest-rate futures" contracts actively traded in 1984. Vehicles ranged from short-term (Treasury bills, certificates of deposit, Eurodollar and sterling time deposits) to long-term (U.S. Treasury bonds and Government National Mortgage Association pass-through contracts).

GNMA futures provide a convenient device for hedging by institutions active in the mortgage market. Mortgage bankers can short hedge to offset exposure to interest-rate fluctuations arising from the issuance of mortgages not yet assembled into a pool for subsequent resale. Savings and loan companies can long hedge to "lock in" current interest rates for funds they expect to receive in the near future. And speculators who believe they can predict interest rates more accurately than others can attempt to exploit such skills in this market.

As shown in Figure 17-10(b), prices are generally stated in terms of "points"—percentages of par value for representative instruments. A yield-to-maturity or discount corresponding to the settlement price is also shown.

Stock Index Futures

Figure 17-10(c) shows quotations for *futures contracts on stock indices*. Each such contract involves the delivery at settlement of *cash* in an amount equal to a *multiplier* times the difference between (1) the value of index at the close of the last trading day of the contract and (2) the price of the futures contract. If the index is *above* the futures price, those with *short* positions pay those with *long* positions. If the index is *below* the futures price, those with *long* positions pay those with *short* positions.

In practice, of course, a clearing house is used, and all contracts are marked to market every day. In a sense, the settlement day differs from other days in only one respect—all open positions are marked to market for the last time and then closed.

Cash settlement provides results similar to those associated with delivery of all the stocks in the index. It avoids the effort and transactions costs associated with (1) the purchase of stocks by people who have taken short futures positions, (2) delivery of these stocks to people who have taken long futures positions, and (3) the subsequent sale of the stocks by those who receive them.

Major Contracts   In 1984 four index futures were available. The most popular, based on Standard and Poor's 500-stock index, was traded at the Index and Option Market of the Chicago Mercantile Exchange.

The CME also offered a futures contract based on a 100-stock index "adopted" by Standard and Poor's. Second in importance was a contract based on the New York Stock Exchange Composite Index, traded at the New York Futures Exchange. The original stock index future was that based on the Value Line Index, traded at the Kansas City Board of Trade.

For all contracts but the Value Line Index Futures, the multiplier was 500; for the Value Line contract, it was 200. Thus the purchase of an S&P 500 contract for 150 and subsequent sale for 155 would result in a profit of $2,500 (500 × $5).

Trading Volume   The volume of trading in futures contracts is very large. To assess its importance, the number of contracts can be multiplied by the total dollar value represented by one contract. As shown in Figure 17-10(c), estimated volume on May 25, 1984, for the S&P 500 was 41,442 contracts. At a value of $151 per contract, this is equivalent to 41,442 × 500 × $151, or over $3.1 billion! To compare this with an equivalent number of shares, one can divide by $35 (a rough estimate of the average value per share for stocks on the New York Stock Exchange at the time). The result indicates that there were thus approximately 89 million *futures equivalent shares* for this contract alone—greater than the total share volume on the New York Stock Exchange for the day (which was slightly over 78 million shares).

This is not unusual. On many days the value involved in trades of stock index futures exceeds that of trades of stocks per se.

Indices   Three of these contracts are based on *value-weighted* indices. Standard and Poor's 500-stock index is based on the total outstanding value of 500 stocks, Standard and Poor's 100-stock index on the total value of 100 stocks, and the New York Stock Exchange Composite Index on the total value of all the stocks listed on the New York Stock Exchange. Each of these indices can, in principle, be matched with a low-turnover portfolio of the included stocks, held in proportion to amounts outstanding.

The Value Line Index is based on approximately 1,700 stocks covered by Value Line. The change in the index is computed by taking the *geometric mean* of the relative changes in the prices of the underlying securities. Since the stocks are *equally weighted*, small stocks are relatively more important than in the other indices. However, the performance of the Value Line index cannot be replicated exactly by an actual portfolio—even one requiring considerable turnover every day. A portfolio rebalanced daily to have equal dollar values of every stock would change by an amount (prior to transactions costs) equal to the *arithmetic* mean of the percentage changes in the prices of the included stocks. This would *exceed* the value of the geometric mean as long as there were any differences in returns across stocks. In this sense, the Value Line Index gives a *downward-biased* measure of the change in value of "the average stock." This contrasts with value-weighted indices, which give *unbiased* measures of the change in value of "the average dollar" invested in the included stocks.

Correlations   Table 17-1(A) shows correlations among the three major indices and associated futures contracts during the latter half of 1982. Not surprisingly, the two value-weighted indices (NYSE and S&P 500) are highly correlated. The NYSE index, which includes more small stocks, is more highly correlated with the Value Line Index than is the S&P 500.

Despite their differences, all the index-to-index correlations exceed .90. Not so the correlations of the futures contracts with their own indices. The S&P 500 index future is most highly correlated with its index (.882), with the Value Line futures the least highly correlated with its index (.744).

On the other hand, the futures contracts *are* highly correlated with one another. The lowest futures-to-futures correlation coefficient is .949.

TABLE 17-1

The Major Indexes and Associated Futures Contracts: Correlations and Standard Deviations[a]

(A) CORRELATIONS						
	S&P 500		NYSE		Value Line	
	Index	Future	Index	Future	Index	Future
S&P 500 Index	1.000	.882	.998	.879	.919	.875
S&P 500 Future	.882	1.000	.865	.967	.723	.967
NYSE Index	.998	.865	1.000	.857	.942	.862
NYSE Future	.879	.967	.857	1.000	.697	.949
VL Index	.919	.723	.942	.697	1.000	.744
VL Future	.875	.967	.862	.949	.744	1.000

(B) STANDARD DEVIATIONS (% PER DAY)		
	Index	Futures
S&P 500	1.34	1.82
NYSE	1.25	2.02
VL	1.00	1.74

SOURCE: Gregory M. Kipnis and Steve Tsang, *Donaldson, Lufkin & Jenrette Futures Service*, Dec. 17, 1982.
[a] Based on daily percentage changes, June 16–December 10, 1982. Futures contracts are for delivery in December.

Interestingly, during this period the Value Line futures contract was more highly correlated with the S&P 500 and NYSE indices than with the Value Line index itself.

Table 17-1(B) shows the standard deviations of the daily percentage changes in (1) the indices and (2) the prices of the associated futures contracts. In every instance there was greater variability in the latter than in the former.

Hedging What accounts for the popularity of stock index futures? Simply put: they provide relatively inexpensive and highly liquid positions similar to those obtained with diversified stock portfolios.

Instead of purchasing 500 stocks, one can invest an equivalent amount of money in U.S. Treasury bills and take a *long* position in S&P 500 futures.

Instead of trying to take short positions in 500 stocks in anticipation of a market decline, a speculator can take a *short* position in S&P 500 futures, posting margin in U.S. Treasury bills.

An investor holding one or more stocks can *hedge* much of the associated *market risk* by taking a *short* position in a stock index futures contract.

An investor who is short one or more stocks can hedge much of the associated market risk by taking a *long* position in a stock index futures contract.

And so on.

Evidence that much index futures activity comes from hedgers can be found in the financial press. On a typical day, reported volume will be very similar to the open interest at the end of the day. This contrasts with other futures contracts, for which open interest is several times as large as the daily volume, as examination of Figures 17-1 and 17-10 will indicate.

A key role served by index futures is the provision of *liquidity* to investors as a result of the ability of brokers and dealers to hedge market risk associated with temporary positions.

When someone wishes to sell a large block of a stock, a broker or dealer can agree to purchase the stock immediately, then spend the requisite time to "line up" buyers. In the interim, however, economic news might cause the market to fall, and with it the stock. To compensate for this risk, brokers and dealers traditionally offered low bid prices for purchase of stock in such circumstances.

Conversely, when someone wishes to buy a large block of a stock, a broker or dealer can agree to provide it, then go about the task of lining up "the other side." Traditionally, the asking price was "marked up" to cover the risk that the market would go up in the interim.

Now the situation is different. A broker or dealer can agree to purchase a large block of stock at a fixed price and immediately take a short position in an index futures to hedge against an adverse move in the stock market. As the block is sold, the futures position can be covered by reversing trades. Conversely, a broker or dealer can agree to sell a large block at a fixed price, taking a long position in index futures to hedge against an adverse stock market move.

Given competition among brokers and dealers, this will lead to lower bid-ask spreads for investors—i.e., greater liquidity.

The fact that volume is large relative to open interest indicates that many positions are reversed on the *same* day that they are opened. This undoubtedly reflects a great deal of intraday transactions by brokers and dealers hedging positions resulting from their normal trading activities.

Correlation between stock index futures contracts and "the stock market" makes such contracts attractive hedging vehicles for a great many investors. However, the fact that the correlations are not perfect (as Table 17-1 shows) indicates that there will be *basis risk* even if a futures contract is used to hedge a highly diversified stock portfolio. Moreover, the fact that futures tend to be more variable suggests that an appropriate hedge position may not involve a one-for-one match between such a portfolio and an equal value of index futures.

When index futures are used to hedge a nondiversified portfolio, the disparity between values of the two "sides" can, of course, be quite large.

Arbitrage   When stock index futures were first proposed, a number of analysts predicted that at long last there would be an indication of investors' expectations about the future course of the stock market. It was said that the value of such a futures contract would indicate the consensus opinion of investors concerning the future level of the associated index: in times of optimism it might be much higher than the current level of the market, while in times of pessimism it might be much lower.

Such predictions were naive, to say the least. If the price of a futures contract on a "commodity" held in inventory diverges too far from an "appropriate" relationship with the price of the commodity and the associated carrying costs, opportunities for arbitrage profits will present themselves. If and when this happens, clever arbitrageurs can be expected to make trades designed to capture the profits. And such trades can be expected to rapidly bring the futures and spot prices back "in line."

Stocks are certainly held ("in inventory"). Thus the price of a stock index futures contract should stay close to an appropriate relationship with the current level of its associated index. But what relationship is appropriate? To find the answer, we can examine two ways to achieve the same goal.

On the day shown in Figure 17-10(c), Standard and Poor's 500-

stock index stood at 151.62. A December S&P 500 futures contract sold for 156.75. Consider the following investment strategies:

1. Purchase the stocks in the S&P 500 index, hold them until December, then sell them.
2. Purchase a December S&P 500 futures contract and U.S. Treasury bills maturing in December. Hold the futures contract until the settlement date in December.

For comparability, the stocks purchased under strategy 1 would be sold on the settlement date for the futures contract in strategy 2.

Strategy 1 would cost $151.62 (in "index terms") at the outset. In return, it would provide: (1) dividends for which stocks "went ex-dividend" prior to the settlement date, and (2) an amount of money equal to the value of the index on the settlement date.

Assume that $151.62 is invested in Treasury bills in strategy 2. Thus it would also cost $151.62 at the outset. In return, it would provide (1) the face value of the Treasury bills on the settlement date and (2) an amount of money equal to the difference between the value of the index and $156.75 on the settlement date.

By design, both strategies require the same initial outlay. How do the inflows compare?

For generality, denote:

$P_f =$ the current futures price
$P_s =$ the initial spot price (level) of the index
$\tilde{P}_I =$ the price (level) of the index on the settlement date
$y =$ the dividend yield of the index
$i =$ the riskless interest rate

Then:

$yP_s =$ the total dollar value at settlement obtained from all dividends for which ex-dates fall prior to the settlement date

$(1 + i)P_s =$ the total dollar value obtained at the settlement date by investing P_s dollars now

Strategy 1 provides a settlement-date value of:

$$yP_s + \tilde{P}_I \tag{17-7a}$$

while strategy 2 provides a settlement-date value of:

$$(1 + i)P_s + (\tilde{P}_I - P_f) \tag{17-7b}$$

Both strategies have the same cost and are subject to precisely the same uncertainty (due to the unknown level of the index at settlement).

If there were no transactions costs, any disparity of these two values would provide an opportunity for riskless arbitrage. Consider a "long position" in strategy 1 and a "short position" in strategy 2. The end-of-period value would be the difference between (17-7a) and 17-7b):

$$yP_s + \tilde{P}_I - [(1 + i)P_s + \tilde{P}_I - P_f] = yP_s - P_s - iP_s + P_f$$

Note that (1) this is a *certain* amount and (2) no funds are required, since the short position will finance the long position. If the end-of-period value were positive, one could literally get something for nothing—an unlikely possibility.

If the end-of-period value for this strategy were negative, the obvious solution would be to take a "long position" in strategy 2 and a "short position" in strategy 1. The result would again be something for nothing.

In the absence of transactions costs, arbitrage would insure that:

$$yP_s - P_s - iP_s + P_f = 0$$

Simplifying:

$$P_f - P_s = (i - y)P_s \tag{17-8}$$

The amount on the left-hand side of equation (17-8) is the *basis* for the contract. The amount on the right-hand side indicates that the basis should depend *only* on (1) the current level of the index and (2) the difference between the interest rate and the dividend yield on the index.

In practice, of course, the situation is not this simple—for a number of reasons.

Positions in futures, stocks, and Treasury bills involve *transactions costs*. Thus arbitrage will not take place unless the basis diverges far enough from the amount shown in (17-8) to warrant such costs. The futures price, and hence the basis, can be expected to move within a *band* around the "theoretical value," with the width of the band determined by the costs of those who can engage in transactions most efficiently.

To add to the complexity, both dividends and the relevant interest earned are subject to some uncertainty. Neither the amounts of dividends to be declared nor their timing can be specified completely in advance. And, since futures positions must be marked to market daily, the amount of cash required for strategy 2 may have to be varied via additional borrowing or lending.

Leaving uncertainty aside, there will be predictable variation in the "theoretical value" for the basis. As settlement nears, the magnitudes of both interest and yield payments diminish, as does their difference. At settlement, the theoretical basis must, of course, equal zero.

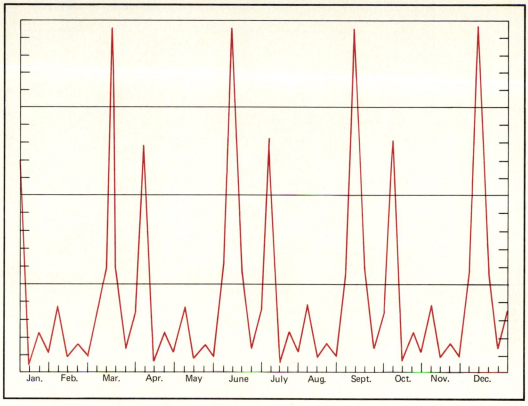

SOURCE: *Futures contracts on Stock Indexes*, Salomon Bros. Stock Research—Strategy Systems, July 13, 1982.

FIGURE 17-12
S&P 500: Dividend Distributions for a 52-Week Period

Dividends provide another source of predictable variation. Figure 17-12 shows that the typical pattern of distributions is far from even.

Figures 17-13(a) and (b) contrast actual values with theoretical values for the basis on two S&P 500 futures contracts. In each case, a "band" is shown, bounded by points at which it could pay a low-cost arbitrageur to exploit a disparity. Neither diagram shows periods of persistent mispricing large enough to provide significant profits for average investors. There is some indication of increased efficiency—in 1984, actual values diverged less from theoretical values and also varied less from previous actual values.

Stock index futures are used extensively by professional brokers, dealers, and institutional investors. As a result, prices of such contracts are likely to track their underlying indices very closely, taking into account both dividends and current interest rates. It is unlikely that a private investor will be able to exploit "mispricing" of such a contract

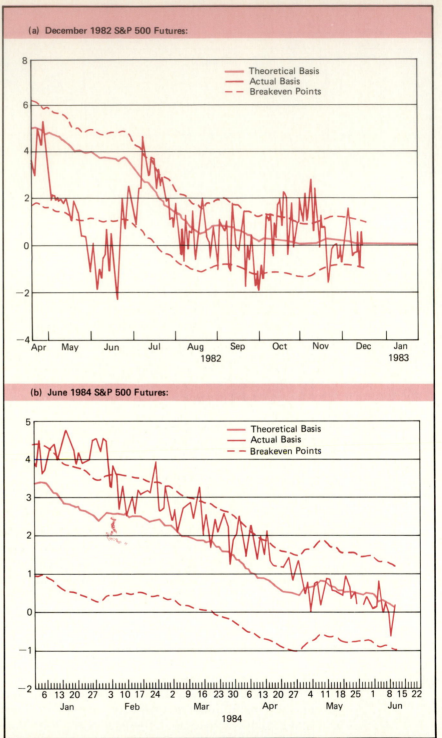

(a) December 1982 S&P 500 Futures:

(b) June 1984 S&P 500 Futures:

SOURCE: Gregory M. Kipnis & Steve Tsang, *Donaldson, Lufkin and Jenrette, Stock Index Strategies*, June 1984.

560   FIGURE 17-13
Theoretical versus Actual Values of the Basis.

relative to its index. But stock index futures can provide inexpensive ways to take positions in the stock market or to hedge portions of the risk associated with other positions. And their use by brokers and dealers can lower transactions costs for investors who may never take direct positions in such contracts.

Synthetic Futures   For some stock indices, no futures contracts are traded, but both put and call options are available. In such cases, an investor can create a *synthetic futures contract*.

The clearest example involves European options. As shown in Chapter 16, the *purchase* of a European call option and the *sale* of a European put option at the same exercise price will provide a value at expiration that will be related dollar-for-dollar to the stock price at the time. This is shown in Figures 17-14(a), (b), and (c).

Figures 17-14(a) and (b) show the payoffs associated with (a) the purchase of a call at an exercise price of E and (b) the sale of a put at the same exercise price. The results obtained by taking *both* positions are shown by the solid line in Figure 17-14(c).

Depending on the prices of the call and put, this strategy may either require a net outlay of cash or provide a net inflow. For comparability with the purchase of a futures contract, this may be offset with borrowing or lending as required to bring the net investment to zero. The dashed line in Figure 17-14(c) shows a case in which the call option costs more than is provided by the sale of the put option. The difference is borrowed, requiring the end-of-period payment shown in the figure. The dashed line thus indicates the *net* end-of-period payoffs for a strategy requiring no initial outlay. These are equivalent to the payoffs from a futures contract with a contract price equal to F. We have thus constructed a "synthetic" futures contract.

In practice, the equivalence is not perfect. Listed options are American, not European, raising the possibility that the buyer of the put will exercise it prematurely. Moreover, the synthetic combination is really a *forward* contract, since no marking to market is required.

Despite these differences, the existence of well-functioning markets for options on an index greatly reduces the attractiveness of comparable futures contracts. Given the success of options on the S&P 100 index, this may explain the relatively small volume in S&P 100 futures contracts shown in Figure 17-10(c).

Given sufficient interest, almost anything can be the subject of futures trading. Where there is risk, there will be a demand for insurance. Futures markets accommodate this demand and facilitate speculation as well. In the future, as in the past, new markets will open and old ones will close as dictated by the interests of hedgers and speculators.

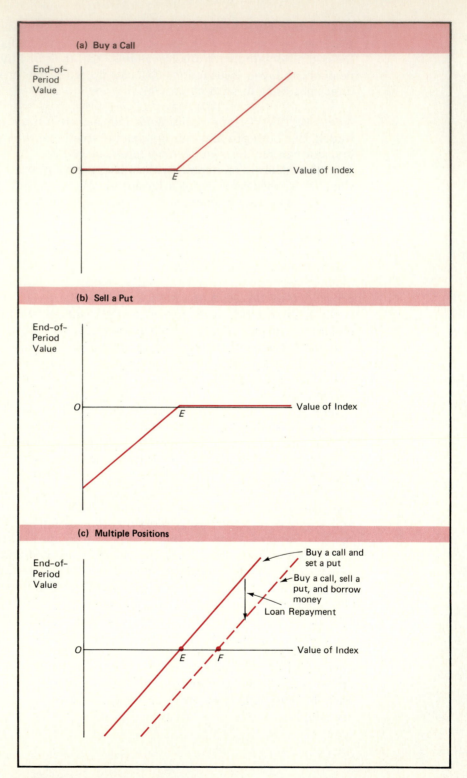

FIGURE 17-14
Synthetic Futures Contracts

Problems

1. Do exchange-imposed price limits protect the futures trader from losses that would result in the absence of price limits?

2. Is a contango relationship consistent with the thesis that, on net, hedgers hold short positions?

3. With reference to futures trading, explain what long hedging is and give an example. Also give an example of short hedging. Cite the occupations of the hedgers in your examples.

4. What are some differences between a futures contract and a call option?

5. In early 1980 the spot and one-year forward rates for Swiss francs were $.6968 and .6700, respectively. What risk-free interest rate on Swiss francs would be consistent with the interest-rate-parity theorem if the one-year risk-free rate on U.S. dollars was 15% at the time?

6. Based on the information in Figure 17-10, what can be said about investors' opinions on May 25, 1984, concerning:
   a. The prospects for near-term inflation in West Germany relative to the prospects in the United States?
   b. Interest rates on U.S. Treasury bonds in 1986?
   c. Interest rates on GNMA pass-through certificates in 1986?
   d. Interest rates on three-month U.S. Treasury bills at the end of 1984?

7. In December 1979 it was possible to buy a January 1980 contract in gold at the New York Commodity Exchange for $487.50 per ounce and sell an October 1981 contract for $614.80 on the same day. Would this have been profitable? Exactly what could you have done if you had taken these positions? Is the rate of interest at the time relevant in this context?

8. Assume you are convinced that the spread between long- and short-term interest rates is going to narrow within the next few months but do not know whether rates in general will be higher or lower than they are at present. Other investors disagree with your prediction: they expect the spread to remain constant. How could you profit from your superior predictive ability by using the markets for futures in financial instruments?

9. A publication used by farmers provides diagrams of the typical annual patterns of "cash prices" for a number of seasonal commodities. Should one expect that the price of a futures contract will follow the same pattern as the cash price of the commodity for which it is written? Why or why not? What kind of pattern might one expect a futures price to follow? Why?

18

Investment Companies

INVESTMENT COMPANY FUNCTIONS

Investment companies are *financial intermediaries*. They obtain money and invest it in financial assets (e.g., stocks, bonds, commercial paper). The people who provide the money are given claims on the assets and the earnings from them. The process typically involves the *packaging* of a set of assets into a single combination. If only one type of claim is issued, each claimant owns a proportionate share of the package of assets. However, some companies (such as real estate investment trusts) issue two or more types of claims. In effect, the assets originally packaged together are *repackaged*.

Investment companies can:

1. *Administer* an account: prepare tax records, reinvest dividends, and so on.
2. *Diversify* a portfolio: hold many different securities.
3. *Tailor* a portfolio: select investments meeting a specified set of conditions (e.g., high yield, medium risk, and so on).
4. *Control* a portfolio: insure that the specified set of conditions continues to be met.
5. *Select* securities that seem to be mispriced, in an attempt to "outperform"—i.e., achieve a higher return relative to risk than available elsewhere.

Economies of scale make it possible for a firm to perform the first four functions at a lower cost per dollar of investment than would be incurred by a small investor. Given a sufficiently large number of investors with similar objectives, the potential advantages to be gained from joint investment through an investment company may well outweigh any disadvantages.

The fifth function is subject to more dispute. Many investment company managers hope to identify areas of inefficiency in the market, exploit them, and share the resultant abnormal gains with investors by charging less for their services than they add in value. Unfortunately, they may instead fail to find abnormal situations while incurring additional costs in the form of increased management fees, transactions costs resulting from continuing turnover of the portfolio, and inadequate diversification.

Investment companies differ in many ways, and classification is difficult. We will follow common practice and restrict the term to apply to financial intermediaries that do not obtain money from "depositors." Thus the traditional operations of savings and loan companies and banks will be excluded. However, the process of deregulation is rapidly breaking down previous barriers. In 1984, banks and savings and loan companies offered retirement savings vehicles that were equivalent to investment company shares. Future changes in regulations may provide even more competition among traditional depository institutions, traditional investment companies, brokerage firms, and others in this arena.

MAJOR TYPES OF INVESTMENT COMPANIES

The United States Investment Company Act of 1940 classifies investment companies as follows:[1]

Unit investment trusts
Management companies
—closed-end companies
—open-end companies

Unit Investment Trusts

In the United Kingdom a "unit trust" is an open-end investment company (described in a later section). In the United States the term is used in a more limited sense to refer to a *fixed* unit trust—i.e., a company with a portfolio that is, in essence, fixed for the life of the fund.

To form a unit trust, a *sponsor* (e.g., a large brokerage firm) purchases a specific set of securities, deposits them with a *trustee* (e.g., a bank or trust company), and receives in turn a number of shares representing proportional interest in those securities. These shares,

---

[1] Another classification covers certain companies that issue "face-amount certificates" promising specific payments. This type of company is rare and will not be discussed here.

known as *redeemable trust certificates*, are then sold to investors by the sponsor. All income received from the portfolio is paid out by the trustee to shareholders, as are any repayments of principal. Only in exceptional circumstances is the portfolio altered. There is no active management of a unit trust, only the custodial and administrative services provided by the trustee. Correspondingly, fees charged during the life of the trust are low (e.g., $1.50 per year per $1,000 of asset value).

Most U.S. unit trusts hold fixed-income securities and expire after the last one has been paid off (or, possibly, sold). Durations range from six months for unit trusts of "money market" instruments to over twenty years for trusts of "bond market" instruments. Some trusts include only federal government bonds, others only corporate bonds, others only municipal bonds, and so on.

The sponsor of a unit trust will, of course, wish to be compensated for the effort and risk involved. This is accomplished by setting a selling price for the shares that exceeds the cost of the underlying assets. For example, a brokerage firm might purchase $10 million worth of bonds, place them in a unit trust, and issue 1 million shares. Each share might be offered for $10.35. If all were sold, the sponsoring organization could cover the cost of the portfolio and have $350,000 left for selling expenses and profit. Markups, or *load charges*, of this sort range from less than 1% for short-term trusts to 3.5% for long-term trusts.

Dealers in fixed-income securities generally quote both bid and ask (offer) prices. The bid price is the amount the dealer will pay for a security; the ask, or offer, price is the amount an investor must pay to purchase the security. Most unit trusts redeem shares at *net asset value* calculated on the basis of *bid* prices. First the value of the portfolio is determined, using dealers' bid quotations; then this amount is divided by the number of shares outstanding to obtain the net asset value per share. When a share is presented for redemption, the trustee simply sells one or more securities to raise the required cash.

Many fund sponsors make a market in the shares of the trusts they create. Shares are purchased at prices above the net asset value used by the fund for redemption. Typically the sponsor's price is determined by valuing the fund's securities using dealers' ask (offer) quotations. Shares acquired in this manner, and any left over from the initial offering, are offered for sale by the sponsor at a still higher price— usually the current purchase price plus a load charge equal to that in effect at the time the trust was created.

Management Companies

A unit trust has no board of directors and no managers as such. Other investment companies have both. In theory, the board of directors, elected by shareholders, hires a firm—the "management company"—

to manage the fund for a fee, based at least in part on the total value of the fund. In practice, however, the management company is usually the business entity that started and promoted the fund. One management company may have contracts to manage a number of funds, each of which is a separate corporation with its own board of directors. Boards of directors of funds rarely fire management companies, and management companies sometimes sell the "right" to manage a fund to other firms. In form, directors choose managers; in substance, the reverse is often closer to the truth.

Annual management fees range from less than ¼ of 1% of the value of net assets to well over 1% of net assets. Fees are usually based on the market value of the fund's total assets, with the percentage sometimes declining as the value increases. This provides management a certain amount of incentive to perform well; the better the fund's performance, other things equal, the larger the value of its assets.

In addition to the fee paid by a fund to its management company, there are administrative and custodial expenses. These services are usually provided by the management company, but the costs are charged to the fund. Total annual expenses, including the management fee per se, average well below 1% of the value of all assets for large investment companies. Many funds require their management company to cover all costs over a specified amount, effectively limiting total expenses, typically to 1% to 2% of the net asset value.

Funds may be managed by independent management companies, investment advisers, firms associated with brokers, or insurance companies.

Closed-End Funds

Unit trusts are *closed* in one direction—the number of shares outstanding cannot be increased. However, they are *open* in the other direction—the number can be reduced whenever someone decides to redeem shares.

Investment companies that do not stand ready to redeem shares continuously are termed *closed-end funds*. Most (but not all) have unlimited lives. Dividends and interest obtained from the portfolio are paid out to shareholders, as are realized capital gains, less realized capital losses. However, most funds allow (and encourage) the reinvestment of such payments. The fund keeps the money and sends the investor additional shares based on the net asset value per share obtained by computing the market value of all assets, subtracting any liabilities, and dividing by the number of shares outstanding. For example, immediately after a dividend of $1 per share, if net asset value were $15 per share, the holder of 30 shares would be given the option to receive either $30 (30 × $1) or 2 shares (= $30/$15). This feature allows a

Investment Companies

fund (and its management) to increase in size and makes it partially open-ended in one direction.

Closed-end funds are corporations whose assets are invested in other securities. Like other corporations, most such funds can issue new shares via stock offerings. However, this is done infrequently, not continuously, and the corporation's capital structure is "closed" most of the time.

Most closed-end funds can repurchase their own shares in the open market. Whenever market price falls well below net asset value, repurchase of shares will increase the fund's net asset value per share. For example, if net asset value per share were $20 and shares could be purchased for $16, the managers could sell $20 worth of securities from the fund's portfolio, buy back one of the fund's outstanding shares, and have $4 left over. If the $4 were burned, the net asset value of the remaining shares would still be $20; if it were added to the fund, the net asset value per share would increase.

Managers of closed-end funds seldom seize opportunities of this sort, perhaps because their fee is a function of the total value of assets managed. However, some do reinvest shareholders' dividends by purchasing shares in the open market when the price falls below net asset value.

In the 1930s, closed-end funds in the United States engaged in highly creative financing. Money was obtained via bank loans and by issuing bonds, preferred stocks, and warrants, as well as by selling common stock. This made the valuation of the various claims on a fund an interesting exercise and provided otherwise unavailable investment opportunities. Restrictions incorporated in the Investment Company Act of 1940 put a damper on such activities. Perhaps equally important, investors' interest in managed funds using diverse forms of financing appears to have waned, and most closed-end funds now have few if any claims outstanding besides those of their common stock holders.

Shares of closed-end funds are traded through brokers at prices agreed upon by the parties involved. Some are listed on national exchanges and are fairly actively traded. Others change hands only rarely. There is no necessary relationship between the *price* of such a share and its net asset value. If a fund does not stand ready to redeem shares or to buy them in the open market at net asset value, there is no obvious floor under the price. And if new shares cannot be purchased from the fund at the net asset value, there is no obvious ceiling.

At the end of 1982 there were 48 closed-end funds in the United States, managing portfolios worth approximately $7.1 billion.[2]

---

[2] Wiesenberger Investment Companies Services, *Investment Companies 1983*. By permission from the *Wiesenberger Financial Service* © 1983, A Division of Warren, Gorham and Lamont Inc. All Rights Reserved.

Publicly Traded Funds

Friday, July 13, 1984

Following is a weekly listing of unaudited net asset values of publicly traded investment fund shares, reported by the companies as of Friday's close. Also shown is the closing listed market price or a dealer-to-dealer asked price of each fund's shares, with the percentage of difference.

	N.A. Value	Stk Price	% Diff		N.A. Value	Stk Price	% Diff
Diversified Common Stock Funds				Castle	27.89	26⅝ −	4.5
AdmExp	16.47	15¼ −	7.4	CentSec	12.80	11½ −	10.2
BakerFen	37.88	31½ −	16.9	Claremont	33.96	28¼ −	16.8
GenAlnv	16.09	16⅛ +	0.2	CLAS		17	1 13/16
Lehman	13.50	13⅞ +	2.8	CLAS Pfd	39.40	...	...
NiagaraSh	15.62	16⅝ +	6.4	Engex	a14.12	10 −	29.1
OceasSec	5.94	7¼ +	22.1	EqtyStrat	b10.08	9¾ −	3.3
Source	30.61	28⅝ −	6.5	Japan	11.87	10⅞ −	8.4
Tri-Contl	22.68	22½ −	0.8	Mexico	b2.95	2¾ −	6.8
Specialized Equity and Convertible Funds				Nautilus	27.22	30 +	10.2
				NewAmFd	41.26	33½ −	18.8
AmCapCv	23.73	27½ +	15.9	Pete&Res	27.10	27¼ +	0.1
ASA	b52.82	50¾ −	3.9	Z-Seven	12.17	14¾ +	21.2
BancrftCv	z	...	...	a-Ex-dividend. b-As of Thursday's close. z-Not available.			

FIGURE 18-1
Closed-End Fund Net Asset Value
and Price Quotations

SOURCE: Reprinted with permission of *The Wall Street Journal*. © Dow Jones and Company, Inc., July 16, 1984. All Rights Reserved.

The net asset values of closed-end fund shares, based on security values computed using Friday's closing market prices, are published in the financial press. Figure 18-1 provides an example. Both the net asset value and the last price at which the fund's shares traded on the day in question are shown (if no trade price is available, the last dealer's asked price is indicated). The final column indicates the associated percentage discount (if negative) or premium (if positive).

Closed-end shares listed on exchanges or actively traded over the counter are included in daily summaries of stock prices and volumes. However, net asset values are published only once each week.

Open-End Funds

A management investment company that stands ready to redeem shares at or near net asset value at all times is termed an *open-end fund* or, more commonly, a *mutual fund*. All such companies are open in at least one direction, since outstanding shares may be redeemed at the shareholders' discretion. Most are also open in the other direction. The fund continuously offers new shares for a price at or near net asset value.

When old shares are redeemed, securities in a fund's portfolio may be sold to raise the needed cash. Conversely, when new shares are issued, the proceeds may be used to purchase new securities for the portfolio. When some shares are redeemed and others sold in a single day at the same net asset value, only the net amount paid out or received need be used for the sale or purchase of securities in the fund's portfolio. To avoid excessive brokerage fees, most funds main-

Investment Companies

tain a small average cash balance to cushion some of the day-to-day fluctuations in these flows.

A few funds charge a redemption fee (e.g., 2% of net asset value), but the vast majority redeem shares for their full net asset value.

Some open-end companies, known as *no-load funds*, sell their shares at net asset value. Others, known as *load funds*, offer shares through brokers or other selling organizations, which add a percentage *load charge* to the net asset value. The percentage charged is usually smaller, the greater the amount invested. For example, a selling organization receiving $1,000 to be invested in a fund might retain $85, leaving $915 to be used to purchase the fund's shares at the current net asset value per share. This is usually called a load charge of 8.5%, but it is actually 9.3% (85/915 = .093) of the amount ultimately invested. Load charges of this magnitude are levied by many funds for small purchases.

The performance of no-load funds as a whole does not differ in any systematic way from that of load funds. This is not surprising. The load charge, which goes to the selling organization, represents the cost of education and persuasion. Mail-order firms often sell items for less than stores. Salespersons who work in stores and those who sell mutual funds provide service and require compensation. Buyers who consider such services worth less than they cost can and should avoid paying for them.

Shares of load funds may not be resold by dealers at prices below that based on the stated schedule of load charges. Such resale price maintenance seems relatively harmless, since there are a great many similar open-end funds and an adequate number of no-load funds for those who prefer self-education.

At the end of 1982 there were 1,396 open-end investment companies with assets worth $283.4 billion.[3] Of these, 497 were no-load funds, which held about $220 billion worth of assets.[4]

Figure 18-2 shows a portion of the quotations for mutual funds provided for each trading day in the financial press. The net asset value, based on closing prices for the fund's securities on the day in question, is shown first. This is followed by the "offer" price—the net asset value plus the load charge applicable to the smallest possible purchase; for no-load funds this column contains the letters "NL." The final column indicates the difference (in dollars) between the day's net asset value per share and that computed at the close of the previous trading day.

[3] Investment Company Institute, *1983 Mutual Fund Fact Book*.

[4] Wiesenberger Investment Companies Services, *Investment Companies 1983*. By permission from the *Wiesenberger Financial Service* © 1983, A Division of Warren, Gorham and Lamont Inc. All Rights Reserved.

```
                    Offer NAV                          Offer NAV
               NAV  Price Chg.                     NAV  Price Chg.
ABT  Family Funds: ......      DodgC Bal  23.69 N.L.+ .13
  A Birthrt 11.22 12.26+ .03   DodgC Stk  21.91 N.L.+ .19
  Emrg Gr   10.25 41.20+ .01   Drx Burnh x16.10 16.68– .12
  Sec  Inc  10.23 11.18+ .03   Dreyfus  Group:
  Tax Mgt   13.13 14.35+ .08     A Bonds  12.00 N.L.+ .08
Acorn Fnd   27.50 N.L.+ .09      CalT Ex  12.68 N.L.+ .06
ADV Fund    17.64 N.L.+ .03      Drevf Fd 11.17 12.21+ .08
Afuture Fd  10.83 N.L.+ .03      Dreyf Lv 15.12 16.52+ .06
AIM  Funds:                      Growth    9.33 N.L.+ .05
  Conv Yld  11.29 12.07– .02     Infrmd   12.04 N.L.+ .04
  Grnway     8.04  8.60+ .02     NYT  Ex  12.87 N.L.+ .07
  HiYld Sc   9.56 10.22 ...      Spl Incm  6.97 N.L.+ :03
  Summit     4.68  (z)+ .04      Tax ExB  10.51 N.L.– .05
Alliance  Capital:               Third Ch  5.68 N.L.+ .07
  Alli Intl  9.08  9.92+ .05   Eagle Gth  6.50  7.10+ .02
  Alli Mtge  9.10  9.58+ .02   Eaton Vance Funds:
  Alli Tech 15.64 17.09+ .06     EH  Bal   6.92  7.46+ .03
  Alpha  Fd 18.98 20.74+ .03     EH  Stk  10.58 11.41+ .05
American Capital Group:          Growth    6.07  6.63+ .05
  Comstk    12.26 13.40+ .06     High Yld  4.31  4.71+ .01
  Corp Bd.   6.25  6.83+ .01     Inc Bost  8.02  8.77+ .03
  Enterpr   10.26 11.21+ .06     Invests   7.15  7.81+ .04
  Exch Fd   41.53 N.L.+ .11      Spc Eqty 17.23 18.58+ .06
  Fd Amer   10.93 11.95+ .04     Tax Mge  12.94 14.14+ .04
  Growth    22.09 N.L.+ .05      VS Specl 10.74 11.74+ .05
  Harbor    11.58 12.66– .01   Eberstadt Group:
  High Yld  x8.96  9.61– .09     Chem Fd   8.56  9.36– .01
  Muni  Bd x16.68 17.51– .13     Enrgy R  10.95 11.97+ .06
  O T C      8.89  9.72+ .02     Surveyr  12.65 13.83+ .02
  Pace  Fd  18.53 20.25+ .06   Empir Bld  14.95 15.70+ .03
  Prov Inc   4.49  4.84+ .02   Energy Utl 18.93 N.L.+ .04
  Venture   13.55 14.81+ .09   Evergrn  r 36.17 N.L.+ .17
AE Growth   13.91 N.L.– .04    Evrgrn TR  13.57 N.L.+ .04
American Funds Group:          Farm B Gr  12.44 N.L.+ .03
  Am  Bal    9.09  9.93+ .06   Federated  Group:
  Amcap F    7.43  8.12+ .02     Am Lead   9.59 10.26+ .05
  Am Mutl   13.15 14.37+ .02     Exch Fd  31.22 N.L.+ .16
  Bnd FdA   11.70 12.79+ .05     GNMA      9.80 N.L.+ .09
  Eupac     13.05 14.26– .01     Hi Incm  11.03 11.80+ .02
  Fund Inv  10.22 11.17+ .05     Incm Tr   9.64 N.L.+ .01
  Gth FdA   11.76 12.85+ .03     Infrmd    9.15 N.L.+ .04
  Inc FdA    9.61 10.50+ .04     SIMT     10.08 N.L.+ .01
  I C A      9.73 10.63+ .07     Stock Tr 13.93 N.L.+ .06
  Nw Econ   12.55 13.72+ .05     Tax Free  8.36  8.75+ .05
  Nw Prsp    7.45  8.14+ .04     US Gvt S  7.96  8.34+ .07
  Tax  Ex    9.16  9.62+ .04   Fidelity Investments: ....
  Wash Mt    8.29  9.06+ .04     Bd Corp   6.14 N.L.+ .01
  Am Grwth   8.19  8.94 ...      Congr St 48.27 N.L.– .04
  Am Heritg  3.00 N.L.+ .03      Contra    8.94 N.L.+ .02
  Am Invest  7.04 N.L.+ .06      Discovr  16.78 N.L.+ .11
  AmInv Inc  8.77 N.L.+ .03      Eq Incm  21.33 21.77+ .05
  Am MedAs  26.88 N.L.+ .04      Exch Fd  39.20 N.L.+ .10
  AmNat Gw   3.69  4.03+ .02     Fidel Fd 13.44 N.L.+ .06
  AmNtl Inc 17.40 19.02+ .08     Freedm   10.98 N.L.+ .03
  Amway Mt   5.24  5.60+ .01     Govt Sec  8.76 N.L.+ .05
  Analytic 131.56 N.L.+ .72      Hi Incm   8.11 N.L.+ .02
  Armstrng   7.22 N.L.+ .04      High Yld 10.75 N.L.+ .03
Axe-Houghton:                    Ltd Muni  7.88 N.L.+ .05
  Fund B     8.64  9.39+ .03     Mageln   29.37 30.28+ .15
  Income     4.10  4.46+ .03     Mass TF   9.42  9.52+ .08
  Stock Fd   6.14  6.71+ .05     Mercry   10.90 11.24+ .01
Babson  Group:                   Muncpl    6.40 N.L.+ .01
  Bond  Tr   1.41 N.L. ...       Puritan  11.27 N.L.+ .03
  Grwth     10.62 N.L.+ .01      Sel Ergy  9.59  9.79+ .04
  UMB  Bd    9.20 N.L.+ .01      Sel Finl 15.92 16.24+ .07
  UMB Stk    9.96 N.L.+ .04      Sel Hlth 15.61 15.93+ .06
  BLC Gwth  15.42 16.86+ .08     Sel Metl 11.70 11.94+ .17
  BLCInc Fd 14.70 16.07+ .03     Sel Tech 19.11 19.50 ...
  Beacon Gr 12.92 N.L.+ .09      Sel  Util 14.28 14.57+ .04
  Beacon Hil 15.39 N.L.+ .01     Specl Sit  9.91 10.22+ .07
BenhamCapital Mgmt: ....         Thrift Tr  9.10 N.L.+ .04
  CalTF In   9.37 N.L. ...       Trend    33.64 N.L.+ .01
  CalTF  L   9.36 N.L.+ .04    Fidu CapG  16.52 N.L.+ .03
  Cap TNT    9.82 N.L.+ .01    Financial Programs:
Berger Group Funds:              Bond Shr  5.91 N.L.+ .01
  100 Fund  14.75 N.L.– .01      Dynam     6.42 N.L.– .04
  101 Fund  12.93 N.L.+ .03      Industl   3.73 N.L.+ .01
Boston Company:                  Income    7.30 N.L.+ .03
  Cap Apr   22.75 N.L.+ .15      Tax Free 13.37 N.L.+ .05
  Govt Inc  10.21 N.L.+ .03      Wld Tch   6.92  7.28– .01
  Spcl Grw  15.54 N.L.+ .01    First Investors Fund:
  Bos Found 12.24 13.38+ .08     Bond Ap  11.98 12.92+
  Bowser GF  2.80 N.L. ...       Discovr  11.8' 12.91–
  Bruce Fnd 185.51 N.L.+ .12     Gro 'h    '    7.3'
Bull & Bear Group:               In        '
  Cap Grw   12.07 N.L.+ .04
  Eq Incm   10.08 N.'.+ '
  Golcnd    10.60  '  +
  'High     13.7'
```

FIGURE 18-2
Mutual Fund Net Asset Value Quotations

RELATED INVESTMENT MEDIA

A number of investment-company-like institutions exist. This section describes some of the more important types.

Variable Annuities

In 1952 the College Retirement Equities Fund, which serves as an investment medium for the faculty and staff of a number of academic and nonprofit institutions, pioneered the concept of a variable annuity. Since then a number of insurance companies have developed similar plans.

Two quite different aspects are involved in such a plan. During an *accumulation period* the investor in effect contributes money periodically (e.g., monthly) to an open-end mutual fund, withdrawing nothing. Typically some sort of life insurance (e.g., a policy guaranteed to pay an amount equal to the total dollar value contributed) is included. The premium for this insurance is deducted from each contribution, along with any load charge, and the remainder used to purchase shares (or "units") of the fund.

At the end of the accumulation phase (usually upon retirement), the investor will hold shares with some current market value. He or she might cash in the shares and spend the money in any desired way (although many plans do not allow this). Alternatively, the money might be used to purchase a *fixed annuity*. This is a contract in which an insurance company promises to pay a given amount each month to the purchaser, until the latter dies. If a *joint survivor option* is included, payments continue (perhaps at a reduced amount), until the purchaser's spouse dies.

For rate-setting, insurance companies utilize *mortality tables*, which indicate the probabilities, based on experience, that persons of various ages will die within a year. While no one can predict the day on which a specific individual will die, it is possible to determine with reasonable accuracy how many of a large number of people in a given age group will die in each future year. When a group of 65-year-olds is sold a set of annuities, the insurance company that sells the policies can estimate the amount of cash required in each future year to meet its resulting obligations. This can be converted into a *present value* in one of two ways. The simplest procedure is to find the cost of a portfolio of default-free bonds that will produce cash on the required dates. If the insurance company were to buy such bonds, it could completely hedge its bets; thus the annuities could be sold for this amount plus commissions, sales charges, and so on.

In practice this is rarely done. Instead, the present value of the annuity obligation is computed by discounting the expected payments, using some low rate of interest. The insurance company hopes to earn a higher return on its portfolio but must make up the difference if there is a shortfall. *Reserves* are maintained to cover the latter possibility. If and when actual returns exceed the assumed interest rate, some of the excess may be paid the insurance company's stockholders or returned to policyholders. *Mutual* insurance companies are owned (in principle) by policyholders, so good investment returns will, in time, result in higher payments to annuitants. Thus many "fixed" annuities may, in fact, be *variable*, with the amounts paid depending to at least some extent on investment performance.

A *variable annuity* is variable by design, with annuity payments dependent directly on investment performance. All investment risk is borne by the annuitant; moreover, assets are usually invested in common stocks instead of bonds, so there is more risk to be borne.

The procedure is best described with an example. Assume that at retirement the present value of a fixed annuity of $1 per month for a particular individual will be $100, based on an assumed rate of interest of 4%. If the person's account is worth $50,000 at the time, a fixed annuity paying $500 (= $50,000/$100) can be purchased. Alternatively the money can be used to buy units of a variable annuity. If the unit value falls to $4.50, the monthly check will fall to $450; if the value of a unit rises to $5.50, the check will rise to $550, and so on.

The value of an annuity unit is determined by the experience of an investment fund. The procedure is straightforward. The percentage change in the value of the fund—including dividends, interest received, capital gains and/or losses (realized or not), less any expenses—is computed. From this the interest rate assumed in the original annuity valuation is subtracted. The value of each annuity unit is then increased or decreased by the difference. In effect, the insurance company pays itself a dividend equal to the amount required to cover the interest the company assumed it would receive when the annuities were priced; and this dividend is paid no matter what the experience of the fund might have been. Thus the risk is shifted from the insurance company to the purchasers of the annuities.

The lower the assumed interest rate, the greater the relative benefits received by those who live longer and the smaller the relative benefits received by those who die early. Correspondingly, those holding variable annuities based on lower interest rates can expect greater increases in monthly payments over time than can those holding similar annuities based on higher interest rates.

To implement a variable annuity, an insurance company must set up a *separate account*, which may be invested directly in a diversified portfolio or simply used to purchase shares in an open-end mutual fund—usually one run by the same company. The separate account typically backs both *accumulation units*, similar to the shares of an open-end fund that pays no dividends, and *annuity units*. The former are relevant to the investor during the accumulation phase; the latter during the payout phase, after retirement.

The choice between a variable and a fixed annuity is similar to that involved in most investment decisions. To what extent is a person willing to take on added risk to get a higher expected return? Although professional advisers can help assess the magnitudes involved, the final decision must rest with the individual who will bear the risk.

Commingled Funds

Banks and insurance companies invest money for individuals and organizations. Banks manage personal trust funds; both banks and insurance companies manage individual retirement funds. Any such fund can be invested on an individual basis, with specific securities selected and held in a separate account. This is often done for large accounts, but to capture economies of scale, small accounts are often *commingled*, allowing joint participation in one or more large pools of securities.

The vehicle utilized in this process is the *commingled fund*. In form (but not in law), it is similar to an open-end mutual fund. The securities in the fund are valued periodically, and the total value is divided by the current number of *units* to determine a *net asset value per unit*. On any valuation date, money from an account may be used to purchase units at this value. Alternatively, units purchased previously may be redeemed at the current unit value.

A bank or insurance company may offer several commingled funds. One fund may hold only short-term money market instruments; another, long-term bonds; yet another, common stocks. A commingled fund investing in mortgages may be offered, as may one investing in real property.[5] When a complete menu of this sort is available, money from a given trust or retirement account can be invested in two or more commingled funds and/or in individual securities.

Real Estate Investment Funds

The real estate investment trust (REIT), although not classified as an investment company for legal purposes, is similar to a closed-end fund. Like an investment company, it can serve as a conduit for earnings on investments, passing them on to claimants and avoiding corporate taxation.

REITs must invest primarily in real estate or loans secured by

---

[5] Real property commingled funds may be only partially open-ended; owing to the illiquidity of the assets, some sponsoring organizing reserve the right to limit the redemption of units, either temporarily or until sale of the underlying property.

real estate. They can obtain capital by issuing stock, bonds (convertible or not), and even warrants. They can also borrow from banks, issue mortgages on some or all of their property, and issue commercial paper.

Like managed investment companies, REITs "hire" a management firm for a fee—typically about 1% of the value of assets per year. Most trusts are affiliated with banks, life insurance companies, or mortgage firms, which set them up and serve as their investment managers.

The stocks of many real estate investment trusts are listed on major exchanges. Price and volume quotations are listed with those of other stocks in the financial press.

There are two major types of REITs. *Mortgage trusts* invest primarily in mortgages and construction and development loans. The latter, which constitute the bulk of the assets of many trusts, are loans made to the builder or developer of a project, with the property serving as collateral. The loans, generally fairly short-term, are made on the premise that the property will be finished on time and sold for an amount sufficient to allow the developer to pay off the loan on time and in full. *Equity trusts* invest in real estate property directly; in effect, they serve as landlords. The property may be financed in part by issuing mortgages. A few firms, termed *mixed* or *hybrid* trusts, are neither predominantly mortgage nor equity trusts, but combine the two modes.

Most REITs are highly levered. A typical trust might issue fixed claims worth 70% of its total assets. Any fall in the value of the property held by such a firm will generally cause a greater percentage change in the value of its common stock, as will an adverse shift in the relationship between the interest paid on its short-term debt and that earned on its assets.

In the recession of 1973-1974 the construction industry was particularly hard hit. This caused a large number of defaults on construction and development loans and on some long-term mortgages. Many REITs were left with half-finished buildings. Moreover, short-term interest rates, at which REITs traditionally obtain substantial amounts of capital, climbed above mortgage interest rates. From October 25, 1973, to August 19, 1974, the Dow Jones Industrial Average fell 27%; an index of the prices of shares in equity REITs fell more than 50%; and an index of the prices of shares in mortgage REITs fell over 70%.[6] Many trusts went bankrupt, including some associated with extremely well-known (and reputedly conservative) financial institutions.

The experience of the early 1970s undoubtedly diminished the enthusiasm of those who invested heavily in REITs (especially those who failed to appreciate the fact that leverage increases risk as well

---

[6] "Real Estate Investment Trusts: A Background Analysis and Recent Industry Developments, 1961-1974," Economic Staff Paper 75, No. 1, Office of Economic Research, U.S. Securities and Exchange Commission (1975).

as expected return). However, the poor initial results should not cause the rejection of the concept. Such trusts provide a vehicle for the inclusion of important types of assets in a portfolio. Owing to their specialized investment policies and typically high leverage, of course, only a portion of an individual's assets should be invested in such securities. Properly utilized, however, they should be desirable investment media.

INVESTMENT POLICIES

Different funds follow different investment policies. Some funds are designed as substitutes for an investor's entire portfolio; others expect their investors to hold other securities, and possibly shares in other funds. Some restrict their domain and/or selection methods severely; others give their managers wide latitude. Many engage in highly active management, with substantial portfolio changes designed to exploit hoped-for superior investment predictions; others are more passive, concentrating instead on tailoring a portfolio to serve the interests of a particular clientele.

While categorization is difficult, and many funds pursue mixed strategies, broad classes can be identified.

Money market funds hold short-term (typically less than one year) fixed-income instruments such as bank certificates of deposit, high-grade commercial paper, bankers' acceptances, and U.S. Treasury bills. These open-end funds make it possible for small investors to move in and out of the short-term market. The fund manager will extract a fee for this service, of course—usually between ¼ of 1% and 1% of the average asset value per year. There are usually no load charges, and money may be added to or removed from an account at almost any time. Dividends are usually declared daily. Arrangements with a cooperating bank often make it possible to write a check on an account—the bank obtains the amount involved by redeeming "shares" in the fund when the check clears.

Bond funds invest in fixed-income securities. Some go farther, specifying that only particular types of instruments will be purchased. There are high-grade bond funds, medium-grade bond funds, corporate bond funds, government bond funds, convertible bond funds, and so on. Some are organized as open-end companies, others as closed-end bond funds. A number of the latter are run by subsidiaries of banks and insurance companies.

As indicated earlier, the predominant type of unit trust in the United States is the *bond unit trust*. Some are based on government issues, others on corporate issues, and still others on specialized types. Municipal bond unit trusts, like open-end municipal bond funds, make it easier for those in high tax brackets to obtain diversification and, possibly, increased liquidity while taking advantage of the exemption of such securities from personal income taxation.

Bond unit trusts typically hold securities with different coupon payment schedules and pay roughly equal dividends every month.

A few open-end companies and some unit trusts are restricted to holdings of *preferred stocks*. Others include both bonds and preferred stocks in their portfolios.

Many open-end companies consider themselves managers for the bulk of the investment assets of their clients. Funds that hold both equity and fixed-income securities particularly fit this description. Wiesenberger Investment Companies Service's annual *Investment Companies* manual classifies such companies as belonging to one of two groups. *Income funds* wish to "provide as liberal a current income from investments as possible."[7] *Balanced funds* wish to "minimize investment risks so far as this is possible, without unduly sacrificing possibilities for long-term growth and current income."[8] Some funds hold relatively constant mixes of bonds, preferred stock, convertible bonds, and/or equities; others alter the proportions periodically in attempts to "time the market."

A *diversified common stock fund* invests most of its assets in common stocks, although short-term money market instruments may be held to accommodate irregular cash flows and/or to engage in some market timing.

In 1983, Wiesenberger's manual classified the majority of diversified common stock funds as having one of three types of objectives: (1) maximum capital gain, (2) growth, (3) growth and income.[9] Two factors appear to be involved in this classification: the relative importance of dividend income versus capital gains and the overall level of risk to be taken. The classifications "are arranged in descending order of emphasis on capital appreciation and, consequently, in ascending order of the importance placed on current income and relative price stability."[10] Since high-yield portfolios are generally less risky than those with low yields, relatively few major conflicts arise, although two rather different criteria are involved.

Borderline cases remain: "The difference between a Capital Gain Fund and a Growth Fund is a matter of degree, and in some cases little distinction may exist. Similarly, there is no sharp line of demarcation between a Growth Fund and a Growth and Income Fund."[11] Classi-

---

[7] Wiesenberger Investment Companies Services, *Investment Companies 1983*, By permission from the *Wiesenberger Financial Services* © 1983, A Division of Warren, Gorham and Lamont Inc. All Rights Reserved.

[8] *Ibid.*

[9] A fourth category ("specialized") covered funds not highly diversified.

[10] Wiesenberger, *op. cit.*

[11] *Ibid.*

fication is difficult because the official statement of objectives in a fund's prospectus is usually fuzzy, to say the least.

The Investment Company Act of 1940 defines a *diversified investment company* as one that invests at least 75% of its funds in a diversified manner: within this portion of the portfolio, no single issuer's securities may account for more than 5% of the fund's assets nor more than 10% of the value of such securities outstanding. Funds not meeting this standard are classified as *nondiversified investment companies*. Some choose the latter classification simply to maintain flexibility. Others do so to *specialize* in certain types of securities.

A few specialized funds concentrate on the securities of firms in a particular *industry*; there are chemical funds, aerospace funds, electronic funds, gold funds, and so on. Others deal in securities of a particular type; for example, there are funds that hold restricted (letter) stock, over-the-counter stock funds, and so on. Others provide a convenient means for holding the securities of firms in a particular *country*—for example, the Japan Fund, Mexico Fund, various Canadian funds, etc. Specialized funds may be either open-end or closed-end.

Open-end *tax-free municipal bond funds* were first offered in 1976. *Municipal bond unit trusts* have been available longer. Some municipal bond investment companies hold issues from many states. Others specialize in the issues of governmental units in one state to provide a vehicle for residents of that state who wish to avoid paying state taxes on the income.

An *index fund* attempts to provide results similar or identical

TABLE 18-1
Mutual Funds, Classified by Investment Policy (as of December 31, 1982)

Type of Fund	Number of Funds	Combined Assets ($ billions)
Common stock:		
Maximum capital gain	92	11.1
Growth	157	22.8
Growth and income	108	20.4
Specialized	22	.9
Balanced	24	3.1
Income	126	12.9
Bond and preferred stock	13	2.3
Money market	214	180.5
Tax-exempt municipal bond	53	8.2
Tax-free money market	25	8.8

SOURCE: Wiesenberger Investment Companies Service, *Investment Companies 1983*, By permission from the Wiesenberger Financial Service © 1983, A Division of Warren, Gorham and Lamont, Inc. All Rights Reserved.

to those computed for a specified market index, such as Standard and Poor's 500-stock index. A number of banks have established commingled index funds, and corporations and other organizations have set up index funds for their own employee retirement trust funds. The *Vanguard Index Trust*, a no-load investment company, provides a vehicle for small investors who wish to obtain results similar to those of Standard and Poor's 500-stock index.

Table 18-1 provides an indication of the number of mutual funds of various types and the amount of assets under their control.

MUTUAL FUND ACCOUNTS

The United States Internal Revenue Code allows an investment company to avoid corporate income taxation. A unit trust, closed-end or open-end fund can qualify as a *regulated investment company* by meeting certain standards concerning diversification[12] and paying out at least 90% of its net income, exclusive of capital gains, each year. Net realized capital gains may be distributed or retained. If the company chooses the latter course, it must pay a tax calculated at the maximum rate applied to capital gains for personal income taxes. Shareholders are then given credit for having paid tax at this rate on the gains on their shares.

Most mutual funds "pay out" both income (dividends and interest) and net realized capital gains. However, at a shareholder's option, payments may be made in shares rather than in cash. In either event, the shareholder must pay personal income tax on the dividends and capital gains distributions on his or her holdings.

While an investor can purchase shares in a fund and receive all distributions in cash, this is only one of many possible arrangements. Mutual funds offer plans of several types to satisfy investors' desires for different patterns of contributions and withdrawals over time.

Accumulation plans are designed for those who prefer to make no withdrawals over some period of time. The simplest procedure involves automatic reinvestment of all dividends and capital gains. As with other plans, this often results in positions involving fractional shares, but, since most accounts are maintained via computerized records, this poses no problem.

Voluntary accumulation plans allow an investor to add to an account as desired, subject only to some minimum amount that must be invested each time. Alternatively, a fixed dollar amount may be invested at periodic intervals—in some cases via automatic bank transfers.

---

[12] At least 50% of the company's assets must be diversified: within this portion, no more than 5% of total assets can be invested in the securities of any one issuer. Moreover, no more than 25% of total assets may be invested in any one company.

Contractual accumulation plans call for a fixed amount to be contributed regularly (usually monthly) over a relatively long period (often five or more years). Sales charges may or may not be lower than those applicable to a voluntary plan. The investor is not legally bound to make all the payments, but since a large proportion of early contributions typically goes toward sales charges, commitment to a contractual plan should not be considered if cancellation is at all likely.

The Investment Company Amendment Act of 1970 placed limits on the load charges for contractual plans. The total amount may not exceed 9%, and no more than 50% of the first year's contribution may be allocated to sales charges (i.e., at least half must be invested in fund shares). Moreover, if a 50% "front-end" load charge is assessed in the first year, cancellation of the plan within 18 months entitles the investor to a refund reducing the effective charge to 15% of the amount paid in.

Accumulation of funds for retirement may also be accomplished via an *individual retirement account* (*IRA*) or a *Keogh plan*. In 1983 anyone could contribute up to $2,000 of his or her earned income to an individual retirement account, deducting the amount contributed from gross income when calculating personal income tax. If the income-earner's spouse had no earned income, a total of $2,250 could be contributed to two IRAs.

Self-employed individuals can contribute 15% of their net earnings from self-employment, up to a maximum ($15,000 in 1983), to a Keogh plan account, with such contributions also deductible from gross income for tax purposes. Either type of account is maintained by a *custodian*— usually a bank. Contributions and any cash received from investments are invested in accordance with the investor's desires. Funds may be withdrawn beginning at age 59½ and withdrawals must begin by age 70½.

All money taken out of a custodial account is taxable income, but there is no additional tax on dividends and interest received during the accumulation period, and the investor may be in a lower tax bracket after retirement. Thus the "tax shelter" aspect of such plans can be quite attractive.

Many institutions have made arrangements for custodial accounts with investment restricted to their offerings. There are, for example, bank plans, savings and loan company plans, security broker's plans, and investment company plans. Many allow the investor to direct the custodian to switch money among separate vehicles with no additional charges.

It is increasingly common to find several investment companies operating as a *family of funds*. An investor may purchase shares in one or more of the funds under common management and also switch money from one to another. Sales charges are typically lower than those applicable to similar transactions involving funds managed by different companies; in some cases transfers within a family may be made without charge. In any event, a single account is usually maintained, with all contributions, withdrawals, and tax information included in one statement.

Many mutual funds offer voluntary *withdrawal plans*. The investor instructs the fund to pay out either a fixed amount or a specified percentage of the account's value periodically (e.g., monthly). When payments exceed regular distributions, the number of shares is decreased.

A few funds offer *insurance*. A contractual accumulation plan may include a provision that contributions will be completed if the investor dies or is disabled. The premium for such insurance is, in effect, added to the sales charge.

Even more exotic arrangements are offered by some funds. The convenience of centralized accounting and preparation of needed tax documents, coupled with arrangements conforming to individuals' particular situations, allow mutual funds to effectively fill the role of an investment manager for small (and some not-so-small) investors.

MUTUAL FUND PERFORMANCE

The need to compute net asset values daily, and the public nature of such figures (and the amounts distributed to shareholders), make open-end investment companies ideal candidates for studies of the performance of professionally managed investment funds. United States mutual funds have frequently been the subject of extensive (and sometimes unwelcome) study. Open-end funds in other countries have also been examined, as have U.S. closed-end funds.

Recently, data on professionally managed pension funds and bank commingled funds have become available. The performance of the managers of such funds appears to be similar to that of mutual fund managers: they do reasonably well tailoring portfolios to meet clients' objectives, but few seem to be able consistently to "beat the market." While the following sections deal only with U.S. investment companies, many of the results apply to other professionally managed funds, both in the United States and in other countries.[13]

---

[13] For evidence on funds outside the United States see, for example: James R. F. Guy, "The Effect of International Diversification on the Historical Performance of British Mutual Funds," University of California Graduate School of Business Administration (Berkeley Working Paper No. 36, July 1975); John G. McDonald, "French Mutual Fund Performance: Evaluation of Internationally Diversified Portfolios," *Journal of Finance*, XXVIII, no. 5 (December 1973), 1161-80; Juan A. Palacios, "The Stock Market in Spain: Tests of Efficiency and Capital Market Theory" (Ph.D. dissertation, Stanford University, June 1973); G. Pogue, B. Solnik, and A. Rousselin, "The Impact of International Diversification: A Study of the French Mutual Fund Industry" (MIT Working Paper 658-73, June 1973); and Michael A. Firth, "The Investment Performance of Unit Trusts in the Period 1965-75," *Journal of Money, Credit and Banking*, November 1977.

Risk Control

One of the functions that a mutual fund can perform for its investors is the maintenance of a particular risk posture. Formal statements of objectives provide some idea of a fund's intended posture, but typically the wording is (perhaps intentionally) vague. Nonetheless, there is a relationship between portfolio risk and stated objectives.

Figure 18-3 summarizes information on the standard deviations of monthly excess returns over a ten-year period for funds with similar objectives, using classifications assigned by Wiesenberger at the beginning of the period. Each bar plots the range of values obtained. Mean values, included in the figure, are shown by squares. On average, funds that promised low risk provided it. However, some funds with conservative objectives took on more risk than others with less conservative objectives: the bars in Figure 18-3 overlap considerably.

Perhaps it is too much to expect a fund to state a specific risk target once and for always. Some managers like to change market exposure periodically in attempts at market timing. Others wish to avoid the possibility of stockholders' suits claiming that objectives were not met. In either case, past risk exposure may be a better guide to future risk exposure than the rather general statements found in a fund's prospectus.

Figure 18-4 shows that this is often the case. Each point plots the beta values for a fund in two different periods. While the points do not plot neatly along a 45-degree line from the origin (which repre-

FIGURE 18-3
Risk versus Fund Objectives: 123 Mutual Funds, 1960-69.

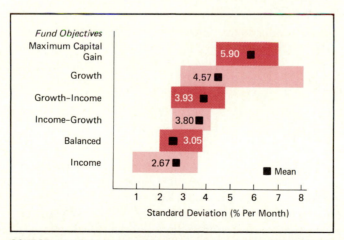

SOURCE: John G. McDonald, "Objectives and Performance of Mutual Funds, 1960-1969," *Journal of Financial and Quantitative Analysis*, IX, no. 3 (June 1974), 316.

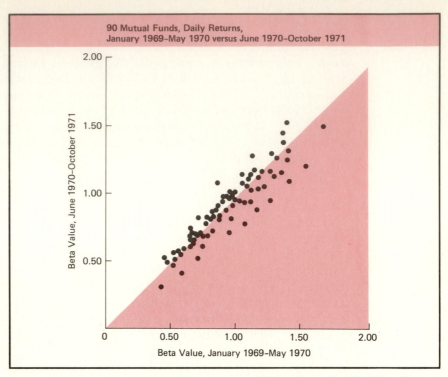

90 Mutual Funds, Daily Returns,
January 1969–May 1970 versus June 1970–October 1971

Beta Value, June 1970–October 1971 (y-axis)

Beta Value, January 1969–May 1970 (x-axis)

SOURCE: Gerald A. Pogue and Walter Conway, "On the Stability of Mutual Fund Beta Values" (unpublished working paper, MIT Sloan School of Management, June 1972).

FIGURE 18-4
Past versus Future Beta Values: 90 Mutual Funds, January 1969–May 1970 versus June 1970–October 1971.

sents equal beta values in both periods), there is a clear relationship between "past beta" and "future beta." Most funds do control risk at least within limits.

Diversification

An important task for any investment manager is the provision of an appropriate degree of portfolio diversification. The correct amount depends on the proportion of clients' funds managed and on the likelihood that superior abnormal returns can be obtained by sacrificing diversification. Since most mutual funds are intended to be a major component of a shareholder's portfolio, one would expect them to be well diversified. Figure 18-5 shows that many are. Quarterly excess returns over a five-year period were computed for 100 funds and compared with corresponding values for Standard and Poor's 500-stock index. For each

584   Investment Companies

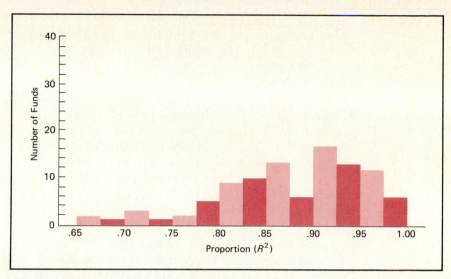

SOURCE: Merrill Lynch, Pierce, Fenner, and Smith, Inc. *Investment Performance Analysis, Comparative Survey, 1970-1974*.

FIGURE 18-5
Proportion of Variation in Quarterly Returns Attributable to Market Fluctuations: 100 Mutual Funds, 1970-1974.

fund a value of *R-squared* was computed. This indicates the proportion of the variation in a fund's returns that can be attributed to variations in returns on the index. As the figure shows, approximately 90% of the quarter-by-quarter variation in a typical fund's return was associated with swings in the value of the S&P 500 index during this period, but the values ranged from 66% to 98%.

Average Returns

To measure a fund's ability to "beat the market," one must compare its performance with that which could have been obtained in some simple or passive manner. If average return is examined, a *comparison portfolio* or *benchmark* of *equal risk* should be used. In choosing such a benchmark, a measure of risk relevant for the investor in question should be used.

Many studies compare the performance of each investment company with that of a combination of (1) a market index such as Standard and Poor's 500-stock index and (2) Treasury bills. The particular combination is chosen to have a risk equal to that of the investment company. The "bottom line" measure of performance is the difference between the average return on the fund and the average return on the "comparison mix." This amount, the *average differential return*, is typically (and misleadingly) called the fund's *alpha value*. To avoid confusion with nonequilibrium *expected* returns, we will term such measures *ex post alpha values*.

Many analysts select a "comparison mix" with an equal *beta value*, where beta is measured relative to the stock index in question. Thus if the estimated average beta of a fund relative to the S&P 500 is .80, its performance is compared with that of a mix with 80% invested in the market index and 20% in Treasury bills each period.[14]

A fund can obtain a positive ex post alpha value by market timing (moving to higher-than-average beta levels prior to market rises and to lower-than-average beta levels prior to market declines) or by security selection (purchasing securities that return more than others with the same beta levels).

Ex post alpha values of this type consider only market risk and thus do not penalize funds for taking on nonmarket risk, although they do include any reward (in higher returns) such risk may entail. Further discussion of such aspects is included in Chapter 21. For present purposes it suffices to indicate that such values are commonly employed performance measures, and they provide useful insights concerning professional investment management in general and that of mutual funds in particular.

Figure 18-6(a) shows the distribution of ex post alpha values for 70 funds, based on annual returns from 1955 through 1964. The average value was −.09% per year (continuously compounded). Thus, net of expenses (other than load charges), the typical fund provided approximately the same return as a market-based passive fund with a constant beta value equal to the fund's average beta value. Of the 70 funds, 40 had positive ex post alpha values.

Different periods give slightly different results. Figure 18-6(b) shows the distribution of ex post alpha values based on monthly returns for 125 funds from 1960 through 1969. The average value was .05% per month, or about .6% per year. During this period the typical fund outperformed a passive fund of similar average beta by slightly more than ½ of 1% per year, and slightly over half (53%) of the funds had positive ex post alphas.

Figure 18-6(c) provides a third example. It shows returns for 100 funds based on quarterly returns from 1970 through 1974. The average ex post alpha value was −.5% per quarter, or approximately −2% per year, and only 20 of the funds had positive alphas.

These results suggest that, net of expenses, the average mutual fund does not significantly outperform an equal-beta passive alternative

---

[14] The procedures actually utilized make the comparisons with such "benchmark portfolios" implicitly, rather than explicitly. Details are given in Chapter 21.

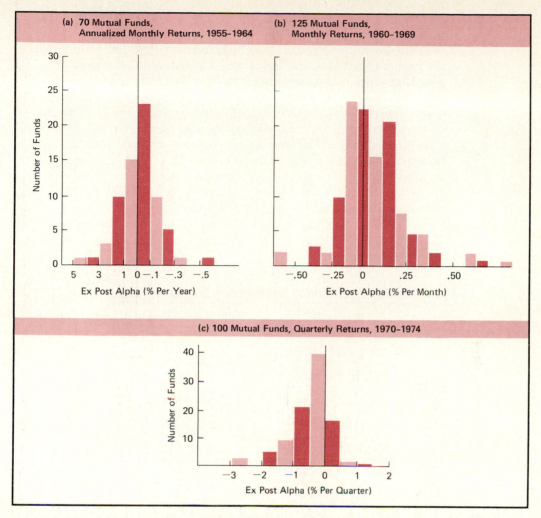

(a) 70 Mutual Funds, Annualized Monthly Returns, 1955–1964

(b) 125 Mutual Funds, Monthly Returns, 1960–1969

(c) 100 Mutual Funds, Quarterly Returns, 1970–1974

SOURCE: (a) Norman E. Mains, "Risk, the Pricing of Capital Assets, and the Evaluation of Investment Portfolios: Comment," *Journal of Business*, July 1977. By permission of the University of Chicago Press © 1977. (b) United States Securities and Exchange Commission, *Institutional Investor Study Report*, March 10, 1971 (U.S. Government Printing Office). (c) Merrill Lynch, Pierce, Fenner and Smith, Inc., *Investment Performance Analysis, Comparative Survey, 1970-1974*.

FIGURE 18-6

Mutual Fund Performance: Ex Post Alpha Values

over any extended period. This is not too surprising. After all, the market's performance is itself an average of the performance of all investors. If, on average, mutual funds could beat the market, some other investors would have to be beaten. With substantial professional management in today's stock market it is difficult to conjure up the image of a likely group of victims.

Consistency of Performance

Despite the rather negative results described thus far, there remains the possibility that a few funds may consistently beat the market by reason of superior management. If funds with, say, a run of four superior years are identified, some will be included because of good luck and others (potentially) because of skill. The former have a 50-50 chance of above-average performance in the next year; the latter, a better than 50-50 chance. The greater the number of consistently superior managers, the greater the proportion of such a group that will turn in an above-average performance in the fifth year.

Unfortunately, the record provides little support for the thesis that a significant number of mutual managers can consistently outperform a passive portfolio with equal market risk. The following results were obtained using a measure of annual differential returns for 115 funds from 1955 through 1964.[15]

Number of Consecutive Years Funds' Performance Exceeded That of a Passive Portfolio with Equal Beta	Proportion of Group with Performance Exceeding That of a Passive Portfolio with Equal Beta in the Subsequent Year (%)
1	50.4
2	52.0
3	53.4
4	55.8
5	46.4

If there are superior mutual fund managers, they either extract an amount equal to their superior returns in salaries or move from fund to fund often enough to make it difficult to verify their existence.

Expenses

Funds incur two kinds of expenses. Management fees and administrative expenses are direct and generally reported. Transactions costs are only partly measurable: brokers' commissions are reported, but bid-ask spreads and the price impacts of trading are usually not even estimated.

By adding back management and administrative expenses and explicit transactions costs one can obtain an estimate of a fund's perfor-

---

[15] Michael C. Jensen, "Risk, the Pricing of Capital Assets, and the Evaluation of Investment Portfolios," *The Journal of Business*, 42, no. 2 (April 1969), 167-247.

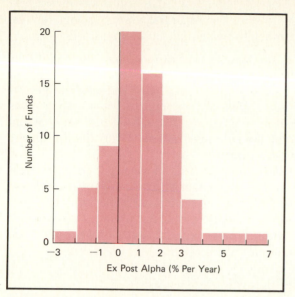

FIGURE 18-7
Mutual Fund Performance: Ex Post Alpha
Values Based on Gross Returns.

SOURCE: Norman E. Mains, "Risk, the Pricing of Capital Assets, and the Evaluation of Investment Portfolios: Comment," *Journal of Business*, July 1977.

mance net of only implicit transactions costs. Figure 18-7 shows the distribution of ex post alpha values based on this measure of "gross" performance for the funds covered in the analysis previously summarized in Figure 18-6(a). While ex post alpha values *net* of all expenses averaged —.09% per year, the values based on *gross* performance averaged 1.07% per year. Moreover, 50 of the 70 funds had positive ex post alpha values based on this measure of performance.

A study[16] by the United States Securities and Exchange Commission attempted to estimate the impact of turnover and several other factors on performance. Ex post alpha values were computed for 132 mutual funds using monthly returns from 1965 through 1969. Then these values were compared with various measures, including turnover, measured by the ratio of (1) the smaller of purchases or sales during a month divided by (2) the month-end asset value. Performance was not significantly related to *any* of the other factors. For example:

> Large funds did no better, other things equal, than small funds.
>
> Funds with load charges did no better, other things equal, than those with no load charges (and therefore investors in such funds did worse, net of load charges, than those in funds with no load charges).

---

[16] United States Securities and Exchange Commission, *Institutional Investors Study Report* (March 10, 1971), U.S. Government Printing Office.

Funds managed by firms with substantial assets under management did no better, other things equal, than others.

But performance net of costs *was* related to turnover—negatively so. The analysis indicated that, on average, a 10% increase in the rate of turnover (e.g., from 50% per year to 60% per year) reduced net performance by .3% to .6% a year. This corresponds to transactions costs of 3% to 6% for the sale of a security and the subsequent purchase of another (e.g., 1.5% to 3% for the sale and 1.5% to 3% for the purchase), with no improvement in performance.

The results of this study suggest that, on average, portfolio revisions lowered net performance (as measured by ex post alpha values). Alterations in a fund's portfolio may be desirable to maintain a desired posture vis-à-vis risk and/or dividend yield. But changes intended to exploit supposed market inefficiencies will, for the average investment manager, prove undesirable net of all costs.

Market Timing

To achieve superior portfolio performance one must either select securities that outperform others of comparable risk or switch from risk class to risk class at appropriate times. The latter strategy is often called *market timing*. The idea is to hold high-beta securities prior to market rises and low-beta securities prior to market declines. An all-equity fund can change its beta level by switching among stocks with different beta values; a balanced fund can also alter its bond/stock mix.

Successful market timing will eventually be reflected in a positive alpha value based on long-term performance. Overall performance may also be separated into parts—for example, one part attributed to security selection and another to market timing. Details of such procedures are given in Chapter 21.

In a study[17] of the performance of 57 mutual funds over the period from 1953 through 1962, only one was found with a record suggesting any significant ability to time the market. A later study[18] of the performance of 116 funds from February 1968 through June 1980 found only one fund with a record indicating significant market-timing ability in both the first and the second half of the period.

Such results are not surprising. If many funds were consistently successful at market timing, they would show up in tests for superior overall performance, unless they were consistently engaging in inferior security selection and thus losing the fruits of their ability to predict

[17] Jack L. Treynor and Kay Mazuy, "Can Mutual Funds Outguess the Market?" *Harvard Business Review*, 44, no. 4 (July–August 1966), 131–36. Copyright © 1966 by the President and Fellows of Harvard College. All Rights Reserved.

[18] Roy D. Henriksson, "Market Timing and Mutual Fund Performance: An Empirical Investigation," *The Journal of Business*, 57, no. 1, pt. 1 (January 1984), 73–96.

the market. The latter situation seems highly improbable. More likely, investment managers find it as difficult to time the market as to select underpriced securities. Such is the lot of a participant in a highly efficient market.

CLOSED-END FUND PREMIUMS AND DISCOUNTS

Several studies[19] have shown that the performance of managers of diversified closed-end investment companies in the United States is similar to that of open-end fund managers. When returns are measured by changes in *net asset values* (plus all distributions), closed-end funds appear to be neither better nor worse than open-end funds. Risk is controlled reasonably well, funds formed to provide diversification do so, and there is little evidence that managers can either select underpriced securities or time the market successfully. Performance gross of expenses is roughly equal to that of comparable passive portfolios and performance net of expenses somewhat lower.

But there is more to be said about closed-end funds. An investor can purchase an open-end fund's shares for their net asset value (plus any required load charge) and sell them later at the subsequent net asset value. Except for any load charges, the performance of the *management* of such a fund, based on net asset values, is equal to that of the *shareholders*. Not so with closed-end funds. Owners buy and sell shares at prices determined on the open (secondary) market. Shareholders' returns depend on these prices, which may nor may not equal net asset values.

A closed-end fund's shares may sell for the current net asset value per share, for more (i.e., at a *premium*, or, more commonly, for less (i.e., at a *discount*).

Figure 18-8 shows the *ratio* of (1) the market value of all outstanding claims (stock and any bonds, warrants, and so on) for a group of diversified closed-end funds to (2) the total value of the assets held by these funds at the end of each year from 1933 through 1982. With rare exceptions the ratio was less than 1.0: on average, the funds sold at discounts. Equally noticeable is the substantial variation from year to year.

The fact that the price of a closed-end fund differs from its net asset value, with the magnitude of the difference varying from time to time, introduces an added source of risk and potential return. By

---

[19] See, for example: William F. Sharpe and Howard B. Sosin, "Closed-end Investment Companies in the United States: Risk and Return," *Proceedings, 1974 Meeting of the European Finance Association*, ed. B. Jacquillat (Amsterdam: North-Holland Publishing Co., 1975); Antonio Vives, "Analysis of Forecasting Ability of Closed-end Fund's Management," Carnegie-Mellon University, September 1975 (unpublished), and "Discounts and Premiums on Closed-end Funds: A Theoretical and Empirical Analysis," Carnegie-Mellon University, 1975 (unpublished).

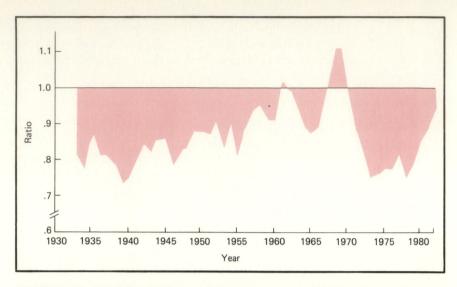

SOURCE: 1933–1972: William F. Sharpe and Howard B. Sosin, "Closed-End Investment Companies in the United States; Risk and Return," *Proceedings, 1974 Meeting of the European Finance Association*, ed. B. Jacquillat (Amsterdam; North-Holland Publishing Co. 1975); 1973–82: Wiesenbergel Investment Companies Services, *Investment Companies 1983*.

FIGURE 18-8

The Ratio of the Value of Claims to the Value of Assets for a Group of Diversified Closed-End Funds, 1933–1982.

purchasing shares at a discount, an investor may be able to increase his or her return. Even if the discount remains constant, the effective dividend yield will be greater than that of an otherwise similar no-load open-end company. If the discount is substantial when the shares are purchased, it may subsequently narrow (i.e., the ratio will increase) and the return will be even greater. On the other hand, if the discount increases (i.e., the ratio falls), overall return may be less than that of an otherwise comparable open-end fund. This latter possibility makes closed-end fund shares riskier than those of similar open-end funds.

Some of the risk associated with varying discounts can be reduced by holding a *portfolio* of shares in several closed-end funds. Discounts on different funds move together, but not perfectly. For example, past data suggest that the standard deviation of the percentage change in the ratio of price to net asset value for a portfolio of 10 to 12 funds is likely to be approximately half that of a typical investment in the shares of a single fund.[20]

---

[20] Sharpe and Sosin, "Closed-end Investment Companies in the United States."

Investment Companies

Explanation of the behavior of closed-end fund prices provides a challenge for the person who believes that capital markets are perfectly efficient. For one not firmly committed to such a view, the purchase of shares of closed-end companies at prices sufficiently below net asset values may provide an opportunity for superior performance.

Problems

1. Explain fully the differences between closed-end and open-end investment companies. Include a discussion of the determination of share purchase price and of the extent to which the number of shares outstanding may be varied for each of these two forms of investment companies.

2. Referring to Figure 18-2, what are the load charges for (a) the Acorn Fund and (b) the Alpha fund? What percentage of *value* is the load charge for ICA (Investment Company of America)—a fund offered by the American Funds Group?

3. Referring to Figure 18-1, how many diversified common stock funds were selling for premiums on the date in question? What was the discount on Japan Fund? Did this offer an opportunity for riskless arbitrage? Why or why not?

4. Some have suggested that closed-end fund discounts do not follow a random walk but tend instead to be mean-reverting (i.e., a discount is more likely to move toward some sort of historic average than it is to move away from it). If this were true, how might you "play" a fund's discount to increase your expected return? What about the risk involved? If discounts did not behave in this manner and you could buy either a no-load open-end fund or a closed-end fund at a discount, which would you do? Why? Would your answer depend on the length of time you planned to keep your money invested?

5. Why should anyone pay management fees to those who operate a tax-exempt municipal bond fund when bonds of this type can be purchased directly?

6. Some have argued that the apparently average performance of the average mutual fund provides a test more of arithmetic than of market efficiency. They point out that many funds appear in the right-hand portions of Figures 18-6(a), (b), and (c) because they outperformed comparable passive strategies. In what sense is "ex post alpha" only a partial measure of performance for such funds? Even if this were a completely adequate measure of performance, is the fact that some funds achieve a positive ex post alpha in a given period inconsistent with market efficiency?

7. Under what conditions might it make sense to invest all one's money in a mutual fund specializing in stocks of companies in the energy sector? In a fund specializing in stocks with above average earnings growth? In a diversified common stock fund? In a balanced fund?

8. Could a money market fund ever provide its investors with a negative return (e.g., over a period as short as a day)? What would be a reasonable way for such a fund to compute its net asset value and dividend each day? What problems

might arise if the value of each holding were computed by "amortizing" the value from its purchase price to the amount it is scheduled to pay at maturity?

9. Wiesenberger's *Investment Companies* provides data on the *expense ratio* (the total amount spent on management fees and administrative costs during a year divided by total asset value) for each of a number of open-end and closed-end investment companies. Does this cover all the costs borne by investors in such funds? What other costs may be relevant? How does an expense ratio differ from a load charge? Is the length of time one plans to keep one's money in a fund relevant for assessing the cost associated with an expense ratio? A load charge?

19

Financial Analysis

THE FINANCIAL ANALYST

In the broadest sense, financial analysis involves determining the values of financial assets, levels of risk and return, and the relationship between risk and return in financial markets. An alternative definition is more pragmatic: financial analysis is what financial analysts do.

The *Financial Analyst's Handbook*[1] defines the term *financial analyst* as synonymous with security analyst or investment analyst—"one who analyzes securities and makes recommendations thereon."[2] Such people may be called economists, market analysts, technical analysts, chartists, industry analysts, or security analysts. A broader interpretation (and the membership of the Financial Analysts Federation) includes those who manage portfolios and/or exercise general responsibility for the investment of funds.

Some restrict the term financial analysis to cover persons who provide inputs for the portfolio management process; those who manage portfolios and guide the overall investment of funds are described as *investment managers*. This chapter deals primarily with financial analysis in this narrower sense; the next, with investment management.

Professional Organizations

In the United States and Canada, those who belong to a local society of financial analysts automatically belong to the Financial Analysts Federation. Among other things, this entitles them to a subscription

---

[1] Sumner N. Levine, ed., *Financial Analyst's Handbook* (Homewood, Ill.: Dow Jones-Irwin, Inc., 1975).

[2] William C. Norby, "Overview of Financial Analysis," in Levine, *Financial Analyst's Handbook,* p. 3.

to the *Financial Analysts Journal*, a major source of information on basic research done by other analysts and members of the academic community. In 1984 there were about 14,500 members in the 52 societies of the Federation.

In 1962 the *Institute of Chartered Financial Analysts* was formed by the Financial Analysts Federation to award the professional designation of *Chartered Financial Analyst* (C.F.A.). Twenty years later 7,257 analysts had qualified. To become a C.F.A. one must have several

FIGURE 19-1

General Topic Outline, C.F.A. Candidate Study and Examination Program

Candidate Level
I II III

Techniques of Analysis—Fixed Income Securities

Bond Instruments and Credit Evaluation

Fixed income instruments:
taxable, tax exempt, corporate, government conventional, mortgage–backed, convertible security, contractual obligation fixed coupon, floating coupon, call protection;
sinking fund, put, extensible, retractable, fixed maturity;
average life, half life of amortizing, mortgage–backed bonds;
Credit quality: bond ratings; earning power tests, asset tests

Credit Markets: yield curve; yield spread; investor expectations; relative value; interest rate forecasting

Mathematical Properties of Bonds
Yield and duration
Bond swapping

Comparative Returns: Stocks vs Bonds

Bond Management, Policy, Implementation
Utilization of the bond basics, investor expectations and client objectives to frame bond policy in terms of maturity, quality, diversification, coupon, and unit commitments

Techniques of Analysis—Equity Securities

I II III

Financial Instruments
Stocks, warrants, rights, options

Sources of Information

Characteristics of the Stock Market
Market indicators; comparative returns
Relationship of stock market to economy

Industry Appraisal and Evaluation
Analysis of demand: growth (nominal and real), end–uses, cyclicality, exports
Analysis of supply: existing plant, capital spending needs, barriers to entry, foreign competition
Industry profitability: supply/demand balance, pricing, raw materials, capital and labor, learning curve, research
External factors: political, regulatory, social, demographic
Security market evaluation of profits

Company Appraisal and Evaluation
Sales analysis: growth (nominal and real), position within industry, vertical/horizontal integration
Earnings analysis: cost structure, operating leverage, return on equity, sources of earnings growth, non–operating factors
Balance sheet analysis: financial leverage, intangibles, flow of funds analysis
Dividend analysis: payout policy, dividend growth, internal and external funding
Management appraisal: planning, diversification, technical expertise, marketing, reputation, ethics

Risk analysis: company versus industry, stock versus market, qualitative factors
Valuation analysis: earnings multiples, discounted dividend model, growth stock valuation

Technical Analysis
Contrary opinion, stock price and volume, stock trading characteristics

Security Analysis and the Efficient Market
Weak, semi–strong and strong, implications for fundamental and technical analysis

Stock Investment Philosophy

Objective of Analysis—Portfolio Management

I II III

Principles of Financial Asset Management
Definition of portfolio management, basic concepts—return, risk, diversification, portfolio efficiency
Evolution of portfolio management—traditional and recent developments

Investor Objectives, Constraints and Policies
Liquidity requirement
Return requirement
Risk tolerance
Time horizon
Tax considerations
Regulatory and legal considerations
Unique needs, circumstances and preferences
Determination of portfolio policies

Expectational Factors
Social, political and economic
Capital markets
Individual financial assets

Integration of Portfolio Policies and Expectational Factors
Portfolio construction—asset allocation, active/passive strategies
Monitoring portfolio and responding to change—objectives, constraints and policies, expectational factors
Execution—timing, commission costs, price effects

Portfolio Performance Appraisal
Performance criteria—absolute performance, relative to portfolio objectives and risk level, relative to other portfolios with similar objectives
Measurement of performance—valuation of assets, accounting for income, rates of return and volatility
Evaluation of results—relationship to performance criteria, sources of results

FIGURE 19-1 (*continued*)

years of practical experience and pass three examinations. Figure 19-1, which shows the subjects covered in each of the tests, provides a good summary of the types of knowledge the successful financial analyst needs.

Societies of financial analysts have been formed elsewhere. Those of eleven European countries constitute the European Federation of Financial Analysts Societies. There are also societies in Australia, Japan, Brazil, and other countries.

Estimating Security Characteristics

Financial analysts may attempt to achieve either or both of two possible goals. The first goal is to determine the *characteristics* of a security, a group of securities, or the market as a whole. For example, an analyst may wish to estimate the yield of a security over the next year in order to determine its suitability for portfolios in which yield per se is relevant (owing to, say, tax or legal restrictions). Careful analysis of a company's dividend policy, likely future cash flows, and so on should lead to better estimates than can be obtained by simply dividing last year's dividends by the current stock price.

Another analyst may wish to estimate a security's future beta value and nonmarket risk, both of which are relevant for the management of any portfolio not simply invested in "the market."

In many cases it may be desirable to know more about the sources of a security's risk and return. If a portfolio is being managed for a Texas oil man, one might want to minimize the sensitivity of its return to changes in oil prices. Careful analysis of a company's business, and perhaps the business of its customers and suppliers, is required to estimate key *attributes* of securities (and hence of portfolios).

Financial analysis is also needed to estimate expected returns and their relationships to important security attributes (e.g., the location of a Capital Asset Pricing Model security market line, plane, or hyperplane; the "lambda values" of the Arbitrage Pricing Theory; and so on).

Attempting to Identify Mispriced Securities

The second possible goal is to find *mispriced* securities. Naive versions assume that some securities are so overpriced that no one should hold them, and other securities are so underpriced that everyone should hold them. Such situations are, of course, improbable. More sophisticated versions assume that some securities are sufficiently underpriced to make larger-than-normal holdings desirable, and others sufficiently overpriced to make smaller-than-normal holdings (including zero) desirable, where a "normal" holding is that which would be recommended were the stock priced correctly.

A search for a mispriced security is, in essence, a search for an area in which the financial analysts' estimates of future earnings, dividends, and so on:

1. differ from consensus estimates,
2. are generally closer to correct values, and
3. will (preferably) eventually be reflected in security prices.

Two rather different approaches may be taken in the search for mispriced securities. Valuation analysis attempts to determine the appropriate "intrinsic value" for a security, then compares this with the current price (which represents the consensus of market opinion). This may be done in great detail, using estimates of all major factors (e.g., the economy, industry sales, firm sales, capitalization ratios, and growth rates). Alternatively, a short-cut method may be utilized—for example, an estimate of earnings may be multiplied by a "justified" or "normal" price-earnings ratio. A related method attempts to estimate the return expected from a security over a specified period, given its current price, then compares this with the "appropriate" return in the market for stocks with similar attributes.

Another approach considers only one or two aspects and compares estimates directly with the consensus estimates. For example, next year's earnings for each of a group of stocks may be estimated. If an analyst's estimate for a stock exceeds the consensus of other analysts' estimates, the stock may be considered attractive: he or she expects the actual earnings to provide a happy surprise for the market, which will bring a greater-than-normal year-end price and thus a greater-than-normal annual return. Conversely, when an analyst's estimate of earnings is below that of the market, a smaller-than-normal year-end price and thus annual return is expected.

At a more aggregate level, an analyst or investment organization may be more (or less) optimistic about the economy than the consensus of other investors. A more bullish (or less bearish) opinion could suggest that a larger-than-normal position in equities be taken; while a less bullish (or more bearish) opinion calls for a smaller-than-normal position.

Alternatively, an organization might agree with the market's views on the economy and the individual characteristics of specific securities but feel that others have misjudged the prospects for particular industries. In such cases larger-than-normal holdings may be taken in stocks representing industries with prospects that the market is thought to have underestimated, and smaller-than-normal holdings in stocks representing industries with prospects that the market is thought to have overestimated.

Beating the Market

Other examples could be given, but the difference between the two possible goals should be clear. Financial analysis may be used to *understand* the market or to try to *beat* it.

Many books and articles have been written that assertedly show how analysis can be used to beat the market. Unfortunately, no prescription that has been in print for long is likely to work without fail.

Even if an approach has worked in the past, as more and more investors apply it, prices will be driven to levels at which it will not work in the future. Any system designed to beat the market, once known to more than a few people, carries the seeds of its own destruction.

There are two reasons for not including advice on *guaranteed* ways to "beat the market" in this book. First, to do so would make a successful system public and hence unsuccessful. Second, the author knows of no such system. Some apparent anomalies and possible inefficiencies have been described in previous chapters. But any book that purports to open the door to the *certainty* of abnormally high returns for those who follow its advice should be regarded with the greatest skepticism.

FINANCIAL ANALYSIS AND MARKET EFFICIENCY

The concept of an efficient market may appear to be firmly founded on a paradox. If financial analysts carefully analyze the prospects for the economy, various industries, and individual companies, security prices will efficiently reflect values. But if this is the case, why should anyone do financial analysis?

There are two responses to this question. First, people should engage in financial analysis only to the point at which the added benefits cover the added costs. Those who help create market efficiency must earn a living. Barring government support of such praiseworthy activity, one would expect that in a completely free market, prices would be close enough to intrinsic values to make it worthwhile for only the most skillful analysts to search for mispriced securities. The market would thus be nearly, not perfectly, efficient.

The other response to the question focuses on the less controversial goal of financial analysis. Even in a perfectly efficient market there is work to be done. Investors do differ in circumstances, portfolios should be *tailored* to accommodate such differences, and successful performance of this task generally requires estimation of security attributes and the sources and magnitudes of risk and return.

NEEDED SKILLS

To understand and estimate the risk and return of the overall market, specific types of securities (e.g., bonds versus stocks), industries, sectors, and/or individual securities, one must understand financial markets and the principles of valuation. Much of the material required for such an understanding can be found in this book. But, as Figure 19-1 indicates, much more is required. Future prospects must be estimated (perhaps probabilistically) and interrelationships assessed. This requires the skills of the economist and an understanding of industrial organization. And to process relevant historical data, one should have some command of quantitative methods and understand the nuances of accounting.

This chapter cannot provide all the material one needs to become a successful financial analyst. Books on accounting, economics, industrial organization, specific industries, and quantitative methods are required. Instead, we will discuss some techniques used by financial analysts, some of the pitfalls involved, and useful sources of investment information.

EVALUATING INVESTMENT SYSTEMS

. . . switch from bonds to stocks after the growth rate of the money supply has risen for two months; switch from stocks to bonds after the growth rate of the money supply has been below its most recent peak for 15 months. Historically, such a policy would have produced over twice the return obtained by simply holding stocks.

. . . this simple formula predicted over 95% of the quarterly variation in Standard and Poor's 500-stock index over the period studied.

. . . A portfolio of the 25 stocks with the greatest historical relative strength would have outperformed a portfolio of the 25 stocks with the smallest relative strength in 8 months out of 12.

. . . This completely objective stock selection procedure, which can be performed without error on a microcomputer, would have outperformed 80% of the professionally managed portfolios during the period in question.

Statements such as these have been made in the past and will be made in the future. All assert that a mechanical *system*, using only available historical data, can provide results superior to those obtained via sensible but passive portfolio management. Some simply provide predictions of the (stock) market; others prescribe a complete set of instructions for portfolio management. All present impressive statistics based on "as if" tests using data from some past period.

Advocates of such systems may well believe they have found the path to instant affluence. But their proofs often rest on shaky ground. When considering any system, it is imperative that one be certain that none of several sins has been committed.

Failure to Adjust for Risk

According to versions of the Capital Asset Pricing Model, any procedure that, *de facto*, selects high-beta stocks is likely to produce above-average returns in bull markets, below-average returns in bear markets, and above-average returns over the long run.

Properly adjusted for risks, systems that simply select high-beta stocks are less likely to outperform sensible passive strategies. Some systems do little more than this, and their advocates often publicize only average returns, with no consideration given to risk.

Failure to Consider Transactions Costs

Systems that rely on constant trading may possibly produce *gross* returns that exceed those of passive strategies of comparable risk. But this is not the ultimate test. Returns *net* of required transactions costs should be considered. Only trades that increase performance by more than their cost can be justified.

Failure to Consider Dividends

When the performance of a system is compared with that of some passive but sensible strategy, dividends (and interest payments) are often ignored. This may seriously bias the results. For example, a system may be advocated that, in effect, selects low-yield (high-growth) stocks. The prices of such stocks *should* increase at a faster rate than those of stocks in a broadly based index. When yields differ significantly, it is important to compare total returns.

Nonoperational Systems

To be useful, a system must not require information about the future.

Many systems require action after some series of values has reached a "peak" or "trough." But it is rarely obvious until well after a peak or trough has been reached that it was in fact a peak or trough.

A similar situation arises when an equation is *fitted* to a body of data. For example, a system might posit a relationship between the money supply at time $t-1$ and stock prices at time t. The general relationship might be:

$$SP_t = a + bM_{t-1} \qquad (19\text{-}1)$$

where:

SP_t = stock price index at time t

M_{t-1} = money supply at time $t-1$

a, b = constants

To make such a system operational, specific numeric values for a and b are needed. A "test" of such a system might involve fitting the equation to a body of data. The predictive ability of the equation would then be assessed. But the values for *a* and *b* found in this manner could not have been known in advance. A true test must use values that do not require advance knowledge of the results.

Spurious Fits

Given a set of data from a past period, it is not too difficult to find a system that would have worked at the time. For example, an equation with many constants can be fitted to stock data statistically; with the values thus obtained, the system would have worked well. Alternatively, simple systems can be tried, in turn, until one is found that would have worked well.

If 100 irrelevant systems are tried with a set of data, one of them is likely to give results that are "statistically significant at the 1% level." This should not cause undue excitement. But what if the system in question were the first one tried? Its author might be forgiven for a certain amount of enthusiasm. However, subsequent experience would show that the success was in fact due to chance and not likely to be repeated.

A high correlation has been found between births in Sweden and the sighting of storks in the area. Similarly, stock prices in the United States have been shown to be correlated with sunspot activity and with women's skirt lengths. Few would associate causal relationships with such phenomena; coincidental correlations abound. Without solid reasons to believe that a relationship is due to underlying forces, it would be foolish to predict its continuation in the future.

Comparisons with Easily Beaten Systems

Often a predictive system is said to "explain" a large part of the variation in some stock index. Figure 19-2 shows the quarterly level of Standard and Poor's 500-stock index over a ten-year period (the solid curve) and the levels predicted by a system based on historic values of the money supply (the dotted curve). The two sets of values are clearly quite similar.

Impressive? Not very. An extremely simple set of predictions, shown by the dashed curve in Figure 19-2, is even better. This procedure predicts that each quarter's index will equal that of the preceding one:

$$SP_t = SP_{t-1} \qquad \textbf{(19-2)}$$

Any system that is purported to be able to beat the market must predict *returns*, not price levels, since returns determine profits and losses. A good test is thus the extent to which predicted returns conform to actual returns. Figure 19-3 shows the price-change portion of return

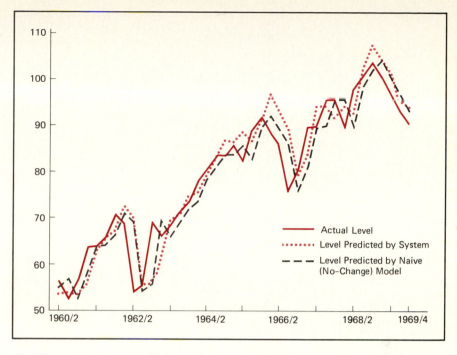

SOURCE: Kenneth E. Homa and Dwight M. Jaffee, "The Supply of Money and Common Stock Prices," *The Journal of Finance*, XXVI, no. 5 (December 1971), 1045–66.

FIGURE 19-2
Actual and Predicted Levels, Standard and Poor's 500-Stock Index, Second Quarter 1960 through Fourth Quarter 1969.

predicted by the system analyzed in Figure 19-2, along with the actual amount for each quarter. The relationship is tenuous, at best.

Ex Post Selection Bias

Many studies describe a stock selection procedure that outperformed standard stock market indices. Some of these avoid the sins considered thus far, but another factor may be involved. To facilitate computer processing, a standard set of data is usually employed. For example, an investigator might use a data tape prepared in 1985 with statistics relating to the period from 1975 through 1984. The stocks included on the tape were probably chosen because they existed and were important (i.e., had substantial market value) in 1985. Any system that could have selected stocks in 1975 that were certain to be alive, well, and important in 1985 should have done well.

Implicitly, studies of this type commit the sin described earlier—

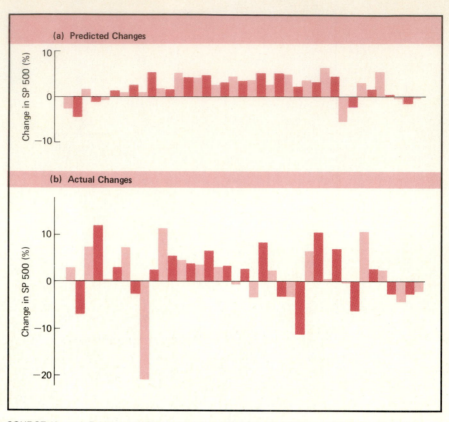

SOURCE: Kenneth E. Homa and Dwight M. Jaffee, "The Supply of Money and Common Stock Prices," *The Journal of Finance*, XXVI, no. 5 (December 1971), 1045–66.

FIGURE 19-3
Predicted and Actual Quarterly Percentage Changes, Standard and Poor's 500-Stock Index, Second Quarter 1960 through Fourth Quarter 1969.

they require some information not available in advance. Their security selection is based in part on performance after (ex post) the selection date.

Failure to Use Out-of-Sample Data

Can *any* evidence concerning a system's ability to beat the market be persuasive? Probably not to one who firmly believes in market efficiency. But an appropriate test can be undertaken.

The *search* for a system should be conducted using one set of data, and the *test* of its efficacy performed using an entirely different set of data. To be complete, such a test should involve the (simulated) management of a portfolio and be designed so that each investment decision is based solely on information available at the time the decision is made. Finally, the performance of the system should be measured in the way one would measure the performance of any investment manager, and the probability that results were due to chance rather than inherent superiority should be estimated.

Figure 19-4 shows how sobering such an exercise can be. Values forecast by three predictive systems for quarterly percentage changes in Standard and Poor's 500-stock are shown, along with the subsequent actual values. Each of the predictive systems fits *past* data extremely

FIGURE 19-4

Predicted and Actual Quarterly Percentage Changes, Standard and Poor's 500-Stock Index, Third Quarter 1970 through Second Quarter 1972

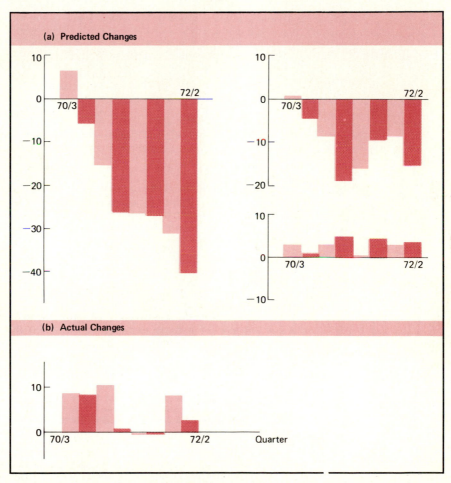

SOURCE: James E. Pesando, "The Supply of Money and Common Stock Prices: Further Observations on the Econometric Evidence," *The Journal of Finance*, XXIX, no. 3 (June 1974), 909–22, Table 2.

Financial Analysis

well. The same could not be said for their predictions about *future* data. Presumably, the proponents of the systems had hoped for something better.

Reliance on Misleading Visual Comparisons

Occasionally the proponent of a system will produce a graph that plots both the levels of an indicator intended to predict future market moves and the levels of the market itself. Visual comparison of the two curves may suggest that the indicator has indeed predicted changes in the market. However, the eye cannot easily differentiate between a situation in which changes in a market "predictor" *follow* the market and one in which the changes *precede* the market. But the distinction is crucial, for only a situation of the latter type can bring superior investment performance.

FUNDAMENTAL VERSUS TECHNICAL ANALYSIS

One of the great divisions in the ranks of financial analysts is that between the fundamentalists and the technicians. The fundamentalist tends to look forward, the technician backward. The fundamentalist is concerned with future earnings and dividends, risk, and the appropriate rate at which to discount future prospects. The technician thinks little if at all about such things:

> Technical analysis is the study of the internal stock exchange information as such. The word "technical" implies a study of the market itself and not of those external factors which are reflected in the market. . . . [A]ll the relevant factors, whatever they may be, can be reduced to the volume of the stock exchange transactions and the level of share prices; or more generally, to the sum of the statistical information produced by the market.[3]

The technician's emphasis on price is not entirely inconsistent with market efficiency:

> The current market price is assumed to represent the total knowledge of the investment community about any given security at a particular moment; that price discounts all the good news and all the bad. The sum of the knowledge which has led to the determination of price is greater than that available to any individual investor or to any group of investors.[4]

In fact, technical analysis is often termed *demand and supply* analysis, since these are the forces that determine price.

---

[3] Felix Rosenfeld, ed., *The Evaluation of Ordinary Shares*, a summary of the proceedings of the Eighth Congress of the European Federation of Financial Analysts Societies (Paris: Dunod, 1975), 297.

[4] *Ibid.*, p. 297.

The technician usually attempts to predict short-term price movements and thus makes recommendations concerning the *timing* of purchases and sales (of specific stocks or of stocks in general). It is sometimes said that fundamental analysis is designed to answer the question "What?" and technical analysis to answer the question "When?"

While much of the basis for technical analysis can be justified in the context of market efficiency, the key concept cannot:

> . . . the methodology of technical analysis . . . rests upon the assumption that history tends to repeat itself in the stock exchange. If a certain pattern of activity has in the past produced certain results nine times out of ten, one can assume a strong likelihood of the same outcome whenever this pattern appears in the future. *It should be emphasized, however, that a large part of the methodology of technical analysis lacks a strictly logical explanation.*[5] [Italics added]

Even this statement can be interpreted charitably. For example, the use of past data to estimate a future beta value is based on stock market data, assumes that history tends to repeat itself, and has some empirical validity. But technicians go beyond this to assert that study of past patterns of price, volume, and so on can identify times when certain stocks, or stocks in general, are overpriced or underpriced:

> Like a medical thermometer, [technical analysis] is a signalling device; sometimes a false indication is given when there is no cause for alarm, but when there is cause for alarm, the signal will almost invariably be flashed.[6]

Much of this book is concerned with the principles of fundamental analysis, for such analysis is essential if capital markets are to be efficient. Technical analysis is given less attention, for it rests on a *non sequitur*. If current prices reflect all that can be known about the future, including whatever can be deduced from the past behavior of prices, volumes, and so on, it will be impossible to identify mispriced securities using technical analysis. Not surprisingly, there is little evidence showing the efficacy of technical methods. Many "proofs" have been offered, but most are based on studies in which at least one of the sins described earlier has been committed.

METHODS OF TECHNICAL ANALYSIS

Most (but not all) technical analysts rely on charts of prices and trading volumes. Virtually all employ colorful, and sometimes even mystical, terminology. Thus a price rise on large volume may be termed an *accumulation*, in which stock is moving from "weak hands" to "strong

---

[5] *Ibid.*, pp. 297–98.

[6] Robin J. Russo, *Compare—A Technical Timing System* (New York: Dean Witter & Co. Inc., 1976).

hands." On the other hand, a price decline on large volume may be described as a *distribution*, in which stock is moving from "strong hands" to "weak hands." When price rises, demand is said to be stronger than supply, and when price falls, supply is said to be stronger than demand. Large volume may be considered a sign of a sustainable move, while small volume indicates a transitory change. Periods in which price moves within a narrow band are *consolidation phases*; prices through which stocks move with difficulty are *resistance levels*; and so on.

Such statements may sound profound, but they fail to pass the tests of simple logic. A price will change when the consensus estimate of value changes. Large volume associated with a price change reflects a substantial difference of opinion concerning the impact on value of new information. Small volume reflects less disagreement. If price or volume data could be used to predict future short-term price moves, investors would rush to exploit such information, moving prices rapidly enough to make the information useless.

Chartists (technicians who rely on chart formations) nonetheless believe that certain patterns carry great significance, although chartists often disagree on the significance of a pattern or even its existence on a particular chart. Figure 19-5 shows some of the more popular forms. Those in Figure 19-5(a) rely primarily on price activity, while those in Figure 19-5(b) require that price moves be "confirmed" by appropriate changes in trading volume.

Many chartists use "bar charts," such as those shown in Figure 19-5, which plot each day's price range as a vertical bar, along with the corresponding volume. Others use "line charts," which simply connect points representing daily closing prices. Still others believe that the future can be predicted only by analyzing "point and figure" charts.

Details of construction of point and figure charts vary, but the idea is to plot prices constituting a trend in a single column, moving to the next column only when the trend is reversed. For example, prices might be rounded to the nearest dollar and the chart begun by plotting a beginning rounded price. As long as the (rounded) price does not change, nothing is done. When a different price is recorded, it is plotted. As long as new prices continue in the same direction, they are plotted in the same column. When there is a reversal, a new column is started.

Point and figure enthusiasts find all sorts of patterns in their charts. As with all chartist techniques, the idea is to recognize a pattern early enough to profit from one's ability to foresee the future course of prices—a neat trick, if one can do it.

Many other approaches are used by technicians. Some construct *moving averages* to assess "intermediate" and "long-term" trends, which can then be compared with each other and/or with current prices. For example, prices over the previous 30 weeks may be averaged; if price is currently above this amount, it may be considered "too high."

Alternatively, a long-term average may be compared with a short-term average. When the latter crosses the former, a "signal" is said to have been given; the action recommended will depend on whether the averages are rising or falling, the direction from which the short-term average crosses the long-term, and so on.

Moving averages are widely used for speculation in commodity futures. As indicated in Chapter 17, it may be desirable to detect the

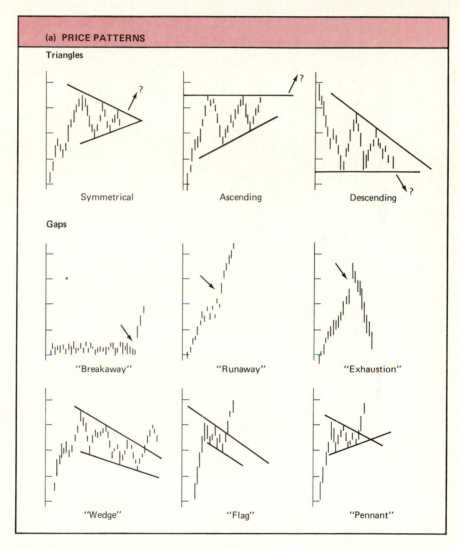

(a) PRICE PATTERNS

Triangles

Symmetrical   Ascending   Descending

Gaps

"Breakaway"   "Runaway"   "Exhaustion"

"Wedge"   "Flag"   "Pennant"

SOURCE: Alan R. Shaw, "Technical Analysis," in Sumner N. Levine, ed., *Financial Analyst's Handbook* (Homewood, Ill.: Dow Jones-Irwin, Inc., 1975) 1, 944–88.

FIGURE 19-5
Chartists' Patterns.

Financial Analysis

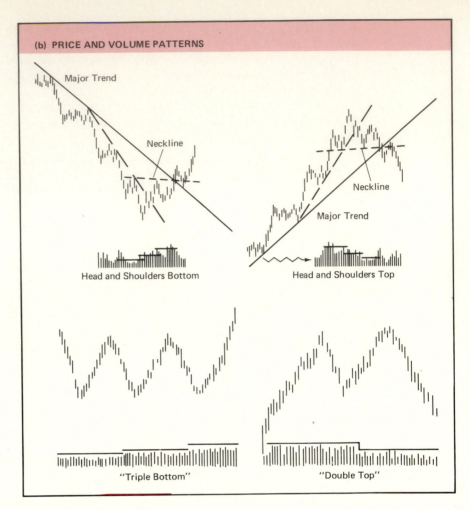

(b) PRICE AND VOLUME PATTERNS

Major Trend

Neckline

Head and Shoulders Bottom

Neckline

Major Trend

Head and Shoulders Top

"Triple Bottom"

"Double Top"

FIGURE 19-5 (*continued*)

side of a market on which there is net hedging, since only by taking the other side might a speculator expect to be compensated for any risk borne. If prices do follow a seasonal pattern as hedging shifts from short to long, a moving-average strategy may help keep the speculator on the appropriate side of the market.

Another procedure used by technicians measures *relative strength*. For example, a stock price may be divided by an industry price index to indicate the stock's movement relative to its industry; an industry index may be divided by a market index; or a stock price price may be divided by a market index.

Often the rate of change of a stock price or market index over some recent period is measured; this is typically termed *momentum*.

Some technical analysts focus on relationships among different indexes. For example, the venerable *Dow theory* requires that a pattern in the Dow Jones Industrial Average be "confirmed" by a required movement in the Dow Jones Railroad (now Transportation) Average before action be taken.

Some technicians compute a cumulative index of the difference between the number of issues advancing and the number declining each day and compare this *advance-decline line* with the Dow Jones Industrial Average.

A whole host of technical procedures is based on the idea of *contrary opinion*. The idea is to determine what the losers are doing, then do the opposite. For example, one might see whether the "odd-lotters" (those who buy and sell in lots of less than 100 shares each) are buying or selling. If "the little investor is usually wrong," this is a certain way to be (usually) right. Fortunately for the little investor, and unfortunately for the contrary-opinion technician, the premise has not been established.

A different approach is taken by other technicians. Their idea is to identify the winners, then follow their example. Thus one might watch for situations in which specialists (market-makers) have large short positions in a stock (i.e., have borrowed and sold stock they do not own). This suggests that they think its price will go down and "they must know something." Perhaps so, but by the time the specialists' positions are made public, it may be too late to share their profits.

Some technicians believe that large short positions are a bearish signal (since the short-sellers are pessimistic); others regard them as a bullish signal (since the short-sellers will eventually have to buy stock to return it to the lender). Neither hypothesis has been confirmed.

The widespread availability of personal computers and "dial-up" services with data on stock prices, volumes, and so on has made it possible for amateur investors to practice technical analysis in the privacy of their own homes. Producers of software have been quick to provide programs to perform such analyses, complete with multi-colored graphs.

Many regard technicians as members of the lunatic fringe of the investment world. Descriptions of their activities are felt to be a suitable subject for anthropologists, but inappropriate in a book intended for the serious investor.

Fundamentalists far outnumber technicians, a situation that may be expected to continue in the future.

FUNDAMENTAL ANALYSIS

Fundamental analysts forecast future levels of the economy, industry sales and earnings, company sales and earnings, and so on. Eventually such forecasts have to be converted to estimates of likely returns: those obtained from holding general types of securities (e.g., stocks versus bonds), the securities of firms in different industries, and/or the securities of specific firms. In some cases the conversion is made explicitly—for example, an estimate of next year's earnings may be multiplied by a projected price/earnings ratio to estimate price a year hence, or a set of dividend projections may be compared with current price to determine an internal rate of return. In other cases the conversion is implicit—for example, stocks with projected earnings exceeding consensus estimates may be placed on an "approved" list.

Top-Down versus Bottom-Up Forecasting

A single individual analyzing investment prospects has no organizational problems. Consistent assumptions may be maintained with no need to explicitly structure the prediction process. Organizations in which two or more people divide the task of making predictions lack this advantage. Procedures are required to coordinate predictions, including any made outside the organization.

Some investment organizations follow a sequential approach. Forecasts are made first for the economy, next for industries, and finally for companies. The industry forecasts are *conditional* on the economic forecasts, and the company forecasts are conditional on both the industry and economic forecasts. Such *top-down* approaches may also provide estimates of the prospects for particular securities markets or segments thereof.

Other organizations begin with estimates of the prospects for companies and/or industries, then build to estimates of the prospects for the economy, securities markets, and so on. Such *bottom-up* approaches may (implicitly) involve inconsistent assumptions. Top-down systems are less susceptible to this danger.

In practice, a combination of the two approaches is often employed. Forecasts are made for the economy and securities markets in a "top-down" manner. These provide a setting within which security analysts make "bottom-up" forecasts for individual companies. The sum of the individual forecasts should be consistent with the original "macroforecasts." If not, the process is repeated (perhaps with additional controls) to insure consistency.

Probabilistic Forecasting

Explicit probabilistic forecasting often focuses on economic forecasts, since uncertainty at this level is of the greatest importance for the performance of diversified portfolios. A few alternative economic scenarios may be forecast and accompanying projections made of the prospects for industries, companies, and securities. Such an exercise provides an idea of the likely sensitivities of different securities to surprises concerning the economy. By assigning probabilities to the different scenarios, risks may also be estimated.

Econometric Models

An *econometric model* provides a means for estimating future levels of one or more *endogenous* variables, based on the assumed future levels of one or more *exogenous* variables. The model may be extremely complex (and regarded by many of its users as a mysterious "black box"), or it may be a simple formula computed with a desk calculator. In any event, it should reflect a happy marriage in which *economics* is used to suggest the forms of relevant relationships and *statistical procedures* are applied to historic data to estimate the quantitative magnitudes involved.

Some investment organizations utilize large-scale econometric models to translate predictions about such factors as the federal budget, expected consumer spending, and planned business investment into predictions of future levels of gross national product, rates of inflation, amounts of unemployment, and so on. Several firms and nonprofit organizations maintain such models, selling outputs and/or the use of computer programs to investment organizations, corporate planners, public agencies, and others.

Producers of such a large-scale model usually provide several "standard" projections, based on judgments about exogenous variables; some also assign probabilities to alternative scenarios. Models are computerized, and users may substitute their own assumptions to estimate the implications of different predictions.

Large-scale econometric models of this type employ one or more equations and from several to several hundred quantitative estimates of important relationships. Estimates of the magnitudes of such relationships (*parameters*) obtained from historic data may or may not enable a model to work well in the future. When predictions turn out to be poor, it is sometimes said that there has been a *structural change* in underlying economic relationships. However, the failure may be due to the influence of factors omitted from the model. In any event, such a situation necessitates changes in the values of parameters and/or the basic form of the econometric model. Rare indeed is the user who does not "fine-tune" (or completely overhaul) such a model from time to time as further experience is accumulated.

Input-Output Analysis

One firm's output may be another's input. The interdependence of firms and industries makes it difficult to do analysis in isolation. The use of different models for various industries may thus yield forecasts inconsistent with *interindustry* relationships, even if each model is utilized in conjunction with a single large-scale model of the economy.

Input-output analysis can help in this regard. Interindustry relationships are considered explicitly to determine, for example, the dollar value of industry A's output required for industry B to produce one dollar's value of output. This makes it possible to obtain consistent estimates of the sales of different industries, given projections of the levels of various aggregate variables.

The U.S. government prepares input/output tables every few years, as do other governments. Since such tables are based on past relationships (and are updated infrequently), projections using input-output analysis typically incorporate modifications. Econometric models and the judgments of experts may be used to make adjustments to reflect changes in relative amounts of inputs made in response to changes in relative input prices.

Financial Statement Analysis

For some, the image of a typical investment analyst is that of a gnome, fully equipped with green eyeshade, poring over financial statements in some back room. This is rarely accurate, but security analysts do study such statements. Some try to dissect and rearrange them; most try to project them into the future.

A company's financial statements can be regarded as the output of a model of the firm—a model designed by management, the company's accountants, and (indirectly) the tax authorities. Different companies use different models and treat similar events in different ways. Examples include: the valuation of pension liabilities (which actuarial method? what assumed rate of interest?), inventory valuation (FIFO or LIFO?), the treatment of products leased to customers (as inventory with rental income, or immediate sales?), and so on.

To fully understand a company, and to compare it with others that use different procedures, one must be a financial detective, looking for clues in footnotes and accompanying text. Those who take bottom-line figures (e.g., earnings) on faith may be more surprised by future developments than those who try to look behind the accounting veil.

The ultimate goal of the fundamental analysis of a corporation is, of course, to determine the values of the outstanding claims on its income. First, the firm's income must be projected, then the possible distributions of that income among the claimants must be considered and relevant probabilities assessed.

In practice, short-cut procedures are often used. Many analysts focus on reported accounting figures, even though such numbers may not adequately reflect true economic values. In addition, simple measures are often used to assess complex relationships. For example, some analysts attempt to estimate the probability that short-term creditors will be paid in full and on time with the ratio of liquid assets to the amount of short-term debt; the probability that interest will be paid to bondholders with the ratio of earnings before interest charges to the amount of such charges; and the prospects for a firm's common stock with the ratio of earnings to the book value of equity.

The use of *ratios* for such purposes is widespread. Some ratios use items from the same statement (e.g., a particular balance sheet or income statement). Some use items from two different types of statements, others use items from two or more statements of the same type (e.g., this year's balance sheet and last year's balance sheet), and still others incorporate data on market values.

Ratios may be used in several ways. Some analysts apply absolute standards, on the grounds that a substandard ratio indicates a need for further analysis. Others compare a company's ratios to those of the "average" firm in the same industry to detect differences worthy of further consideration. Yet others analyze trends in a company's ratios over time, hoping thereby to better predict future changes.

One use of ratios is illustrated in Figure 19-6. If the future value of every ratio shown could be forecast, one could compute the implied forecast for the price of the firm's stock. The reciprocal of the turnover ratio equals the sum of the reciprocals of the four ratios to its right; every other value equals the product of the two items to its right. The problem with such an approach is the lack of a simple way to obtain independent estimates of such interrelated elements: for example, a stock's *P/E* ratio is typically related to the firm's current earnings and estimated future earnings growth.

Ratio analysis can be very sophisticated, but it can also be overly simplistic. Routine extrapolation of a present ratio (or its recent trend) may produce a poor estimate of its future value (for example, there is no reason for a firm to maintain a constant ratio of inventory to sales). Moreover, a series of simple projections may produce inconsistent estimates—e.g., predictions of balance sheet items that would not even balance.

Electronic Spreadsheets

To project future financial statements, one should build a model (or models) of the relationships among the items on such statements and (usually) outside factors. Traditional ratio analysis does this, albeit crudely. A much better procedure uses modern microcomputer hardware and spreadsheet software.

A *spreadsheet* is, at base, an arrangement of information in *rows* and *columns*. Each *cell* on a traditional ("paper") spreadsheet typically contains a *number* or a *label*. Some of the numbers (e.g., sales) are

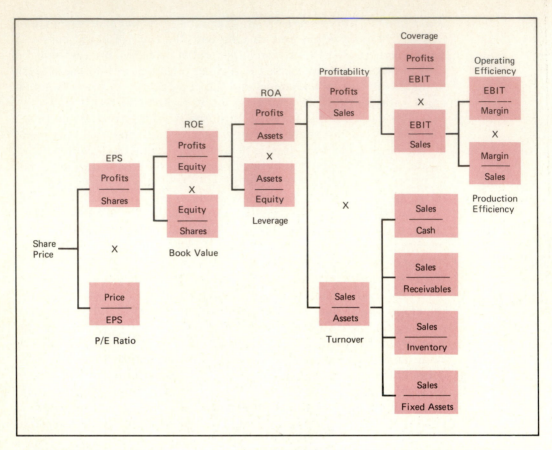

SOURCE: Samuel S. Stewart, Jr., "Corporate Forecasting," in Sumner N. Levine, ed., *Financial Analyst's Handbook* (Homewood, Ill.: Dow Jones-Irwin, Inc., 1975), I, 912.

FIGURE 19-6
The Use of Predicted Ratios to Compute Predicted Price.

entered directly, others (e.g., Earnings Before Interest and Taxes) are computed from numbers in other cells.

An *electronic spreadsheet* simulates a traditional spreadsheet on a computer screen. There are, however, profound differences. Most important: cells can contain *formulas*. For example, the cell for Earnings Before Interest and Taxes (EBIT) could contain both the formula for calculating the value *and* the value produced by the formula. Normally only the value would be displayed, giving an outward appearance similar to that of a traditional spreadsheet. However, any change in the number in the cell for sales would immediately change the value of EBIT.

The ability to rapidly explore the implications of changes in key values (prices, quantities, costs, and so on) makes it possible to perform *sensitivity analyses* (termed *what-if analyses* by users of spreadsheet programs).

Many security analysts build detailed models of firms and industries using advanced spreadsheet software. Figure 19-7 outlines a general approach.

First, balance sheet and income statement data for the current year (0) and several preceding years (−1, −2, . . .) are entered (in blocks A and B). From such information, earnings and dividends per share are computed (in block C). Then ratios and other derived values of interest are produced (in block D) for each of the years, with formulas that use balance sheet and income statement data as inputs.

Given historic values, key summary measures useful for making predictions can be obtained. In some cases, simple averages of yearly values will be helpful; in others, growth rates based on trend lines fit to the yearly values will be important. These values, derived primarily from information in block D, are contained in block E.

Blocks A through E are concerned with *analyzing the past*. The remainder of the spreadsheet deals with *projections of the future*.

FIGURE 19-7
Projections Using Electronic Spreadsheets

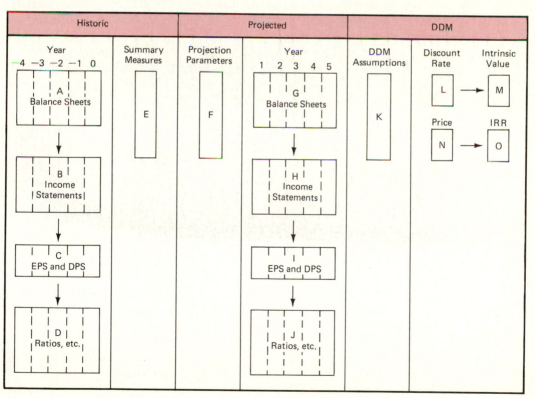

The major goal is to project future balance sheets (block G) and income statements (block H) for several years into the future. From these can be derived earnings and dividends per share (block I) and ratios and other values of interest (block J).

Projections of future values are based on *formulas* and *parameters*. For example:

> Sales might be assumed to start at a given *base* level and grow by a constant *percentage* each year.
>
> Accounts receivable might be assumed to be a constant *percent* of sales each year.
>
> Long-term debt might be assumed to remain at a constant level (e.g., start at that base and "grow" by zero percent each year).
>
> Inventory might be assumed to equal a constant times the square root of sales.

Formulas for calculating the values in blocks G and H will be contained in the appropriate cells. Choice of such formulas is a major part of the process of *building a model* of the firm. The remaining part is the choice of specific values for the parameters in the formulas.

Such "projection parameters" are contained in block F. Some can equal corresponding values in block E; others can be chosen independently. Given these values, the information in blocks G through J is computed automatically.

In a typical model of this sort, block I will contain projected dividends per share and earnings per share for the next five years. With advanced spreadsheet software it is a simple matter to go beyond this and to compute all the information needed by a *dividend discount model*.

In Figure 19-7, block K contains values concerning (1) the length of time before "maturity," (2) growth rates of earnings from year 5 to maturity, (3) payout ratios from year 5 to maturity, and (4) conditions after maturity is reached. These may be entered directly (as assumptions) or computed from values in prior blocks.

Given the assumptions in block K, the information in blocks M and O can be computed. Based on an "appropriate" discount rate (entered in block L), an *intrinsic value* for the stock is calculated (in block M). Based on the current price (entered in block N), an *internal rate of return* is calculated (in block O).

A more detailed analysis could break sales (revenues) into indices of price per unit and number of units sold (e.g., sales = price times quantity). Explicit estimates of demand conditions (quantities sold at different prices) and supply conditions (quantities produced with various amounts of plant, labor, and so on) could be obtained and potentially more accurate projections made. Predictions could also be tied to macroeconomic variables.

With this type of "analytic engine" it is straightforward to estimate the sensitivity of a stock's intrinsic value or implied rate of return to changes in key external variables (e.g., GNP, oil prices, interest rates). The calculations may also be performed for many alternative values, with the probabilities of the alternative *scenarios* being used to obtain estimates of risk, expected return, and so on.

Financial statement analysis can help an analyst understand what a company is, where it may be going, the factors likely to affect it, and the sensitivity of its prospects to such factors. If other analysts are doing such analysis and doing it well, it will be difficult to find mispriced securities in this manner. But it should be possible to better identify firms likely to go bankrupt, those with higher or lower beta values, those with greater or lesser sensitivities to major factors, and so forth. Increased understanding of such aspects may well provide ample reward for the effort entailed.

Analysts' Recommendations and Stock Prices

When a security analyst decides that a stock is mispriced, he or she tells clients about it, at least some of whom act on the information. As they do so, the price of the security is likely to be affected. As news of the analyst's recommendation spreads, more investors will act, and the price will react even more. At some point the analyst's information will be "fully reflected" in the stock price.

If it is considered that a stock is underpriced and the analyst's clients then purchase it, the stock's price will tend to rise. Conversely, if a stock is considered overpriced and the analyst's clients then sell it, the stock's price will tend to decline. If the analyst's views were well founded, no subsequent "counterreaction" should be expected. Otherwise, the price is likely to return to its prerecommendation level at some later stage.

An interesting example of the impact of analysts' recommendations is provided by the behavior of prices of stocks mentioned in *The Wall Street Journal's* "Heard on the Street" column, which periodically summarizes recent stock recommendations.

An analyst's opinion is typically published in "Heard on the Street" some time after it is first given to clients. The analyst's view is thus "somewhat public" for several days before publication, but when the column appears the opinion becomes "very public," since it then reaches a substantially larger audience.

Figure 19-8(a) shows the reactions of security prices to publication in "Heard on the Street" of positive opinions about 597 stocks in 1970 and 1971. Figure 19-8(b) summarizes the reactions to negative opinions about 188 stocks during the same period. In each diagram the vertical axis plots the average cumulative "abnormal return"—return adjusted

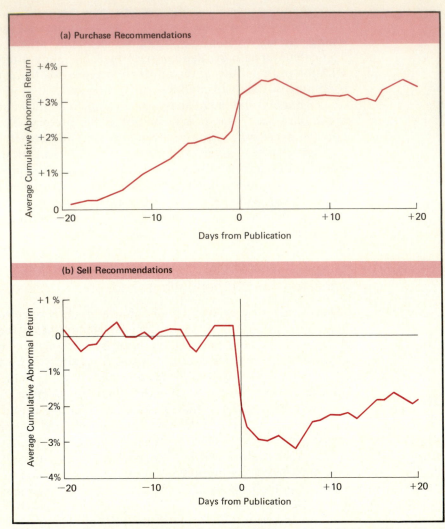

SOURCE: Peter Lloyd Davies and Michael Canes, "Stock Prices and the Publication of Second-Hand Information," *Journal of Business*, 51, no. 1 (1978). By permission of the University of Chicago Press. © 1978.

FIGURE 19-8
Effect on Stock Prices of Stock Recommendations in "Heard on the Street": 1970 and 1971.

for normal reactions to overall market moves. The horizontal axes indicate trading days, relative to the date of publication of the recommendation. The cumulative abnormal returns are expressed relative to dates twenty trading days prior to publication.

As the figures indicate, on average the publication of such a recommendation does affect a security's price. After adjusting for market moves, on the date of publication the average stock recommended for purchase rose .923%, while the average stock recommended for sale fell 2.374%. After adjustments for changes in the overall market, of the 597 stocks recommended for purchase, 70% rose on the date of publication; of the 188 recommended for sale, 90% fell.

Both types of recommendation appear to contain information: twenty trading days after publication, prices were not significantly different (after adjustment for market moves) than they were at the end of the day they were published.

The upward moves in Figure 19-8(a) prior to day zero are consistent with the impact of prior purchases by clients of the analysts. An alternative hypothesis would hold that analysts simply recommended purchase of stocks that had recently risen in price. Note, however, that Figure 19-8(b) is quite different: there is no distinct pattern prior to the date of publication of a sell recommendation. The analysts did not tend to recommend the sale of securities that had recently fallen in price. And on average any prior actions by their clients had little effect on price. This is consistent with the fact that to take advantage of a negative opinion one has to hold the stock initially or incur the extra costs associated with a short sale. Thus negative information known to relatively few investors may well impact stock prices more slowly than positive information.

SOURCE OF INVESTMENT INFORMATION

Virtually any information that affects the value of an investment can be considered "investment information." The serious financial analyst must thus be truly well informed. Even an analyst who specializes in one or two industries must cope with a staggering array of information sources, some on paper ("hard copy"), some in computer-readable form.

Publications

Space precludes a detailed listing here of industry-related publications. An excellent bibliography of such sources, compiled by the New York Society of Security Analysts, can be found in the *Financial Analyst's Handbook*.[7] Periodical literature of interest to the investment analyst is indexed by industries, products, and companies in the *Predicasts F&S Index*.

Figure 19-9 presents a selected bibliography of general sources, based on the holdings in the Jackson Library of the Stanford University Graduate School of Business.[8] Nothing can substitute for a careful pe-

---

[7] *Ibid.*, pp. 883–926.

[8] The bibliography was prepared by the reference librarians of Jackson Library.

FIGURE 19-9
Sources of Investment Information

I. GENERAL INFORMATION ON BUSINESS AND FINANCIAL DEVEL-
OPMENTS

A. Economic Data Handbooks

1. Economic Statistics Bureau of Washington, D.C. *Handbook of Basic Economic Statistics*.
2. Standard and Poor's *Statistical Service*, *Current Statistics*.
3. U.S. Bureau of the Census. *Statistical Abstracts of the U.S.*
4. U.S. Office of Business Economics. *Business Statistics*.

B. Daily Newspapers

1. *American Banker*.
2. *Daily Commercial News*.
3. *Financial Times* (British—London).
4. *Journal of Commerce*.
5. *New York Times*.
6. *Wall Street Journal*.
7. *Washington Post*.

C. Weekly Newspapers

1. *Barron's*.
2. *Commercial and Financial Chronicle*.
3. *Financial Post* (*Canadian*).
4. *Market Chronicle*.
5. *Vie Francais l'Opinion*.
6. *Wall Street Transcript*.
7. *Weekly Bond Buyer*.

D. Weekly Periodicals

1. *Business Week* (see especially "Finance" section).
2. *EDP Industry Reports*.
3. *Financial World*.
4. *Investment Dealers' Digest*.
5. *Japan Stock Journal*.
6. *California Business*.
7. *Newsweek* (especially "Business and Finance" section).
8. *San Francisco Business*.
9. *Time* (especially "Business" or "Economy and Business" section).
10. *United States Banker*.
11. *U.S. News & World Report*.
12. *World Business Weekly*.

E. Biweekly Periodicals

1. Chase Manhattan Bank. *International Finance*.
2. *Forbes*.

F. Monthly Periodicals

1. *Across the Board*.
2. Bank letters: issued by various banks, e.g., Cleveland Trust

FIGURE 19-9 (*continued*)

Company, First National City Bank of New York, Morgan Guaranty, Chase Manhattan, Bank of America, Wells Fargo.
3. *Business Conditions Digest*
4. *Conference Board Statistical Bulletins.*
5. *Donoghue's Money Fund Report.*
6. *Dun's Business Month.*
7. *Economic Indicators.*
8. Federal Reserve Bank Reviews (monthly reviews are issued by all the Federal Reserve Banks).
9. *Federal Reserve Bulletin.*
10. *Federal Reserve Chart Book.*
11. *Financial Executive.*
12. *Fortune.*
13. *Going Public* (looseleaf service lists initial public offerings).
14. *Institutional Investor.*
15. *Market Value Index.*
16. *Nation's Business.*
17. *OTC Review.*
18. *Stock Market Magazine.*
19. *Survey of Current Business.*
20. *Venture Capital.*

G. Bimonthly Periodicals

1. *Financial Analysts Journal.*
2. *Financial Planner.*
3. *Harvard Business Review.*

H. Quarterly Periodicals

1. *Business Starts.*
2. *Journal of Business.*
3. *Journal of Finance* (five issues a year).
4. *Journal of Financial and Quantitative Analysis* (five issues a year).
5. *Journal of Money, Credit and Banking.*
6. *Mergers and Acquisitions.*

I. Annual Economic Reviews

1. U.S. Bureau of Domestic Commerce. *U.S. Industrial Outlook.*
2. U.S. Congress. Economic Joint Committee. *The . . . Economic Report of the President*; *Hearings* (i.e., hearings held to consider the *President's Economic Report*).
3. U.S. Congress. Economic Joint Committee. *Joint Economic Report* (i.e., the committee's report on their hearings on the *President's Economic Report*).
4. U.S. Office of Business Economics. *Business Statistics.*
5. U.S. President. *Economic Report . . . together with the annual report of the Council of Economic Advisers.*

II. INDUSTRY INFORMATION

A. Business and Financial Journals and Periodicals (See Section I above)

FIGURE 19-9 (*continued*)

B. Government Publications and Documents; see especially:

1. Annual reports of regulatory commissions such as the F.P.C., F.T.C., I.C.C., and S.E.C.
2. *Survey of Current Business* (monthly periodical).
3. *Treasury Bulletin* (monthly periodical).
4. U.S. Census Bureau. *Census of Manufacturers*.
5. ————. *Annual Survey of Manufacturers*.
6. ————. *Census of Retail Trade*.
7. ————. *Census of Service Industries*.
8. ————. *Census of Wholesale Trade*.
9. ————. *Current Industrial Reports*.
10. ————. *Statistical Abstracts of the U.S.*
11. U.S. Industry & Trade Administration. *U.S. Industrial Outlook*.
12. U.S. Mines Bureau. *Minerals Yearbook*.
13. U.S. Office of Business Economics. *Business Statistics*.

C. Reports of Investments and Business Services

1. Arnold Bernhard & Co.
   a. *Value Line Investment Survey*.
   b. *Value Line Options and Convertibles*.
   c. *Value Line OTC Special Situations Service*.
2. Howard & Company. *Going Public*.
3. Kidder, Peabody and Co. *Research Service*.
4. Moody's
   a. *Manuals*.
   b. *Industry Review*.
   c. *Bond Survey*.
   d. *International Bond Review*.
5. Smith Barney, Harris Upham and Co. *Research Service*.
6. Standard and Poor's
   a. *Industry Survey*.
   b. *Outlook*.
   c. Statistical Service. *Current Statistics*.

D. Special Bibliographies (indexes to periodicals)

1. *Business Periodicals Index*.
2. *DISCLOSURE Journal* (indexes SEC filings of 10-K's, Registrations, etc.).
3. Predicasts *F&S Index* (U.S., Europe, International—abstracts periodicals by company, product and industry).
4. ————. *F&S Index of Corporate Change*.
5. ————. *Forecasts* (abstracts periodicals which contain forecasts for various industries).
6. ————. *Worldcasts* (forecasts by region).
7. Public Affairs and Information Service. *Bulletin*.
8. *Wall Street Journal Index*.

FIGURE 19-9 (*continued*)

E. Special Reports of Private Agencies
1. Audit's Investment Research, Inc.
   a. *Healty Stock Review*.
   b. *Real Estate Disclosure Digest*.
2. Creative Strategies Inc.
   a. *Industry Analysis Service*.
   b. *Retail Automation Report*.
3. SRI International *Long Range Planning Service Reports* (includes Index).

F. Acquisitions and Mergers
1. *Announcements of Mergers and Acquisitions* (monthly publication by The Conference Board).
2. Financial Stock Guide Service. *Directory of Obsolete Securities*.
3. Predicasts. *F&S Index of Corporate Change*. Quarterly.

G. Reports and Brochures of Brokerage and Banking Firms
1. Bank of America
   a. Daily Quotation Sheets: *U.S. Government Securities, Federal Agencies and Other Securities*.
   b. *Small Business Reporter*.
   c. *Weekly Monetary Summary*.
2. Bankers Trust. *Current Business Picture*.
3. Goldman Sachs. *Risk, Return and Equity Valuation* (quarterly).
4. Kidder Peabody & Co.
   a. *Current Investment Policy and Strategy Implementation*.
   b. *Emerging Growth Stocks*.
   c. *Money and Capital Markets*.
   d. *Monthly Earnings Summary*.
   e. *Monthly Valuation Information*.
   f. *Portfolio Manager's Review*.
5. Merrill Lynch, Pierce, Fenner and Smith. *Quantitative Analysis*.
6. Siegel Trading Company. *Weekly Market Letter*.
7. Salomon Brothers
   a. *Analytical Record of Yields and Yield Spreads*.
   b. *Bond Market Roundup*.
   c. *Bond Portfolio Analysis*.
   d. *Comments on Credit*.
   e. *Monthly Stock Review*.
   f. *Preferred Stock Guide*.
   g. *Prospects for Financial Markets*.
   h. *Strategy Systems*.
   i. *Total Rate-of-return Indexes*.
8. Smith, Barney, Harris Upham & Co., *Analysts Roundtable*.
9. Thomson and McKinnon Auchincloss Kohlmeyer
   a. *Commodity Letter*.
   b. *Technical Analysis*.

FIGURE 19-9 (*continued*)

10. *Wall Street Transcript* (weekly newspaper, most of whose contents are reprints of brokerage house reports).

H. Trade Association Publications (Especially Annual Review Numbers)

1. *ADP Symbol Guide*.
2. *Dow Jones Investor's Handbook*.

I. Trade Journals (Especially Annual Statistical Numbers)

III. COMPANY INFORMATION

A. Corporation Reports

1. *Annual reports to shareholders*.
2. *Disclosure Journal* (indexes annual reports to shareholders, 10-K reports, registration statements).
3. Financial Stock Guide Service. *Directory of Obsolete Securities*.
4. *10-K reports*.
5. *Prospectuses*.
6. *Registration statements*.

B. Financial and Business Journals (see Section II above; the Predicasts *F&S Index* indexes most of these extensively by S.I.C. code and by company name)

C. Publications of Brokerage and Banking Firms

D. Manuals

1. *Moody's Manuals*. (*Banks and Finance*; *Industrial*; *International*; *Municipals and Governments*; *OTC Industrials*; *Public Utility*; *Transportation*)
2. Standard and Poor's *Standard Corporation Descriptions*.
3. Standard and Poor's *Stock Reports* (American Stock Exchange; New York Stock Exchange; Over-the-Counter and Regional Exchanges).
4. *Walker's Manual of Western Corporations*.

E. Publications of Financial Services

1. Arnold Bernhard & Co.

   a. *Value Line Investment Survey*.
   b. *Value Line Options & Convertibles*.
   c. *Value Line OTC Special Situations Service*.

2. *Financial Dynamics* (see also its *Debt Analysis Supplement*).
3. Goldman Sachs. *Risk*, *Return and Equity Valuation* (quarterly).
4. Hambrecht and Quist Institutional Research

   a. Weekly Report
   b. Monthly Statistical Research Summary

5. Moody's
   a. *Bond Record*.
   b. *Bond Survey*.

FIGURE 19-9 (*continued*)

    c. *Dividend Record*.
    d. *Handbook of Common Stocks*.
    e. *Industry Review*.
    f. *International Bond Review*.
    g. *Manuals* (see Section III, above; note especially the semi-weekly supplements and the blue sections in the center of annual volumes).
    h. *Stock Survey*.
6. *Quote* (American; New York; Over-the-Counter).
7. *R.H.M. Survey of Warrants, Options & Low-priced Stocks*.
8. Standard and Poor's
    a. *Analysts Handbook* (annual, with monthly supplements).
    b. *Bond Guide*.
    c. *Called Bond Record*.
    d. *Commercial Paper Rating Guide*.
    e. *Corporation Records*.
    f. *Creditweek*.
    g. *Dividend Record*.
    h. *Earnings Forecaster*.
    i. *Industry Surveys*.
    j. *Outlook*.
    k. *Standard Corporation Descriptions* (note especially the daily supplements).
    l. Statistical Service. *Current Statistics*.
    m. *Stock Guide*.
    n. *Stock Reports* (NYSE, ASE, OTC).
9. United Business Service. *United Business & Investment Report*.
10. *Vickers Guide to Investment Company Portfolios*.

IV. SECURITIES MARKET INFORMATION: INVESTMENT ADVICE

A. Bond and Stock Ratings

1. Moody's *Manuals*.
2. Moody's *Bond Record*.
3. Salomon Brothers. *Preferred Stock Guide*.
4. Standard and Poor's *Bond Guide*.
5. Standard and Poor's *Commercial Paper Ratings Guide*.
6. *Value Line Investment Survey*.
7. *Value Line Options and Convertibles*.

B. Beta Factors

1. Goldman Sachs. *Risk, Return and Equity Evaluation*.
2. Merrill Lynch, Pierce, Fenner and Smith, Inc. *Quantitative Analysis*.
3. *Value Line Investment Survey*.

C. General Market Condition and Outlook

1. Moody's *Bond Survey*.
2. Moody's *Stock Survey*.

FIGURE 19-9 (*continued*)

3. Publications of brokerage and banking firms (see Section II).
4. Standard and Poor's *Outlook*.
5. United Business Service. *United Business and Investment Report*.

D. Recommendations and Appraisals of Securities

1. Brokerage and banking house reports and brochures (see Section II).
2. Goldman Sachs. *Risk, Return and Equity Valuation*.
3. Merrill Lynch. *Quantitative Analysis*.
4. Reports of financial reporting agencies and investment services, especially:

   a. Kidder Peabody & Co. *Research Department Service*.
   b. Moody's *Bond Survey*.
   c. Moody's *Stock Survey*.
   d. Standard and Poor's *Creditweek*.
   e. Standard and Poor's *Outlook*.
   f. United Business Service. *United Business & Investment Report*.
   g. *Value Line Investment Survey*.

V. SECURITY PRICE QUOTATIONS

A. Daily Range and Close

1. *Commercial and Financial Chronicle* (Monday issue contains high and low, but not the close, for each day of the preceding week).
2. *New York Times*.
3. *San Francisco Chronicle*.
4. Standard and Poor's *Daily Stock Price Record*.
5. *Wall Street Journal*.

B. Weekly Range and Close

1. *Barron's*.
2. *Financial Post* (Canadian).

C. Monthly Range

1. *Bank and Quotation Record*.
2. *Capital International Perspective*.
3. Standard and Poor's *Daily Stock Price Record* (ASE, NYSE, OTC).

D. Annual Range

1. *Bank and Quotation Record* (January issue has range for preceding year; other issues have range for current year to date).
2. *Barron's* (first issue in January has range for preceding year).
3. *Commercial and Financial Chronicle* (Monday issue).
4. Dow Jones *Investor's Handbook* (annual).
5. Standard and Poor's

   a. *Bond Guide*.
   b. *Standard Corporation Descriptions*.

FIGURE 19-9 (*continued*)

---

      c. *Stock Guide*.

      d. *Stock Reports* (ASE, NYSE, OTC, and regional exchanges)

E. Other Compendia of Price Quotations

    1. *Daily Stock Price Record* (ASE, NYSE, OTC; each quarterly volume lists range for each stock for each day of the quarter).

    2. National Quotation Bureau. *Monthly Bond Summary*.

    3. National Quotation Bureau. *Monthly Stock Summary*.

VI. SECURITY PRICE INDEXES AND AVERAGES

A. Daily and Financial Newspapers

B. Periodicals

    1. *Barron's*.

    2. *Commercial and Financial Chronicle* (Monday issue).

    3. *CPI Detailed Index*.

    4. *Federal Reserve Bulletin*.

    5. *Producer Prices and Price Indexes*.

    6. *Survey of Current Business*.

C. Special Services

    1. Standard and Poor's

      a. *Outlook*.

      b. Statistical Service. *Current Statistics*.

      c. *Daily Stock Price Index*.

    2. Moody's

      a. *Manuals* (blue section).

      b. *Bond Survey*.

      c. *Stock Survey*.

D. Other Compendia of Price Indexes and Averages

    1. *Capital International Perspective*.

    2. *Dow Jones Averages 1885-1980* (averages for each day since the series began).

    3. L. Fisher and J. H. Lorie, *A Half Century of Returns on Stocks and Bonds*.

    4. Roger G. Ibbotson and Rex A. Sinquefield, *Stocks, Bonds, Bills and Inflation: the Past and the Future, 1982 edition*.

    5. *Wall Street Journal Index* (pages at the back list the Dow Jones averages for each day of the month covered in that volume of the index).

VII. DATA ON MONEY MARKETS

A. *Weekly Bond Buyer*.

B. Salomon Brothers

    1. *Analytical Record of Yields and Yield Spreads*.

    2. *Bond Market Roundup* (weekly).

FIGURE 19-9 (*continued*)

3. *Bond Portfolio Analysis*.
4. *Comments on Credit*.
5. *Prospects for Financial Markets* (annual).
6. *Total Rate-of-Return Indices*.

C. *Euromoney* (monthly periodical).

D. Lehman Brothers, Kuhn Loeb. *The Lehman Indices*.

VIII. DATA ON MUTUAL FUNDS

A. Computer Directions Advisors
1. *Spectrum 1*: *Investment Company Stock Holdings Survey*.
2. *Spectrum 2*: *Investment Company Portfolios*.

B. *Donoghue's Money Fund Directory*.

C. *Donoghue's Money Fund Report*.

D. *Institutional Investor* (monthly periodical).

E. Investment Company Institute. *Mutual Fund Fact Book*.

F. Investment Dealers' Digest. *Mutual Fund Directory*.

G. *Johnson's Investment Company Charts*.

H. *Lipper Mutual Fund Investment Performance Average*.

I. *Mutual Funds Almanac*.

J. N-1R Reports (annual reports of mutual funds to SEC).

K. United Business Service. *United Mutual Fund Selector*.

L. *Vickers Guide to Investment Company Portfolios*.

M. Wiesenberger Investment Companies Service, Inc. *Investment Companies* (annual).

N. Wiesenberger Investment Companies Service, Inc. *Mutual Funds Panorama*.

IX. INSIDERS TRANSACTIONS AND HOLDINGS

A. Computer Directions Advisors. *Spectrum 6*: *Insider Holdings*.

B. Corporate Data Exchange. *CDE Stock Ownership Directories*.
1. *Agribusiness*.
2. *Banking and Finance*.
3. *Energy*.
4. *Fortune 500*.

C. U.S. Securities and Exchange Commission. *Official Summary of Security Transactions & Holdings*.

rusal of these (and other) publications, and no attempt will be made here to describe each one. Instead, some of the more essential sources of information will be discussed.

Anyone planning to invest in anything but mutual funds should read *The Wall Street Journal*. It provides extensive statistical data, financial news, and even a bit of humor. An alternative is the financial section of *The New York Times*. Most other daily newspapers contain financial information, but much less than found in the *Journal* or the *Times*. A weekly publication with a wealth of statistical data is *Barron's*.

A useful source of daily price and volume figures for both stocks and mutual funds is Standard and Poor's *Daily Stock Price Record*. Each volume covers one calendar quarter, and all values for a given stock or fund are listed in a single column.

Dividend information, listed by stock, can be found in either *Moody's Dividend Record* or *Standard and Poor's Dividend Record*.

Historic beta values, adjusted for mean reversion, are shown for approximately 1,700 stocks in the *Value Line Investment Survey*.

Some brokerage houses provide their major clients with the monthly *Stock Guide* and *Bond Guide* published by Standard and Poor's. Figures 19-10 and 19-11 illustrate the contents of these useful publications.

The most comprehensive source of information about mutual funds in general, and the characteristics of individual funds, is Wiesenberger Investment Service's *Investment Companies* (annual). The standard source of information on virtually any important security is the most recent annual *Moody's Manual* (Bank and Finance, Industrial, International, Municipal and Government, OTC Industrial, Public Utility, or Transportation).

Historic data and analyses for 1,700 stocks and most major industries can be found in the *Value Line Investment Survey*. The *Value Line Options and Convertibles* covers both convertible bonds and options. Both publications offer Value Line's estimates of the relative attractiveness of the investments at current prices.

Current forecasts of company earnings are published in Standard and Poor's weekly *Earnings Forecaster*.

Publications of major security analysts' societies are the *Financial Analysts Journal* (U.S.), *Analyse Financiére* (France), and *The Investment Analyst* (United Kingdom). Academic journals that emphasize aspects of investments are the *Journal of Business*, the *Journal of Finance*, the *Journal of Financial and Quantitative Analysis*, and the *Journal of Financial Economics*.

Anyone interested in the management of money for institutional or corporate investors (especially pension funds) should read the *Journal of Portfolio Management*, which publishes the views of both practitioners and academicians. A biweekly periodical widely read by institu-

16 Abb-Ala STANDARD & POOR'S CORPORATION

Title-Industry Code & Co. Finances (In Italics) / Individual Issue Statistics Exchange	Ind / Interest Dates	Chgs. 1981 / S&P Quality Rating	Eligible	Times Earn. 1982 / Bond Form	1983 Yr. End / Legality M N N	Cash &Eqv / Redemption Provisions Refund Earliest/Other	Current Assets / Call Price For S.F.	Liabs Date / Call Price Regular	L. Term Debt (Mil $) / Out-st'd'g (Mil $)	Debt % Prop / Underwriter Firm	Year	Interim Times Earn. Period / Price Range 1972-82 High	1972-82 Low	1982 / 1983 High	1983 / 1983 Low	1984 High	1984 Low	Mo. End Price Sale(s) or Bid	Curr Yield	Yield to Mat.
Abbott Laboratories	*21a*	*4.19*		*5.16*	*5.48 Dc*	*213*	*1293*	*677 12-83*	*484*	*45.3*										
• SF Deb 6¼s '93	Jj15	AA+	X	R	- ✓ -	....	100	±101.15	9.74	G1	'68	93½	54⅛	77¼	72	81	76	80⅛	7.75	9.58
• SF Deb 7⅝s '96	Ms	AA+	X	R	✓ ✓ -	....	100	±102.492	25.4	L5	'71	106	80	83¾	75½	84	84	82⅞	9.23	10.18
• SF Deb 9.20s '99	aO15	AA+	X	R	✓ ✓ -	[1]104.60	[2]100	±105.06	72.2	G2	'74	111½	58½	88	78⅝	81⅞	72⅛	73	12.60	13.37
• SF Deb 11.80s 2013	Fa	AA+	X	R	✓ ✓ -	[3]105.90	[4]100	±111.21	150	G2	'83	....	....	101¼	98⅛	No Sale		87⅛	13.54	13.59
• Nts 11s '93	Fa	AA+	X	R	- ✓ -	....	....	[5]100	100	G2	'83	....	....	104	95½	95½	94¾	A93⅛	11.78	12.25
ACF Indus	*55*	*1.94*		*1.62*	*.... Dc*	*6.68*	*313*	*150 9-83*	*408*	*54.1*		*9 Mo Sep*		*1.81*	*0.98*					
Eq Tr Ctf 14⅛s '92	fA	A+	X	R	- ✓ -	....	[6]100	NC	30.0	B1	'82	113	99⅞	115¾	97	109	103⅞	103⅞	14.32	14.06
Eq Tr Ctf 14½s '96	jD	A+	X	R	- ✓ -	....	[7]100	NC	30.0	B1	'81	112⅛	91⅛	114½	105½	107½	101⅛	101⅛	14.30	14.26
Eq Tr Ctf 11.60s 2000	Mn15	A+	X	R	- ✓ -	....	[8]100	NC	37.5	B1	'80	103½	69⅝	97½	90½	93⅛	85⅛	85⅛	13.59	13.89
Action Industries	*59*	*1.23*		*1.93*	*3.10 Je*	*0.03*	*73.1*	*39.2 12-83*	*10.3*	*75.6*		*6 Mo Dec*		*3.28*	*3.36*					
◆Sr SF Deb[9] 11¼s '92	mS15	NR	Y	R	- - -	....	100	±105.90	2.69	d1	'77	100	61¼	79	79	81⅛	81	81⅛	13.87	15.32
Aetna Life & Casual	*35*	*9.14*		*7.63*	*7.98 Dc*				*421*											
• Deb 8⅛s 2007	aO15	AAA	X	R	✓ ✓ -	....	[10]100	[11]104.58	250	M10	'77	101½	51¼	81½	65	70⅛	63	s63	12.90	13.29
Affiliated Bankshrs[12]Colo[13]	*10a*	*1.17*		*1.16*	*1.17 Dc*				*74.2*											
Nts 11⅝s '93	Ao	A	X	R	- ✓ -	....	....	[14]100	50.0	M10	'83	....	....	100	93⅞	96½	91	91	12.77	13.38
After Six	*68c*	*1.02*		*1.13*	*1.70 Je*	*5.89*	*37.5*	*5.66 9-83*	*22.2*	*399*		*3 Mo Sep*		*1.04*	*1.10*					
◆ws SF Deb 11¼s '95	Mn15	B	Y	R	- - -	[15]100	[16]100	102	[17]25.0	D10	'83	....	....	100	84	87	87	82	14.33	15.15
Air Products & Chemicals	*14b*	*5.87*		*3.63*	*3.27 Sp*	*85.8*	*559*	*460 12-83*	*★496*	*25.8*		*3 Mo Dec*		*2.98*	*3.80*					
• SF Deb 11⅝s 2010	Mn15	A+	X	R	- ✓ -	[18]106.60	[19]100	109.24	70.1	L5	'80	101	74½	95½	91½	91	91	A89	13.06	13.12
• Nts 14⅝s '87	fA	A+	X	R	- ✓ -	....	....	NC	100	L5	'82	104	99½	110½	107	106½	106¼	105	13.93	12.69
Nts 12⅜s '94	Ao15	A+	X	R	- ✓ -	....	....	[20]100	100	L5	'84	....	....	....	....	99	97¼	97¼	13.11	13.25
Airco, Inc.	*14b*	*Subsid of BOC Int'l*																		
SF Deb 9⅛s 2000	aO	A-	X	R	- ✓ -	[21]104.33	[22]100	±105.19	75.0	D5	'75	106½	59⅛	93½	71	75⅛	68½	69⅞	13.51	14.24
[23]Alabama Bancorporation	*10a*	*1.14*		*1.15*	*1.17 Dc*				*81.3*											
• Flt'g Rt Nts[24] 10¼s '99	mS	AA	X	R	- ✓ -	[25]Z100	....	[26]100	15.4	F2	'74	104½	96	101⅛	98	100½	99⅜	99⅜	10.29	....
• Nts 9½s '84	jJ	AA	X	R	- ✓ -	....	....	100	35.0	F2	'75	108¾	80	100½	97.5	100½	99.28	99.53	9.54	12.55
Alabama Gas Corp[27]	*73b*	*2.48*		*2.82*	*2.83 Sp*	*1.32*	*67.9*	*79.7 12-83*	*25.8*	*22.2*		*3 Mo Dec*		*1.94*	*2.07*					
1st E [28]5⅞s '84	fA	A+	X	CR	- ✓ ✓	....	100	100	1.60	H2	'59	90	66	97⅛	90	98⅜	97¼	98¾	5.95	11.08
1st F [29]8s '94	Fa	A+	X	R	- ✓ ✓	....	100	±103.84	7.50	W7	'69	97⅛	53¼	79¼	73½	76	71	71	11.27	13.41
1st G [30]9½s '96	Jj	A+	X	R	- ✓ ✓	....	100	±106.31	12.8	W7	'71	108½	58⅛	86⅛	76	82¼	77	77⅛	12.32	13.43
Alabama Power Co.[31]	*72a*	*1.68*		*1.94*	*2.25 Dc*	*144*	*664*	*499 12-83*	*2421*	*55.1*										
1st 3½s '85	Jd	A-	X	CR	- ✓ ✓	....	100	100	15.0	B10	'55	79½	54¼	90	79½	91½	89⅝	91⅛	3.83	12.26
1st 3½s '86	Ms	A-	X	CR	- ✓ ✓	....	±100.29	±100.29	13.7	U3	'56	73¾	52½	84½	73¾	86½	84⅛	86	4.07	12.27
1st 4⅜s '87	Mn	A-	X	CR	- ✓ ✓	....	±100.27	±100.43	14.5	M10	'57	75¼	53	80	70⅛	80¾	79⅛	80	5.78	12.87
• 1st 8⅝s '87	aO	A-	X	R	- ✓ ✓	....	100	±102.71	75.0	B1	'77	99½	66	93	85½	91	87½	s87½	9.86	13.30
1st 3⅞s '88	Jj	A-	X	CR	- ✓ ✓	....	±100.10	±100.45	23.0	L5	'58	68⅛	47⅛	74	64¼	75⅛	73¾	74⅛	5.23	12.97
1st 4⅞s '89	Mn	A-	X	CR	- ✓ ✓	....	±100.11	±100.73	20.0	M10	'59	75¾	48⅛	72¼	64¾	71⅞	69½	69⅝	7.00	13.40
• 1st 18¼s '89	aO	A-	X	R	- ✓ ✓	[32]103.05	[33]100	±112.17	98.0	M6	'81	121	98⅛	128	110	115¼	108	s112	16.29	14.93
1st 5s '90	Ao	A-	X	CR	- ✓ ✓	....	±100.11	±100.92	6.96	B10	'60	76¼	46½	69¼	62⅞	68⅝	66⅛	66⅛	7.53	13.42
• 1st 14¾s '91	Jj	A-	X	R	- ✓ ✓	[34]106.56	[35]100	±109.84	98.0	B1	'81	110	87½	111⅛	103⅜	109⅛	102	103⅛	14.30	14.01
1st 4½s '91	Ms	A-	X	CR	- ✓ ✓	....	±100.60	±101.28	13.0	E1	'61	70⅛	42⅛	64⅛	58⅛	63	60¾	60¾	7.41	13.46
1st 4⅜s '92	Jd	A-	X	CR	- ✓ ✓	....	100	101.03	14.4	B10	'62	68¾	39⅛	60	54½	58½	56	56	7.81	13.47
1st 4⅜s '93	Mn	A-	X	CR	- ✓ ✓	....	100.04	±101.23	13.8	L5	'63	67⅞	38	57¾	52¼	55⅞	53⅛	53¼	8.22	13.50
1st 4⅝s '94	Mn	A-	X	CR	- ✓ ✓	....	±100.60	±101.82	24.1	F2	'64	70⅛	37¼	57	51¼	54¾	51⅞	52	8.89	13.51
1st 4⅞s '95	mS	A-	X	CR	- ✓ ✓	....	±100½	±102.14	33.3	B10	'65	71⅞	37	55⅛	50	53⅛	50½	50½	9.65	13.54
1st 6¼s '96	aO	A-	X	CR	- ✓ ✓	....	±100.89	±103.15	29.4	B10	'66	87	43⅛	62⅞	56⅛	60	56⅜	56⅝	11.04	13.57
1st 6½s '97	aO	A-	X	CR	- ✓ ✓	....	100	±102.92	28.0	L5	'67	89⅛	43⅝	63⅛	57⅛	60½	56¾	56¼	11.45	13.59

Uniform Footnote Explanations—See Page 1. Other: [1]Red rest'n(9.2%)to 10-15-84. [2]Fr 10-15-84. [3]Red rest'n(11.80%)to 2-1-93. [4]Fr 2-1-94. [5]Fr 2-1-90. [6]Fr 8-1-88. [7]Fr 12-1-87. [8]Fr 5-15-86. [9]Int incr fr 11% 5-15-82. [10]Fr 10-15-88. [11]Fr 10-15-87. [12]Plan mgr w IntraWest Fin'l. [13]Plan name chge,aft mgr,to 1st Natl Bancorp. [14]Fr 4-1-90. [15]Red rest'n(13.875%)to 5-15-88. [16]Fr 5-15-88. [17]Incl disc. [18]Red rest'n(11.7%)to 5-15-90. [19]Fr 5-15-91. [20]Fr 4-15-91. [21]Fr 10-1-85. [22]Fr 10-1-86. [23]Now AmSouth Bancorp. [24]Thru 8-31-84,aft for T-Bill rate. [25]Also repayable at hldr's option on int dates. [26]Fr 9-1-84. [27]Subsid of Alagasco. [28]Incr fr 5 1/2% 8-1-82. [29]Incr fr 7 1/4% 8-1-82. [30]Incr fr 8 3/4%,1-1-83. [31]Subsid of Southern Co. [32]Red rest'n(18.44%)to 10-1-86. [33]Restricted to $1M yearly to 1987. [34]Red rest'n(14.89%)to 1-1-86. [35]Restricted to $1M yearly to 1986.

FIGURE 19-10
Standard and Poor's *Bond Guide*.

tional investors and money managers is *Pensions and Investment Age*. *Institutional Investor*, a periodical full of "inside information" on the investment industry, is published monthly.

While a company's annual report provides useful information, the annual business and financial report (10-K) filed with the Securities and Exchange Commission usually includes more details. A similar report, the N-1R, is filed by management investment companies.

Computer-Readable Data

The rapid increase in the use of microcomputers by both professional and amateur investors has led to a major expansion in the availability of *computer-readable investment data*.

Fundamental and market data for thousands of stocks are provided on magnetic tape to professional investors by *Standard and*

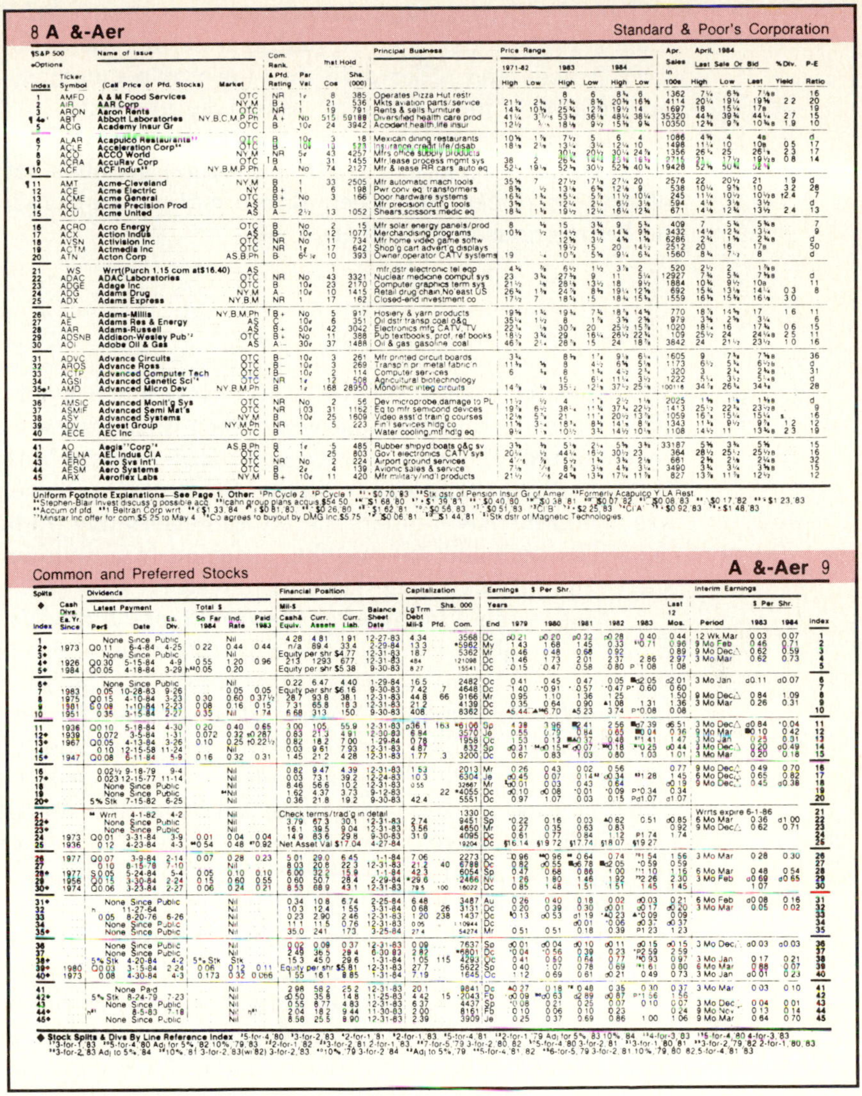

FIGURE 19-11
Standard and Poor's *Stock Guide*.

Poor's Computstat Services and *Value Line, Inc*. These data bases are also available on a dial-up basis via time-shared computer services and on disks for use in microcomputers.

Information on the performance of mutual funds, investment advisors, and bank and insurance company funds is available on a time-shared basis from *Computer Directions Advisors*.

Extensive fundamental and market data are provided on a dial-

Financial Analysis

up basis by *Compuserve*, *Dow Jones News/Retrieval*, and *The Source*. Each service is designed so that users of microcomputers can "download" prices and other data into their own machines easily, rapidly, and relatively inexpensively (especially at night).

Many data bases are available on "floppy disks" for direct use in microcomputers. The *Isys Corporation* supplies several major sets of data on prices, fundamental information, and predictions made by brokerage houses and others.

MARKET INDICES

What did the market do yesterday? How much would an unmanaged portfolio have returned last year? Such questions are often answered by examining the performance of a *market index*. Many are available. Some correspond to explicit portfolio strategies; others do not. Some are comprehensive, others merely representative. Indices differ in the securities included, the weights assigned to individual securities, and the computational procedures employed.

Most widely followed is the *Dow Jones Industrial Average*, computed by simply summing the prices of 30 large-value stocks, then dividing the total by a constant (the "divisor"). The performance of the index thus corresponds to that of a portfolio in which the relative value of each holding is proportional to the price of the stock relative to that of the full set of 30 stocks. When one of the stocks splits, extra shares are assumed to be sold and the proceeds invested in equal numbers of shares of all 30 stocks (formally, this is accomplished by adjusting the divisor). Small stock dividends are ignored, making the index slightly biased downward.

Similar procedures are used to compute two other Dow Jones Averages: one uses 20 transportation stocks, the other 15 utility stocks.

Levels of the Dow Jones Averages are reported in virtually every newspaper. Historical data and quarterly dividends and earnings figures are published from time to time in *Barron's*.

A more representative measure, used by most institutional investors, is Standard Poor's Composite 500-stock index, a market-value-weighted average of 500 stocks.

The S&P 500 corresponds to a portfolio in which the relative value of each holding is proportional to the value of all the company's shares relative to the total value of all companies' shares. Except on occasions when the stocks used to compute the index are changed, the only rebalancing required to maintain an equivalent portfolio is that needed to accommodate new issues of stock, tender offers, and so on. Reinvestment of dividends can, of course, cause problems, owing to the absence of fractional shares, but the S&P 500, like any market-value-weighted index, corresponds to a low-cost unmanaged portfolio strategy.

Market-value-weighted indices are *macroconsistent*: every investor could hold a portfolio invested in the same manner, and everything would add up. This is not true for indices such as the Dow Jones averages (since there are different numbers of shares of various corporations' stocks) or equal-dollar-weighted indices (since there are different numbers of dollars invested in various corporations). Market-value-weighted indices represent the average *dollar* (or franc, pound, or whatever) invested in the stocks included. They thus conform to a portion of the overall *market portfolio*.

In addition to its composite 500-stock index, Standard and Poor's also computes market-value-weighted industry indices. Indices for the 400 industrials, 20 transportation, 40 utilities, and 40 financial stocks used to make up the composite index are also prepared. Values for all indices, along with quarterly data on dividends, earnings, and sales, may be found in Standard and Poor's *Analysts' Handbook* (annual) and *Analysts' Handbook Supplement* (monthly).

More comprehensive market-value-weighted indices for U.S. stocks are also computed. The New York Stock Exchange publishes a composite index of all stocks listed on that exchange, as well as four subindices (industrials, utilities, transportation, and finance). The American Stock Exchange computes an index of its stocks. The National Association of Securities Dealers, using its automated quotation service (NASDAQ), computes indices based on the market value of approximately 3,000 over-the-counter stocks (industrial, bank, insurance, other finance, transportation, utilities, and a composite index). And Wilshire Associates computes the *Wilshire 5000 equity index*, which indicates the total market value of all stocks listed on the New York and American Stock Exchanges plus those "actively traded over-the-counter." Levels of all these indices are published weekly in *Barron's*, but dividend values are not included, limiting their usefulness for some applications.

Capital International Perspective publishes market-value-weighted indices using various combinations of 1,200 stocks from 19 different countries.

The *Dow Jones 20-Bond Index* is computed by averaging the prices of ten utility and ten industrial bonds. More satisfactory are the *Salomon Brothers Bond Total Rate of Return Indices* and the *Shearson-Lehman Bond Indices*.

All the indices discussed thus far can be computed by taking an *arithmetic* average (weighted or unweighted, depending on the index) of the percentage changes in the prices of the included securities. Thus each corresponds to a feasible portfolio strategy. One popular set of indices is not constructed in this manner. Each of four *Value Line Averages* (industrials, rails, utilities, and composite) is computed daily by multiplying the previous day's index by the *geometric mean* of the daily price relatives (today's price divided by yesterday's) of the relevant stocks in the Value Line Investment Survey. Each day's performance is therefore worse than that which would have been obtained using an arithmetic average of the same values. But an arithmetic average corresponds to the performance that would be achieved by a portfolio rebalanced daily to have equal dollar values of each of the included stocks. Thus the Value Line Averages are biased downward and correspond to no achievable portfolio policy.

Market indices play an important role in portfolio management and the measurement of investment performance; these aspects of investment management are covered in subsequent chapters.

Problems

1. Explain the reasoning behind the sentence: "Any system designed to beat the market, once known to more than a few people, carries the seeds of its own destruction."

2. A phrase one often hears is "Buy low, sell high." Why is the system suggested by this phrase not operational?

3. Explain why the Dow Jones Industrial Index is not macroconsistent.

4. A brochure describes "a computerized system based on extensive analysis of the last 40 years of stock price movements." The firm selling the service says that it can provide "solid statistical evidence" that the system picks stocks that return 35% per year. Would you pay for its recommendations? Why or why not?

5. Compare picking stocks that will "beat the market" with (a) predicting rainfall, and (b) detecting the locations of enemy submarines. Would you expect methods developed for predicting rainfall to work well for picking mispriced stocks? What about methods designed to detect the locations of enemy submarines?

6. Is the evidence in Figure 19-8 consistent with market efficiency? If your sole source of security analysis were the "Heard on the Street" column, would your investment decisions be affected by it? If so, how would you use the information?

7. Assume that a detailed study of recent market history has shown that a change in the ratio of (1) a specialist's short position in a stock to (2) the amount held by mutual funds west of the Mississippi River is followed by a change in the price of the stock in the opposite direction. Does this prove that the ratio is a useful indicator for stock selection?

8. Would an input-output table prepared when crude oil cost $3 per barrel be especially helpful if crude oil now costs $30 per barrel?

9. It is commonly asserted that the Value Line Stock Index is more representative of the stock market than Standard and Poor's 500-stock index. What is an appropriate definition of "representative" in this context? How do the two indices differ? Which of the differences make the Value Line index more representative? Which make the Standard and Poor's index more representative?

10. A company's return on assets is defined as the ratio of profits to assets. This can, in turn, be considered the product of two ratios:

$$\frac{\text{profits}}{\text{assets}} = \frac{\text{profits}}{\text{sales}} \times \frac{\text{sales}}{\text{assets}}$$

(ROA) (profitability) (turnover)

If you know with certainty what a firm's profitability and turnover will be, can you predict its return on assets? If you only have estimates of *expected* turnover and *expected* profitability and measures of the likely deviations of the two from these estimates (i.e., the standard deviation of profitability and the standard deviation of turnover), what can you say about the return on assets?

20

Investment Management

INTRODUCTION

Investment management is the process by which money is managed. It may be active or passive, use explicit or implicit procedures, accord with the assumptions of market efficiency or not, be controlled or uncontrolled. The trend is toward more highly controlled operations consistent with the notion that capital markets are relatively efficient. However, approaches vary, and many different investment "styles" can be found.

TRADITIONAL INVESTMENT MANAGEMENT ORGANIZATIONS

Few like to be called "traditional." However, many investment management organizations follow procedures little changed from those popular decades ago and thus deserve the title. Figure 20-1 shows the major characteristics of a typical organization of this type.

Projections concerning the economy, security and money markets, and so on are made (often qualitatively) by *economists*, *technicians*, or other market experts within or outside the organization. The projected environment is communicated via briefings, reports, and so on—usually in a rather implicit and qualitative manner—to the organization's *security analysts*. Each analyst is responsible for a group of securities, often those in one or more industries (in some organizations, analysts are called *industry specialists*). Often a group of analysts reports to a senior analyst responsible for a sector of the economy or market.

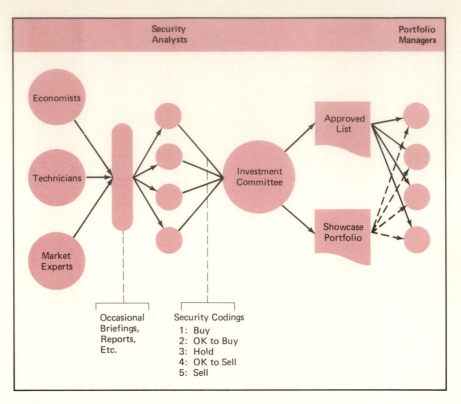

FIGURE 20-1
A Traditional Investment Management Organization

The analysts, often drawing heavily on reports of others (e.g., "street analysts" in brokerage houses), make predictions concerning securities for which they are responsible. In a sense, such predictions are conditional on the assumed economic and market environments, although the relationship is loose, at best.

Analysts' predictions seldom specify an expected return (either total return or return relative to that of securities with similar attributes) or the time over which predicted performance will take place. Instead, an analyst's feelings about a security are summarized by assigning it one of five codes, as indicated in Figure 20-1 (some organizations reverse the numbers, so that 5 represents a buy recommendation and 1 a sell recommendation; and some Europeans favor +, 0+, 0, 0−, and −).

Security codings constitute the information formally transmitted to the *investment committee*, which typically includes the senior management of the organization. In addition, analysts occasionally brief the investment committee on their feelings about various securities.

The investment committee's major formal output is the *approved* or *authorized list*, which includes the securities deemed worthy of accumulation in portfolios. The rules of the organization typically specify that any security on the list may be bought, while those not on the list should be either held or sold, barring special circumstances.

The presence or absence of a security on the approved list constitutes the major information transmitted explicitly from the investment committee to *portfolio managers* (including, in banks, trust officers). In some organizations senior management supervises a "showcase portfolio" (e.g., a bank's major commingled equity fund), the composition of which indicates to portfolio managers the relative intensity of management's feelings regarding different securities.

In many ways this description is a caricature of an investment organization—even one run along traditional lines. But many of these attributes can be observed in practice. Traditional organizations may deal with uncertainty only obliquely, utilize inconsistent estimates, and fail to fully take into account the relative efficiency of modern capital markets.

PORTFOLIO MANAGEMENT FUNCTIONS

Figures 20-2(a), (b), and (c) show the key ingredients required for each of the three major tasks associated with modern investment management. The three functions are:

1. *Portfolio analysis*—the determination of a portfolio's risk, expected return, and utility for the client in question.
2. *Portfolio revision*—the selection of a set of security purchases or sales.
3. *Performance measurement and attribution*—the determination of the actual performance of a portfolio, the reasons for that performance, and comparison with a preselected "benchmark."

The three functions are designed to answer three questions: What *is* the portfolio, what *should* it be, and how *has* it done? The remainder of this chapter deals with the first two functions; the next chapter deals with the third.

Ingredients for Portfolio Analysis and Revision

To estimate a portfolio's risk and expected return one must have estimates of the expected returns of individual securities and their risks as well as estimates of the correlations among security returns. To determine the utility of a portfolio for a specific client (an individual, institution, or group of individuals) one must know the relevant characteristics of the client—for example, tax status, risk tolerance, and other

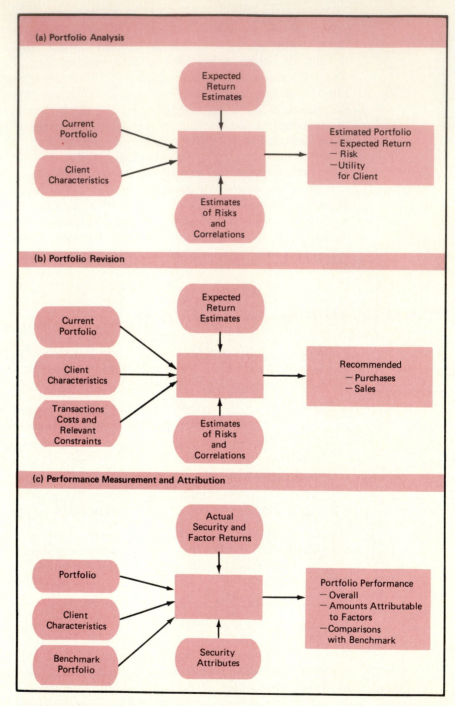

FIGURE 20-2
Three Portfolio Management Functions

assets and liabilities. To determine an appropriate set of revisions, one must also take into account transactions costs and any constraints on holdings.

Selecting a "Normal" Bond/Stock Mix

One of the key characteristics that differentiates clients from one another concerns attitudes toward risk vis-à-vis expected return. The greater a client's *risk tolerance*, the greater should be the risk and expected return of the overall portfolio.

Determining the extent to which a client is willing to accept greater risk in order to get greater expected return is not a simple task. In practice it is often done indirectly. The likely implications of investments in alternative *stock/bond mixes* are presented to the client, who then chooses a preferred mix. This provides guidance concerning the "normal" ("strategic," "target") mix of such assets. It also provides information about the client's risk tolerance—information that can be

FIGURE 20-3
Average Excess Return and Standard Deviation of Excess Return for Different Stock/Bond Mixes, 1926-1983

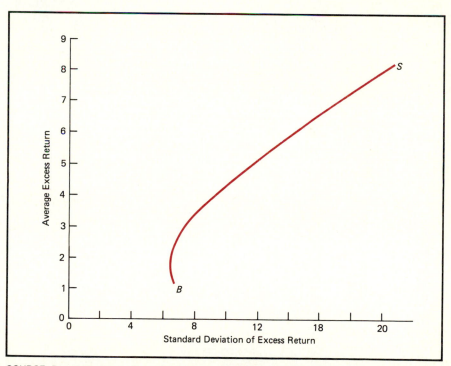

SOURCE: Based on data in Roger G. Ibbotson, *Stocks/Bonds, Bills and Inflation*, *1984 Yearbook*, R. G. Ibbotson Associates, Inc. Chicago, Ill., February 1984.

used to make "tactical" changes in holdings when opportunities are "abnormal."

The starting point is a set of estimates of the risks and expected returns for different bond/stock mixes. Figure 20-3 provides an example based on historic excess return (return minus the Treasury bill rate)

FIGURE 20-4
Effect of the Bond/Stock Mix on the Real Value of an Endowment Fund

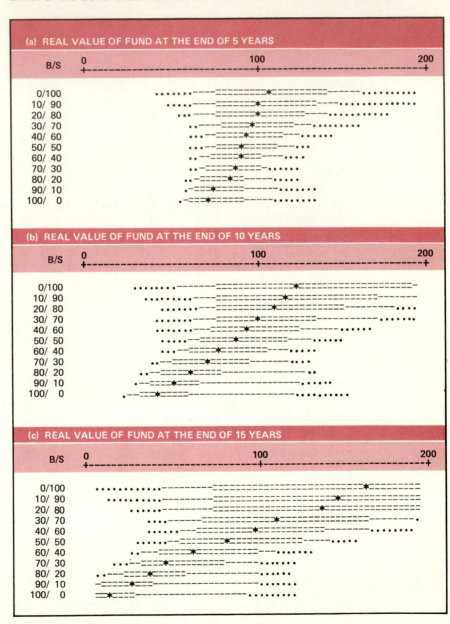

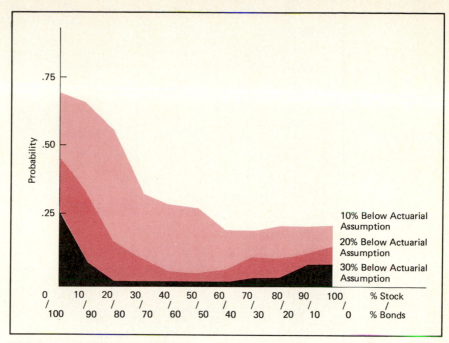

SOURCE: Peter O. Dietz and H. Russell Fogler, "The Debt/Equity Dilemma," Frank Russell Co., Inc., Capital Placement Division, 1975.

FIGURE 20-5
Effect of the Bond/Stock Mix on the Internal Rate of Return of a Pension Fund

from 1926 through 1983. The vertical axis plots the average excess return and the horizontal axis the standard deviation of excess return. Point *B* represents investment in long-term corporate bonds, point *S* investment in common stocks, and intermediate points combinations of the two.

In practice historic experience, judgment, or a combination of the two may be used to estimate the risks and returns of different stock/bond mixes. In any event, given a range of opportunities, an investor should choose the combination of risk and expected return that best suits his or her objectives, circumstances, and so on. When the choice is made on behalf of others (e.g., by a trustee for one or more beneficiaries), the task is much more difficult, but a decision is still required.

Investment managers and advisory organizations have developed various procedures for helping clients understand the trade-off between risk and return so they can make reasonable decisions in this regard. Figures 20-4, 20-5, and 20-6 illustrate some of these methods.

Figure 20-4 is taken from a study done for a small college. At the time an amount equal to 6% of the market value of the college's

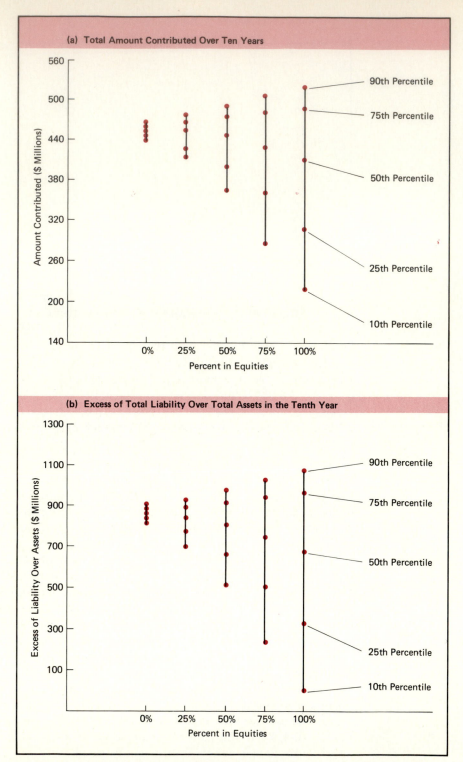

SOURCE: Frank C. McLaughlin, "Using Simulation to Chart the Way," *Pension World*, September 1975 (based on a study performed by Willshire Associates, Inc).

FIGURE 20-6
Effect of the Bond/Stock Mix on a Pension Fund's Cost and Value

endowment fund was being spent. The study assumed that in future years the amount spent would be the same in *real dollars*. Given this, what might be the *real* value of the fund at the end of 5, 10, or 15 years, and how might this be affected by the stock/bond mix?

To answer the question, historic *real* returns from representative portfolios of bonds and stocks were used. For example, to construct the bar graph at the top of Figure 20-4(a) a mix of 0% in bonds and 100% in stocks was assumed. The value of the fund was assumed to equal 100 at the beginning of 1926, and year-by-year results were computed for the period from 1926 through 1930, using the assumed spending rule and the actual real returns in each year. The real value of the fund at the end of 1930 was then determined. The procedure was repeated using returns from 1927 through 1931, 1928 through 1932, and so on. The bar graph summarizes the frequency distribution of the end-of-period real values produced in this way, as follows:

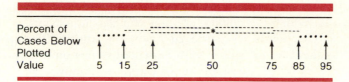

Figure 20-5 is taken from a study designed for a pension fund. Here the focus was on the probabilities that the ending asset value might be 10%, 20%, or 30% below the amount that would be obtained if returns equaled the rate projected by the fund's consulting actuary (6% per year). The figure plots such probabilities for various stock/bond mixes. In this study, actual returns on indices of bonds and stocks were used in a manner similar to that employed in the endowment study.

Figure 20-6 shows some of the results from a more detailed study of a pension plan. This analysis took into account the fact that the amount contributed by a corporation to its pension fund each year usually depends on the performance of the fund's investments. Under such circumstances, two aspects are uncertain: the contributions in each year, and the value of the fund at the end of any given number of years. Figure 20-6(a) shows the estimated distribution of the total amount contributed over ten years, and Figure 20-6(b) the estimated distribution of the difference between the plan's obligations and the value of the assets in the fund in the tenth year. Not shown is the relationship between the two aspects—i.e., the extent to which good outcomes in one figure are associated with bad (or good) outcomes in the other figure.

This study differed from the previous ones in another way. Instead of using year-by-year returns, *Monte Carlo simulation* was employed. Expected returns and standard deviations of return were specified for each of the investment media, along with the correlation between their returns. Then many cases were analyzed, with returns drawn randomly from the associated joint probability distribution. The diagrams summarize the results from all the cases. This is a more versatile procedure and makes it easy to assume that the future will be different from the past.

Risk Tolerance

After a client has selected a normal stock/bond mix, what can be said about his or her risk tolerance? One would, of course, like to identify all the indifference curves that represent a client's attitude toward risk and expected return. However, in practice a more modest goal is usually adopted—to obtain a reasonable representation of the shape of such curves in the likely region of risk and expected return within which the client's optimal choices should fall.

The points in Figure 20-7 plot the alternative mixes presented to a client in a diagram with expected return on the vertical axis and *variance* on the horizontal axis. Curve *BCS* shows the risk-return characteristics of all possible stock/bond mixes, and point *C* identifies the attributes of the mix chosen by the client.

If all the possible mixes had been presented to the client and point *C* had been chosen, we could infer that the slope of the client's indifference curve that goes through *C* is precisely equal to that of curve *BCS* at this point. This follows from the nature of indifference curves. If the curve through point *C* cut curve *BCS*, other points on the curve would have been preferred to *C*, as shown in Figure 20-8 for point *X*.

In principle the choice of a stock/bond mix provides only information about the slope of an indifference curve at one point. To go beyond

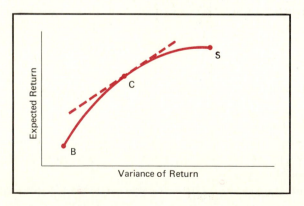

FIGURE 20-7
Inferring Client Risk Tolerance

Investment Management

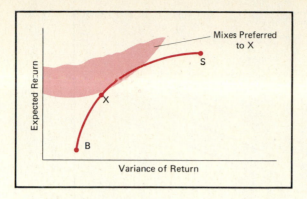

FIGURE 20-8
A Nonoptimal Mix

this one must make an assumption about the general shape of client indifference curves. An assumption commonly made is that of *constant risk tolerance* over a range of alternatives in the neighborhood of the point originally chosen.

Figures 20-9(a) and (b) show the nature of the assumption. As indicated in Figure 20-9(a), indifference curves in a diagram with *variance* on the horizontal axis are assumed to be linear and parallel over the range in question. Figure 20-9(b) plots the same curves in a more familiar diagram—one with *standard deviation* on the horizontal axis. As shown, the curves have the conventional shape—they indicate that the investor requires more return to compensate for an additional unit of standard deviation as the risk of the portfolio increases.

Utility

The equation of an indifference curve with constant risk tolerance can be written as:

$$E_p = U_{pc} + \frac{V_p}{T_c} \qquad \textbf{(20-1)}$$

where

E_p = the expected return of the portfolio
V_p = the variance of return of the portfolio
T_c = the client's risk tolerance
U_{pc} = the *utility* of the portfolio for the client

Graphically, U_{pc} is the vertical intercept if the indifference curve (line) in Figure 20-9(a) is extended to the vertical axis. If this indifference curve were, in fact, linear throughout, U_{pc} would be the portfolio's *certainty equivalent return*. Thus in Figure 20-9(a) portfolio P' is as desirable for this particular client as a portfolio with an expected return of U'_{pc} and no risk—i.e., one providing U'_{pc} with certainty.

Investment Management

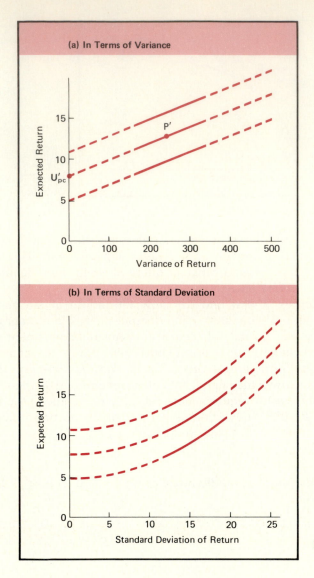

FIGURE 20-9
Constant Risk Tolerance

Since there is no reason to assume that indifference curves have the same form all the way to the range of zero risk, it is preferable to interpret U_{pc} as simply an indicator of the height of an indifference curve. We will use the term *utility* for this purpose. Rewriting (20-1):

$$U_{pc} = E_p - \frac{V_p}{T_c}$$

(20-2)

$$\underset{\text{utility}}{} \quad \underset{\substack{\text{expected} \\ \text{return}}}{} \quad \underset{\substack{\text{risk} \\ \text{penalty}}}{}$$

This shows that the utility of portfolio p for client c is a *risk-adjusted expected return*. From the expected return we subtract a *risk penalty* that depends on the portfolio's risk and the client's risk tolerance. The greater the portfolio's risk and the smaller the client's tolerance for risk, the smaller the utility of the portfolio.

A client's *risk tolerance* (T_c) indicates the *added variance he or she is willing to accept in order to get an added unit of expected return*. More formally— it is his or her *marginal rate of substitution of variance for expected return*.

The procedure is illustrated with a series of "worksheets" in Tables 20-1 and 20-2. In each case, three values are *input*: the expected return and standard deviation of a portfolio and the client's risk tolerance. All other values are *derived*, using the formulas shown in the third column.

TABLE 20-1
Portfolio Utility for a Client with Risk Tolerance = 80

(a) PORTFOLIO A		
Item	Value	Source
Portfolio characteristics:		
(a) Expected return	14.00	Input
(b) Standard deviation	20.00	Input
Client characteristic:		
(c) Risk tolerance	80.00	Input
Risk penalty:		
(d) Variance	400.00	(a) squared
(e) Risk penalty	5.00	(d)/(c)
Utility:		
(f) Expected return	14.00	from (a)
(g) Risk penalty	5.00	from (e)
(h) Utility	9.00	(f) − (g)

(b) PORTFOLIO B		
Item	Value	Formula
Portfolio characteristics:		
(a) Expected return	19.00	Input
(b) Standard deviation	30.00	Input
Client characteristic:		
(c) Risk tolerance	80.00	Input
Risk penalty:		
(d) Variance	900.00	(a) squared
(e) Risk penalty	11.25	(d)/(c)
Utility:		
(f) Expected return	19.00	from (a)
(g) Risk penalty	11.25	from (e)
(h) Utility	7.75	(f) − (g)

TABLE 20-2

Portfolio Utility for a Client with Risk Tolerance = 120

(a) PORTFOLIO A

Item	Value	Formula
Portfolio characteristics:		
(a) Expected return	14.00	Input
(b) Standard deviation	20.00	Input
Client characteristic:		
(c) Risk tolerance	120.00	Input
Risk penalty:		
(d) Variance	400.00	(a) squared
(e) Risk penalty	3.33	(d)/(c)
Utility:		
(f) Expected return	14.00	from (a)
(g) Risk penalty	3.33	from (e)
(h) Utility	10.67	(f) − (g)

(b) PORTFOLIO B

Item	Value	Formula
Portfolio characteristics:		
(a) Expected return	19.00	Input
(b) Standard deviation	30.00	Input
Client characteristic:		
(c) Risk tolerance	120.00	Input
Risk penalty:		
(d) Variance	900.00	(a) squared
(e) Risk penalty	7.50	(d)/(c)
Utility:		
(f) Expected return	19.00	from (a)
(g) Risk penalty	7.50	from (e)
(h) Utility	11.50	(f) − (g)

Table 20-1 computes the utilities of two portfolios for an investor with a risk tolerance of 80. Portfolio A is clearly preferable—its utility for him or her is 9.00%, while that of portfolio B is only 7.75%.

Table 20-2 computes the utilities of the same two portfolios for an investor with a risk tolerance of 120. In this case, portfolio B is preferable, giving a utility of 11.50%, compared to 10.67% for portfolio A.

The first investor is more conservative (has a lower tolerance for risk) than the second. Not surprisingly, the lower-risk, lower-expected return portfolio A is better. For the less conservative second investor, the higher-risk, higher-expected return portfolio B is better.

The goal of portfolio management is to *maximize* the *utility* of a portfolio for a client.

PASSIVE AND ACTIVE MANAGEMENT

Within the investment industry a distinction is often made between those who manage portfolios *passively*—holding securities for relatively long periods with small and infrequent changes—and those who take an *active* stance. Passive managers generally act as if the security markets were relatively *efficient*. Put somewhat differently, their decisions are consistent with the acceptance of *consensus* estimates of risk and return. The portfolios may be surrogates for the market portfolio or they may be *tailored* to suit clients with characteristics that differ from those of the average investor. But passive portfolio managers do not try to "beat the market."

Active managers believe that from time to time there are mispriced securities or groups of securities. They do not act as if they believe that security markets are efficient. Put somewhat differently, they use *deviant* predictions—their estimates of risks, returns, and correlations differ from consensus opinions. Of course, if some are more bullish than average about a security, others must be more bearish. The former will hold "more-than-normal" proportions of the security while the latter will hold "less-than-normal" proportions.

It is useful to think of a portfolio as composed of three components: (1) a market portfolio, (2) deviations designed to tailor holdings to reflect client characteristics, and (3) deviations designed to take advantage of security mispricing. For example, a portfolio might break down as follows:

	Percent in Market	Percent in Tailored Portfolio	Percent in Actual Portfolio
ABC	3.5	4.5	7.0
DEF	1.1	.5	.2
.	.	.	.
.	.	.	.
.	.	.	.

The first column indicates the percentages in a broadly representative market portfolio—the holdings that might be best for an average client in a perfectly efficient market. The second column shows the proportions that would be optimal for a specific client in such a market. The third column shows the actual proportions in the actively managed portfolio.

The differences between the proportions in the first two columns are motivated by considerations of client *utility*, circumstances, and so on. They reflect *tailoring* to account for differences between the characteristics of the investor in question and those of the "average investor."

The *active positions* are represented by the differences between the last two columns:

	Active Position
ABC	+2.5
DEF	− .3
.	.
.	.
.	.

Such differences arise because active managers disagree about risks, correlations, and expected returns. Deviations of this type represent *bets* such managers place against one another.

SECURITY SELECTION, ASSET ALLOCATION, AND MARKET TIMING

In principle, one should make predictions of expected returns, risks, and correlations for all available securities, then determine an optimal portfolio (mix of securities) for the investor in question. Such a (one-stage) *security selection* process is illustrated in Figure 20-10(a).

In practice, this is rarely (if ever) done. Excessive costs would be incurred to obtain detailed predictions of individual security risks, returns, and correlations and to process them adequately. Instead, the overall decision is made in two or more stages.

Figure 20-10(b) illustrates a two-stage procedure. In this case, a portfolio of stocks is formed, along with a portfolio of bonds and one of cash-equivalent securities (e.g., Treasury bills, certificates of deposit). The *security selection* process used in each of these *groups* is *myopic*. For example, differences in the sensitivities of various stocks to movements in the bond market are not taken into account in selecting the stock portfolio. The second stage of the process allocates the investor's funds among the three *asset-class portfolios* chosen in the first stage. Such a process is generally termed *asset allocation*.

Figure 20-10(c) shows a three-stage process. In the first stage (*security selection*), combinations of securities in each of several stock groups and in each of several bond groups are selected. The second stage (*group selection*) involves the determination of an appropriate combination of the stock-group portfolios and an appropriate combination of the bond-group portfolios. The final stage is devoted to *asset allocation*, using the bond and stock portfolios as asset-class portfolios. In every stage but the last, decisions are made myopically, considering only a subset of the available securities. In every stage but the first, groups of securities are "locked together" in fixed proportions determined in prior stages.

Active or passive management may be used in any stage (or portion of stage). For example, "active bets" might be placed on individual securities with assets allocated across security classes based on consensus expected returns for such classes. Alternatively, passive portfolios of individual securities might be constructed, with deviant predic-

FIGURE 20-10
Investment Styles

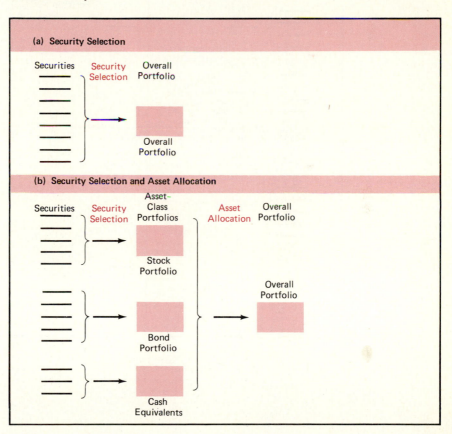

FIGURE 20-10 (*continued*)

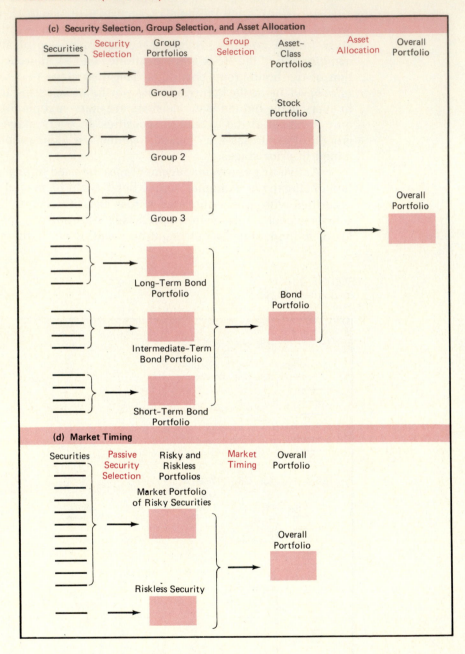

tions used to allocate assets actively among major classes. Organizations that engage in the former type of activity are said to have a *security-selection style*. Those that engage in the latter are said to have an *asset-allocation style*. Firms that place active bets on groups of securities (e.g., those from different industries or economic sectors) are said to employ a *group-rotation style*. And so on.

Figure 20-10(d) portrays a "pure" *market timer*. A passive portfolio of risky securities is constructed to serve as a surrogate for the market portfolio. The only active decision concerns the appropriate allocation of funds between this portfolio and riskless assets (i.e., borrowing and lending). An organization following this philosophy changes its mix of risky and riskless assets based on predictions of the risk and expected return of "the market."

Some investment organizations use relatively pure "styles." Others employ combinations of approaches, making it difficult to classify them into neat "style" categories.

RISKY VERSUS RISKLESS SECURITIES

Some of the key aspects of investment management can be illustrated with a setting in which only risk and return matter, clients differ only in risk tolerance (e.g., there are no tax effects), and investors can borrow or lend at a single risk-free (Treasury bill) interest rate. If all investors agreed about security risks and expected returns, this would be the world of the original Capital Asset Pricing Model, and all efficient strategies would involve mixtures of the market portfolio and (possibly) borrowing or lending. In a world in which investors disagree about risk and return, such strategies will be considered desirable by those who adopt consensus estimates of risk and return but not by those with deviant beliefs.

Passive Management

A passive manager adopts consensus estimates of risk and return. In the situation being considered here, such a manager would only have to choose the appropriate mixture of the market portfolio and Treasury bills. The best combination would, of course, depend on the client's risk tolerance.

Figure 20-11 provides an illustration. Point *T* plots the return offered by Treasury bills, and point *M* the risk and expected return of the market portfolio, using consensus estimates. Combinations of the two investments plot along line *TM*. The client's attitude toward risk and return is shown by the set of indifference curves, and the optimal position (*P*) lies at the point where an indifference curve is tangent

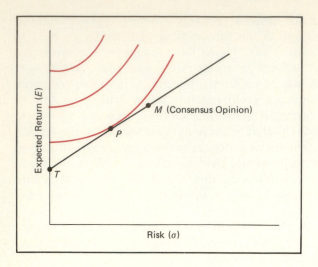

FIGURE 20-11
Passive Investment Management

to line *TM*. In this case the best mix uses both Treasury bills and the market portfolio. In other situations only one might be chosen, or the market portfolio might be levered up via borrowing.

When management is passive, the overall mix is altered only when (1) the client's preferences change and/or (2) the consensus opinion about the risk and return of the market portfolio changes. The manager must continue to assess the latter and keep in touch with the client concerning the former. But no additional activity is required.

The Supply of Risk-Bearing

Every investment manager should have as accurate a view as possible concerning the current consensus opinion of the risk and return associated with investment in the market as a whole. For the active manager this is an important input; for the passive manager it is all-important.

When estimates of overall economic uncertainty increase, security prices will usually adjust so that the risk and expected return of the market portfolio both increase. But what about the return per unit of risk?

Figure 20-12 shows a likely situation. In Figure 20-12(a) the market's prospects are initially those shown by point *M*. Given this alternative, plus the ability to borrow and lend at the interest rate shown by point *T*, investors collectively choose to hold all available risky securities.

Now, imagine that some unforeseen event causes investors' opinions about market risk and return to change, so that the market portfolio plots at point *M'*. Since the excess return per unit of risk is unchanged, everyone will want the same amount of risk and return as before.

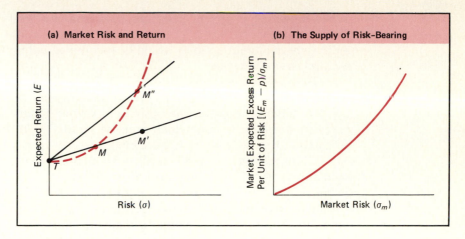

FIGURE 20-12
Changes in Market Risk and Return

But this will require the sale of some of everyone's now more risky securities. This cannot be done (who will buy?). Instead, the prices of risky securities will fall, increasing their expected returns.[1] Eventually the market portfolio will plot at a point such as M'' on a line with a higher slope (excess return per unit of risk).

The dashed line in Figure 20-12(a) shows the points at which the market portfolio is likely to plot as the assessment of risk changes, given investors' attitudes toward risk. Of course, changes in the society's average attitude toward risk and return can alter the relationship in any direction, but such variations are likely to be small and less frequent than changes in estimates of economic uncertainty.

Figure 20-12(b) summarizes the situation in a slightly different manner. It shows the *excess return per unit of risk* (vertical axis) required to induce investors to accept various amounts of risk (horizontal axis). As shown, this *supply of risk-bearing curve* is upward-sloping.

Both the dashed line in Figure 20-12(a) and the curve in Figure 20-12(b) show that a change in the risk of the market portfolio is likely to be accompanied by a more-than-proportionate change in its expected excess return.

Market Timing

Passive portfolio managers estimate the consensus opinion of market risk and return and accept it as correct. Market timers also estimate the consensus opinion but reserve the right to consider it incorrect.

---

[1] And generally changing risk per dollar of price as well.

When selecting a mix of Treasury bills and the market portfolio, a market timer would use his or her own opinion and thus might choose a different combination than would be recommended to the same client by a passive manager.

This is illustrated in Figure 20-13. Point M plots the consensus opinion concerning the market's prospects and point M^* the manager's opinion. Given the latter, the optimal mix with Treasury bills for the client in question is that which plots at point P^* (in this case, a 50-50 combination of the two ingredients).

If the manager is correct, all is well. But what if the consensus opinion is right? Then the appropriate mixture is that shown by point P (here, one with 30% stocks and 70% Treasury bills). The manager has made two mistakes. First, the mixture is inappropriate. Second, both the client and the manager are misinformed about the true prospects—here, they believe that the selected mix plots at point P^* when in fact it plots at point P'. This error might cause the client to make incorrect decisions in other domains (e.g., business, marriage). Of course, errors of the same type can arise when a passive manager misestimates the consensus opinion of the market, but they are likely to be less severe.

A market timer will generally alter the mix of risky and riskless securities when his or her opinion about market prospects changes, even if there is no change in the consensus opinion or the client's attitude toward risk and return. The amount of the change will depend on the client's preferences, but the fact that such changes may occur

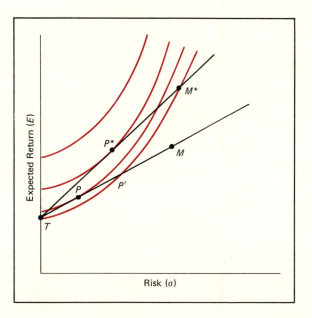

FIGURE 20-13
Market Timing

frequently and be large makes market timing an *active* management style.

CHOOSING A STOCK/BOND MIX

Pure market timing involves a choice between two assets—one risky, the other riskless. *Asset allocation* involves a choice among two or more asset classes, most or all of which are risky. In practice, emphasis is often placed on the selection of an appropriate mix of stocks and risky bonds.

When a choice is to be made between two investments, simple formulas may be used. When three or more investments are available, more complex procedures (quadratic programming) should be employed.

To allocate assets between stocks and bonds, one needs values for:

E_s = the expected return on stocks
E_b = the expected return on bonds
S_s = the standard deviation of return on stocks
S_b = the standard deviation of return on bonds
ρ_{bs} = the correlation of returns of bonds and stocks

The appropriate mix is given by:

$$X_s = \frac{V_b - C_{bs}}{V_b - 2C_{bs} + V_s} + \frac{E_s - E_b}{2(V_b - 2C_{bs} + V_s)} T_c \qquad \textbf{(20-3)}$$

where:

X_s = The optimal proportion invested in stocks
V_s = The variance of return on stocks $(= S_s^2)$
V_b = the variance of return on bonds $(= S_b^2)$
C_{bs} = the covariance of returns of bonds and stocks $(= \rho_{bs} S_b S_s)$

Figure 20-14 plots this relationship, with investor risk tolerance on the horizontal axis and the proportion that should be invested in stocks on the vertical axis. In this example, historic values from 1926 through 1983 are taken as predictions of future expected returns, risks, and correlation.

Note that the relationship between risk tolerance and the appropriate stock/bond mix is *linear*. Of course, the *location* of the line depends on predicted expected returns, risks, and correlation. As shown in Chapter 12 (Figure 12-12), corresponding historic values have varied considerably. It is thus important that all relevant information be used to obtain the best possible estimates of *future* values.

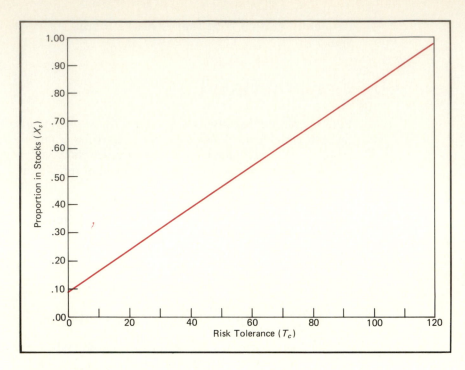

FIGURE 20-14
Risk Tolerance and Stock/Bond Mix

Equation (20-3) shows that, given risk tolerance, there is a linear relationship between the appropriate proportion invested in stocks and the *spread* between the expected return on stocks and that on bonds. Figure 20-15 shows this relationship, using 1926-1983 values for predictions of risks and correlation, for investors with different levels of risk tolerance.

Estimating Expected Returns

It is important to make the best possible predictions of stock and bond expected returns. Many investment managers use yield-to-maturities of representative bonds or sets of bonds as a surrogate for expected return. The expected return on stocks is estimated using either a *bottom-up* or a *top-down* approach.

A number of organizations forecast earnings and dividends on a stock-by-stock basis, then utilize a *dividend discount model* to compute an internal rate of return for each security, based on current price. Such values can be aggregated to obtain a bottom-up forecast for the expected return on a portfolio of stocks.

Others predict the expected return on a diversified portfolio of

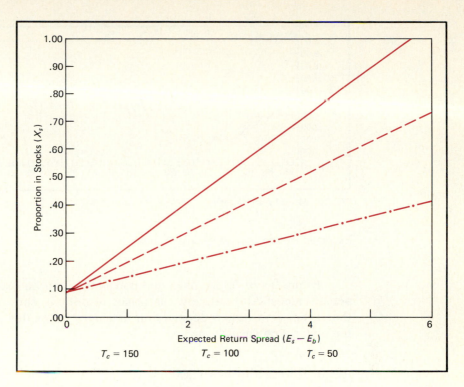

FIGURE 20-15
Expected Return Spread and Stock/Bond Mix

stocks directly. Past dividends and earnings for stock indices, levels of macroeconomic variables such as gross national product and corporate profits, are analyzed. Projections of such aggregate values provide the basis for a *top-down* estimate of the expected return on "the stock market."

The difference between the expected return on stocks and that on bonds is often called the *risk premium*. Figure 20-16 shows a set of projections made by one brokerage firm. Values for periods prior to December 1980 were made using a top-down approach; subsequent values are based on a bottom-up analysis.

Estimating Risks and Correlation

In Figure 20-16 the spread between expected returns on bonds and stocks varies substantially. There is no reason to believe that predicted risks and correlations do not change also. The substantial variability in the *actual* standard deviations and the correlation between bond and stock returns may also reflect changes in *predicted* values.

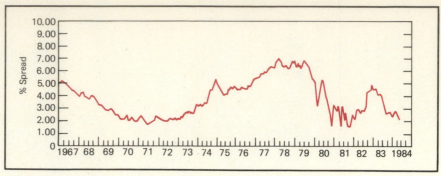

SOURCE: Merrill Lynch, *Quantitative Analysis*, May/June 1984.

FIGURE 20-16
Expected Return Spread: Stocks-Bonds

Estimates of future risks and correlation can be based on recent actual values. Alternatively, the prices of *options* can be used, since the value of an option depends on investors' estimates of the risk of the underlying security.

Asset Allocation in Practice

Some investment organizations that estimate risks and correlation change such predictions infrequently. Given a set of such predictions, for every change in the "risk premium" (expected return spread), there should be a corresponding change in the stock/bond mix, as shown in Figure 20-16.

Other organizations use procedures that "map" expected return spreads to appropriate stock/bond mixes directly. When the spread is "normal," a "normal" mix is adopted. Any departure from the normal spread is multiplied by a specified value to determine an appropriate departure of the mix from its normal level. Figure 20-17 provides an example.

SECURITY SELECTION

Many investment managers concentrate on *security selection*. The consensus opinion of prospects for the market as a whole may be accepted as correct, but the prices of individual securities are questioned. On average, security prices are assumed to equal intrinsic values, but the selector believes that he or she can identify at least a few securities that are overpriced and others that are underpriced. Typically the manager estimates the expected return of an overpriced security to be

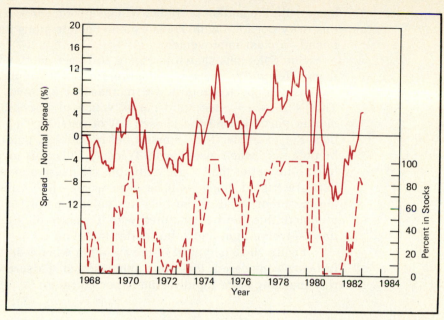

SOURCE: Steven G. Einhorn and Patricia Shaugnasy, "Using the Dividend Discount Model for Asset Allocation," *Financial Analysis Journal,* May/June 1984.

FIGURE 20-17
Abnormal Expected Return Spread and Stock/Bond Mix

less than the consensus estimate and the expected return of an under-priced security to be more than the consensus estimate. In some cases risk estimates that differ from consensus values are also employed. The net result is a decision to hold overpriced securities in less-than-normal (tailored passive portfolio) proportions and to hold underpriced securities in more-than-normal (tailored passive portfolio) proportions.

To focus on key issues, we will again assume that borrowing and lending are available without limit at a single rate of interest. In such a setting, differences in investors' risk tolerances are best accommodated by combining a single portfolio of risky securities with riskless borrowing or lending. Given consensus predictions of expected returns, risks, and correlations, the optimal combination of risky securities will, of course, be the market portfolio.

The security selector adds bets to the market portfolio, adding risk as holdings are moved away from market proportions. If, on net, the bets are good, expected return will also increase.

Figure 20-18 illustrates this. As before, points M and T indicate the prospects of the market portfolio and Treasury bills, respectively. Passive strategies can be used to obtain any point on line 1. In this case, however, the manager has selected a set of bets that, when combined with the market portfolio, will give point $(M + B)$. By combining this risky portfolio with Treasury bills, points along line 2 can be obtained—a clear improvement.

Since the bets shown in Figure 20-18 are good, why not increase them? This will increase expected return, but it will also increase risk. Moreover, expected return will increase at a slower rate than risk. This is shown by the solid curve, which plots combinations of the market portfolio and the chosen set of bets, varying the size of the bets. For example, if the amount bet is doubled, point $(M + 2B)$ will be obtained: when mixed with Treasury bills, this gives points along line 1—no better than those available via passive management. If the bets are tripled, things will be even worse—line 4 lies below line 1. On the other hand, if the bets are halved, point $(M + .5B)$ will be obtained; this can be combined with Treasury bills to give points on line 3—worse than line 2, but better than line 1.

Figure 20-18 is typical of the situation when a series of good bets is being considered: the curve increases at a decreasing rate, with risk changing more rapidly than expected return.[2]

FIGURE 20-18
Security Selection: Optimal Use of Good Bets

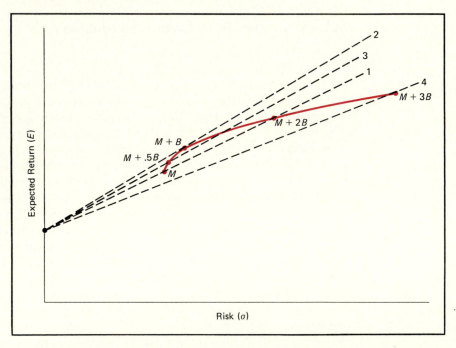

[2] This is generally the case when risky assets (such as M and B) with less-than-perfectly positively correlated returns are combined. For details, see W. F. Sharpe, *Portfolio Theory and Capital Markets* (New York: McGraw-Hill Book Company, 1970).

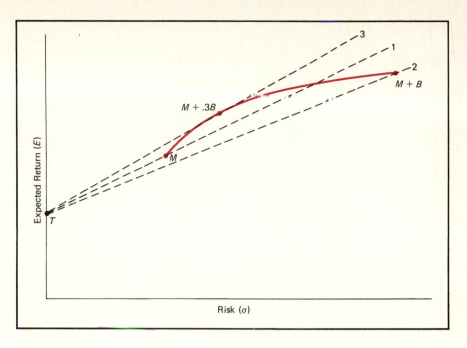

FIGURE 20-19
Security Selection: Suboptimal Use of Good Bets

In the case shown in Figure 20-18 the manager has chosen the right amount to bet. This can be seen graphically—point $(M + B)$ lies on the ray from point T tangent to the curve. If either less or more is bet, a poorer set of combinations will be obtained when the risky portfolio is mixed with Treasury bills.

Figure 20-19 shows a very different situation. Here the manager has selected a good set of bets—properly used, they can improve performance. But excessive zeal has led the manager to bet too much, actually decreasing likely performance. Combinations of Treasury bills and the selected portfolio $(M + B)$ lie on line 2—below line 1, available via passive management. But a portfolio in which bets are reduced to 30% of the amounts selected by the manager will do much better, allowing points along line 3.

This idea can be generalized. The optimal portfolio can be characterized as $(M + wB)$, where w is the proportion of the manager's desired bets that will provide the best risk-return combination. In Figure 20-19 the optimal value of w is .30.

Figure 20-19 shows a situation in which superior security analysis is misused, leading to a portfolio that is actually inferior to an "index fund." However, there is hope: in such a case smaller bets can produce a portfolio superior to the market.

Investment Management

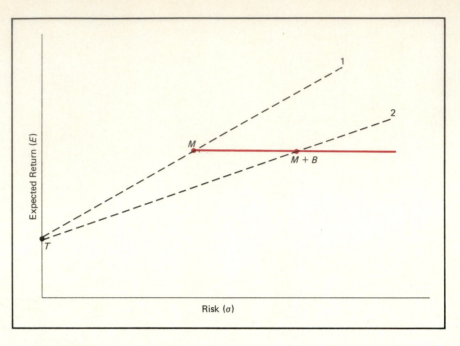

FIGURE 20-20
Security Selection: Average Bets

Figure 20-20 shows a more gloomy situation. Here the bets are neither good nor bad. Security analysis is average. The recommended bets add risk but do not change expected return. The curve of the previous figure becomes a horizontal line, and potential performance is lowered (from line 1 to line 2) if the manager's choice of bets is adopted. The situation will not be as bad if the bets are reduced. But the best value of w is zero!

Security selectors are generally very active portfolio managers, for they will consider a change in holdings whenever they believe that the relative amounts by which different securities are mispriced have changed.

Reports comparing proportionate holdings of various securities in a portfolio with the proportions in an alternative passive portfolio are prepared by many investment management organizations. In some reports, holdings in the two portfolios are compared on a security-by-security basis. In others, proportionate holdings of securities within each economic sector are compared. Yet others focus on the total amounts invested in different sectors.

The goal of any such analysis is to show how the organization has placed its "active bets" relative to an appropriate passive port-folio.

ADJUSTING PREDICTIONS

Many organizations use security analysis to estimate expected returns, leaving the estimation of risks and correlations to computer departments instructed to assume that the future will be more or less like the past. Such estimates of risk may be wrong, but they are as likely to err in one direction as another.

This may not be the case for estimates of expected returns. An analyst may be (1) optimistic or pessimistic and (2) likely to exaggerate or understate. An entire organization may have similar characteristics. The appropriate value to use for a security is not necessarily the estimated value of its expected return but rather the expected return when such an estimate is given.

Typically the focus is on the *difference* between an organization's estimate of expected return and the consensus (efficient market) estimate. This difference, which may be estimated in a number of ways (e.g., by deviations from a security market line, plane, or hyperplane) can be considered a (predicted) *alpha*. To obtain an unbiased estimate of expected return one needs to add to the consensus (equilibrium) value the *best estimate* of alpha when this sort of prediction is made. Historic data may be used to determine the average ex post, alpha obtained when a similar value of alpha was predicted.

The idea can be extended. Given one or more types of prediction (e.g., unanticipated earnings changes, security codings), ex post alphas can be examined to find the typical relationship between predictions and outcomes. This relationship can then be used with current predictions to estimate (expected) alphas, which can then be added to consensus expected returns to obtain the best estimates of overall expected return.

The principle applies as well to estimates used for market timing and choice of stock/bond mixes. The appropriate values for the expected returns and risks of broad asset classes are those which summarize the likely distribution of such returns, given the current prediction. For example, assume that an organization simply predicts each year's market as being "bullish" or "bearish." To know how to act, given such a prediction, one would like a century or two of data on such predictions, made by the same people, using the same procedures. If this information were available, all the market returns in years predicted to be bullish could be analyzed and a mean and standard deviation obtained. These values could be used to estimate market prospects when the organization feels bullish. Similarly, the mean and standard deviation of market returns in years previously predicted to be bearish could be used when the organization feels bearish.

It may be possible to obtain a detailed record for calibrating security analysts, since predictions for many securities can be made at one time. But a comparable record for market analysis is out of the question, since there is only one market to predict.

Without a definitive record of predictive accuracy, it behooves any analyst to be humble about his or her ability to detect errors in the consensus opinion regarding either the market as a whole, groups of securities, or specific securities. Overestimation of predictive ability leads to less-than-optimal performance and can lead to performance that is worse than that obtained via passive strategies. Underestimation also leads to less-than-optimal (but better than passive) performance. If predictors lack adequate humility, their enthusiasm can be tempered by directives from above reducing the size of the bets on individual securities and/or the amount of turnover allowed for the portfolio.

TRANSACTIONS COSTS

Thus far the unpleasant subject of *transactions costs* has been avoided. At any time the best available price at which someone will buy a security (the *bid* price) is likely to be less than the best available price at which it can be purchased (the *asked* price). Moreover, any agents involved in the transaction (brokers, and so on) will require compensation (commissions), and there may be taxes to pay as well.

As indicated in Chapter 2, the difference between sale proceeds and purchase cost may exceed 1% for many securities and can range as high as 5% to 10%.

The existence of transactions costs greatly complicates the life of any investment manager, and the more active the manager, the greater the complications. The hoped-for advantage of any move must be weighed against the cost of making it. Moreover, it is difficult to know how much of the cost to consider. Any move away from a long-term norm (for risky versus riskless assets, the relative proportions of risky asset classes or holdings of individual securities) is likely to be temporary and should be charged the cost of both getting there and getting back. In general, the desirability of the move will depend on the length of time the position is likely to be maintained as well as the advantage it is expected to give per unit of time while maintained.

PORTFOLIO REVISION

Figure 20-2(b) summarized the key ingredients required for rational portfolio revision decisions. Simply put:

The goal is to improve the utility of the portfolio for the client, net of an appropriate portion of the required transactions costs.

Sophisticated procedures (quadratic programming) and computer processing are required if this is to be accomplished efficiently. However, improvements in procedures and dramatic decreases in the cost of computers have made such approaches economically feasible for many investment managers. *Asset allocation programs* capable of analyzing dozens of asset classes within a minute on an inexpensive micro computer are widely available within the professional investment community.

The "bottom-line" number to be maximized is *utility net of transactions costs*:

$$NU_{pc} = E_p - \frac{V_p}{T_c} - C_p \qquad \text{(20-4)}$$

where:

E_p = the expected return of the portfolio

V_p = the variance of return of the portfolio

C_p = the appropriate portion of the transactions costs incurred in the revision of the portfolio

T_c = the client's risk tolerance

NU_{pc} = the *net utility* of the portfolio for the client

Key to the approach is the concept of *marginal net utility*:

The marginal net utility of asset i (MNU_{ip}) is the change in the net utility of portfolio p per unit change in the holding of asset i if a small amount of asset i is purchased or sold.

For example, assume a $1,000 portfolio has a net utility of 10%. If $1 worth of security i with a marginal net utility of 8.0% is sold and the proceeds used to buy $1 worth of security j with a marginal net utility of 12.0%, the resulting portfolio's net utility will be greater:

$$
\begin{aligned}
\$1,000 \times 10.0\% &= 10,000 \\
-\$1 \times 8.0\% &= \quad -8 \\
+\$1 \times 12.0\% &= \underline{\quad +12} \\
&\quad\; 10,004
\end{aligned}
$$

$$NU_{pc} = \frac{10,004}{\$1,000} = 10.004\%$$

In general:

If one security has a higher marginal net utility than another, a *swap* in which the former is purchased and the latter sold can increase the portfolio's net utility.

Figure 20-21 shows the typical relationship between the improvement and the *size* of the swap. If feasible, S' dollars worth of the

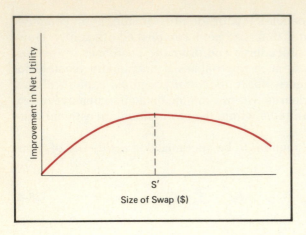

Improvement in Net Utility

S'

Size of Swap ($)

FIGURE 20-21
Portfolio Improvement versus Swap Size

two securities should be swapped. If not (e.g., if this would require a disallowed short sale of the security being sold), the largest feasible swap should be made.

It is a relatively simple matter to compute the marginal net utility of every security in a portfolio.[3] Having done this, we can find the best swap and calculate the optimal swap size. This will give a revised portfolio. Then the marginal net utilities can be recalculated and the procedure repeated. It is easy to know when to stop:

> The optimal set of revisions has been found when the largest marginal net utility of the securities that can be purchased is not greater than the smallest marginal net utility of the securities that can be sold.

---

[3] Formally, marginal net utility is the derivative of NU_{pc} with respect to X_i:

$$MNU_{ip} = \frac{\delta NU_{pc}}{\delta X_i}$$

where:

X_i = the proportion of portfolio p invested in security i

From (20-4):

$$MNU_{ip} = \frac{\delta E_p}{\delta X_i} - \frac{1}{T_c} \frac{\delta V_p}{\delta X_i} - \frac{\delta C_p}{\delta X_i}$$

$$= E_i - \frac{1}{T_c} \frac{\delta V_p}{\delta X_i} - C_i$$

where:

C_i = the change in the appropriate amount of transactions cost associated with a change in X_i:

The definition of variance implies that:

$$\frac{\delta V_p}{\delta X_i} = 2C_{ip}$$

where:

C_{ip} = the covariance of security i's return with that of portfolio p

$$C_{ip} = \sum_j X_j C_{ij}$$

Thus:

$$MNU_{ip} = E_i - \frac{2}{T_c} \sum_j X_j C_{ij} - C_i$$

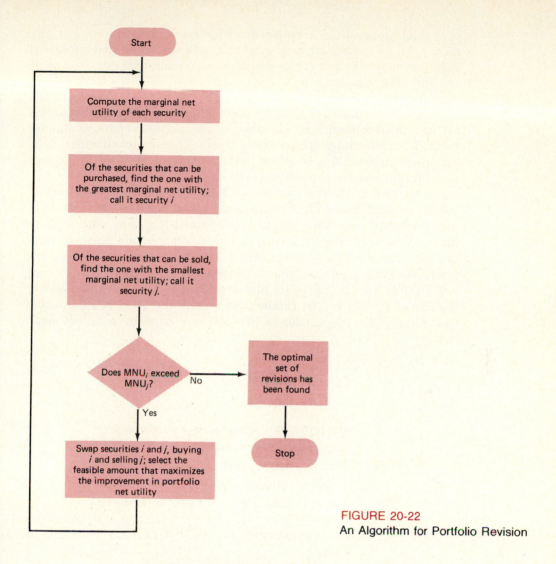

FIGURE 20-22
An Algorithm for Portfolio Revision

Figure 20-22 provides a flow diagram of the *algorithm* (procedure). Other features are often added. *Upper and lower bounds* on holdings may be specified. Desired levels of *portfolio attributes* may be taken into account, by specifying *targets* and *penalties* for divergences from the targets. And so on.

PROCEDURES FOR SECURITY SELECTION

Portfolio revision algorithms are particularly suitable for asset allocation. Explicit estimates of all covariances are used, and computer costs are small.

Such approaches are also used for security selection. For efficiency, *factor models* are employed and covariances treated implicitly. Solutions may take five minutes or more on a microcomputer, but costs are still very low.

As indicated earlier, many investment managers use formal portfolio revision procedures only for asset allocation (if at all). Securities are combined to form asset classes or group portfolios using a simpler method. Such methods are generally *myopic* (i.e., do not consider interactions with securities in other asset classes or groups). They may also be significantly *suboptimal*.

One method proceeds as follows. First, an *alpha value* and *nonfactor risk* are estimated for each security in a group. The nonfactor risk may be based on a very simple factor model (e.g., one with a stock index as the only relevant factor) or a very complex one. Next, optimal *passive proportions* are determined (often, relative market values are used). The bet placed on a security (divergence from passive proportion) will be related directly to its alpha value. For a given alpha value, the size of the bet will be smaller, the greater the security's nonfactor risk. Finally, the magnitudes of the bets will depend on a "bet size" factor:

$$X_{ig} = X_{ig}^p + k_{bs} \left[\frac{\alpha_i}{NFR_i} - \text{Avg}\left(\frac{\alpha_i}{NFR_i} \right) \right] \qquad \textbf{(20-5)}$$

where:

X_{ig} = the proportion of security i in group g

X_{ig}^p = the passive proportion of security i in group g

k_{bs} = the "bet-size" factor

α_i = security i's alpha value

NFR_i = the *variance* of security i's nonfactor risk

$\text{Avg}\left(\dfrac{\alpha_i}{NFR_i} \right)$ = the average value of (α_i / NFR_i) for the securities in group g

The greater the confidence in the deviant beliefs, the greater should be k_{bs}. And the greater k_{bs}, the greater will be the bets.

MANAGER-CLIENT RELATIONS

The larger the amount of money managed, the more communication there is likely to be between investment manager and client. Not surprisingly, corporate, union, and government officials responsible for pension funds spend a great deal of time with those who manage their money. Such officials also concern themselves with a number of prior questions: who should manage the money, how should it be managed, and how should the managers be instructed and constrained?

Many of the aspects of manager-client relations can be characterized as responses to a difference of opinion concerning a manager's abilities to make good bets.

For example, assume that a client thinks that a manager is betting too much. In the terms used earlier, the manager is choosing a portfolio of $(M + B)$, while the client prefers to have, say, $(M + .5B)$. One way to accomplish this is to invest half the funds in a passive (or latter doesn't compensate for the change, the total portfolio will be invested in $(M + .5B)$.

A related situation occurs when a client is considering two managers who appear to have good ideas but exaggerated opinions concerning their abilities. The first manager invests funds in $(M + B_1)$; the second in $(M + B_2)$. By splitting the fund between the two, one can obtain $(M + .5B_1 + .5B_2)$—as long as the managers don't compensate for the change by increasing their bets.

This type of *split-funding* is used by most pension funds. Two reasons are given. First, it allows the employment of managers with different skills and/or different styles. Second, the impact of erroneous bets can be reduced by diversifying across different bettors. As more investment managers are used, the overall portfolio is likely to appear more like the market portfolio.

Split-funding reduces the money placed with one bettor, lowering both the risk and the possible return associated with betting. It is also likely to increase transactions and investment management costs. Moreover, substantial coordination is required to insure overall risk control, and so on.

Extensive use of split-funding can give results similar to those obtained with an explicit passive fund, but at considerably greater cost, owing to the expenses associated with transactions and management fees.

Whether or not split-funding is used, a client who feels that a manager is betting too much would, if possible, like to simply reduce the size of the bets. For example, one might ask a manager to diverge only half as much as he or she normally would from passive proportions of individual securities, to change the bond/stock mix only half the normal amount, etc. But since there is no simple way to determine the normal response, compliance is difficult to monitor. Instead, a relatively inefficient approach is employed: limits are placed on changes in the bond/stock mix, the holdings in any single security, the proportion invested in any single industry, the estimated degree of diversification of the portfolio, and so on.

Institutional investors (pension funds, endowment funds, etc.) typically use more than one investment manager and provide each with a set of *objectives* (*target* or *normal* positions) and a set of *constraints* on allowed divergences from such normal positions. Individual investors who employ investment managers tend to give such instructions implicitly, if at all. This may reflect less sophistication, a less formal relationship with the manager, or the fact that the management fee for a small account is not large enough to cover the cost of dealing with a series of objectives and constraints.

Problems

1. In a world with no transactions costs what could you say about the marginal net utilities of all the securities in an optimal portfolio, if no legal or practical upper or lower limit were imposed on any holding?

2. A mutual fund manager is assessing the fund's portfolio. He estimates transactions costs to be 1% for a "round trip"—i.e., the purchase of one security and the sale of another. Legal restrictions require that no more than 5% of the portfolio be invested in any one security; short sales also are precluded by law. The current holdings and marginal utilities (i.e., *before* transactions costs) of five securities are:

	Percent Invested	Marginal Utility
GM	5.0	12.3%
ATT	3.0	9.1
HON	2.1	9.5
IBM	4.0	9.8
XRX	0	5.2

Can you find a swap using these five stocks that would improve the portfolio? Why or why not?

3. Should an "overpriced" stock definitely be excluded from one's portfolio? Why or why not?

4. "When it comes right down to it, portfolio analysis involves only risk, expected return, client characteristics, and transactions costs." How does the notion of *market efficiency* fit into this scheme?

5. An investment advisory firm has estimated the prospects for bonds and stocks as follows:

Expected returns:
  Bonds   10%
  Stocks   18%
Standard deviations:
  Bonds   5%
  Stocks   22%
Correlation coefficient, bonds and stocks: .5

Using these estimates, the firm has run a number of simulations, tracing out the implications of different bond/stock mixes for a client's future financial situation. After much thought the client has indicated that of the mixes considered, she would prefer a combination with 60% invested in stocks and 40% in bonds. What can you say about her risk tolerance? [Hint for those who do not or cannot use calculus: Write an equation for the utility of a 60/40 mix, using T_c as the client's risk tolerance. Then do the same for a 61/39 mix. Finally, find the value of T_c that makes the two amounts the same.] Why is this an adequate measure of her risk tolerance? Over what range are these values likely to represent her feelings?

7. The shorter the period during which a security is likely to be held, the shorter should be the period over which the transactions costs associated with its purchase should be amortized. Yet if a high proportion of transactions costs are "charged" for portfolio revision, the amount turned over will tend to be small. And the smaller the turnover, the longer the period over which the typical stock will be held. How might one achieve a consistent approach toward the amortization of transactions costs?

8. What problems are involved in helping an individual investor select a "normal" bond/stock mix? What about the officers in charge of a corporation's pension fund? What should be the objective of such officers? If the corporation will definitely meet the required pension payments, aside from possible tax effects does the investment strategy of the fund matter? If so, for whom does it matter?

9. Is it possible for more than half the managers of institutional portfolios to "beat" Standard and Poor's 500-stock index in a given year? If so, does this contradict the assertion that the "average dollar invested" cannot "beat the market?" Why or why not?

10. If there were no transactions costs, would the average dollar under active management provide inferior performance to the average dollar passively managed over one month? What about the prospects (in terms of expected return and risk) of these two approaches over the next twelve months? Explain.

21

Performance Measurement and Attribution

INTRODUCTION

In one sense the measurement of investment performance is the last stage of the investment management process; in another sense it is simply part of a continuing operation.

An investor who pays someone to actively manage a portfolio, in the hope of achieving superior performance, has every right to insist on knowing what sort of performance is actually obtained. Such information can be used to alter the constraints placed on a manager, the objectives stated for the account, or the amount of money allocated to the manager. Perhaps more important: by measuring performance in specified ways, a client can forcefully communicate his or her interests to an investment manager and, in all likelihood, affect the way in which a portfolio is managed. Moreover, an investment manager, by measuring and diagnosing his or her own performance, can help isolate sources of strength or weakness.

Unfortunately, it is very difficult to separate performance due to skill from that due to luck. In this context, as in any other, a change should be made only when there is adequate reason to expect the advantages to outweigh the costs. Switching from one manager to another on the basis of minor differences in short-term performance will certainly incur transactions costs (as the new manager replaces old holdings with new ones that conform to his or her "style"), but there may or may not be any improvement in future performance. Differences in managers' past performance should be treated as interesting data, suggesting areas for more detailed examination and discussion. But drastic changes in management based solely on recent history should usually be avoided.

Superior past performance may well have been due to good luck;

if so, it should not be expected to continue in the future. Inferior past performance may have been due to bad luck, but it may also have resulted from excessive turnover, management fees, or other costs. If so, more detailed diagnostic performance measurement may identify areas in which changes can improve performance. Only if a manager is reluctant to make such changes may it make sense to take one's money elsewhere.

Many investment management organizations measure the performance of individual employees and departments for internal purposes. The effectiveness of a trading department may be measured by comparing the prices at which securities are bought and sold with the highest and lowest prices recorded during the day. The usefulness of security analysts' codings may be measured by computing the performance of recommended securities relative to the performance of similar securities and comparing the average results for securities coded "1" with the results for those coded "2," and so on. An investment committee's effectiveness may be measured by comparing the performance of a portfolio composed of all stocks on the approved list with one composed of all stocks recommended by security analysts but rejected by the committee. And so on.

The most widely publicized type of measurement is that used for external reporting to clients. Such *bottom-line* measurement is concerned primarily with the results obtained by the organization as a whole, with little concern for the manner in which the results were produced. Some investment managers routinely measure their own performance in this way; some sophisticated investors (e.g., corporate pension fund officials) measure their fund's performance; and a number of third parties provide measurement services for both investors and investment managers.

MAKING RELEVANT COMPARISONS

The essential idea behind performance measurement is to compare the returns obtained through active management with those of one or more appropriate alternatives. In some cases the focus is on the returns from "similar" actively managed funds; in others, "similar" naive or passive strategies are considered.

With either approach it is important to choose relevant alternatives. *Benchmark portfolios* should be *feasible* and should represent alternatives that might have been employed if the portfolio being measured had not been held. Moreover, dimensions of performance relevant for the decision being considered should be chosen. *Return* is a key aspect of performance, of course, but some way must be found to account for differences in funds' exposures to *risk*. A single measure that takes both elements into account may be employed. Alternatively, the comparison may be restricted to funds with similar exposure to risk, and their returns compared directly.

It is important to analyze risk appropriately. The impact of a portfolio on the investor's overall risk is relevant. If the ultimate beneficiary of a fund has many other assets, and if the other assets are invested in "the market," the *market risk* of the fund provides a good estimate of its impact on overall risk. If, however, the fund provides its beneficiaries' sole support, its *total risk* is relevant.

Risk-adjusted performance measurement is generally based on one of these two extremes: taking either market risk or total risk into account.

MEASURES OF RETURN

Most performance measurement covers a period of at least five years, broken into a number of subperiods—usually calendar quarters. This provides a fairly adequate sample size for statistical evaluation while avoiding the examination of ancient history.

FIGURE 21-1
Comparing Equity Rates of Return

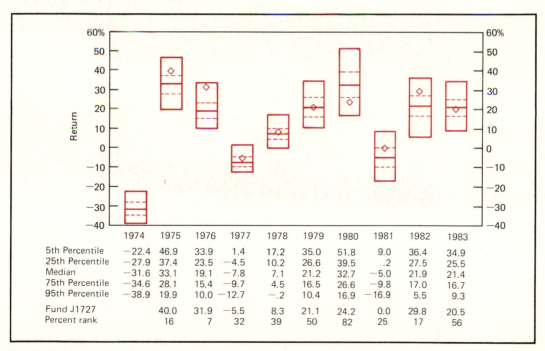

	1974	1975	1976	1977	1978	1979	1980	1981	1982	1983
5th Percentile	−22.4	46.9	33.9	1.4	17.2	35.0	51.8	9.0	36.4	34.9
25th Percentile	−27.9	37.4	23.5	−4.5	10.2	26.6	39.5	.2	27.5	25.5
Median	−31.6	33.1	19.1	−7.8	7.1	21.2	32.7	−5.0	21.9	21.4
75th Percentile	−34.6	28.1	15.4	−9.7	4.5	16.5	26.6	−9.8	17.0	16.7
95th Percentile	−38.9	19.9	10.0	−12.7	−.2	10.4	16.9	−16.9	5.5	9.3
Fund J1727		40.0	31.9	−5.5	8.3	21.1	24.2	0.0	29.8	20.5
Percent rank		16	7	32	39	50	82	25	17	56

SOURCE: SEI, *Funds Evaluation Service*.

Performance Measurement and Attribution

Two measures of return are utilized in such analyses: total return and excess return (the fund's return during a quarter minus the return on, e.g., a 90-day Treasury bill over the same period). Such figures may be averaged or cumulated to obtain annual or five-year measures of return.

Often a fund receives or distributes cash one or more times during a quarter. If possible, calculations are made as if unit (net asset) values had been determined each time a cash flow occurred, with units (shares) purchased or sold as needed at the time. The return on one unit for the quarter can then be calculated directly. This is often termed the fund's *time-weighted return*; it measures the manager's performance, without extraneous influences due to the timing of cash flows not under his or her control.

If the data needed to compute a time-weighted return (the market values of the fund prior to every cash flow) are not available, an internal rate of return (sometimes termed a *dollar-weighted return*) may be used to compute the return for a quarter.

Figure 21-1 shows a comparison between an equity fund's return each year and the returns of a group of managed equity funds.

FIGURE 21-2
Comparing Equity Funds' Variabilities

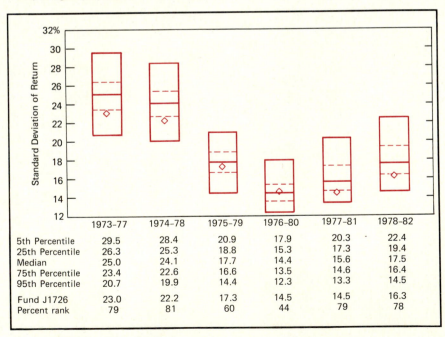

	1973–77	1974–78	1975–79	1976–80	1977–81	1978–82
5th Percentile	29.5	28.4	20.9	17.9	20.3	22.4
25th Percentile	26.3	25.3	18.8	15.3	17.3	19.4
Median	25.0	24.1	17.7	14.4	15.6	17.5
75th Percentile	23.4	22.6	16.6	13.5	14.6	16.4
95th Percentile	20.7	19.9	14.4	12.3	13.3	14.5
Fund J1726	23.0	22.2	17.3	14.5	14.5	16.3
Percent rank	79	81	60	44	79	78

SOURCE: SEI, *Funds Evaluation Service*.

684   Performance Measurement and Attribution

MEASURES OF RISK

Two measures of ex post performance are typically used as surrogates for ex ante risk.

The standard deviation of quarterly returns (or excess returns) can serve as an estimate of a fund's average total risk over the period covered.

Figure 21-2 compares the standard deviation of return for the equity portion of a fund with similar values for the equity portfolios of a group of funds.

The returns or excess returns of a fund may also be regressed on those of a market measure, such as Standard and Poor's 500-stock index, to determine the fund's *historic beta* level during the period covered. Alternatively, the historic beta of each security may be determined and a weighted average based on current market values used as an estimate of the fund's beta. Figure 21-3 compares such estimates for the equity portion of a fund with those of the equity portions of a sample of funds of similar size.

FIGURE 21-3
Comparing Equity Funds' Beta Values

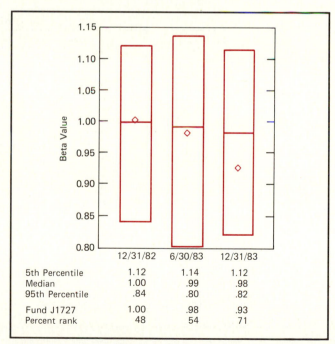

	12/31/82	6/30/83	12/31/83
5th Percentile	1.12	1.14	1.12
Median	1.00	.99	.98
95th Percentile	.84	.80	.82
Fund J1727	1.00	.98	.93
Percent rank	48	54	71

SOURCE: SEI, *Funds Evaluation Service*.

EX POST CHARACTERISTIC LINES

Figure 21-4 shows an ex post characteristic line fitted with standard linear regression techniques using the excess returns from an equity portfolio and a stock market index over 20 quarters. Three measures of performance are reported.

Market sensitivity is the fund's average beta level over the period. In this case the fund's equities were aggressive—the average beta value was 1.16.

The *alpha value* is the vertical intercept—i.e., the ex post value of alpha. The value was positive—approximately 0.4% per quarter or

FIGURE 21-4
An Ex Post Characteristic Line

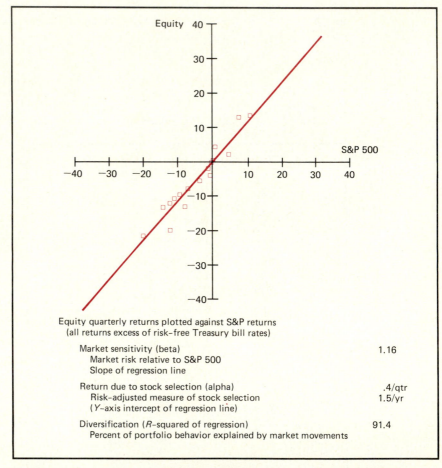

Equity quarterly returns plotted against S&P returns
(all returns excess of risk-free Treasury bill rates)

Market sensitivity (beta)	1.16
Market risk relative to S&P 500	
Slope of regression line	
Return due to stock selection (alpha)	.4/qtr
Risk-adjusted measure of stock selection	1.5/yr
(*Y*-axis intercept of regression line)	
Diversification (*R*-squared of regression)	91.4
Percent of portfolio behavior explained by market movements	

SOURCE: Merrill Lynch, Pierce, Fenner and Smith, Inc., Investment Performance Analysis.

Performance Measurement and Attribution

1.5% per year (the latter is not exactly four times the former, owing to rounding).

The third measure is 100 times the value of *R-squared*. In this case, 91.4% of the variance in the fund's excess returns could be attributed to variation in the excess returns on Standard and Poor's 500-stock index.

DIFFERENTIAL RETURNS

It is relatively simple to compare a fund's returns, quarter by quarter, with those of a relevant benchmark portfolio (e.g., a passive portfolio with similar risk exposure). Figure 21-5 shows an example. First, the fund's average beta value was detemined from an ex post characteristic line (the one shown in Figure 21-4). Then the fund's total return in each period was compared with that of a fund invested only in Standard and Poor's 500-stock index and Treasury bills, with proportions of the

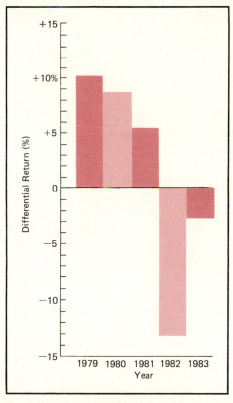

SOURCE: Merrill Lynch, Pierce, Fenner and Smith, Inc., *Investment Performance Analysis*.

FIGURE 21-5
Differential Returns

two chosen to provide a constant beta value equal to the average value obtained by the fund.

Differential returns are generally computed by comparing a fund's returns with those of a benchmark portfolio of similar risk. The usual procedure, illustrated in Figure 21-5, is based on market risk. But if desired, a mix with the same *total* risk can be employed.

EX POST ALPHA VALUES

When comparison with an equal-beta portfolio of Treasury bills and a stock index is employed, the average differential return equals the fund's *ex post alpha value*—i.e., the vertical intercept obtained when an ex post characteristic line is fit using excess returns. Thus a fund's ex post alpha value can be interpreted as the average difference between its return and that of a passive strategy of equal (and constant) market risk.

If an equal-total-risk combination of (1) Treasury bills and (2) a security index is used as a comparison portfolio, a different average differential return will be obtained. This measure (an *ex post total-risk alpha*) indicates the average difference between a fund's return and that of a passive strategy of equal (and constant) total risk.

THE REWARD-TO-VARIABILITY RATIO

An alternative "bottom line" measure of performance indicates the *reward* (mean excess return) per unit of *variability* (standard deviation of excess returns). Such a measure, called the *reward-to-variability ratio*,[1] has an obvious intuitive appeal. It can also be justified on more formal grounds.

Figure 21-6 plots the average excess return (vertical axis) and standard deviation of excess return (horizontal axis) for a fund (point *F*), a benchmark portfolio (point *B*), and Treasury bills (point *T*). Line *TB* shows the results that could have been obtained by combining Treasury bills and the benchmark portfolio, while line *TF* shows the results that could have been obtained by combining Treasury bills with investment in fund *F*. In each case, borrowing at the Treasury bill rate is assumed to be feasible.

As shown in Figure 21-6, fund *F* can be said to have outperformed the benchmark, in the sense that for any desired risk exposure an investor could have done better with a combination of Treasury bills and the fund than with a combination of Treasury bills and the bench-

---

[1] And, by some, the Sharpe ratio.

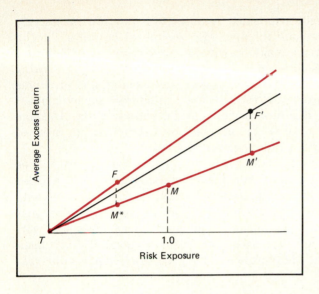

FIGURE 21-6
Reward-to-Variability Ratios

mark. Graphically: line *TF* is steeper than line *TB*. But the slopes of these lines *are* the reward-to-variability ratios. Putting it in reverse: any risky investment's reward-to-variability ratio can be considered the slope of the line showing the results that could have been obtained by combining it with borrowing or lending.

The relationship between a fund's reward-to-variability ratio and its ex post total-risk alpha value is also illustrated in Figure 21-6. Point *B** shows the results that could have been obtained via a passive strategy with the same risk as the fund. The distance *FB** is the difference in the average returns of funds *F* and *B** or, equivalently, the average difference in their returns. But the latter *is* the fund's ex post total-risk alpha value.

Figure 21-6 also shows that alpha values may prove misleading when two funds are compared. The performance of fund *F'* was inferior to that of fund *F*, as the slopes of lines *TF* and *TF'* and the reward-to-variability ratios indicate. But fund *F'* has a larger alpha value (distance *F'B'*) than fund *F* (distance *FB**). Clearly, the alpha values of funds with significantly different exposures to risk may not be directly comparable. This is true for both total-risk and the more common beta-risk alpha values.

RELATIVE AND ABSOLUTE MEASURES

In any comparison it is important to use a relevant alternative. If a comparison portfolio with positive amounts of both Treasury bills and stocks is used, some would argue that the contest has been arranged so that a fund can easily win, since Treasury bills provide excessively low returns to compensate for their high degree of liquidity. On the other hand, a comparison portfolio with negative amounts of Treasury bills assumes that it is possible to lever up stock holdings by borrowing at the Treasury bill rate; some would argue that realistic alternatives in this range of risk are less attractive, and that in this case the contest has been arranged so that it is very difficult for a fund to win. *Absolute* values of differential returns are thus said to discriminate in favor of conservative funds and against aggressive ones.

One way to meet such criticism is to compare the *relative* values of performance measures for funds of similar risk. Figure 21-7 provides both absolute and relative comparisons. Each point represents the beta value of a fund (horizontal axis) and its actual return in one year (vertical axis). Mutual funds, banks commingled equity funds, and market indices are included. The line plots results that could have been obtained by combining Standard and Poor's 500-stock index with Trea-

FIGURE 21-7
Measuring Relative Performance

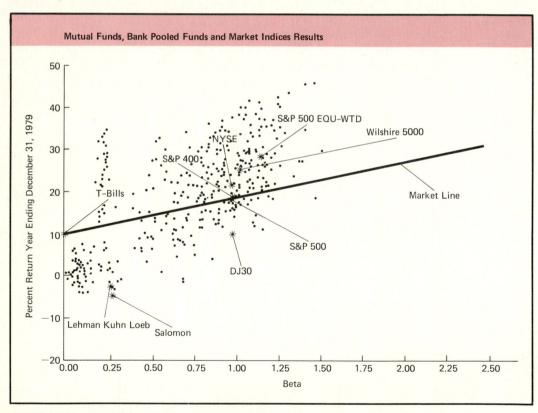

SOURCE: Wilshire Associates.

sury bills. The vertical distance from a fund's point to the line indicates its differential return relative to an equal-beta benchmark combination of Treasury bills and the S&P 500. This may be compared visually with the differential returns for other funds. Alternatively, the line may be ignored, and a fund's return compared directly with the returns of other funds with similar betas (i.e., those plotting above and below its point).

MARKET TIMING

A successful *market timer* positions a portfolio to have a higher beta value prior to market rises and a lower beta value prior to market declines. If the benefits are not outweighed by added costs, overall performance will be superior to that of a benchmark portfolio with a constant beta equal to the average beta of the timer's portfolio.

An unsuccessful market timer alters a portfolio's beta in ways unrelated to subsequent market moves, adding costs but not benefits.

To "time the market," the beta value of the equity portion of the fund can be changed, or the mix of fixed-income and equity investments can be altered.

In Figure 21-8 the excess returns of two hypothetical funds are plotted (on the vertical axes) against those of a market index (on the horizontal axes). Straight lines fit via standard regression methods give

FIGURE 21-8
Superior Fund Performance

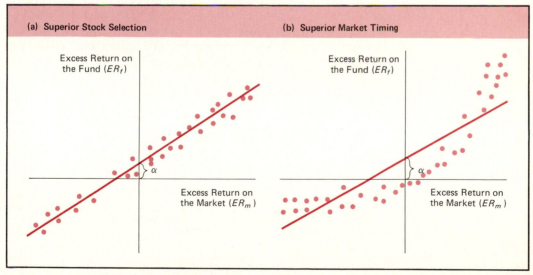

(a) Superior Stock Selection

Excess Return on the Fund (ER_f)

α

Excess Return on the Market (ER_m)

(b) Superior Market Timing

Excess Return on the Fund (ER_f)

α

Excess Return on the Market (ER_m)

positive ex post alpha values in each case. But the causes differ. The fund shown in Figure 21-8(a) held securities with roughly the same beta value at all times but managed to find some that were underpriced. The fund shown in Figure 21-8(b) held securities with high beta values in periods in which the market return was high and securities with low beta values in periods in which the market return was low or negative.

Characteristic Curves

To measure the ability of an investment manager to successfully time the market one can fit something more complex than a straight line in diagrams such as those shown in Figure 21-8.

One procedure fits a *quadratic curve*. Multiple regression analysis is used to estimate the parameters in

$$ER_f = a + b(ER_m) + c(ER_m^2)$$ (21-1)

where:

ER_f = the excess return on the fund

ER_m = the excess return on the market index

ER_m^2 = the excess return on the market index, squared

a, b, c = values to be estimated by regression analysis

The "characteristic curve" shown in Figure 21-9(a) plots such an equation. The value of c is positive, indicating that the curve becomes steeper as one moves to the right—i.e., that the fund successfully timed the market.[2]

An alternative procedure fits two straight lines, as shown in Figure 21-9(b). Periods in which risky securities outperform riskless securities (i.e., the excess return on the market portfolio is positive) can be termed "up markets." Periods in which risky securities underperform riskless securities (i.e., the excess return on the market portfolio is negative) can be termed "down markets." A successful market timer selects a high *up-market beta* and a low *down-market beta*. Graphically: the slope of the characteristic line for positive excess market returns exceeds that of the line for negative excess market returns.

To estimate such a relationship, multiple regression analysis can be used to estimate the parameters in:

$$ER_f = a + bER_m - cZ$$ (21-2)

---

[2] For details of the method, see Jack L. Treynor and Kay Mazuy, "Can Mutual Funds Outguess the Market?," *Harvard Business Review*, 44, No. 4 (July-August 1966), 131-36, Copyright © 1966 by the President and Fellows of Harvard College. All Rights Reserved.

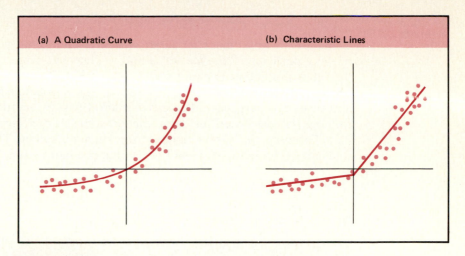

(a) A Quadratic Curve	(b) Characteristic Lines

FIGURE 21-9
Characteristic Curves

where:

$$Z = \begin{cases} 0 & \text{if } ER_m \geqq 0 \\ ER_m & \text{if } ER_m < 0 \end{cases}$$

To see why this works, consider the effective equation for different values of ER_m:

Value of ER_m	Equation
< 0	$ER_f = a + (b - c)ER_m$
0	$ER_f = a$
> 0	$ER_f = a + bER_m$

Clearly, b is the "up-market beta" and $(b - c)$ is the "down-market beta." The value of c indicates the difference between the two values. For a successful market timer, c will be positive.

In either equation (21-1) or (21-2), the value of c provides an estimate of market-timing ability. Its statistical significance indicates the likelihood that the results were due to skill rather than luck.[3]

---

[3] For details, see R. D. Henriksson and R. C. Merton, "On Market Timing and Investment Performance. II. Statistical Procedures for Evaluating Forecasting Skills," *Journal of Business,* 54 (October), 513–33.

Predictions of Market Direction

Consider an investment manager who considers only a combination of risky securities ("the market") and riskless securities. Prior to each period, a prediction is made about the market. If an up market (risky securities outperforming riskless securities) is predicted, some risky securities are purchased. If a down market (risky securities underperforming riskless securities) is predicted, some risky securities are sold.

Table 21-1(a) shows results from such a strategy. There are four relevant classifications, based on (1) the prediction and (2) the actual

TABLE 21-1
Predictions of Market Direction

(a) MARKET TIMER A			
	Actual		
	Up	Down	Total
Prediction: Up	40	30	70
Down	18	12	30
Total	58	42	
Proportion right	.52		
Predictive accuracy	.69	.29	
PA(up) + PA(down)	.98		

(b) AN ETERNAL OPTIMIST			
	Actual		
	Up	Down	Total
Prediction: Up	58	42	100
Down	0	0	0
Total	58	42	
Proportion right	.58		
Predictive accuracy	1.00	.00	
PA(up) + PA(down)	1.00		

(c) MARKET TIMER B			
	Actual		
	Up	Down	Total
Prediction: Up	34	20	54
Down	24	22	46
Total	58	42	
Proportion right	.56		
Predictive accuracy	.59	.52	
PA(up) + PA(down)	1.11		

outcome. Results from 100 periods are shown: in 58 of them, the market was "up"; in 42 it was "down." This conforms to actual experience—Standard and Poor's 500-stock index outperformed U.S. Treasury bills in 58% of the months from 1926 through 1983.

It is tempting to consider this record successful. In 52 of the 100 periods, the prediction was correct—40 "up" predictions were followed by up markets and 12 "down" predictions were followed by down markets. But this is not a very useful measure of performance. Table 21-1(b) shows the record of an eternal optimist, who always predicts that stocks will do well. Such a prediction will generally be right more than half the time. In this case, it was right 58% of the time. No predictive ability is required to achieve such a record.

More relevant are tests of the ability of a manager to predict different kinds of markets. As shown in Table 21-1(a), manager A "called" 40 of the 58 up-market periods correctly. Predictive accuracy thus equalled .69 (= 40/58). On the other hand, only 12 of 42 down markets were called correctly, for a predictive accuracy of .29 (= 12/42). As shown in Table 21-1(b), an eternal optimist is perfectly correct in up markets and perfectly incorrect in down markets.

A summary measure should take into account ability to make good predictions in both kinds of markets. One method simply adds the two predictive accuracies. Anyone can achieve a value of 1.0 for this score by always predicting the more common outcome. A perfect market timer will make a score of 2.0. Imperfect but valuable market timers will obtain scores between 1.0 and 2.0. The greater the score, the more valuable the manager. And the greater the statistical significance of the difference between the score and 1.0, the less likely it is that the difference was due to luck.[4]

As Table 21-1(a) indicates, market timer A fell short of the mark, with an overall score of .98. Table 21-1(c) shows a more satisfying set of results. Market timer B was right 59% of the time in up markets and 52% of the time in down markets, for an overall score of 1.11. If this reflects skill rather than luck, he or she can add value in the future—value that can result in higher management fees, greater utility for clients, or both.

PERFORMANCE ATTRIBUTION

Bottom-line performance measurement concentrates on the question of *how* a portfolio did, both absolutely and relative to a benchmark. *Performance attribution* attempts to determine *why* it did what it did, both absolutely and relative to a benchmark.

---

[4] For details, see Henriksson and Merton, op. cit.

Attributes, Factors, and Effects

The starting point is the estimation of an appropriate *factor model* of security returns. Such a model can be written as:

$$\tilde{R}_i = b_{i1}\tilde{f}_1 + b_{i2}\tilde{f}_2 + \cdots + b_{iM}\tilde{f}_M + \tilde{d}_i \qquad (21\text{-}3)$$

where:

$$\tilde{R}_i = \text{the return on security } i$$
$$b_{i1}, b_{i2}, \ldots, b_{iM} = \text{attributes } 1, 2, \ldots, M \text{ of security } i$$
$$\tilde{f}_1, \tilde{f}_2, \ldots, \tilde{f}_M = \text{factors } 1, 2, \ldots, M$$
$$\tilde{d}_i = \text{security } i\text{'s nonfactor return}$$

For a particular *review period*, cross-section regression analysis will provide a value for every term. Thus for period t:

$$R_{it} = b_{i1_t}f_{1_t} + b_{i2_t}f_{2_t} + \cdots + b_{iM_t}f_{M_t} + d_{i_t} \qquad (21\text{-}4)$$

where:

$$R_{i_t} = \text{the return on security } i \text{ in period } t$$
$$b_{i1_t}, b_{i2_t}, \ldots, b_{iM_t} = \text{attributes } 1, 2, \ldots, M \text{ of security } i \text{ in period } t$$
$$f_{1_t}, f_{2_t}, \ldots, f_{M_t} = \text{factors } 1, 2, \ldots, M \text{ in period } t$$
$$d_{i_t} = \text{security } i\text{'s nonfactor return in period } t$$

In effect, the total return on security i is *decomposed* into $M + 1$ components:[5]

$$R_{i_t} = E_{i1_t} + E_{i2_t} + \cdots + E_{iM_t} + d_{i_t} \qquad (21\text{-}5)$$

where:

$$E_{ij_t} = b_{ij_t}f_{j_t}$$
$$= \text{the effect on security } i \text{ of factor } j \text{ in period } t$$

Each of the first M components represents the joint *effect* of a security *attribute* and an actual *factor* value. Such a component can be considered a *factor-related return*. The final term is the security's *non-factor-related return* for the period.

Table 21-2 illustrates the procedure with a 12-factor model. Three of the attributes are *common* to all stocks analyzed: (1) historic beta relative to Standard and Poor's 500-stock index, (2) current dividend yield, and (3) a measure of size (logarithm of the current market value of shares outstanding). Each of the associated factors is termed a *common factor*. The remaining nine attributes are "zero-one" variables.

---

[5] In the version shown, there is no intercept (constant) term. Instead, each sector factor plays the role of an intercept for all the securities in the sector. Since the nonfactor return (d_{i_t}) for a given security need not be zero in every period (or on average over many periods), it plays the role of a security-specific intercept.

TABLE 21-2
Performance Attribution for a Stock

	(a) Attribute	(b) Factor	(c) = (a) × (b) Effect
Common factors:			
Beta	.80	1.20	.96
Yield	6.00	.50	3.00
Size	4.00	−.40	−1.60
Sector factors:			
Basic industries	0.00	10.50	0.00
Capital goods	0.00	10.14	0.00
Consumer staple	0.00	9.55	0.00
Consumer cyclical	0.00	9.60	0.00
Credit cyclical	0.00	9.15	0.00
Energy	0.00	10.34	0.00
Finance	1.00	9.03	9.03
Transportation	0.00	10.80	0.00
Utilities	0.00	9.77	0.00
Nonfactor return			1.22
		Total return:	12.61

For each security, one such attribute equals 1.0; all others equal 0.0. In this case, the attributes represent nine economic *sectors*. The corresponding factors are termed *sector factors*.

In this period, high-historic-beta stocks outperformed low-historic-beta stocks, other things equal—the beta factor was positive. High-yield stocks outperformed low-yield stocks, other things equal—the yield factor was positive. And large stocks underperformed small stocks, other things equal—the size factor was negative.

This was a good period for transportation stocks—the transportation factor was the largest of all the sector factors. It was a relatively bad period for finance stocks—the finance factor was the smallest of the sector factors. And so on.

The third column in Table 21-2 shows the effects of the attribute and factor values. For example, .96% of the security's total return of 12.61% can be attributed to the joint effect of (1) its historic beta value of .80 and (2) the actual beta factor value of 1.20. Similarly, 3.00% of the total return can be attributed to the joint effect of its yield (6.00) and the yield factor (.50). The security's total return was reduced by 1.60% by the joint effect of its large size (4.00) and the fact that large stocks did poorly (the size factor was −.40).

Since this is a finance stock, its "base" return in the period was 9.03%. Happily, it did relatively well compared to stocks with similar attributes—its nonfactor return was 1.22%.

Performance Attribution for a Portfolio

Equations (21-4) and (21-5) can be used to decompose a portfolio's return. The relevant attributes are those of the portfolio, each of which is, in turn, a value-weighted average of the values of the corresponding attribute of the component securities. Table 21-3 provides an example.

Note the positive values for most of the sector attributes. For example, Table 21-3 shows that 10% of the value of the portfolio was invested in stocks in the basic industries sector, 13% in capital goods stocks, and so on.

The third column shows the joint effects of the portfolio attributes and the actual factor values. As before, the sum of such effects plus the nonfactor return equals the portfolio's total return (10.57%).

The nonfactor return of a portfolio can be calculated in either of two ways. A value-weighted average of the nonfactor returns of the component securities can be used. Alternatively, the sum of the factor-related effects can be subtracted from the portfolio's total return.

There is no evidence in Table 21-3 of successful *security selection*, since the nonfactor return was virtually zero. Some securities in the portfolio may have had large positive nonfactor returns; if so, they were offset by others with large negative nonfactor returns. For a manager whose style does not include "stock picking," this may be taken as evidence of a job well done. For a stock picker, it shows lack of success.

TABLE 21-3
Performance Attribution for a Portfolio

	(a) Attribute	(b) Factor	(c) = (a) × (b) Effect
Common factors:			
Beta	.60	1.20	.72
Yield	4.00	.50	2.00
Size	5.00	−.40	−2.00
Sector factors:			
Basic industries	.10	10.50	1.05
Capital goods	.13	10.14	1.32
Consumer staple	.04	9.55	.38
Consumer cyclical	.06	9.60	.58
Credit cyclical	0.00	9.15	0.00
Energy	.25	10.34	2.59
Finance	.30	9.03	2.71
Transportation	.05	10.80	.54
Utilities	.07	9.77	.68
Nonfactor Return			.01
		Total return:	10.57

Comparative Performance Attribution

Absolute performance is interesting. But in many cases *comparative* performance is more relevant. A manager may do poorly in a bad market. But if he or she provides a higher return than would have been obtained otherwise, the client is clearly better off.

The overall return of a portfolio can be compared with that of one or more *benchmark* portfolios to determine the *difference* in the two returns. Moreover, one can determine the *sources* of the difference via *comparative performance attribution*.

Assume that the *i* in equation (21-4) refers to a portfolio. Letting *j* refer to the return on a benchmark portfolio:

$$R_{j_t} = b_{j1_t}f_{1_t} + b_{j2_t}f_{2_t} + \cdots + b_{jm_t}f_{M_t} + d_{j_t} \qquad \text{(21-6)}$$

Subtracting equation (21-6) from equation (21-4) gives:

$$R_{i_t} - R_{j_t} = (b_{i1_t} - b_{j1_t})f_{1_t} + (b_{i2_t} - b_{j2_t})f_{2_t} \\ + \cdots + (b_{iM_t} - b_{jM_t})f_{M_t} + (d_{i_t} - d_{j_t}) \qquad \text{(21-7)}$$

Each of the first *M* terms represents a *differential effect* equal to the product of (1) the *difference* in the attributes of the two portfolios and (2) the actual value of the related factor. The last term in the equation indicates the difference in the nonfactor returns of the two portfolios. The sum equals the difference in the total returns of the two portfolios.

Table 21-4 provides an example. Overall, the portfolio underperformed its benchmark by 2.18%. Security selection played virtually no role: the nonfactor returns were similar and small (0.1% for the portfolio and −.01% for the benchmark). On net, *sector selection* lowered returns slightly—the sum of the values in the last column for the nine sectors was −.21%. In the portfolio, capital goods, consumer cyclical, energy, finance, and utility stocks were *overweighted* relative to the benchmark, while the remaining sectors were *underweighted*. A successful "sector picker" would place bets *on* (overweight) sectors with high factor values and place bets *against* (underweight) sectors with low factor values, leading to a net positive "sector-bet effect." In this period, at least, this manager was not a successful sector bettor.

In Table 21-4, the major sources of the relative underperformance of the portfolio were those associated with common factors. The manager had lower-beta stocks than those in the benchmark in a period when high-beta stocks did better than low-beta stocks, other things equal. He or she had lower-yield stocks in a period in which high-yield stocks outperformed low-yield stocks, other things equal. The stocks in the portfolio were also larger than those in the benchmark in a period when large stocks tended to do poorly. All three differences lowered returns relative to the benchmark, with the effect of the "low-yield bet" the largest and the effect of the "big-stock" bet the smallest.

TABLE 21-4
Comparative Performance Attribution

	(a)	(b) Attributes	(c) = (a) − (b)	(d)	(e) = (c) × (d)
	Portfolio	Benchmark	Difference	Factor	Differential Effect
Common factors:					
Beta	.60	1.10	−.50	1.20	−.60
Yield	4.00	6.00	−2.00	.50	−1.00
Size	5.00	4.00	1.00	−.40	−.40
Sector factors:					
Basic industries	.10	.20	−.10	10.50	−1.05
Capital goods	.13	.03	.10	10.14	1.01
Consumer staple	.04	.10	−.06	9.55	−.57
Consumer cyclical	.06	.01	.05	9.60	.48
Credit cyclical	.00	.05	−.05	9.15	−.46
Energy	.25	.20	.05	10.34	.52
Finance	.30	.18	.12	9.03	1.08
Transportation	.05	.19	−.14	10.80	−1.51
Utilities	.07	.04	.03	9.77	.29
Nonfactor return	.01	−.01	.02		.02
				Total return:	−2.18

ESTIMATING THE SIGNIFICANCE OF PAST PERFORMANCE

Most performance measurement concentrates on historic values. But what are the values likely to be in the future? Putting it another way: To what extent was a historic value due to luck (good or bad) and to what extent was it due to skill or the lack thereof?

The issue can be illustrated by considering a "bottom-line" measure of fund performance. How much attention should one pay to an average differential return?

Examination of the pattern of differential returns can provide some help in this regard. If a fund provided a differential return of exactly +1% every quarter, one might reasonably assume that such performance might continue in the future. But if the differential returns had ranged from −9% to +10%, even though the average value might have been + 1%, one might reasonably assume that future performance would be virtually as likely to be positive as negative.

The variability of a measure from period to period can be used to compute the *standard error of the mean* (average) value, to be used in this connection.[6] For example, the average differential return might

---

[6] The standard error of the mean equals the standard deviation divided by the square root of $N − 1$, where N equals the number of observations.

Performance Measurement and Attribution

be +1.0% per quarter and its standard error .8% per quarter. Roughly, this means that the chances are (a) two out of three that the fund's "true" ex ante expected differential return lies within the range from +.2 (= 1.0 − .8) to + 1.8 (1.0 + .8) and (b) 95 out of 100 that it lies within the range from −.6 (= 1.0 − 2 × .8) to + 2.6% (= 1.0 + 2 × .8). The latter range includes the possibility that the value is really zero; thus a *classical* statistician would say that "at the 95% confidence level" the hypothesis that the manager has no skill cannot be rejected. A *Bayesian* statistician would say that the *sample* of historic data should lead to a revision of one's assessment: from a *prior* expectation, e.g., that the fund's true expected differential return is zero, to a *posterior* expectation that it is larger. The extent of the revision will depend on the ex post average value and its standard error, and the conviction with which one holds the prior belief. The appropriate estimate of expected future results should, in this view, lie between the prior estimate and the historic performance measure; and it should be closer to the latter, the smaller its standard error.

In pragmatic terms: superior performance *on average* is interesting, but *consistently* superior performance is very interesting indeed.

Statistical procedures can be applied to virtually any performance measure, including specific effects in a comparative performance attri-

FIGURE 21-10
Comparing the Performance of Fixed-Income Investments

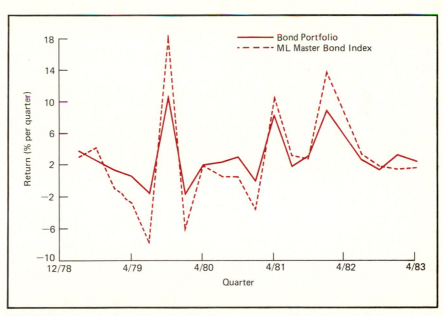

SOURCE: Merrill Lynch, Pierce, Fenner and Smith, Inc., *Investment Performance Analysis*.

bution analysis. The better the average value of a measure, and the smaller its variability from period to period, the more relevant it is for the future.

THE PERFORMANCE OF FIXED-INCOME INVESTMENTS

Analysis of the performance of the nonequity portion of a fund may be limited to a quarter-by-quarter comparison of the total returns from such investments with those of an index representing a particular class of bonds; Figure 21-10 is typical.

Figure 21-11 illustrates a different approach. Here return is related to *duration*, with the return on the fund ("Manager A") compared with the returns of bond portfolios with similar durations.

Much more could be said about performance measurement. It suffices to indicate that, although some investment managers may not like it, performance measurement appears to be here to stay.

FIGURE 21-11
Return versus Duration for Bond Portfolios

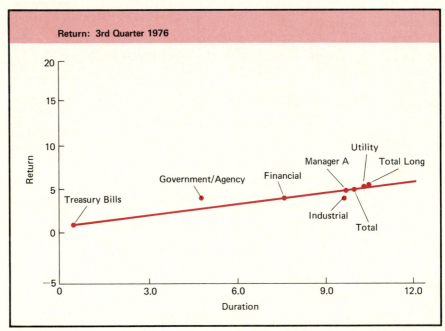

SOURCE: Wayne H. Wagner and Dennis A. Tito, "Definitive New Measures of Bond Performance and Risk," *Pension World*, May 1977.

Problems

1. Why is the reward-to-variability ratio measure of performance more appropriate than the ex post alpha measure if the fund being assessed represents its beneficiary's entire investment portfolio?

2. Does a fund's ex post alpha [the vertical intercept of a characteristic line fitted to points representing the fund's excess returns (on the vertical axis) versus those of a market index (on the horizontal axis)] measure gains and losses due to security selection, marketing timing, or both?

3. The performance of the commingled fund of a local bank over a ten-year period compared with that of Standard and Poor's 500-stock index was as follows:

	Fund	SP 500
Average quarterly excess return	.6%	.5%
Standard deviation of quarterly excess returns	9.9%	6.6%
Beta	1.1	1.0

The William Mathews Trust Fund, which is the sole support of an elderly widow, was invested partly in Treasury bills (about 70% of the total), with the remainder in this fund. The bank has started a new fund, intended to match the SP 500 index. Based solely on past performance, would it be desirable to use the new fund for this trust instead of the original commingled fund?

4. A major brokerage firm provides a performance measurement service in which the "bottom line" measure of a fund's performance is ex post alpha—the intercept in a regression equation of the form:

$$R_f - p = \alpha + \beta(R_s - p) + \epsilon$$

where

R_f = the return on the fund

p = the return on a U.S. Treasury bill

R_s = the return on Standard and Poor's 500-stock index

α = alpha, a constant fitted by regression analysis

β = beta, a constant fitted by regression analysis

ϵ = a random error term

Provide an interpretation of this measure in terms of the difference between the return on the portfolio and that of some other investment strategy. Exactly what does this alternative strategy involve? Under what conditions is ex post alpha a sufficient measure of performance? Under what conditions is it not?

Performance Measurement and Attribution

5. A mutual fund changed its beta value from year to year in an attempt to "time the market." The accompanying table shows the values of the fund's beta in each of ten years, along with the return on the fund, the return on Standard and Poor's 500-stock index, and the return on Treasury bills.

Year	Fund Beta	Return on Fund	Return on SP 500	Return on Treasury Bills
1969	.90	−2.99%	−8.50%	6.58%
1970	.95	.63	4.01	6.53
1971	.95	22.01	14.31	4.39
1972	1.00	24.08	18.98	3.84
1973	1.00	−22.46	−14.66	6.93
1974	.90	−25.12	−26.47	8.00
1975	.80	29.72	37.20	5.80
1976	.75	22.15	23.84	5.08
1977	.80	.48	−7.18	5.12
1978	.85	6.85	6.56	7.18

Assume that the beta value shown for each year was the fund's true beta during the entire year.
a. What was the fund's average beta over the ten-year period?
b. Compute the year-by-year returns for a fund made up of Treasury bills and the SP 500 in the proportions required to have a constant beta value equal to the value found in (a).
c. Compute the year-by-year returns for a fund made up of Treasury bills and the SP 500 in the proportions required to have a beta value equal to that of the fund in *each year*.
d. Compute the year-by-year amounts of the fund's returns attributable to *market timing*. Does the fund's record suggest an ability to time the market?
e. Compute the year-by-year amounts of the fund's returns attributable to *security selection*. Does the fund's record suggest an ability to select securities?
f. Compute the average *total* return and standard deviation of *total* return on (1) the fund, (2) the SP 500, (3) the "policy fund" considered in (b), and (4) the "timing only" fund considered in (c). Which fund would have been best for an investor who had a risk tolerance of 100? Why?

22

Extended Diversification

INTRODUCTION

A major theme of modern portfolio theory concerns the merits of *diversification:* in an efficient capital market sensible investment strategies will include holdings of many different assets. Previous chapters have considered traditional securities such as stocks and bonds and some less traditional ones, such as commodity and financial futures and options. We have yet to deal with diversification that extends beyond the borders of one's own country and with the holding of tangible assets. After completing these tasks, we turn briefly to a less lofty subject: sports and horse race betting. As indicated in previous chapters, active investment management can be considered a form of betting. It is instructive to contrast this rather subtle form of wagering handled by security brokers and dealers with the more explicit form handled by race tracks and legal and illegal "bookmakers."

INTERNATIONAL INVESTMENT

If the world were under a single political jurisdiction, having one currency and complete freedom of trade among areas, one might think of "the market portfolio" as including all capital assets in the world, each in proportion to its market value. Limiting one's investments to securities representing firms domiciled in one area could, in such a situation, decrease return per unit of risk. Few advocate that Californians own only shares of firms with headquarters located in California. And in a world without political boundaries, few would advocate that, say, Americans own only shares of American firms.

But political boundaries do exist, as do different currencies and

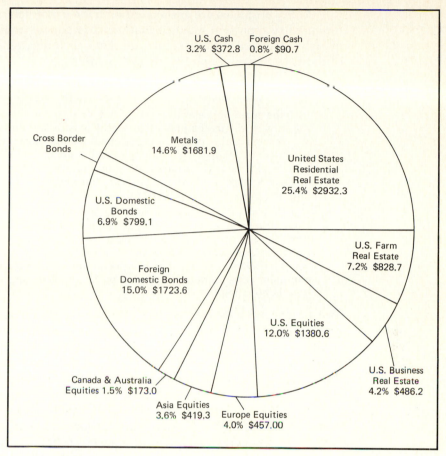

SOURCE: Roger G. Ibbotson and Laurence B. Siegel, "The World Market Wealth Portfolio," *Journal of Portfolio Management,* Winter 1983.

FIGURE 22-1
The World Market Wealth Portfolio, Year-end 1980

restrictions on trade and currency exchange. Such unpleasantries diminish, but do not destroy, the advantages to be gained from international investment.

The World Market Wealth Portfolio

Figure 22-1 provides an estimate of the *world market wealth portfolio,* defined to include those "capital market securities that are most marketable and most readily identifiable . . . the securities that make up the opportunity set faced by most investors."[1]

---

[1] Roger G. Ibbotson and Laurence B. Siegel, "The World Market Wealth Portfolio," *Journal of Portfolio Management,* Winter 1983.

Extended Diversification

Many problems are associated with the construction of a portfolio designed to represent a single market. It is almost impossible to adequately represent *all* investment markets, as indicated by the authors of the paper from which Figure 22-1 is taken:

> We have left huge categories out of the portfolio, while at the same time we have included categories that are not wealth at all.
>
> . . . the most important omission is human capital, which is probably the largest single component of world wealth. We have also excluded . . . foreign real estate . . . proprietorships and partnerships . . . many small corporations . . . [and] personal holdings such as automobiles, cash balances, and various consumer capital goods. We have not only omitted a large proportion of wealth, but we also have little idea as to how large the omitted proportion is.
>
> Our inclusions may misrepresent the market even more than our omissions. We have included U.S. and foreign government debt that is almost certainly not backed dollar-for-dollar by government-owned assets such as parks and bridges. More likely, it is backed by claims on a future tax base. Other inclusions in our portfolio also misrepresent wealth. For example, some corporations own parts of other corporations, causing double counting.[2]

The latter problem can be quite important. Differences in financial practices across industries and countries may lead to serious distortions when market values of equity are obtained by multiplying price per share by total shares outstanding. According to one estimate "only about 5 to 7% of outstanding Japanese bank shares are available to ordinary investors, compared with 30 to 35% for other Japanese issues. . . ."[3] If so, (1) some indices of performance of Japanese stocks may overweight the bank sector, and (2) some estimates of the relative sizes of components of the world market portfolio may overstate the importance of Japanese stocks vis-à-vis stocks of countries with less extensive intercorporate holdings.

Figures 22-2(a), (b), and (c) provide breakdowns of the values of bonds and stocks. As shown in Figure 22-2(a), U.S. bonds and stocks made up about half the value of "world" bonds and stocks at the end of 1980.

Figure 22-2(b) provides estimates of values of non-U.S. equities by the country of the issuer.[4]

Figure 22-2(c) provides estimates of the values of non-U.S. bonds. For this purpose, a bond is considered to be *domestic* if "(1) the currency of a bond is the currency of the borrower's home country and (2) the bond is primarily bought by nationals of the borrower's home country."[5]

---

[2] *Ibid.*

[3] Richard J. Gillespie, "Managers Trail Index," *Pensions and Investment Age,* April 30, 1984, p. 116.

[4] Owing to double counting, the importance of Japanese stocks may have been overstated; moreover, some companies traded in two locations may have been counted twice.

[5] Roger G. Ibbotson, Richard C. Carr, and Anthony W. Robinson, "International Equity and Bond Returns," *Financial Analysts Journal,* July/August 1982.

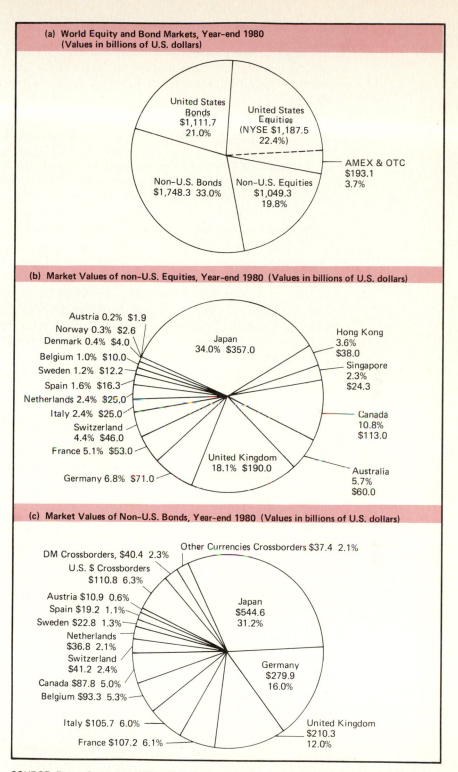

(a) **World Equity and Bond Markets, Year-end 1980**
(Values in billions of U.S. dollars)

- United States Bonds $1,111.7 21.0%
- United States Equities (NYSE $1,187.5 22.4%)
- AMEX & OTC $193.1 3.7%
- Non-U.S. Bonds $1,748.3 33.0%
- Non-U.S. Equities $1,049.3 19.8%

(b) **Market Values of non-U.S. Equities, Year-end 1980** (Values in billions of U.S. dollars)

- Austria 0.2% $1.9
- Norway 0.3% $2.6
- Denmark 0.4% $4.0
- Belgium 1.0% $10.0
- Sweden 1.2% $12.2
- Spain 1.6% $16.3
- Netherlands 2.4% $25.0
- Italy 2.4% $25.0
- Switzerland 4.4% $46.0
- France 5.1% $53.0
- Germany 6.8% $71.0
- Japan 34.0% $357.0
- Hong Kong 3.6% $38.0
- Singapore 2.3% $24.3
- Canada 10.8% $113.0
- Australia 5.7% $60.0
- United Kingdom 18.1% $190.0

(c) **Market Values of Non-U.S. Bonds, Year-end 1980** (Values in billions of U.S. dollars)

- DM Crossborders, $40.4 2.3%
- Other Currencies Crossborders $37.4 2.1%
- U.S. $ Crossborders $110.8 6.3%
- Austria $10.9 0.6%
- Spain $19.2 1.1%
- Sweden $22.8 1.3%
- Netherlands $36.8 2.1%
- Switzerland $41.2 2.4%
- Canada $87.8 5.0%
- Belgium $93.3 5.3%
- Italy $105.7 6.0%
- France $107.2 6.1%
- Japan $544.6 31.2%
- Germany $279.9 16.0%
- United Kingdom $210.3 12.0%

SOURCE: Roger G. Ibbotson, Richard C. Carr, and Anthony W. Robinson, "International Equity and Bond Returns," *Financial Analysts Journal*, July/August 1982.

FIGURE 22-2
Equity and Bond Values

All others are considered *crossborder bonds*. In Figure 22-2(c), such crossborder bonds are classified on the basis of the currency in which payments are made (U.S. dollars, German deutsche marks, and other currencies).

International Equity Indices

In most countries there are indices of overall (domestic) stock values and of the values of stocks within various industry or economic sectors. Such indices can be used for assessing "market moves" and, more importantly, for comparative performance measurement.

On the international level, the indices produced by Capital International Perspective are widely used for such purposes. Monthly values are calculated for the the levels of three international indices, 19 national indices, and 38 international industry indices. Each index represents the value of a market-weighted portfolio of stocks (using total shares outstanding). Values for each of the 19 national indices are given both in the local currency and in U.S. dollars based on exchange rates at the time. Values of the other indices are stated only in U.S. dollars. Over 1,200 stocks are included, representing approximately 60% of the aggregate market value listed on the 19 covered stock exchanges.[6]

All 1,200 stocks are used to compute the "World" index. The "Europe" index includes approximately 450 companies representing 12 European countries. The "Europe, Australia, Far East" (EAFE) index, representing a portfolio of over 750 stocks, is widely used by U.S. investors as a benchmark when evaluating the performance of international investment managers.

Exchange Risk

Investment abroad brings all the risks associated with investment at home, plus at least two more.

First, there is *political risk*. Governments may restrict, tax, or completely prohibit the exchange of one currency for another. Since such policies change from time to time, the ability to repatriate one's foreign investments may be subject to some uncertainty. There may even be a possibility of complete expropriation, making political risk very large.

Second, there is *exchange risk*. The return in U.S. dollars from a French security depends on both the security's return in francs and the rate at which francs can be exchanged for dollars in the future, and this latter rate is generally subject to at least some uncertainty.

---

[6] *Capital International Perspective*, July 1984.

Hedging Exchange Risk. To an extent, exchange risk can be reduced by hedging in the market for forward exchange. In the case of default-free fixed-income investment it may be possible to completely eliminate such risk in this way. For example, a one-year discount bond paying 1,000 British pounds might be purchased and a forward contract made to deliver £1,000 a year hence in return for, say, $1,300. If the current (spot) exchange rate were $1.35 per pound, and the bond cost £850, the return in dollars would be 13.29%:

current cost: £850 × $1.35 per £ = $1,147.50
(spot rate)

proceeds: £1,000 × $1.30 per £ = $1,300
(forward rate)

return in dollars: $\dfrac{1,300 - 1,147.50}{1,147.50} = .1329$

Except for political risk, this is a certain return. The exchange risk has been completely removed by hedging.

Unfortunately it is not possible to *completely* hedge the exchange risk associated with risky investments. Forward contracts can be made to cover *expected* cash flows, but if the *actual* cash flows are larger or smaller than expected, some currency may have to be exchanged at the spot rate prevailing at the time. Since future spot rates usually cannot be predicted with complete certainty, this will affect overall risk.

As a practical matter, this "unhedgeable" risk is likely to be small. Moreover the cost of hedging foreign investments may exceed the benefit—perhaps by a large amount.

Foreign and Domestic Returns. Changes in exchange rates can cause major differences between the returns obtained by domestic investors and the returns obtained by unhedged foreign investors.

Consider an American investor and a Swiss investor, both of whom purchase shares in a Swiss stock traded only in Switzerland. Let the price of the stock in Swiss francs be P_0 at the beginning of a period and P_1 at the end of the period. If r_d is the *domestic return:*

$$1 + r_d = \frac{P_1}{P_0} \tag{22-1a}$$

For example, if $P_0 = 10$ SF and $P_1 = 12$ SF, then $r_d = .20$ or 20%.

For the Swiss investor, r_d is the stock's return. Not so for the U.S. investor.

Assume that at the beginning of the period the *price* (in dollars) of one Swiss franc is $.50. When considering investments, it is preferable to state exchange rates in this manner (units of domestic currency per unit of foreign currency) rather than with the more common ratio of units of foreign currency per units of domestic currency.

Denoting this exchange rate at the beginning of the period as X_0, the cost of a share of the Swiss stock will be:

$$X_0 P_0$$

In the example, the cost will be .50 × 10 SF, or $5.

Now, assume that the exchange rate rises to $.55 per Swiss franc at the end of the period. Denoting this by X_1, the ending value of the stock for the American investor will be:

$$X_1 P_1$$

In the example, the value will be .55 × 12 SF, or $6.60.

If r_f is the *foreign return* (i.e., return to the foreign investor):

$$1 + r_f = \frac{X_1 P_1}{X_0 P_0} \tag{22-1b}$$

In the example, $1 + r_f = 6.60/5$, so $r_f = .32$ or 32%.

In effect, the American citizen made *two* investments: (1) an investment in a Swiss stock and (2) an investment in the Swiss franc. To analyze the result, it is convenient to separate the two effects. If the American investor had purchased a Swiss franc at the beginning of the period, hidden it somewhere, then sold it at the end of the period, the *return on foreign exchange* (r_x) would be given by:

$$1 + r_x = \frac{X_1}{X_0} \tag{22-1c}$$

In the example, $1 + r_x = .55/.50$, so $r_x = .10$ or 10%.

Comparison of equations (22-1a) and (22-1c) with equation (22-1b) indicates that:

$$1 + r_f = (1 + r_d)(1 + r_x)$$

or:

$$r_f = r_d + r_x + r_d r_x \tag{22-1d}$$

In the example:

$$.32 = .20 + .10 + (.20 \times .10)$$

The last term will generally be smaller than the two preceding ones, since it equals their product, and both are generally less than 1.0. Thus it will be approximately the case that:

$$r_f \approx r_d + r_x \tag{22-2}$$

In words:

> The foreign return on an investment will approximately equal the domestic return plus the return on foreign exchange.

Foreign and Domestic Expected Returns   Equation (22-2) leads directly to the proposition that the *expected* return on a foreign investment will approximately equal the *expected* domestic return plus the *expected* return on foreign exchange:

$$E_f = E_d + E_x \qquad (22\text{-}3)$$

The expected domestic returns of bonds in countries with high expected inflation rates should be correspondingly high. However, a foreign investor in a country with a lower inflation rate should expect a *negative* return on foreign exchange, as his or her currency *strengthens* relative to that of the country with the higher inflation rate. In evaluating the foreign investment there is thus good news (a high expected domestic return) and bad news (an expected loss on the foreign currency). If markets were completely integrated, one might even expect the two values to net to an amount equal to the expected return on an equivalent bond in the foreign investor's own country.

Foreign and Domestic Risks.   Equation (22-2) also leads to a relationship among the relevant risks:

$$S_f^2 = S_d^2 + S_x^2 + 2\rho_{dx} S_d S_x \qquad (22\text{-}4)$$

where:

S_f = the standard deviation of r_f
S_d = the standard deviation of r_d
S_x = the standard deviation of r_x

Note that before summing, the standard deviations on the right are squared, leading in most cases to less-than-proportional increases in the standard deviation on the left. For example, assume:

$$S_d = 15\%$$
$$S_x = 5\%$$
$$\rho_{dx} = 0$$

then:

$$S_f^2 = (15)^2 + (5)^2$$
$$= 225 + 25$$
$$= 250$$

and the standard deviation of foreign return equals the square root of 250, or 15.8%—only slightly greater than that of domestic return (15%).

Note also that the smaller the correlation between returns on foreign exchange and returns on foreign investments, the smaller will be the difference between foreign and domestic risk. A study[7] using data from 17 countries over the period from January 1971 through December 1980 found an average correlation of .034—effectively, zero.

Table 22-1 provides evidence on the relative magnitudes of the three types of risk. Standard deviations of monthly values over the period from December 1970 through December 1980 are shown for domestic risk (corresponding to S_d), exchange risk (corresponding to S_x), and foreign risk (corresponding to S_f), with the latter two measured from the perspective of an American investor. As shown in the last column, with the exception of Hong Kong stocks, fluctuations in exchange rates increased risk (i.e., the realization of S_f exceeded that of S_d). Differences tended to be proportionately relatively small for stocks and proportionately relatively large for bonds.

The importance of exchange risk can easily be exaggerated. Calculations such as those in Table 22-1 assume that investors purchase only domestic goods and services and thus convert all proceeds from foreign investments into their own currency before engaging in any spending for consumption purposes. But most people buy foreign goods, and many buy foreign services as well (e.g., as tourists). The cheaper another country's currency relative to one's own, the more attractive purchases of its goods and services will be. Other things equal, it may make sense to invest more in countries whose products and scenery one admires, for the effective exchange risk is likely to be smaller there than elsewhere.

Multinational Firms

Firms operating in many countries provide international diversification at the corporate level. One might expect that investment in the stocks of such *multinational* corporations could serve as a good substitute for investment in stocks of foreign ("national") companies.

A number of studies have shown that this may not be the case. In one,[8] returns on portfolios of stocks of multinational firms headquartered in each of nine countries were calculated for the period from April 1966 through June 1974. Then each portfolio's returns were regressed on the returns on the market index for its country. The middle column in Table 22-2 shows the proportion of variance explained by movements in the "domestic" markets. Finally, each portfolio's returns

[7] Bruno Solnik and Eric Nemeth, "Asset Returns and Currency Fluctuations: A Time Series Analysis," paper presented at the second tagung, Geld Banken und Versicherungen, Universität Karlsruhe, December 1982.

[8] Bertrand Jacquillat and Bruno Solnik, "Multinations Are Poor Tools for Diversification," *Journal of Portfolio Management,* Winter 1978.

TABLE 22-1
Risks for Domestic and U.S. Investors Based on Historic Values, December 1970–December 1980

	(1) Domestic Risk	(2) Exchange Risk	(3) Foreign Risk	(3)/(1) Foreign/ Domestic Risk
Stocks				
Australia	24.62	9.15	27.15	1.10
Belgium	13.28	11.02	18.76	1.41
Canada	18.92	4.16	20.29	1.07
Denmark	15.41	10.28	17.65	1.15
France	22.00	10.24	25.81	1.17
Germany	13.87	11.87	18.39	1.33
Hong Kong	47.95	5.63	45.80	.96
Italy	24.21	8.58	26.15	1.08
Japan	16.39	10.42	19.55	1.19
Netherlands	16.37	10.97	18.91	1.16
Norway	28.61	8.89	29.92	1.05
Singapore	35.82	6.52	36.03	1.01
Spain	16.71	9.10	20.26	1.21
Sweden	15.05	8.89	18.06	1.20
Switzerland	16.80	14.67	21.40	1.27
United Kingdom	28.94	8.84	31.61	1.09
United States	16.00	.00	16.00	1.00
Bonds				
Canada	6.16	4.16	7.93	1.29
France	4.39	10.24	11.80	2.69
Germany	6.91	11.87	14.35	2.08
Japan	6.53	10.42	14.36	2.20
Netherlands	7.16	10.97	13.61	1.90
Switzerland	4.33	14.67	15.33	3.54
United Kingdom	12.30	8.84	16.29	1.32
United States	8.96	.00	8.96	1.00

SOURCE: Bruno Solnik and Bernard Noetzlin, "Optimal International Asset Allocation," *Journal of Portfolio Management,* Fall 1982.

were regressed simultaneously on the returns on market indices in eight countries. The final column in Table 22-2 shows the proportion of variance explained by movements in *both* domestic and foreign markets.

During the period covered in Table 22-2, the returns on multinational firms based in the United States appeared to be relatively unrelated to those of foreign stocks. Such firms were thus a poor substitute for direct investment in foreign firms by an American investor. The

Extended Diversification

715

TABLE 22-2
Proportions of Returns on Stocks of Multinational Firms Explained by Stock Market Indices

Headquarters Country of Multinational Firms	PROPORTION OF VARIANCE IN RETURNS EXPLAINED BY	
	Domestic Market Index	Domestic and Other Market Indices
Belgium	45	58
France	45	62
Germany	65	74
Italy	47	51
Netherlands	50	63
Sweden	42	50
Switzerland	52	75
United Kingdom	44	49
United States	29%	31%

SOURCE: Bertrand Jacquillat and Bruno Solnik, "Multinationals Are Poor Tools for Diversification," *Journal of Portfolio Management,* Winter 1978.

situation was somewhat better for investors in other countries, perhaps because multinational corporations in their countries had more extensive foreign operations.

Correlations Between Equity Markets

If all economies were tied together completely, stock markets in different countries would move together, and little advantage could be gained through international diversification. But this is not the case. Table 22-3 shows the correlations of returns on diversified "market" portfolios of equities in various national stock markets with the returns on an index of equities in all the included countries. The value for the United States is large, owing primarily to the importance of the United States in the world index. The striking feature is, however, that many of the figures are very small (and some are even negative), even though each of the national indices represents a well-diversified domestic equity portfolio. Clearly, the potential advantages from international diversification are large.

Factor Models of International Security Returns

Relationships among security returns are difficult to determine in a domestic context and even harder to analyze in an international setting. But the possibility of holding an international portfolio requires that such a setting be considered.

Extended Diversification

TABLE 22-3
Correlations of Annual U.S. Dol-
lar-Adjusted Total Equity Returns
with World Total Equities, 1960–
1980

Country	Correlation
Australia	.753
Austria	−.042
Belgium	.483
Canada	.716
Denmark	.358
France	.384
Germany	.322
Hong Kong	.848
Italy	.281
Japan	.385
Netherlands	.804
Norway	−.045
Singapore	.700
Spain	−.015
Sweden	.470
Switzerland	.557
United Kingdom	.703
United States	.967

SOURCE: Roger G. Ibbotson, Richard C.
Carr, and Anthony W. Robinson, "Interna-
tional Equity and Bond Returns," *Financial
Analysts Journal,* July/August 1982.

Figure 22-3 shows a simple structure that models some relationships of this type. Each country's market is assumed to be sensitive
to a change in the world market, with the sensitivities measured by
"country-world" beta values. The world market factor is risky, and
each country market factor has two types of risk—one due to the world
factor and another specific to the country. A security's return is sensitive to changes in its own country's market factor and, through it,
indirectly to the world market factor. The degree to which a stock
moves with its country market factor is indicated by a "stock-country"
beta value, and the sensitivity of a stock to the world market factor
is obtained by multiplying the two relevant beta values:

$$\beta_{sw} = \beta_{sc} \times \beta_{cw}$$

where:

β_{sw} = percentage change in the return on stock s per unit of
percentage change in the world market factor

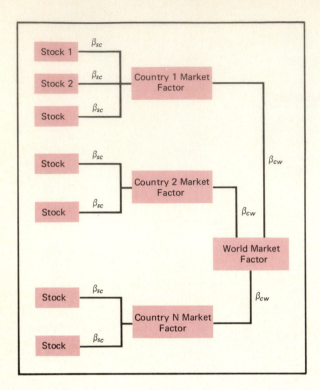

FIGURE 22-3
A Simple Model of International Security Returns

β_{sc} = percentage change in the return on stock s per unit of percentage change in the country market factor of country c

β_{cw} = percentage change in the country market factor of country c per unit of percentage change in the world market factor

The model in Figure 22-3 is overly simplistic, however, and fails to account for a number of phenomena. For example, the returns of at least some multinational firms are affected to an extent by the economic fortunes of several countries. This can be modeled by tying the security of such a firm to several country factors. More simply, its return can be related directly to the world market factor and to its own country factor (which is also related to the world market factor).

Also missing in Figure 22-3 are industry or economic-sector effects. One could focus exclusively on such effects by replacing country market factors with international industry factors. However, such a drastic step would not be desirable—the average security's return appears to be more closely related to prospects for its domestic economy than to prospects for its worldwide industry.[9]

[9] Donald R. Lessard, "World, Country and Industry Relationships in Equity Returns: Implications for Risk Reduction Through International Diversification," *Financial Analysts Journal,* 32, no. 1 (January–February 1976), 32–38.

A more general model could capture both country and industry or economic-sector effects. A factor would be introduced for each industry-country combination. Thus there might be a British finance factor, a French consumer goods factor, a Swiss capital goods factor, and so on. Correlations among the factors could capture both country-related and industry-related aspects.

Another promising alternative would incorporate macroeconomic factors. Thus there might be a French inflation expectations factor, a Japanese industrial production factor, and so on. Correlations among the factors could capture both within-country and between-country relationships among macroeconomic variables.

Equilibrium in International Capital Markets

Tests of any sort of *International Arbitrage Pricing Theory* require the identification of an adequate international factor model. Since such a model is lacking at present, it is impossible to say whether or not arbitrage pricing relationships hold internationally.

If international capital markets were completely *integrated,* a type of *International Capital Asset Pricing Model* might describe the relationship between expected returns and relevant attributes of securities. In particular, each security's expected return might be proportional to its beta value relative to the world market wealth portfolio.

On the other hand, if capital markets were completely *segmented,* a different Capital Asset Pricing Model might hold in each country. Within a country, each security's expected return might be proportional to its beta value relative to the market portfolio of its own country, but the relationship between expected returns and beta values might be different in each country. Assuming similar societal tolerance for risk in different countries, however, one might expect there to be a relationship between expected returns and total risks of "market portfolios" across countries.

Table 22-4 provides some evidence. The first two columns show the average return and standard deviation of return in U.S. dollars for equity indices of each country from 1960 to 1980. The third column shows the beta value of the excess return on each index relative to that of a "World" equity index (with all values measured in U.S. dollars). The final column indicates the ex post alpha for each country index relative to the world equity index. Of course, such indices cover only equities and thus may be poor proxies for national "market portfolios." Nonetheless, their performance is of interest.

While the alpha values in Table 22-4 vary considerably, none was statistically significantly different from zero. Therefore, this evidence does not disconfirm the possibility that international capital markets are totally integrated. On the other hand, the relationship between average return and total risk (standard deviation of return) across coun-

TABLE 22-4
Equity Returns, 1960–1980

	Average Return	Standard Deviation of Return	Beta	Alpha
Australia	12.20	22.80	1.02	1.52
Austria	10.30	16.90	.01	4.86
Belgium	10.10	13.80	.45	2.44
Canada	12.10	17.50	.77	2.75
Denmark	11.40	24.20	.60	2.91
France	8.10	21.40	.50	.17
Germany	10.10	19.90	.45	2.41
Italy	5.60	27.20	.41	−1.92
Japan	19.00	31.40	.81	9.49
Netherlands	10.70	17.80	.90	.65
Norway	17.40	49.00	−.27	13.39
Spain	10.40	19.80	.04	4.73
Sweden	9.70	16.70	.51	1.69
Switzerland	12.50	22.90	.87	2.66
United Kingdom	14.70	33.60	1.47	1.76
United States	10.20	17.70	1.08	−.69

SOURCE: Roger G. Ibbotson, Richard C. Carr, and Anthony W. Robinson, "International Equity and Bond Returns," *Financial Analysts Journal,* July/August 1982.

tries was approximately as strong as that between average return and beta. Thus the evidence does not disconfirm the possibility that international capital markets are completely segmented.

Clearly, this sort of evidence is simply not powerful enough to reject either extreme hypothesis (or, *a fortiori,* one lying between the two extremes).

As indicated in earlier chapters, it has proven very difficult to assess the extent to which a particular equilibrium theory holds within the United States, which is still the largest capital market in the world. *A fortiori,* it is difficult to reach strong conclusions concerning equilibrium conditions in international capital markets. The presence of exchange and political risks, transportation costs, restrictions on trade, differences in national preferences, and so on makes it unlikely that returns will conform strictly to an "International Capital Asset Pricing Model." On the other hand, there *are* flows of capital across borders, so it also seems unlikely that international markets are completely segmented.

Since added risks may be associated with foreign investing, and since markets are certainly segmented to an extent, it may make sense for an investor to hold a more-than-proportionate share of domestic securities vis-à-vis the world market portfolio. Nonetheless, even when these risks are taken into account, both theory and history suggest that *some* international investment is still likely to give higher returns per unit of risk than an all-domestic portfolio, even for an investor in the United States.

TANGIBLE ASSETS

In the first half of the 1970s, marketable securities such as stocks and bonds provided returns that were relatively disappointing, especially in real terms. And, as shown in Chapter 10, neither bonds nor stocks have served as hedges against unanticipated inflation in recent years. Overall, *tangible assets* have been better hedges against inflation, although differences in relative price changes prevent any given asset from serving as a perfect hedge against changes in the cost of purchasing other assets. As shown in Chapter 10, owner-occupied real estate has been especially attractive in recent years. And, as shown in Chapter 17, commodity futures have proved to be desirable as well.

Collectible Assets

Not surprisingly, disenchantment with returns on marketable securities has led some investors to examine a host of tangible assets normally considered only by "collectors." Table 22-5 shows geometric mean returns over three five-year periods for several assets of this type.

Some of the figures in Table 22-5 are quite dazzling. But none of the assets provided *consistently* dazzling results over all three periods—a fact that should come as no surprise to one who has read the previous chapters in this book.

TABLE 22-5
Annual Returns on Tangible Assets, Five-Year Periods Ending June 1

	1969–1974	1974–1979	1979–1984
Chinese ceramics	31.1	−3.1	15.7
Coins	9.5	32.4	11.3
Diamonds	11.6	13.6	6.1
Old masters	7.3	17.3	1.5
U.S. stamps	14.1	24.9	9.8

SOURCE: Based on data in R. S. Salomon, Jr., and Mallory J. Lennox, "Financial Assets—A Temporary Setback," *Stock Research Investment Policy,* Salomon Brothers, Inc., June 8, 1984.

Collectible assets provide income in the form of consumption. One can admire a Rembrandt, sit on a Chippendale, play a Stradivarius, and drive a Morgan. Value received in this manner is not subject to income taxation and is thus likely to be especially attractive for those in high tax brackets. However, the value of such consumption depends strongly on one's preferences. If markets are efficient, collectible assets will be priced so that those who enjoy them most will find it desirable to hold greater-than-market-value proportions, while those who enjoy them least will find it desirable to hold less-than-market-value proportions (and, in many cases, none at all).

Institutional funds and investment pools have been organized to hold paintings, stamps, coins, and other assets. Such arrangements are subject to serious question if they involve locking such objects in vaults where they cannot be seen by those who derive pleasure from this sort of consumption. On the other hand, if the items are rented to others, the only loss may be that associated with the transfer of a portion of the consumption value to the government in the form of a tax on income.

Gold

In the United States, private holdings of gold bullion were illegal before the 1970s. In other countries, investment in gold has long been a tradition. According to one estimate,[10] at the end of 1980 gold represented over 14% of the World Market Wealth Portfolio.

Table 22-6 contrasts returns from gold for a U.S. investor with those from U.S. equities over the period from 1960 through 1980. Gold

TABLE 22-6
Characteristics of Returns, 1960–1980, Gold and U.S. Equities

	Arithmetic Mean Annual Return	Standard Deviation of Annual Returns
U.S. Equities	10.23%	17.68%
Gold	17.59	29.21
Correlation, gold and U.S. equities:	−.142	
Correlation, gold and U.S. cash equivalents:	+.683	

SOURCE: Roger G. Ibbotson and Laurence B. Siegel, "The World Market Wealth Portfolio," *Journal of Portfolio Management,* Winter 1983.

---

[10] In Ibbotson and Siegel, "The World Market Wealth Portfolio."

is clearly a risky investment, but in this period, at least, it also provided high average returns.

For any single investment, of course, risk and return are only parts of the story: correlations of an asset's total return with the returns on other assets are also relevant. In the period covered in Table 22-6, gold price changes were slightly negatively correlated with stock returns. Similar results have been obtained for other periods. Gold thus appears to be an effective *diversifying asset* for an equity investor. Table 22-6 also shows that gold prices were highly correlated with returns on U.S. cash equivalents (Treasury bills, commercial paper, and so on). This is consistent with gold's traditional role as a hedge against inflation, since higher inflation generally brings higher short-term interest rates.

SPORTS BETTING

Throughout the world large amounts of money are wagered on the outcomes of sporting events. In the United States betting on horse races is conducted legally at race tracks in many states and via legal off-track betting establishments in some states. In addition, illegal "bookmakers" in every state accept bets on horse races. Bets on other events—most notably professional football games—are made legally in Nevada and illegally with bookmakers almost everywhere.

A security dealer typically wishes to operate with a small average inventory and thus little exposure to loss through price fluctuations. To do this he or she usually sets a bid price and an ask price that will bring roughly equal orders for purchases and sales in, say, a week's time. The bid/ask spread represents the dealer's profit margin and the trader's transactions costs.

In sports betting the bookmaker acts as dealer and wishes to have relatively little "inventory" (exposure to loss). Two major methods are employed to achieve this: *spread betting* and *odds betting*. The former is used for bets on games such as football and basketball and the latter for bets on contests such as horse races and presidential elections.

Spread Betting

A professional football example will illustrate spread betting. The San Francisco 49ers are scheduled to play the Seattle Seahawks. It is widely felt that the 49ers are likely to win. Thus the bookmaker establishes a *spread*. For example, if the 49ers are "favored by 7 points," the final score will, in effect, be modified by subtracting 7 points from the 49ers score, then paying those who bet on the "winner" using that adjusted score. People who bet on San Francisco bet that the team will "beat the spread"; those who bet on Seattle bet that San Francisco will not beat the spread.

The point spread serves as an equilibrating mechanism. Other things equal, the greater the spread, the smaller will be the amount bet on San Francisco and the larger the amount bet on Seattle. At some level the "books will be balanced." Given local prejudices, this may be accomplished by San Francisco bookmakers' "laying off" excess money bet on the 49ers with Seattle bookmakers who have excess money bet on the Seahawks.

How does the bookmaker make a living? With a range that corresponds to the security dealer's bid/ask spread. Typically, the bettor puts up $11 for a $10 bet; in other words, a winner will receive $10 (plus his or her initial bet, if paid in advance) while a loser is out $11. If the books are balanced, the bookmaker will pay out $10 for every $11 taken in.[11]

While bookmakers generally set point spreads to balance their books, in an efficient market such spreads would provide good estimates of the expected differences in points scored (and by and large the evidence is consistent with market efficiency).

Odds Betting

A goal of many "dealers" in bets is to be reasonably certain that after the contest is over, less will be paid out than is taken in. To do this, terms must be set so that bets on underdogs are attractive. Spreads are one way; *odds* are another.

An example from horse racing will illustrate the procedure. Assume that Doonesbury is favored to win the sixth race at Golden Gate Fields, while the other seven horses are considered inferior but of roughly equal speed. If the payoff per dollar bet were the same for all eight horses, most of the bets would be placed on the favorite. To spread the betting over the contenders, a larger amount must be paid per dollar bet if a long-shot wins.

Assume that the odds are set at 7-to-1 for each of the seven slow horses. This means that if $1 is bet on one of them, and the horse wins, the bettor will receive his or her $1 back plus $7 more.[12] Assume also that the odds on Doonesbury are set at 5-to-3, so that every $3 bet on the favorite will return $8 (the original $3 plus $5) if the horse wins. Now imagine that the amounts bet, given these odds, are as shown in Table 22-7. The total *pool* (amount bet) is $1,000, but no matter which horse wins the race, only $800 will be paid out, leaving

---

[11] Unless the ending score equals the spread, in which case the general procedure is to return all the money bet.

[12] Such odds are sometimes termed 8-for-1.

TABLE 22-7
Odds, Amounts Bet, and Payouts for a Horse Race

Horse	Amount Bet	Odds	Amount Paid Out if Horse Wins
#1 (favorite)	$ 300	5-to-3	$800
2	100	7-to-1	800
3	100	7-to-1	800
4	100	7-to-1	800
5	100	7-to-1	800
6	100	7-to-1	800
7	100	7-to-1	800
8	100	7-to-1	800
Total amount bet =	$1,000		

$200 (or 20% of "the handle") for the track, the government, and/or the bookmaker.

The figures in Table 22-7 may seem contrived, but they represent the kind of situation achieved automatically by *parimutuel betting*. In this form of wagering (used at most horse race tracks) the actual payoff odds for a horse are determined *after all betting has finished* by subtracting the total take (typically about 20%) from the amount bet, then dividing this amount by the amount bet on that horse.[13] Thus the "dealer" is always assured of a fixed percentage in "transactions costs."

Betting on horses, like betting on stocks, is a negative-sum game: owing to transactions costs, the amount paid out is less than the amount paid in. The expected return on the average bet will therefore be negative. Since it is difficult to justify most such activity on the basis of hedging, bettors either (1) erroneously believe that they are all superior predictors, (2) are willing to pay in this manner for entertainment, or (3) prefer risk. Undoubtedly all three aspects play a role. One attribute that makes betting entertaining is the suspension of one's usual mind set and the taking of risks with relatively small amounts of money. In such an environment and with limited exposure, even a conservative investor may take pleasure in acting like a riverboat gambler.

Evidence consistent with risk preference of this sort has been found in many analyses of the expected returns from bets on horses with different probabilities of winning races. Figure 22-4 summarizes a number of such studies. The horizontal axis indicates closing odds (on a logarithmic scale)—favorites plot at the left end of the scale

[13] This applies only to bets that a horse will win the race. More complex procedures are used for *place* (second or better) and *show* (third or better) bets. In addition, the actual payoff is usually rounded down to the nearest multiple of, say, 10 cents per $2 bet.

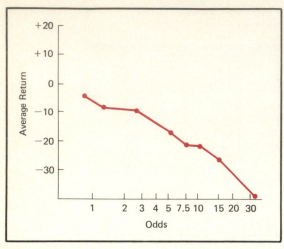

FIGURE 22-4

Average Return Versus Odds in Horse Race Betting

SOURCE: Wayne W. Snyder, "Horse Racing: Testing the Efficient Markets Model," *Journal of Finance*, September 1978.

and extreme long-shots at the right end. The vertical axis indicates average returns. All are negative, but the returns on favorites are considerably better than those on long-shots. "Investors" at the track are apparently willing to give up some expected return to get more risk—in this domain they appear to prefer risk.[14]

The Efficiency of Horse Race Betting

Investors in stocks can avail themselves of the results of financial analysis, both fundamental and technical. However, the high degree of efficiency of the stock market diminishes the value of such information for a single investor, since much of it is already reflected in security prices.

A similar situation prevails in the market for horse race betting. Fundamental analyses of the abilities of horses and trainers, the effects of weather, and so on abound, as do technical analyses of trends, reversals, and other changes in "form." If the market is efficient, reasonably public information provided by such analysts ("handicappers") will be reflected in prices ("closing odds").

A succinct statement of this hypothesis is the following:

$$\text{Prob. (win|track odds)} = \text{Prob. (win|track odds and publicly held information)}$$

---

[14] However, there is some evidence that a high-risk bet made up by "parlaying" bets on favorites in successive races (i.e., betting all winnings for horse 1 on horse 2, betting all winnings on horse 2 on horse 3, and so on) may offer higher expected returns than an equally risky single bet on a long-shot. For discussion of this point, see Richard N. Rosett, "Gambling and Rationality," *Journal of Political Economy*, December 1965. By permission of the University of Chicago Press, © 1979.

Extended Diversification

In words: the probability that a horse will win, given the information on the track odds, is the same as the probability given the odds *and* other information. Put somewhat differently, widely reported handicapping information does not *add* to the information incorporated in the track odds (but it well may have influenced the odds).

In one test[15] the hypothesis was found to be roughly consistent with data for bets placed at Belmont track in New York State. The odds at the track appeared to incorporate the information contained in published "picks" by fourteen handicappers. However, this did not seem to be the case in the less "professional" (and higher-transaction-cost) off-track betting market—a fact that may give some solace to those who invest in small and little-followed stocks.[16]

It is appropriate that we end this chapter and the book on this note. For the positive economist the relatively efficient nature of security and betting markets is heart-warming, for it shows once more the efficacy of competition. For the investor or bettor it provides a challenge, to say the least.

Problems

1. What types of political risks are relevant only for a foreign investor? What types are relevant for both foreign and domestic investors? To what extent and in what manner would you expect each of these two types of risks to be taken into account in the current prices of securities?

2. How might a U.S. citizen or company use currency futures to partially hedge against exchange-rate risk?

3. When a U.S. citizen is attempting to estimate the expected return and variance of return for a foreign security, what factors, in addition to those recognized in domestic security analysis, should be considered?

4. Is low correlation between the percentage changes of market indices of two countries a sufficient condition to ensure that a portfolio containing securities of both countries dominates a portfolio containing only domestic securities?

5. Assume that the model in Figure 22-3 captures all the aspects of the risks of securities worldwide. If capital markets were completely integrated internationally, with a single currency, would the expected returns on the securities in a single country be related to their beta values relative to that country's stock market

---

[15] Stephen Figlewski, "Subjective Information and Market Efficiency in a Betting Market," *Journal of Political Economy*, 87, no. 1, February 1979. By permission of the University of Chicago Press, © 1979.

[16] There is some evidence that information is better reflected in the win pool than in the show and place pools. For details of a "system" designed to exploit such discrepancies, see Donald B. Hausch, William T. Ziemba, and Mark Rubenstein, "Efficiency of the Market for Racetrack Betting," *Management Science*, December 1981.

factor? If so, what would determine the nature of this relationship? What if each country's capital market were completely isolated from that of every other country?

6. Should gold bullion be considered part of the "market portfolio"? If the beta of gold relative to a stock market is negative, does this imply that its beta relative to world market wealth portfolio is also negative?

7. One sometimes finds a variation of the following statement in a newspaper: "The bookmakers took a terrible beating this week, since 80% of the underdogs beat the point spread." Does this seem likely? Why or why not?

8. According to Figure 22-4 the returns on horses with odds of 1-to-1 appear to have averaged −8%, while those on horses with odds of 3-to-1 appear to have averaged −12%. The diagram below illustrates these situations:

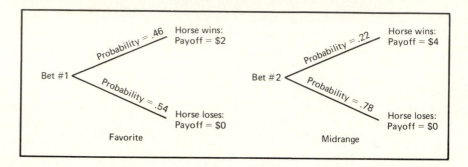

a. Show a comparable diagram for a bet of $1 on one favorite, with all the winnings (if any) bet on another favorite with the same odds and expected return. Would this *parlay* be better than a single bet of $1 on a midrange horse? Why or why not?

b. The returns for horses with odds of 7-to-1 appear to have averaged about −20%. What is the probability that such a "long-shot" will win a race? How does a bet on such a horse compare with a parlay of three favorites?

9. Does the fact that some handicappers' picks do not add to the information in track odds mean that they can't pick winners? Does it mean that their work is of no value? What aspects of security markets are comparable? In what way?

INDEX

Tax shelters, 229-30
Technical financial analysis, 608-13
Technical insolvency, 300
Technicians, 641, 642
Tender offers, 358
Terada, Noboru, 404n
Term loan, 300
Term structure, 313, 317-26
Third market, 34
Time-series analysis, 383
Time-series behavior of earnings, 458-62
Time spread, 516
Time value, option, 515
Time-weighted return, 684
Toevs, Alden, 327n
Tokyo Stock Exchange, 26
Top-down forecasting, 614
Total return, 684
Total risk, 683
Transaction costs, 41-43, 558
   failure to consider, 603
   portfolio revision and, 672, 673
Transfer agent, 357
Treasury bills, 280, 282-83
   annual returns on, 9-10
   interest rate on, 77
Treasury bonds, 280, 284
Treasury Bulletin, 90
Treasury Investment Growth Receipts
   (TIGRS), 289, 290
Treasury notes, 280, 283-84
Treasury stock, 360
Treynor, Jack L., 447n, 590n, 692n
True interest rate, 87-88
Trustees, 297, 566
Trust indenture, 297
Trust Indenture Act of 1939, 50
Truth-in-lending law, 87
Truth-in-securities law, 49

U

Uncorrelated returns, 132-34
Underlying security, 471
Underpriced securities, 163, 164
Underwriters, 44-45, 295
Unfunded liability, 329
Uniform Securities Acts, 52
U.S. Commodity Futures Trading Com-
   mission, 534
U.S. government agency securities, 285-89
U.S. government securities, 278-85, 708, 709
Unit investment trusts, 566-67
Univariate analysis, 347, 348
Unsecured loans, 4
Up-market beta, 692
"Upstairs dealer market," 31, 34, 41-42
Up-tick, 25

Urwitz, Gabriel, 334n
Utility, portfolio:
   determination of, 643, 651-54
   improvement of, 672-75
Utility functions, 514
Utility net of transactions costs, 673

V

Valuation analysis, 600
Value Line, Inc., 635
   Averages, 637-38
   futures contract, 554, 555
   Index, 553-54
Value Line Investment Survey, 368, 464-66, 633
Value Line Options and Convertibles, 633
Vanguard Index Trust, 580
Variable annuities, 573-75
Variable-rate mortgage, 307
Variability, 11
Variance, marginal, 155-60, 177
Variance in return:
   international, 716
   portfolio revision and, 663
   portfolio risk and, 126-30
   risk tolerance and, 650-51
Visual comparisons, reliance on mis-
   leading, 608
Vives, Antonio, 591n
Voluntary accumulation plans, 580
Voluntary bankruptcy, 300, 301
Voting, stockholder, 357-58
Voting bonds, 299

W

Wall Street Journal, The, 283, 633
Warrants, 481-82, 484-85
Watts, Ross, 421
Weekend effect, 407-8
Wert, James, 331
West, R. R., 339n
What-if analyses, 619
Wiesenberger Investment Services *In-
   vestment Companies*, 633
Williams, John Burr, 138
Wilshire 5000 equity index, 637
Wire houses, 20
Withdrawal plans, 582
World market wealth portfolio, 707-10

Y

Yield curve, 89-91
Yield factor, 379-81
Yield spread:
   defined, 314
   determinants of, 338-40
   yield-to-maturity and, 314, 321-22